Library Use Only

DRAMA
for Students

DRAMA
for Students

Presenting Analysis, Context, and Criticism on
Commonly Studied Dramas

Volume 12

Elizabeth Thomason, Editor

Detroit
New York
San Francisco
London
Boston
Woodbridge, CT

National Advisory Board

Drama for Students

Staff

Editor: Elizabeth Thomason.

Contributing Editors: Anne Marie Hacht, Michael L. LaBlanc, Ira Mark Milne, Jennifer Smith.

Managing Editor: Dwayne D. Hayes.

Research: Victoria B. Cariappa, *Research Manager.* Cheryl Warnock, *Research Specialist.* Tamara Nott, Tracie A. Richardson, *Research Associates.* Nicodemus Ford, Sarah Genik, Timothy Lehnerer, Ron Morelli, *Research Assistants.*

Permissions: Maria Franklin, *Permissions Manager.* Debra J. Freitas, Jacqueline Jones, Julie Juengling, *Permissions Assistants.*

Manufacturing: Mary Beth Trimper, *Manager, Composition and Electronic Prepress.* Evi Seoud, *Assistant Manager, Composition Purchasing and Electronic Prepress.* Stacy Melson, *Buyer.*

Imaging and Multimedia Content Team: Barbara Yarrow, *Manager.* Randy Bassett, *Imaging Supervisor.* Robert Duncan, Dan Newell, *Imaging Specialists.* Pamela A. Reed, *Imaging Coordinator.* Leitha Etheridge-Sims, Mary Grimes, David G. Oblender, *Image Catalogers.* Robyn V. Young, *Project Manager.* Dean Dauphinais, *Senior Image Editor.* Kelly A. Quin, *Image Editor.*

Product Design Team: Kenn Zorn, *Product Design Manager.* Pamela A. E. Galbreath, *Senior Art Director.* Michael Logusz, *Graphic Artist.*

Copyright Notice

Table of Contents

The Study of Drama

We study drama in order to learn what meaning others have made of life, to comprehend what it takes to produce a work of art, and to glean some understanding of ourselves. Drama produces in a separate, aesthetic world, a moment of being for the audience to experience, while maintaining the detachment of a reflective observer.

Drama is a representational art, a visible and audible narrative presenting virtual, fictional characters within a virtual, fictional universe. Dramatic realizations may pretend to approximate reality or else stubbornly defy, distort, and deform reality into an artistic statement. From this separate universe that is obviously not "real life" we expect a valid reflection upon reality, yet drama never is mistaken for reality—the methods of theater are integral to its form and meaning. Theater is art, and art's appeal lies in its ability both to approximate life and to depart from it. By presenting its distorted version of life to our consciousness, art gives us a new perspective and appreciation of reality. Although, to some extent, all aesthetic experiences perform this service, theater does it most effectively by creating a separate, cohesive universe that freely acknowledges its status as an art form.

And what is the purpose of the aesthetic universe of drama? The potential answers to such a question are nearly as many and varied as there are plays written, performed, and enjoyed. Dramatic texts can be problems posed, answers asserted, or moments portrayed. Dramas (tragedies as well as comedies) may serve strictly "to ease the anguish of a torturing hour" (as stated in William Shakespeare's *A Midsummer Night's Dream*)—to divert and entertain—or aspire to move the viewer to action with social issues. Whether to entertain or to instruct, affirm or influence, pacify or shock, dramatic art wraps us in the spell of its imaginary world for the length of the work and then dispenses us back to the real world, entertained, purged, as Aristotle said, of pity and fear, and edified—or at least weary enough to sleep peacefully.

It is commonly thought that theater, being an art of performance, must be experienced—that is, seen—in order to be appreciated fully. However, to view a production of a dramatic text is to be limited to a single interpretation of that text—all other interpretations are for the moment closed off, inaccessible. In the process of producing a play, the director, stage designer, and performers interpret and transform the script into a work of art that always departs in some measure from the author's original conception. Novelist and critic Umberto Eco, in his *The Role of the Reader: Explorations in the Semiotics of Texts,* explained, "In short, we can say that every performance offers us a complete and satisfying version of the work, but at the same time makes it incomplete for us, because it cannot simultaneously give all the other artistic solutions which the work may admit."

Thus Laurence Olivier's coldly formal and neurotic film presentation of Shakespeare's *Hamlet* (in which he played the title character as well as directed) shows marked differences from subsequent adaptations. While Olivier's Hamlet is clearly entangled in a Freudian relationship with his mother, Gertrude, he would be incapable of shushing her with the impassioned kiss that Mel Gibson's mercurial Hamlet (in director Franco Zeffirelli's 1990 film) does. Although each of the performances rings true to Shakespeare's text, each is also a mutually exclusive work of art. Also important to consider are the time periods in which each of these films were produced: Olivier made his film in 1948, a time in which overt references to sexuality (especially incest) were frowned upon. Gibson and Zeffirelli made their film in a culture more relaxed and comfortable with these issues. Just as actors and directors can influence the presentation of drama, so too can the time period of the production affect what the audience will see.

A play script is an open text from which an infinity of specific realizations may be derived. Dramatic scripts that are more open to interpretive creativity (such as those of Ntozake Shange and Tomson Highway) actually require the creative improvisation of the production troupe in order to complete the text. Even the most prescriptive scripts (those of Neil Simon, Lillian Hellman, and Robert Bolt, for example), can never fully control the actualization of live performance, and circumstantial events, including the attitude and receptivity of the audience, make every performance a unique event. Thus, while it is important to view a production of a dramatic piece, if one wants to understand a drama fully it is equally important to read the original dramatic text.

The reader of a dramatic text or script is not limited by either the specific interpretation of a given production or by the unstoppable action of a moving spectacle. The reader of a dramatic text may discover the nuances of the play's language, structure, and events at their own pace. Yet studied alone, the author's blueprint for artistic production does not tell the whole story of a play's life and significance. One also needs to assess the play's critical reviews to discover how it resonated to cultural themes at the time of its debut and how the shifting tides of cultural interest have revised its interpretation and impact on audiences. And to do this, one needs to know a little about the culture of the times which produced the play as well as the author who penned it.

Drama for Students supplies this material in a useful compendium for the student of dramatic theater. Covering a range of dramatic works that span from the fifth century B.C. to the 1990s, this book focuses on significant theatrical works whose themes and form transcend the uncertainty of dramatic fads. These are plays that have proven to be both memorable and teachable. *Drama for Students* seeks to enhance appreciation of these dramatic texts by providing scholarly materials written with the secondary and college/university student in mind. It provides for each play a concise summary of the plot and characters as well as a detailed explanation of its themes and techniques. In addition, background material on the historical context of the play, its critical reception, and the author's life help the student to understand the work's position in the chronicle of dramatic history. For each play entry a new work of scholarly criticism is also included, as well as segments of other significant critical works for handy reference. A thorough bibliography provides a starting point for further research.

These inaugural two volumes offer comprehensive educational resources for students of drama. *Drama for Students* is a vital book for dramatic interpretation and a valuable addition to any reference library.

Source: Eco, Umberto, *The Role of the Reader: Explorations in the Semiotics of Texts,* Indiana University Press, 1979.

Carole L. Hamilton
Author and Instructor of English
Cary Academy
Cary, North Carolina

Introduction

Purpose of **Drama for Students**

The purpose of *Drama for Students* (*DfS*) is to provide readers with a guide to understanding, enjoying, and studying dramas by giving them easy access to information about the work. Part of Gale's "For Students" literature line, *DfS* is specifically designed to meet the curricular needs of high school and undergraduate college students and their teachers, as well as the interests of general readers and researchers considering specific plays. While each volume contains entries on "classic" dramas frequently studied in classrooms, there are also entries containing hard-to-find information on contemporary plays, including works by multicultural, international, and women playwrights.

The information covered in each entry includes an introduction to the play and the work's author; a plot summary, to help readers unravel and understand the events in a drama; descriptions of important characters, including explanation of a given character's role in the drama as well as discussion about that character's relationship to other characters in the play; analysis of important themes in the drama; and an explanation of important literary techniques and movements as they are demonstrated in the play.

In addition to this material, which helps the readers analyze the play itself, students are also provided with important information on the literary and historical background informing each work.

This includes a historical context essay, a box comparing the time or place the drama was written to modern Western culture, a critical overview essay, and excerpts from critical essays on the play. A unique feature of *DfS* is a specially commissioned overview essay on each drama by an academic expert, targeted toward the student reader.

To further aid the student in studying and enjoying each play, information on media adaptations is provided, as well as reading suggestions for works of fiction and nonfiction on similar themes and topics. Classroom aids include ideas for research papers and lists of critical sources that provide additional material on each drama.

Selection Criteria

The titles for each volume of *DfS* were selected by surveying numerous sources on teaching literature and analyzing course curricula for various school districts. Some of the sources surveyed included: literature anthologies; *Reading Lists for College-Bound Students: The Books Most Recommended by America's Top Colleges;* textbooks on teaching dramas; a College Board survey of plays commonly studied in high schools; a National Council of Teachers of English (NCTE) survey of plays commonly studied in high schools; St. James Press's *International Dictionary of Theatre;* and Arthur Applebee's 1993 study *Literature in the Secondary School: Studies of Curriculum and Instruction in the United States.*

Input was also solicited from our expert advisory board (both experienced educators specializing in English), as well as educators from various areas. From these discussions, it was determined that each volume should have a mix of ''classic'' dramas (those works commonly taught in literature classes) and contemporary dramas for which information is often hard to find. Because of the interest in expanding the canon of literature, an emphasis was also placed on including works by international, multicultural, and women playwrights. Our advisory board members—current high school teachers— helped pare down the list for each volume. If a work was not selected for the present volume, it was often noted as a possibility for a future volume. As always, the editor welcomes suggestions for titles to be included in future volumes.

How Each Entry Is Organized

Each entry, or chapter, in *DfS* focuses on one play. Each entry heading lists the full name of the play, the author's name, and the date of the play's first production or publication. The following elements are contained in each entry:

- **Introduction:** a brief overview of the drama which provides information about its first appearance, its literary standing, any controversies surrounding the work, and major conflicts or themes within the work.

- **Author Biography:** this section includes basic facts about the author's life, and focuses on events and times in the author's life that inspired the drama in question.

- **Plot Summary:** a description of the major events in the play, with interpretation of how these events help articulate the play's themes. Subheads demarcate the plays' various acts or scenes.

- **Characters:** an alphabetical listing of major characters in the play. Each character name is followed by a brief to an extensive description of the character's role in the plays, as well as discussion of the character's actions, relationships, and possible motivation.

  Characters are listed alphabetically by last name. If a character is unnamed—for instance, the Stage Manager in *Our Town*—the character is listed as ''The Stage Manager'' and alphabetized as ''Stage Manager.'' If a character's first name is the only one given, the name will appear alphabetically by the name.

Variant names are also included for each character. Thus, the nickname ''Babe'' would head the listing for a character in *Crimes of the Heart*, but below that listing would be her less-mentioned married name ''Rebecca Botrelle.''

- **Themes:** a thorough overview of how the major topics, themes, and issues are addressed within the play. Each theme discussed appears in a separate subhead, and is easily accessed through the boldface entries in the Subject/Theme Index.

- **Style:** this section addresses important style elements of the drama, such as setting, point of view, and narration; important literary devices used, such as imagery, foreshadowing, symbolism; and, if applicable, genres to which the work might have belonged, such as Gothicism or Romanticism. Literary terms are explained within the entry, but can also be found in the Glossary.

- **Historical and Cultural Context:** This section outlines the social, political, and cultural climate *in which the author lived and the play was created.* This section may include descriptions of related historical events, pertinent aspects of daily life in the culture, and the artistic and literary sensibilities of the time in which the work was written. If the play is a historical work, information regarding the time in which the play is set is also included. Each section is broken down with helpful subheads.

- **Critical Overview:** this section provides background on the critical reputation of the play, including bannings or any other public controversies surrounding the work. For older plays, this section includes a history of how the drama was first received and how perceptions of it may have changed over the years; for more recent plays, direct quotes from early reviews may also be included.

- **Further Reading:** an alphabetical list of other critical sources which may prove useful for the student. Includes full bibliographical information and a brief annotation.

- **Sources:** an alphabetical list of critical material quoted in the entry, with full bibliographical information.

- **Criticism:** an essay commissioned by *DfS* which specifically deals with the play and is written specifically for the student audience, as well as excerpts from previously published criticism on the work.

In addition, each entry contains the following highlighted sections, set separate from the main text:

- **Media Adaptations:** a list of important film and television adaptations of the play, including source information. The list may also include such variations on the work as audio recordings, musical adaptations, and other stage interpretations.

- **Compare and Contrast Box:** an ''at-a-glance'' comparison of the cultural and historical differences between the author's time and culture and late twentieth-century Western culture. This box includes pertinent parallels between the major scientific, political, and cultural movements of the time or place the drama was written, the time or place the play was set (if a historical work), and modern Western culture. Works written after the mid-1970s may not have this box.

- **What Do I Read Next?:** a list of works that might complement the featured play or serve as a contrast to it. This includes works by the same author and others, works of fiction and nonfiction, and works from various genres, cultures, and eras.

- **Study Questions:** a list of potential study questions or research topics dealing with the play. This section includes questions related to other disciplines the student may be studying, such as American history, world history, science, math, government, business, geography, economics, psychology, etc.

Other Features

DfS includes ''The Study of Drama,'' a foreword by Carole Hamilton, an educator and author who specializes in dramatic works. This essay examines the basis for drama in societies and what drives people to study such work. Hamilton also discusses how *Drama for Students* can help teachers show students how to enrich their own reading/viewing experiences.

A Cumulative Author/Title Index lists the authors and titles covered in each volume of the *DfS* series.

A Cumulative Nationality/Ethnicity Index breaks down the authors and titles covered in each volume of the *DfS* series by nationality and ethnicity.

A Subject/Theme Index, specific to each volume, provides easy reference for users who may be studying a particular subject or theme rather than a single work. Significant subjects from events to broad themes are included, and the entries pointing to the specific theme discussions in each entry are indicated in **boldface.**

Each entry has several illustrations, including photos of the author, stills from stage productions, and stills from film adaptations.

Citing Drama for Students

When writing papers, students who quote directly from any volume of *Drama for Students* may use the following general forms. These examples are based on MLA style; teachers may request that students adhere to a different style, so the following examples may be adapted as needed.

When citing text from *DfS* that is not attributed to a particular author (i.e., the Themes, Style, Historical Context sections, etc.), the following format should be used in the bibliography section:

''Our Town,'' *Drama for Students.* Ed. David Galens and Lynn Spampinato. Vol. 1. Farmington Hills: Gale, 1997. 8–9.

When quoting the specially commissioned essay from *DfS* (usually the first piece under the ''Criticism'' subhead), the following format should be used:

Fiero, John. Essay on ''Twilight: Los Angeles, 1992.'' *Drama for Students.* Ed. David Galens and Lynn Spampinato. Vol. 1. Farmington Hills: Gale, 1997. 8–9.

When quoting a journal or newspaper essay that is reprinted in a volume of *DfS*, the following form may be used:

Rich, Frank. ''Theatre: A Mamet Play, 'Glengarry Glen Ross'.'' *New York Theatre Critics' Review* Vol. 45, No. 4 (March 5, 1984), 5–7; excerpted and reprinted in *Drama for Students,* Vol. 1, ed. David Galens and Lynn Spampinato (Farmington Hills: Gale, 1997), pp. 61–64.

When quoting material reprinted from a book that appears in a volume of *DfS*, the following form may be used:

Kerr, Walter. ''The Miracle Worker,'' in *The Theatre in Spite of Itself* (Simon & Schuster, 1963, 255–57; excerpted and reprinted in *Drama for Students,* Vol. 1, ed. Dave Galens and Lynn Spampinato (Farmington Hills: Gale, 1997), pp. 59–61.

We Welcome Your Suggestions

The editor of *Drama for Students* welcomes your comments and ideas. Readers who wish to suggest dramas to appear in future volumes, or who have other suggestions, are cordially invited to contact the editor. You may contact the editor via

E-mail at: **ForStudentsEditors@galegroup.com.**

Or write to the editor at:

Editor, *Drama for Students*
The Gale Group
27500 Drake Rd.
Farmington Hills, MI 48331-3535

Literary Chronology

1809: Nikolai Vasilyevich Gogol, named after Saint Nikolai, is born in the small town of Velikie Sorochintsy, in the Ukraine, part of Russia at this time. His parents, Maria Ivanovna and Vasily Afanasevich Gogol-Yanovsky, are landowners.

1836: Nikolai Gogol's *The Government Inspector* is brought to the attention of Tsar Nicholas I, who likes it so much that he insists on its production. *The Government Inspector* premieres at the Alexandrinsky Theatre in Saint Petersburg.

1852: Gogol dies at the age of forty-two as the result of a religious fast.

1860: Anton Chekhov is born on January 17 in Taganrog, a Russian seaport village on the Black Sea. His grandfather was an emancipated serf who had managed to buy his own freedom. His father, Pravel Yegorovitch Chekhov, a cruel and dictatorial taskmaster who made his children's lives miserable, runs a small grocery store.

1874: Hugo Laurenz August von Hofmannsthal is born on February 1 in Vienna, Austria, the only child of Ann Maria Josefa Fohleutner and Hugo August Peter, the director of an investment bank.

1888: Eugene O'Neill is born on October 16 in New York City to James and Mary Ellen O'Neill.

1890: Marcus Cook Connelly is born on December 13 in McKeesport, Pennsylvania. His father, Patrick Joseph Connelly, is an actor and hotel owner, while his mother, Mabel Louise (maiden name Cook), is an actress.

1892: Elmer Rice is born Elmer Leopold Reizenstein in New York City on September 28. He is the son of Jacob Reizenstein and his wife Fanny (maiden name Lion), German-Jewish immigrants.

1896: Anton Chekhov's *Chayka* or *The Seagull* is produced. It is the first play in the author's second period of writing for the theater—that of the last few years of his life—in which he is considered to have penned his widely acknowledged dramatic masterpieces.

1904: Anton Chekhov dies.

1911: Tennessee Williams is born Thomas Lanier Williams on March 26 in Columbus, Mississippi. He is the son of Cornelius Coffin and Edwina (maiden name Dakin) Williams.

1914: Jan de Hartog is born on April 22 in Haarlem, the Netherlands. His father, Arnold Hendrik, is a minister and theology professor, and his mother, Lucretia (maiden name Meijjes), is a lecturer in medieval mysticism.

1921: Eugene O'Neill's *Anna Christie* goes through several revisions before its Broadway debut at the Vanderbilt Theatre on November 2 of this year. O'Neill's first version was a four-act play entitled *Chris*, which opened in Atlantic City, New Jersey, on March 8, 1920. Anna's father dominated this play and Anna and Mat were minor roles. O'Neill called his second version *The Ole Davil*, which provided the outline for the final version. O'Neill's last revisions strengthened the character of Anna, and reworked the plot to focus on her. The success of *Anna Christie* helped reinforce O'Neill's reputation as one of the finest American dramatists.

1925: Hugo von Hofmannsthal's five-act play *Der Turm* (*The Tower*) is first published in book form. A revised version of *The Tower* is first performed on stage in 1927.

1927: Neil Simon (full name Marvin Neil Simon) is born on July 4 in the Bronx, New York City. Simon grows up here and makes it the setting for nearly all of his plays.

1929: Marc Connelly's *The Green Pastures* appears. This Pulitzer Prize-winning play is a reenactment of stories of the Old Testament in which all the characters (including God) are African American and speak in a black southern dialect. The play is first performed at the Mansfield Theatre in New York City in 1930.

1929: Elmer Rice's *Street Scene* debuts on January 10 of this year at The Playhouse on Broadway in New York City. It has been considered one of Rice's most successful works and has cemented his reputation as a serious playwright. Rice himself directs the original production, which runs for 602 performances. *Street Scene* wins the 1929 Pulitzer Prize for drama.

1929: Hugo Laurenz August von Hofmannsthal dies of a stroke on July 15, just before he was to attend the funeral of his eldest son.

1935: Joseph A. Walker is born on February 23 in Washington, D.C., to Joseph (a house painter) and Florine Walker.

1936: Paul Zindel is born in Staten Island, New York, on May 15. He is the son of Paul, a New York policeman, and Betty Zindel.

1937: Lanford Wilson is born on April 13 in Lebanon, Missouri, the town in which he sets *Talley's Folly* and two other plays.

1938: Caryl Churchill is born on September 3 in London, England, the daughter and only child of Robert Churchill and his wife. Churchill's father is a political cartoonist; her mother works as a model, secretary, and actress.

1939: Jason Miller is born on April 22 in Long Island City, New York. He is the only child of John and Mary Claire Miller, an electrician and a teacher respectively.

1947: David Mamet is born on November 30 in Chicago, Illinois. He is the son of Bernard Mamet, a labor lawyer, and his wife, Leonore.

1951: Jan de Hartog's *The Fourposter*, his most successful play, is first produced at the Ethel Barrymore Theatre. It runs for 632 performances on Broadway. The play earns de Hartog the 1952 Antoinette Perry (Tony) Award.

1953: Eugene O'Neill dies of pneumonia on November 27 in Boston, Massachusetts.

1959: Tennessee Williams's *Sweet Bird of Youth* is produced. Although it becomes his biggest box office success since *Cat on a Hot Tin Roof* (1955), the play comes to be regarded as an example of the playwright in decline. It is his second-to-last big success.

1964: Paul Zindel's *The Effect of Gamma Rays on Man-in-the-Moon Marigolds*, his best-known play, is first produced at the Alley Theatre in Houston, Texas. It eventually opens off-Broadway in 1970 and in 1971 makes a brief jump to Broadway. Overall, the play enjoys a very successful New York run of 819 performances. It is an autobiographical drama loosely based on Zindel's experiences growing up in a single-parent household.

1967: Elmer Rice dies of a heart attack on May 8 in Southampton, England, survived by five children from three different marriages.

1972: Joseph A. Walker's *The River Niger*, a loosely autobiographical play, is first performed by the Negro Ensemble Company in New York City. The play is first published in 1973, and is adapted to the screen by Walker in the 1976 production starring Cicely Tyson and James Earl Jones.

1972: Jason Miller's *That Championship Season* makes its debut off-Broadway at the Estelle Newman/Public Theatre on May 2, where it runs for 144 performances. The production is then moved to the Booth Theatre on Broadway, where it runs for an additional 844 performances. The play runs for a total of 988 performances before it closes on April 21, 1974.

1977: David Mamet's *A Life in the Theatre* is produced and proves to be one of his early successes.

1979: Lanford Wilson's romantic comedy *Talley's Folly* is produced. It is the second of three plays in what come to be known as Wilson's Talley Family series. The play is nominated for several Tony Awards and wins the Pulitzer Prize and other awards in 1980.

1980: Marcus Cook Connelly dies in New York City on December 21.

1982: Since its premiere on August 28 of this year, Caryl Churchill's *Top Girls* has been regarded as a unique, if difficult, play about the challenges working women face in the contemporary business world and in society at large. Premiering in the Royal Court Theatre in London before making its New York debut on December 28, 1982, in the Public Theatre, *Top Girls* wins an Obie Award in 1983 and is the runner-up for the Susan Smith Blackburn Prize.

1983: Tennessee Williams chokes to death on February 24 in his New York hotel suite.

1985: Neil Simon's *Biloxi Blues* becomes the twenty-first play by Simon to reach the Broadway stage in twenty-four years. In the 1980s, the author, already an established comedic playwright, turns to his own life for inspiration and produces a trilogy of semi-autobiographical plays. He first introduced Eugene Morris Jerome, the hero of *Biloxi Blues*, in the widely acclaimed *Brighton Beach Memoirs*. *Biloxi Blues* is a Broadway hit and is honored with a Tony Award for the best play of 1985.

Acknowledgments

The editors wish to thank the copyright holders of the excerpted criticism included in this volume and the permissions managers of many book and magazine publishing companies for assisting us in securing reproduction rights. We are also grateful to the staffs of the Detroit Public Library, the Library of Congress, the University of Detroit Mercy Library, Wayne State University Purdy/Kresge Library Complex, and the University of Michigan Libraries for making their resources available to us. Following is a list of the copyright holders who have granted us permission to reproduce material in this volume of *Drama for Students (DfS)*. Every effort has been made to trace copyright, but if omissions have been made, please let us know.

COPYRIGHTED MATERIALS IN *DfS*, VOLUME 12, WERE REPRODUCED FROM THE FOLLOWING PERIODICALS:

Ball State University Forum, v. 20, Spring, 1979. © 1979 Ball State University. Reproduced by permission.—*Eugene O'Neill Review,* v. 13, Spring 1990. © Copyright 1990 by Eugene O'Neill Review. Reproduced by permission.—*Hudson Review,* v. 25, Winter, 1972–73. Copyright © 1972 by The Hudson Review, Inc. Reproduced by permission.—*Melus,* v. 7, Spring 1980. Copyright © MELUS: The Society for the Study of Multi-Ethnic Literature of the United States, 1980. Reproduced by permission.—*Modern Drama,* v. 12, December 1969; v. 30, September 1987. Copyright © 1969, 1987 University of Toronto, Graduate Centre for Study of Drama. Reproduced by permission.—*The Nation,* New York, v. 178, May 29, 1954. Copyright © 1954 The Nation magazine/ The Nation Company, Inc. Reproduced by permission.—*The New Leader,* v. 68, Arpil 8, 1985. Copyright © 1985 by The American Labor Conference on International Affairs, Inc. Reproduced by permission.—*The New Republic,* v. 3823, April 25, 1988. © 1988 The New Republic, Inc. Reproduced by permission of The New Republic.—*The New York Times,* April 19, 1970. Copyright © 1970 by The New York Times Company. Reproduced by permission.—*The New Yorker,* v. XLVI, No. 9, April 18, 1970; v. 70, July, 1994. Copyright © 1970 by The New Yorker Magazine, Inc. ©1994 by John Lahr. Originally published in The New Yorker. All rights reserved. Reproduced by permission of the authors.—*Slavic Review,* v. 47, Fall 1988. Copyright (c) 1988 by American Association for the Advancement of Slavic Studies. Reproduced by permission.—*The Southern Review, Louisana State University,* v. 21, No. 3, Summer 1985 for "Mother, Sister, Wife: A Dramatic Perspective," by Anthony Barthelemy. Copyright ©1985, by Anthony Barthelemy. Reproduced by permission of the author.—*Studies in American Drama, 1945-Present,* v. 6, 1991. Reproduced by permission.—*Theatre History Studies,* v. 20, June 2000. Copyright © 2000 by Theatre History Studies. Reproduced courtesy, Theatre History Studies.—*Theatre Journal,* v. 35, March, 1985. Theatre

Journal: © 1985, University and College Theatre Association of the American Theatre Association. Reproduced by permission of The Johns Hopkins University Press.

COPYRIGHTED MATERIALS IN *DfS*, VOLUME 12, WERE REPRODUCED FROM THE FOLLOWING BOOKS:

Adler, Thomas P. From *Mirror on the Stage: The Pulitzer Plays as an Approach to American Drama.* Purdue University Press, 1987. Reproduced by permission.—Barnett, Gene A. From *Lanford Wilson.* Twayne Publishers, 1987. Copyright © Macmillan Library Reference. Reproduced with the permission of Macmillan Library Reference USA, a division of Ahsuog, Inc.—Carpenter, Frederick Ives. From *Eugene O'Neill.* Twayne Publishers, 1964. © Macmillan Library Reference, 1964. Reproduced with the permission of Macmillan Library Reference USA, a division of Ahsuog, Inc.—Dean, Anne. From *David Mamet: Language as Dramatic Action.* Associated University Presses, 1990. Copyright © 1990 by Associated University Presses. Reproduced by permission.—Demastes, William W. From *Beyond Naturalism.* Greenwood Press, 1988. Copyright © Greenwood Publishing Group, Inc. Reproduced by permission.—Griffin, Alice. From *Understanding Tennessee Williams,* edited by Matthew J. Burccoli. Copyright © 1995 by University of South Carolina Press. Reproduced by permission.—Hirsch, Foster. From *A Portrait of an Artist: The Plays of Tennessee Williams.* Copyright © Kennikat Press. Reproduced by permission of author.—Hogan, Robert. From *The Independence of Elmer Rice.* Southern Illinois University Press, 1965. Copyright © 1965 by Southern Illinois University Press. All rights reserved. Reproduced by permission.—Jain, Jasbir. From "Feminist Drama: The Politics of the Self: Churchill and Keatley," in *Women's Writing: Text and Context,* edited by Jasbir Jain. Rawat Publications, 1996. Reproduced by permission.—Nolan, Paul T. From "The Green Pastures," in *Marc Connelly.* Twayne Publishers, 1969. Copyright © Macmillan Library Reference. Reproduced with the permission of Macmillan Library Reference USA, a division of Ahsuog, Inc.

PHOTOGRAPHS AND ILLUSTRATIONS APPEARING IN *DFS,* VOLUME 12, WERE RECEIVED FROM THE FOLLOWING SOURCES:

Act I from a Moscow Art Theater production of "The Seagull" by Anton Chekhov, 1905, photograph. From Konstantin Stanislavsky: Selected Works, compiled by Oksana Korneva. Raduga Publishers, Moscow, 1984.—Act III of a Moscow Art Theater production of "The Seagull" by Chekhov (with Stanislavsky, Lilina and Roksanova), 1905, photograph. From Konstantin Stanislavsky: Selected Works, compiled by Oksana Korneva. Raduga Publishers, Moscow, 1984.—Chekov, Anton, photograph. International Portrait Gallery/Library of Congress.—Churchill, Caryl, photograph. © Jerry Bauer. Reproduced by permission.—Connelly, Marc, photograph. AP/Wide World Photos. Reproduced by permission.—de Hartog, Jan, photograph. Copyright © Marjorie de Hartog. Reproduced by permission.—Elliott, Denholm (l), holding balance bar, as Samuel West watches him, scene from theatrical production of David Mamet's "A Life in the Theatre," at Theatre Royal. © Donald Cooper. Reproduced by permission.—Field, Betty, standing near bed along with Burgess Meredith, (illustration, upper corner) newlywed couple kissing at window, playbill cover from Jan de Hartog's theatrical production of "The Fourposter," directed by Jose Ferrer, at Ethel Barrymore Theatre, photograph. Performing Arts Books. Reproduced by permission of Performing Arts Books and Playbill Inc.—Garbo, Greta, with Clarence Brown, photograph. The Kobal Collection. Reproduced by permission.—Goddard, Beth (l), as Kit, sitting next to Lesley Sharp, as Angie, scene from theatrical production of Caryl Churchill's "Top Girls," at Royal Court Theatre. © Donald Cooper. Reproduced by permission—Gogol, Nikolai (thin mustache, in dark coat), illustration. Corbis-Bettmann. Reproduced by permission.—Goody, Bob (l), as Osip, leaning over Timothy Spall, scene from theatrical production of Nikolai Gogol's "The Government Inspector," at Greenwich Theatre. © Donald Cooper. Reproduced by permission.—Hofmannsthal, Hugo von, photograph.—Joanne Woodward, in a scene from the film "Effect of Gamma Rays on Man-in-the-Moon Marigolds," 1972, photograph. Twentieth Century Fox. The Kobal Collection. Reproduced by permission.—Kaye, Danny, wearing general's uniform, standing at table with Walter Sklezak and others, scene from the film "The Inspector General," photograph. The Kobal Collection. Reproduced by permission.—Kelly, Janis (with Kristine Ciesinski) in "Street Scene," photograph. © Donald Cooper/PHOTOSTAGE. Reproduced by permission.—Lam, Sarah, as Nijo, gathered at table with Deborah Finalay, as Isabella Bird, Lesley Sharp, as Dull Gert, and Lesley Manville, as Marlene, scene from theatrical production of Caryl Churchill's "Top

Girls," at Royal Court 91. © Donald Cooper. Reproduced by permission.—Mamet, David, photograph. AP/Wide World Photos. Reproduced by permission.—Miller, Jason, photograph. AP/Wide World Photos. Reproduced by permission.—Newman, Paul, photograph. The Kobal Collection. Reproduced by permission.—O'Neill, Eugene G., photograph. The Library of Congress.—People relaxing in front of apartment building, scene from the film "Street Scene," 1931, photograph. United Artists. The Kobal Collection. Reproduced by permission.—Playbill from theatrical production of Joseph A. Walker's "The River Niger," directed by Douglas Turner Ward, at Brooks Atkinson Theatre, title page. Performing Arts Books. Reproduced by permission of Performing Arts Books, and Playbill Inc.—Playbill text page of cast, from theatrical production of Joseph A. Walker's "The River Niger," directed by Douglas Turner Ward, at Brooks Atkinson Theatre, photograph. Performing Arts Books. Reproduced by permission of Permforming Arts Books, and Playbill Inc.—Playbill title page from theatrical production of Jan de Hartog's "The Fourposter," directed by Jose Ferrer, at Ethel Barrymore Theatre, magazine cover. Performing Arts Books. Reproduced by permission of Performing Arts Books and Playbill Inc.—Rex, Ingram, photograph. The Kobal Collection. Reproduced by permission.—Rice, Elmer (wearing patterned tie, round black framed glasses), New York City, 1931, photograph. AP/Wide World Photos. Reproduced by permission.—Richarson, Natasha, and Chris Christopherson, scene from theatrical production of Eugene O'Neill's "Anna Christie," at Young Vic Theatre. © Donald Cooper. Reproduced by permission.—Robert Knepper, being embraced by Clare Higgins, scene from theatrical productions of Tennessee Williams' "Sweet Bird of Youth," at Royal National Theatre, photograph. © Donald Cooper. Reproduced by permission.—Simon, Neil, photograph. AP/Wide World Photos. Reproduced by permission.—Sorvino, Paul, standing with Richard A. Dysart ©, Charles Durning (2nd from r), Walter McGinn, Michael McGuire on

playbill cover from theatrical production of Jason Miller's "That Championship Season," at the Booth Theatre, directed by A. J. Antoon, cover illustration by R. Kursar. Performing Arts Books. Reproduced by permission of Performing Arts Books, and Playbill Inc.—Sperdakos, George, dancing with Kerrie Keane, scene from theatrical production of "Talley's Folly," at Theatre Plus, photograph by Mr. Robert C. Ragsdale. Reproduced by permission.—Sperdakos, George, sitting with Kerrie Keane, scene from theatrical production of Lanford Wilson's "Talley's Folly," at Theatre Plus, photograph by Mr. Robert C. Ragsdale. Reproduced by permission.—Walken, Christopher, standing in rain with Matthew Broderick, scene from the film "Biloxi Blues," photograph. The Kobal Collection. Reproduced by permission.—West, Samuel, standing behind Denholm Elliott, scene from theatrical production of David Mamet's "A Life in the Theatre," at Theatre Royal. © Donald Cooper. Reproduced by permission.—White man pointing to black man as two black women look on, playbill cover from theatrical production of Marc Connelly's "The Green Pastures," at Forty-Fourth Street Theatre, photograph. Performing Arts Books. Reproduced by permission of Performing Arts Books, and Playbill Inc.—Williams, Tennessee (wearing dark tie with metallic polka dots), 1955, photograph. AP/Wide World Photos. Reproduced by permission.—Wilson, Lanford (hair blowing in the breeze), New York City, 1980, photograph. AP/Wide World Photos. Reproduced by permission.—Woodward, Joanne with Nell Potts, in a scene from the film "Effect of Gamma Rays on Man-in-the-Moon Marigolds," 1972, photograph. Twentieth Century Fox. The Kobal Collection. Reproduced by permission.—Woolfe, Eric, sitting, holding book, watching four others actors, scene from theatrical production of Neil Simon's "Biloxi Blues," at The Grand Theatre, photograph by Mr. Robert C. Ragsdale. Reproduced by permission.—Zindel, Paul, photograph. AP/Wide World Photos. Reproduced by permission.

Contributors

Cynthia Bily: Bily teaches writing and literature at Adrian College in Adrian, Michigan, and writes for various educational publishers. Entry on *Talley's Folly*. Original essay on *Talley's Folly*.

Liz Brent: Brent has a Ph.D. in American Culture, specializing in cinema studies, from the University of Michigan. She is a freelance writer and teaches courses in American cinema. Entries on *The Fourposter, The Government Inspector, The Green Pastures, The River Niger*, and *The Tower*. Original essays on *The Fourposter, The Government Inspector, The Green Pastures, The River Niger*, and *The Tower*.

John W. Fiero: Fiero holds a Ph.D. degree. He formerly taught drama and playwriting at the University of Louisiana at Lafayette and is now a freelance writer and consultant. Entry on *The Seagull*. Original essay on *The Seagull*.

Beth A. Kattelman: Kattelman has a Ph.D. and specializes in modern drama. Entry on *The Effect of Gamma Rays on Man-in-the-Moon Marigolds*. Original essay on *The Effect of Gamma Rays on Man-in-the-Moon Marigolds*.

David J. Kelly: Kelly is Professor of English, College of Lake County (IL). Original essays on *The Fourposter* and *The Tower*.

Rena Korb: Korb has a master's degree in English literature and creative writing and has written for a wide variety of educational publishers. Entry on *Biloxi Blues*. Original essays on *Biloxi Blues, Talley's Folly*, and *That Championship Game*.

Tara L. Mantel: Mantel is a freelance writer and editor based near Boston. Original essay on *Street Scene*.

Ryan D. Poquette: Poquette has a B.A. in English, and specializes in writing drama and film. Original essay on *The Seagull*.

Wendy Perkins: Perkins is Assistant Professor of English, Prince George's Community College, MD; Ph.D. in English, University of Delaware. Entry on *Anna Christie*. Original essays on *Anna Christie, The Seagull*, and *Street Scene*.

Annette Petrusso: Petrusso is a freelance author and screenwriter, Austin, TX. Entries on *A Life in the Theatre, Street Scene, Sweet Bird of Youth, That Championship Season*, and *Top Girls*. Original essays on *A Life in the Theatre, Street Scene, Sweet Bird of Youth, That Championship Season*, and *Top Girls*.

Kathy A. Smith: Smith is a Ph.D. specializing in writing and American literature. Original essay on *The Fourposter*.

Anna Christie

EUGENE O'NEILL

1921

Anna Christie went through several revisions before its Broadway debut at the Vanderbilt Theatre on November 2, 1921. O'Neill's first version was a four-act play entitled *Chris,* which opened in Atlantic City, New Jersey on March 8, 1920. Anna's father dominated this play, and Anna and Mat were minor roles. O'Neill called his second version *The Ole Davil,* which provided the outline for the final version. O'Neill's last revisions strengthened the character of Anna and reworked the plot to focus on her. The success of *Anna Christie* helped reinforce O'Neill's reputation as one of the finest American dramatists.

The play focuses on the problematic relationship between a sailor and the daughter he has not seen for almost twenty years. Their relationship becomes complicated by her romantic involvement with another man of the sea and her unveiling of her troubled past. In this compelling account of a young woman's decline and subsequent salvation, O'Neill presents a realistic and painful exploration of family conflict and the harsh reality of women's lives in the early part of the twentieth century. Yet, audiences and critics also praised the play's confirmation of the power of love and forgiveness. Frederic I. Carpenter, in his study of O'Neill's plays, comments that *Anna Christie* is "a serious study of modern life, which dramatizes that mixture of comedy and tragedy most characteristic of life."

Anna Christie was successfully adapted to the screen three times. The second version starred Greta

Garbo and is considered by film critics to be one of Hollywood's finest motion pictures.

AUTHOR BIOGRAPHY

Eugene O'Neill was born on October 16, 1888, in New York City to James and Mary Ellen O'Neill. The O'Neill's led a transient life as the family followed James's stage career. James was a celebrated actor who became famous for his performance in *The Count of Monte Cristo*. The constant traveling and the life of the theatre caused tensions between O'Neill's parents, which were exacerbated by Mary's addiction to morphine, a habit she started after her son's difficult delivery. Their decidedly dysfunctional family had an enormously negative effect on Eugene and his brother Jamie. After surviving his expulsion from Princeton, a suicide attempt, a bout of tuberculosis, and a failed marriage, O'Neill determined to devote his life to writing for the theatre. Familial tensions would become the subject of several of O'Neill's plays, including his most successful, *Long Day's Journey into Night* and *Anna Christie*.

In 1914, with his father's help, O'Neill published *Thirst and Other One Act Plays*. The first staging of one of his plays did not occur until after his involvement with the Provincetown Players in Massachusetts in the summer of 1916. The summer theater premiered his *Bound East for Cardiff*, which enjoyed solid reviews. O'Neill's successful playwriting continued for three decades and secured him the reputation as one of the world's greatest dramatists. When he died of pneumonia on November 27, 1953, in Boston, Massachusetts, he had earned several awards for his work including the Pulitzer Prize in 1920 for *Beyond the Horizon,* in 1922 for *Anna Christie,* in 1928 for *Strange Interlude,* and in 1957 for *Long Day's Journey into Night;* the Gold Medal from the National Institute of Arts and Letters in 1923; a Litt.D. (Doctor of Letters) from Yale University in 1923; the Nobel Prize in literature in 1936; and the New York Drama Critics Circle Award in 1957, for *Long Day's Journey into Night.*

PLOT SUMMARY

Act 1

The play opens in Johnny-The-Priest's saloon in New York City, one afternoon in the fall. Barge captain Chris Christopherson receives a letter from Anna, his daughter, who writes that she is coming to see him. Chris explains that he hasn't seen her since she was five and lived in Sweden. Since he was a sailor who rarely saw his family, Anna's mother brought her to Minnesota to live with her cousins on a farm. When her mother died, she stayed on. Chris insists that it was "better Anna live on farm, den she don't know dat ole davil, sea, she don't know fa'der like me."

When Chris leaves to get food, Anna appears in the bar, "plainly showing all the outward evidences of belonging to the world's oldest profession." She immediately demands of the bartender, "Gimme a whisky—ginger ale on the side. And don't be stingy, baby." As she drinks, she relates details of her past to Marthy, the woman who has been staying on the barge with Chris. Anna explains that when the police raided the house where she worked in Saint Paul, she was thrown in jail, and then she was sent to the hospital. She has come to see her father to get rest but does not expect much from him, since men, she claims, "give you a kick when you're down, that's what all men do." She admits that she hated the farm where her cousins worked her to death "like a dog." After one of her cousins raped her, she escaped to Saint Paul, where she found work as a nanny. She soon became tired of taking care of other women's children, and so she drifted into prostitution. When Chris returns to the bar, the two have an awkward reunion. Chris is thrilled when she agrees to stay with him on the barge.

Act 2

Ten days later, Anna walks on the deck of the barge, "Simeon Winthrop," anchored in the Provincetown harbor, looking healthy and "transformed." She admits to her father that she loves the sea, which angers him. He does not want her to be ruined by her association with it, but she claims it has made her feel "clean." Chris worries that she will marry a sailor, and then experience the extreme loneliness her mother felt.

That night, they rescue four shipwrecked sailors. Anna brings one of them, Mat Burke, a drink, and the two begin to talk. She impresses him when she aggressively holds off his advances, and he soon declares he will marry her. When Chris finds the two together, he becomes angry and vows to keep them apart.

Act 3

When Chris tries to convince Anna that Mat would make a terrible husband, she insists, ''it's me ain't good enough for him.'' Later, Chris attacks Mat during an argument over Anna, but Mat quickly subdues him. Anna declares her love for Mat, but tells him she can never marry him. When Mat and Chris battle over her fate, Anna, who feels as if she is being treated like ''a piece of furniture,'' explodes and tells them about her past. Chris in ''a stupor of despair'' and Mat ''livid with rage'' fall silent with condemnation, which goads Anna into ''a harsh, strident defiance.'' She blames Chris's abandonment of her for her descent into prostitution. She tells Mat that she wanted to keep her past a secret from him, but she loved him too much to deceive him. Insisting that she has changed, and that the sea and his love have cleansed her, she pleads with Mat not to reject her. Mat, however, thinking she has made a fool of him, physically threatens her and then leaves, swearing never to see her again. Chris, recognizing Anna's great love for Mat and her present predicament, is determined to force Mat to marry her. He tells her ''dat ole davil sea'' is to blame.

Act 4

Two days later, when Chris returns to the barge, drunk, Anna is packed and ready to go back to her life in Saint Paul. Chris admits, ''Ay guess it vas all my fault—all bad tangs dat happen to you,'' and he asks for her forgiveness. Chris tells her he has signed onto a steamer that sails the next morning for South Africa, so he can send money to her. Soon Mat appears wanting to have ''a last word'' with Anna. When he begs her to admit she had lied about her past, Anna swears that she has changed, and that she hated all the men she was with. Eventually, Mat is able to believe her and to forgive her. The two happily embrace and decide they will marry in the morning. When Anna discovers Mat has signed up for duty on the same ship as Chris, Mat assures her that she will not be lonesome for long, since ''with the help of God'' they will have children.

When Chris discovers that both he and Mat will be leaving the next morning on the same ship, he again blames the sea. Anna tries to reassure them that ''we're all fixed now.'' She offers a toast to the sea ''no matter what.'' The play ends with the ''mournful wail of steamers' whistles.''

Eugene O'Neill

CHARACTERS

Mat Burke

Chris Christopherson, Anna's father, rescues Mat at sea. Mat is employed as a stoker (a person who tends a ship's furnace and supplies it with fuel) aboard ocean liners. Thirty-year-old Mat is ''a powerful, broad-chested six-footer, his face handsome in a hard, rough, bold, defiant way . . . [and is] in the full power of his heavy-muscled, immense strength.'' He has very traditional attitudes about women and their place in society, but he loves Anna enough to accept her past. Unlike Chris, Mat believes that his destiny is shaped by his own strength and courage, coupled with the will of God.

Anna Christie

See Anna Christopherson.

Anna Christopherson

When Anna Christopherson (also called Anna Christie) first arrives at Johnny-The-Priest's Saloon, she plainly shows ''all the outward evidences of belonging to the world's oldest profession. Her youthful face is already hard and cynical.'' Her hard exterior shields her need for love, which she slowly

MEDIA ADAPTATIONS

- The first film version of *Anna Christie* was a silent production in 1923, which was directed by John Griffith Wray, written by Bradley King, and starred Blanche Sweet as Anna.

- The 1930 Hollywood version was advertised with the tag line, "Garbo Talks!" It was directed by Clarence Brown, written by Frances Marion, and starred Greta Garbo as Anna and Charles Bickford as Mat.

- A German film of the play was also produced in 1930 starring Greta Garbo. Jacques Feyder, using a German version of Frances Marion's script, directed this movie. Theo Shall played Mat.

allows to surface, after she determines that she has been cleansed through her contact with the sea.

Christopher Christopherson

Anna's father Chris is captain of a coal barge and has spent his life on the sea. He is "a short, squat, broad-shouldered man of about fifty, with a round, weather-beaten, red face," twinkling eyes, and "a simple good humor." While his face reveals a nature that is "childishly self-willed and weak," it also shows his "obstinate kindliness." Chris loves his daughter, but he has been too weak to resist the lure of the sea; consequently, he has not taken responsibility for raising her. He is deeply superstitious about the power of the sea, and uses it as an excuse for his poor parenting. However, when Anna is threatened, first by the possibility of marriage to a sailor and then by rejection, Chris's love for her emerges and makes him bold.

Johnny-The-Priest

Johnny-The-Priest owns the bar where Anna and Chris reunite. Johnny is an ironic foil for Anna, whose outward, hard appearance masks her vulnerability.

Marthy Owen

Marthy is a weathered, older woman who exhibits a youthful love of life. She has been living on the barge with Chris. When she understands that Chris is worried about Anna's response to their relationship, Marthy agrees to leave, accepting his rejection and her own relocation with a generous heart.

THEMES

Identity

In O'Neill's masterpiece, *Long Day's Journey into Night,* Mary Tyrone insists, "None of us can help the things life has done to us. They're done before you realize it, and. . . . they make you do other things until at last everything comes between you and what you'd like to be, and you've lost your true self forever." Like *Long Day's Journey into Night, Anna Christie* focuses on the search for identity. But, unlike those in the Tyrone family, Anna Christie is able to discover a new sense of self through her contact with the sea and through a loving relationship.

Appearances and Reality

Closely related to the theme of identity in the play is that of appearances versus reality. Both Chris and Anna, at times, appear to be what they are not. Even though when Anna walks into Johnny-The-Priest's, "plainly showing all the outward evidences of belonging to the world's oldest profession," she appears to her father as the innocent child he left behind in Sweden. Mat initially thinks she is Chris's woman, as is apparent when he asks her, "What would [a lady] be doing on this bloody hulk?" He soon, however, decides that he is not fit "to be kissing the shoe-soles of a fine, decent girl" like her. When Anna is honest with Chris and Mat about her past, Chris refuses to hear, telling her, "Don't talk dat vay, Anna! Ay go crazy! Ay von't listen!" Mat, however, immediately accepts what she is saying, and he reacts by rejecting her.

Chris refuses to consider the reality of Anna's past because he loves her and because he is unable to face his role in her descent into prostitution. He admits that he has not been the perfect father to Anna, but he will not take full responsibility for his abandonment of her. That "ole davil sea" gives him an excuse for leaving Anna and her mother and for letting her stay on the farm after her mother dies. Thus, he tries to appear to Anna as a man who wanted to be a good father but was prevented from doing so by the overpowering force of the sea. Mat's rejection of Anna reveals his inability to accept a woman who does not fit the ideal of a wife and illuminates society's restrictive attitudes toward women.

Courage and Cowardice

Throughout most of the play, Chris is afraid to face his responsibility for Anna's harsh life. Anna, however, shows herself to be much more courageous than her father. Rather than deceive the man she loves, she is willing to leave him. Finally, though, when Mat refuses to let her go, she garners the courage to admit to her father and to Mat the sordid details of her past.

Change and Transformation

After living with her father for a while on the barge, Anna experiences a transformation. Later, she tries to explain to Mat that "yust getting out in this barge, and being on the sea changed me. . . . and made me feel different about things, 's if all I'd been through wasn't me and didn't count and was yust like it never happened." She explains that the sea and Mat's love have cleansed her of her past. When Mat abandons her, she considers going back to her former life as a prostitute, but she cannot return to prostitution.

Atonement and Forgiveness

All three characters are faced with the choice of whether or not to forgive themselves and each other. After Chris finally admits his failings, he begs Anna's forgiveness. She offers it without hesitation, and she tries to ease his mind by suggesting that fate, not free will, rules their lives. She tells him, "It ain't your fault, and it ain't mine, and it ain't his neither. We're all poor nuts, and things happen, and we yust get mixed in wrong, that's all."

Mat's act of forgiveness is more problematic. Because of his rigid attitudes toward women and their place, he must be convinced that Anna was forced to be with other men, and that she did not have feelings for any of them. Only after Anna swears that she hated all of the men she was with

TOPICS FOR FURTHER STUDY

- Read O'Neill's *The Hairy Ape* and compare its themes to those in *Anna Christie*.

- Explore biographical details about O'Neill, especially those that concern his life on the sea and his relationship with his family. What autobiographical elements can you find in the play?

- Investigate common attitudes toward prostitution in the first few decades of the twentieth century. How similar are those attitudes to today's attitudes?

- How does the relationship between Anna and Mat reflect the changing role of women in the early part of the twentieth century?

will he forgive her and accept her as worthy of his love.

STYLE

Realism

O'Neill's first plays were melodramas. He soon rejected the flat characterizations and unmotivated violent action typical of melodrama, and instead he adopted the tenets of realism, a new literary movement that took a serious look at believable characters and their sometimes problematic interactions with society. O'Neill began to use settings and props that reflect his characters' daily lives and to write realistic dialogue that replicates natural speech patterns.

O'Neill's new type of realism rejects traditional forms and digs beneath the surface of everyday reality. In *Anna Christie*, O'Neill incorporates realistic depictions of men at sea and of the interactions between family members. The play explores the tensions that can arise between family members as a result of feelings of abandonment and guilt. It also illuminates the harsh reality of women's lives in the early part of the twentieth century. O'Neill creates in the play a lyrical realism in the problematic romance between Anna and Mat.

Setting

While the play depicts the harsh life of men who live and work at sea, O'Neill also uses the setting symbolically. The sea becomes almost a character in the play as it affects the lives of Chris, Anna, and Mat. Chris claims that the sea is an "ole davil" that controls the lives of men. He tells Anna that a sailor's life is "hard vork all time. It's rotten. . . . for to go to sea" and that sooner or later that "ole davil . . . [will] svallow dem up." Chris conveniently uses the sea as an excuse for his abandonment of Anna, claiming that it continually lured him away from her. He warns Anna not to marry a sailor who would also be tempted by that "ole davil" to be apart from his family for long periods of time. When he finds Anna and Mat together, he vows, "dat's your dirty trick, damn ole davil, you . . . but py God, you don't do dat! Not while Ay'm living! No, py God, you don't!"

Anna, however, regards the sea in a completely different light. After a short time living on the barge with her father, the sun and fresh air out on the water restores her health. The sea also rejuvenates her spiritually, as she notes, when she claims that it has cleansed her of her old life. Anna tells Chris, "I feel so . . . like I'd found something I'd missed and been looking for—'s if this was the right place for me to fit in . . . and I feel happy for once . . . happier than I ever been anywhere before!" The sea also brings Mat to Anna. Mat insists, "the sea's the only life for a man with guts in him isn't afraid of his own shadow. 'Tis only on the sea he's free."

HISTORICAL CONTEXT

The Emergence of the American Theatre

At the end of the nineteenth century, a group of playwrights that included James A. Herne, Bronson Howard, David Belasco, Augustus Thomas, Clyde Fitch, and William Vaughn Moody started breaking away from traditional melodramatic forms and themes. As a result, American theatre began to establish its own identity. These and other playwrights in the early part of the twentieth century were inspired by the dramatic innovations of Henrik

Ibsen, August Strindberg, and George Bernard Shaw. During this period, experimental theatre groups made up of dramatists and actors encouraged new innovative American playwrights. In 1914, Lawrence Langner, Helen Westley, Philip Moeller, and Edward Goodman created the Washington Square Players in New York, and in 1915, playwright Susan Glaspell helped start the Provincetown Players in Massachusetts. The goal of both of these groups was to produce plays that the more conservative Broadway theatres rejected. The most important member of this latter group was Eugene O'Neill, who wrote plays with a uniquely American voice. George H. Jensen, in the *Dictionary of Literary Biography,* notes that "before O'Neill began to write, most American plays were poor imitations or outright thefts of European works." Jensen insists that O'Neill became the "catalyst and symbol . . . of the establishment of American drama."

Realism

In the late nineteenth century, playwrights turned away from what they considered the artificiality of melodrama to a focus on the commonplace in the context of everyday contemporary life. They rejected the flat characterizations and unmotivated, violent action typical of melodrama. Their work, along with much of the experimental fiction written during that period, adopts the tenets of realism, a new literary movement that supported the creation of believable characters with sometimes problematic interactions with society. Dramatists, like Henrik Ibsen, discard traditional sentimental theatrical forms as they chronicle the strengths and weaknesses of ordinary people confronting difficult social problems, like the restrictive conventions nineteenth-century women endured. Writers who embraced realism use settings and props to reflect their characters' daily lives as well as realistic dialogue that replicates natural speech patterns.

O'Neill's long career reflected the shifting styles of the American theatre at the end of the nineteenth century and the beginning of the twentieth. His early plays were unsuccessful attempts at melodrama. He then turned to realistic depictions of men at sea and later of the interactions between family members. In *Anna Christie,* O'Neill creates a lyrical realism in the problematic romance between Anna and Mat. O'Neill's new type of realism rejects traditional forms, digging beneath the surface of everyday reality. Following the new American doctrine of "Art Theatre," O'Neill incorporated philosophical themes and unusual forms in his plays. In

COMPARE
&
CONTRAST

- **Early 1920s:** Some Americans consider the Russian Revolution an important humanitarian development. Others, however, fear it to be a communist threat to American democracy.

  1926: Joseph Stalin becomes dictator of the Soviet Union. His reign of terror will last for twenty-seven years.

  1991: President Mikhail Gorbachev orders the dissolution of the Soviet Union, and a new Commonwealth of Independent States is formed by the countries that formerly made up the Soviet Union.

- **1921:** Margaret Sanger founds the American Birth Control League. Other important social changes for women include the ability to vote, to receive higher forms of education, to smoke and drink, and to wear clothes that do not restrict their movements.

Today: Women are guaranteed equal rights under the law.

- **1921:** Approximately 900,000 immigrants enter the United States in the fiscal year ending June 30. After World War I, Americans are afraid of the influx of immigrants who are willing to work for lower wages and so could threaten American jobs.

  Today: Americans' concern over the economic impact of immigrants continues.

- **1921:** As a result of overproduction by American farmers, prices fall eighty-five percent below 1919 highs.

  Today: Many small farms are going bankrupt or being swallowed up by large farming conglomerates.

the 1920s, he experimented with expressionism, most notably in *Emperor Jones* and *The Great God Brown.*

CRITICAL OVERVIEW

Anna Christie earned mostly positive reviews when it opened on Broadway in 1921, which helped it run successfully for 117 performances. The play also earned O'Neill a Pulitzer Prize. Over the years, its critical reputation has remained strong. Critics praise the play's realistic characterizations, especially of Anna and her father Chris. Percy Hammond, in his opening night review of the play for the New York *Tribune,* writes that *Anna Christie* presents the audience with a "veracious picture of some interesting characters in interesting circumstances." Frederic I. Carpenter, in his book on O'Neill, claims that "the character of Chris, 'childishly self-willed and

weak, of an obstinate kindliness,' is one of O'Neill's minor triumphs." Several critics have considered Anna a realistic portrait of a street-wise, yet vulnerable, young woman. James Whittaker in his article for the New York *News,* insists that in Anna "O'Neill has his first concrete heroine." Travis Bogard, in his *Contour in Time: The Plays of Eugene O'Neill,* praises O'Neill's characterization of Mat, whom he calls "a true citizen of the sea." Bogard comments that Mat is crucial to the play's naturalistic themes, since he serves as a personification of the sea.

Opinions about the play's ending, however, are mixed. An opening night review in the New York *Sun* voices the sentiments of many critics who find the last act too conventional. Leo Marsh in the New York *Telegraph* praises the play's vitality but criticizes the "apparent compromise" at the end. J. Ranken Towse in his review for the New York *Post* insists that the "incredible" happy ending is "disastrous." In his article for *Freeman,* Ernest Boyd offers the harshest criticism in his conclusion that the play's ending is the "worst anti-climax in the theatre.'' Ironically, H. Z. Torres in the New York *Commercial* complains that the last act is not happy enough due to the ''ugliness and morbidness'' of the plot.

Others, however, defend the play's conclusion. John Gassner in his article on O'Neill's plays comments that *Anna Christie*'s ending possesses a ''raffish mordancy that suited the subject and tone of the work, and did not impair the effectiveness of this justifiably popular play.'' In *Eagle,* Arthur Pollock insists that the resolution at the end of the play is a natural extension of the plot. George H. Jensen, in his article on O'Neill for the *Dictionary of Literary Biography,* determines that O'Neill has been ''wrongly criticized'' for the play's last act, noting the ambiguous future the main characters have in store for them. However, Carpenter contends that *Anna Christie* is ''one of the most perfectly romantic of O'Neill's early works,'' and most audiences and scholars agree on O'Neill's ability to present a realistic portrait of compelling characters in *Anna Christie.*

CRITICISM

Wendy Perkins

Perkins, an Associate Professor of English at Prince George's Community College in Maryland, has published articles on several twentieth-century authors. In this essay, she examines O'Neill's exploration of the naturalistic themes in Anna Christie.

> *[The wind-tower] was a giant, standing with its back to the plight of the ants. It represented in a degree . . . the serenity of nature amid the struggles of the individual—nature in the wind, and nature in the vision of men. She did not seem cruel to him then, not beneficent, not treacherous, not wise. But she was indifferent, flatly indifferent.*

This famous passage from Stephen Crane's short story ''The Open Boat,'' which focuses on four men in a small dinghy struggling against the current and trying to make it to shore, is often quoted as an apt expression of the tenets of naturalism, a literary movement in the late nineteenth and early twentieth centuries in France, America, and England. Writers included in this group, like Crane, Émile Zola and Theodore Dreiser, expressed in their works a biological and/or environmental determinism that prevented their characters from exer-

cising their free will and thus controlling their destinies. Crane often focused on the social and economic factors that overpowered his characters. Zola's and Dreiser's work included this type of environmental determinism (economic, social, and political forces that restrict our lives, often interfering with our attempts to exercise free will and to shape our own destinies) coupled with an exploration of the influences of heredity in their portraits of the animalistic nature of men and women engaged in the endless and brutal struggle for survival. Eugene O'Neill explores similar naturalistic tendencies in *Anna Christie* in the harsh lives of the play's main characters. Through his story of a reformed prostitute and her relationships with the men in her life, O'Neill raises important questions about how much influence we have over our destinies.

In *Anna Christie* O'Neill presents a naturalistic impression of the forces that continually frustrate human will and action. The naturalistic view proposes that humans are controlled by their heredity and environment, and so they cannot exercise free will. O'Neill questions the validity of this view in his portrait of Anna, who has been shaped by forces beyond her control, but who also may have the will and the ability to change her life.

Several environmental factors contributed to Anna's descent into prostitution. When Chris frequently left Anna and her mother alone in Sweden, her mother transplanted them to her cousins' farm in Minnesota. After her mother died, she was forced to stay on the farm where she was made to work ''like a dog,'' since her father never came for her. After her cousin raped her, she left the farm and took a job in Saint Paul as a nanny. Soon, however, biological and environmental influences propelled her into a life of prostitution.

Anna admits that her need for freedom compelled her to leave her position as a nanny. She explains, ''I was caged in, I tell you—yust like in yail—taking care of other people's kids—listening to 'em bawling and crying day and night—when I wanted to be out—and I was lonesome—lonesome as hell. So I give up finally.'' Her need for freedom, combined with the sexual needs of the men she encounters in the city, contributes to her downfall. She ridicules her father's assumption that there would be ''all them nice inland fellers yust looking for a chance to marry'' in Saint Paul, when she confesses, ''Marry me? What a chance! They wasn't looking for marrying.'' Anna admits that loneliness prompted her to give in to their sexual advances. As

Natasha Richardson as Anna Christopherson and John Woodvine as Chris Christopherson in a scene from a theatrical production of Anna Christie.

a result of her experiences in the city, she claims that she does not expect much from her father, since men ''give you a kick when you're down, that's what all men do.'' She tries to force her father to admit his responsibility for her fate, when she demands, ''and who's to blame for it, me or you? If you'd even acted like a man—if you'd even had been a regular father and had me with you—maybe things would be different.''

While O'Neill presents convincing evidence that forces beyond her control have damaged her, he challenges Anna's opinion about ''all men'' when she comes to live with her father on the sea. Chris welcomes his daughter with open arms and gives her the opportunity to find a new identity. After a short time on the sea, Anna feels cleansed of her old life. She admits, ''I feel so ... like I'd found something I'd missed and been looking for—'s if this was the right place for me to fit in ... and I feel happy for once ... happier than I ever been anywhere before!''

Chris, however, believes the sea contains an overwhelmingly demonic force. He continually rants about how ''dat ole davil sea'' has ruined lives, including his own and Anna's. The sea, thus, becomes an effective excuse for shirking his responsi-

bilities to his daughter. When Chris has a sense of foreboding about Anna, he concludes that the sea has a will of its own. He insists the sea is ''hard vork all time. It's rotten ... for go to sea. ... Dat ole davil, sea, sooner, later she svallow [everyone] up'' who comes in contact with her. Determined, however, to fight the power of the sea when he finds Anna and Mat together, he vows, ''dat's your dirty trick, damn ole davil, you ... but py God, you don't do dat! Not while Ay'm living! No, py God, you don't!'' Later, as Anna despairs over losing Mat, Chris tells her that her predicament is not her fault:

> it's dat ole davil sea, do this to me. ... She bring dat Irish fallar in fog, she make you like him, she make you fight with me all time. If dat Irish fallar don't never come, you don't never tal me dem tangs, Ay don't never know, and everytang's all right. Dirty ole davil.

O'Neill exposes the weakness in Chris's attitude toward the sea as he presents irrefutable evidence that Chris's abandonment of Anna contributed to her downfall. Another challenge to Chris's belief comes from Mat, who echoes Anna's feelings about the sea when he tells Chris,

> you know the truth in your heart, if great fear of the sea has made you a liar and a coward itself. The sea's the only life for a man with guts in him isn't afraid of

WHAT DO I READ NEXT?

- In the expressionistic *The Hairy Ape* (1922), O'Neill explores naturalistic themes in his depiction of the disillusionment of a seaman.

- Stephen Crane's short story, ''The Open Boat,'' (1898) depicts the struggles of four shipwrecked seamen to reach shore.

- *Long Day's Journey Into Night*, first performed in 1956, is O'Neill's finest study of domestic interaction and offers insight into O'Neill's own tragic relationship with his family.

- Stephen Crane's novel *Maggie: A Girl of the Streets* (1896) presents a harrowing account of the effects of poverty and prostitution.

- Kate Chopin's *The Awakening* (1899) chronicles the tragic life of a young woman who rebels against puritanical social doctrines.

---

his own shadow. 'Tis only on the sea he's free . . . the sea give you a clout once, knocked you down, and you're not man enough to get up for another, but lie there for the rest of your life howling bloody murder.

Anna appears to take control of her own destiny while she is living on the barge. She enters freely into a relationship with Mat, even against her father's wishes, and she stands up to both of them when they threaten her freedom. When Mat uses physical force to try to convince her to marry him, telling her ''I'll make up your mind for you bloody quick,'' Anna is ''instinctively repelled by his tone,'' and tells him, ''say, where do you get that stuff.'' As Mat and Chris battle over her fate, Anna, who feels as if she is being treated like ''a piece of furniture,'' explodes. She insists: ''You was going on 's if one of you had got to own me. But nobody owns me, see?—'cepting myself. I'll do what I please and no man, I don't give a hoot who he is, can tell me what to do.'' Yet environmental determinism soon reexerts its influence over her. After she tells Chris and Mat about her past, Mat rejects her, unable to break free of the social stigma of prostitution.

In the last act, O'Neill continues his questioning of free will and determinism as Anna and Mat reunite. Environmental and biological forces seem to be held at bay when Mat decides that he will marry Anna. Several critics find this apparent ''happy ending'' to be too forced and conventional. For example, Leo Marsh in the New York *Telegraph* praises the play's vitality but criticizes the ''apparent compromise'' at the end. In his article for

Freeman, Ernest Boyd offers the harshest criticism in his conclusion that the play's ending is the ''worst anti-climax in the theatre.''

Others, however, note the play's ambiguous resolution. John Gassner in his article on O'Neill's plays comments that *Anna Christie*'s ending possesses a ''raffish mordancy that suited the subject and tone of the work, and did not impair the effectiveness of this justifiably popular play.'' George H. Jensen, in his article on O'Neill for the *Dictionary of Literary Biography,* determines that O'Neill has been ''wrongly criticized'' for the play's last act, noting the ambiguous future the main characters have in store for them.

The ending does, in fact, perfectly compliment O'Neill's explorations of the question of free will and destiny. Just as he seems to present a traditional, romantic ending to Anna's story, he imbues it with a sense of doom. When Mat insists to Anna, ''I've a power of strength in me to lead men the way I want, and women, too, maybe, and I'm thinking I'd change you to a new woman entirely,'' Anna agrees, ''yes, you could.'' Yet, her fierce sense of independence and her aversion to feeling caged may create problems in their marriage. Also, Mat and Chris are both sailing the next day for South Africa, leaving Anna alone again. While Mat assures Anna that he will return safely, Chris, looking out into the foggy night with a sense of foreboding, insists, ''Fog, fog, fog, all bloody time. You can't see where you was going, no. Only dat old davil, sea—she knows.'' O'Neill seems to echo Chris's sense of doom when he ends the play with the "mournful wail of steamers' whistles."

In *Anna Christie* O'Neill refuses to provide a definite answer to the questions of free will and destiny. He does suggest that environmental and biological influences can sometimes overwhelm us. Anna reinforces this viewpoint when Chris asks for her forgiveness, and she gives it freely, admitting, "It ain't your fault, and it ain't mine, and it ain't his neither. We're all poor nuts, and things happen, and we yust get mixed in wrong, that's all." Yet Anna has also demonstrated that courage, love, and forgiveness can sometimes help shape destinies.

Source: Wendy Perkins, in an essay for *Drama for Students,* Gale Group, 2001.

John V. Antush

John Antush's essay discusses O'Neill's approach to modernism and postmodernism and how his experimentation challenges the form and in the case of Anna Christie *'explodes' the traditional love story.*

When we pause to reassess Eugene O'Neill's contribution to American theatre, what astonishes us is not just the sustained dramatic achievement through the period that we now call "modern" (1920–1956 in America), but the multiple ways he anticipates and lays the foundations for a postmodern dramatic aesthetic. O'Neill spent most of his literary career chipping away at those stage conventions that dominated the nineteenth-century theatre and the popular imagination. From his realistic depiction of man's desire to belong to nature in *Beyond the Horizon,* to his expressionistic portrayal of a possessive god in *The Emperor Jones,* to the naturalism of operative destiny in *Desire Under the Elms,* to the surrealistic symbolism of sex in *Strange Interlude,* to the existential isolation in *Long Day's Journey Into Night,* O'Neill's double-barreled critique of the theatre's superficial realism and tawdry artifice underlies his most daring experiments in subject matter and dramaturgy. This sustained attack contains his most important contribution to modernism and anticipates most of the components of postmodernism.

Every new age calls itself "modern," and modernism always represents a revolt from traditional techniques, forms, ways of thinking. What we have grown used to calling "modern" for the last eighty years, however, no longer fits our present situation. So, for want of a better word, we call

> THE NATURALISTIC VIEW PROPOSES THAT HUMANS ARE CONTROLLED BY THEIR HEREDITY AND ENVIRONMENT, AND SO THEY CANNOT EXERCISE FREE WILL."

contemporary dramatic experiments "postmodern." By about 1950 the wartime sense of militant purpose had been diluted by a postwar feeling of drift, random sequence, instinctive response, and chance. This self-canceling interplay of rational purpose, defect, and ignorance seems to inform the meaning and technique of the postmodern dramatic aesthetic. However, the new dramatists, such as Edward Albee, Sam Shepard, Arthur Kopit, David Rabe, Lanford Wilson, and David Mamet, among others, in their need for new forms of expression in the postmodern world, are not so much making radical breaks with established traditions as synthesizing techniques and philosophies from movements as diverse as expressionism and epic theatre to surrealism and existentialism.

The two basic varieties of postmodernism, radical and reactionary, hold up for examination the mimetic purposes of realistic modernism. The more radical postmodernism questions the codes, myths, techniques of modernism. Reactionary postmodernism mines past forms to celebrate them; sometimes it mixes modernist stylistic devices in the name of rebellion, but it reaffirms their value. In the final analysis both radical and reactionary postmodernism deconstruct modernism. Samuel Beckett's strategic use of the familiarizing and stabilizing vaudeville routines in *Waiting for Godot,* for example, self-consciously entertains the audience; but the routines' trajectories, which exist only as reflections of the self-canceling circularity of language, systematically affirm the instability of linguistic constructs, especially as applied to the prevailing social *mythos.* What Beckett does so radically in this play, O'Neill had begun to do less obviously in his early plays. O'Neill's literary career spans the modern period, and his substantial contributions reflect the fertile diversity of modernism even as his dramatic experiments undermine modernism itself from the very beginning.

> " MASKED IN THE RHETORIC OF COMPLEMENTARY HALVES, THE MODERN THEATRE STILL PORTRAYS MEN AND WOMEN AS FUNDAMENTALLY OPPOSITE, INSTEAD OF SIMPLY DIFFERENT, SEXUAL BEINGS NEEDING EACH OTHER FOR COMPLETION."

In one of his earliest plays, *Anna Christie,* O'Neill successfully makes the sea the occasion of a postmodernist inquiry into the possibilities and limitations of moral judgment, of the traditional love plot, and of dramatic form itself. This apparently realistic text methodically explodes the premises of the traditional modern sea story in which the sea is the neutral backdrop of moral struggle isolating and clarifying man's heroic efforts in an indifferent universe. It also explodes the premises of the traditional love story in which love finds a way over parental opposition and conflicting religious beliefs. O'Neill's relentless probing into the American myths of middle-class morality and romantic love involved him in an elaborate critique of the ways in which popular beliefs are embodied in dramatic structures that encode and propagate those myths. Buried under the theatricalism of his father's theatre is a reductive ideology of morality and sexuality whose entire network of meanings, values, and presuppositions unraveled under O'Neill's close scrutiny. Thus, O'Neill's experimentalism, more than an Oedipal rebellion of realistic modernism, offers an informing postmodern vision that requires careful discriminations of judgment and unsettles the audience.

Anna Christie turns on a pivotal reversal in our perception of the morality of Chris's decision to leave his family and go to sea—an epiphany not shared by Chris himself. Toward the end of the first act, Chris explains to his twenty-year-old daughter Anna, whom he has not seen in fifteen years, why he never came home.

> Ay tank, after your mo'der die, ven Ay vas away on voyage, it's better for you you don't never see me!... Ay don't know, Anna, vhy Ay never come home Sveden in old year. Ay vant come home end of every voyage. Ay vant see your mo'der, your two bro'der before dey vas drowned, you ven you vas born-but-Ay-don't go. Ay sign on oder ships—go South America, go Australia, go China, go every port all over world many times—but Ay never go aboard ship sail for Sveden. Ven Ay gat money for pay passage home as passenger den—(*He bows his head guiltily*) Ay forgat and Ay spend all money. Ven Ay tank again, it's too late.... Ay don't know vhy but dat's vay with most sailor fallar, Anna. Dat ole davil sea make dem crazy fools with her dirty tricks. It's so.

In Act One Anna (and the audience) tends to judge Chris harshly, seeing his non-decision as a decision of passive weakness, of succumbing to immediate pleasure and evading responsibility for his faraway family. However, Chris's obvious happiness at seeing his daughter, his strong love for her, his desire to make amends and to care for her, and his blindness to the ravages of her ill-spent youth: these tone down Anna's (and the audience's) condemnation. She feels some sympathy as she sees Chris struggle with his guilt; later she feels superior as she witnesses his scruples, rationalizations and evasions. Nevertheless, Chris's own morality, the standard by which he secretly judges himself, calls for him to resist the sea, to prove his manhood and find redemption in a decisive moral commitment to his family. Only in such heroic rationality of purpose can he take charge of his life and shape his individual destiny. Consciously and publicly Chris excuses himself, saying, "Dat ole davil, sea, she make me Yonah man ain't no good for nobody." But unconsciously gnawing at him is that unspoken standard—the conventional standard by which the audience first tends to judge him—which causes him so much pain and guilt and reinforces other bad decisions.

Through the first of the three major versions of this play, *Chris Christophersen,* this is nearly as far as O'Neill got in his moral vision of men and women in relation to nature and to each other. The reversal occurs gradually as the audience becomes aware of the defect in Chris's morality. His superstitious rationalization of "dat ole davil, sea" to account for deep conflicting inner urges had also led him to believe that after her mother's death five-year-old Anna was better off inland with uncaring relatives than near him and the sea. Ironically this moral blindness to Anna's true interests also leads him to excuse Anna's faults. He accepts her unconditionally at the beginning and does not reject her towards the end when he discovers her scandalous past.

Chris's specious morality might pass for an acceptable standard except for Anna. The beginning of Act Two, ten days after her arrival, as Anna, *"healthy, transformed"* and *"with an expression of awed wonder,"* appears on the deck of the barge, *Simeon Winthrop,* hints that O'Neill is playing with a different, more complicated morality in Anna's discovery of the sea.

> It's like I'd come home after a long visit away some place. It all seems like I'd been here before lots of times-on boats-in this same fog. . . . But why d'you s'pose I feel so—so—like I'd found something I'd missed and been looking for—'s if this was the right place for me to fit in? . . . And I feel clean, some-how—like you feel yust after you've took a bath. And I feel happy for once—yes, honest!—happier than I have ever been anywhere before!

In *Beyond the Horizon* O'Neill had already suggested an elemental sense of belonging whether to the land or to the sea as an important variable of moral commitment. In *Anna Christie* he elaborates the moral wellsprings of belonging to some such external power, a mystical force, a totem, that brings man into unique relationship with the rhythms of the universe and the source of his being.

Anna and Chris belong to the sea by accidents of geography and genealogy. Raised in a small port town on the Swedish coast, Chris went to sea because there was nothing else for him to do. The sea is in his blood, bred into his and Anna's genes by generations of seafaring ancestors. All the men in Chris's village went to sea. Chris's own father, whom he hardly knew, died and was buried at sea, as were two of Chris's three older brothers and his two sons. The nature of the place where they were born provides only one opportunity to make a living, one outlet for growth, one direction along which the lines of their lives can be charted. In the end Anna comes to realize that she is united to the sea by the blood of generations, and that her true fulfillment can come only by accepting that rela-tionship and living it fully.

Anna has already taken the measure of Chris's morality and recognized her own more intuitive morality when Mat Burke, the shipwrecked sailor, rises like Proteus from the sea. Mat, the true "citi-zen of the sea," defines in his personality the complex morality of bringing his deepest natural urges into creative harmony with the external force of the sea. Mat identifies with the sea, sees himself as part of it, and boasts that his great physical strength as well as his strength of character issues from the sea. "And if 'twasn't for me and my great strength, I'm telling you—and it's God's truth—

there'd been mutiny itself in the stokehole." And a few lines later, "I'm a divil for sticking it out when them that's weak give up." With the appearance of Mat, Chris's more conventional morality of resist-ing the external pull of the sea gives way completely to a more perplexing intuitive belief in the vital force Mat shares with the sea. Anna responds to the vitality in Mat's nature and to his instinctive belief in the power he shares with the sea. Mat, in his turn, intuits the same cleanness and *élan vital* of the sea in Anna and is immediately drawn to her. The sea has brought them together and Mat sees that as his destiny. "I'm telling you there's the will of God in it that brought me safe through the storm and fog to the wan spot in the world where you was!"

Anna and Mat have known only abusive sexual relationships during their formative years, so they have serious handicaps to overcome. Seduced by her own cousin on the farm in Minnesota and driven to prostitution, Anna has been exploited by men since her tender years. Mat has known only the cheap waterfront prostitutes that prey on sailors. Both are contemptuous of and defensive toward the opposite sex; both inhabit limiting conventions of gender and project one stereotype after another on each other. Mat's perception of Anna ranges over the gamut of his imagination from angel to hooker to "fine decent girl" whose shoe-soles he is not fit to kiss and back to whore again. Finally he surren-ders to her as woman and, with her help, reconciles his role as husband to his vocation as sailor. Anna's reaction to Mat moves from resentment at his intru-sion on her idyll, to repulsion at his masculine presence, to contempt for his egotism, to repug-nance at his crude advances, to perplexity at his early passion and candor, to amusement at his boyish boasting, to admiration and love, to anger at his possessiveness and ultimately surrender to him and to her destiny as a sailor's wife. Both lovers move through the conventional stages of the roman-tic love plot of excitation, deferral, and release; but then the sea adds a further dimension of moral skepticism and uncertain possibility.

Just as Chris's very weakness prevents him in the end from doing worse damage to his daughter than he has already done, so Mat's egotism, which originally made impossible his acceptance of Anna's past, rescues him in the end. When Anna tells Mat that he is the first and only man she has ever loved—that not only did she not love all those other men who paid for sex but hated them—Mat finds a face-saving excuse that soothes his bruised ego. "If 'tis truth you're after telling, I'd have a right, maybe, to believe you'd changed—and that I'd changed you myself till the thing you'd been all your life wouldn't be you any more at all.'' Mat makes Anna swear this is true on a cross given him by his mother; but when he finds out Anna isn't Catholic, he concludes, ''If your oath is no proper oath at all, I'll have to be taking your naked word for it and have you anyway, I'm thinking—I'm needing you that bad!'' The love plot comes to its conventional close when Mat finds out that Anna is not just an ordinary pagan; she is ''wan of them others,'' a Lutheran. ''Luthers, is it? . . . Well, I'm damned then surely. Yerra, what's the difference? 'Tis the will of God, anyway.''

For the first three acts early audiences could respond to Anna as the stereotypical ''golden-hearted whore'' from nineteenth-century melodrama who nobly sacrifices her one chance to marry the man she loves by telling him the truth about her past. Those same audiences could respond to Mat as the conventional reformed womanizer, the sailor with a girl-in-every-port who is transformed by the love of a fallen but virtuous woman. However, the irresolution and ambiguity of the final act express an ambivalent vision of married life beyond the ''happy end'' of conventional drama, even modern drama (as opposed to postmodern drama).

As a story, the play is rich in poetry and colloquial dialogue; it is ironic and funny but not very interesting, with its stock characters and conflicts, until Chris and Mat fight for possession of Anna in Act Three. Chris tries to validate his claim to Anna as a loving father, genuinely (although mistakenly) concerned for her welfare in preventing her marriage to a ''no good fallar on sea.'' If one looked hard enough one might detect faintly incestuous undertones in Chris's not completely disinterested notions of making up for lost time with Anna. He tells Mat frankly, ''Ay don't vant for Anna get married. . . . Ay'm a ole man. Ay don't see Anna for fifteen year. She vas all Ay gat in vorld. And now ven she come on first trip—you tank Ay vant her leave me 'lone again?'' The rivalry Chris feels with Mat is paternal, not sexual; the domestic intimacy Chris yearns for is not sexual either. However, the quasi-incestuous insularity of Chris's overprotectiveness shares with Mat the romantic ideal of women as docile child-wives and men as paternal husbands. Mat feels entitled to Anna by the lover's imperative to free her from the obsolete bonds of her misguided father. When Anna refuses to marry Mat but will not give her reasons, Mat tries bullying her. ''I'm thinking you're the like of them women can't make up their mind till they're drove

to it. Well, then, I'll make up your mind for you bloody quick.'' In the ensuing argument, Mat tells Chris, ''She'll do what I say! You've had your hold on her long enough. It's my turn now.'' As the two men, even in the heat of their disagreement, slip easily into their common assumption about the social hierarchy and the sexual inequality of women, Anna herself looks on in disbelief.

> CHRIS (*Commandingly*) You don't do one tang he say, Anna! (*Anna laughs mockingly.*)
>
> BURKE She will, so!
>
> CHRIS Ay tal you she don't! Ay'm her fa'der.
>
> BURKE She will in spite of you. She's taking my orders from this out, not yours.

The dialogue exposes the underlying assumptions of woman's inferiority and her need to capitulate to man's whims and power. Chris and Mat may argue about whose orders Anna should take from here on out, but they agree that she should take orders from one of them.

The historical response to arranged marriages was a blend of passion and pragmatism in romantic wedlock that was raised to the level of cultural icon in the West by the late nineteenth century. This ideal of romantic marriage based on erotic love has persisted in the drama at least from the Renaissance well into the modern theatre. Novels, plays and films have increasingly touted the loving companionate marriage as necessary for personal and social well-being; and the sexual hierarchy within marriage thus becomes the foundation for a balanced social order. But encoded in the conventions of even the modern theatre's treatment of sexual relationships is the persistent notion of men and women as hierarchical opposites. Masked in the rhetoric of complementary halves, the modern theatre still portrays men and women as fundamentally opposite, instead of simply different, sexual beings needing each other for completion. Such mutually exclusive depictions of masculinity and femininity reinforce popular notions of dominance and subordination in a patriarchal hierarchy. Implicit in this pattern of thinking is the assumption that Anna, a grown woman, will pass normally from the father/child authority of Chris to the husband/wife-child domination of Mat. O'Neill evolves a devastating commentary on the ideological abuses underlying male/female relationships by making Anna herself draw attention to the sexual division that locks men and women into antagonistic roles without access to each other's subjective thoughts, feelings and needs. In this scene, Anna, refusing to be trapped any longer in Chris's and Mat's limiting social definitions of gender, rejects the role of subservient child-wife. ''Gawd,'' she says, ''you'd think I was a piece of furniture! . . . You was going on 's if one of you had got to own me. But nobody owns me, see?—'cepting myself.'' Then she proceeds to destroy all the other illusions the two men have about her by revealing her past prostitution. Everything in her past experience—even her rejection and humiliation in past encounters with men, and her subsequent acceptance by her father and love of Mat—all conspire to help Anna make the excruciatingly tough choice between individual identity and maritally prescribed role. She forces Mat and Chris to accept or reject her as she is, not filtered through the lenses of their popular misconceptions. Anna's repudiation of this role and her later redefinition of her relationships to both her father and her future husband expose the limitations of a socially determined identity, rooted in sexual differentiation, that too easily transforms the love relationship into a battle for mastery and possession. By this means O'Neill, following the lead of Shaw, opens a fissure in the prison wall of the deadlocked sexual ideology of marriage by suggesting, not a sexual hierarchical complementariness, but a more precarious balance between sexual equals.

As we will shortly see, O'Neill hit upon a structural device that would complement this perspectival innovation. But an advance glance at traditional marriage-plot structure will help to show that innovation's appropriateness.

Modern marriage plots, whether they focus on courtship or marital discord, have traditionally employed the same structural dynamics. Courtship plots commonly follow the pattern of attraction, opposition, and resolution ending in marriage. (Boy finds girl, boy loses girl, boy gets girl.) And marital discord plots confront the marriage partners with a series of internal and external obstacles that must be overcome before the partners can live ''happily every after.'' Of course that ideal stasis is not always achieved. Ibsen's *A Doll's House* creates an uneasy awareness of marital abuses; Strindberg's *The Father* complicates the pattern by reducing the institution of marriage to total war-to-the-death for mastery; and Pirandello's *Six Characters in Search of an Author,* emphasizing the ''locked'' condition of wedlock, proceeds to chart the psychological distance between the mismatched mates whose conflict can never be resolved because their author, lacking the imaginative capacity to ameliorate their impossible situation, abandoned them to the limbo of an unfinished work. However, whether the spe-

cific marriage is salvageable or not, the *institution* of marriage is still held up as an ideal. Even in apparent satires on the married state, it is individual weakness and not the gender-related issues of marriage per se that is questioned. O'Neill's very different agenda could not be accommodated within the thesis-antithesis-synthesis structure of the traditional, formulaic marriage trajectory. And the aforementioned solution, a device that O'Neill uses to notable effect, is the open-ended conclusion—a technique often utilized by modernist writers in response to the nineteenth century's modes of closure.

The open-ended text does not satisfactorily resolve the issues it poses, because ambiguity is part of its meaning; instead, it passes its tension on to the viewer or reader, who must actively respond to the disturbing questions left unsolved. The intended consequence is to unsettle the audience and make them critics of, rather than unwitting perpetuators of, the thinking implicit in the marriage plot convention. The viewer who unconsciously accepts such fictional representations as natural or unproblematic becomes a victim of the text's underlying ideology. This strategy deflects the viewer's attention from the seductive satisfaction of emotional release to the more painful contradiction of patriarchal marriage that the text of the play offers up for critique. Thus O'Neill's structural and perspectival techniques might be seen as a proto-postmodernist inquiry into the assumptions of the modern marriage plot.

Anna's problematic optimism at the end of the play illustrates a singularly postmodernist opening up of traditional concepts of marital identity roles. After the reconciliation of the three principals, Anna announces the astounding news that Mat and Chris have signed on to the same ship. She assures them that it is all right, that she will not be lonely, that being a sailor's wife runs in the family. ''I'll get a little house somewhere,'' she says, ''and I'll make a regular place for you two to come back to—wait and see.'' The three drink to their future together—Anna and Mat drink happily, but Chris is subdued. Soon Chris's gloom begins to infect Mat. ''It's funny,'' says Chris. ''It's queer, yes—you and me shipping on same boat dat vay. It ain't right. Ay don't know—it's dat funny vay ole davil sea do her vorst dirty tricks.'' When Mat concedes he may be right, Anna puts her arm around Mat and says ''*with determined gaiety,*'' ''Aw say, what's the matter? Cut out the gloom. We're all fixed now, ain't we, me and you? . . . Come on! Here's to the sea, no matter what! Be a game sport and drink to that!''

She and Mat defiantly drink her toast to the sea. Chris, however, has the last word. As the other two stare at him he mutters, ''Fog, fog, fog, all bloody time. You can't see vhere you vas going, no. Only dat ole davil, sea—she knows!''

On the surface, Anna's role as wife and daughter seems conventional enough by social and literary standards alike. This play is not an instance of wild but unessential gender role reversals, like Anna going to sea as a stoker while Mat stays home to care for the children. Rather, the socially prescribed gender roles are more subtly undermined, in their subordination to more important individual drives, and in their adaptation to meet the sometimes conflicting requirements of the newly emerged, tripartite psychic relationship. Both Chris and Mat perceive their love of the sea as a masculine trait: Chris as masculine weakness, Mat as masculine strength. In sharing her love of the sea with her men, Anna manifests the bisexuality C. G. Jung claims we all inhabit. Not only do men and women physiologically secrete both male and female hormones; they also share masculine and feminine psychological archetypes called the *animus* and the *anima*. Conditioned by the sex glands and chromosomes, these archetypes make it possible for us to understand and respond to members of the opposite sex: they exist in us at birth as a predisposition formed by the racial memory of ancestral experiences between the sexes. Man intuits something of the nature of woman through his *anima*; woman apprehends man through her *animus*. However, the *animus* and the *anima* may sow confusion if the archetypal image is projected onto the partner without perceiving the discrepancies between this ideal and the actual person, as Mat and Anna both did at first. Mat and Anna's gradual adjustment of the demands of their collective unconscious to the actualities of their individual differences is a process of sexual maturation.

In dismantling the traditional roles of wife and daughter, Anna has redesigned these roles to fit her own individual needs for personal fulfillment. By telling them the truth about herself, Anna has gambled and won; but her victory—a victory over self rather than the two men—is not a question of marital supremacy. It is victory of her own authentic relationship *to* the two men. However, the role that Anna assumes in playing out her own marriage drama must still take into consideration the relative blindness of Mat and Chris to their new roles. Out of this restructuring of marital roles along the lines of equality, mutual respect and affection, a tiny wedge

has been driven into their socially constructed identities based on sexual differentiation, and this validates the possibility of a happy ending.

O'Neill knew he had to give the play its happy ending. As he wrote in a letter to the *New York Times,*

> In the last few minutes of *Anna Christie* I tried to show the dramatic gathering of new forces out of the old. I wanted to have the audience leave with a deep feeling of life flowing on, of the past which is never the past—but always the birth of the future—of a problem solved for the moment but by the very nature of its solution involving a new problem. . . . It would have been so obvious and easy—in the case of this play, conventional even—to have made my last act a tragic one. It could have been done in ten different ways, any one of them superficially right. But looking deep into the hearts of my people, I saw it couldn't be done. It would not have been true. They were not that kind. They would act in just the silly, immature, compromising way that I have made them act; and I thought that they would appear to others as they do to me, a bit tragically humorous in their vacillating weakness.

However, instead of an ending with a sense of closure and consequent stasis about it, O'Neill made the text a living affair with a sense of life going on beyond the end. Yes, there will be life after marriage for Anna and Mat; but such happiness as they may find will only be achieved by the same kind of openness and good sense they have shown in getting this far. Writing in the *New York Times* on November 13, 1921, Alexander Woollcott summed up the dissatisfaction of the critics with the ambiguity of what they felt was a ''faint-hearted'' ending. ''It is,'' he wrote, ''a happy ending with the author's fingers crossed''—which is exactly the truth about marriage that the critics could not accept but which audiences applauded through a highly successful (for its day) Broadway run of 177 performances, a blockbuster road tour, numerous revivals, and several movie versions.

This play is only one example of how O'Neill took elements from his father's Victorian theatre, transmuted them in the modernist experimentations of his day, and plotted the direction for much of the postmodern drama that followed him. His innovations in dramatic form helped close the gap between life and plot. His example inspired others, like Arthur Miller in *After the Fall* and Edward Albee in *A Delicate Balance,* to explore married life beyond the traditional happy ending as a means of exposing myths of gender and enlarging the boundaries of the theatre.

Source: John V. Antush, ''Eugene O'Neill: Modern and Postmodern,'' in *Eugene O'Neill Review,* Vol. 13, No. 1, Spring 1990, pp. 14–25.

Winifred L. Frazer

In the following essay, Winifred Frazer looks at the influence the sea and the sea god, Poseidon, have on Anna Christie's *characters, their lives and fate.*

Eugene O'Neill, more than any other American playwright of his time, had a feeling for myth and its enactment in ritual and drama. Witness his use of masks, his recognition of the power of a syncopated drum beat, his understanding of Oedipal family relationships, his satirical outlook on man's worship of the machine rather than of his essential Dionysian or Appolonian nature, his intuitive feeling for choric responses, his clear portrayal of the life-God Eros and the death-God Thanatos in conflict and collusion, his worship of the earth mother, his awe of the primal father, his feeling for resurrection in both Biblical and pagan mythology, his sense of the timeless and the cyclic, and his comprehension of the rites of passage to manhood.

But perhaps Poseidon presided over his psyche more than any other God. As a young boy, in a widely reproduced photograph, he gazes winsomely to sea from his seat on a large rock near the O'Neill's New London waterfront home. And the last house the dying playwright owned was at Marblehead on the rocky Massachusetts coast, where the eye had a vast wide-angle view of the Atlantic Ocean and the ear was assaulted by the battering of the waves against the concrete sea wall below the house. In between, O'Neill lived on the sand dunes at the tip of Cape Cod in a remodeled Coast Guard Station which the waves eventually carried into the sea, and in a mansion-sized "cottage" on the Georgia coast at Sea Island, where the sea was murky and warm. His sea voyages in the years 1910 and 1911 to Argentina, Africa, and England affected him deeply. According to the Gelbs, he learned to stand watch on the highest yardarms and found it the most exalting experience of his life. Also, the only physical activity he seems to have enjoyed was swimming—which he could do for long distances far from shore in icy water.

O'Neill's effusions about the ocean are among the most lyrical in his plays. Paddy in *The Hairy Ape* remembers with a holy joy the clipper ship days when men who were sons of the sea sailed the ships, until sons, sea, and ship became one. And in *Long Day's Journey into Night* written two decades later, Edmund can hardly find words to express his ecstasy: "I became drunk with the beauty and singing rhythm

Greta Garbo and Clarence Brown in a scene from the 1930 film adaptation of Anna Christie.

of it [the ship on the sea], and for a moment I lost myself—actually lost my life. I was set free! I dissolved in the sea. . . ." Swimming in the sea was also a religious experience: "When I was swimming far out . . . I had the same experience. . . . Like a saint's vision of beatitude." And O'Neill at one time had expected "the grand opus" of his life to be an autobiographical play called *Sea-Mother's Son.*

To the Greeks, Poseidon, the God of the Sea, and brother of Zeus, was second only in importance to this God of Gods. A sea-faring people honored Poseidon by a great temple at Sunion, the rocky cape at the tip of the coast, south of Athens. The Earth-Shaker could calm the waves by riding upon them in his golden car, and in his three-pronged trident lay the power to shatter cities. This Bull-God secretly fathered Theseus, who had a special feeling for coming earthquakes created by his God-father. Poseidon, at Theseus' command, destroyed the falsely accused Hippolytus as he drove his chariot along the rocky coast of Greece. God of salt waters and of fresh, Poseidon contended with other Gods for domains of earth, could send sea-monsters and tidal waves inland, and was a power to be reckoned with by all the peoples of the Aegean.

> " TO A SEA-FARING MAN LIKE CHRIS CHRISTOPHERSON, THE GOD OF THE WATERS IS THE POWER THAT RULES HIS LIFE. BELIEVING IT DEVILISH, STILL HE IS UNABLE TO KEEP AWAY FROM THE SEA."

To a sea-faring man like Chris Christopherson, the God of the waters is the power that rules his life. Believing it devilish, still he is unable to keep away from the sea. Claiming that carrying coal on a barge between New York and Boston is not a sea job, nevertheless he is upon the waters. And further emphasizing his paradoxical attitude, he extols life on the barge for its sun, fresh air, good food, moonlight, and beautiful sights of passing schooners under sail, while in almost the same breath cursing the sea. O'Neill himself, in "Ballard [*sic*] of the Seamy Side," written after his sea voyages, complains about the hardships of a sailor's life, but makes the refrain of each stanza: "They're part of the game and I loved it all." And in *The Iceman Cometh* the derelicts are sunk in a Bottom-of-the-Sea Rathskellar, which is also a haven. The Gods change form also in *The Great God Brown*. The Dionysian part of Dion Anthony becomes continually more sneering and Mephistophelian, while the Christian part becomes more strained, tortured, and ascetic.

But the Fate which the Gods mete out is inevitable. Larry, the bartender, in the play's opening scene, listens skeptically to Chris's denunciation of the sea and his tale of protecting his daughter from its malevolent influence through her inland upbringing. "This girl, now," he prophesies, "'ll be marryin' a sailor herself, likely. It's in the blood." Generations of sea-faring men cannot produce a daughter who is not attracted to it. As surely as the Mannons are cursed by their Fate as New England Puritans, so are the Christophersons by the Sea. Chris's ardent hope that Anna will marry some "good, steady land fallar here in East" is obviously not in the cards. In fact Chris himself belies the wish by singing in expectation of that happy event. "My Yosephine, come board the ship,"—a most unlikely song for a "land fallar."

When Anna enters, she intimates that the open sea is the world for her by revealing that she "never could stand being caged up nowheres." The Fate of the characters is thus exposed in the opening scene, and as in Greek tragedy, the play consists of its unfolding. Old Marthy, in spite of her admiration for Chris, does agree that he is nutty on the one point of avoiding the sea and bursts into "hoarse, ironical laughter" when she learns that it is living on a farm that has made Anna a prostitute. But when Chris later learns the truth, far from seeing the irony, *he* attributes her fall in some mysterious way to the old devil sea. And he is perhaps not far wrong, for although she first exclaims, "Me? On a dirty coal barge! What do you think I am?" and Larry also exclaims, "On a coal barge! She'll not like that, I'm thinkin'" still it turns out that Anna experiences a magical transformation under the Sea God's spell.

> It's like I'd come home after a long visit away some place. It all seems like I'd been here before lots of times—on boats.... I feel so—so—like I'd found something I'd missed and been looking for—'s if this was the right place for me to fit in.... I feel clean.... And I feel happy for once. (II)

Chris has forebodings, but Anna chides him for his fear that he is a fool for having brought her on the voyage and comments satirically that whatever happens is God's will. Chris "starts to his feet with fierce protests," shouting, "Dat ole davil sea, she ain't God."

But Chris is unavailing against Poseidon's potency, for at that moment, with the full irony of Fate, an incarnation of the Sea God arises out of the fog to board the barge. Michelangelo couldn't have portrayed him better. Mat Burke, dressed in nothing but a pair of dungarees, is a "powerful, broad-chested six-footer, ... in the full power of his heavy-muscled, immense strength." He is "handsome in a hard, rough, bold, defiant way," and "the muscles of his arms and shoulders are lumped in knots and bunches." Like Poseidon, he is not backward about proclaiming his strength. With scorn for the other sailors who went out of their minds with fear and weakness, he tells Anna that they would all be at the bottom of the sea except for "the great strength and guts is in me." When one storm after another raked the seas over the leaking ship from bow to stern, he alone prevented mutiny in the stokehole. By a "kick to wan and a clout to another," which they feared more than the sea itself, he kept the men going beyond human endurance. Now, in spite of going without food and water for two days and two nights and rowing continuously with the others lying in the lifeboat, Mat boasts, "I can lick all hands on this tub, wan by wan, tired as I am!'' (II) Mortal man could hardly fit the role of the Earth-Shaker better than Mat Burke.

Anna, he first thinks, is ''some mermaid out of the sea,'' and later a Goddess, whose ''fine yellow hair is like a golden crown on your head,'' but in either case, he was destined to find her: ''I'm telling you there's the will of God in it that brought me safe through the storm and fog to the wan spot in the world where you was!'' In spite of having been placed in the wilderness to die, Oedipus meets Laius at the appointed crossroads. Anna's inland upbringing does not thwart her predistined encounter with Mat. Admitting to a ''bit of the sea'' in her blood, which Mat senses, Anna announces with some pride that all the men in her family have been sailors and that all the women have married sailors too. Mat's response is fervent: ''It's only on the sea you'd find rale men with guts is fit to wed with fine, high-tempered girls the like of yourself.'' Chris hears words of courtship with open-mouthed desperation. Then recognizing his old antagonist, he shakes his fist with hatred at the sea, and illustrating the dramatic irony of man pitted against the Gods, swears, ''Damn your dirty trick, damn ole davil, you! But py God, you don't do dat! Not while Ay'm living!'' (II) Anna, fathered by generations of sea men, can not be reclaimed by the land. ''Digging spuds in the muck from dawn to dark,'' Mat and Anna agree, is for the sodden in spirit. It is not a fruits-of-the-vineyard God which they worship, but the uncontrolled, violent, yet clean, God Poseidon. The same is true of Chris in reality. He had become sick in a land job and had had to go back to the ''open air'' of the sea to regain his health.

Criticism of the play has been that it is Chris's play through the first two and a half acts and Anna's and Mat's play thereafter, that Mat Burke is a somewhat comic Irishman, and that the ending is a happy one, which distorts the theme of the inevitable fate of those who live on and by the sea, which Synge so well shows in *Riders to the Sea*. But in spite of its critics, *Anna Christie* survives as a popular play (and musical and movie). Perhaps, looked at in the light of Greek myth, it has a unity which it seems to lack if viewed merely as a naturalistic American drama.

Acts II, III, and IV take place on the barge at sea, where actors and audience feel surrounded by this salty medium in the breeze, the fog, and the sounds of steamers and fog-horns. Mat emerges from the Sea itself, and if he is seen as an Irish

Poseidon, he holds together the theme of the old devil sea as fate and the theme of Anna's rejuvenation by sea and love. And after all, there is a good bit that is comic about the Gods—at least Aristophanes thought so—and many a playwright has regaled us with the tale of Zeus and Amphitryon. So the fact that O'Neill's God speaks with an Irish lilt—''Isn't it myself the sea has nearly drowned . . . and never a groan out of me till the sea gave up and it seeing the great strength and guts of a man was in me'' (III) should not mean he is not to be taken seriously. Like Zeus in the form of Amphitryon, or Poseidon when he came to Theseus' mother in a sea cove, Mat is determined to father heroes. What you are ''needing in your family,'' he tells Chris, is a man like himself, ''so that you'll not be having grandchildren would be fearful cowards and jackasses the like of yourself.'' (III) Anna does become the central figure in the second half of the play, fought over ''like a piece of furniture'' by Chris and Mat and there is considerable humor in Mat's dismay that she, ''wan of the others,'' has taken an oath upon his sacred Catholic crucifix. Emphasis on the young characters, however, does not lessen the importance of Chris, whose happiness depends upon his daughter's welfare. Chris suffers the tragic effect of her revelation that she has been a prostitute. It is he who comes to a self-understanding (admittedly not of the soul-shaking proportions of the Greek hero) that he has not avoided the fate of the Christophersons.

As for the happy ending—Act IV closes, like Acts II and III, with Chris cursing that ''ole davil, sea.'' And his foreboding words, with which Mat agrees, ''I'm fearing maybe you have the right of it for once, divil take you'' seem more like the ''comma'' with which O'Neill said he intended to close than a period declaring a happy marriage for Anna and Mat. Anna has so confounded her father and suitor by the story of her past that they have stumbled ashore for a two-day orgy with the God Dionysius. She has been tempted to leave for New York, but the sea has pulled her back—its power and cleansing effect an antidote to her misery. It has also had its effect on the men: Chris, having decided that he is a no-good ''Yonah'' has offered himself as a propitiating sacrifice by signing on as bosun of the *Londonderry,* a steamer sailing next day for Cape Town, half a world away, whereas Mat has unknowingly signed on the same ship as stoker— thus leaving Anna alone again.

Added to the presentiment of the play's last lines—''Fog, fog, fog, all bloody time. You can't see where you vas going, no. Only dat ole davil, sea—she knows!''—is the ''muffled, mournful wail of steamers' whistles.'' (IV) It is a sombre mood on which the curtain falls. The fact that Mat and Anna seem momentarily destined for happiness does not make them less dependent on whatever fate the God Poseidon metes out to them. O'Neill knew that Driscoll, the stoker on whom he had modeled Mat and Yank in *The Hairy Ape,* had drowned himself at sea. And the original Chris had drowned by falling between the piles of the dock one night on his way to the barge. Just as Poseidon sent his sea-son Mat Burke out of the depths into Anna's life, so he will remove him and Chris from it according to his will. As in the Greek dramatic trilogies, no more than a comma is needed at the end to indicate the inevitably tragic continuation of the story of a House.

In *Anna Christie* it makes no difference whether one is Swedish or Irish, Lutheran or Catholic, bosun or stoker, if he goes to the sea in ships, Poseidon controls his life. Since the early version called *Chris* was on a road tryout in early 1920, at the same time that *Beyond the Horizon* was on trial in New York, O'Neill must have concluded that neither the land, which ruins Robert Mayo, nor the sea, which ruins Chris, bestows favors on human kind, and Anna seems destined for destruction by both. In plays like *Bound East for Cardiff, The Long Voyage Home, Ile,* and *The Hairy Ape,* the characters, although buffeted or ruined by the sea, do not blame their fate upon it. And it has been claimed that Chris uses the sea as a scapegoat for his own irresponsibility. But if, as Thomas Mann says, myth is ''the pious formula'' into which human traits flow from the unconscious, then Poseidon is as real as the psyche in determining man's fate. Whatever defect *Anna Christie* may seem to have because of Mat's overpowering presence in the last part of it is countered by his being an agent of the same powerful God who rules the Christophersons.

Source: Winifred L. Frazer, ''Chris and Poseidon: Man Versus God in *Anna Christie,*'' in *Modern Drama,* Vol. 12, No. 3, December 1969, pp. 279–85.

Frederick Ives Carpenter

In the following excerpt, Frederick Carpenter theorizes on Anna Christie*'s popularity despite its flaws and suggests that its acclaim comes from its genuine mix of comedy and tragedy.*

Anna Christie, produced exactly one year after *The Emperor Jones,* proved almost as popular. It was enthusiastically reviewed, and it ran for 117 performances, and it won for its author his second Pulitzer Prize. It was quickly made into a silent movie, and in 1929 was remade into a ''talkie,'' with Greta Garbo in the title role. Thirty-three years later a large jury of film critics at the Seattle World's Fair voted this one of the fourteen best motion pictures ever produced in America. And this cinematic excellence suggests a reason for the play's popularity: it is one of the most perfectly romantic of O'Neill's early works. But the fact that both *Beyond the Horizon* and *Anna Christie* won Pulitzer Prizes, while two much better plays of the same period—*The Emperor Jones* and *Desire Under the Elms*—were passed by, suggests an ironic commentary on official taste.

In spite of its popularity *Anna Christie* suffers from obvious faults, which were emphasized by George Jean Nathan before the play was produced. Written by fits and starts, it lacked unity. Two years before final production an earlier version had been tried out in Atlantic City under the title of *Chris.* In this play the character of Anna's father had dominated, while both Anna and her lover remained minor. After several attempts at revision, O'Neill finally withdrew the early play, and later rewrote it with a newly conceived Anna in the title role. But in the process the center of action had shifted, the characters had changed, and the ending had become doubtful. Popular critics, of course, were delighted to find an O'Neill play that seemed to end happily. But many condemned its ''sentimentalism,'' and O'Neill, after several attempts to defend it, finally decided against the play. In 1932 he stipulated that it must not be included in the selection of his best *Nine Plays.*

The main plot describes the conflict of Chris Christopherson, the captain of a small barge, and his daughter Anna. He has tried to protect her from ''dat ole davil, sea,'' by having her brought up by cousins far inland in Minnesota. But, unknown to him, one of these cousins has seduced her, and she has drifted into prostitution. Now she visits him in New York for the first time, and he sees with dismay that she loves the sea. He tries bitterly to prevent this love and also her love for a young Irish sailor, Mat Burke. Finally she tells him the truth about her own past, and he reacts by getting drunk and signing on an ocean-going ship. Like his prototype, the ''square-'ead'' Olson of the *S. S. Glencairn,* he succumbs to his destiny as homeless child of the sea.

Meanwhile the sub-plot describes the love affair of Anna and Mat Burke, the sailor. Immediately attracted to him, she nevertheless realizes that he may cease to love her if he learns about her past. But she forces herself to tell him, as well as her father, declaring that she has never really loved anyone before him. He also reacts by getting drunk and signing (by chance) on the same ship as her father. But, when Mat finally returns to confront her again, he becomes convinced of her true love. At the conclusion they go off to marry, knowing that on the next day he must leave on "the long voyage" away from home. Love triumphs, but the future remains bleak.

The character of Chris, "childishly self-willed and weak, of an obstinate kindliness," is one of O'Neill's minor triumphs. Without any understanding of himself and without any realistic love or responsibility for this daughter whom he has never seen for fifteen years, he yet imagines that merely by shielding her from the sea he can protect her. In his "obstinate kindliness" he seems the perfect foil for the earlier "emperor" Jones, with his equally obstinate worldliness. But the character of Mat Burke, at the other extreme, is that of a romantic Irishman whose primitive innocence and blind love for Anna never seem quite credible. The romantic unreality of Mat weakens the play.

Between the realistic Chris and the unrealistic Mat stands Anna Christie. Unlike Chris, her character had developed very slowly in O'Neill's imagination; but, unlike that of Mat, it is now fully realized. Its complexity foreshadows the later characters of O'Neill's major plays, who seem both realistic and archetypal. Moreover, Anna is that typical figure of modern literature—the prostitute with a heart of gold. She possesses a clear intelligence which sees through the childish illusions of her father, and a perfect integrity which will not let her deceive her lover. Like Dostoevski's ideal prostitute in *Crime and Punishment,* Anna seems to stand above the sordid world and to become an instrument for its salvation. Also like Dostoevski's heroine, she has been called "sentimental." Why should a girl so pure in heart have taken to prostitution in the first place?

The character of Anna is crucial. She is drawn from life, but is larger than life. Like Dostoevski, O'Neill knew his prostitutes: her speech and her mannerisms are wholly convincing. And the actual details of her regeneration from the effects of her past are copied from letters of the former mistress of O'Neill's best friend, Terry Carlin. But beyond this, the deeper motivation of Anna's prostitution is derived from O'Neill's own psychological experi-

ence. Her childhood neglect by her father, her loneliness in alien surroundings, her seduction by a relative, and her drifting into prostitution—all reflect O'Neill's own feeling of desertion by his own parents, his loneliness at boarding school, the influence of his own brother, and the resulting profligacy of his own youth. The central theme of the play is the irresponsibility of Anna's father, which for a time drove the heroine into prostitution, but it did not destroy her.

Like the character of Anna, the ending of the play has been criticized for its mixed nature. It is not tragic, but it is true to life. Replying to criticism, O'Neill wrote: "It would have been so obvious and easy . . . to have made my last act a tragic one. It could have been done in ten different ways. . . . But looking deep into the hearts of my people, I saw that . . . they would act in just the silly, immature, compromising way that I have made them act." The play is not a tragedy, and should not be damned for its "failure" as one. Like the later *Strange Interlude,* it is a serious study of modern life, which dramatizes that mixture of comedy and tragedy most characteristic of life. Even for O'Neill, life was not always pure tragedy.

The apparent confusion and destiny of *Anna Christie* may be resolved by considering it as a serious romantic drama of character. The three central characters are all children of the sea, and each grows to understand and to accept his destiny. Anna has not only become regenerated by the sea, but has learned to accept her own past. Chris has stopped fighting the sea, and mutely accepts Anna's final assurance: "It's all right, Mat. That's where he belongs." And Mat agrees: "'Tis the will of God, anyway." At the end they all drink: "Here's to the sea, no matter what!" Obviously none of them is happy, and none expects happiness. Chris exclaims at the end: ''Fog, fog, fog, all bloody time!'' But they remain true to their inner natures, and they at last ''belong.''

Source: Frederick Ives Carpenter, ''The Early Plays: Romance,'' in *Eugene O'Neill,* Twayne Publishers, 1964, pp. 93–96.

SOURCES

Bogard, Travis, *Contour in Time: The Plays of Eugene O'Neill,* Oxford University Press, 1972.

Boyd, Ernest, Review in *Freeman,* Vol. 4, December 7, 1921, p. 304.

Carpenter, Frederic I., ''Chapter 3: The Early Plays: Romance,'' in *Twayne's United States Authors Series Online,* G. K. Hall, 1999.

Gassner, John, ''Eugene O'Neill,'' in *American Writers,* Vol. 3, Scribner's, 1974, pp. 385–408.

Hammond, Percy, Review in the New York *Tribune,* November 3, 1921.

Jensen, George H., ''Eugene O'Neill,'' in *Dictionary of Literary Biography, Volume 7: Twentieth-Century American Dramatists,* edited by John MacNicholas, Gale Research Inc., 1981, pp. 139–65.

Marsh, Leo, Review in the New York *Telegraph,* November 3, 1921.

Pollock, Arthur, Review in *Eagle,* November 3, 1921.

Review in the New York *Sun,* November 3, 1921.

Torres, H. Z., Review in the New York *Commercial,* November 3, 1921.

Towse, J. Ranken, Review in the New York *Post,* November 3, 1921.

Whittaker, James, Review in the New York *News,* November 13, 1921.

FURTHER READING

Hackett, Francis, Review in *The New Republic,* November 30, 1921, p. 20.
    This review focuses on the play's style and its mixture of ''pathos and romance.''

Macgowan, Kenneth, Review in the New York *Globe,* November 3, 1921.
    Macgowan comments on the style and structure of the play in this opening night review.

Mantle, Burns, Review in the New York *Mail,* November 3, 1921.
    This reviewer analyzes the play's realism.

Biloxi Blues

NEIL SIMON
1985

Biloxi Blues was the twenty-first play by Neil Simon to reach the Broadway stage in twenty-four years. In the 1980s, the author, already an established comedic playwright, turned to his own life for inspiration and produced a trilogy of semi-autobiographical plays. He first introduced Eugene Morris Jerome, the hero of *Biloxi Blues,* in the widely acclaimed *Brighton Beach Memoirs.* That play depicted Eugene's close-knit Brooklyn Jewish family, as seen through Eugene's diary entries. In *Biloxi Blues* Simon follows Eugene as he gets sent to army training camp in Biloxi, Mississippi. There, the naïve Eugene, who has never before left home, is forced to confront difficult issues and his own reactions to them. These experiences inform his development as a writer.

Biloxi Blues was a Broadway hit. Not only was it honored with a Tony Award for the best play of 1985, but also audiences warmed to the humor that filled each scene, indeed, almost every line. Critics noted that Simon, as he had done so many times previously, was able to draw his audience together with his relatively simple words. Despite the strongly comedic bent, the play also holds a more serious message as Eugene comes to learn about the wide world around him. More importantly, for Eugene's personal development and his development as a writer, he comes to learn what his place in the world can, and should, be.

AUTHOR BIOGRAPHY

Neil Simon (full name Marvin Neil Simon) was born on July 4, 1927, in the Bronx, New York City. He grew up there and made it the setting for nearly all of his plays. *Brighton Beach Memoirs,* the first in the trilogy that includes *Biloxi Blues,* is a semi-autobiographical rendering of his childhood.

When he was 16, Simon graduated from DeWitt Clinton High School. Shortly thereafter, he entered New York University under the U.S. Army Air Force Reserve Training Program. He eventually attained the rank of corporal. In 1945, he was sent to Colorado on active duty. While there, he attended the University of Denver.

In 1946, the same year that he was discharged from service, Simon went to work for Warner Brothers in New York, where his older brother Danny also worked. He and Danny teamed up to write comedy sketches for the radio star Goodman Ace. In the 1950s, the Simons began to work for television programs. They wrote for famous personalities such as Sid Caesar, Phil Silvers, and Jackie Gleason. Collaboratively, they also wrote sketches for camp shows. Some of these sketches were later adapted as a stage play and contributed material to a stage musical.

In 1956, Danny left the Simon team to work as a television director. Neil continued to write for television for five more years. Eventually, he tired of the medium. In 1961, his first play, *Come Blow Your Horn,* became a hit, running on Broadway for eighty-four weeks. His second play, *Barefoot in the Park,* ran for over 1,500 performances on Broadway.

Since these initial successes, Simon has been a mainstay of the theater scene. Most of his plays draw on his New York background and focus on familial relations and domestic concerns. Simon also established his own Neil Simon Theater.

In the early 1980s *Brighton Beach Memoirs* introduced Simon's alter ego, Eugene. In 1985, Simon followed up this effort with *Biloxi Blues,* the second play in the trilogy that culminated in *Broadway Bound. Biloxi Blues* was Simon's twenty-first play to appear on Broadway in twenty-four years. It won Simon his first Tony Award for best drama. In the years since, Simon has continued to write plays for Broadway, and he has averaged a new comedy every theatrical season.

Simon has also written many popular films. These include screen adaptations of many of his own popular plays, including *Barefoot in the Park, The Odd Couple,* and *The Sunshine Boys.* Original screenplays include *Murder by Death* and *The Goodbye Girl.*

PLOT SUMMARY

Act 1

Act 1 of *Biloxi Blues* opens on the coach of an old railroad train. It is 1943, and inside the coach are five soldiers, new recruits from the Northeast, who are being transferred to boot camp in Biloxi, Mississippi. After basic training, they will be sent to fight in World War II. The soldiers are grumbling, unhappy, and apprehensive about what the future holds.

The new recruits arrive at the camp and enter their barracks. Almost right away, Sergeant Toomey, who is in charge of their company, comes in. He begins harassing the soldiers, who have not received army training and do not act appropriately. The privates immediately begin to learn how Sergeant Toomey's army works. He punishes randomly and unfairly. He stirs dissent among the privates by making everyone but Eugene do push-ups. Early on, Arnold emerges as the rebel. He refuses to eat the food served at the mess hall, although he knows he will be punished.

One evening, Eugene proposes that each soldier share his fantasy of what he would do if he only had a week to live. They each contribute five dollars, and Eugene chooses the winner. Eugene selects Arnold's fantasy as the best—making Sergeant Toomey do two hundred push-ups in front of the platoon. However, the privates argue about whose fantasy is the best. Wykowski makes derogatory comments about Jews. Arnold refuses to allow Wykowski to talk that way. As the two men are about to fight, Sergeant Toomey comes in and breaks it up. He says he will tolerate no racial slurs. After he is gone, Eugene feels badly because he didn't stand up for Arnold, a fellow Jew.

In the next scene, the soldiers are about to go on a forty-eight-hour leave. Wykowski realizes that somebody has stolen all his money from his wallet. He declares that Arnold is the thief. Toomey comes into the barracks and demands that the thief step forward, or no one will be allowed off the camp. Arnold takes sixty-two dollars out of his wallet. Toomey asks why Arnold decided to return the money knowing that he could be severely punished. Then Toomey tells the privates that it was *he* who stole the money, not Arnold. He wanted to teach Wykowski a lesson about not leaving valuables around to tempt his fellow soldiers. Because Arnold confessed to a crime he did not commit, however, he is confined to barracks. The other soldiers don't understand why Arnold ''confessed.'' Arnold explains that he would have been punished anyway, because Toomey is trying to break his spirit. Wykowski appreciates that Arnold stuck his neck out for the platoon. Eugene admires Arnold for his principles, but Arnold tells Eugene that he needs to stop being a spectator and get involved in what is going on around him.

Act 2

On their leave, the other soldiers visit a prostitute, Rowena. Wykowski spends half an hour with her. Selridge is only with her for a minute or so. Carney decides to stay faithful to his girlfriend. A nervous Eugene chats with her and then goes on to lose his virginity to her.

Meanwhile, the other privates have returned to the barracks, where they have discovered Eugene's journal and are reading it aloud. They learn Eugene's private thoughts about them—that Carney is not to be trusted, that Selridge calls out his mother's name in his sleep, and that Wykowski is ''pure animal but will likely win a Medal of Honor.'' When Eugene returns, they do not tell him they have his notebook, but he quickly realizes that it is missing. Wykowski begins reading from the journal. Eventually, the notebook comes to Arnold, whom Eugene begs not to read it. Arnold does, however, and discovers that although Eugene has a high regard for Arnold, he believes he is gay, and that makes him uncomfortable.

In the next scene, Toomey comes into the barracks in the middle of the night and wakes everyone up. He reports that two soldiers were caught in a sexual act in the latrine, but that one escaped through the window. Toomey wants the guilty party to step forward. When no one does, he suspends everyone's base privileges and weekend leave. The soldiers all believe that the other man was Arnold, and for the first time, Eugene learns the power of the written word. The next morning, however, Toomey announces that he has learned the other man's name, James Hennesey. The private faces up to five years in army prison.

Neil Simon

Soon thereafter, Eugene goes on his quest to find a girl to fall in love with. At a USO dance, he meets Daisy and falls for her. She attends a local Catholic school. Eugene declares his intention of writing her.

Meanwhile, at the camp, Toomey is getting drunk, because he is being sent to the Veterans Hospital the next day. He calls for Arnold and tells him he would like to turn him into a disciplined soldier. To do so, Toomey holds a loaded gun on Arnold and forces Arnold to take it from him. Then Toomey has Arnold call in the platoon to charge Toomey before witnesses with threatening the life of an enlisted man. Toomey seems determined that Arnold will turn him in, but accepts Arnold's offer of dropping the charges in exchange for Toomey's completing two hundred push-ups.

The next day, a man whom Eugene refers to as sane, logical, and decent replaces Toomey. Eugene continues corresponding and visiting with Daisy. On their last date, before he ships out overseas, he tells her that he loves her and kisses her for the first time. As the play ends, the soldiers are again aboard a train, and they are talking about Hennesey, who only got three months in jail and then will be dishonorably discharged. At the conclusion of the play, Eugene shares the fates of his bunkmates with the audience: Selridge became a sergeant and trained new recruits at Biloxi; Wykowski lost a leg in battle but was cited for outstanding courage; after six months of enemy attack, Carney was hospitalized for severe depression; Arnold was listed as missing in action; and Daisy married a Jewish doctor. As for Eugene, he hurt his back on his first day in England and served out the war as a reporter for the army publication *Stars and Stripes*.

CHARACTERS

Donald Carney

Don Carney is a private from New Jersey. He mistakenly thinks of himself as a crooner and irritates his bunkmates with his singing. Eugene, the narrator of the play, believes that Carney's most noteworthy trait is his indecisiveness. Because of this, Eugene does not entirely trust him.

Arnold Epstein

Arnold Epstein is a Jew from New York. He has a sensitive mind and an equally sensitive stomach. He is well read and intelligent. He feels he does not belong in the army, and he refuses to allow his spirit to be broken by Sergeant Toomey. Instead, Arnold rebels; for example, he refuses to eat food from the mess hall even though it means days of latrine duty. He shows himself to be responsible to a higher moral calling by taking the blame for the theft of Wykowski's money so that the other soldiers can go on leave. Eugene admires Arnold's steadfastness and his pursuit of truth and justice. Of all the soldiers, Arnold is able to keep calm, despite the problems presented by camp life and his fellow recruits.

Daisy Hannigan

Eugene meets Daisy at a USO dance. She attends a local Catholic school. They only meet again twice, yet they declare their love for one another right before Eugene ships out. They never see each other again, but Eugene learns that Daisy ends up marrying a Jew.

James Hennesey

James Hennesey is a private in the platoon. He forces Wykowski to reveal his prejudice by claiming to be part African American. At the end of the play, Hennesey's participation in a homosexual act is revealed. He is sent to prison for three months, after which he will be given a dishonorable discharge.

Eugene Morris Jerome

Eugene is the narrator of the play. He is from Brooklyn, New York, and his army experience represents his first time away from home. He is Jewish. He has three goals for the war: he wants to become a writer, not get killed, and lose his virginity. All his actions during training are focused on the achievement of these goals. As part of becoming a writer, Eugene keeps a journal in which he records his thoughts. This habit suggests that Eugene is more interested in observing what goes on around him than in participating in it. Eugene recognizes this fact; for example, he chastises himself for not standing up for Arnold when Wykowski harasses him for being Jewish. Eugene's eventual army assignment—as a journalist for an army publication—also reinforces the way that Eugene interacts with the world—writing about it instead of being someone who makes things happen.

Kowski

See Joseph Wykowski.

Rowena

Rowena is the prostitute to whom Eugene loses his virginity. She gives Eugene a "freebie," and he is greatly disappointed when he returns, and she does not even remember him.

Roy Selridge

Roy Selridge is a private from New York who demonstrates little unique personality. Instead, he follows Wykowski's lead.

Sergeant Merwin J. Toomey

Sergeant Toomey is the company's sadistic leader. He often hands out grueling and unpleasant punishments for mild infractions. He constantly tests the soldiers and tries to teach them hard lessons; in one instance he steals Wykowski's money. Toomey dislikes Arnold's questioning the army's authority and his refusal to follow orders. Toomey's most important goals are to break Arnold's spirit and to make a real soldier of him. Toomey is relieved of his duties before the ten-week training is up and sent to a veteran's hospital.

Joseph Wykowski

Joseph Wykowski (also called Kowski) is a private from Connecticut. Wykowski is a belligerent loudmouth who is prone to arguing, fighting, and bragging. Because he is the most aggressive of the privates, he becomes the company's unofficial spokesperson. However, he does not represent all the men, for he is prejudiced, casting aspersions on Jews—including his bunkmates—as well as African Americans. Wykowski is a bully and a ringleader; for example, he is the man who encourages the reading of Eugene's diary despite objections from others.

MEDIA ADAPTATIONS

- *Biloxi Blues* was adapted as a film with the same name by Ray Stark. Neil Simon wrote the screenplay and Mike Nichols directed. The film is available from MCA Home Video.

THEMES

Prejudice and Anti-Semitism

One of the most important themes in the play is prejudice. Many of the characters show prejudice toward other groups of people. Wykowski is the most obvious, openly expressing his derogatory feelings toward Jews and African Americans. His prejudice toward Jews is more obvious as Jewish soldiers are in the company, providing Wykowski with an outlet for his feelings. By contrast, in the early 1940s, white and African-American soldiers were segregated, thus there are no African-American privates to incite racial slurs. A brief dialogue points out the segregation of the U.S. military as well as some of the feelings of the privates about it. When Hennesey claims to be "Half mick, half nigger," Selridge protests, "You can't be colored. They wouldn't let you in with us." Wykowski, on the other hand, rushes to this opportunity, "... I guessed it. It was something I couldn't put my finger on but I knew something was wrong with you." Only then does Hennesey reveal that his statement was only a lie to find out Wykowski's true feelings.

Anti-Semitism, on the other hand, haunts the play. Wykowski subscribes to the stereotypes that surround Jews. When Arnold wins Eugene's "fantasy" game, and thus the prize money, Wykowski responds, "It never fails. It's always the Jews who end up with the money." Wykowski asserts that his name-calling doesn't matter. As he tells Hennesey, "Where I come from we're all polacks, dagos, niggers and sheenies. That stuff doesn't mean crap to me. You're a mick, what do I care?" Other army personnel also demonstrate prejudice. The soldiers who refuse to flush the toilets that Arnold has just scrubbed call him a "New York Jew Kike."

However, Eugene is also guilty of prejudice. He reveals—though privately—his doubts about Arnold in his notebook. Although Eugene holds Arnold in extremely high regard—calling him "the most complex and fascinating man I've ever met"—he also is wary of his fellow soldier because he thinks Arnold is gay.

Ironically, the sadistic Toomey demands that his men not express their prejudice while he himself uses stereotypes. He tells the company, "If I hear any more racial slurs from this platoon, some dumb bastard is going to be shoveling cow s—t. . . . Especially if I hear it from a Polack!"

Jewishness

Simon portrays the otherness of Jews in predominantly Christian-American society. In Arnold Epstein, Simon has created a character who fits a common American stereotype of a Jew. Arnold is an intellectual from New York City. He is physically weak and prone to illness. He bemoans his digestion, his health, and the food that is served. The other members of the company, those who do not show open anti-Semitism, demonstrate their lack of familiarity with Jews. As Selridge points out, "I never met a Jew before the army." This statement emphasizes the true minority status of the American Jew.

Military Life

Military life in *Biloxi Blues* is presented in a largely comedic manner; its difficulties are exaggerated, especially by Sergeant Toomey's sadistic

TOPICS FOR FURTHER STUDY

- Think about an event you think would add to the play's message. Then write an additional scene for the play, imitating Simon's style and humor.

- Conduct research to find out about the racial and ethnic makeup of the U.S. Army during World War II. How does it differ from today's army? Write a few paragraphs comparing and contrasting the two armies.

- Wykowski is a blatant bigot. How might Eugene have better responded to him, if he were participating in life instead of merely witnessing it? Write a monologue in which Eugene expresses his true feelings for Wykowski and his bigotry.

- Do you agree with Eugene's assessment that he should have stood up for Arnold against Wykowski? Should the other men have stood up for Arnold even though they are not Jewish? Explain your answer.

- Homosexuality is one of the important issues raised in the play. In recent years, the question of whether or not gays should serve in the military has created political divisions. Find out about the status of gays in the military today. Write a paragraph explaining the recent policy changes that have taken place about this subject.

- One of Simon's defining characteristics is his humor. Imagine that *Biloxi Blues* was strictly a drama. Rewrite one of the scenes of the play as a drama instead of a comedy.

- Read either *Brighton Beach Memoirs* or *Broadway Bound*. Compare Eugene's character in either of these plays with his character in *Biloxi Blues*. Which Eugene do you like better? Why?

---

streak. Despite such elements, the play contains real truths about military life and the experience of young soldiers. On a more superficial level, certain details do accurately represent military life, such as the inedible food and the cramped quarters. The privates forge quick bonds that are not necessarily the most lasting. More compelling, however, is the transformation that the privates undergo as they learn about army life. Through their training, Eugene and the others become more mature people.

Rites of Passage

For Eugene, army training is his rite of passage into adulthood. Two of the goals he sets for himself foreshadow his transformation. He wants to become a writer, which implies that true development must take place, and he wants to lose his virginity. In the army, Eugene accomplishes both of these goals. He has sex with the prostitute Rowena, and his role in the army ends up being as a journalist for an army newspaper.

In his personal development, Arnold learns about himself and the kind of man he wants to be. For example, he realizes that he is ashamed of himself for not defending Arnold—a fellow Jew— from Wykowski's attacks. His analysis of his bunkmates also indicates a sense of introspection, one that is necessary for a writer, and one that signifies a certain level of growth.

STYLE

Point of View and Narration

Although *Biloxi Blues* is a play, it is essentially structured around Eugene's point of view—despite the fact that he is not present at some scenes, most notably the culminating one between Toomey and Arnold. Though Simon examines other characters in as much depth, perhaps even greater depth, as he does Eugene, this still remains Eugene's story—the story of a formative experience in Eugene's progress to become a writer (which he does in the final play of the trilogy, *Broadway Bound*).

The events that are portrayed are filtered through Eugene's point of view, his journal entries, and ultimately his memory. Several narrative devices emphasize this perspective. Throughout the play, Eugene steps away from the action and directly addresses the audience. His brief monologues allow him the opportunity to share what he feels about what is happening in his life. Another emphatic device is his reporting the fate of the play's characters at the end. Eugene knows what has happened to everyone. Recounting several of the characters' fates reminds the reader that the play is really Eugene's remembrance—it does not take place in real time. As such, Eugene's point of view and perception direct the play.

Comedy

Like all of Simon's plays, *Biloxi Blues* is a comedy. Though it deals with several serious issues (such as homosexuality, anti-Semitism, and sadism), and it essentially centers on the life-and-death events of World War II, Simon treats his narrative humorously. The dialogue is filled with jokes, puns, gags, and one-liners. Almost anything can become the subject of Simon's comedy: chipped beef, a deck of dirty cards, even the invasion of Italy. However, the humor that abounds does not obscure the greater meaning underneath—that of Eugene trying to understand his place in the world as well as what it means to be a writer. Eugene goes on to become a comedic playwright himself (in *Broadway Bound*), thus his use of numerous comedic turns in the relating of his army experience is entirely appropriate.

Characterization

Biloxi Blues has many characters, but most of them are not complexly developed. The majority represent certain types of people. For example, of the privates, Wykowski is a loud-mouthed bully, and Arnold is a stereotypical New York Jew. Toomey is the sadistically typical army drill sergeant who takes personally his role of shaping scared and immature boys into men and soldiers. The play's two women represent polar opposites. Rowena is the good-natured prostitute who does not feel demeaned by her profession. Daisy, on the other hand, is the virgin schoolgirl whom Eugene idealizes. While some critics have objected to such oversimplification of the characters, for Eugene, they actu-

ally do represent the way that certain types of people contributed to his greater understanding and his development as a writer. Eugene's time among these people—only ten weeks—is so brief that in his recollection of the period, they all come to stand for some facet of his development rather than existing as real, living people. The oversimplification is in keeping with the way that Eugene perceives these people and his experiences with them.

Structure

Biloxi Blues takes place over the period of the ten weeks when Eugene is in training camp. While the action is chronological, only the important events that occur are highlighted—those that show the development of individual characters as well as the conflicts they meet. These individual scenes flow smoothly, with a sense of continuity. Issues that are brought up in earlier scenes are resolved in later ones. By the end of the play, Eugene has demonstrated that he has achieved all of the goals he set for himself on the train ride to Mississippi. This is only one example of the sense of completion the play imparts.

HISTORICAL CONTEXT

The Outbreak of World War II

Although World War II broke out in Europe in 1939, the United States did not join the fight until 1941. At the outbreak of the war, however, the United States contributed arms and other supplies to the Allied war effort. In response to the war, the United States also passed the first peacetime draft in U.S. history.

By 1941, the German army had captured most of Europe. Only Britain remained completely free, and Germany had established a bombing campaign intended to force Britain's surrender. On December 7, 1941, the Japanese bombed Pearl Harbor in Hawaii. The next day, the U.S. Congress declared war on the Axis Powers—Germany, Japan, and Italy. The entry of the United States into the war brought much-needed forces and supplies to the British army.

The United States and the War

For the rest of the war, U.S. troops fought along with the Allied troops in North Africa, Europe, the

COMPARE & CONTRAST

- **1940s:** In the year that World War II breaks out, 1939, there are 334,473 Americans on active military duty in the Army and Navy. These numbers grow dramatically during the war years. By 1943, there are over nine million Americans on active military duty. By the end of the war, in 1945, that number has risen to twelve million.

   1990s: In 1999, there are about 1.1 million active duty military personnel serving in the United States and its territories. The great majority of these are based in the continental United States.

- **1940s:** In 1943, the United States is deeply involved in World War II. American soldiers participate in all the major regions of the war.

   1990s: In the 1990s, U.S. troops are involved in UN peacekeeping missions throughout the world. In 1991, U.S. soldiers lead a multinational force in the Persian Gulf War to free Kuwait from an Iraqi invasion.

- **1940s:** The U.S. Army is segregated. Almost one million African-American soldiers are relegated to their own companies.

   1990s: Since 1948, when the order desegregating the army came down from President Harry S Truman, African Americans have served side by side in the army with white soldiers.

- **1940s:** In 1948, there are about five million Jews living in the United States.

   1990s: In 1997, America's six million Jews represent about 2.3 percent of the national population. The highest percentage of Jews live in New York State.

Mediterranean, and the Pacific. After forcing a surrender in North Africa, Allied troops invaded Sicily, and, later, Italy. By June 1944, the Allies had captured Rome, making it the first Axis capital to fall.

One main campaign of the war was the Allied invasion of German-occupied France. On June 6, 1944, known as D-Day, the Allies landed 150,000 U.S., British, and Canadian soldiers in Normandy, France. By August of that year, these forces had liberated Paris. As the soldiers continued westward toward Germany, Soviet troops pressed on Germany from the east. On May 7, 1945, Germany surrendered.

However, the Allied forces had to continue to fight the Japanese. A campaign in the Pacific, intended to lead to the capture of Japan, was hard-fought and bloody. Then, on August 6, 1945, the United States dropped the atomic bomb on Hiroshima, Japan. This devastating attack was followed three days later by another atomic bomb on Nagasaki, Japan. Japan surrendered on September 2, 1945. World War II was over.

The Homefront

In 1943, when the play takes place, the United States had already been at war for two years. The war effort united the American people. Called upon to serve their country, Americans helped in many ways. Families grew ''victory'' gardens to provide themselves with vegetables, so that farm crops could be sent overseas to feed the soldiers. Children collected scrap metal that could be melted down and used in ammunition factories. Women worked in these factories, performing jobs traditionally held by men, who were now serving in the army. People bought Liberty bonds as a way of providing the government with the money needed to carry out the war effort. The American people were called upon to make many sacrifices. For example, meat and gasoline were rationed. Overall, a sense of solidarity developed during the war years as Americans worked together to fight a common enemy.

Social Problems

Despite the relative solidarity the war effort brought to the United States, many Americans were treated unfairly. Japanese Americans suffered greatly. Perceived as a threat to U.S. security, more than 110,000 people of Japanese descent were forcibly removed from their West Coast homes and relocated to internment camps. Many remained there until 1945. Hawaii, whose Japanese population was too large to relocate, was placed under martial law.

Not all American leaders agreed with this policy. One member of the Supreme Court referred to it as legalized racism, but this scathing indictment had no effect on the events of internment. Many Japanese-American families ended up losing their homes and belongings. Despite this prejudicial treatment, about 33,000 Japanese Americans served in the U.S. military.

Social discrimination also took place against African Americans. Although many African Americans were able to move into better-paying jobs because of the demand for workers, other war plants would not hire them or would employ them only as janitors. In 1941, President Franklin D. Roosevelt created the Fair Employment Practices Committee to make sure that all applicants, regardless of race, were considered for job openings.

Within the U.S. Army, as well, social discrimination existed. African-American soldiers were segregated from white soldiers, and most were kept out of combat. Black soldiers were often assigned to low-level work. The Tuskegee Airmen was one of the few all-black units that actually fought in the war. These fighter pilots launched their first combat mission against Italy in 1943. Over the next two years, they played a key role in the successful Allied air campaign.

CRITICAL OVERVIEW

Biloxi Blues is one of Simon's most successful plays. Simon won his first Tony Award for best play in 1985, and Matthew Broderick, playing the role of Eugene, won the Tony for leading actor. Following on the heels of *Brighton Beach Memoirs,* which opened Simon's autobiographical trilogy of plays, *Biloxi Blues* represented a turning point in the critical reception of Simon's work.

First and foremost, many reviewers commented on Simon's new and readily apparent interest in examining his own past, including his emergence as

a writer. Indeed, Simon's representation of Eugene's army career is almost identical to Simon's own, as is the family background presented in *Brighton Beach Memoirs.* As William A. Henry III writes in his review in *Time,* ''Neil Simon has seemed in recent writing to seek a greater resonance between his plays and his most personal recollections, and to yearn for the respect that accrues to a creator who examines himself.''

Simon's capability as a comic writer is aptly demonstrated. As with Simon's previous works, audience and critics hold differing opinions about his use of comedy. Theater-goers, on the whole, appreciate Simon's comedic strains more than critics, responding to them on a personal level rather than analyzing them on an intellectual level. Paul Berman of *The Nation* notes Simon's ''formidable'' skill at humor. ''You see it even when he plucks an old string like the funny quality of Jewish names.'' However, Berman also asserts that while you do a lot of laughing, ''the author would have done better to recognize [that] as the purpose of this play,'' rather than the development of a young writer.

For Robert Brustein of *The New Republic,* although the play ''carries some authentic moments of tension and electricity,'' Simon makes a mistake in choosing to package them in ''a conventional service comedy.'' Brustein further criticizes ''the very jokes that unite the audience'' as serving to ''disunite the play.'' Again, this commentary illustrates the basic disparity between the way a critic views a piece of art and the way the average viewer does.

Critics also discuss the play's characters and plot. Henry writes, ''Inevitably, the sequel lacks some of the roundedness and universality of *Brighton Beach:* a military stopover cannot encompass the complex, cumulative relationships of a family.'' Berman writes that Eugene's progress toward becoming a writer is never seen in great enough depth and believes for this reason that Arnold is the more compelling character.

Overall, however, many critics agree with the audience's positive assessment. Reviewers comment on the realism of the army setting. Howard Kissel writes in *Women's Wear Daily* that it ''is certainly Simon's best play, to my mind the first in which he has had the courage to suggest there are things that matter more to him than the reassuring sound of the audience's laughter. My admiration for the play is deep and unqualified.'' Kissel, thus, refutes other critics' opinions of Simon's use of humor in the play. Henry finds it to be among "the most telling statements of the World War II generation, or any generation that loses many of its young in battle, about how much of life is luck." He concludes that it "ranks as among the best new American plays of the Broadway season." Many critics also admiringly remark on the quality of the play's first staging. Brustein notes that the audience at the play showed remarkable "spirit" and was "more lively, more engaged, more at home than any Broadway crowd in years"—surely an enormously important indicator of a play's ultimate success.

CRITICISM

Rena Korb

Korb has a master's degree in English literature and creative writing and has written for a wide variety of educational publishers. In the following essay, she discusses the comedy of Simon's play and its underlying dramatic aspects.

Neil Simon had been a successful comedic playwright for close to twenty-five years when his play *Biloxi Blues* opened on Broadway in 1985. The semi-autobiographical *Biloxi Blues,* closely modeled on Simon's own experience in the army, was the second in what would become a trilogy of plays that brought the author widespread acclaim, both from critics and audiences. The trilogy centers on Eugene Morris Jerome, an insightful, introspective Jewish boy from New York who grows up to become a writer. *Biloxi Blues* takes place in 1943, at an army training camp in Biloxi, Mississippi. Eugene, a new recruit, is sent there along with other young men from the East Coast. There he encounters a sadistic sergeant, an anti-Semitic member of the platoon, and the specter of homosexuality. He also loses his virginity and falls in love for the first time. Through these experiences, and the conflicts they engender, Eugene learns about his own relationship to the human drama that takes place on a daily basis. He also takes important steps to becoming a writer.

First and foremost to Simon's audience, *Biloxi Blues* is successful because of its comic element. Numerous critics note the positive way the audience responds to Simon's jokes. The dialogue is filled with gags, puns, and one-liners. Anything is subject to Simon's humor: army food ("They oughta drop this stuff [chipped beef] over Germany. The whole country would come out with their hands up."); accusations of homosexuality ("It's like an Agatha Christie story. *Murder by Fellatio.* Title's no good. Sounds like an Italian ice cream. . . . How about *Murder on the Fellatio Express*?"); and first sex ("My first time? . . . Are you kidding? That's funny . . . Noo . . . It's my second time . . . The first time they were closed."). The new privates respond to one another with sarcasm, flippancy, and physical humor.

Another main focus of humor is Eugene's journal entries, through which he frames the play. In the opening scene, while everyone around him attempts to sleep, Eugene takes part in the dialogue, at the same time as he is chronicling his thoughts about his new colleagues. This device allows Eugene the opportunity to infuse the play with humor by commenting on the people around him. The play opens with Eugene's description of his fellow recruits, including Wykowski, who has what seems to be a permanent erection; Carney, who thinks he's a singer but really isn't; Selridge, who smells "like a tuna-fish sandwich left out in the rain"; and Arnold Epstein, whose digestion problems lead to his often-noted flatulence. In his journal, Eugene sums up what he sees "If the Germans only knew what was coming over, they would be looking forward to this invasion."

Often in his journal entries, Eugene mixes humor with essential truths. These truths would be mundane, even sentimental, if rendered in straight language. For instance, in writing about Arnold Epstein, whom he calls "the worst soldier in World War Two and that included the deserters," Eugene notes, "His major flaw was that he was incapable of digesting food stronger than hard-boiled eggs. . . I didn't think he'd last long in the army because during wartime it's very hard to go home for dinner every night." Eugene's observation, while funny, also points out the more serious truth: these boys, none of whom is older than twenty years, are being forced to leave the safety and security of their homes and sent onto the dangerous field of war.

Eugene's narrative also comments on the very nature of the army and its intense discipline. Arnold's rebellion is punished with KP duty, while the other privates endure what Eugene considers to be a worse fate: a fifteen-mile midnight march through the swamps of Mississippi. "But maybe Toomey was right," Eugene later muses. "If nobody obeys

Christopher Walken as Sergeant Toomey and Matthew Broderick as Eugene Morris Jerome in the 1987 film adaptation of Biloxi Blues.

orders, I'll bet we wouldn't have more than twelve or thirteen soldiers fighting the war . . . We'd have headlines like, 'Corporal Stanley Leiberman invades Sicily.'''

The constant comic element in *Biloxi Blues* does not mask the play's more serious elements: the potentially violent conflict between Toomey and Arnold; the anti-Semitic degradation that Wykowski inflicts upon Arnold; Eugene's attempts to learn how to become a writer; and the essential life-and-death issue of World War II. Through the conflict between Arnold, Toomey, and Wykowski, Eugene

comes to learn about the place he chooses to occupy in the world.

Eugene first questions his own actions when Wykowski launches an anti-Semitic attack on Arnold. Angry that Eugene has selected Arnold's fantasy—making Toomey perform two hundred push-ups—for the prize money, Wykowski retaliates with a series of derogatory remarks that center on stereotypes held about Jews: Jews always ''end up with the money,'' and they have distinguishable ''Jew'' noses. He then proceeds to point out the Jews—Arnold and Eugene—whom he declares are ''easy

WHAT DO I READ NEXT?

- Simon's *Brighton Beach Memoirs* (1984) first introduces Eugene Morris Jerome. Set in Brooklyn in 1937, it tells of a Jewish family and their financial troubles during the Great Depression.

- Simon's *Broadway Bound* (1987) completes his semi-autobiographical trilogy. It centers on Eugene and his older brother as they leave home to become writers for a radio show. Meanwhile, their parents break up, and their family resists their new profession. Eugene comes to realize that life does not contain the happy endings he is able to write into his comedy.

- Doris Kearns Goodwin's biography *No Ordinary Time: Franklin and Eleanor Roosevelt: The Home Front in World War II* is a compelling biography that provides interesting perspectives and details about the home-front society in the United States during World War II. In particular,

it takes the reader further into the events happening inside the Roosevelt White House and the dynamics of the many people living, working, and visiting there during this historic time.

- David Guterson's novel *Snow Falling on Cedars* (1994) describes the internment of Japanese Americans in Washington State during World War II. Set both in the 1940s and 1990s, it explores the devastating and long-term effects of racism.

- Tim O'Brien's *The Things They Carried* (1990) is a collection of related short stories about young recruits serving in the Vietnam War. O'Brien fought in Vietnam, and his work evocatively and movingly presents this difficult period in American history, particularly for the young men who were sacrificed to the war.

---

to spot.'' After Toomey prevents the potential fight between Arnold and Wykowski, Eugene faces the audience, sharing his journal entry.

> . . . I never liked Wykowski much and I didn't like him any better after tonight. . . . But the one I hated most was myself because I didn't stand up for Epstein, a fellow Jew. Maybe I was afraid of Wykowski, or maybe it was because Epstein sort of sometimes asked for it, but since the guys didn't pick on me that much, I figured I'd just stay sort of neutral . . . like Switzerland.

Although Eugene recognizes the negative aspect of his passivity, he does nothing to change it. After Arnold is involved in yet another conflict—this time with Toomey—Eugene is again forced to acknowledge his essential nature. He says to Arnold, who has just taken the blame for a crime he did not commit in order to ensure that the rest of the men will be allowed to go on their leave, ''I admire what you did back there, Arnold. You remind me of my brother, sometimes. He was always standing up for his principles too.''

> EPSTEIN: Principles are okay. But sometimes they get in the way of reason.

EUGENE: Then how do you know which one is the right one?

EPSTEIN: You have to get involved. You don't get involved enough, Eugene.

EUGENE: What do you mean?

EPSTEIN: You're a witness. You're always standing around *watching* what's happening. Scribbling in your book what other people do. You have to get in the middle of it. You have to take sides. Make a contribution to the fight.

EUGENE: What fight?

EPSTEIN: *Any* fight. The one you believe in.

EUGENE: Yeah. I know what you mean. Sometimes I feel like I'm invisible. Like The Shadow. I can see everyone else, but they can't see me. That's what I think writers are. Sort of invisible.

EPSTEIN: Not Tolstoy. Not Dostoyevsky. Not Herman Melville.

EUGENE: Yeah. I have to read those guys.

Simon ends this serious exchange with a dollop of humor. When Toomey calls from offstage that he doesn't hear Arnold getting to his assigned punishment of cleaning the latrines, Arnold says, "I'd better go. I have to get involved with toilet bowls."

Eugene, however, continues to choose not to get involved. For example, instead of telling his bunkmates his thoughts, he writes them down in his journal. Eugene wrote about his bunkmate Carney that he found him to be untrustworthy. Carney admits that his girlfriend also told him that "she didn't think I was someone she could count on." Carney's self-revelation to Eugene confirms the keenness of Eugene's perceptions.

Significantly, Eugene is not present at the most dramatic, harrowing scene of the play—the final confrontation between Toomey and Arnold. This scene is the only one in which the threat of real violence is present. Toomey is "piss drunk" with a "loaded .45 pointed at the head of dung that the piss-drunk sergeant hates and despises." In Arnold's words, the situation is "Delicate . . . extremely delicate." Only after Arnold has successfully wrestled the gun away from Toomey are the other recruits allowed to join the scene, "*in various states of undress.*" Their lack of clothing indicates their relative innocence as compared to Arnold, who has just faced down the man who has made their collective lives miserable.

Eugene sums up the essential incompatibility between him and Arnold in his address to the audience immediately following this scene. "Epstein won the fantasy game fair and square because *his* really came true." Arnold makes the fantasy game his actual life. This is the difference between observing life and living life.

Eugene's difficulties with living life manifest in his parting scene with Daisy. He admits that he is "having a lot of trouble with words," to which Daisy replies, "That doesn't sound like Eugene the Writer to me." But Eugene is "not writing now." He is instead "Eugene the Talker," the Eugene who must take part in an important life event—a first love—rather than analyze it. He finds the courage to tell Daisy his feelings, and thus he creates his most important connection in the play to another person. For a writer, however, the accomplishment of successfully observing and recording life is no small matter. By the end of the play, Eugene realizes that although he is an apt and careful observer, he is still unable to take his experiences and successfully translate them into words. After his final goodbye to Daisy, he "knew at that moment I was a long way from becoming a writer because there were no words I could find to describe the happiness I felt in

> OFTEN IN HIS JOURNAL ENTRIES, EUGENE MIXES HUMOR WITH ESSENTIAL TRUTHS. THESE TRUTHS WOULD BE MUNDANE, EVEN SENTIMENTAL, IF RENDERED IN STRAIGHT LANGUAGE. FOR INSTANCE, IN WRITING ABOUT ARNOLD EPSTEIN, WHOM HE CALLS 'THE WORST SOLDIER IN WORLD WAR TWO AND THAT INCLUDED THE DESERTERS,' EUGENE NOTES, 'HIS MAJOR FLAW WAS THAT HE WAS INCAPABLE OF DIGESTING FOOD STRONGER THAN HARD-BOILED EGGS. . .'"

those ten minutes with Daisy Hannigan." The fact that Eugene has gone on to produce this play is testament to his eventual ability to express himself in the exact words he chooses.

Source: Rena Korb, in an essay for *Drama for Students,* Gale Group, 2001.

Stanley Kaufmann

Stanley Kaufmann discusses the film version of Neil Simon's play Biloxi Blues, *praising its director, Mike Nichols, for his refreshing take on familiar scenes and its principal actors for the 'delight' they bring to their roles.*

One of America's premier comic talents is on glittering display in *Biloxi Blues,* a craftsman whose skill approaches the level of serious work as long as he sticks to lightweight work. I mean, of course, Mike Nichols. I first saw his directing in the Broadway production of Neil Simon's *Barefoot in the Park* (1963), a soufflé in the hands of a new, masterly pastry chef. Since then, in more Simon pieces and in other plays—excepting a misguided venture into Chekhov—Nichols has invariably evoked the best in his actors and has been subtly

A scene from the theatrical production of Biloxi Blues *at The Grande Theatre in London, Ontario.*

ingenious with rhythm, timing, movement. Since then, Nichols has also made films—ten, I believe— and, to his theater gifts, has added cinematic dexterity.

He shows it again in *Biloxi Blues,* from the opening shot. That shot isn't novel (one very much like it was in Brando's film *Morituri*), but Nichols uses it well to set mood and motion. We see the hero, Matthew Broderick, through the window of a moving train. He is in World War II Army uniform, in a car crowded with soldiers. The camera then pulls back and up to show us the whole train, steaming across a railroad bridge. From Broderick's face up to the panorama, the camera's movement incises a feeling of wistful adventure, of progress into the unwished-for.

Later, Nichols refreshes a moment that was old when it happened to Andy Hardy—the stripling falling in love for the first time. Broderick, on his first leave from the boot camp training that occupies most of the film, goes to a dance in nearby Biloxi and meets a girl his own age, the delightful Penelope Ann Miller. As they dance, the camera gently circles them in the sparkling ballroom light, as if the film itself were sharing the youngsters' wonder.

In Broderick and Miller and Matt Mulhern, who plays a tough trainee, Nichols started with an advantage: these three had been in the Broadway production of the original play, which was well directed by Gene Saks. For that advantage, I assume that Nichols was grateful. But for the drill sergeant, Nichols made a surprising choice of his own: Christopher Walken, not everyone's idea of a hard-as-nails drill sergeant. Walken, whose speech sometimes sounds a bit coarse in genteel roles, here sounds a bit too silken; but once we understand that we're not going to get the sergeant stereotype, he creates his own brand of strict professionalism, of loneliness, of hate.

The script is pure Neil Simon, which is to say impure. Gags, very funny, frequently replace credible dialogue. Sharp observation is tinged with sentimentality. Structure consists of invention— there isn't much structure, really, just a series of scenes, some of which are linked. This last factor is common in Simon's plays and screenplays and is somewhat more tolerable in *Biloxi Blues* because here he is turning the pages of an album (his own Army experience) rather than trying to develop a cogent comedy. Simon's colorings of nostalgia, for a time that was clearly discomfiting, apparently rise because these experiences were part of his youth.

It's hard to imagine a viewer being bored or unamused by *Biloxi Blues.* It's easier to imagine a viewer finally dissatisfied with it.

Source: Stanley Kaufmann, ''Stanley Kaufmann on Films: Variously Clever,'' in *New Republic,* Vol. 3823, No. 198, April 25, 1988 p. 26.

Leo Sauvage

This review by Leo Sauvage describes Simon's Biloxi Blues *as a 'well-made' piece full of laughter, if not originality, while exploring the institutions of love and the military.*

Almost all of the flags on the Great White Way have gone up to salute Neil Simon's *Biloxi Blues* as the first ''comedy hit'' of the current season. The latest installment of the famous playwright's so-called autobiographical series is precisely that—largely, alas, because the current season has been extremely poor.

The play, a droll recounting of Simon's basic training at an Army camp in Mississippi, is certainly well-made. It has funny lines and situations—some genuinely witty, some designed to win automatic laughter of a rather low sort—and a story whose unequal episodes are fashioned into a whole without excessively visible stitches. The problem is that only rarely does the work achieve dramatic originality. Even so, *Biloxi Blues* is quite likely to survive at least as long as its predecessor, *Brighton Beach Memoirs*—recently moved from the Neil Simon Theater to make room for the new production, yet in its third year still entrenched on Broadway at the 46th Street Theater.

Eugene Morris Jerome (Matthew Broderick), the hero and ''author'' of *Brighton Beach Memoirs,* is now six years older, or of conscription age. The time is 1943, we are told. To any normal human being that means World War II. In *Biloxi Blues,* though, the war appears to be a very minor item of conversation and concern among the soldiers drafted to fight it. Granted, they are far from the bombed-out cities, the countries being invaded by Hitler's panzer divisions, the refugees and murdered millions of Europe. Nevertheless, the United States had been engaged in the conflict for over a year; thousands of Americans had already been killed, wounded or captured. The bad news surely must have reached Biloxi, not to mention Brooklynite Eugene Jerome and his knowledgeable buddy Arnold Epstein (Barry Miller).

The sole suggestion of what these young men will soon confront, however, comes in a sort of postscript: On a train bringing Eugene and his comrades to the embarkation port, he tells us their respective fates. Otherwise the play is not about war; it is about how different types of individuals react when put into a military uniform and forced to accept someone else's absolute authority for no better reason than the stripes on his sleeves. In fact, whatever the author may have intended, *Biloxi Blues* becomes first of all an attack on militarism. Simon may well have been conscious of this, for he apparently tried to blunt the thrust by making Sergeant Toomey (Bill Sadler) exceptional—a man clearly in need of psychiatric treatment, not your typical noncom in charge of teaching blind obedience to civilians he professionally despises.

Simon's second focus is Eugene's unfolding love life: the nice Jewish boy's initial sexual experience with a prostitute (Randall Edwards), and his subsequent affection for Daisy Hannigan (Penelope Ann Miller), a church-going virgin. I do not object in principle to the playwright's recourse to old-fashioned devices, but it strains credulity that at age 19 Eugene should be so embarrassed at the prospect of making love to a hooker. His nervous behavior is

> ''. . . NICHOLS HAS INVARIABLY EVOKED THE BEST IN HIS ACTORS AND HAS BEEN SUBTLY INGENIOUS WITH RHYTHM, TIMING, MOVEMENT.''

particularly surprising if we remember that as a young teenager in *Brighton Beach Memoirs* he was eager to get to the bottom of these matters. The very attractive Randall Edwards, incidentally, is much too elegant, and too patient, to be convincing as a woman turning tricks on weekends for waiting soldiers. If the author can be believed, in 1943 Biloxi had both the nastiest sergeant and the sexiest whore in the country.

Upon losing his virginity Eugene falls for the innocent Daisy, who hesitates to allow a first kiss not only because of her mother's warnings but also because it is Good Friday. Although Penelope Ann Miller nicely prevents her character from drowning in absurdity, such scruples were outdated before the end of World War I. Since the girl is Catholic and the boy Jewish, one is not surprised to learn in the last scene that she is married to someone else. Indeed, one wonders why it was thought necessary to mention the expected. Then Simon comes up with the punch line that gets the biggest laugh of the evening: The pious young Catholic is now a Mrs. Goldstein, or some equally obvious Jewish name. Clever, albeit not terribly far above the level of an average standup comic's gambit, and perhaps a little too pat in its pandering to the desires of a Broadway audience. The scenes involving the troops, happily, display a deeper humor.

Biloxi Blues has been directed well by Gene Saks and performed well by an ensemble of excellent actors, several of whom play outstanding characters outstandingly. Interestingly, neither Matthew Broderick nor his Eugene Morris Jerome head either category. Broderick is very good when he is feeling his way around in the barracks, but in his two big conventional scenes tailor-made to amuse the audience he gets carried away and resorts to even easier gimmicks. The true central figure of *Biloxi Blues* is Arnold Epstein, a Jewish intellectual, masterfully delineated by Barry Miller. Epstein is the sort of rational philosopher who seems utterly unfit, if not for fighting a war, certainly for life in a training camp under military—that is, stupid—discipline. Still, he develops an attitude toward authority that in effect amounts to a new model of passive resistance, based not on instinct or peasant shrewdness (like the Good Soldier Schweik's) but on sophisticated thinking which builds up to a strategy. His scenes with the sadistic Sergeant Toomey—a role Bill Sadler expertly pushes precisely to the limit of tolerance—culminate in a final confrontation where mad brutishness is rendered helpless and intellectual preparedness triumphs. This duel between two kinds of power is a powerful moment of theater.

Source: Leo Sauvage, ''On Stage: Life Along the Mississippi,'' in *The New Leader,* Vol. 68, No. 5, April 8, 1985, pp. 20–21.

SOURCES

Berman, Paul, Review in *The Nation,* April 20, 1985, p. 474.

Brustein, Robert, Review in *The New Republic,* May 20, 1985, p. 26.

Henry, William A., III, Review in *Time,* April 8, 1985, p. 72.

Kissel, Howard, Review in *Women's Wear Daily,* March 29, 1985, p. 72.

FURTHER READING

Johnson, Robert K., *Neil Simon: A Casebook,* Twayne, 1983. This is an in-depth discussion of Simon's earlier career and the plays he wrote up through the early 1980s. Johnson analyzes individual plays as well as traces common themes among them.

Konas, Gary, *Neil Simon: A Casebook,* Garland, 1997. A discussion of Simon's career.

Simon, Neil, *A Memoir,* Simon & Schuster, 1996. Simon recalls his life and the influences that shaped him as a writer.

The Effect of Gamma Rays on Man-in-the-Moon Marigolds

PAUL ZINDEL

1964

The Effect of Gamma Rays on Man-in-the-Moon Marigolds is Paul Zindel's best-known play. It is an autobiographical drama loosely based on his experiences growing up in a single-parent household. The play's main character, Beatrice, is modeled on Zindel's mother, who became a bitter and disillusioned woman after the departure of her husband. The play was first produced in 1964 at the Alley Theatre in Houston, Texas. It eventually opened off-Broadway in 1970, and in 1971 made a brief jump to Broadway. Overall, the play enjoyed a very successful New York run of 819 performances. Zindel's portrayal of the painful side of family life struck a chord with audiences who found they could easily relate to the themes of loneliness and shattered dreams. The play was critically acclaimed and earned several awards, including an Obie Award for best play of the season (1970), the New York Drama Critics Circle Award for best American play of the year (1970), and the Pulitzer Prize for drama (1971). It was so popular that in 1972 Twentieth Century-Fox released a film version starring Joanne Woodward.

The Effect of Gamma Rays on Man-in-the-Moon Marigolds has been widely read and performed up to the present day. Its realistic portrayal of the struggles of young adults still resonates with audiences, even though it was written more than thirty-six years ago. An edition with a new introduction by Zindel was published in 1997. In it Zindel talks about the direct parallels between the charac-

ters and his own family, and notes how pleased he is that the play still speaks to modern audiences.

AUTHOR BIOGRAPHY

Paul Zindel was born in Staten Island, New York, on May 15, 1936. He is the son of Paul, a New York policeman, and Betty Zindel. He also has an older sister, Betty. His father left the family when Paul was two years old, and from then on, Zindel was raised by his mother. Betty Zindel moved the family from town to town and worked at various odd jobs to support them. Zindel's mother was a troubled woman who was bitter and very distrustful of men. She constantly threatened suicide. Her despair and disappointment in life is found in the character of Beatrice Hunsdorfer in *Gamma Rays*. For a time, Betty worked as a private duty nurse, and this is directly reflected in the play, as Beatrice rents out her spare room to invalids to make extra money.

At the age of fifteen, Zindel was diagnosed with tuberculosis and confined to an adult sanatorium for eighteen months. This period of isolation gave him time for a great deal of introspection and contributed to his ability to sit back and observe the world around him. Zindel received a Bachelor of Science in chemistry and education from Wagner College in 1958, and went on to receive a Master's of Science in 1959. In college, he attended a lecture given by playwright Edward Albee. It inspired him so much, he decided to sign up for a playwriting course taught by Albee, who eventually became his mentor. Zindel wrote his first play, *Dimensions of Peacocks*, in 1959 under Albee's tutelage. During his early years as a playwright, 1959 to 1969, Zindel also taught chemistry at Tottenville High School in Staten Island. He wrote plays in his spare time and attended as many professional productions as he could.

In 1964 *Gamma Rays* had its premier at the Alley Theatre in Houston. Nina Vance, head of the Alley Theatre, liked the play so well she invited Zindel to be a playwright-in-residence during the 1967 season. During this time, he wrote his second-most popular play, *And Miss Reardon Drinks a Little,* which was produced at the Mark Taper Forum that same year. In 1970 *The Effect of Gamma Rays on Man-in-the-Moon Marigolds* opened in New York to overwhelmingly positive reviews. Zindel won the Pulitzer Prize and was finally able to devote himself to writing plays full-time. In 1973, Zindel married Bonnie Hildebrand. The couple even-

tually had two children, David Jack and Elizabeth Claire.

Zindel has also had a successful career writing fiction for young adults. In 1966 Charlotte Zolotow, an editor at Harper and Row Publishers, saw a televised version of *The Effect of Gamma Rays* and contacted him to see if he would be interested in writing a novel for teenagers. He agreed and published the *The Pigman* in 1968. The book was extremely well received. He followed this with many successful young adult novels, which have won numerous awards. Zindel also continues to write plays, though none of his subsequent plays has gained quite the popularity or critical acclaim of *The Effect of Gamma Rays on Man-in-the-Moon Marigolds.* His most recent play (published by Dramatists Play Service in 2000) is *Every Seventeen Minutes the Crowd Goes Crazy*, about a family of children who are left to fend for themselves.

PLOT SUMMARY

Act 1

The Effect of Gamma Rays on Man-in-the-Moon Marigolds opens with a voice-over of Tillie talking about how the same atoms now in her hand were once contained in different parts of the Earth throughout history. The scene then shifts to Beatrice Hunsdorfer talking on the phone with Tillie's science teacher, Mr. Goodman, explaining why Tillie is absent from school so often. Beatrice doesn't tell him that it is because she often keeps Tillie at home to do household tasks. She is very complimentary to Mr. Goodman, and thanks him for the pet rabbit he has allowed Tillie to bring home. Once Beatrice hangs up the phone, however, her kind demeanor changes, and she angrily berates Tillie for putting her in the position of having to call the school. Tillie's sister Ruth enters, ready for school. She tells Beatrice how Tillie became the laughingstock of the entire school during an assembly when she was up on stage cranking a model of an atom. Ruth then tells Beatrice that there is a file of the family's history kept in the school office. Beatrice voices her concern about this file. The stage goes dark, and Tillie's voice is heard describing a science experiment in which a small piece of metal placed in a cloud chamber started to smoke. Tillie is enthralled when Mr. Goodman tells her this fountain of atoms could go on for eternity. The lights then come up on the stage. Tillie is preparing boxes of dirt in which to plant marigolds for a science experiment. The marigold seeds have been exposed to cobalt-60, and Tillie is going to study the effect this has. Beatrice enters and talks about her wish to transform the house into a teashop. She asks Tillie about the science experiment, and Tillie explains the concept of half-life to her. Suddenly, Nanny begins to shuffle into the room with her walker. She is very old, and moves extremely slowly over to the table. Beatrice reluctantly serves Nanny hot honey-water, all the while making nasty comments behind her back and yelling sarcastically into her face as if she were a deaf child. Beatrice then relates the story of how Nanny's career-minded daughter brought her to the Hunsdorfer's because she didn't want to bother with taking care of her. The scene ends with Beatrice bemoaning her life, ''Half-life! If you want to know what a half-life is, just ask me. You're looking at the original half-life!''

In the next scene, Beatrice is again talking on the phone to Mr. Goodman. She tells him she is worried about the effect the radioactive marigolds may have on Tillie. Mr. Goodman assures her there is no danger. The stage then goes dark, and a thunderstorm begins. Ruth is heard screaming from her room upstairs. She is having an epileptic seizure. She stumbles onto the stairs just as Beatrice runs out and catches her. Tillie also rushes in, but Beatrice sends her back to her room. Ruth's seizure finally runs its course, and Beatrice sits on the couch with her to calm her. She tells Ruth her favorite story, about a happier time when Beatrice used to ride on her father's produce wagon. During this story, Beatrice gives insight into how her world fell apart when her father became so ill he had to be confined to a sanatorium. The scene ends with Beatrice in despair, wondering if life has anything good left in store for her. The stage goes dark again, and the lights come up with Nanny seated at the table. Beatrice is madly cleaning out the upstairs rooms, throwing paper and junk everywhere. The audience discovers that Beatrice has had a revelation and has decided to take immediate action to turn the house into a teashop. She is also drinking whiskey and is slightly inebriated. Beatrice rants about how she is finally taking stock of her life and is going to make some changes. She is going to throw Nanny out, and tells Tillie she must get rid of the rabbit. Ruth bounds in and relates the news that Tillie is a finalist in the science fair. For once, Ruth is proud of her sister. The phone rings, and it is Dr. Berg, the principal, asking that Beatrice be present to sit on stage for the finals of the science fair. She

Paul Zindel

screams at Dr. Berg on the phone, ''I SAID I'D THINK ABOUT IT!'' and then hangs up and begins screaming at Tillie. Tillie begins to cry, and Beatrice suddenly realizes how cruel she has been to Tillie. She moves toward Tillie to hug her as the act ends.

Act 2

As act 2 begins, Beatrice, Tillie, and Ruth are all getting ready to go to the science fair. Tillie readies her project while Ruth babbles on about Tillie's main competition, Janice Vickery. Ruth drops a bombshell when she mentions that the teachers are anxious to see what Beatrice will wear to the science fair. Many of them knew her as a strange outcast in high school whom they used to call ''Betty the Loon.'' Tillie begs Ruth not to tell Beatrice this. She agrees only after Tillie gives the rabbit to her. Beatrice comes in. She is dressed up in an outfit that is described as ''strange, but not that strange, by any means.'' She acts annoyed at having to go, but it is clear that she is proud. The taxi arrives, and they start out the door. Ruth begins to put her coat on, but Beatrice tells her she must stay home to look after Nanny. Ruth gets very angry and nastily calls her mother ''Betty the Loon.'' The words hit Beatrice like a shot. Her world crumples.

She stops, totally defeated, and tells Ruth to go with Tillie. Ruth hesitates at first, but Beatrice screams at her, "GET OUT OF HERE." Ruth exits and Beatrice begins sobbing as the lights go down.

The lights then come up on the science fair. Janice Vickery gives her presentation standing next to the skeleton of a cat. She describes how she got a dead cat from the ASPCA and boiled the skin off to get the skeleton out and reconstruct it. Janice's speech provides some much-needed comic relief at this point in the play. The scene then switches to Beatrice on the telephone. She is drunk. She telephones the school to give a message to the principal and teachers, "Tell them Mrs. Hunsdorfer called to thank them for making her wish she was dead." Beatrice also phones Nanny's daughter to tell her Nanny must be out by tomorrow. Beatrice then spies the pet rabbit in his cage. She picks up the cage, a towel, and a bottle of chloroform and slowly walks upstairs as the lights fade. The scene switches back to the science fair, where Tillie is giving her presentation. She describes the past, present, and future of her experiment with man-in-the-moon marigolds. During this speech, as in her voice-overs throughout the play, the audience can see Tillie's true brilliance and optimism. The lights go down and come back up on the Hunsdorfer household. Ruth rushes in announcing that Tillie won the science fair. Beatrice does not greet her with the expected happiness, but numbly informs her that the rabbit is dead in her room. This news sends Ruth into a seizure. Beatrice and Tillie get Ruth through her seizure as Nanny begins to shuffle into the room. At the end of the scene Beatrice weakly announces, "I hate the world." The play concludes with Tillie's voice-over describing how the science experiment with man-in-the-moon marigolds has made her feel important. The play ends on an optimistic note as Tillie ponders the possibilities science can open up for mankind.

CHARACTERS

Beatrice Hunsdorfer

Beatrice is the central figure around whom the play revolves. She is a single mother who was left by her husband years ago. This event has fostered a deep distrust of men. She still lives in the same house in which she grew up and has become increasingly reclusive over the years. Beatrice still mourns the loss of her father, a man whom she was forced to confine to a sanatorium years ago. The world has caused her a lot of pain, and she takes it out on those around her. She vents her hostility primarily upon her two teenage daughters. Beatrice has always yearned to be popular, but she has always been an outcast. She is desperate to escape her circumstances and constantly dreams of a better life.

Ruth Hunsdorfer

Ruth is Beatrice's older daughter. She is an epileptic whose seizures are brought on by anxiety or stress. Ruth is somewhat promiscuous and is very concerned about her appearance. She constantly worries about Tillie, her younger sister, embarrassing her at school. Ruth is very fickle in her relationship to Tillie. She often makes fun of her, but as soon as Tillie wins the science fair and becomes somewhat of a school celebrity, Ruth is very quick to brag, "That's my sister." Ruth has a quick temper and is not afraid to talk back to her mother. Her attempts to lash out and hurt her mother are what drive much of the action of the play.

Tillie Hunsdorfer

Tillie is Beatrice's younger daughter. She is an outcast at school and is teased by the other students. Tillie is very intelligent, and her teacher, Mr. Goodman, encourages her interest in science. The title of the play comes from the experiment Tillie enters in the school science fair. Tillie is a dreamer who yearns for a better world. She is quiet and thoughtful. She is also somewhat awkward and is often chastised by her mother for this.

Nanny

Nanny is the boarder who lives in the spare room. She is nearly blind, deaf, and can barely walk with the aid of a walker. Nanny's daughter has given up responsibility for her care.

Janice Vickery

Janice is Tillie's main competitor at the science fair. She gives a gruesome but funny presentation in which she describes boiling a cat and collecting the bones to reconstruct the skeleton. Janice's speech provides comic relief right before the dramatic climax of the play.

THEMES

Triumph in the Face of Adversity

The characters in *The Effect of Gamma Rays on Man-in-the-Moon Marigolds* all face adversity, but each reacts very differently. Beatrice has allowed the difficulties and bad luck she has encountered throughout life to defeat her. She attempts to better her life, but her bitterness presents a barrier. Beatrice is so caught up in the negative, unfair aspects of life that she is unable to see any goodness around her. Tillie, however, is able to prevail, even in the worst circumstances. She can find beauty in the smallest detail. No matter how many times she is chastised or disappointed, she gets back up and tries again. She is a survivor.

Self-Image

Beatrice and Ruth are very concerned with how they appear to others. Ruth is constantly worried about how she looks. She wears tight sweaters and refuses to go to school without first putting on makeup. Ruth wants to fit in and is very fickle in her relationship to Tillie. Most of the time she considers Tillie an embarrassment and doesn't want to be associated with her. Ruth quickly changes her mind, however, when Tillie wins the science fair, because she wants to boost her own image by bragging about Tillie's accomplishments. Beatrice is also trapped by a need to fit in. She talks about how popular she was in high school, but eventually the audience discovers that this wasn't true at all. Beatrice was an outcast in high school who was constantly teased. This caused her a great deal of pain and was a factor in her withdrawal from the world. Tillie is the only one of the family who is secure in her self-image. Although she is teased and made fun of, she continues to be true to herself. She doesn't try to change and fit in with the crowd, but instead pursues the things that are important to her. This ultimately leads to her success in the science fair, and the playwright suggests that it will help Tillie succeed in life.

Dreams

Dreams are a very important theme in *The Effect of Gamma Rays on Man-in-the-Moon Marigolds.* Beatrice, Tillie, and Ruth all share their dreams or tell of dreams they have had at some point in the play. In act 1, Ruth has a seizure brought on by a nightmare. Beatrice also relates a recurring nightmare about her father and his vegetable wagon.

MEDIA ADAPTATIONS

Throughout the play, Beatrice is constantly talking about her dreams of opening a tea shop, of becoming a dancer, and of escaping her dreary existence. Tillie's dreams are sparked by her discoveries in science class. Because Tillie can still find good in the world, the possibility exists for her dreams to come true.

Life versus Death

Images of death and decay are prominent in the play. Beatrice kills most things around her. She chloroforms the rabbit, and she tries to kill her daughters' spirits by constantly berating and belittling them. Nanny is nothing more than a walking corpse. Even the room looks as if it is decaying, with its piles of newspaper and objects strewn everywhere. Tillie is the only one who connects to a life force. She plants the marigold seeds that eventually grow into many strange and wonderful mutations.

The Inability to Make Meaningful Human Connections

Just as Nanny is shut out from the outside world through hearing loss and the thick cataracts that cover her eyes, Beatrice is shut out from the outside world through her fear. She has covered the large window of the front room with newspaper so passersby cannot see in. She doesn't want the family to interact with the outside world. Beatrice is just as

TOPICS FOR FURTHER STUDY

- What do you think Beatrice, Ruth, and Tillie will be doing ten years after the play ends? What societal influences might contribute to the characters' futures? Consider such elements as increased opportunities for women, advances in scientific research, changes in the American family, and so on.

- *The Effect of Gamma Rays on Man-in-the-Moon Marigolds* has often been compared to Tennessee Williams's play *The Glass Menagerie*. Both have been described as *memory plays*. How do memories influence the action in each play? Do the characters always relate past memories truthfully? If not, what insight does this provide into their current situation?

- Tillie and Ruth are made fun of because they are growing up without a father. Does society have the same view of single-parent households today that it had in 1964? What changes in society have influenced the current view of a "typical American family"?

- Tillie sees atomic energy as a discovery that opens up vast wonderful possibilities for mankind. Do you agree with her? Support your answer with examples that cite good and/or bad uses of atomic energy. What has atomic energy allowed mankind to do that was previously impossible?

- In what ways could the Hunsdorfers improve their current family situation? Consider such elements as communication and honesty.

- Nanny's daughter has given up responsibility for her mother's care to focus on her own career. Was she right in doing this? Is society's view of aging different than it was in 1964? Why or why not? Have things gotten better or worse for people who need special care?

---

trapped within her own self-made prison as Nanny is within her aging and failing body. Also, Beatrice, Ruth, and Tillie are unable to truly connect and share with one another. Most of the communication between Beatrice and Ruth consists of yelling and bickering, while Tillie chooses to remain silent. None of the three is willing to really open up and share their true feelings with their family members.

Half-life

The half-life of the radioactive isotopes that Tillie explains to Beatrice symbolizes numerous things about the family. Beatrice uses the words "half-life" literally to describe the unfulfilled potential she feels in her own life. Also, just as the radioactivity will go on forever, so will the unfortunate situations and bitterness that Beatrice is caught in. Half-life also symbolizes hope for Tillie, however. She relates to the concept in a positive way, recognizing the magic potential of something that never ends. To Tillie, half-life represents new areas

just waiting to be explored, filled with wonder and fantastic possibilities.

STYLE

Setting

The Effect of Gamma Rays on Man-in-the-Moon Marigolds is a drama. The exact year is not indicated, however, the style and content of the play indicate that it is set in relatively modern times, probably during the early 1960s. Most of the action takes place in the front room of the Hunsdorfer house, a wooden structure that was once a vegetable shop run by Beatrice's father. The house is rundown and is strewn with clutter, symbolizing the broken bits and pieces of Beatrice's dreams. Beatrice has lived here her entire life. She feels trapped in her current circumstances and, to symbolize this, the playwright keeps her "trapped" in this room. Beatrice does not go out of the house during the entire course of the play.

Voice-overs

The play is framed by Tillie's voice-overs. This gives the impression that we are seeing the story through her eyes. Tillie's voice-overs help set up the themes of the play and give the audience a glimpse into Tillie's true self as she talks about the wonders of the atom and how science has opened her eyes to the possibilities of the world. At home Tillie is constantly stifled and berated. Zindel uses her voice-overs to allow her to speak her true feelings and dreams. This technique helps audiences to understand that Tillie is an optimist and a dreamer who can find good in the world no matter what her current circumstances.

Comic Relief

Zindel uses comic relief at various points in the play to break the tension for the audience. If the tension was sustained too long without a break, it would become too uncomfortable, and audiences would not want to continue following the story. The first scene with Nanny provides comic relief and serves to show that Beatrice has a sense of humor, although it is very sarcastic and biting. Janice Vickery's presentation at the science fair is also an important point of comic relief. It follows the very intense, climactic scene of the play. This is a place where the audience needs a "breather" before moving into the strong emotions of the last scene.

Telephone Calls

In *The Effect of Gamma Rays on Man-in-the-Moon Marigolds* the telephone represents the intrusion of the outside world. Beatrice remains in the house throughout the entire play. The only time she is seen interacting with the outside world is when she is on the telephone. During her telephone conversations, the audience can see how uncomfortable and inadequate Beatrice feels. This technique provides a way for the playwright to expand Beatrice's character without having to put her in multiple settings or bring a lot of other characters into the play.

Plot Structure

The play follows a standard linear, climactic structure, which means it has a beginning, a middle,

and an end that follow in chronological order and lead to a climax, or moment of greatest intensity, near the end of the play. Act 1 precedes act 2 in time. Each event follows in sequence, except for Tillie's voice-overs, which are timeless. It is not important for the audience to know when Tillie is speaking these voice-overs, because they are there to give insight into Tillie's character and to develop the themes of the play, not to move the story along.

HISTORICAL CONTEXT

In the early 1960s, nuclear arms began to play a big part in world relations. The Cold War between the United States and the Soviet Union was in full force. In 1962, the Cuban missile crisis brought the world to the brink of disaster when the Soviet Union placed nuclear missiles aimed at the United States in Cuba. President John F. Kennedy demanded that the missiles be removed and warned that, if the missiles were launched, the United States would retaliate, resulting in an all-out nuclear war. The Soviets withdrew the missiles, but the incident deeply shattered Americans sense of well-being. Many citizens no longer felt safe. Families began to build bomb shelters in their backyards, and schools began holding regular bomb safety drills. In 1963, the United States and the U.S.S.R. agreed to install a "hotline" from the White House to the Kremlin to try to avoid nuclear disaster. That same year the two countries and Great Britain signed a nuclear testing ban.

During this time, there was also a great deal of scientific activity and experimentation, particularly in the areas of radioactivity and nuclear energy. Scientists recognized the power that atomic energy provided, and they continued to look for ways to harness this energy for positive means. The effects of radioactivity weren't widely known, and experiments such as the one conducted by Tillie in the play provided new information on the uses and dangers of this mysterious force. The growing interest in the use of nuclear energy also sparked the rise of the environmental movement. Many citizens became concerned that tampering with the destructive force of nuclear energy would destroy the Earth's ecological systems. Some were afraid mankind would destroy the planet.

On the American political scene, 1963 was a year of crisis. It is often considered the year in which the United States "lost its innocence," when

COMPARE & CONTRAST

- **1960:** About 36 percent of women have jobs outside the home.

  Today: 60 percent of women are in the work force.

- **1962:** The Cuban missile crisis puts the United States on the verge of an all-out nuclear war with the Soviet Union. Schools conduct bomb safety drills.

  Today: The Cold War is over and the Soviet Union no longer exists. A great deal more is known about the effects of nuclear war.

- **1962:** The Telstar communications satellite relays the first trans-Atlantic television pictures.

  Today: Many people own personal satellite dishes that allow them access to hundreds of channels.

- **1964:** The United States space probe *Ranger 7* takes the first clear, close-range photographs of the moon.

  Today: The moon has been walked on, and Mars has been photographed. Space travel is increasingly common.

- **1964:** Less than 13 percent of families are headed by a single parent. There is a strong stigma associated with living in a single-parent household.

  Today: More than 27 percent of families are headed by a single parent. It is no longer unusual and does not carry the same stigma it once did.

President John F. Kennedy was assassinated in Dallas. It was a tumultuous time, as many Americans began questioning long-held beliefs. The civil rights movement was gaining momentum, as African Americans voiced their demands for equal rights. In 1963, riots broke out during civil rights demonstrations in Birmingham, Alabama. That same year the Reverend Dr. Martin Luther King, Jr., led 250,000 people to Washington, D.C., in a march for freedom where he gave his famous ''I have a dream'' speech. At this time, women's views of themselves also started changing. They had been taught that they were to stay home, raise families, and be dependent upon their husbands, but they began to discover that this type of life left them feeling unfulfilled. Many women longed for experiences apart from home and family, just as Beatrice longs to escape her circumstances in the play. In 1963, Betty Friedan published *The Feminine Mystique,* a book that discussed the way women were feeling and contributed to the start of the women's movement. More and more women began to look for work and opportunities outside of the home, and the typical American family started to undergo drastic changes.

CRITICAL OVERVIEW

Paul Zindel's *The Effect of Gamma Rays on Man-in-the-Moon Marigolds* was first produced in 1964 by the Alley Theatre in Houston, Texas. It launched his career as a serious playwright. Nina Vance, head of the Alley Theatre, was so impressed with the play that she took an immediate option on Zindel's next work. The play was also presented on television in October 1966 by the National Educational Television as part of its *New York TV Theatre* series. The televised version was not very well received, however. In the *Dictionary of Literary Biography,* Ruth Strickland notes, ''Reviewers of the television drama found little to praise.'' The version shown on television had been cut, however, and this may have caused the unenthusiastic reception.

The *Effect of Gamma Rays on Man-in-the-Moon Marigolds* opened off-Broadway on April 7, 1970, at the Mercer-O'Casey Theatre. This time the reviews were overwhelmingly positive. Zindel was hailed as a promising new playwright. Audiences and critics appreciated his ability to create believable teenage characters and found the story of the

Hunsdorfer family very poetic and moving. Many critics compared the play to Tennessee Williams's *The Glass Menagerie,* noting its sensitive portrayal of human relationships. As Ruth Strickland writes, "many critics found the play old-fashioned in the best sense of the word, praising its realism, yet moved by its poetry." In *American Theatre 1969–1970,* Clive Barnes gives the play very high praise, writing, "One of the greatest, probably the greatest, hit of the current off-Broadway season, Paul Zindel's *The Effect of Gamma Rays on Man-in-the-Moon Marigolds,* would clearly have made it equally as well on Broadway." The play continued off-Broadway until a fire forced it to move into the New Theatre on Broadway. The play remained there until May 14, 1972, when it closed after 819 performances. The play won numerous prestigious awards, including a 1970 Obie Award as best play of the season, a 1970 New York Drama Critics' Circle Award as best American play of the year, and the Pulitzer Prize for Drama in 1971.

Some critics felt that *The Effect of Gamma Rays on Man-in-the-Moon Marigolds* was so widely accepted by audiences because it hearkened back to a more traditional format than had been seen recently on many off-Broadway stages. In the late 1960s there was a wild explosion of experimental theatre off-Broadway. Many shows had little or no story line and were not much more than a collection of random acting exercises. While some audiences appreciated the experimentation and innovation, many found it hard to make sense of these performances. Plays with a story line were easier for audiences to understand. *The Effect of Gamma Rays on Man-in-the-Moon Marigolds* provided a story, and therefore appealed to a wider audience. A play with a well-crafted story line is sometimes known as a "well-made play." Zindel's play can be considered a well-made play, and Clive Barnes notes this feature in *American Theatre 1969–1970* as part of its appeal: "The off-Broadway show that was most successful was Paul Zindel's *The Effect of Gamma Rays on Man-in-the-Moon Marigolds.* Interestingly, it is almost completely a model of the well-made play, a family drama of the kind we thought had gone out with Arthur Miller and Tennessee Williams."

One criticism that has been leveled against the play is that it is melodramatic and overly sentimental. While most critics have appreciated the gentle tone of the piece, some feel that Zindel is a bit too sappy in his presentation of the family's situation. Ruth Strickland notes that Zindel's "weaknesses are lapses into melodrama" and, in the *Concise*

Dictionary of American Literary Biography, Jack Forman describes the piece as "a domestic melodrama with an occasional lapse into sentimentality." Overall, though, the response of audiences and critics alike has been positive. In his recent book *Hot Seat: Theater Criticism for the New York Times, 1980–1993,* Frank Rich notes that he finds the play "compassionate," and he appreciates that Zindel avoids "simple moral judgments." The play is still performed in regional theatres throughout the country, a testament to its quality and the universality of its themes.

CRITICISM

Beth A. Kattelman

Kattelman has a Ph.D. and specializes in modern drama. In this essay, she discusses the theme of the triumph of the human spirit in Zindel's play.

The Effect of Gamma Rays on Man-in-the-Moon Marigolds presents the themes of alienation and man's inhumanity to man played out in the microcosm of the family. Life has not been kind to Beatrice Hunsdorfer, and she takes her frustration and hatred of the world out on those around her. Beatrice has been deeply hurt and has developed an instinct to lash out at others before they get the chance to do the same to her. She lives by the rule, *Do unto others before they do unto you.* She is particularly abusive to her daughters. Throughout the course of the play she calls them names, makes fun of them, and does whatever she can to thwart their dreams and desires. Beatrice constantly reminds her daughters that they are nothing more than a burden to her: "Marry the wrong man and before you know it he's got you tied down with two stones around your neck for the rest of your life." She shows little warmth or affection and uses her children as scapegoats for her anger at the world.

Yet, even though the play presents the bleak situation created by Beatrice's frustration and despair, it also offers a glimmer of hope in the character of Tillie who, despite her mother's cruelty, refuses to be defeated. Tillie embodies the spirit of the survivor. Tillie is an outcast at school. She is awkward and is considered strange and unattractive by her classmates. Yet Tillie is able to appreciate what life has to offer because she has discovered something more important than external appearances, something more lasting. She has discovered

Joanne Woodward as Beatrice Hunsdorfer in a film adaptation of The Effect of Gamma Rays on Man-in-the-Moon Marigolds.

that she is important. This knowledge gives her an inner strength. As Beverly A. Haley and Kenneth L. Donelson note in their essay ''Pigs and Hamburger, Cadavers and Gamma Rays,'' ''Tillie emerges a potential winner, for her thirst for knowledge and her scientific experiment with the marigolds have given her confidence in her own self-worth.'' In the play, Zindel gives the message that if one can hold on to one's faith and can see past the immediate ugliness to the beautiful potential in the world, there is the possibility not only to survive but also to triumph. Tillie's realization that all things are interconnected inspires her. ''Most important, I suppose, my experiment has made me feel important—every atom in me, in everybody, has come from the sun—from places beyond our dreams.'' She knows that there is life beyond her mother's household and that there is a huge world out there filled with possibilities. Tillie remains true to herself and her vision and is thus able to succeed. There is a sense that her victory at the science fair is just the first in a string of great accomplishments.

Zindel has captured an important theme of the play in its title. Although Clive Barnes of the *New York Times* once called the title ''one of the most discouraging titles yet devised by man,'' it is nonetheless appropriate. This phrase provides a clue as to what the play is about. The title of the play refers to not only the science project Tillie is working on, but also the larger theme of the influence human beings can have on one another and the different ways people can react under the same circumstances. Beatrice's tirades and her constant negative pronouncements about the world are the ''gamma rays'' which bombard Tillie and Ruth. Throughout the play, Beatrice sends out almost nothing but negative energy, and it works to slowly damage many of those around her. But not everyone in the environment succumbs. Although Beatrice treats both her daughters with cruelty and abuse, their reactions are quite different. Tillie remains quietly true to her own vision and thus counteracts some of Beatrice's damaging effects. Ruth, on the other hand, tries desperately to fight back, but with little success. She is ultimately on a path of self-destruction, perhaps destined to repeat Beatrice's mistakes. Just as the gamma rays destroy some of the marigolds while bringing about wonderful mutations in

WHAT DO I READ NEXT?

- *The Glass Menagerie*, a play by Tennessee Williams written in 1945, also deals with shattered dreams and a mother who is unable to appreciate her children for what they really are. Her inability to face reality keeps the family trapped in the past, unable to truly communicate with each other.

- *100 Amazing Make-It-Yourself Science Fair Projects,* written and illustrated by Glen Vecchione in 1989 is a collection of winning science fair projects for students. It contains projects on a wide variety of subjects. Specific steps to create each project and illustrations are included.

- *My Darling, My Hamburger* is a novel written by Paul Zindel in 1969. It deals with how parental influence can affect the boyfriend-girlfriend relationships of teenagers.

- *The Miracle Worker* is a play written by William Gibson in 1956. It tells the story of how Helen Keller, a young girl who was blind, deaf, and dumb was taught to communicate with the world by her brilliant teacher Annie Sullivan.

- *Respect for Acting* was written by Uta Hagen in 1973. It is a handbook that gives very good, practical advice for anyone interested in becoming an actor. The book introduces acting concepts and terminology and provides exercises that can be used by the student to develop his or her craft.

- *Surviving High School* is a book written by Mike Riera in 1997. It provides a straightforward discussion of the challenges and problems teenagers encounter in high school. Each chapter discusses ways young adults can meet these challenges. The book contains many quotes and firsthand experiences from teens.

---

others, one daughter succumbs, while the other becomes even stronger in her determination to succeed. As Ruth Strickland notes in the *Dictionary of Literary Biography,* ''The message is clear: Tillie is the mutant who has emerged from a horrifying environment with faith and potential intact—she is the double bloom. . . . Ruth is a victim of her mother's despair.''

Numerous critics have praised *The Effect of Gamma Rays on Man-in-the-Moon Marigolds* for its realistic portrayal of young adults and the perseverance they can possess. There are many examples throughout history of young adults who have faced adversity with courage and spirit. One of the most extreme examples, but one that has some parallels to the play, is the way in which the young Anne Frank was able to persevere during the two years she and her family were forced to hide from the Nazis in the attic of an Amsterdam house. Although Anne's circumstances were much more dire than those Tillie finds herself in, there is a similarity in

the way both young girls are able to reach deep within themselves to find the courage and strength to carry on. Even the words they use have a similar ring. In her diary, Anne Frank wrote, ''in spite of everything, I still believe that people are really good at heart. I simply can't build up my hopes on a foundation consisting of confusion, misery and death. . . . [I]f I look up into the heavens, I think that it will all come right, that this cruelty too will end, and that peace and tranquillity will return again.'' Tillie also finds strength by looking beyond her current situation to the possibilities of what might be: ''I believe this with all my heart, THE DAY WILL COME WHEN MANKIND WILL THANK GOD FOR THE STRANGE AND BEAUTIFUL ENERGY FROM THE ATOM.'' Both girls are able to hold onto their faith in the human spirit despite the odds. Tillie and Anne are optimists, and that is their ultimate triumph.

Although Tillie is definitely the heroine of the play, she is not perfect. In a way, she may be too

> BEATRICE HAS BEEN DEEPLY HURT AND HAS DEVELOPED AN INSTINCT TO LASH OUT AT OTHERS BEFORE THEY GET THE CHANCE TO DO THE SAME TO HER. SHE LIVES BY THE RULE, *DO UNTO OTHERS BEFORE THEY DO UNTO YOU*."

optimistic. For instance, in her exploration and discussion of radioactivity, she all but ignores the bad potential atomic energy may hold. Only one time in the play does she briefly mention the destructive potential of the atom, saying "My experiment has shown some of the strange effects radiation can produce . . . and how dangerous it can be if not handled correctly." Tillie downplays the negative and chooses to see the world her way. Ironically, this actually gives her some similarities with Beatrice. Each of these characters sees what she wants to see. Beatrice is determined to find the bad side of everything. Tillie is determined to find the good. Irony is an incongruity between what might be expected and what actually occurs, and there is irony in Tillie's one-sided attitude toward atomic energy. This aspect has been mentioned by some critics who found it interesting that Zindel would embed this celebration of atomic energy in the play. An uncredited author in *Types of Drama* notes, "Somewhat unfashionably, Zindel takes science and the atom not as symbols of man's alienation and death, but as symbols of man's heavenly origin or his link with the sun." Zindel does not rely on the typical or expected way of presenting issues and families. That is one thing which makes the play so intriguing and powerful.

Paul Zindel writes from personal experience. He knows what it is like to grow up in a difficult situation and to come out on top. Zindel's youth was spent in the shadow of an abusive, slightly mad mother. He found a way to survive, and he wants his audience, particularly young people, to find a way to do the same. In an interview for *Top of the News,* Zindel told Audrey Eaglen, "I'm telling the kids that I love the underdog and sympathize with his struggle because that's what I was and am in many

ways still. I want my kids to feel worthy, to search for hope against all odds." Zindel's message is clear: Find a way to believe in yourself; you are important.

The Effect of Gamma Rays on Man-in-the-Moon Marigolds gives audiences a lot to consider. It raises many more questions than it answers. Some of these questions were consciously written into the play, while others came as a surprise, even to Zindel. In his new introduction to the most recently published edition of the play he writes, "I found questions lurking in the shadows of Beatrice Hunsdorfer's vegetable store that I hadn't even known I'd asked. What is it, really, to grow up in a home without a loving, competent father or mother? Do we yet understand the pain and loneliness and disability of kids who do? And from where do survivors of such homes conjure the magic to insist that, despite everything, their dreams will stay alive?" These are important questions, and Zindel hopes that by raising them he opens up the opportunity for audiences to make some discoveries about themselves. In his new introduction Zindel also states, "It's important, too, that those who read and hear our stories find answers for their own lives."

The Effect of Gamma Rays on Man-in-the-Moon Marigolds is a play about the triumph of the human spirit that still resonates with audiences today because it ultimately deals with universal concepts. But the thing that has sustained its appeal is its optimistic message of hope. After sharing some painful, yet funny moments in the lives of these characters, the audience is left with an upbeat, positive message summed up in Tillie's final declaration, "Atom. Atom. What a beautiful word."

Source: Beth A. Kattelman, in an essay for *Drama for Students,* Gale Group, 2001.

Jeffrey B. Loomis

In the following essay, Loomis extols the anti-sexist message of The Effect of Gamma Rays on Man-in-the-Moon Marigolds *and points out the correlation between Zindel's play and Dante's Divine Comedy.*

Already preparing a bridge to such a recent male feminist play as Robert Harling's *Steel Magnolias,* Paul Zindel, in *The Effect of Gamma Rays on Man-in-the-Moon Marigolds,* gave us, two full decades ago, a strong indictment of sexism. In Zindel's revisionary Dantesque play, the frumpy housewife

Beatrice Hunsdorfer may look like an illusion-frustrated female transplanted into a Northern urban landscape from the barren Mississippi River towns of Tennessee Williams. Beatrice's tantrum in Act Two, turning her house into a chaos, may seem fully explained when she declares "I hate the world"; she thus appears at first no more positive a rebel than Kopit's Madame Rosepettle in *Oh Dad, Poor Dad, Mamma's Hung You in the Closet and I'm Feeling So Sad.* But Beatrice's rebellion does not seek merely to hiss venom toward dominant patriarchs, in the manner adopted by La Rosepettle, and she surely does not demonstrate strength (like Williams's Serafina Delle Rose and Maggie Pollitt) only while working out an alliance with males on whom she remains dependent. If Beatrice is like a Williams character, the model seems Big Mama. Like that Mississippi matriarch by the end of her play, Beatrice fully intends to create a freer, more dignified life for herself and the children she loves—including, in her case, a highly intelligent daughter, Tillie, who, if she fully grasps her evident educational opportunities, might eventually live a life of considerable success.

Whatever the superficial resemblances one might remark between *Gamma Rays* and Williams's *Glass Menagerie,* the "hopeful" philosophy apparent in Zindel seems a radical departure from Tennessee Williams. Williams's most famous heroines, in *Menagerie* and *Streetcar,* remain, for all their vividness of personality, resolutely trapped in all the illusions imposed on them by patriarchal culture. His heroines surely often enough prove sexually liberated—but still, frequently, remain encaged. Perhaps the ideal Williams heroine is one of calm spiritual liberation—a person like Hannah in *Iguana,* Yet Hannah, despite her spiritual liberty, remains economically starving; Big Mama is more amply fed, but only because she inherited a wealthy man's estate. Even though Hannah and other Williams heroines might become, like Big Mama, capable businesspersons, few even dare think of seeking economic self-determination, as Zindel's Beatrice finally does.

Gamma Rays may ultimately appear too much a product of late Sixties social optimism; Zindel does not seem aware of how harshly even educated Tillies must struggle for independence. Yet the main power of this play still remains its long-unrecognized anti-sexist vision. That vision makes it clearly a historically prophetic work; it is not, as multiple critics have narrowly claimed, a mere tired echo of earlier writers.

> IT IS, OF COURSE, TILLIE WHO VOICES THIS PLAY'S MOST DANTESQUE SENTIMENTS; SHE SHARES DANTE'S BELIEF THAT ALL EARTHLY ATOMS ARE CONNECTED WITH ORIGINATING STARS OF LOVE; THAT THEY WERE, AS SHE SPECULATES, 'FORMED FROM A TONGUE OF FIRE [THE HOLY SPIRIT?] THAT SCREAMED THROUGH THE HEAVENS UNTIL THERE WAS OUR SUN.'"

Gamma Rays ends with the rhapsodic teenage scientist Tillie Hunsdorfer declaring that

> . . . [T]he effect of gamma rays on man-in-the-moon marigolds has made me curious about *the sun and the stars,* for the universe itself must be like a world of great atoms—and I want to know more about it. But most important, I suppose, my experiment has made me feel important—every atom in me, in everybody, has come *from the sun*—from places *beyond our dreams.* The atoms of our hands, the atoms of *our hearts* . . . (emphasis mine).

Surely, whether consciously or not, these lines—like Tillie's earlier response to a wondrous atomic cloud-chamber—call to mind both the imagery and the visionary fervor which conclude Dante's *Paradiso:*

> . . . [L]ike to a wheel whose circle nothing jars,
> Already on my desire and will prevailed The Love
> that moves the sun and the others stars.

Zindel's play—if by accident, nonetheless with uncanny regularity—demonstrates remarkable affinity with Dante's *Divine Comedy.* The clearest hint of such affinity is Zindel's choice of the two main characters' names: Beatrice and Matilda. Obviously, Beatrice Hunsdorfer does share the name of Dante's central female character, although she markedly differs from her namesake, the medieval icon of spiritually quiescent splendor. Tillie Hunsdorfer, the incipient teenage intellectual, bears more direct resemblance to the Dantesque character she recalls. Matilda of Tuscany, the likely historical model for the character Matelda whom readers meet at the height of Purgatory near Dante's Beatrice, was "a wise and powerful woman . . . splendid, illustrious . . . surpassing all others in her brilliance . . . educated, [with] a large collection of books. . . . "

At least in Tillie Hunsdorfer, then, Zindel has a character who closely recalls an analogous character in Dante's great poem. It is, of course, Tillie who voices this play's most Dantesque sentiments; she shares Dante's belief that all earthly atoms are connected with originating stars of Love; that they were, as she speculates, "formed from a tongue of fire [the Holy Spirit?] that screamed through the heavens until there was our sun."

But the Dantesque affinities of Zindel's text do not cease with Beatrice's name and Tillie's name and personality. Zindel's earliest stage directions in the play set the action in "a room of wood," "once a vegetable store." The mention of "wood" and "vegetation," and, most of all, the note that this place was once "a point of debarkation for a horse-drawn wagon to bring its wares to a small town," all summon to my mind Dante's *selva oscura,* the "dark wood" which serves, in *Inferno* 1, as Dante's own "point of debarkation" for a pilgrimage toward the starry multifoliate rose of Paradise. According to Dante, he completed the visionary journey which young Matilda Hunsdorfer hopes, in her lifetime, to share.

But Matilda's mother Beatrice seems long ago to have lost any chance for a meaningful pilgrimage through life. Even as a child, she thought herself proven unworthy to take over her father's vegetable business—to sit atop its wagon, as if clothed in the radiant garb of Dante's own Edenic chariot-rider Beatrice, and be a woman recognized (independently of any male mate) for her talents. She might, given other life circumstances than those she knew, have imitated Dante's successful pilgrimage. But—because her father truly was not, as she mistakenly still wants to believe, one who "made up for all other men in this whole world"—she encountered in him her primal "bogey man." He made her think that she, as a woman, was inferior to all men, that she could not care for his vegetable business either before or after his death, that she needed instead to "marry . . . [and] be taken care of." As a result, by the time of the play's scenes Beatrice has become a perpetual "widow of confusion," much as Dante began (but only began) the *Commedia* as one whose "way was lost."

Like Dante, too, Beatrice Hunsdorfer has dream-visions. But her visions do not foresee an attainable future bliss; they recall, instead, a "nightmare" of past denial. Her dreams, also like Dante's, contain ghosts of lost loved ones. Yet Dante's lost Beatrice still beckons ahead of him; she there pledges to teach him "nobility, . . . virtue, . . . the Redeemed Life," his soul's "ordained end." By contrast, Beatrice Hunsdorfer's lost earthly father, as a ghost, continues to deny her the self-esteem he first refused her long ago:

> And while he was sleeping, I got the horses hitched up and went riding around the block waving to everyone. . . . I had more nerve than a bear when I was a kid. Let me tell you it takes nerve to sit up on that wagon every day yelling "Apples!" . . .
>
> . . . . .
>
> Did he find out? He came running down the street after me and started spanking me right on top of the wagon—not hard—but it was embarrassing—and I had one of those penny marshmallow ships in the back pocket of my overalls, and it got all squished. And you better believe I never did it again. . . .
>
> Let me tell you about my nightmare that used to come back and back: Well, I'm on Papa's wagon, but it's newer and shinier, and it's being pulled by beautiful white horses, not dirty workhorses—these are like circus horses with long manes and tinsel—and the wagon is blue, shiny blue. And it's full—filled with yellow apples and grapes and green squash.
>
> . . . . .
>
> Huge bells swinging on a gold braid [are] strung across the back of the wagon, and they're going DONG, DONG . . . DONG, DONG. And I'm yelling "APPLES! PEARS! CUCUM . . . BERS!"
>
> . . . . .
>
> And then I turn down our street and all the noise stops. This long street, with all the doors of the houses shut and everything crowded next to each other, and there's not a soul around. And then I start getting afraid that the vegetables are going to spoil . . . and that nobody's going to buy anything, and I feel as though I shouldn't be on the wagon, and I keep trying to call out.
>
> But there isn't a sound. Not a single sound. Then I turn my head and look at the house across the street. I see an upstairs window, and a pair of hands pull the curtains slowly apart. I see the face of my father and my heart stands still. . . .
>
> Ruth . . . take the light out of my eyes.

Convinced by her sexist father that she had no gifts for managing her own meaningful career—"afraid that [if guarded only by her] the vegetables would spoil . . . and . . . nobody . . . [would] buy anything"—Beatrice has ever since been trapped in her own everyday earthly Inferno: on a "long street," "everything crowded," "not a soul around."

Although she is like Zindel's own mother in her concocting ''charmingly frantic scheme[s] . . . to get rich quick,'' she is, not surprisingly, highly jealous of her invalid boarder Nanny's daughter, ''Miss Career Woman of the Year.'' She also envies her own daughters, refusing to admit that they have gifts which could lead them to careers even semi-professional. She can't believe that her daughter Ruth can even use a typewriter; at one point, she proclaims that Tillie should forget about her scientific ambitions and instead go to work in a dime store.

And Tillie might have been behind that dime store sales counter the next week had she not suddenly become a finalist in her high school's Science Fair. Her science teacher Mr. Goodman—himself typically sexist, at least in his shock that ''he never saw a girl do anything like that before''—was convinced of her promise. As a slightly inattentive Ruth reports to her mother, Mr. Goodman said that Tillie ''was going to be another Madame Pasteur.''

So Tillie is spared the dime store, and Beatrice as her mother seems simultaneously spared her sense of being a complete ''zero,'' ''the original half-life!'' Once it reaches her consciousness that Tillie has achieved what Ruth calls ''an honor,'' Beatrice can declare, as she embraces her brainy child, an expletive which almost briefly approaches a creedal statement of faith: ''Oh, my God. . . .'' And, as she tells Ruth in the next act, ''Somewhere in the back of this turtle-sized brain of mine I feel just a little proud! Jesus Christ!''

Indeed, it does not seem altogether fanciful to suggest that Act Two of *Gamma Rays* becomes (although not at all in a traditional Dantesque manner) Beatrice Hunsdorfer's encounter with a personal purgatory. As Act One ends, the school principal Mr. Berg (translation from the German: ''Mr. [Purgatorial?] Mountain'') invites Beatrice to the Science Fair competition ceremonies. At the opening of the play's second act she has dressed for that event in a feathery costume, leading Ruth to quote some gossip from one of her mother's childhood companions: ''[Mama's] idea of getting dressed up is to put on all the feathers in the world and go as a bird. Always trying to get somewhere, like a great big bird.'' Has Beatrice always frustratingly hoped that an eagle would lift her, as it lifted Dante, up to higher purgatorial crests?

Beatrice, after all, recalls her own youth as being something like Tillie's youth now. She might have advanced toward a better life had she not been intimidated (as Tillie herself is not) by others' disparagings. As Ruth tells Tillie, Beatrice as a girl ''was just like you and everybody thought she was a big weirdo''; ''First they had Betty the Loon, and now they've got Tillie the Loon.''

Unfortunately, the selfish Ruth who utters these words eventually comes close to ruining her mother's chances for any sort of purgatorial experience. In brattish rage because she herself is being asked to skip the Science Fair and replace her mother as guardian of Nanny the Boarder, Ruth screeches ''Goodnight, Betty the Loon'' at a Beatrice who is finally escaping, if still somewhat timidly, her fear of the outside world in order to attend Tillie's school ceremonies. Ruth's vicious ploy does gain her what she wants: Beatrice now immediately returns (or so it seems) to the agoraphobic terror of life which has for so long characterized her; she ''helplessly'' sends Ruth off with the Science Fair paraphernalia that she herself was to carry, and she then ''breaks into tears that shudder her body, and the lights go down on her pathetic form.''

Yet Act One had already prepared the way for Beatrice's doing something (in an earthly purgatory) with the insights which her memories (like Dante's in non-earthly Inferno) were giving her. She said then that she had ''almost forgot[ten] about everything [she] was supposed to be.'' Still, Zindel built irony into such of her statements as ''Me and cobalt-60! Two of the biggest half-lifes you ever saw!'' Zindel's stage-directions soon afterwards say that Beatrice was forming ''mushroom cloud'' smoke rings with her cigarettes; thus, her ''half-life,'' like that of cobalt-60, always perhaps could, in its ''mushroom cloud'' explosion, hold positive mutation within it.

And, in the last scenes of *Gamma Rays,* Beatrice does lunge after such positive mutation. She tears newspapers off from the house's windows, then rearranges tables and places tablecloths and napkins on them. She calls Nanny's daughter, ordering her to take the old boarder away. Sitting down, guffawing over that conquest, and hitting her daughter's pet rabbit cage with her foot, she decides to chloroform the creature—which is, in Hugh Hefner's America, not only a children's pet, but an unfortunate symbol of female suppression.

No mere self-centered cruelty leads Beatrice to these behaviors. She is striving to make meaningful mutation occur in her (and in her daughters') life. Thus, when the girls start to express a fear that she may truly have killed their bunny, she doesn't directly respond to them. She matter-of-factly pronounces broader concerns: "Nanny goes tomorrow. First thing tomorrow"; "I don't know what it's going to be. Maybe a tea shop. Maybe not."

So long trapped in a hellish rut because not daring to lead a business-woman's produce-wagon off from "a point of debarkation," pilgrim Beatrice now seeks to redirect her life. For her, "hat[ing] the world" has not meant a spiritual leap beyond that world, in the manner of Dante's original Beatrice. She has, instead, made a ramshackle earthbound leap into self-assertion. And yet a certain level of spiritual other-centeredness has allied itself with that self-assertion. Even though she will force her daughters to "work in the [tea-shop] kitchen," she will not any longer seek to deny them an education for future self-determination. They will have "regular hours" in the business, but those hours will be scheduled "after school." She will no longer live so much in the shadow of her father that she tries to limit others in the way he limited her.

In introductory comments to the *Gamma Rays* script, which are really an unofficial dedication of the play to his mother, Zindel makes it clear that he considered that woman a beautiful mutation: someone who had at least striven, in her limited way, to become like the liberated modern mom he described in a short children's piece written for *Ms.* in 1976:

> . . . She says "Absolutely not," when I want to drive the car, and "Have a good time," when I tell her I'm running away to Miami. She doesn't want me to know when we don't have enough money. . . . If I see her crying she says, "It's just something in my eye." She tells me secrets like she's lonely. When I tell her I miss my father she hugs me and says he misses me too. I love my mother. I really do.

("I Love My Mother")

Zindel has given the reader enough information to show his own mother's clear resemblances to Beatrice Hunsdorfer. One thus chuckles at his jocose offhand comment: "I suspect [the play] is autobiographical." Besides, autobiography may extend past the characterization of Beatrice to a character (unseen onstage) who may in some ways markedly suggest Paul Zindel himself: Mr. Goodman, Tillie's high school chemistry teacher.

Zindel taught high school chemistry for ten years and only left Staten Island, where he had taught, after the Pulitzer Prize award for *Gamma Rays.* Despite that fact, one of course would not claim that he deliberately insults himself when he has Beatrice at first describe Mr. Goodman as a "delightful and handsome young man" but then refer to him, a few minutes later, as "a Hebrew hermaphrodite." After all, the "hermaphrodite" reference is not ultimately intended as a physical description—at least not in the play's thematic undertext. A statement which at first seems only to exemplify Beatrice's crude-mouthed bitterness more importantly helps introduce the play's revisionist Hebrew theology, viewing all humankind as androgynous.

Zindel's anti-sexist thoughts of 1970 might be challenged now by such radical feminists as Mary Daly. She considers "androgyny" to be "a vacuous term," "expressing pseudo-wholeness" as an example of one of those "false universalisms (e.g., humanism, people's liberation) . . . which Spinsters must leap over, . . . must span" in order to affirm their own "intuition of integrity" [*Gyn/Ecology: The Metaethics of Radical Feminism* (1978)]. And, it is true, Zindel's androgyny still has a patriarchal sound; his anti-sexist thesis emphasizes the pun "Adam"/ "atom," and he thus does recall for us the name of the first legendary Hebrew patriarch. Still, even Daly would grant "deceptive" but hard-to-avoid concepts of androgyny some relative value in progress to a non-sexist world. And others would remain more encouraged than she by Zindel's androgynous creed.

That creed is voiced throughout a play which has appeared to invite regular misreading. For instance, despite her obvious affection for the character's gutsy energy, Edith Oliver claims that Beatrice "is as much a victim of her own nature as she is of circumstance" [*New Yorker,* 18 April 1970]. Yet, given Zindel's pointed indictment of her father's sexism, why should we be assigning Beatrice herself with a heavy load of blame? Adler does perceive, without explaining why, that Beatrice's father caused her psychological problems. And yet he, too, does not seem at all to sense that this is a feminist play; he does not discuss it in his mildly feminist chapter "Nora's American Cousins," and he indeed rates Beatrice's plan to open a tea-shop as "slightly outrageous."

I do not believe for a moment, as Adler implies and as Brustein shouts, that *Gamma Rays* simply clones the illusion-ridden mother-daughter encaging atmosphere of *The Glass Menagerie* [Thomas P. Adler, *Mirror on the Stage: The Pulitzer Plays as an Approach to American Drama* (1987); Robert Brustein, *The Culture Watch: Essays on Theatre and Society, 1969–1974* (1975)]. Jack Kroll approaches closer to the truth about the play when he says that "The calculus of love, jealous vengefulness, remorse, flaring hatred, and desperate reconciliation[,] among these three people fighting for spiritual life, is the point and merit of Zindel's affecting play" [*Newsweek,* 27 April 1970]. And Harold Clurman, that ever-trustworthy sage, adds that "In *Gamma Rays* . . . a real person [he means Tillie, but I think Beatrice also fits the description] flowers from the compost of abject defeat and hysteria" [*Nation,* 15 March 1971].

In the play's very opening monologue, Tillie expresses indomitable faith in human androgynous potential as she tells of how Mr. Goodman, in chemistry class, helped her sense that in adamic atoms of origin all human beings are equal:

> He told me to look at my hand, for a part of it came from a star that exploded too long ago to imagine. This part of me was formed from a tongue of fire that screamed through the heavens until there was our sun.
>
> . . . When there was life, perhaps this part of me got lost in a fern that was crushed and covered until it was coal. And then it was a diamond as beautiful as the star from which it had first come.
>
> . . . . And he called this bit of me an atom. And when he wrote the word, I fell in love with it.
>
> Atom.
>
> Atom.
>
> What a beautiful word.

For all its potential Dantesque echoes, Zindel's beautiful play finally shines with the ameliorative twentieth-century hope of an original, deeply sensitive, and highly enlightened modern good man. Paul Zindel, that man, is distant from the norm, even in our own age, as he rebuffs the patriarchal sexism which was not absent even from Dante's enlightened Renaissance Christianity. Neither Beatrice Hunsdorfer nor Paul Zindel wants to idealize only "GOODY-GOODY GIRLS" like Dante's Beatrice Portinari dei Bardi. Both believe, or at least want to believe by their play's conclusion, that, by "hat[ing] the world" which limits women to roles as men's slaves (or even sacred muses), they may recreate that world—in Zindel's words, "bring innovation to civilization, to institutions, . . . make contributions . . . [toward a] world which is a better place to live" [interview with Paul Janeczko, *English Journal 66,* No. 7 (October 1977)]. Zindel's revised Genesis myth (perhaps his own creatively revisionist response to the very different Garden of Eden scenes which culminate Dante's *Purgatorio*) suggests how hard a non-sexist world is to create, and

even to define. But such a world—in which we would recreate the meaning of "Adam" by finding our common personhood as "atom"—still seems to him a necessary earthly paradise, one always meant to be.

Source: Jeffrey B. Loomis, "Female Freedoms, Dantesque Dreams, and Paul Zindel's Anti-Sexist *The Effect of Gamma Rays on Man-in-the-Moon Marigolds,*" in *Studies in American Drama, 1945–Present,* Vol. 6, 1991, pp. 123–33.

Thomas P. Adler

In the following excerpt, Adler notes flaws in The Effect of Gamma Rays on Man-in-the-Moon Marigolds *and comments on the themes of the play.*

For critics to call *The Effects of Gamma Rays on Man-in-the-Moon Marigolds,* Paul Zindel's Off-Broadway work and the 1971 prize winner, "honest" or "engaging" creates the impression that here is a work which pretends to be nothing other than what it is: a stark if overly familiar family-problem play about life's ability to sustain itself against great odds—doing for a particular family something of what [Thornton] Wilder does for the universal family of man in [*The Skin of Our Teeth*]. Zindel, though, appears to have pretensions to something more, attempting to impart additional weight to his basically simple characterization and content through overblown stage trickery. Originally produced at Houston's Alley Theatre, *Effects* too obviously recalls Williams's *Glass Menagerie* in its character configurations and stylistic techniques: both concern a mother, who lives mostly on dreams, and two children, one healthy, the other not; both households lack a father, through either death or desertion; in both, a gentleman from the outside world helps, or thinks he helps, one of the children. The stylistic similarities are even more pronounced: in both, the stage setting, while essentially realistic—an apartment in St. Louis, a vegetable store in New York—is used in a nonillusionistic fashion, particularly as regards lighting and music. In *Menagerie,* the nonrealistic elements, including the images and legends flashed on a screen, are integral to the play as "memory" occurring in Tom's mind. In *Marigolds,* however, such devices as recorded voice-overs (sometimes used pretentiously as when a character's voice reverberates electronically) and blackouts and spotlighting of characters (equivalent to cinematic fade-outs and close-ups) seem superimposed upon a fragile content that cannot support them, as if the form could supply a weightiness the content does not itself merit. Zindel seems inter-

A scene from the 1972 film adaptation of Effect of Gamma Rays on Man-in-the-Moon Marigolds.

ested in the techniques in and for themselves, simply as a means of avoiding straight realism.

Furthermore, perhaps because Zindel usually writes novels for adolescents, the abundant symbolism in *Marigolds* frequently lacks subtlety. The mother, Beatrice, for example, to assuage her guilt over having sent her own father off to a sanatorium, cares for the senile Nanny who, with her "smile from a soul half-departed" and her "shuffling motion that reminds one of a ticking clock," serves as a walking personification of death and of how affluent Americans (her daughter is "Miss

Career Woman") mistreat their aged parents. More compellingly, the once orderly vegetable store now symbolically reflects the clutter and refuse of Beatrice's psychic and emotional life. With her motto "just yesterday," Beatrice lives on reminiscences of things *past*—a word prominently displayed on a placard at the high school science exhibit—on would-have-beens and should-have-beens. All her life she has romantically dreamed and schemed, yet she has seldom carried through on her plans, some of them, like turning the run-down store into a neighborhood tea shop, slightly outrageous. Like Willy Loman [in

Arthur Miller's *Death of a Salesman*], Beatrice tends to blame something outside herself for her failure, though she accurately assesses the way that a competitive, success-oriented society attempts to force everyone into a predetermined mold, decrying the lack of tolerance and the levelling down to sameness and mediocrity that, paradoxically, is a part of the American system: ''If you're just a little bit different in this world, they try to kill you off.'' Difference may threaten the status quo and not be easily handled or accommodated, yet Zindel argues not only that some differences are beneficial but that variation rather than sameness is essential for there to be progress.

Although Zindel's exposition leaves some past events annoyingly obscure, it seems to have been criticism by the father she idolized that began Beatrice's descent into a present condition she characterizes as ''half-life'' and ''zero.'' One day she hitched up the horses and rode through the streets selling fruit, to be met by her father's stern rebuke; ever since, she has dreamed of riding a shiny wagon pulled by white horses, only to see the forbidding figure of her father look on disapprovingly. She married badly, merely to please her father, but then no man could live up to her dream. After she took her father off to the hospital, she had the horses ''taken care of''—a cycle of failure, guilt, and still more failure.

The cycle of parent destroying child continues in Beatrice's erratic relationship with her daughters, shifting suddenly between compassion and bitterness—in much the way that the pet rabbit is alternately loved and then hurt. Beatrice's older daughter, the mentally disturbed Ruth who was traumatized by contact with death and violence, tells tales, craves the attention of men by flaunting her sexuality, and appears just as destructive and vindictive as her mother; when she cannot have what she desires, she ruins it for everyone else. The younger Tillie, in her awkwardness and unprettiness and firm grasp on reality, stands as Ruth's opposite and a living denial that one need be determined by heredity and environment. Tillie discovers a much-needed father figure in her high school teacher (unfortunately named Mr. Goodman), who introduces her to the word *atom,* which she comes to love. The notion that everything in the universe, herself included, is somehow connected with every other thing from the moment of creation enthralls her; it provides a fixed point of reference and a feeling of importance. For her science project, she exposes marigold seeds to radiation, which need not produce sterility and may

> DIFFERENCE MAY THREATEN THE STATUS QUO AND NOT BE EASILY HANDLED OR ACCOMMODATED, YET ZINDEL ARGUES NOT ONLY THAT SOME DIFFERENCES ARE BENEFICIAL BUT THAT VARIATION RATHER THAN SAMENESS IS ESSENTIAL FOR THERE TO BE PROGRESS."

even yield a positive effect: while those that receive little radiation are normal and those exposed to excessive radiation (like Beatrice and Ruth) are killed or dwarfed, those subject to only moderate radiation produce mutations, some of which (like Tillie, who has experienced very detrimental influences but has emerged relatively unscathed) are good and wonderful things. Against all odds, Tillie not only survives but actually thrives.

Finally, though, Zindel's optimism does not grow organically from the play. Some might argue that Tillie's (and the playwright's) optimism, because it is won with so much difficulty and is so at variance with the adverse and negative atmosphere from which she arises, is therefore all the more impressive and no more facile or unwarranted than Wilder's. The widely divergent perspectives of the two writers, however, militate against this: where Wilder discerns a pattern of ultimate success after repeated failures over the entire sweep of human history, Zindel ties his faith and hope to a specific—and atypical rather than representative—household that he then proposes as symbolic and universally applicable. Though Zindel seems to find little difficulty in asserting this optimism, an audience might have a considerably harder time assenting to it.

Source: Thomas P. Adler, ''The Idea of Progress,'' in *Mirror on the Stage: The Pulitzer Plays as an Approach to American Drama,* Purdue University Press, 1987, pp. 127–41.

Walter Kerr

Kerr is an American essayist, playwright, and Pulitzer Prize-winning drama critic. Below, he recounts the memorable aspects of The Effect of

Gamma Rays on Man-in-the-Moon Marigolds *and probes the desperate lives of the characters.*

Whenever I think of Paul Zindel's *The Effect of Gamma Rays on Man-in-the-Moon Marigolds,* I am going to think of three things, not one of them the title (the title, by the way, makes perfect sense and you will remember it readily once you have seen the play). The first is the sound, the sheer weighted sound, of a load of old newspapers being dumped from a balcony landing. Sada Thompson [who is playing Beatrice], slatternly mother of two and savior of none, is at her house-cleaning again, which means that she is picking up the accumulated refuse of her life and hurling it to another, though no better, spot. The bundle comes down like a dead heart; the force of the drop is shattering. And familiar. You seem to have heard it before.

The second memory that keeps coming back is the tactile, naked terror with which Miss Thompson, at midnight during a thunderstorm, brushes a prying flashlight away from her face. Her older daughter has long ago had a breakdown, for very good reasons, and is now desperately fearful of lightning; Miss Thompson has crawled out of bed to console her, a motherly duty she is perfectly willing to perform. But in the dark the daughter has discovered a flashlight, and she is using it to find the face that will reassure her. Suddenly, to Miss Thompson, the probing, isolating, totally revealing finger of light becomes a spider seeking out the seams of failure in her face; without warning she is flailing at it, attacking it as though the truth itself were something to be killed.

The moment continues, but in another vein altogether, arriving at one of the most evocative conjunctions of performing, staging and writing that we have had in the theater, on Broadway or off, in some years past. Miss Thompson must suppress her own terrors to help ease those of her daughter. To do it she passes from her sharp alarm and irritation to making girlish funny faces, conjuring up the child she once was and the way—perhaps—she once made her father laugh.

From that she passes to telling stories of her father, of his vegetable wagon that she sometimes rode through the streets, of the rhythmic cries he made to advertise his wares, of the singsong warmth that so long ago promised her a golden life. As she talks, the daughter becomes calm, pleased, half-drugged with delight, so much so that at last the two of them are musically whispering "apples—pears—

cuc*um*bers!" into the night while the flashlight swings as lazily as the clapper of an old bell. The image is morose and singularly charming; it is also essential to the cruel body of the play.

The third thing I'll remember is the play's ending, a coming-together of harshness and hope that exactly summarizes, without preachment of any sort, the meanings Mr. Zindel wishes his compressed and honest little play to carry. The brief lyricism of the wagon-bell-at-midnight passage is necessary if we are to endure, and understand, the venom that overtakes Miss Thompson in her relationship with a younger daughter.

This daughter, played plainly and plaintively and very well indeed by Pamela Payton-Wright, is as bright as she is rumpled. We first meet her alone, idly stroking a pet rabbit, staring at her hand, mouthing thoughts to herself about what the universe has had to go through—the tongues of fire, the explosions of suns—to produce her own five fingers. A knobby-kneed schoolchild with thin blond hair and a dress that bunches up in the back, she has a gift for scientific speculation; she is, at the moment, engaged in growing and studying marigolds that have been exposed to radiation, and she may just possibly win a competition her teacher has urged her to enter at school. Precisely because she is intelligent, because others are interested in her, because some sort of future may open itself to her, her mother cannot abide her. "I hate the world," Miss Thompson seethes as she stares at all the dreams that have emptied out before her. No one else is going to find it fascinating. Miss Payton-Wright is not even going to go to school all that often.

When a teacher phones to ask why the child is not at school, Miss Thompson descends a cluttered staircase in a shapeless robe—toweling with the nap all gone—that contains both her despair and her cigarettes. She snatches up the ringing instrument with such brisk indifference that you know she can only parody conversation, never truly enter it. Her eyes are wide, darting, expectant: they expect insult. Her body moves restlessly beneath the robe: it is a fencer's body, wary of attack and ready for evasion or assault. The woman is ordinary, recognizable; and half-mad.

On the phone, she is four or five persons at once. She is a plain bully: she will keep her daughter home when she pleases. She is a plausible, painful flirt. The teacher will either respond to her coy gestures or get himself classified a fag. She is all motherly concern: she cares so much for her children's studies that she "provides them with 75-watt light bulbs right there at their desks." Her eyes search the room for the nonexistent desks as she prattles on: the room is almost nothing but empty cartons and sagging bureaus; she sees the desks.

She sees, when she wishes, the carefree creature she might have become; she was, after all, elected "Best Dancer of the Class of 19-bootle-de-doo." (No one alive could manage this fey cop-out as well as Miss Thompson.) She sees the husband who first got a divorce and then a coronary. ("He deserved it," she parenthesizes, swiftly, meanly.) She sees her older daughter, tight sweater unbuttoned enticingly, turning into a fierce repetition of herself. She sees where they all are now, all except the gifted one. Their only source of income is a "$50-a-week corpse," an abandoned crone for whom they care, without caring. She sees "zero" wrapping its arms around her, and she repeats the word in a run-on babble that sounds like steam bubbling up from a lava bed. She is greedy, cynical, jealous, clever, irresponsible, vicious and lost.

In the play's last sequence, we are permitted to hear the schoolgirl's shy, halting, but determined brief lecture on the effects of radiation. Displaying her flowers in the high school contest—some of them blighted, some richer through mutation, all the product of those first exploding suns—she voices, tremulously, but insistently, her own stubborn confidence that "man will someday thank God for the strange and beautiful energy of the atom."

That is half of the final stage image. The other half is of Miss Thompson, near-mindless now, endlessly folding napkins for a tearoom she will never open, face-to-face with the half-paralyzed crone, aware of the presence of that other, older, sick and sensual daughter.

The play is thus framed. The mother is the wrong and right mother for these children, as the children are wrong and right sisters to each other. They all hurt one another simply by existing; the damage can never be repaired. But they constitute the situation as given, the human mutations thrown off; there is no dodging the gamma rays, there is only disaster for some and double-blooms for some others.

The ending doesn't press the point. It just expands to it, and bitterly—but gently—leaves the matter there. The play itself is one of the lucky blooms; it survives, and is beautiful. With it, Mr. Zindel becomes one of our most promising new

> THEY ALL HURT ONE ANOTHER SIMPLY BY EXISTING; THE DAMAGE CAN NEVER BE REPAIRED. BUT THEY CONSTITUTE THE SITUATION AS GIVEN, THE HUMAN MUTATIONS THROWN OFF; THERE IS NO DODGING THE GAMMA RAYS, THERE IS ONLY DISASTER FOR SOME AND DOUBLE-BLOOMS FOR SOME OTHERS."

writers. In it, Sada Thompson calls clear attention—perhaps more emphatically than ever before—to the fact that she is one of the American theater's finest actresses.

Source: Walter Kerr, "Everything's Coming up Marigolds," in *New York Times,* April 19, 1970, pp. 1, 3.

Edith Oliver

Oliver began her career as an actress and television writer and producer. Here, she regards Beatrice as the central figure in The Effect of Gamma Rays on Man-in-the-Moon Marigolds.

The title *The Effect of Gamma Rays on Man-in-the-Moon Marigolds* is a false clue to a touching and often funny play that, whatever its faults, is not nonsensical or verbose or pretentious or way-out flashy. Actually, it is a rather old-fashioned domestic drama (old-fashioned is no insult from me) in that it is about people—and interesting ones at that—whose behavior, while outlandish at times, is made as comprehensible as anybody's behavior ever can be made. The play, which was written by Paul Zindel and opened last week at the Mercer-O'Casey, is more than anything else the study of a woman. Her name is Beatrice Hunsdorfer, and she has been all but destroyed by a life that so far has consisted of one disappointment after another. With all her expectations crushed but with plenty of energy left, much of it spent on wreaking a kind of petty vengeance on everybody around her, she is as much a victim of her own nature as she is of

" HER NAME IS BEATRICE HUNSDORFER, AND SHE HAS BEEN ALL BUT DESTROYED BY A LIFE THAT SO FAR HAS CONSISTED OF ONE DISAPPOINTMENT AFTER ANOTHER."

circumstance. There is, however, nothing bleak or whiny about Mrs. H. She is the fierce, embittered, wise-cracking mother of two young daughters. One of them, Ruth, is a highly strung, rather bratty girl subject to convulsions, and the other, Matilda, is an awkward, dim-looking but not dim, science prodigy. It is Matilda's gamma-ray experiment with marigolds at the local high school that gives the play its bumpy title, eventually wins her a prize, and, indirectly, almost finishes off her mother and sister and the rickety life they have built.

The plot is the least of it. The character of Mrs. H. is all, or nearly all. We learn that the only man she ever loved was her father, that her husband never amounted to anything and left her penniless in the horrible mess of a house where the action takes place, that she considers her daughters millstones around her neck (or she says she does; she is capable of sudden, remorseful tenderness and pride), and that there is no one on earth that she hates as much as she hates herself. She makes fifty dollars a week ("I'd be better off as a cabdriver") by providing minimum care for a decrepit old woman boarder. She is very intelligent. She is also, wandering around in a shabby bathrobe with a cigarette in one hand and a glass of whiskey in the other, a holy terror, and she is so convincingly played by Sada Thompson that it is all but impossible to separate the role from the actress. The first and by far the better of the two acts is a series of vignettes and conversations: Mrs. H., all offhand iron courtesy and cutting explanations, talking on the telephone to a science teacher who is looking for Matilda; the girl herself, clutching her pet rabbit, listening to the conversation in frozen apprehension; Mrs. H. berating her daughter for not doing the housework ("This house is going to ferment"); Mrs. H., behind a glittery smile, raining down insults on her poor old boarder, who is as deaf as she is feeble; Mrs. H., impulsive

and loving, soothing her edgy Ruth, who has had a nightmare. The second act, in which events and crises take over, and in which incidents are given more significance than they appear to warrant, seems artificial, and even melodramatic, after the first one, but the play stands up pretty well, all the same. The performances, under Melvin Bernhardt's direction, are all that any dramatist could wish for. Pamela Payton-Wright is the shy, inspired Matilda, Amy Levitt is Ruth, and Judith Lowry is the tottery paying guest. Sara Brook designed the good costumes, and the good set is by Fred Voelpel.

Source: Edith Oliver, "Why the Lady Is a Tramp," in *New Yorker,* Vol. XLVI, No. 9, April 18, 1970, pp. 82, 87–88.

SOURCES

Barnes, Clive, "Off-Broadway and Off-Off 1969–70," *American Theatre 1969–1970,* Charles Scribner's Sons, 1970. pp. 63–74.

Barnet, Sylvan, Morton Berman, and William Burto, eds., *Types of Drama: Plays and Essays,* Little Brown and Company, 1972, pp. 640–641.

Eaglen, Audrey, Interview with Paul Zindel, in *Top of the News,* Vol. 34, No. 2, Winter 1978, pp. 178–85.

Forman, Jack, "Paul Zindel," in *Concise Dictionary of American Literary Biography Supplement: Modern Writers, 1900–1998,* Gale Research, 1998.

Frank, Anne, *Anne Frank: The Diary of a Young Girl,* Bantam Books, 1993, p. 263.

Haley, Beverly A., and Kenneth L. Donelson, "Pigs and Hamburger, Cadavers and Gamma Rays: Paul Zindel's Adolescents," in *Elementary English,* Vol. 51, No. 7, October 1974, pp. 940–945.

Hipple, Theodore, in *Dictionary of Literary Biography, Volume 52: American Writers for Children since 1960: Fiction,* edited by Glenn E. Estes, Gale, 1986, pp. 405–410.

Rich, Frank, "Amulets Against the Dragon Forces," in *Hot Seat: Theater Criticism for the New York Times, 1980–1993,* Random House, 1998, pp. 665–656.

Strickland, Ruth L., "Paul Zindel" in *Dictionary of Literary Biography: Volume 7: Twentieth-Century American Dramatists,* edited by John MacNicholas, Gale, 1981, pp. 368–373.

Zindel, Paul, *The Effect of Gamma Rays on Man-in-the-Moon Marigolds,* Bantam Books, 1973.

———, Introduction to *The Effect of Gamma Rays on Man-in-the-Moon Marigolds,* Bantam Books, 1997.

FURTHER READING

Asimov, Isaac, *Atom: Journey Across the Subatomic Cosmos,* Dutton, 1991.
  Asimov discusses the properties of the atom in easily understandable terms. This book was deemed ''a masterpiece'' by *Omni Magazine.*

Meadows, Jack, *The Great Scientists,* Oxford University Press, 1989.
  This book is profusely illustrated and is about the lives of twelve great scientists and their discoveries. Of particular interest is the chapter on Albert Einstein.

Raymond, Gerard, ''The Effects of Staten Island on a Pulitzer Prize-Winning Playwright,'' *Theater Week,* Vol. 2, No. 37, April 24, 1989, pp. 16–21.
  Raymond discusses the influence of Zindel's experiences as a child on his writing.

Wetzsteon, Ross, ed., *The Obie Winners: The Best of Off-Broadway,* Doubleday, 1980.
  This book contains the complete texts of ten plays that have won an Obie Award. It also includes a complete listing of the Obie Award winners through 1979.

The Fourposter

JAN DE HARTOG

1951

The Fourposter, Jan de Hartog's most successful play, was first produced at the Ethel Barrymore Theatre in 1951; it ran for 632 performances on Broadway. The play earned de Hartog the 1952 Antoinette Perry (Tony) Award. *The Fourposter* was adapted to the screen in a 1952 film produced by Columbia Pictures. A musical rendition, entitled *I Do! I Do!* opened on Broadway in 1966.

The Fourposter features two characters, Agnes and Michael, and spans the years 1890 to 1925, as key moments in their marriage are played out around their four-poster bed. In act 1, scene 1, they have just returned from their wedding ceremony, anxious and nervous about consummating their marriage. In scene 2, Agnes begins to feel the labor pains of their first child. In act 2, scene 1, Michael, who has become a highly successful writer, reveals to Agnes that he has been having an affair. In scene 2, Michael has just discovered what he thinks is a bottle of liquor in their son's bedroom. In act 3, scene 1, they have just returned from their daughter's wedding. In scene 2, they are moving out of their house to live in a smaller apartment.

De Hartog's play charts the ups and downs of a long-lasting marriage that is punctuated by moments of crisis and reconciliation. It maintains a balance in perspective between the special concerns and complaints of the woman and those of the man, as a function of their traditional societal roles. The ''four-poster'' bed, in and around which these mo-

ments of crisis are played out, symbolizes the lasting quality of the marriage bond, which remains steady throughout several decades of love and conflict.

AUTHOR BIOGRAPHY

Jan de Hartog was born on April 22, 1914, in Haarlem, the Netherlands. His father, Arnold Hendrik, was a minister and theology professor, and his mother, Lucretia (maiden name Meijjes), was a lecturer in medieval mysticism. De Hartog left home at the age of ten to work as a sailor on fishing boats, steamers and tugboats, becoming an adjunct inspector with the Amsterdam Harbor Police. He attended the Amsterdam Naval College from 1930 to 1931. From 1932 to 1937, he worked at the Amsterdam Municipal Theatre. During this period, de Hartog wrote a number of popular detective novels under the pseudonym F. R. Eckmar. From the late 1930s through the 1960s, de Hartog worked steadily as a successful playwright and novelist.

His 1940 novel *Hollands Glorie* was based on de Hartog's own experiences as a sailor, but it became a symbol of Dutch resistance against the Nazi occupation of World War II and was banned. Wanted by the Nazis, De Hartog hid in an Amsterdam home for senior citizens, disguised as an old woman. *The Fourposter,* his most successful play, was written during this period of hiding. Escaping to England, he became a correspondent for the Netherlands Merchant Marines in 1943. In 1946, he married the daughter of the English writer J. B. Priestly, Angela Priestly, with whom he had four children. *The Fourposter* opened on Broadway in 1951, earning de Hartog the 1952 Antoinette Perry (Tony) Award.

In 1961, he married Marjorie Eleanor Mein, with whom he adopted two children. De Hartog and his second wife became known for their many humanitarian efforts throughout the world. In 1962, he was writer-in-residence and lecturer in playwriting at the University of Houston. While there, he published a nonfiction book, *The Hospital,* based on his and his wife's volunteer work at the hospital in Houston, which attracted national attention to the quality of hospital care. In 1963, he and his wife aided survivors of a flood in Holland, out of which came his book *The Little Ark.* In 1966, they advo-

Jan de Hartog

cated the adoption of Vietnamese and Korean orphans, adopting two children themselves. De Hartog's book, *The Children: A Personal Record for the Use of Adoptive Parents,* was based on this experience.

PLOT SUMMARY

Act 1

The Fourposter takes place in the bedroom of Agnes and Michael, a married couple, who are the only characters in the play. Act 1, scene 1 takes place in 1890, at night. They have just come home from their wedding. Agnes's mother has placed a pillow with ''God Is Love'' embroidered on it on the bed. Michael is amorous, but Agnes is shy and nervous about consummating their wedding, even threatening to walk out on Michael. Soon, however, she feels comfortable enough to get into bed with him.

Act 1, scene 2 takes place in 1891, in the late afternoon. Agnes is pregnant with their first child. Michael complains that he is having labor pains and worries that Agnes is neglecting him in favor of the coming child. When she goes into labor, Michael leaves to get the doctor for her delivery.

Act 2

Act 2, scene 1 takes place in 1901, at night. Michael has become a very successful writer, and they are now quite wealthy. They have just returned from an evening out at a party, and they begin to bicker and argue. Agnes accuses him of being self-centered, and Michael reveals that he has been having an affair. Agnes responds by hinting that she may also be having an affair. They make up, however, when Michael asks if he can read to her from his most recent writing.

Act 2, scene 2 takes place in 1908, from four A.M. until dawn. Michael has just discovered what he thinks is a bottle of liquor in the bedroom of their son, Robert, who is now seventeen. Michael claims he is going to beat the boy when he returns home. He and Agnes argue; she accuses him of favoring their daughter, while he accuses her of favoring their son. Agnes reveals to Michael that their daughter, Lizzie, is engaged. They then discover that the bottle does not contain alcohol, but cod liver oil, which Michael had poured into it years earlier to hide the fact that he was not swallowing it, as prescribed by his mother.

Act 3

Act 3, scene 1, takes place in 1913, in the late afternoon. Michael and Agnes have just returned from their daughter's wedding. They argue, and Agnes informs Michael that she no longer loves him and is going to leave him. She criticizes Michael for discouraging a young aspiring poet who had asked for advice on his poems. Michael agrees to look at the poems again but is still critical. Agnes accuses him of not needing her any more, but he tells her, "It's you who make me sing . . . and if I sing like a frog in a pond, it's not my fault." Upon hearing this, Agnes simultaneously laughs, cries, and embraces him.

Act 3, scene 2 takes place in 1925, at dawn. Michael and Agnes are moving out of their house to live in a smaller apartment. Agnes wants to place their pillow, on which the words "God Is Love" are embroidered, under the bedcovers for the newlywed couple who will be moving into their house, but Michael protests. They bicker over the pillow, each in turn surreptitiously removing it and replacing it. Finally, Michael leaves the pillow where Agnes has placed it in the bed, setting a bottle of champagne next to it.

CHARACTERS

Agnes

Agnes is the wife of Michael. Over the course of their marriage, Agnes goes through several phases in her feelings for her husband. As a newlywed bride, she is nervous and anxious about consummating their marriage. As an expectant mother, she becomes more focused on the arrival of their child than on her husband. As the wife of a wealthy and successful writer, she is resentful toward her husband, who has become self-centered, and who, she learns, has been having an affair with another woman. Agnes and Michael face many hardships throughout their marriage, but their love sees them through. For Agnes, their love and enduring marriage can also be seen as an extension of God's love and blessing on them, as is evidenced by the "God Is Love" pillow that she places on the bed in the final scene of the play.

Michael

Michael is the husband of Agnes. Like her, he experiences their marriage over a period of decades as a series of crises and reconciliations between husband and wife. As a newlywed husband, he is anxious to consummate his marriage, but first he must contend with the fears and anxieties of his innocent bride. As a successful writer, he becomes self-centered and takes a mistress because he feels neglected by his wife. In the end, Michael reaffirms his love for his wife and his commitment to their marriage. Though Michael does not seem to share his wife's religious convictions, he finally acquiesces in letting her leave the pillow on the bed. He then adds a bottle of champagne, in his own way leaving a token of love to the new couple that is to move into his and Agnes's old home.

THEMES

Marriage

The central theme of this play is marriage. Each of the six scenes takes place in the bedroom of Agnes and Michael, a married couple, during key moments of crisis and reconciliation in their marriage. The first scene takes place on their wedding night. The second scene takes place just as she is experiencing labor pains before the birth of their first child. In the following scene, seven years later, he reveals that he has been having an affair. In the next scene, they argue over how to raise their children, he favoring the daughter, and she favoring the son. In the following scene, they have just returned from their daughter's wedding. Agnes informs Michael that she no longer loves him and is leaving him, but they soon reconcile. In the final scene, they are moving out of their house to a smaller space in an apartment building. The play thus charts the patterns of conflict and resolution over thirty-five years of a marriage. This large-scale overview presents the marriage as rocky but ultimately stabilized by the strong basis of mutual love between husband and wife. In the end, Agnes concludes that they have been ''happy'' together, and that ''marriage is a good thing.''

Gender Roles

In portraying the marital relationship between Agnes and Michael, de Hartog explores issues of conflict over traditional gender roles within the family. On their wedding night, Michael, as a man, is eager to consummate their marriage, while Agnes, as an innocent and naive young woman, is extremely anxious and nervous about getting into bed with him. She complains that she wants to go home and hints that he has gotten her drunk to more easily undress her. Soon enough, however, she overcomes her initial fears and becomes comfortable getting into bed with him.

During the scene in which Agnes is about to give birth to their first child, Michael complains that she has neglected him while she has been preparing for the coming child. As a man, he feels jealous of the expected child, whom he fears will supplant him in his wife's affections. When she attempts to tease him, calling him a ''baby,'' he bursts out, ''That's right! Humiliate me! Lose no opportunity of reminding me that I'm the male animal that's done its duty and now can be dismissed! . . . A drone, that's what I am! The one thing lacking is that you should devour me. The bees. . . .'' Michael then admits that he fears losing her to the baby and even wishes that he himself were ''lying in the cradle,'' receiving her attentions. He fears ''that cuckoo''—meaning the child—is going to push him ''out of the nest.'' He complains that, since she became pregnant, he has become, ''miserable, deserted, alone,'' and that ''You do nothing else all day but fuss over that child.'' He goes on to assert that he feels, as a man, usurped by the coming child. He tells her, ''I retired into the background as becomes a man who recognizes that he is one too many.'' However, she reassures him that she could not have done it

MEDIA ADAPTATIONS

- *The Fourposter* was adapted to the screen in a 1952 production of the same name by Columbia Pictures. It starred Rex Harrison and Lili Palmer, and it was directed by Irving Reis.

without the support of a loving husband, telling him, ''You helped me more than all model husbands put together.''

During a scene that takes place seventeen years later, Agnes expresses her sense of discontent and oppression in the role of wife and mother. She tells Michael, ''I can't . . . die behind the stove, like a domestic animal.'' She goes on to compare the restrictions placed on women to the freedoms allowed men, telling Michael, ''You are a man. You'll be able to do what you like until you are seventy.'' Agnes then expresses her rage and frustration with the restrictions placed upon her in her role as wife and mother:

> I want to live, can't you understand that? My life long I have been a mother; my life long I've had to be at somebody's beck and call; I've never been able to be really myself, completely, wholeheartedly. No, never! From the very first day you have handcuffed me and gagged me and shut me in the dark. When I was still a child who didn't even know what it meant to be a woman, you turned me into a mother.

Through such outbursts as this, de Hartog represents marriage as a series of struggles between man and woman, a push and pull of love and conflict, often based on differences in the emotional needs, as well as the societal expectations, of men and women in their traditional marital roles.

STYLE

Setting

The setting is of central importance in this play. The play's title, *The Fourposter,* refers to the fourposter bed around which key moments of crisis and

TOPICS FOR FURTHER STUDY

- Famous Dutch artists include Rembrandt, Vincent Van Gogh, and Piet Mondrian. Learn more about one of these artists and his influence on other artists.

- Because of the impact of his work on the Dutch resistance movement, de Hartog went into hiding during the Nazi occupation of the Netherlands. Anne Frank was among the many Jews who went into hiding to avoid Nazi persecution, and who eventually perished in the Holocaust. Learn more about Nazi persecution of Jews in the Netherlands during World War II.

- De Hartog was born in the Netherlands, where he lived during the Nazi occupation of World War

II. One of his early novels became a symbol of the Dutch resistance movement and was soon banned. Learn more about the Netherlands during World War II. What were the events and conditions of the Nazi occupation? What was the Dutch resistance movement?

- De Hartog's religion is Quaker. What are the central beliefs of the Quakers? What is the history of the Quakers?

- One of the characters in de Hartog's play makes reference to the German philosopher Arthur Schopenhauer. Who was Schopenhauer? What were the basic tenets of his philosophy? In what ways has he influenced Western thought and culture?

---

reconciliation in the marriage of Agnes and Michael take place. The bed is the site of such events as the consummation of their marriage on their wedding night and the birth of their first child. In their later years, they are moving out of their house into a smaller apartment and have to leave the bed behind because it is too big to fir into their new place. In the final moments of the play, Agnes sums up the significance of the bed to their marriage. She comments, ''It's odd, you know, how after you have lived in a place for so long, a room gets full of echoes. Almost everything we've said this morning we have said before. . . . It's the bed, really, that I regret most. Pity it wouldn't fit.'' The four-poster bed represents the stable base of deep love that remains constant throughout their long and rocky marriage.

The setting is also significant in act 2, as it demonstrates the wealth Michael and Agnes have achieved through his success as a writer. The stage directions describe the changes that have been made in their bedroom furnishings, from modest to extravagant: ''The only piece of furniture left from the preceding scene is the four-poster, but it has been fitted out with new brocade curtains. Paintings hang on the walls; expensive furniture crowds the room. . . .

The whole thing is very costly, very grand and very new.'' In act 3, scene 1, which takes place in 1913, Agnes and Michael are still wealthy, but their furnishings show the signs of established, rather than newly acquired, wealth. The bed canopy, drapes, and furniture in this scene have changed, ''all in more conservative taste now.''

Time Frame

The time frame of the play is significant to its central concerns. The six scenes, divided into three acts, span the years 1890 to 1925. The scenes take place anywhere from one to twelve years apart. The play as a whole thus provides an overview of key moments in thirty-five years of a marriage. Although this leaves large gaps of time in the reader's (or theatergoer's) knowledge of the marriage, it paints a broad, sweeping portrait of the relationship, highlighting the larger patterns of conflict, reconciliation, and change.

Visual Cues

The play includes two sequences that are played out almost entirely through actions rather than dialogue. These two sequences, one in the first scene and one in the final scene, parallel one another, as they play out in pantomime the push and pull of the marital relationship. In the first scene, which takes place on their wedding night, Agnes is so nervous about getting into bed with Michael that she picks up her suitcase and walks out of the room, locking Michael inside. Michael, however, notices that she has left her shoes. The stage directions at this point describe Michael's actions and movements about the room, as he nervously and frantically unpacks his nightshirt, begins to undress, puts on his night-cap and nightshirt, then changes his mind and begins to dress again, without removing his night-shirt or night cap. At this point, Agnes returns, catching Michael in this state of partial dress and undress, an expression of his anxiety and uncertainty as to how he should best proceed with her.

In the final scene, Agnes and Michael act a similar series of moves and countermoves, which express an ongoing ambivalence between the two of them. Agnes wishes to place the ''God Is Love'' pillow on the bed for the incoming bride, but Michael is against the idea, for the sake of the groom. As each walks in and out of the room, Agnes and Michael put on and remove the pillow several times. Finally, Michael leaves the pillow on the bed, but he places a bottle of champagne next to it. Like the series of actions in the first scene, this series of actions plays out in pantomime a point of conflict and a moment of reconciliation between husband and wife—a pattern that continues throughout their marriage.

HISTORICAL CONTEXT

The Netherlands

De Hartog was born in the city of Haarlem in the Netherlands. He also spent an important period of his life in the city of Amsterdam, which is the capital of the Netherlands (although the seat of government is located in the city of the Hague). The nation of the Netherlands, officially called the King-dom of the Netherlands, is often referred to as Holland, after one of the country's major provinces. The language of the Netherlands is Dutch. In 1795, the Netherlands was occupied by the French and, under Napoleon, renamed the Kingdom of Holland. National sovereignty, however, was restored in 1814. During World War I, the Netherlands re-mained neutral. During World War II, although the

Netherlands claimed neutrality, its citizens were largely sympathetic to the Allied cause. In 1940, however, the Germans invaded the region, which they occupied until it was liberated by Canadian forces in 1945. During the period of German occu-pation, a Dutch resistance movement sprang up, which helped de Hartog to escape a death sentence by helping him secretly leave the Netherlands for England. In the postwar era, the Netherlands formed strong ties with the nations of the former Allied forces.

Developments in Twentieth-Century Theater

The late nineteenth century represented the height of realism in drama of the Western world. The Moscow Art Theater, established in 1895 by Russian actor and director Konstantin Stanislavsky, represented the pinnacle of realist theater. The be-ginning of the twentieth century, however, ushered in a variety of avant-garde and experimental efforts to break away from realism. In Italy, the theater of futurism, begun in 1909, initiated this break with the staging of theatrical events designed to break through the ''fourth wall'' separating the events of a play from the audience. From 1910 to 1925, a theater of German expressionism was inspired by the expres-sionist movement in the visual arts. Expressionism was a reaction against societal norms and the aes-thetics of naturalism and impressionism. Experi-mental theater in France during the first half of the twentieth century included the organization of such theatrical companies as the ''Cartel,'' beginning in 1927, and the *Theatre des Quinze,* which, in its brief existence between 1930 and 1934, exerted a strong international influence. In the United States, the Theater Guild was established as an art theater in 1918, becoming the most influential stage in the nation with productions of the works of great play-wrights such as Eugene O'Neill and Elmer Rice. O'Neill, in particular, helped to elevate American theater to a level of literary quality. The post-World War II era, during which *The Fourposter* was first produced on Broadway in New York City, initiated further variety in the development of theater. Per-haps the most internationally influential playwright of this era was the German Bertolt Brecht, whose ''epic theater,'' based on a technique he called the ''alienation effect,'' was intended to break from the illusionary quality of drama to present social com-mentary directly to the audience. Influential pro-ductions on the American theatrical scene during the 1950s included works by O'Neill, as well as by Arthur Miller and Tennessee Williams.

COMPARE & CONTRAST

- **1940–1945:** During World War II, the Netherlands officially maintains neutrality, despite the fact that its citizens are largely sympathetic to the Allied cause, and the country is occupied by Nazi Germany during these years.

    Postwar Era: The Netherlands is liberated from German occupation by Canadian forces in 1945. The nation strengthens ties with former allied nations, joining the North Atlantic Treaty Organization (NATO).

- **Early–Mid-Twentieth Century:** Amsterdam, the capital of the Netherlands, is a center of art and culture and embodies a spirit of open-mindedness.

    1960s–2000: Amsterdam gains a reputation as ''swinging Amsterdam,'' a mecca of permissiveness, individualism, and counterculture freedoms, appealing to many youths and radicals.

- **World War II:** Anne Frank, a German Jewish girl, hides out with her own and another family in Amsterdam in order to avoid Nazi persecution. They are eventually discovered by the Nazis and sent to concentration camps, where Anne Frank dies. In all, some 70,000 Jews are deported from Amsterdam and sent to concentration camps, where many are killed.

    Late Twentieth Century: *The Diary of Anne Frank*, written while the author in hiding, is edited and published by her father, who survived the concentration camp. Her diary is now widely read and taught to school children as an example of the Jewish experience of the Holocaust.

- **1940–1945:** During the Nazi occupation of the Netherlands in World War II, Queen Wilhelmina, her royal family, and the Netherlandic government establish a government in exile in England.

    Postwar Era: Upon liberation from German occupation, Queen Wilhelmina and the legitimate Netherlandic government return to the Netherlands to rule. During this postwar era, the government makes important moves toward increased democratization, such as establishing universal suffrage.

CRITICAL OVERVIEW

The Fourposter, Jan de Hartog's most successful play, was first produced at the Ethel Barrymore Theatre in 1951, and ran for 632 performances on Broadway. This first run starred the famous husband and wife acting duo, Jessica Tandy, as Agnes, and Hume Cronyn, as Michael. *New York Times* drama critic Brooks Atkinson gave the opening night performance hearty applause. In an October 25 review, he hails it as a ''literate and professional work all the way through.'' He describes the writing of the play as ''so compact and simple that you may not realize at once how good it is.'' Atkinson notes that while ''nothing very extraordinary happens'' throughout the play, de Hartog ''has managed to skeletonize it with great understanding and skill.''

His one criticism is that ''Once in a while it seems thin.'' In a somewhat longer review in the *New York Times* a month after the first, Atkinson expands upon his original praise for the play, calling it ''a sparingly written and deftly acted cartoon of marriage.'' He again asserts that it contains sequences that are ''thin and tenuous.'' However, he asserts that ''minute as it is in size and reserved as it is in style, *The Fourposter* is a genuine and original piece of civilized comedy.'' John Gassner, in *Best American Plays* (1958), comments that *The Fourposter,* ''revealed a facet of the author's dramatic talent hitherto unsuspected on Broadway,'' adding, ''It was a warm sense of comedy that made *The Fourposter* one of the pleasantest of Broadway plays.'' Gassner goes on to explain, ''The background of *The Fourposter* is vividly American, but in treating married life, the author dealt with timeless traits and foibles, even while availing himself of elements of period comedy.'' *The Fourposter* earned de Hartog the 1952 Antoinette Perry (Tony) Award. It was adapted to the screen in a 1952 film produced by Columbia Pictures. A musical rendition entitled *I Do! I Do!* opened on Broadway in 1966.

Describing the 1955 revival of *The Fourposter* in New York's City Center, including the original cast of Tandy and Cronyn, Gassner notes, ''it was appreciated no less than on its first appearance on Broadway proper.'' Gassner does point out that ''Dissent was possible on the grounds that the humor and sentiment were rather standardized,'' but defends the play in stating that

> a critic could be mollified on the feeling that familiarity has been a requirement of domestic comedy ever since the ancients, and the standardization of humor in De Hartog's play was certainly mitigated by the rich acting roles provided by the author.

Atkinson said of the 1955 run of *The Fourposter* that ''the comedy seems even brighter'' than in his ''happy memories of the original opening night.'' Calling it ''original and funny,'' Atkinson observes,

> Mr. de Hartog's dialogue is immensely entertaining, his point of view is sardonically humorous and he is never unaware of the fact that his version of the *comédie humaine* is frequently touching.''

De Hartog saw the production of four of his plays between 1939 and 1951 at the Amsterdam Municipal Theater on Broadway and on the West end. Gassner describes de Hartog's appearance on the American theatrical scene:

> [De Hartog] first attracted attention in the American theatre in 1948 with *Skipper Next to God. . .* , the drama of a sea captain who transported Jewish refugees to Palestine and refused to allow international politics to rule his conscience. It was not a play contrived for Broadway, but it attracted attention with its strenuous idealism when staged in New York with the late John Garfield in the role of the skipper.''

CRITICISM

Liz Brent

Brent has a Ph.D. in American Culture, specializing in film studies, from the University of Michigan. She is a freelance writer and teaches courses in the history of American cinema. In the

Playbill cover from the 1952 production of The Fourposter *featuring Betty Field and Burgess Meredith.*

following essay, Brent discusses religious references in de Hartog's play.

Jan de Hartog's Tony Award-winning play, *The Fourposter* (1951), presents key moments of crisis and reconciliation between a married couple over the course of thirty-five years of their marriage. Throughout the play, there are many references to God, spirituality, and religion, which reflect upon the nature of the relationship between Agnes and Michael.

Act 1, scene 1, takes place on Michael and Agnes's wedding night. Michael, who is slightly intoxicated, is amorous toward Agnes, anticipating the consummation of their marriage. Agnes, on the other hand, is extremely nervous and anxious about her first night with her new husband and even threatens to walk out on him. Throughout the scene, Michael expresses his love and desire for Agnes in religious terms. Upon entering the bedroom, Michael, who is carrying Agnes, kisses her, lays her down on the bed, and tries to kiss her again. Self-conscious, Agnes tells him to hurry and to close the bedroom door. As he does this, she gets up from the bed and turns on a light. As she stands there, Michael

WHAT DO I READ NEXT?

- *The Threepenny Opera* (1928), by German playwright Bertolt Brecht, is an operatic social satire by one of the most influential playwrights of the twentieth century.

- *The Iceman Cometh* (1939), by American playwright Eugene O'Neill, was first produced in 1946. O'Neill, who won the Nobel Prize for Literature in 1936, was a central figure in elevating American theater to the quality of literature in the first half of the twentieth century. *The Iceman Cometh*, one of his greatest works, is a tragic play that takes place over the course of one day in the life of a family whose lives are wracked by alcoholism, drug abuse, illness, and personal failure.

- *Captain Jan*, by Jan de Hartog (original title: *Hollands Glorie*, published in 1940; English translation published in 1976), is based on the author's experiences as a tugboat sailor. The novel became a symbol of Dutch resistance during Nazi Occupation and was soon banned.

- *Death of a Salesman* (1949), by American playwright Arthur Miller, is one of the most highly celebrated plays of the post-war era. It concerns an average man done in by his efforts to live up to societal expectations.

- *Waiting for Godot* (1952), by Anglo-Irish playwright Samuel Beckett, is a central work of the Theater of the Absurd. It is set in an unspecified, abstract time and place, in which two men wait indefinitely to meet Godot. Beckett won the Nobel Prize for Literature in 1969.

- *The Little Ark* (1953), by Jan de Hartog, is a play based on the experiences of de Hartog and his second wife, who, during a severe flood in Holland, turned their houseboat into a makeshift hospital.

- *The Hospital* (1964), by Jan de Hartog, is a nonfiction work based on de Hartog's own volunteer experience and advocating improved conditions in American hospitals.

---

removes her gloves and kneels at her feet. When she asks what he is doing, he tells her, ''I'm worshipping you. . . . Can't I worship you?'' When Agnes cautions, ''If our Lord could see you,'' Michael asserts that his expressions of love for her are not contrary to, but in harmony with, the will of God. He replies, ''He could only rejoice in such happiness.'' Further equating his feelings for Agnes with religious sentiment, he calls her, ''Angel!'' as he repeatedly tries to kiss her.

Once they are finally comfortable enough to get into the bed together, Agnes continues to delay further intimacy by expressing concern that the oil lamp might leak. Michael, attempting to calm her anxieties, as well as his own, takes her hand, and tells her, ''Darling, listen. You are an angel, and I'm madly in love with you, and I'm embarrassed to death and so are you, and that's the reason why we . . . Good night.'' Earlier, as he is attempting to take

her shoes off for her, against her protests, Michael equates this romantic gesture with ''heaven,'' telling her, ''Isn't that heaven? I could spend the whole night undressing you.''

But, as they are preparing to get into bed, Michael utilizes swear words to express his frustration over Agnes's many delays and hesitations. Agnes's fear of taking the next step in their relationship, toward the expected sexual encounter, is expressed as a desire that ''everything could stay as it was—before today.'' Wishing in her anxiety to maintain the chastity of their relationship, she tells him, ''I couldn't stand any more—happiness. Could you?'' To which Michael replies, ''God, no.'' But when she manages to find fault with even this assertion of his happiness with her, commenting, ''How coldly you say that!'' Michael blurts out, ''But what the blazing hell do you expect me to say?'' Agnes then chides him for swearing, admonishing him, ''Is that language for the wedding night. . . before going to sleep? You ought to be ashamed of yourself!'' In his mounting frustration, Michael swears again, ''But damn it, Agnes. . . .'' Thus, while equating the wedding night with a religious sentiment, Michael also finds himself swearing in God's name with his frustration over Agnes's efforts to avoid consummating their marriage. Agnes, for her part, continues to scold Michael, both for expressing his love and passion as a religious sentiment and for swearing in God's name on such a sacred occasion as their wedding night.

The love between the newlyweds is also expressed as a sacred sentiment via the small pillow, embroidered with the words, ''God Is Love,'' which Agnes's mother has placed under the bedcovers for them. Agnes exclaims, ''Wasn't that sweet of her?'' But Michael, who, on his wedding night, prefers not to be reminded of his bride's mother or of her chaste religious sentiment, flatly replies, ''Yes, lovely.'' Once in bed, Agnes places the ''God Is Love'' pillow under her head, as if to comfort her anxieties about expressing the physical element of love between herself and her husband.

For Michael, as for Agnes, God is indeed love. But Michael, unlike Agnes, views the physical expression of love as equally sacred as the platonic ideal of love. In act 1, scene 2, a year later, Agnes is just about to go into labor with their first child. To sooth and comfort her, Michael offers to read her the first half page of the new book he has started writing. In the passage he reads, Michael once again equates the physical expression of love, as symbolized by a double bed, with religious worship. A romance, it describes a woman entering an attic to look at an old double bed as if she were entering a temple to regard a religious shrine:

> When she entered the attic with the double bed, she bent her head, partly out of reverence for the temple where she had worshipped and sacrificed, partly because the ceiling was so low. It was not the first time she had returned to that shrine. . . .

The ''God Is Love'' pillow later plays a part in a moment of violent conflict between husband and wife. In act 2, scene 1, Michael and Agnes have returned home from a party. They begin to argue, and Michael reveals to Agnes that he has been having an affair. Throughout the scene, the bed has only one bed pillow on it, atop which rests the little ''God Is Love'' pillow. The one bed pillow indicates the separate sleeping arrangements of husband and wife, who have become estranged from one another over the years. Agnes clings to the ''God Is

> " AS SHE STANDS THERE, MICHAEL REMOVES HER GLOVES AND KNEELS AT HER FEET. WHEN SHE ASKS WHAT HE IS DOING, HE TELLS HER, 'I'M WORSHIPPING YOU. . . . CAN'T I WORSHIP YOU?' WHEN AGNES CAUTIONS, 'IF OUR LORD COULD SEE YOU, ' MICHAEL ASSERTS THAT HIS EXPRESSIONS OF LOVE FOR HER ARE NOT CONTRARY TO, BUT IN HARMONY WITH, THE WILL OF GOD.''

Love'' pillow, perhaps an ironic reminder of the loss of faith they have both experienced in regard to their marriage. As they argue, Michael continues to express his anger and frustration by swearing, ''I'll be damned. . . .'' He tells her that he has ''lived through hell'' while hiding his affair. Agnes, on the other hand, expresses her anger and frustration by invoking heaven and the name of God.

However, when she finally expresses concern over the announcement of the affair, Michael bursts out, ''At last! Thank God, a sign of life.'' He explains to her that she has neglected him for years, despite his attempts to gain her attention. But as the argument heats up, Agnes tells him, ''You're the vilest swine God ever created!'' As they continue to argue, she hits him with the ''God Is Love'' pillow. He then grabs it out of her hands and throws it. From that point the argument turns into a minor physical struggle, but soon it becomes an expression of mutual love as they reconcile with one another. This marital quarrel, like all of the conflicts between Agnes and Michael, ends with reconciliation and a reaffirmation of their love for one another. The use of the ''God Is Love'' pillow in the course of their fight is in part meant to be ironic. The pillow represents an ideal of holy matrimony, yet ends up being used for the physical expression of anger between husband and wife. But the use of the pillow in their fight is also a confirmation that the higher spiritual quality of their lifelong love for one another never disappears, even amidst their most violent conflicts.

In act 3, scene 2, Agnes and Michael are about to move out of their house and into a smaller apartment. The ''God Is Love'' pillow once again symbolizes the strong bond of love that underlies the cycle of conflict and reconciliation that characterizes their marriage. They have left the four-poster bed for the new homeowners, a newlywed couple, because it won't fit in their new place. As Michael packs their last suitcase before leaving, Agnes enters the bedroom with the ''God Is Love'' pillow hidden behind her back. Noticing it, Michael asks, ''We don't have to take that little horror with us, do we?'' Agnes explains that she plans to leave the pillow on the bed for the new occupants, ''as a surprise.'' Describing exactly the scenario of their own wedding night, Michael pictures the ''surprise'' as ''Two young people entering the bedroom on their first night of their marriage, uncovering the bed and finding a pillow a foot across with 'God Is Love' written on it.'' Tossing the pillow off the bed, he cynically mocks, ''God Is Love!'' But as soon as he leaves the room, Agnes puts the pillow back on the bed and covers it with the spread.

The pillow also comes to represent the male-female conflict within marriage. From Agnes's perspective, it is meant to be a comfort to the new bride, a ''message'' from one woman to another to reassure her about the anxieties of consummating her wedding night. From Michael's perspective, however, the pillow represents a union of women, ''the biggest trade union in the world,'' conspiring against the man's excitement over consummating his marriage and confronting him with the ''horror'' of a life of restricted ''freedom,'' as represented by marital commitment. Reentering the room, Michael discovers that the pillow has been put back on the bed. He asks Agnes why she has done this, and she explains, ''I wanted to leave something . . . friendly for that young couple . . . a sort of message.'' When Michael asks her what the message is, she replies, ''I'd like to tell them how happy we've been—and that it was a very good bed . . . I mean, it's had a very nice history, and that . . . marriage was a good thing.'' Michael responds, ''Well, believe me, that's not the message they'll read from this pillow. . . . I won't let you do this to that boy.'' Taking the pillow, she tells him, ''When I found this very same little pillow in this very same bed on the first night of our marriage, I nearly burst into tears!'' Michael replies, ''Oh you did, did you? Well, so did I! And it's time you heard about it! When on that night, at

that moment, I first saw that pillow, I suddenly felt as if I'd been caught in a world of women. Yes, women! I suddenly saw loom up behind you the biggest trade union in the world, and if I hadn't been a coward in long woolen underwear with my shoes off, I would have made a dive for freedom. . . . I'm not going to let you paralyze that boy at a crucial moment.'' Agnes retorts, ''She would find it before, when she made the bed. That's why I put it there. It is meant for her, not for him, not for you, for her, from me!''

Ultimately, this conflict over the pillow symbolizes the gender-based conflicts that arise between husband and wife throughout the course of a marriage, as well as the strong basis of spiritual love on which the marital bond is based. In the final moments of the play, Michael once again removes the pillow from the bed, but, when he is not looking, she replaces it under the covers. Reentering the room, Michael pulls back the covers, places a bottle of champagne next to the ''God Is Love'' pillow, and pulls up the covers again. Michael then picks Agnes up, kisses her, and carries her out of the room. It seems that, from the perspective of Jan de Hartog, God is indeed love.

Source: Liz Brent, in an essay for *Drama for Students,* Gale Group, 2001.

David Kelly

Kelly is an instructor of literature and creative writing at Oakton Community College and the College of Lake County. In the following essay, he explores the ways in which de Hartog has the characters in his play struggle for their freedom from each other, even as the play makes it clear that they belong together.

Much can be said for the range of human interaction that Jan de Hartog packs into his small play, *The Fourposter.* The play's scope is small, with only two characters and one set, but it captures thirty-five years of the struggles of a marriage, swooping easily between the extremes of joy and bitterness, anger and compassion. It is a comedy in the strictest sense of the word because everything turns out fine in the end, but even so it leaves open the question of whether or not its subjects, Michael and Agnes, have built their contentment with each other on unstable ground. From the first scene to the last, these two characters express deep ideological differences, giving viewers good reason to suspect that their marriage might be based on a selfish drive for comfort instead of on true, profound love. While vagueness is a sign of weak writing, this unanswered question is one that thoughtful romances are almost always forced to raise.

Audiences of the early 1950s, when the play first ran on Broadway, might have been content to think of *The Fourposter* as a sweet triumph of love, but time has shown the play to be more resilient and complicated, with a greater depth of understanding of the human condition than popularity alone requires. Ironically, the script tends to make Michael and Agnes seem like they were meant to be generalized, hazy representations of their social roles, referring to them as ''He'' and ''She,'' which denies the clearness of the personalities that de Hartog establishes so well. Despite the way these pronouns mask them, the individual traits of these characters show through, providing dramatic tension between their roles within the marriage and their own personalities.

The play can be interpreted as presenting the struggle for simplicity in the face of life's complications, which become more twisted and indecipherable over the course of a marriage. To make the distinction, de Hartog takes measures to establish a solid base of serenity over which to layer the problems of human identity. For instance, he set the play fifty years before the time he wrote it (a hundred years ago from now), pushing it back to the nineteenth century, before both world wars, before airplanes and automobiles, before electrical connections modernized the world with appliances that are meant to save time. Writing about an earlier generation can give an author a chance to explain large events with the benefit of hindsight, but in a domestic comedy like *The Fourposter* the distance of years serves to wrap the action in a shroud of nostalgia, reminding viewers that the action takes place in a simpler, more manageable, time.

Another way that stability is asserted is in the play's central image, the four-poster bed itself. Huge, and always looming in the middle of the set, the bed serves to remind viewers that there is a firm base anchoring Michael and Agnes's marriage, in spite of the changes that occur over the course of thirty-five years.

Having established this core of stability, de Hartog is free to present aspects of these two characters that make them struggle against the confines of marriage. In doing this, he presents a case for understanding marriage as being, by its nature, at odds with individual freedom. There is no implication that the conflict between freedom and mar-

> ... HE PRESENTS A CASE FOR UNDERSTANDING MARRIAGE AS BEING, BY ITS NATURE, AT ODDS WITH INDIVIDUAL FREEDOM. THERE IS NO IMPLICATION THAT THE CONFLICT BETWEEN FREEDOM AND MARRIAGE IS NECESSARILY A BAD THING, FOR, AS THE PLAY EVENTUALLY ASSERTS, THE UNION OF 'HIM' AND 'HER' ENDS UP BEING SATISFACTORY FOR THEM BOTH.''

riage is necessarily a bad thing, for, as the play eventually asserts, the union of ''Him'' and ''Her'' ends up being satisfactory for them both.

De Hartog does a superb job of treating the concerns of both Michael and Agnes with the fullest measure of respect, but he has rendered Michael's concerns more clearly. This cannot be read as greater approval for how Michael thinks, but only as a frank acknowledgement that de Hartog, a male writer, was able to understand Michael better. The sexes are so evenly balanced here that it seems unlikely that Michael's resistance to a settled relationship is meant as a statement about all men's view of marriage. Michael is almost matched in his struggle for independence by Agnes, but his struggle is rendered with more complete detail.

One way that Michael struggles against unity is that he drinks throughout the play, although de Hartog makes little use of alcohol's intoxicating effects. As a strict Quaker, it is doubtful that he would have had much insight to offer about intoxication. Instead of filling in much detail, he portrays Michael's relationship with liquor as a by-product of a rebellious streak that becomes frozen in him by his early entry into marriage, a facet of his character that becomes more and more pronounced as his social position becomes more confining. From the start, on their wedding night, he laughs off Agnes's concerns about his drinking, saying that he just appears intoxicated because he is so giddy with love, likening it to his fantasy about undressing her slowly: both are, in his mind, the offbeat products of a creative mind. The play foreshadows his drinking as a problem at this point by creating a link between the smell of liquor on his breath and the dangerous smell of gas from the lamp.

In subsequent acts, Michael continues to drink to rebel, and to distance himself from marriage. A turning point comes in the second act, when he sees his own drinking reflected back at him in his seventeen-year-old son Robert, forcing Michael to take a strong stand against liquor. His promise to someday show Agnes ''the difference . . . between gaiety and delirium tremens'' marks a threshold for his character, an end to any pretense he could have harbored that drinking makes life any more free and easy. This point is punctuated with symbolism when Michael becomes sick from drinking out of the bourbon bottle he has found, discovering only after he has gulped from it that it contains three-year-old cod liver oil.

While Michael's drinking increases through the years, his writing ability diminishes. Instead of heartfelt poetry, he starts producing cheap, sentimental, obvious novels. Writing ceases to be an artistic act, but a financial necessity: ''I have to spend every waking hour making money,'' he tells Agnes just past the play's middle point, in the second scene of act 2. While he does take his responsibility to his family seriously, it blinds him to the needs that he has as an individual. When he talks about the young poet who is supposed to be his protege, Agnes sees a world-weariness in him, represented by the way he has his hands on his head; he is outright hostile to the young man's work. When she forces the issue, Michael comes to see the relationship between his own youthful writing and the idealistic work of the young man who is just starting out; the enthusiasm of the protege's sonnet ''Nocturne Embrace'' is no more naive than Michael's poem from his wedding night, ''The Fountain of the Royal Gardens.'' Remembering the sincerity with which he wrote as a young man, and seeing the passion the unnamed young man has, while writing about Agnes, Michael comes to realize how important she is to his talent, and he therefore sees that his life as an artist is not, as he had thought, separate from his life as a member of their marriage.

Ironically, the least serious threat to the marriage portrayed here is the possibility of other people. When, in the beginning of the second act, Michael talks seriously about leaving Agnes for another woman, she shows little worry, and in fact she responds in a cunning way that makes his own jealousy kick into gear, causing him to abandon his plan to leave her. Whether she has really had an affair is doubtful, given the lack of details she is able to provide. The important thing is that she can read Michael so well, and that she knows that he is not so much in love with the young woman as he is flattered by the attention that she gives him. His description of the young woman shows no sign of his appreciating her for who she is, only of appreciating the fact that she can appreciate him: ''At last I have found a woman who'll live with my work,'' he tells Agnes, ''and a better guarantee of my faithfulness nobody can have.'' Agnes, in fact, finds a better way to guarantee his faithfulness by feigning indifference, and by threatening their marriage, which, it turns out, is more important to him than his work. Marriages are often destroyed by love affairs, but in this play Michael's affair is a relatively minor thing, a brief lapse into narcissism that is quickly brushed aside. De Hartog's point throughout is that the marriage, like the big four-poster bed, is huge and looming; it is more important to the lives of these characters than are their individual concerns.

If it were only Michael who was reluctant about his involvement in the marriage, the lesson for viewers might be one of gender, fitting in with traditions of Western culture that see men as less cooperative, less compelled by love, and less willing to commit. Agnes, however, has her own problems with the marriage, and, although she is more inclined to put her interests aside for the sake of a working domestic relationship, she does reach a point late in the play where she fears that she will lose her individuality completely. *The Fourposter* is never pessimistic about the benefits of marriage, but neither of its characters is entirely committed to it without reservation.

As Michael's job is his writing, Agnes's is the raising of their children. She chastises him for not being more consistently interested in them, refusing to allow Michael to harm the boy when he becomes determined to discipline Robert. She also knows more about the personal life of their daughter, Lizzie, than Michael can guess. Like Michael, who comes to fear that his artistic ability has been squandered for the sake of the family, Agnes ends up fearing that she will have no life when the children are not there to care for anymore. She plans to leave after Lizzie's marriage, to find out who she is as an individual. The scene in which she announces her leaving has some parallels to Michael's announcement in the second act, in that there is a young man involved who is not identified by name. But Agnes has no delusions about having a romantic relationship with the young man. If Michael was interested in his young woman because she was somewhat of a fan, in this case it is Agnes who is a fan, appreciating the young poet for his talent. The same fascination that drew her to Michael attracts her to this young poet, and she in fact forgets about him when Michael becomes like the young poet he once was, drawing upon her for inspiration.

Throughout the play, Agnes' maternal instincts are evident, from the way she cares for Michael when he suffers sympathetic labor pains to the way she worries about the young couple moving into the house at the end. Her fear, in the first scene of act 3, of losing the chance to be a woman before she becomes a grandmother, is much more poignant than any of Michael's concerns because the marriage relationship has seemed, all along, to be her idea, while he has seemed to only be going along with it. The most dangerous moment in the play, where the basic premise of marriage nearly comes apart, is when she shouts out words that seem more appropriate for him:

> —don't you feel yourself that there is nothing between us anymore in the way of tenderness, of real feeling, of love; that we are dead, as dead as doornails, that we move and think and talk like—like puppets?

This brutal evaluation of their situation is shocking because up to that point it had been Agnes's role to nurture the marriage, not tear it down, and Michael's role to do what he could to struggle against their union, trapped by jealousy and the desire to make her happy. When Agnes stops believing in their marriage, audiences know that it is in grave danger.

After Michael sets the order straight again by showing Agnes that he needs her and that his art suffers without her inspiration, the crisis is over. In the play's final scene, de Hartog summarizes the personalities of these two individuals by giving them each a symbolic object to bring to the marriage bed as their commentary on marriage for the next newlyweds. Michael's is a bottle of champagne, because he is enchanted with the idea of showing up at their new apartment drunk at eight in the morning, showing the new landlady, an authority figure, that he is not locked into a conformist lifestyle. His interest in drinking the champagne is slight, and he is easily distracted from doing it. In some ways, his willingness to give up the champagne idea makes it even more unusual that he would be so strongly opposed to her idea, which is to leave the pillow, embroidered with ''God Is Love,'' that her mother gave her on their wedding night. This pillow most strongly captures the differences of their two personalities. Agnes sees the mention of religion as a good, almost necessary thing for the newlyweds. She wants them to have a reminder about how important love is, over and above their individual concerns—for her purpose, the pillow might well say, ''Love is God.'' Michael is strict in his opposition, almost panicking about the responsibility that is being put upon the young groom's shoulders. ''You can burst into tears,'' he tells her, ''you can stand on your head, you can divorce me, but I'm not going to let you paralyze that boy at a crucial moment.''

In the end, Michael gives in: the pillow stays, but he leaves the champagne too. Their legacy to the new couple reflects the tensions of their own marriage, but it can easily be said that these tensions are what has made their marriage work for thirty-five years.

Source: David Kelly, in an essay for *Drama for Students,* Gale Group, 2001.

Kathy A. Smith

Smith has a Ph.D., specializing in writing and American literature. In the following essay, Smith discusses how de Hartog uses elements of comedy, especially how he plays upon the conventional manners and morals of American society, both to make the audience laugh at their own foibles and to reflect upon the value of marriage and love.

In general, comedy written for the stage differs from other dramatic forms such as tragedy or theatre of the absurd in that it combines gaiety and optimism with the subtle working out of a philosophical or moral question. The question—in this case whether the heroic couple will sustain their marriage through the predictable calamities and banalities of everyday life—creates a dramatic tension intended to teach something vital about the human condition. A theater audience may be compelled to wait until the very last scene to discover the playwright's answer to this moral question, but in a well-written comedy at least two things happen: laughter and something that inspires hope for the future.

Comedy is balm for the soul. It lures the audience by its own amusement into a willing collaboration with the playwright. The audience learns to recognize the flaws of the dramatic personae (and

A playbill title page for the 1952 production of The Fourposter *at the Ethel Barrymore Theatre.*

by extension, their own). Laughter provides relief from the hectic workings of human consciousness. Comedy's message implies that it is okay to be human and imperfect. Comedy shares with tragedy the capacity to create a sense of greater community with those who are laughing (or crying). Every joke will yield some truth. If everyone is laughing at the same thing, then something in it must be universally felt.

As Paul Grawe writes in *Comedy in Space, Time, and the Imagination,* comedy assures the audience that conflicts will be resolved in such a way as to give them cause for optimism about the future, despite loss of innocence; loneliness associated with the dark, existential moments; and the suffering that comes with human loss, humiliation, and change. If tragedy tends to elicit pity and terror in the face of the human condition, comedy builds faith in the imaginative and skillful art of human survival. Indeed, comedy not only strengthens faith in survival, it dramatizes, writes Grawe, "the conditions" under which the future "can be assured."

The Fourposter combines elements of romantic comedy with a comedy of manners. It teaches about the universal nature of love through the idiosyncra-

sies of its characters and the social codes of a particular period in history. In romantic comedy, as David Grote writes in *The End of Comedy,* "we are more concerned with the experience of the love than with the result of it," for it is expected that love will conquer all, but the pleasure as well as the revelation come from discovering how. Unlike the typical romantic comedy whose action revolves around the heroic couple wooing and finally winning one another (such as Shakespeare's *As You Like It,* or a more contemporary Hollywood film example, *The Runaway Bride*), the hero and heroine in *The Fourposter* are already married when they first appear on stage. Moreover, as the prologue states, the marriage stays intact for thirty-five years. There is, then, none of the usual suspense or intrigue as boy plots to get girl. Nor is there any clever maneuvering or hijinks on the part of friends and family to bring the shy and unwitting couple together. No mistaken identities, parental fears, or obstacles of class or religion interfere with the lovers. In fact, no other characters appear on stage throughout the three-act play but the heroic couple Agnes and Michael; the action depends completely on the dialogue between these two, and the tension ebbs and flows with the pitfalls and small miracles of married life itself.

The play's comic effects spring as much from the mannerisms and social conventions of the times as they do from the private conversations and interactions between the couple that the audience "overhears." In his 1939 doctoral thesis, *The Development of American Social Comedy,* John Geoffrey Hartman suggests that often comedy will "reveal for our amusement the embarrassment individuals suffer because of the very conventions and institutions which they themselves have built up and supported." It certainly holds true here. The action takes place between 1890 and 1925, an era which is often referred to as "the Gilded Age." Many classics of American literature have chronicled turn-of-the-century social life from the so-called Gay Nineties to the Roaring Twenties, most notably, perhaps, F. Scott Fitzgerald's *The Great Gatsby.* Agnes and Michael share with Fitzgerald's Gatsby "an extraordinary gift for hope, a romantic readiness" that characterized a national mood, a yearning for fashionability and success within a strict social code that the "old money" American families had maintained against the "vulgar" industrialists and the *nouveau riche.* Gentlemen were chivalrous; ladies, discreet. Among the fashionable, intrigue was good if you could carry it off without scandal, and marriage was (ho-hum) ''so'' bourgeois. The ''glittering aura'' of the Gilded Age was, of course, not all it was cracked up to be. In *The Great Gatsby,* that recognition comes too late and ends in tragedy; in *The Fourposter,* it is cause for mirth and for recommitment to married life.

When the play opens, it is the couple's wedding night, and Michael is carrying Agnes over the threshold of their new home. Both their conversation and their movements make it clear that they have had too much to drink, although the chivalry and romance of the moment resist their admitting it. So much of the play's effect depends on staging, and the reader feels it immediately. When he gets her inside, he throws her on the bed before even closing the outside door; then there is a flurry of straightening hair and dress and uncertainty as to where to put his top hat and gloves. Romance battles with propriety and with the after-effects of alcohol. Michael is euphoric. He drops to his knees in an outburst of feeling, and when she asks what he's doing, says, ''I'm worshipping you.'' She gets the first laugh with her response: ''Are you out of your senses?'' (Which of course he is.) ''If our Lord could see you. . . ,'' she adds, as if God were the landlord, or as if He had carelessly turned His eyes away for a moment.

The couple's awkward but touching sentiment and the humor that arises from it continue to escalate during the first scene. When she gets close to him to say something ''shocking,'' she discovers he has not washed his ears. In a classically romantic gesture, he offers to take off her shoes, but all she can think of is how much her feet hurt. She begins to tell him to get undressed, but she cannot say that word and finally orders him to take off his hat. Finally, he reads her a (very amateurish) poem that he has been working on. This drives her into the bathroom with her suitcase, where she feels it is safe to change. Meanwhile, with her offstage, he rips off his clothes, puts on his nightshirt, and then pulls his trousers and coat back on over the nightshirt, of course, still wearing his shoes. All the while, he is desperately afraid she will emerge from the bathroom before he is ''prepared.'' Frantically, at the last minute, he finds a towel, wets it, and begins to clean his ears. The audience can feel the suspense and the terrible awkwardness; when she reenters, they are ready for more hilarity.

Sex, the one word on everyone's mind in the first scene, is the one word that can never be broached. In the comic genre, the sexual innuendo

> THE 'GLITTERING AURA' OF THE GILDED AGE WAS, OF COURSE, NOT ALL IT WAS CRACKED UP TO BE. IN *THE GREAT GATSBY*, THAT RECOGNITION COMES TOO LATE AND ENDS IN TRAGEDY; IN *THE FOURPOSTER*, IT IS CAUSE FOR MIRTH AND FOR RECOMMITMENT TO MARRIED LIFE.''

works by ''surprise.'' In *The Dark Voyage and the Golden Mean,* Albert Cook writes, ''We are continually delighted that the wit can plunge headlong against the mores at every turn and dodge aside just in time with an unexpected nonsexual word.'' Laughter both releases tension and serves to preserve the social norms or mores without which the innuendo would have no power. De Hartog knows this instinctively and uses it to his best advantage here. As the scene winds down, everyone is acutely aware that the couple must end up in the bed. They cannot even look at one another until both are fully covered by darkness and sheets. He wants to sleep, seemingly exhausted by the evening's activities and emotional stress, but she thinks she smells gas leaking from the lamps. She insists on smelling his breath, again and again, to see if it might be alcohol. By her smelling his breath, they cleverly conquer their fears of intimacy, embrace, and the scene ends.

The first scene establishes the essential patterns of interaction between Agnes and Michael that will be repeated, with variations, throughout the play. They achieve a delicate stability characterized by playful give-and-take despite the strangeness that marriage confers between even the most compatible of people. One of the most charming ''exchanges'' occurs in the second scene of act 1, when Agnes is pregnant with their first child, but it is actually Michael experiencing the labor pains. They have traded places and, unwittingly, supported each other by doing so. Her constant care of him has taken her mind off her own fears, and he has been able to enter into the process by being ill. Their interactions are affectionately amusing and endearing because they are both still innocent, in love, and fearful of the future. As in the first scene, when the fear is greatest, the humor is, too. When her pains come in earnest, she starts to sing ''Yankee Doodle Dandy.'' He, thinking she is ''going mad,'' slaps her cheeks several times. She slaps back, and they are once more on level ground. She was singing on doctor's orders, a kind of early Lamaze breathing practice.

As the action builds and the first act ends, a darker note is introduced, and the shape of the conflict that will emerge between Michael's sense of worth in his family and his work as a writer is apparent. Their unfinished phrases hint at trouble ahead. He fantasizes about taking the unborn child on adventures, and she reminds him, ''First, there will be years of crying and diapers and bottles.'' He responds, ''I don't mind, darling. Honestly, I don't. I'll—find something to do. I'll work and—and go fishing alone. You're never going to have to worry.'' But lest the looming difficulties of the married condition become overwhelming too soon, de Hartog again interjects a comic note. To distract Agnes from her labor, Michael reads from ''a new book'' he's started. It bears the ridiculously sentimental title, *Burnt Corn, the Story of a Rural Love.* He reads, ''When she entered the attic with the double bed, she bent her head, partly out of reverence for the temple where she had worshipped and sacrificed, partly because the ceiling was low.'' Appropriately enough, it begins with a bed, and it suggests, as does their life together, both a sentimental romance and an earthy pragmatism. Clearly, the romance must make allowances for the practical, here represented by the height of the ceiling.

Only twice in the play is the delicate balance of their marriage truly threatened. In the second act, Michael tells Agnes he has been unfaithful with a woman who makes him feel young and who appreciates him for who he is. In act 3, it is Agnes who experiences the dark existential moment. She tells Michael that she wants to leave the marriage, feeling she no longer loves him, that their life is dull and flat, and that her role as mother and wife has ended. The episodes are real enough; the audience feels the confusion, the pain of betrayal, and the possibility that the marriage may fail. But in both episodes, they come to one another's rescue. Both Agnes and Michael know that his popular book, the one that has gained them entrance into fashionable society and led to his affair, is sentimental tripe. She won't pander to him to gain him back, but instead she turns the tables on him and hints that she, too, has a lover. While the audience suspects that she probably does

not (she never says so, but skillfully avoids telling him anything), he is burning with jealousy. He is mad to know the truth, and he realizes, as she packs her suitcase to leave, that he still wants and needs her love. Similarly, when Agnes expresses the emptiness she feels after the marriage of her daughter, and the reason she ''must'' leave (he has become coarse, harshly criticizing the poetry of a younger man under his tutelage), he humors her by reading some of the young man's poetry. It is every bit as bad as his was as a youth. And, as the playfulness threatens to dampen her enthusiasm for leaving, she discovers that he still needs her, she is palpably relieved, and they embrace.

The Fourposter leaves the audience smiling, as Agnes and Michael quibble over what to leave behind for the new couple that is to occupy their home and their bed. Unable to stop herself, and in defiance of Michael, Agnes sneaks the ''God Is Love'' pillow (it has stayed on their bed for thirty-five years) under the bedspread at the last minute. The pillow is more than a sentimental gesture; it is a morally apt symbol that represents and confirms the source and value of wedded life as well as her own sacrificial love for Michael. It is funny because Agnes thinks she has pulled one over on Michael. But he finds the pillow, and in a fine moment of husbandly compromise, he places a bottle of champagne on the groom's side of the bed, a kind of balancing act, thinking it will bolster the new man's courage on his wedding night. The interaction, of course, brings the audience back full circle to the opening scene, when the embarrassment and awkward shyness of the heroic couple nearly result in a wedding night fiasco. De Hartog's instincts are perfect. Michael can do nothing better than to sweep Agnes off her feet and carry her over the threshold.

It is, of course, the bed that signifies the couple's love and sacrifice for one another. And it is precisely this predictable and yet, as theatre critic Brooks Atkinson wrote in a 1951 review for the *New York Times,* ''ludicrous . . . downright impossible'' love that answers the basic question of the play; that is, what is marriage really good for anyway? All of the couple's vanities and peccadilloes, as well as their irritations and manipulations, are held in balance with the wonderful unconscious playfulness; the tender expression of emotions; the joyful and difficult sacrifices; and the comforts of the thirty-five-year marriage bed. Agnes and Michael are about as middle-class and ''ordinary'' as they are likely to get, and somehow they, and the audience, take comfort in that.

Source: Kathy A. Smith, in an essay for *Drama for Students,* Gale Group, 2001.

Hartman, John Geoffrey, ''The Development of American Social Comedy 1787–1936,'' Ph.D. diss., University of Pennsylvania, 1939, p. 1.

SOURCES

Atkinson, Brooks, *New York Theatre Critics' Reviews,* Vol. 12, No. 22, Critics' Theatre Reviews, October 29, 1951, p. 191.

Cook, Alfred, *The Dark Voyage and the Golden Mean,* Norton, 1966, p. 43.

de Hartog, Jan, ''The Writer in Violent Times: The Dutch Underground Theatre,'' a transcript of a talk given at Weber State College, November 17, 1986.

————, *The Fourposter: A Comedy in Three Acts,* Samuel French, Inc., 1980.

Fitzgerald, F. Scott, *The Great Gatsby,* Charles Scribner's Sons, 1925, p. 2.

Gassner, John, *Best American Plays,* Crown Publishers, 1958, p. 480.

Grawe, Paul, *Comedy in Space, Time, and the Imagination,* Nelson-Hall, 1983, pp.17–8.

Grote, David, *The End of Comedy,* Archon Books, 1983, pp. 36–7.

FURTHER READING

Astro, Alan, *Understanding Samuel Beckett,* University of California Press, 1990.
    Astro gives an introduction to the major works of Beckett, with discussion of the Theater of the Absurd, as well as central themes and stylistics elements of his plays.

Moore, Bob, *Victims and Survivors: The Nazi Persecution of the Jews in the Netherlands, 1940–1945,* Arnold, 1997.
    This text provides a history of the treatment of Jews in the Netherlands during Nazi occupation of World War II.

Moorton Jr., Richard F., ed., *Eugene O'Neill's Century: Centennial Views on America's Foremost Tragic Dramatist,* Greenwood Press, 1991.
    Moorton's book is a collection of essays by various critics discussing the significance of O'Neill to the development of twentieth-century American theater.

Stott, Annette, *Holland Mania: The Unknown Dutch Period in American Art and Culture,* Overlook Press, 1998.
    Stott's book discusses the influence of Dutch artists on nineteenth- and twentieth-century American art.

The Government Inspector

NIKOLAI GOGOL

1836

The Government Inspector, by Nikolai Gogol, has also been translated into English under the titles *The Inspector General,* and *The Inspector.* The written play was brought to the attention of the Tsar Nicholas I, who liked it so much that he insisted on its production. *The Government Inspector* premiered at the Alexandrinsky Theatre, in Saint Petersburg, in 1836. The tsar, who was among the first to see the play, was said to have commented that the play ridiculed everyone—most of all himself.

The plot of *The Government Inspector* hinges on a case of mistaken identity, when a lowly impoverished young civil servant from Saint Petersburg, Hlestakov, is mistaken by the members of a small provincial town for a high-ranking government inspector. The town's governor, as well as the leading government officials, fear the consequences of a visit by a government inspector, should he observe the extent of their corruption. Hlestakov makes the most of this misconception, weaving elaborate tales of his life as a high-ranking government official and accepting generous bribes from the town officials. After insincerely proposing to the governor's daughter, Hlestakov flees before his true identity is discovered. The townspeople do not discover their mistake until after he is long gone and moments before the announcement of the arrival of the real government inspector.

The Government Inspector ridicules the extensive bureaucracy of the Russian government under

the tsar as a thoroughly corrupt system. Universal themes of human corruption and the folly of self-deception are explored through this drama of Russian life. The governor's famous line, as he turns to address the audience directly, "What are *you* laughing at? You are laughing at yourselves," illustrates this theme, which is summed up in the play's epigraph, "If your face is crooked, don't blame the mirror."

AUTHOR BIOGRAPHY

Nikolai Vasilyevich Gogol, named after Saint Nikolai, was born in 1809, in the small town of Velikie Sorochintsy, in the Ukraine, then part of Russia. His parents, Maria Ivanovna and Vasily Afanasevich Gogol-Yanovsky, were landowners. Gogol enrolled in the High School for Advanced Study in Nezhin, in 1821, where his classmates, observing his various physical and social peculiarities, nicknamed him "the mysterious dwarf." In school, he developed an interest in literature and acting. In 1825, when Gogol was sixteen years old, his father died. In 1828, Gogol arrived in Saint Petersburg, intent on becoming a civil servant. Obtaining a disappointingly low-level, low-paying post in the government bureaucracy, Gogol focused his ambitions on writing.

His very first publication, in 1829, was mostly ignored; it was given scathing reviews by the critics who did, however, make note of it. Humiliated and discouraged by this reception, Gogol purchased all the remaining copies of his work and burned them. After an equally unrewarding stint at a second government post, Gogol began teaching history at a girl's boarding school in 1831. *Evenings on a Farm near Dikanka,* Gogol's two-volume collection of stories derived from Ukrainian folklore, was published in 1831 and 1832. The collection was instantly well received. Gogol soon gained the attention of Aleksandr Pushkin, Russia's leading literary figure, who provided him with ideas for two of his most important works.

In 1834, he began a position as assistant professor of medieval history at Saint Petersburg University. Gogol quickly proved himself a resounding failure as a professor, in part because he was not sufficiently knowledgeable in his subject, and left this post after only one year. During that year,

Nikolai Gogol

Gogol, while generally neglecting his teaching duties, published two books of short stories, *Mirgorod* and *Arabesques;* a collection of essays; as well as two plays, *Marriage* and *The Government Inspector* (also translated variously as *The Inspector General,* and *The Inspector*). *The Government Inspector* was brought to the attention of the tsar, who liked it so much that he requested the first theatrical production, which was performed in 1836.

Gogol, reacting to heavy criticism by the government officials his play lampooned, declared that "everyone is against me" and left Russia. He spent the next twelve years in self-imposed exile. During this time, Gogol traveled extensively throughout Europe, staying in Germany, Switzerland, and Paris, eventually settling primarily in Rome. After Pushkin died in 1837, Gogol inherited the mantle of the leading Russian writer of the day. Gogol's literary masterpiece *Dead Souls* and the first edition of his collected works were published in 1842. In 1848, he returned to Russia, settling in Moscow.

Gogol became increasingly preoccupied with religious concerns, eventually taking council from a fanatical priest who influenced him to burn his manuscript for the second volume of *Dead Souls.* Gogol died at the age of forty-two in 1852 as the result of a religious fast.

PLOT SUMMARY

Act 1

The play is set in a small town in provincial Russia, in the 1830s. Act 1 takes place in a room in the governor's house. The governor has called together the town's leading officials—including the judge, the superintendent of schools, the director of charities, the town doctor, and a local police officer—to inform them that a government inspector is due to arrive from Saint Petersburg. The governor explains that this government inspector is to arrive "incognito" with "secret instructions" to assess the local government and administration of the town. The governor, in a panic, instructs his officials to quickly cover up the many unethical practices and general corruption of the local town authorities. The brothers Bobchinsky and Dobchinsky, two local landowners, rush in to inform the governor and his officials that they have seen the government inspector staying at the local inn. As the governor is leaving to greet the "Very Important Person" at the inn, his wife and his daughter, Marya, enter, asking about the inspector.

Act 2

Act 2 takes place in Hlestakov's room at the inn. Ossip, the middle-age servant of Hlestakov, muses that his master, a young man of about twenty-three years, is a government clerk of the lowest rank, who has lost all of his money gambling, and is unable to pay his bill for two weeks' food and lodging at the inn. The governor enters, assuming that Hlestakov is indeed the government inspector. He offers to show Hlestakov the local institutions, such as the prison, whereupon Hlestakov thinks he is being arrested for not paying his bill. The confusion continues, however, until the governor invites Hlestakov to stay at his home, and the young man goes along with this apparent generosity without understanding that he is being mistaken for someone else.

Act 3

Act 3 takes place in the governor's house. The governor's wife and daughter are eagerly awaiting the arrival of the government inspector. Hlestakov and the governor enter, the governor having given him a tour of the hospital and a hearty meal. Finally catching on that he is being mistaken for a high-ranking government official, Hlestakov launches into an elaborate fantasy of his luxurious and privileged life in Saint Petersburg. When Hlestakov retires to his room in the governor's house, the governor's wife and daughter bicker over which of them he was flirting with.

Act 4

Act 4 also takes place in the governor's house. The governor sends in each of his town officials to give Hlestakov as much money as he asks of them. The governor hopes this bribe money will keep Hlestakov from reporting them to the officials in Saint Petersburg. Hlestakov makes the most of this opportunity, asking each man for increasingly extravagant amounts of money. When they have all left, Hlestakov writes a letter to his friend, Tryapichkin, in Saint Petersburg, describing the situation for the sake of amusement. A group of local shopkeepers arrive to speak to Hlestakov regarding the extensive corruption and bribery that takes place on the part of the governor. When they have left, Hlestakov proceeds to flirt with Marya, the governor's daughter; however, the minute she leaves the room, he flirts with the governor's wife. But, when Marya walks in to find Hlestakov pleading his love to the governor's wife, he immediately proposes marriage to her (Marya). When the governor enters, he does not initially believe Hlestakov has proposed marriage to his daughter, but he is soon convinced. At this point, Ossip enters, having made plans for Hlestakov to leave the town as quickly as possible, before his deception is discovered. Hlestakov tells the governor and his wife and daughter that he is leaving town for only a few days, but he will return soon to marry Marya.

Act 5

Act 5 continues in the governor's house. The governor and his wife boast of the luxurious and privileged life they will lead in Saint Petersburg once their daughter has married this high-ranking official. The postmaster arrives, having intercepted and read Hlestakov's letter to his friend in Saint Petersburg, revealing that he has deceived the entire town, and cheated them out of large sums of money. Calling himself an "idiot," the governor wonders that he could have been so foolish as to mistake the young man for "an illustrious personage." At this point, the governor turns to the theater audience and utters the famous line, "What are *you* laughing at? You are laughing at yourselves." Just then, a gendarme (a soldier who serves as an armed police force) enters with the announcement that the real "inspector authorized by the Imperial government" has arrived, and awaits the governor at the inn. The play ends with a famous "tableau vivant," in which each character remains frozen in a posture of surprise and fear upon the announcement that the real government inspector has arrived.

CHARACTERS

Anna Andreyevna

Anna Andreyevna is the governor's wife. In his notes on the characters, Gogol describes her as "still tolerably young, and a provincial coquette," who "displays now and then a vain disposition." Her concern with appearance is indicated by the stage direction that "she changes her dress four times" during the play. The governor's wife flirts shamelessly with Hlestakov. When he informs her of his engagement to Marya, she approves, imagining the benefits she will enjoy in Saint Petersburg as a result of the marriage.

Bobchinsky

Bobchinsky, along with his brother Dobchinsky, is a landowner in the town. In his notes describing the characters, Gogol states that the brothers are "remarkably like each other." They are both "short, fat, and inquisitive . . . wear short waistcoats, and speak rapidly, with an excessive amount of gesticulation." Gogol distinguishes them by noting that "Dobchinsky is the taller and steadier, Bobchinsky the more free and easy, of the pair."

Dobchinsky

Dobchinsky, along with his brother Bobchinsky, is a landowner in the town. It is Bobchinsky and Dobchinsky who first see Hlestakov at the inn and mistake him for the government inspector. They immediately run to tell the governor that the government inspector has arrived, thus initiating the case of mistaken identity that propels the entire play.

The Governor

The governor of the town has the most to fear from the arrival of the government inspector because he has the most power of anyone in the town and is the most corrupt. In his notes on the characters, Gogol describes the governor as "a man who

MEDIA ADAPTATIONS

- *The Government Inspector* was adapted to the screen in a 1949 American film entitled *The Inspector General*. It starred Danny Kaye as the character of Hlestakov and was directed by Henry Foster.

has grown old in the state service," who "wears an air of dignified respectability, but is by no means incorruptible." When Hlestakov announces that he has become engaged to the governor's daughter, the governor immediately indulges himself in fantasies of the luxurious, high status life he will enjoy in Saint Petersburg as a result.

Hlestakov

Hlestakov, also spelled Khlestakov, is a young man of about twenty-three. He is a government clerk of the lowest rank and is traveling through the small town accompanied by his servant, Ossip. Hlestakov has lost all of his money gambling and is unable to pay his food and lodging bill at the inn. The people of the town mistake him for the government inspector, who was set to arrive there incognito to check up on the workings of the local government. Hlestakov at first thinks the governor intends to arrest and imprison him for not paying his bill but eventually realizes that he is being treated as an honored guest of the town. Hlestakov makes the most of this opportunity, weaving elaborate lies about his life in Saint Petersburg, gorging himself at a feast they have provided, milking the local government officials for all of the bribery money he can, and offering a false proposal of marriage to the governor's daughter. Hlestakov leaves town just before a letter posted to his friend and revealing his chicanery is intercepted and read by the town's postmaster—who brings it before the governor. By this time, Hlestakov is far gone; he is out of reach of any revenge that the townspeople may have wished to exact upon him. Gogol insisted that the character of Hlestakov is not calculatingly deceitful but an opportunist, merely making the most of the case of mistaken identity into which he has fallen.

Marya

Marya is the governor's daughter. She and her mother rush to the inn to meet the reputed government inspector. She responds to Hlestakov's flirtations and accepts his marriage proposal. Hlestakov, however, flees the town, telling her that he will return in several days to get her, but he has no intention whatsoever of doing so or of following up on his proposal.

Ossip

Ossip is Hlestakov's servant. Gogol describes him as a middle-aged man who "is fond of arguing and lecturing his master." Gogol notes that Ossip is cleverer than Hlestakov and "sees things quicker." Ossip muses aloud to himself, informing the audience of Hlestakov's true identity and destitute financial circumstances. Ossip wisely hurries Hlestakov out of the town as soon as possible, fearing that his deception will soon be found out.

Postmaster

The postmaster is described as "an artless simpleton." He abuses his station by opening and reading the letters of others, occasionally keeping those that he finds most interesting. His role is minor, but key to the plot, because he intercepts Hlestakov's letter to his friend, which reveals that Hlestakov is not the government inspector.

THEMES

Russian Bureaucracy

As was readily apparent to Gogol's contemporaries, *The Government Inspector* is a satire of the extensive bureaucracy of nineteenth-century Russian government. According to D. J. Campbell, writing in the forward to the *The Government Inspector,* Gogol once stated that "In the *Government Inspector* I tried to gather in one heap all that was bad in Russia." Through the regular practices of "bribery and extortion," according to Beresford in his introduction to Gogol's *The Government Inspector: A Comedy in Five Acts,* most public officials

"tyrannized over the local population" of Russian towns. Beresford goes on to characterize Russia under the yoke of this vast bureaucratic system: "The whole of this immense empire was strangled by red tape, cramped by administrative fetters, and oppressed by a monstrous tyranny of paper over people." Nigel Brown in his *Notes on Nikolai Gogol's The Government Inspector* states that, in *The Government Inspector,* "Gogol was the first Russian writer to examine the realities of the official world in literature, exposing it to hilarious satire." In Gogol's play, Hlestakov, the young man mistaken for the government inspector, belongs to the lowest of fourteen possible levels within the hierarchy of the Russian civil service. The fact that he successfully poses as a public official occupying a much higher level in the bureaucracy thus demonstrates both the ignorance of the townspeople he has duped, and his own sense of self-importance. The chaotic atmosphere of the office of the governor in the opening scene immediately establishes the image of small town Russian bureaucracy as ridiculously inefficient and unprofessional. Nothing of any value seems to get accomplished by the masses of paper and the proliferation of characters holding official government titles. The lack of communication between the small town and the government center in Saint Petersburg also indicates that the Russian bureaucracy was so geographically extensive there was no means of regulating the behavior of civil servants or the effectiveness of local government offices.

Corruption

All of the public officials in the town are thoroughly corrupt. The judge "openly admits to taking bribes"; the postmaster indiscriminately opens and reads letters addressed to others; and the police are drunken, brawling, and given to flogging women. Most corrupt of all is the highest ranking official of the town, the governor: he regularly takes bribes, spends money allotted to the building of a church for his own purposes, and seizes money from the local shopkeepers. In satirizing the corruption within the Russian bureaucracy, Gogol addressed more universal themes of human corruption. Beresford asserts that the play is "an attack on all forms of moral depravity, of which bribery and corruption are but examples." Because of this universal theme, Beresford insists that, "Gogol's play is thus as relevant to the world of the twentieth century as it was to its own time, and it points to a perennial evil of civilized societies." In essence, according to

TOPICS FOR FURTHER STUDY

- Gogol lived and wrote in Russia during the first half of the nineteenth century. Learn more about the history of Russia in the nineteenth century. What were the significant cultural conditions and political events of the time? Learn more about Russia in the present day. How is it different from Russia during Gogol's lifetime?

- Gogol is from a region of Russia that is now the independent nation of the Ukraine. Learn more about the history and culture of the Ukraine in the nineteenth century. Learn more about the Ukraine today. How has the region changed since Gogol's youth?

- In addition to Gogol, important nineteenth century Russian writers include Aleksandr Pushkin, Fyodor Dostoyevsky, Leo Tolstoy, and Anton Chekhov. Learn more about one of these authors. When and where did he live and write? What are his most important literary works? What similarities, if any, can be found between his work and Gogol's?

- The Moscow Art Theater, established in 1895, was a center for innovative techniques in acting and dramatic production in Russia. Learn more about the history of the Moscow Art Theater. What influence do you think these innovative techniques had on productions of Gogol's plays?

Lavrin stating in his book *Gogol,* ''Gogol was really ridiculing a much wider field of rottenness than the officialdom he knew.''

Deception and Self-deception

The Government Inspector is a story of deception and self-deception. The townspeople deceive themselves into believing that Hlestakov is the government inspector, whereupon Hlestakov takes advantage of the case of mistaken identity, further extending the deception to his own advantage. Hlestakov takes such a liking to his assumed role that he almost appears to be convinced by his own deception, imagining himself to be the venerable high official he pretends to be. The townspeople attempt to deceive the government inspector as to the true corruption within the local government, but find that they have only deceived and cheated themselves in the process. Beresford comments that Gogol made use of the plot motif of mistaken identity ''to reveal a fundamental state of chaos in human life.'' Beresford continues,

> It is no accident that the plot of most of his works hinges on a deception, because for him deception was at the very heart of things. He saw human beings as enmeshed in a web of confusion and deceptions, misled not only by appearances but also by their own delusions and lies.

STYLE

Russian Realism and Dramatic Comedy

Gogol has often been dubbed the ''father of Russian realism.'' *The Government Inspector* introduced the principles of dramatic realism to the Russian stage. Lindstrom in his book *Nikolay Gogol* notes that ''the need for greater realism in the theater'' was ''one of Gogol's most pressing concerns.'' Gogol consciously desired to counter the burlesque and sentimentality of popular Russian drama with a play that revealed everyday people in everyday life. Edward Braun in an introduction to *Nikolai Gogol: The Government Inspector* notes that Gogol believed modern drama ''must reflect the problems of modern society,'' and therefore, ''sought with his comedy to bring out the significance of everyday happenings.'' Gogol was thus dissatisfied with the initial production of *The Government Inspector* because the actors had failed to embody the principals of dramatic realism for which the play had been intended. Lindstrom explains that the actors of the day, "did not know how to interpret this new kind of comic realism and gave an appallingly bad performance." In the long run, however, according to Campbell, *The Government Inspector* "contributed a great deal to the evolution of the peculiar Russian realism in acting." Gogol's impact on dramatic realism is also a measure of the use of realistic dialogue in his plays. His lasting influence on Russian literature is in part due to the innovative use of colloquial Russian speech in his literary works. Brown observes that Gogol's plays were innovative in replacing the formal speech of written Russian with dialogue that is "alive with the quality of actual speech." Beresford likewise asserts that Gogol, in *The Government Inspector,* "incorporates . . . all features of everyday speech" in "dialogue such as had never been heard on the Russian stage before and has seldom been equaled since."

The Epigraph and Direct Audience Address

The play's epigraph, taken from a Russian proverb, reads: "If your face is lopsided, don't blame the mirror." This saying is echoed by a line toward the end of the play, whereupon the governor, having learned of his foolish mistake in believing Hlestakov to be the government inspector, turns directly to the audience, demanding: "What are *you* laughing at? You are laughing at yourselves." As a theatrical technique, this is called "direct address," because the actor breaks through the imaginary "fourth wall" of the stage to engage the audience directly in the world of the play. To a Russian audience of the 1830s, when the play was first performed, this line would have constituted a direct confrontation. Most audience members would have belonged to any one of fourteen official levels within the extensive Russian bureaucracy at the time. Because the play ridicules the incompetence and corruption of government officials, many critics and theatregoers were openly offended by it. Gogol's epigraph anticipates this response, warning the spectator that, if the play, like a mirror, reflects a "lopsided" view of Russian society, it is not the play, but the society, that is to blame.

The Tableau Vivant

Gogol placed special emphasis on the "tableau vivant" that ends the play. A "tableau vivant" is equivalent to what in cinema would be a "freeze frame"; the characters freeze for "almost a minute and a half" in a posture that reveals their response to the news that the real government inspector has just arrived. In the stage directions, Gogol specifies the exact posture and facial expression of each character on stage at this point. The governor stands "like a post, arms outstretched, head flung back"; the postmaster "has become a question mark addressed to the audience"; the superintendent of schools is "in a state of innocent bewilderment"; while those characters not specified stand "just like posts." In the notes that precede the printed play, Gogol, asserting that "the actors must pay special attention to the last scene," elaborates upon the mood and effect of the "tableau vivant": "The last word ought to give an electric shock to all present at once. The whole group ought to change its position instantly. A cry of astonishment ought to spring from all the women as though from one bosom." Gogol insisted that "Disregard of these instructions may ruin the whole effect." Victor Erlich comments in his book *Gogol* that this tableau vivant is a "moment of truth," in which, "The lightning which strikes dumb the cast . . . illuminates, in retrospect, the real nature and drift of the proceedings." Richard Peace notes that, in this final moment, "the characters await their fate like the motionless figures of a run-down clock, whose time has suddenly run out."

HISTORICAL CONTEXT

Censorship

Under the reign of Tsar Nicholas I, Russian writers suffered extremely strict censorship of all written material. In 1826, a statute on censorship, according to Beresford, "prohibited the publication of any matter that was deemed to disparage the monarchy or the church or which criticized, even indirectly, the existing order of society." The years 1848–1855, particularly, were referred to as "the age of terror by censorship." Brown describes the crushing power of these censorship practices on Russian society: "Penalties included warnings, rebukes, fines, confiscations of offending books or magazines, police supervision or detention in the guardroom of local military garrisons." Brown concludes that "It was a wonder that anything got into print at all." Braun states that "Genuine Russian masterpieces" of dramatic writing "were suppressed by a pathologically suspicious censor and were destined to wait over thirty years for their first

COMPARE
&
CONTRAST

- **1825–1855:** The reign of Tsar Nicholas I (1796–1855) as Emperor of Russia is characterized by extreme repression and extensive censorship of all printed materials.

  1917–1991: The Russian Revolution of 1917 results in the end of the era of imperial Russia and the formation of the Union of Soviet Socialist Republics (U.S.S.R.)

  1985–1991: The ascendance of Mikhail Gorbachev as president of the U.S.S.R. results in the policies of *Glasnost* (verbal openness) and *Perestroika* (policy of economic and governmental reform), which usher in an era of unprecedented openness as well as the relaxation of censorship and repressive measures. These measures lead to the dissolution of the U.S.S.R. in 1991.

- **1712–1917:** St. Petersburg, located about four hundred miles northwest of Moscow, and founded by order of the Tsar Peter I the Great in 1703, is made the new capital of Russia in 1912. In the eighteenth century, St. Petersburg becomes a center of intellect and the arts. The population of St. Petersburg increases from over 220,000 to one-and-a-half million between 1800 and 1900. In response to anti-German sentiment, the city is renamed Petrograd in 1914.

  1924: Upon the death of Lenin, Petrograd is renamed Leningrad.

  1991: A failed coup attempt waged against president Mikhail Gorbachev, at the seat of Soviet government in Moscow, results in the dissolution of the Soviet Union. The allowance of local elections initiates a series of reforms at the municipal level, including policies to introduce elements of free-market economy. In 1991, voters choose to change the name of the city of Leningrad back to St. Petersburg.

- **Nineteenth Century:** Russian literature in the nineteenth century includes many of the greatest works of prose fiction in world literature to date; authors such as Pushkin, Gogol, Dostoyevsky, Chekhov, and Tolstoy produce some of the most outstanding masterpieces of world literature.

  1917–1980s: During this period, state-sponsored censorship allows only for literature that promotes the government propaganda of the U.S.S.R. By and large, Russian citizens have no access to Western literature, and they have little access to works of Russian literature produced prior to the Revolution of 1917. In 1934, under the rule of Stalin, ''socialist realism'' is declared the only admissible style of literature.

  1985–Present: The beginning of the end of the Soviet era is dated to 1985, when Mikhail Gorbachev became the president of the U.S.S.R. The policies of *Glasnost* and *Perestroika* began effecting a lifting of censorship. The dissolution of the Soviet Union in 1991 marks the end of the era of Soviet Russian literature.

---

public performances.'' Literary historians agree that, had it not been brought to the special attention of the tsar himself, who whimsically approved it, *The Government Inspector* would certainly have been censored from any theatrical production until many years later.

Nineteenth-Century Russian Literature

Despite, or perhaps in spite of, strict censorship under the reign of Tsar Nicholas I, Russian literature flourished in the nineteenth century. Unofficial manuscripts of literary and other written works could be obtained and dispersed among friends and acquaintances without knowledge of the censors. Beresford points out that

> . . . despite the shackles of censorship, literature flourished under Nicholas I. Indeed by a curious paradox of history his reign, which was one of reaction and stagnation in most spheres of life, produced a great ferment of ideas and a remarkable burgeoning of literary talent.

Among such talents were Pushkin, Gogol, and Dostoyevsky. Before Gogol, Aleksandr Pushkin (1799–1837) was the leading Russian writer of the early nineteenth century. Pushkin's masterpiece is the novel *Yevgeny Onegin* (1833), a realistic portrait of Russian life, at all social levels, in both the major cities and the provinces. Pushkin befriended the young Gogol in Saint Petersburg, and is said to have suggested the topic for *The Inspector General* based on his own experience of being mistaken for a high-ranking government official while staying at an inn in a remote town. Pushkin died from a fatal wound incurred during a duel to save his wife's ''honor.'' Gogol, while crushed by the loss of his friend's life, immediately inherited the mantle of leading Russian writer. Fyodor Dostoyevsky (1821–1881), who is among Russia's greatest writers, was greatly influenced by Gogol. Critics often recount the now legendary comment attributed to Dostoyevsky that, as Amy Singleton Adams in the *Dictionary of Literary Biography* offers, all Russian realist writers had emerged ''out from under Gogol's *Overcoat.*'' Dostoyevsky's greatest works include the novella, *Notes from the Underground* (1864), and four novels: *Crime and Punishment* (1866), *The Idiot* (1868–9), *The Possessed* (1872), and *The Brothers Karamazov* (1879–80). Subsequent leading Russian writers of the nineteenth century include Leo Tolstoy and Anton Chekhov.

CRITICAL OVERVIEW

Gogol's lasting influence on Russian literature cannot be underestimated. According to Richard Peace in *The Enigma of Gogol:*

> Gogol exerted an immense influence on the whole course of Russian literature and continues to do so to the present day. There is scarcely a later Russian writer who did not succumb in some measure to his magic, and in many cases (Dostoyevski, Chekhov, Ilf and Petrov) his influence was crucial. In this sense alone, to call Gogol the 'father of Russian prose fiction' is eminently justifiable.

Critics today almost universally agree on the comic and dramatic genius of *The Government Inspector.* Calling the play Gogol's ''comic masterpiece,'' Erlich asserts that it is ''by far the greatest comedy in the Russian language and one of the finest ever written.'' Campbell asserts that it is ''perhaps the greatest comedy ever written for the Russian stage.'' Lindstrom concurs that ''the total effect is one of tremendous dramatic power.''

Beresford comments that ''*The Government Inspector,* a work of enormous comic power, with penetrating shafts of satire and a gallery of unforgettable characters, is the greatest play in the Russian language and one of the acknowledged masterpieces of world drama.''

Because of extremely strict censorship under the reign of the Tsar Nicholas I, Gogol's play might not have been produced in his lifetime. However, the poet Zhukovsky brought the written play directly to the attention of the tsar, who liked it so much that he insisted on a production at the royal theater. *The Government Inspector* opened in 1836, with the tsar in attendance. Nicholas was said to have delighted in the production.

Popular and critical reception of the play, however, has been dubbed by several critics a ''succes de scandale''—meaning that the play's popular success was inextricable from its controversial critical reception. While the tsar himself was not offended by the play's open satire of the Russian bureaucracy, the audience members, most of whom were themselves civil servants, took personal offense. Nigel Brown notes that, ''it is virtually the first work of art to expose to ridicule aspects of the administrative and bureaucratic system of Tsarist Russia.'' As a result, Erlich observes, ''The story of the reception of *The Inspector General* and of Gogol's subsequent reaction is almost as interesting as the play itself.'' He explains:

> The initial impact was explosive. While the audiences' responses were mixed, hardly anyone remained indifferent. The bulk of the theater going public, especially the officials and the sycophants of the bureaucratic establishment, were displeased, indeed often scandalized, by the 'vulgarity' and 'coarseness' of the play, and by its slanderous, not to say subversive tenor.

Janko Lavrin explains that ''The spectators enjoyed the piece, but they were cross with the author. For everyone saw himself personally insulted.'' Yet, ''In spite of all the attacks on Gogol . . . the theatre was always crowded. For even those who disliked it could not help enjoying it.'' Erlich notes, ''The play was making an impact; it was the talk of the town, the focus of a lively and loud controversy,'' thus making Gogol, ''one of the best-known and most talked-about writers of his time.''

Taken aback by the extensive negative reaction to the play, Lindstrom notes that Gogol wrote to a friend, ''Everyone is against me.'' In self-defense, he published an article, ''After the Theater,'' which recounted the overheard dialogue of theatregoers leaving at the end of the play. *After the Theater* was later expanded and published in book form in 1842. Lindstrom comments that, ''Of little artistic merit, it is nevertheless a valuable record of Gogol's increasing insistence on the didactic role of literature and his need to explain his art in terms of moral and social philosophy.'' Gogol, however, was so traumatized by the controversy raised by *The Government Inspector* that he quickly left the country, remaining in self-imposed exile for the next twelve years. He revised the play extensively, publishing a new edition in 1842, which was not performed until 1888. Included was an epilogue entitled, ''The Denouement of the Revizor,'' which attempted to justify the play's meaning by recasting it as a religious allegory. Erlich observes that ''In this ponderous interpretation, the town . . . symbolizes the soul of man, the corrupt officials represent the base passions gnawing at it, while the Inspector serves as an embodiment of man's awakened 'conscience' or sense of guilt.'' Lavrin states unequivocally that ''Such interpretation is of course ridiculous and entirely unconvincing.''

Speaking to the lasting popularity and relevance of *The Government Inspector,* Beresford asserts:

> The Government Inspector is a work of enormous scale, at one extreme an entertaining comedy of errors and, at the other, an illuminating drama of corruption. No single interpretation encompasses all its meaning. . . . It is a play of great originality, that contains the inexhaustible riches of all great art. Its theme is universal and it speaks to the eternal human condition. Its laughter is directed at what is essential and permanent in man. It transcends its own time and people, belonging to all ages and all peoples. It has justly earned for itself the name of immortal comedy.

CRITICISM

Liz Brent

Brent has a Ph.D. in American Culture, specializing in film studies, from the University of Michigan. She is a freelance writer and teaches courses in the history of American cinema. In the following essay, Brent discusses cultural and historical references in Gogol's play.

There are a number of cultural and historical references pertaining to biblical literature and history, as well as ancient Greek mythology and history, in *The Government Inspector,* which may not be familiar to the reader. These references include: King Solomon from biblical history; Alexander the Great from ancient Greek history; the Elysian Fields from Greek mythology; the ancient Greek politician and speechwriter Cicero; and the Tower of Babel from biblical literature. An explanation of some of these references in terms of the central themes found in *The Government Inspector* will facilitate a greater appreciation of Gogol's play.

In act 1, as the governor and other local government officials discuss how to cover up the extent of their corruption, the judge asserts that he is not concerned about the government inspector, because the legal system is too confusing for anyone to comprehend anyway. The Judge states,

> Well, I'm not worried. A person from Petersburg won't be interested in a mere district court. And if he does glance at some legal document, he won't understand it. Solomon himself couldn't understand our documents. I've been on the bench fifteen years, but, as for legal papers, I take one look and throw them in the wastebasket.

The Judge here refers to King Solomon, who is considered the greatest king of biblical Israel. King Solomon, the son of King David and of Bathsheba, is known today by information about him in the Bible. He is renowned for his military strength, his supposed skills as a great lover, his reputedly extensive harem of women (including 700 wives and 300 concubines), his construction of the famous Temple of Jerusalem, and his deep wisdom. The most famous example of his wisdom is described in a story in which two women held a dispute over who is the rightful mother to an infant; Solomon proposed cutting the baby in half, and then, based on each woman's reaction to the suggestion, determined who was the real mother.

In Gogol's play, the reference to Solomon is used to ridicule the Russian legal system. The judge states that even a man as wise as Solomon could not make sense of a single legal document in the Russian court. This comment contributes to Gogol's central theme in this play, which satirizes the Russian government bureaucracy as not only corrupt but also strangled with red tape.

In act 1, the governor calls together the leading town officials to discuss strategies for covering up the extent of corruption, incompetence, and inadequacy in the town's public institutions from the eyes of the government inspector—who is expected to arrive any day. The governor explains to the superintendent of schools that the history teacher will be a problem if observed by the inspector. At one point

Bob Goody as Ossip and Timothy Spall as Hlestakov in a scene from a theatrical production of The Government Inspector.

in the play, the governor alludes to Alexander the Great during a conversation with the superintendent of schools:

> And your history teacher. Clever fellow. I don't deny that. But the man lets his feelings run away with him. I heard one of his lectures. As long as he stayed with the Assyrians and Babylonians, it wasn't so bad, but when he came to Alexander the Great, I thought the house was on fire. He jumped up, took a chair, and smashed it on the floor. . . . Now I know Alexander was a very great hero, but why smash the furniture? The government had to buy a new chair.

Alexander the Great (356–323 BC), a Greek, was King of Macedonia from 336 to 323 BC. A military genius, he lead the invasion of Asia, conquering much of Asia Minor, and overthrowing the Persian Empire. Alexander greatly expanded the boundaries of his empire in the twelve years of his reign. He founded over seventy new cities and spread Greek thought and culture throughout much of Asia. After his death, at the age of thirty-three, lacking the force of his determination and charisma, the empire soon broke up into separate kingdoms.

In Gogol's play, reference to Alexander the Great demonstrates the incompetence and ineffectiveness of the Russian educational system. While most of the local government officials in the play suffer from not taking their jobs seriously enough, the history teacher demonstrates that he takes his job *too* seriously. The superintendent of schools says of the history teacher that he is prepared to give his life ''in the cause of education,'' as if it were a revolutionary effort. The idea that the history teacher gets so excited over historical matters that he is inspired to smash a chair against the floor indicates his loose grasp on contemporary reality.

In act 1, while the governor and his fellow town officials are deliberating about how to prepare for the arrival of the government inspector, the postmaster enters. The governor instructs him to unseal and read every letter, to catch any ''tattle tales,'' who may be writing to Saint Petersburg to complain of the town government. The postmaster assures him that he already opens and reads the letters, but ''not as a security measure''; he explains that he does this because ''. . . I'm curious. I like to know what goes on. It's fun, too. I even learn a lot. More than in the Moscow News.'' When the governor asks if he's read anything about the ''Person from Saint Petersburg,'' meaning the government inspector, the postmaster responds: ''Nothing about Petersburg. . . . You'd love some of the letters. . . . There was a lieutenant the other day, describing a

WHAT DO I READ NEXT?

- "The Nose" (1836) is one of Gogol's best known short stories. It concerns a man whose nose has left his face and taken up an independent life of its own, and the man's efforts to restore the runaway nose to its proper place on his face.

- "The Overcoat" is Gogol's most celebrated short story. It concerns a poor scribe whose heart is broken when his prize possession, a fashionable overcoat, is stolen.

- *Dead Souls* (1842), by Nikolai Gogol, is a comic novel set in feudal Russia. It concerns a man who concocts a get-rich-quick scheme in which he purchases the rights to deceased serfs ("dead souls") to pawn them off for profit.

- *The Captain's Daughter* (1836), by Gogol's contemporary and friend Aleksandr Pushkin, is a historical novel of the Pugachov Rebellion.

- *Evenings on a Farm near Dikanka* (1831 and 1832), by Nikolai Gogol, is a two-volume publication that contains tales drawn from Ukrainian folklore.

- *Nikolay Gogol: Text and Context* (1989), edited by Jane Grayson and Faith Wigzell, is a collection of essays on the works of Gogol discussed in the cultural and historical context of nineteenth-century Russia.

- *The Complete Tales of Nikolai Gogol* (1985) is in two volumes and is edited by Leonard J. Kent. It is an authoritative compilation of Gogol's fiction.

- *Leaving the Theater and Other Works* (1990), edited by Ronald Meyer, is a collection of essays by Gogol.

- *The Theater of Nikolai Gogol: Plays and Selected Writings* (1980) is edited by Milton Ehre. It includes translations of Gogol's dramatic plays.

- *Uncle Vanya* (1896), by the great Russian playwright Anton Chekhov, concerns a man, Uncle Vanya, who has sacrificed his own happiness for the sake of his brother-in-law.

---

ball. He compared it to Elysium: girls, bands playing, banners flying. . . ." Elysium, also called "the Elysian fields," or "the Elysian Plain," is, in Greek mythology, akin to the Christian heaven, a paradise to which heroes and those favored by the gods are sent after death.

The reference to Elysium in Gogol's play is significant in that it alludes to the play's motif of fantasy locations. Once Hlestakov figures out that he is being mistaken for an important person from Saint Petersburg, he weaves an elaborate web of fantasy describing the splendor and prestige of his life in the city. The inhabitants of the town are easily taken in by Hlestakov because of their own eagerness to imagine the far-away city as a sort of paradise, in comparison to their own provincial surroundings. In act 5, after Hlestakov has (insin-

cerely) proposed to the governor's daughter, the governor fantasizes about his future life as the father-in-law of a high-level government official in Saint Petersburg; again, Saint Petersburg resembles a sort of paradise, or Elysium, in the fantasies of a provincial townsman. The postmaster's response to the governor also demonstrates his own simple-mindedness, frivolousness, and ignorance of the severity of his corrupt abuse of a government office. While the other town officials are concerned with every detail that may be observed by the government inspector, the postmaster blithely engages in a frivolous description of a ball, completely unconcerned with the fact that he has illegally opened and kept for himself, a letter intended for someone else.

In act 4, the governor and his local government officials debate over who is to go first in approach-

"THE TOWER OF BABEL IN
GOGOL'S PLAY ECHOES HIS
CENTRAL THEME OF THE GENERAL
INEFFECTIVENESS OF THE RUSSIAN
BUREAUCRACY."

ing Hlestakov, whom they believe to be the government inspector, with the offer of a bribe. The director of charities volunteers the judge to approach Hlestakov first. The judge replies that the director of charities himself should approach the government inspector first, upon which the director of charities replies that the superintendent of schools should go first because he "represents education—enlightenment." The superintendent of schools, however, insists that he becomes completely tongue-tied in the presence of authority. The director of charities responds that, in that case, it should be the judge, after all, who approaches Hlestakov first, because "When you open your mouth, Cicero speaks."

Marcus Tullius Cicero (106–43 BC) was a Roman politician, lawyer, and writer, who became renowned for his powerful speeches and convincing argumentation. Reference to Cicero in Gogol's play is intended to exaggerate the judge's incompetence by means of contrast. The judge, a small-town, provincial government bureaucrat who knows more about hunting dogs than about the law, is compared to one of the greatest public speakers and masters of legal rhetoric in the history of Western culture. This reference builds upon a central theme of Gogol's play, which satirizes the general incompetence among Russian government officials and the general ineffectiveness of the Russian legal system.

In act 4, during a discussion in which the governor and his fellow local officials debate who is to go first in presenting the government inspector with an offer of bribery, the judge is targeted as the most likely candidate. After comparing the judge to Cicero, they continue to praise his speaking powers by insisting that "You can hold forth on the Tower of Babel!"

The Tower of Babel, according to the book of Genesis in the Old Testament, was built in Babylon

after the flood. The story of the Tower of Babel is that the people of Babylon wanted to build a tower that would reach as high as the heavens. To defy this effort, God was said to have created a confusion of languages among the workers building the tower, so that they could not effectively communicate with one another and therefore had to abandon the construction of the tower. The dispersing of these people throughout the world is said to explain the diversity of languages among human cultures.

References to the Tower of Babel usually imply a nonsensical confusion of words. The Tower of Babel in Gogol's play echoes his central theme of the general ineffectiveness of the Russian bureaucracy. The implication is that the extensive web of bureaucracy, which made up the administrative arm of the Russian government, was so confusing and nonsensical that it was a virtual Tower of Babel—a mass of legal documents and verbiage that was ultimately meaningless and ineffective. Furthermore, the local government officials demonstrate their own confusion and ignorance over the meaning of words when they suggest that the Judge is such a skilled speaker that he can "hold forth," or present a powerful speech in a meaningless mass of words. As a mouthpiece for the Tower of Babel, which constituted the Russian bureaucracy, the judge is skilled at generating a mass of nonsensical verbiage upon a meaningless mass of legal documentation.

References to ancient Biblical and Greek history and culture in *The Government Inspector* function to elaborate upon a central theme of corruption, ineffectiveness, and incomprehensibility in the Russian bureaucracy under the reign of Tsar Nicholas I.

Source: Liz Brent, in an essay for *Drama for Students*, Gale Group, 2001.

Daria Krizhanskaya

The following essay by Daria Krizhanskaya, discusses Vsevolod Meyerhold's production of Revisor (The Inspector General) *and how his perspective informs the play as a satire and vehicle for Bolshevik enlightenment.*

On December 9, 1926, after nearly two years of extensive research and rehearsals, Vsevolod Meyerhold premiered his *Inspector General (Revizor)*. Though the production provoked a tempest in the Soviet press and was much discussed by the critics of both liberal and Communist bent, foreign—mostly American—witnesses had no doubt about its artistic value from the very beginning. Meyerhold had created a magnificent and somber spectacle which reflected his pre-revolutionary symbolist past, his tragic world view linked to the philosophy of Russian symbolism, and what appeared to be his apocalyptic warning concerning the future of humanity.

An analysis of newly available archive materials—rehearsal notes recorded by the director's assistants being the most important among them—reveals that the production was a synthesis of the director's aesthetic discoveries made in the pre-revolutionary and post-revolutionary periods. Nevertheless, when placing *Revizor* in the context of Meyerhold's career, critics and historians usually pay scant attention to the essential qualities of the production—the mystical, the tragic and the phantasmagoric. Having dutifully noted them, most scholars then mysteriously leave them unexplained. For Louis Lozowick in 1930, *Revizor,* along with Meyerhold's productions of The *Death of Tarelkin* (1922) and *The Forest* (1924), represented the director's ongoing effort to revamp and reinterpret Russian classics. In 1965, Marjorie Hoover wrote that the production transformed Gogol's comedy of manners into a satire, though one with universally symbolic overtones. Konstantin Rudnitsky in 1969 emphasized ''the aggressive power of the past'' (i.e., the epoch of Tsar Nicholas II) as essential to the meaning of the production. He also mentioned strange ''riddles'' allegedly implicit in or suggested by the historical events of the middle 1920s—riddles that Meyerhold ''heard'' and attempted to reply to in his production. What stands behind this metaphor? What kind of riddles did Rudnitsky have in mind? Throughout his book, he never answers this question, probably because he could not answer it in print. Censorship and self-censorship were still a matter of necessity in the late 60s when Rudnitsky's groundbreaking volume was published in the USSR. By the time of Edward Braun's study in 1995, *Revizor* had become a synthesis of ''realism, hyperbole and fantasy.'' However they characterize it, existing accounts of the production are descriptions rather than interpretations; most of them list *Revizor* under the neutral label of ''revived classic.''

This label derived from critics' convenient and uncomplicated linking of Meyerhold's aesthetics with Bolshevik cultural policies has some historical explanation. At the end of 1922, Lunacharsky, the People's Commissar for Enlightenment, concerned with the growth of purely formal experiments in Soviet art, publicly proclaimed the return to psy-chological literature with the slogan ''Back to Ostrovsky!'' Later, he explained what he meant:

> We, modern playwrights, must observe the life around us sensitively, like Ostrovsky and, unifying profound theatrical effect with precise, penetrating realism, we must present a constructive and explanatory mirror-image of our times.

The quote reveals Lunacharsky's moderately positivistic aesthetics as well as the ideological imperatives of the time. The top party official in charge of Soviet culture was advocating a radical return to the Russian classics. Not yet an order, but a recommendation, this call has been interpreted by Meyerhold scholars as an obvious reason for Meyerhold's staging of Ostrovsky's *A Profitable Post* (1923) and *The Forest* (1924), Gogol's *Revizor* (1926) and Griboedov's *Woe From Wit* (1928). Yet, in the case of *Revizor* this historical coincidence appears to be the simplest part of the truth. A more complete—and complex—reading of the production would take stock of the internal logic of the director's development, viewed as a continuous trajectory from his first directorial efforts in 1903 to his *Revizor* in 1926, and would analyze both the external and internal influences exerting themselves on Meyerhold's artistic consciousness at the time.

Meyerhold and his assistants persistently claimed that *Revizor* was conceived as a condemnation of ''not merely peculation in some miserable little town, . . . but the entire Nicholayan era together with the way of life of its nobility and its officials.'' Even in the ''conversations with the actors,'' he repeatedly announced ''his firm clinging'' to the realistic theater and reiterated his point that ''the grotesque ruins *Revizor.*'' As if casting a spell, he tried to convince everybody, including himself, that by embracing the ultimate good of realism, he would abandon the obvious evil of grotesque. Statements from his theater stressed the production's satirical spirit, directed against the Russian Imperial past, a satire in tune with the Bolshevik's cultural enlightenment program for the masses. Lee Strasberg's observation that ''Meyerhold uncovers the social content of [any] play'' accords with this interpretation only too well. Persuaded by Meyerhold's own declarations, Western scholars frequently forget that Soviet historical documents should not be taken at face value, even if they come from the recently opened post-Communist archives. Meyerhold was keen to manipulate the appropriate Communist vocabulary in the struggles on the ''theater front.'' Most of his conceptual statements concerning the content, ideas, or genre of a production—whether as official speeches or rehearsal notes—must be thoroughly checked against his theater practice.

Interpreted as satire, or a mixture of realism and fantasy, or a revived classic, *Revizor* is rather carefully described but unsatisfactorily interpreted, even in the most trustworthy scholarly writings. But the problem of *Revizor* is contained within the larger problem of the position of Meyerhold vis-a-vis the 1917 October Revolution, which can only be approached with a full understanding of how Meyerhold's previous aesthetic discoveries coalesced in *Revizor.*

Rudnitsky, Braun and Leach, whose books represent the most influential approaches in contemporary Meyerhold scholarship, take it for granted that the director's creative life can be clearly divided into two periods: That of the prerevolutionary, ''decadent,'' modernist Meyerhold, and that of the ardent Bolshevik who, inspired by the Revolution, served it with all his theatrical genius. Indeed, formal historical evidence speaks for this obvious division: Meyerhold joined the party in 1918 and soon came into prominence with the Bolshevik regime, receiving the top artistic title, People's Artist, as early as 1923. Both Russian and foreign witnesses had no doubts about the nature of his postrevolutionary theater practice, with ''its roots deep in our heroic, proletarian struggle.''

With this evidence, and influenced by Rudnitsky, who was the first to bring the director's name back from Stalinist eclipse, most scholarship essentially reiterates the same argument: Meyerhold enthusiastically accepted the Great October, which gave him unprecedented aesthetic ideas together with fresh possibilities for their realization. Meyerhold's theatrical version of constructivism is considered purely a post-revolutionary achievement. Together with Malevich, Mayakovsky, and other avant-garde artists, Meyerhold devoted his genius to the propaganda of the Revolution and followed its cause ''to the very limit.'' Typical of this prevailing view is Camilla Grey's description of these artists, who

> joyfully plunged into the experiment, blissfully regardless of the physical and practical sacrifices involved. . . . It is difficult to believe that they were almost literally starving— . . . living conditions were reduced to the most primitive. They rode lightheaded on the surge of release and the sense of a new-born purpose to their existence; an intoxication drove them to the most heroic feats: all was forgotten and dismissed but the great challenge which they saw before them of changing the world in which they lived.

A seasoned artist in his mid 40s, Meyerhold hardly rode lightheaded. The most turbulent in his turbulent life, his relationship with the Revolution came out of numerous artistic and personal reasons, but not of a pure political intention to change the world. Both in the December 1905 Revolution, and the February 1917 Revolution, he remained politically unengaged, initiating his involvement with the Bolsheviks only when they came to power after the October uprising. Oliver Sayler, who spoke to Meyerhold in the winter of 1917/18, remembered that the director was reticent in their conversation about politics to the point that Sayler was unable to figure out where his political sympathies lay.

However, the image of a Communist artist changing the world for a just social order attracted scholars, especially Western ones, seeking to explain why some members of the left intelligentsia chose to collaborate with the Bolsheviks. The director's later troubles and his downfall at the end of the 30s were attributed to Stalin's embracing of totalitarianism and oppression. Thus, Meyerhold's creative biography offered a deceptively simple picture: until the late 20s, the ''good Revolution'' bestowed on its faithful artist creative freedom and practical benefits, but when it turned ''bad,'' the artist fell as its martyr, shot down in the cells of the NKVD (a predecessor of the KGB). Taken to its logical conclusion, this claim led eventually to the still commonly held belief that Stalin and the degenerated Revolution together are to blame for the death of this great theater genius. Interpreted in this way, Meyerhold's tragic fate may too easily be used to illustrate the maxim about the Revolution that devours its own children.

Until the late 80s, for obvious political reasons, this was the only permissible way of viewing Meyerhold for Rudnitsky and other Soviet scholars. From the time of the thaw through Perestroika, they necessarily had to present him as an ally of Communism whose work met the crude standards of ideology—although only up to a certain point. For Western liberals it was—and still is—a chance to see the whole Revolution, or, at least, its first ''righteous'' decade, as an unparalleled explosion of new proletarian art and mass creativity. The speculations of the Communist leaders responsible for ''cultural construction'' (Lunacharsky, Bogdanov, and Kerzhentsev), official theater documents, Meyerhold's own political statements—all evidence that should be taken at the very least with a grain of salt—has kept Westerners enchanted with the myth of Revolution. This myth helps them to disregard such Bolshevik initiatives as The Red Terror, officially announced in 1918; the revival of the medieval practice of taking hostages; Dzerzhinsky's proclamation of "the infallibility" of Tcheka, which accompanied a mass liquidation of gentry, clergy, merchants, and members of the intelligentsia; and finally the grand opening of the first concentration camp in 1922. It was Trotsky, after all, who held that "terror is a most powerful political instrument," and that "the question of the form or degree of repression, is, of course, by no means one of 'principle.' It's a matter of expediency." And the "new freedom" celebrated in this kind of scholarship has nothing to do with the actual measures taken by the Bolsheviks, including the closing of newspapers and cabaret theaters "in view of their intolerable character" immediately after the October coup, and the expatriation of hundreds of the most prominent Russian scholars and philosophers in 1922. Aimed at erasing individuality, the real Revolution was destructive for Russian culture and Russian society from the very beginning.

The blooming proletarian art of the 20s was mainly created by non-proletarian groups and most certainly did not start from scratch right after October 1917. Moreover the theory which divides Russian art into two disconnected prerevolutionary and post-revolutionary epochs is lazy. Most artists were continuing to explore ideas found and formulated before 1917, during the so-called Silver Age of Russian culture. Tairov founded his Kamerny theater in 1914; at this time, Evgeny Vahtangov and Mikhail Chekhov were enjoying their first success under the auspices of the MAT First Studio, founded in 1913; Fyodor Komissarzhevsky staged his famous *Faust* in 1912; Nikolai Evreinov published his ideas on theatricalization of life between 1908 and 1913 (*An Apologia for Theatricality* in 1908, and a collection of essays, *Theater as Such,* in 1913); finally, the Futurists, Cubists, and Suprematists made their appearance with *The Victory Over the Sun* in 1915.

As for Meyerhold, his "new" and "revolutionary" constructivism emerged from his pre-revolutionary work in general and the experiments in his studio on Borodinskaya (1914–1917) in particular. The molding of his own theatrical methodology led to a liberation of the actor's art through the liberation of the actor's body from the structures of a weary psychological realism, which paradoxically corresponded to the general aesthetics of constructivism and the ideological thesis of shaping "a new man in a new world." A former student of

> INTERPRETED AS SATIRE, OR A MIXTURE OF REALISM AND FANTASY, OR A REVIVED CLASSIC, REVIZOR IS RATHER CAREFULLY DESCRIBED BUT UNSATISFACTORILY INTERPRETED, EVEN IN THE MOST TRUSTWORTHY SCHOLARLY WRITINGS."

Meyerhold's from the Borodinskaya Studio recalled that, during the production of *The Magnanimous Cuckold* (1922!), she thought she was seeing "something familiar"—namely, the visual realization of ideas the director was formulating during the last years of the Studio.

The scholarly fixation on Meyerhold the Bolshevik essentially renders him as nothing more than an artist who, after 1917, became a political director with a constructivist, or expressionist, or some other form of expression. This attitude regards the textual content of his work, i.e., the story, as "dressed up" in avant-garde garb, and thus fails to perceive the aesthetic integrity of the director's best productions. It separates the spoken text from the theatrical one, with its visual, audio, and plastic elements, and obscures a full understanding of Meyerhold's legacy. Suggesting that Meyerhold's principle achievement was in reflecting the burning problems of the day, this view sees his works as formed by external, objective causes that differed from one production to another. In fact, although Meyerhold did reflect his time, he did it more subtly, in a way which was modulated by his own cultivated past and his temperament. If Meyerhold accepted the Great October, it was out of the hope of having his own theater, founded with the blessing and unlimited financial support of the new power. "I don't give a damn about this or that political trend," he used to say before the revolution. "All I want to do is to save the theater." An artist first and foremost, he valued but one thing—to create freely; and he accepted the power that might seem to provide him with the desirable freedom. In the chaotic, hysterical days of the Revolution and the Civil War, he strove to find a niche where he could develop his artistic ideas and train his actors.

Under contract with the Imperial Theatres before 1917, he was unable fully to realize his theatrical ambitions. An influential group of august, veteran actors and top theater patrons were hostile to him and his innovations, and as a result, he never exercised unfettered artistic power on the Alexandrine stage. Sensation and scandal largely characterized his theatrical reputation. ''A celebrity in the modern sense,'' as Paul Schmidt writes, Meyerhold provoked radical opinions, but the ''patrician'' critics—Kugel and Benois in particular—violently attacked his aesthetic principles. The ultra-right *New Time* did not hesitate to remind its readers of his supposedly Jewish origin. *Masquerade* became a target of a particular critical viciousness. Prepared for more than six years, it was presented on the eve of the February revolution. Its allegedly ''mindlessly absurd luxury'' and ''arrogant wastefulness'' outraged Kugel who envisioned ''the hungering crowds,'' ''shouting for bread . . . practically next door'' to the theater. This temperamental description virtually defined a full range of accusations against Meyerhold as a reactionary and even ''a Rasputin in theater.''

Critics aside, he also did not acquire a loyal public. In regard to Meyerhold's relations with pre-revolutionary spectators, a respectful Soviet critic of the 30s, Boris Alpers, was quite right when he wrote:

> For a working class spectator, his art did not exist at all, as it was hidden behind the walls of inaccessible Imperial theaters. And by its very nature, it just couldn't be close to this spectator. . . . For the petty bourgeois intelligentsia, his works were too cold and too rational. . . . Gloomy sarcophaguses that Meyerhold constructed on the stage of Imperial Theaters caused . . . bewilderment and protests among the top Russian aristocracy. That cold, aesthetic pathos with which Meyerhold showed its masks and rituals . . . caused in it unnecessary anxiety.

Always intolerant of an artistic opinion different from his own, he became increasingly defensive and arrogant. The actors, he thought, failed his *Masquerade*—he detested the actors trained in the realistic tradition of the Russian theater. To exercise a new art, he felt he vitally needed new actors trained in his own artistic methods, as well as a theater of his own. Little by little, the idea of his mission—that is, the revolution in the theater—became intermixed with the idea of a revolution in the society. Any change was better for him than no change at all. Considering his conflicts with the old theater to be unresolvable, he longed for a storm that would smash the barriers to his own potential artistic benefits. As a fervent opponent of the old theater system, he came to the Bolsheviks within days of the October Revolution. As if having Meyerhold's case in mind, Kugel wrote in December of 1917 that ''we traded Russia for a ticket to a theater gallery. . . . To reject reality for the sake of phantom theater of one's own imagination—that's the fundamental sickness of Russian mentality.''

After 1917, political, personal, and aesthetic factors became so intertwined in the director's life that it is extremely hard to tease them apart. Even decisions about his personal life were frequently made according to artistic considerations. Establishing theater, not changing the world or enlightening the multitudes, was Meyerhold's ultimate goal. An artist-innovator, Meyerhold never saw the theater as a tool for something else; art of theater had for him its own meaning and value. In his book *On Theatre,* published in 1913, Meyerhold argues that an artistic revolution can come only from an artistic of genius, who is oblivious to the tastes and desires of the masses: ''Some Wagner will overcome the sluggishness of popular mind for Bayreuth to emerge.''

Clearly, then, this sophisticated, essentially apolitical director was not converted in an instant to the mission of producing art according to the needs, or tastes, of the masses. These tastes differed too much from his own. Somebody named Polosikhin, a proletarian correspondent, expressed a common proletarian opinion when he said: ''[I] gave tickets [to one of Meyerhold's productions] to some of our broads [at the factory], and had to hide for a couple of days after that—they wanted to beat me up.'' Unlike Stanislavsky who was fascinated with the similarity between theater and life, Meyerhold sought to discover distinctions between the two, and specifically explore what is immanent to theatrical recreations of reality. For Stanislavsky, life was the first reality, truer than theater; for Meyerhold, theater came first, universalizing life and making it larger.

It is sometimes suggested that Meyerhold exploited the Revolution to propagate his own theatrical reforms. But the issue appears to be more complicated now: He didn't calculate, but he did operate in a revolutionary atmosphere, changing his appearance and vocabulary as actors change their costumes. It is meaningless to accuse him of hypocrisy on these grounds—after all, he didn't change his essential morals and attitudes. Rather, he was a theater person from top to toe to such a degree that nothing but theater had any substantial meaning for him. In September, 1920, Meyerhold arrived in Moscow dressed B la Bolshevik in a soldier's gray coat, but a few years later this coat gave way to a fashionable suit from an expensive tailor.

For Meyerhold the artist, the circumstantial changes of everyday life comprised an external domain—whether it was the proletarian dictatorship, the Civil War chaos, or the society that later ended in fear and hatred. In 1917, the old life collapsed, a new one was born—for better or worse—and he used the cultural form's of this new life, with its new symbols, themes, myths, and vocabulary, to mold the artistic reality of his productions. What changed so drastically in 1917 was the raw material of life—its formulas—but Meyerhold's aesthetics were developing smoothly and consistently.

In his "political" productions in the early '20s, he would insert bulletins on the Civil War (as in *The Dawn,* 1920), or bring onto the stage Red Army detachments together with purely utilitarian objects such as real trucks and motorcycles (as in *Earth Rampant,* 1923). The latter Meyerhold dedicated "to the primary Red Soldier of RSFSR, Lev Trotsky." And yet one should not be misled by these deceptive details: Political statements masked aesthetic ideas; the social was an external form for the aesthetic. Moreover, the aesthetic task Meyerhold attempted to fulfill in these productions had nothing in common with propagandistic zeal.

Thus, the material became revolutionary on the surface—and the transformation of the material was interpreted as a shift in the artist himself. Meanwhile, the artist continued to develop the stage principles he discovered in the first years of Russian modernism. These principles were solely based on the concepts of "*teatral'nost*" and "*uslovnost*"—two terms frequently used in Russian theoretical writings from the Silver Age onwards—where "*teatral'nost*" translates as "theatricality" and "*uslovnost*" is usually rendered as "conditionality," "stylization," or even "conventionality." As Katerina Clark summarizes, *uslovnost* entails a recognition of the impossibility of mimesis, of representing or recreating reality in the theater and of the consequent necessity for conventions, forms unique to the theater and understood as such by audiences. Of major significance in understanding the nature of the theater, *uslovnost* is rooted in a clever observation of Alexander Pushkin made almost a century earlier:

Verisimilitude is still presumed to be the primary condition and basis of dramatic art. What if it were demonstrated that the very essence of dramatic art distinctly precludes verisimilitude? Where is the verisimilitude in an auditorium divided in two parts, one half of which is full of spectators?

Discovered in its new sense in *The Fairground Booth* (1906), theatricality—a miraculous self-revelation of stage and its essential quality which moves beyond style or spectacle—was the foundation of Meyerhold's methodology and an obsessive interest which defined his creative path over the thirty-six years of his career. Through symbolism, "conventionality," commedia dell'arte, traditionalism, constructivism, and the synthetic theater of the grotesque Meyerhold strove always to uncover the nucleus of theatricality. Unlike Stanislavsky, Meyerhold understood it not as a means for revitalizing a dull spectacle but as a specific theatrical language. The grammar of this language—stage time, space, and action—obeyed rules different from those in real life; and a person on stage acted differently from a person in reality. Action in the Meyerhold system was built around an interplay between the actors and the spectators, which emphasized the playful nature of the theater itself through the demonstration of theatrical conventions. The goal of Meyerhold's method, this interaction was never intended to include the direct physical participation of the audience, but it relied on the audience's alert and liberated imagination. Thus, the audience, along with the author, the actor, and the director was considered an equal creator of any theatrical event; the principle of co-activity defined, in turn, notions of space and acting.

Hence the importance of the proscenium, an essential spot of Meyerhold's stage space, to which all the interrelated production elements were linked up. Already in 1913, in the introduction to his collection of articles entitled *On Theater,* Meyerhold wrote:

I, who got into directing in 1902, only by the end of the decade was fortunate enough to touch upon the mysteries of the Theater that are concealed in such primary elements as the proscenium and the mask.

More than merely a frame around the action, the proscenium was understood as a catalyst for the desired spiritual contact between actors and audience. As such, it required the absence of the curtain, which was indeed banned from certain productions of the Fellowship of the New Drama as early as 1906. In 1910 Moliere's *Don Juan* was almost entirely performed on a wide apron jutting out into the auditorium of the Alexandrine Theater. To emphasize the importance of this apron Meyerhold even introduced little blackamoors—the famous proscenium servants—to open the action and to place and remove accessories on the stage between acts.

However, much work was left to be done on the part of the actors. "Doing" instead of "being" became the major principle of Meyerhold's acting technique. The 19th-century focus on the actor who experienced something on stage was now abandoned. The actor was no longer expected "to emanate" feelings; instead, Meyerhold invented for each moment a specific bit of business for the actor based on movement and related to the whole as tile fragments within a mosaic, and it took the audience's creative imagination to perceive all the parts in the artistic totality. With allusions, cross-references, and reflections of all sorts, Meyerhold guided the imagination of his audience to keep the act of perception from being purely subjective.

Bodily movement was considered the core of the actors' "doing" in particular, and the essence of the actors' creative process in general. Convinced that movement *is* development and, therefore, the visual, stage analog of the dramatic action of the play, Meyerhold prioritized it early in his career. As he took his understanding of movement even further, he considered stage emotions and speech as a part of movement and attempted to organize their development in audio-visual ways as well. After the Revolution, when he finally got his own actors, the possibility of the old form of ill-conceived, irregular, movement on stage was completely excluded; the constructivist "apparatuses for playing" (used, for instance, in *The Magnificent Cuckold* and *The Death of Tarelkin*) revealed immediately any sloppy, or cliched gesture, thus celebrating the beauty of functional and expedient movement.

Having formulated this treatment of space and action before 1917, Meyerhold never betrayed it throughout his career. In April of 1917, at a debate entitled "Revolution, Art, War," castigating "the salient, passionless parterre where people come for a rest," Meyerhold asked rhetorically: "Why don't the soldiers come to the theater and liberate it from the parterre public?" In his book, Braun misinterprets this statements as proof of Meyerhold's political radicalism. However, the director was merely voicing once again his desperate desire to establish an interaction between the actors and the audience. He needed an audience different from what he had before, and one better unacquainted with all types of

formal innovations than one contaminated with naturalistic preconceptions. Soldiers, nurses, or nuns, Meyerhold did not really care. Essentially, he remained the same artist who proclaimed as early as in 1913:

> A theater that presents plays saturated in 'psychologism' with the motivation of every single event underlined, or which forces the spectators to rack his brains over the solution of all manner of *social and philosophical problems* [italics added]—such a theater destroys its own theatricality . . . The stage is a world of marvels and enchantment, it is breathless joy and strange magic.

The inner logic of Meyerhold's creative development happened to coincide for a brief moment with the grandiose myth of Revolution. This coincidence was the director's existential tragedy that ended with his physical extermination 23 years later. Back in 1917, however, the myth of Revolution legitimized those means that Meyerhold had already conceived on his own. At the same time, it served as an independent source of new imagery and models that Meyerhold could use for his explorations of theatricality. One of these models, in vogue during the first revolutionary years, was the mass spectacle, such as *Storming the Winter Palace,* staged in 1918 by Nikolai Evreinov. The participants in this repeated storming were supposed to be the same soldiers and workers who did it in 1917, but the Palace Square was decorated with gigantic painted backdrops that introduced a theatrical aspect to the spectacle—an aspect which had evolved directly from Evreinov's pre-revolutionary ideas about the theatricalization of life. Having nothing to do with theater as an aesthetic phenomenon, Evreinov's ideas of recreation of events and emotions had more in common with a theater therapy that would purge people of their passions, whether individual or historical (those of an entire nation).

Yet *the theatricalization of life* and *theatricality* may be considered as counter-currents in the theater history of the 20th century—the former responsible for the extension of theatrical laws into real life, the latter revealing the heart of the theater event, though staying within the boundaries of traditional theater. Theatricality was, of course, Meyerhold's great fascination. Even in *Earth Rampant,* where Meyerhold put on stage real military detachments equipped with field telephones, motorcycles, and automobiles, he did not attempt to bring the mass spectacle into the proscenium theater. Emmanuil Beskin, who greeted with excitement "the destruction of theater" in this production, was quite wrong. In fact, Meyerhold was exploring how real objects would "behave" on stage when plunged into the magnetic field of total theater. Instead of using them merely as realistic props or decorative elements—as prescribed by the realistic tradition—he used them functionally in montage collisions with each other and in an interplay with a live actor—the method he later applied in *Revizor.*

The core of this method lies in the idea that, when placed in a complex stage context, even a simple object such as a chair acquires additional meanings—meanings which may not easily be expressed in words but which exist in relation to the principal meaning of the object, and to each other, most frequently in reciprocal tension. Adrian Piotrovsky referred to this phenomenon as an *objectified metaphor,* where "metaphor" stands for the system of meanings carried by a physical object, and, therefore, objectified. This tension plays into the theatrical system as an extra source of dramatic energy.

As argued above, the specific logic of theater action constituted the basis of Meyerhold's conception of theatricality. This playful, *non-veristic* logic might solely be expressed through rhythm and the pristine physical movements of the actor's body, accompanied by light, color, and sound. As it is by no means the logic of life-like sequences, this new logic calls for the paradoxical and unexpected. But the unfamiliar works on stage only when juxtaposed with the familiar, that is, when the director takes into consideration the audience's common expectations.

From this double-layered structure, in which the unfamiliar paradoxically estranges the familiar, Meyerhold's idea of the grotesque emerged. In effect the director held a special prism up to the eyes of his spectators; this prism contorts shapes and angles, mixes up polarities creating unexpected contradictions, and doesn't distinguish between low and high orders. The sacred and the profane, the beautiful and the ugly, the material and the spiritual—all categories are exploded. Quite early in his career, Meyerhold established the grotesque as a major component of his directorial method. Already in 1912, in the article *Balagan* (*The Fairground Booth*), where he formulated an aesthetic platform for his early period of traditionalism, Meyerhold defined the grotesque as "something familiarly alien," "demonic in its deepest irony," seeking its realization in "mysterious hints, substitutions and metamorphoses." No doubt, this understanding of the grotesque is a modernized version of romantic irony seen in the works of Ludwig Tieck and E. T. A. Hoffman, which should be of no surprise to anyone who remembers that the symbolist movement in Russia, in which Meyerhold participated in his early days, adopted and rejuvenated many romantic concepts. On the other hand, Meyerhold's perspective on the grotesque is also predictive of contemporary aesthetics:

> Grotesque does not know the low and the high . . . it mixes opposites, consciously creating sharp contradictions and playing with its own peculiarity. . . The most important feature of grotesque is a constant intention of the artist to take spectators out of one plane that they had just comprehended to another, which they did not expect.

That the grotesque synthesizes the opposites seems to be the most advanced aspect of Meyerhold's understanding.

Gradually, Meyerhold became convinced that the grotesque is intrinsic to the nature of theater art, that it is theatricality incarnate. In his brochure, *Amplua aktera* (*The Set Roles of the Actor's Art*), written in 1922 together with V. Bebutov and I. Aksyonov, Meyerhold asserted:

> [T]he theater, which is an unnatural combination of natural, temporal, spatial, and numerical phenomena, as such necessarily contradicts our daily experience and is by its very essence an example of the grotesque. Arising from the grotesquerie of the masquerade, it is unavoidably destroyed by any attempt to remove the grotesque from it and to base it on reality.

Analyzed microscopically, the grotesque provides essentially the same unresolved reciprocal tension of different meanings, whether this tension occurs between live bodies in space and props or between elements of stage design, between speaking voices and sound or light, or among all of them altogether. In fact, *tension through interaction* is a formula for Meyerhold's version of the grotesque, though it does not describe the particular emotional coloring of his vision.

That coloring was dark and lurid. Mixing the satirical and the tragic, Meyerhold's productions frequently abandoned harmony, optimism, and joy in favor of restlessness and anxiety. A "dark genius," as Yuri Elagin named him, Meyerhold generally created his works out of twisted forms and shadows, suggesting the presence of an ineffable menace, treading the invisible line between the material world and some other. Although all of these elements represent the basic philosophical concepts of Russian symbolism, the grotesque was innate in Meyerhold's own temperament as well.

Describing the director's temperament, Kugel observed after his encounter with the young Meyerhold:

> his face is not cheerful. He doesn't have enough complacency to laugh, enough peace of mind to be humorous, enough tranquillity and modesty to rejoice. His face is unquiet and uneasy, as if he is startled by life and its enigma.

Emerging, perhaps, from a sensation that a demonic presence is surely concealed beneath the familiar surfaces of common things and events, this anxiety, along with an eagerness to overcome it, haunted Meyerhold throughout his life.

It is now agreed among most contemporary recent Russian scholars that except for seven out of 36 creative years, Meyerhold's art did not reveal its essentially dark nature. This short seven year period extends through the years of Red Terror and War Communism (roughly, 1918–1922) and ends in 1925 with the staging of *Teacher Bubus.* With *Bubus,* critics contemporary to Meyerhold, started to speak about the return of the artist who had staged *The Fairground Booth* and *Masquerade:*

> The tempo of stage action was slowing, anxiety began to fill the space, and the sense of the downfall of high culture . . . recurred as an inner theme in his productions. . . . [Critics] found the chorus in the tragicomedy *The Warrant* "frightening," and envisioned apocalyptic shadows in *Revizor.* In *Woe to Wit* (1928), the piano music played by the man of culture set him apart from the devouring herd of victors. *Commandarm 2* (1931) seemed to be a requiem to those who perished in the legendary times [times of the Civil War]. *The Introduction* (1933) depicted the collapsing, soulless state and the helplessness of a creative individual within it; it was ostensibly set in Germany, but why then did the despair seem so vivid? *Krechinsky's Wedding* dramatized a prevalent horror . . . *The Lady of Camellias* (1934) took the impossibility of living according to human feelings, or of living in general, to its ultimate, tragic end.

In the end, the grim aspect of the grotesque worked its way back up to the surface of Meyerhold's productions. Ironically, his natural predilection towards such a world view was not dissipated by the reality of the Bolshevik state; rather, it was strongly supported by it. After all, this was a state in which the phenomenon of people disappearing in broad daylight was accepted by the general populace as a matter of course. Described by Mikhail Bulgakov in *Master and Margarita* (although with a lighter and more humorous touch) this reality ceased to be defined in terms of causality and linearity. The logic of common sense helped neither to understand nor to survive it; only the absurd and the eerie grotesque could adequately express it. Life was becoming

merely its own empty shell; invisible forces had reduced human beings to the condition of interchangeable mannequins. Having passed through an explosion of hysterical activity from 1917 to 1920, the country was slipping into the lethargy of horror.

These were the very "riddles" of the time that Meyerhold heard and expressed theatrically in his 1926 *Revizor,* and that Rudnitsky was unable to explore fully in his book. The absurdity of modern existence, together with a universal and inevitable doom, pervaded the dark space of *Revizor* and froze the mask-like faces of its characters. It manifested itself in inexplicable doppelgangers and shadows shuddering in the candlelight. The production narrated a story about the living dead, with their empty eyes and cold, distilled eroticism; passions of the flesh were still alive but the needs of soul were long dead. The image of "swinishness in graceful guise"—ugliness and beauty synthesized—became the visual formula of this production, which absorbed naturalistic trends, symbolic motives, grotesque acting based on biomechanical training, and constructivist conceptions, into a sweeping theatrical whole.

Source: Daria Krizhanskaya, "Meyerhold-Revisor-Revolution," in *Theatre History Studies,* Vol. 20, 2000, pp. 157–70.

Ronald D. LeBlanc

In the following essay, author Ronald LeBlanc explores Gogol's gastronomic motif in The Inspector General *and examines the play's metaphorical use of eating for power and pleasure.*

The subject of gastronomy—as it touches upon the significance of what, how, and why man eats—has begun to receive increasing attention in recent years, during which time quite a number of books on the history of food and drink have appeared. Scholars, moreover, have demonstrated a heightened interest lately in the anthropological aspects of this topic. Since eating is a human activity that by its very nature encompasses a social, a psychological, as well as a biological dimension, the depiction of fictional meals in literature allows this ritualistic event to be transformed into a narrative sign with vast semiotic possibilities—not only within the world of the literary work itself (intratextually) but also within a broader cultural context (extratextually). It is not surprising, therefore, that some literary critics have begun to focus their attention quite scrupulously upon the culinary and gastronomical aspects of prose fiction. These

Danny Kaye as Georgi Hlestakov in a scene from the 1949 film adaptation of The Inspector General, *a variant title for* The Government Inspector.

so-called ''gastrocritics'' have examined the various roles played by food and fictional meals in the works of such diverse authors as François Rabelais, Jean-Baptiste Molière, Alain-René Lesage, Jean-Jacques Rousseau, Marquis de Sade, Jacques-Henri Bernardin de Saint-Pierre, Gustave Flaubert, Anton Chekhov, and Lev Tolstoi.

It is perhaps only natural and appropriate that these studies should gravitate toward French literature, since the French have traditionally regarded Paris as the culinary capital of the universe and considered themselves to be inherently fine judges of good taste. Well beyond the borders of France, however, there lived in the nineteenth century a writer from the Ukraine whose obsession with food—both in his own personal life and in his verbal art—is nearly without historical parallel. That writer is, of course, Nikolai Gogol' (1809–1852), perhaps the most famous gourmet and gourmand in all of Russian literature, a man whose preoccupation with the taste of the food he ate and the quantity of the meals he consumed was legendary even in his own day. From his own correspondence as well as from the testimony of acquaintants, we discover that Gogol' was a ''true gastronome,'' who possessed, in addition to a passion for sweets and desserts, a fondness

for Italian macaroni, an item which he insisted on serving up in large, generous portions for his Russian friends. These culinary interests were so serious, in fact, that Sergei Aksakov was led to exclaim that ''if fate had not made Gogol' a great poet, then he would most certainly have become an artist-chef.'' Indeed, the correspondence of Gogol' is replete with lengthy enumerations of his dining experiences in Europe, especially in Rome, where he first discovered the joys of pasta. Gogol' wrote at great length in his letters not only about the culinary aspects of eating, however, but also about the alimentary aspects as well, giving detailed descriptions of the various digestive ailments that plagued him throughout his later life, especially the hemorrhoidal condition that (so he claimed) eventually affected even his stomach. In fact, Gogol' began to complain so frequently about his stomach, the organ which he once referred to as the ''most noble'' in the human body, that his friends complained that they themselves were ''living in his stomach.'' There is indeed a cruel irony implicit in the fact that this notorious gourmand quite possibly died from inflammation of the stomach and intestines due to inanition (*gastroenteritis ex inanitione*). ''In the months preceding his death,'' explains Vladimir Nabokov, ''he had starved himself so thoroughly that he had destroyed the prodigious capacity his stomach had once been blessed with.''

The widespread presence of food and drink in the prose of Gogol' was surely a result, at least in part, of the author's own personal gastronomical obsessions and was noted with obvious disapproval by contemporary critics. They repeatedly complained of the ''Flemish'' quality that such scenes of eating and drinking imparted to the works of Gogol' and several other prose writers from the Ukraine. If nineteenth century Russian critics were apt to assail this use of food and drink in prose fiction as a rather crude and improper violation of artistic decorum, modern critics have preferred to examine the many interesting uses to which an inventive writer, such as Gogol', put gastronomy in his works—whether it be as a way to create a bucolic image of his native Ukraine, to provide local color, to reflect social and religious customs, to reveal the personality of characters, or simply to provide comic effect. Indeed, an entire book has been written on the subject of food and drink in Gogol's works, Alexander Obolensky's *Food-Notes on Gogol* (1972), and Natalia Kolb-Seletski has contributed an article on ''Gastronomy, Gogol, and His Fiction.'' Both these critics roam so broadly across the wide range of the writer's oeuvre in their examination of his use of gastronomical motifs, however, that neither explores at any great depth the semiotics of food and eating within individual works by Gogol'.

It is my intention in this article to restrict my inquiry to *The Inspector General* (1836), a text I have chosen primarily because the gastronomical motifs within it are so prominent. Jan Kott, in a brilliant review of the play, observed that ''in no other of the great comedies is there so much talk about eating.'' My aim is to focus specifically on how the act of eating in this play progresses from a somewhat narrowly ''mimetic'' to a more broadly ''symbolic'' function once the actual physical hunger of the play's main character is satisfied. From the moment Khlestakov is fed, eating begins to operate according to one of the two different semiotic codes that Ronald Tobin, in an illuminating study of Moliére's *L'Ecole des femmes,* has delineated as an opposition between *manger,* or eating as power and violence, and *goûter,* or eating as pleasure. The Mayor, who has mistaken Khlestakov for a powerful inspector general, simply projects the wrong semiotic code (*manger*) upon him and thus ''feeds'' the hero out of a fear of being ''eaten'' himself. The Mayor, in other words, subscribes to Norman Brown's dictum that to live, psychoanalytically

considered, is ''to eat or be eaten.'' The hedonistic Khlestakov, on the other hand, subscribes to the semiotic code of *goûter,* for he indulges an appetite for food—just as he indulges a commensurate ''taste'' for women, cigars, boasting, and even writing—mostly for the pleasure it brings him. ''Khlestakov's philosophy,'' as Vasilii Gippius bluntly puts it, ''is that of vulgar epicureanism.'' In *The Inspector General,* as we shall see, the act of eating ultimately becomes identified with the act of writing, since both activities come to reflect the two main semiotic codes operative within the play. The fear that literature (as *lecture*) inspires in the Mayor at play's end and the pleasure that Khlestakov derives from literature (as *écriture*) mirror the gastronomical opposition between *manger* and *goûter* that underlies the structure of this text.

We can find various purposes for the plethora of gastronomical motifs in the play. At the rudimentary level of story line, food and eating fulfill what we might call a ''structural'' role in *The Inspector General,* generating the initial occurrences of mistaken identity in acts 1 and 2 and thus advancing what meager plot there is in the play. Critics, such as Kott and Obolensky, have already documented quite thoroughly this basic structural role of food and eating in *The Inspector General,* but it might prove helpful to review it briefly here. It begins in act 1 when Bobchinskii, who wishes to tell Dobchinskii the news that an inspector general is expected in town at any time, meets his friend ''near the stall where hot cakes are sold.'' Dobchinskii, however, has already heard this disturbing piece of news from Avdotiia, the Mayor's housekeeper, when she was fetching ''a small keg of brandy'' from Pochechuev. Bobchinskii and Dobchinskii set off together for Pochechuev's house, but en route Dobchinskii's stomach starts to make a ruckus. ''I have not eaten a thing since morning,'' he complains, ''and my stomach is grumbling like an earthquake.'' They decide to stop at the hotel restaurant since Dobchinskii has heard that a shipment of fresh salmon has just recently been delivered there. It is at this same hotel, while they are in the midst of eating the fresh salmon, that Bobchinskii and Dobchinskii first see Khlestakov, mistaking him for an inspector general because, among other things, he runs up a large restaurant bill at the hotel (which he does not pay) and he looks so observantly at their food—staring right into their plates of salmon as they sit there dining. Only an inspector general, they assume, would inspect the local food so carefully, a sentiment echoed a short while later by another townsperson, the director of charities, who voices concern that the bad smell given off by the food at his hospital might ruin an inspection. "Throughout all the corridors," he tells the Mayor, "the smell of cabbage is so bad that you have to hold your nose."

The causal connection between food and the mistaken identity foisted upon Khlestakov by the townspeople continues in act 2, scene 8, where we witness the hilarious initial confrontation between the hero and the Mayor. Khlestakov, who assumes that the Mayor has come to arrest him for his failure to pay the restaurant bill he has run up, blames the innkeeper for serving him such terrible food and for trying to starve him to death by refusing him service: "The beef he gave me is as tough as a log, and the soup—God knows what he threw in there, I should have thrown it out the window. He tried to starve me to death for days on end. . . . The tea tastes strange: It smells like fish rather than tea." The Mayor, who fears that Khlestakov is indeed the inspector general, finds his worst suspicions confirmed by these words. Who else but an inspector general, after all, would complain so vociferously about the food and the service at the local hotel restaurant? The scene closes with the Mayor, who is now thoroughly convinced that this mysterious visitor is indeed the inspector general, setting off together with Khlestakov for dinner at the hospital. There they will consume a delicious meal of fish (*labardan*) and wine, a repast that will not only satisfy Khlestakov's hunger but also loosen his tongue and whet his appetite for other pleasures. Just before leaving for the hospital, however, the Mayor, who wishes to warn his wife beforehand that the inspector general will soon be coming to visit their home, hastily scribbles off a note to her on the only available piece of paper: Khlestakov's unpaid restaurant tab. The resulting letter-bill is a bizarre document which has often been cited as proof of the absurdist and alogical features at work in the play. "I hasten to inform you, my dear," the Mayor's letter reads, "that my situation was highly lamentable, but, trusting on God's mercy, for two pickles and half a portion of caviar a ruble and twenty-five kopecks." This letter-bill with its mélange of fear and power as well as food and money, Kott argues, exposes the latent structure of the play. "In this pretended incongruity there is a whole topography and sociology of this country town," he writes. "There are almost hidden links and connections between the mercy of God, fear and power, between pickles in a restaurant and *labardan* in a hospital, between wine on the Mayor's

table and in a merchant's cellar." This mimetic role of gastronomy in *The Inspector General,* where it serves as an indicator of social status, psychological reality, and personal well-being, is perhaps best demonstrated in the case of the town's two mysterious visitors, Khlestakov and Osip.

Food begins to fulfill this more strictly mimetic function in act 2 of the play, where Gogol' uses it to characterize not only the social status but also the personality of both the master (Khlestakov) and his servant (Osip). In the opening scene of this act, we listen to a long monologue by Osip, who delivers a poor man's soliloquy that both begins and ends with an impassioned, lyrical entreaty for food. He begins the monologue exclaiming, "The devil take it, how I'd like to eat! My stomach is grumbling as if an entire regiment were sounding its trumpets" and concludes it by saying, "Oh if only I could have some cabbage soup! I could eat the entire world." The audience thus learns right away that the desire for food, as far as Osip is concerned, is almost strictly a matter of survival. As had been the case with Lazarillo, Guzmán, Pablos, and other heroes from the Spanish picaresque tradition (as well as with the servants in the stage comedies of Lesage, Moliére, and Pierre-Augustin Caron Beaumarchais), hunger here signals the bitter deprivation such a character as Osip must endure as a result of his lowly social position. Like the traditional Spanish picaro, whose fate it is, as a servant of many masters, to suffer a number of sudden and severe reversals in life, Osip complains here of the numerous vicissitudes of his job: "One day you eat swell but the next you all but pass away from hunger— like now, for instance." Osip's precarious position in life, as emblematized by his hunger, recalls the plight of Lazarillo who—whether he is tricking the blind man for a morsel of sausage and a sip of wine or pilfering crusts of bread at night from the coffers of the stingy priest from Maqueda—is likewise engaged in a constant struggle for physical survival, a battle that forces him continually to fend off starvation. Indeed, Osip's complaints about his impecunious master's compulsion to show off (ordering the best rooms and the finest meals even though he is flat broke) bring to mind Lazarillo's service under the impoverished but honorable squire from Castille, who was likewise greatly obsessed with maintaining appearances at all costs. In any event, the starving Osip exists, like Lazarillo, at a level that gastrocritics would call the *degré zéro alimentaire:* Both these characters clearly eat to live, rather than live to eat.

Osip's master, as we learn from his monologues in scenes 3 and 5 of act 2, exists at the same *degré zéro alimentaire* as does his servant. Like the traditional picaro, he too is starving because of the vicissitudes of fate. Khlestakov's impoverishment has been brought about largely through his own fault, however; it is losses at cards that have reduced him to his present situation. We discover later, in the letter Khlestakov writes to his friend Triapichkin, that this is by no means the first time that the hero has found himself in a situation where he is unable to pay for food as a basic subsistence item. "Remember how, when you and I were broke, we used to sponge our dinners?" Khlestakov writes. "Remember how once a baker was going to toss me out on my ear on account of the pies I'd eaten and charged to the King of England?" What distinguishes Khlestakov's hunger from Osip's, however, is that the master, unlike his servant, would rather starve to death than pawn the Petersburg clothing he values so dearly. His dandified appearance, in other words, seems more important to Khlestakov than life itself. The waiter is finally convinced to bring Khlestakov a meager serving of rather bland soup and meat in scene 6, a humorous scene that provides the audience with a telling revelation of the hero's true personality. Although Khlestakov at first absolutely refuses to accept this modest fare and complains throughout the scene about its quality, he nonetheless proceeds to devour greedily the unappetizing food offered him:

> What kind of soup do you call this? You've simply poured water into a cup: It has no taste at all; it simply reeks. I don't want this soup, bring me another.... My God, what soup! I don't think anyone on earth has ever had to eat such soup. Feathers of some sort are floating around in it instead of fat. Ay, ay, ay. What chicken! Give me the meat! ... What kind of meat is this? This isn't meat.... The devil only knows what it is, but it isn't meat. It's an ax that's been cooked rather than meat.

Khlestakov, whose particular "fervor" is to maintain appearances at all costs, thus feels compelled to criticize this meal as unsuitable for a person of his station, yet he nevertheless eats it.

When the waiter, in reply to the hero's complaints about the food, tells him that this is all that is available, Khlestakov objects strenuously, pointing out that he himself saw two men eating some delicious salmon at the hotel restaurant earlier that day. The waiter explains that decent food—such as salmon, fish, and cutlets—is available only to decent people, to those who are a bit "more respectable" (*pochishche,* literally, "cleaner"); such food,

he adds, is reserved for those who "pay cash." This scene reveals not only the character of Khlestakov, but also the sociology of the world in which he lives. In this society those who are well off are fed salmon, while those who are not well off either do not eat at all or else are reduced to eating watered-down soup and meat that is as hard as wood. It could thus be argued that Gogol' uses gastronomy here in a highly mimetic way, endeavoring to illustrate the socioeconomic disparities existent within contemporary Russian society. This was a traditional way to use food motifs during this period. As James Brown has amply demonstrated in his study of fictional meals in French novels of the late eighteenth and early nineteenth centuries, contemporary writers such as Honoré de Balzac, George Sand, Eugène Sue, and Victor Hugo repeatedly exploited the metonymic possibilities of gastronomy in their fiction. By identifying hunger with poverty and culinary extravagance with wealth, these authors used food and eating as a way to criticize the social and economic inequities of contemporary bourgeois life. What makes the scene between Khlestakov and the waiter so distinctively Gogolian, however, is both the comedy involved in the starving hero's protests about the quality of the food and the irony inherent in the fact that those two supposedly decent respectable members of society (who are allowed to eat salmon while Khlestakov is not) are none other than the buffoons Bobchinskii and Dobchinskii.

The sociology of food in *The Inspector General* is likewise reflected in the fact that while Khlestakov, the master, is led off to a sumptuous banquet at the hospital, his poor servant Osip is left behind to fend for himself. Moreover, when Osip is offered pies, cabbage soup, and oatmeal at the Mayor's house in act 3, he does not turn up his nose and shun such "simple fare" as his master had done earlier at the hotel; instead, he accepts it immediately and gratefully. "Give them here!" he shouts without a moment's hesitation when Mishka, somewhat embarrassed, tells him that such unappetizing items are all that is available at the Mayor's house. Throughout the play, therefore, hunger remains for Osip a very basic physiological appetite that must be satisfied. For his master, however, such is not the case. Once Khlestakov's primitive hunger for food has been satisfied by the feast prepared in his honor at the hospital, a new, more voracious, and more insatiable appetite suddenly begins to manifest itself; a desire for other "pleasures" now begins to make itself felt. With the appearance of this desire for pleasures in Khlestakov, the act of eating in *The*

Inspector General likewise shifts from a mimetic function, as an indicator of social and psychological reality, to a broader, more symbolic role as a paradigm of human desire. As Khlestakov moves from what Roland Barthes calls the "realm of necessity" (*l'ordre de besoin*) to the "realm of desire" (*l'ordre de désir*), a corresponding shift occurs within his psyche; *l'appétit naturel,* in Barthes's terms, is here superseded by *l'appétit de luxe.* Khlestakov, in other words, moves out of the domain of survival, where food indicates deprivation, into the domain of pleasure, where food indicates indulgence. His behavior, accordingly, now begins to follow the semiotic code of *goûter,* where eating signifies a pleasure that one must "taste."

Upon his return to the stage early in act 3, following his brief absence to attend the banquet held in his honor at the hospital, Khlestakov signals very clearly to the audience that his physical hunger has indeed been satisfied. "The meal was very good," he announces. "I have truly eaten my fill." At the same time, however, he signals that an accompanying shift has taken place within him, a shift from the realm of necessity to the realm of pleasure. "I love to eat a good meal," he says. "After all, that is why one lives—to pluck the petals of pleasure. What was the name of that fish we had?." From this point on, Khlestakov begins to manifest a behavior animated almost entirely by the pleasure-seeking principle. Among the many pleasures—all of them decidedly "oral"—which the hero now begins to indulge in *The Inspector General,* none is more memorable than his outrageous boasting. Notice, however, how Khlestakov's bragging, in that celebrated scene (act 3, scene 6) where he tries to impress the two women present—Anna Andreevna and Mariia Antonovna—with outrageous lies about his life in St. Petersburg, both begins and ends with references to food and meals:

> Oh, Petersburg! What a life it is there! You probably think that I am a mere copying clerk. Not at all, I am on friendly footing with the section head. He'll come up and slap me on the shoulder and say, "Come on, old chap, let's go have dinner together."

> Excuse me, I'm ready to take a little nap. That lunch we had, gentlemen, was excellent . . . I am satisfied, I am satisfied . . . Labardan! labardan!

It is safe to assume that Khlestakov's "satisfaction" here derives at least as much from his recent bout of boasting as from his earlier feast at the hospital, both of which have to do, of course, with his mouth. Some of the boasting itself, moreover, directly concerns gastronomical matters. Describing the lavish parties he claims to have hosted in St.

> "'I LOVE TO EAT A GOOD
> MEAL,' HE SAYS. 'AFTER ALL, THAT IS
> WHY ONE LIVES—TO PLUCK THE
> PETALS OF PLEASURE.'"

Petersburg, for instance, Khlestakov asserts that "on the table they serve watermelon—each one costing 700 rubles. Soup is brought in tureens by steamer straight from Paris: They open the lid and steam escapes, steam such as you could never find in nature." In boasting about his life in the capital, Khlestakov thus attempts to create an image of St. Petersburg as a gastronomical paradise of pleasure.

It seems clear enough to what end Khlestakov does all of this boasting: He wishes to impress the local provincials around him, especially the two women present. Like his own creator, Khlestakov seems to be an obsessive liar, who wishes to win the approval and adulation of others. "Both Gogol and Khlestakov," Henry Popkin observes, "lie instinctively, imaginatively, elaborately, and often unnecessarily." What is not so clear, however, is why Khlestakov insists on lying so brazenly and, as Popkin put it, so "unnecessarily." After all, Khlestakov's lying, as Vasilii Gippius has pointed out, does not serve here as the "extrication" device that we find so often in traditional Russian comedies, such as those written by Ivan Krylov, Aleksandr Shakhovskoi, and Gregorii Kvitka-Osnov'ianenko. Khlestakov does not need to lie in order to extricate himself from an unfortunate situation, since the contradictions in his outlandish statements, Gippius notes, "do not disconcert any of the other characters and are obvious only to the audience." Why then does Khlestakov persist in telling such bold-faced lies? Quite simply, he seems to derive enormous pleasure from telling lies. Like the wine at the feast at the hospital, the lies he tells at the Mayor's house seem to make Khlestakov literally "drunk" with pleasure. Iurii Lotman has suggested that Khlestakov tells lies because of a deep-seated feeling of self-contempt; the act of lying makes him so drunk that he ceases to be himself (that is, an insignificant copying clerk of whom he is ashamed). When Khlestakov mocks the copying clerk, Lotman argues, he is inviting others to laugh at the "real" Khlestakov.

Khlestakov, however, may well be attracted to lying not so much by a desire to escape *from* himself, as by an urge to escape *to* something outside of himself: that is, to flee from his loneliness and solitude to the pleasure provided by the company of other people. Khlestakov, in short, may simply be an extremely lonely individual who is merely seeking the warmth provided by human companionship. After all, he has been essentially holed up in his hotel room for the past two weeks, unable to leave town because of his dire financial situation. Suddenly, a fortuitous case of mistaken identity makes him an instant celebrity, surrounded by an entourage of extremely friendly, attentive, and solicitous people. "I love hospitality, and I must admit that I prefer it when people treat me well out of the kindness of their hearts, and not out of self-interest," Khlestakov says early in act 4. "I love pleasant company a lot. . . . I love such people." In addition to gaining him the attention of others, lying provides Khlestakov with many of the same psychological benefits that eating does, since both activities induce a condition that Brown refers to as the "serenity" syndrome: They bring about a state of relaxation and amicability. In psychological terms, Brown explains, "appetite" signals social dislocation, while "eating" signals social rapprochement. In the play a hungry, starving Khlestakov must initially suffer his physical privations and psychological alienation by himself, in solitude and in silence. As the play progresses, however, Khlestakov is able to engage in direct and intimate forms of communication with others through eating and speaking, two essentially oral pleasures. Language and gastronomy are closely related fields, in the sense that the two activities most closely associated with them—eating and speaking—allow man to establish close contact with the world outside himself. "Eating and speaking share the same motivational structure," Brown argues, "language is nothing more than the praxis of eating transformed to the semiosis of speaking: both are fundamentally communicative acts by which man appropriates and incorporates the world." In this respect Khlestakov may be said to be attempting to eat and talk his way into the hearts of those around him, seeking to overcome in the process the existential space that separates his self from the rest of the world. In *The Inspector General* the act of eating, like the act of speaking, may truly be said to constitute the "archetype of intercourse."

Another form of intercourse to which Khlestakov seems drawn, at least ostensibly, is sexual. Eating arouses in him not only the desire to speak—to lie, to boast—but also the desire for sex. His taste for food, he seems to imply, is matched only by his taste for women. Food and sex have, of course, traditionally been located close to each other, both in western culture and in European literature. Indeed, the gastronomical and the sexual are appetites that, contemporary anthropologists assert, are closely associated biologically as well as socially. From a psychoanalytical point of view as well, the table and the bed are never very far apart, since in dreams, as Freud has noted, "a table is very often found to represent a bed." With Gogol', however, characters are seldom allowed to satisfy both their gastronomical and sexual appetites; instead they are usually presented with a choice—*either* a meal *or* a woman. In psychoanalytical terms, such a choice reflects an opposition between "genital" and "oral" modes of libidinal satisfaction. The characters, as one might guess, are invariably encouraged to opt for oral satisfaction; indeed, attempts to derive sexual satisfaction in this fictional world are usually rewarded only with pain and death. Like Gogol', these characters are forced to regress to pregenital (oral) libidinal outlets and thus to embark upon what Hugh McLean has characterized as a "retreat from love."

In *The Inspector General,* Khlestakov first associates gastronomical with sexual pleasures in act 4, scene 2. While commenting on the magnificent feast he enjoyed at the hospital, the hero suddenly switches the topic of his monologue to women, noting to himself that "the Mayor's daughter is not bad." Later in the same act, when he suddenly shifts his romantic attentions from the Mayor's daughter to his wife, Khlestakov refers to her in terms that make the "woman-as-food" motif quite clear. "She is also very nice," he observes, "quite appetizing [*appetichna*]." Similarly, gastronomical and sexual motifs are linked together in Khlestakov's letter to Triapichkin, a letter that, as Kolb-Seletski correctly observes, jumps from mention of the hero's two present paramours to the earlier incident with the baker and his pies in St. Petersburg. In light of the pattern of retreat from love and sex that we discern in the fiction of Gogol'—the regression from genital to anal and oral modes of libidinal satisfaction exhibited by his characters—it comes as no surprise that Khlestakov not only jumps from mention of food to mention of sex (and vice versa), but also digresses easily from talk of women and food to talk of the pleasures provided by a good cigar. This classic Gogolian progression—from food to women to cigars—is illustrated quite nicely by the development of Khlestakov's appetites in *The Inspector General:* First he eats at the hospital (act 2), then he tries to impress the women at the Mayor's house (act 3), and finally he lights up a cigar (act 4). In fine Gogolian fashion, however, this progression from food to women to cigars is no sooner completed, then it is immediately reversed. Once Khlestakov begins to sing the praises of cigars in act 4, he reverts back right away to the pleasures of women and food:

> I see that you are not a cigar fancier. I must admit that cigars are my weakness. I cannot be indifferent to the female sex either.
>
> How about you? Which do you prefer—blonde or brunette? . . . I would really like to know what your taste is.
>
> You fed me well at lunch. I admit that it is my weakness—I love good cuisine.

Of course, Khlestakov cannot talk about cigars or food or women without exaggerating, so he must interject here that, although the cigar he has been given is indeed a "decent" one (*poriadochnaia*), it is not anywhere near as pleasurable as the 25-ruble cigars he is accustomed to smoking in St. Petersburg.

To the list of pleasures that Khlestakov enjoys in *The Inspector General*—eating, boasting, women, cigars—there must be added one final item: literature. To the hedonistic hero of the play, such oral pleasures merely whet his appetite for the aesthetic satisfactions that come from the consumption of literature. Food and eating have often been used in western literature as metaphors for art, especially for reading and writing. Gogol' himself, in his correspondence as well as in one of his essays, links gastronomy with aesthetics by using alimentary metaphors to describe literature. It is not surprising, therefore, to find in his play that the act of eating—both as *manger* and as *goûter*—becomes paradigmatic of the act of writing literature. Khlestakov's own statements about what he "loves" signal to the audience throughout the play that for the hero food and literature serve as paradigms of human desires:

> I love to eat.
> I love to philosophize through prose or verse.
> I love good cuisine.
> I love to read something entertaining.

Moreover, when Khlestakov engages in his outrageous boasting in act 3, scene 6, he brags not only about the food served at his mythical parties, but also about his literary talents and connections. In much the same way that he had earlier boasted of his close personal relationship with his superior at work, Khlestakov brags that he is on a "friendly footing" (*na druzheskoi noge*) with Russia's greatest writer of the time—if not of all time—Aleksandr Pushkin. He proceeds to claim authorship of such foreign works as *Le Marriage de Figaro, Robert-Diable,* and *Norma,* as well as the works of such popular writers in contemporary Russia as Mikhail Zagoskin, Aleksandr Bestuzhev-Marlinskii, Nikolai Polevoi, Osip Senkovskii, and even the notorious Faddei Bulgarin. Carried away by his own literary braggadocio, Khlestakov goes so far as to assert that he exists, not by means of food, but by means of literature (4:49). Indeed, in the letter read to the townspeople assembled at the Mayor's house in the play's climactic finale, Khlestakov writes that he desires to become a writer since he hungers so for "spiritual" food. "Following your example," he writes to Triapichkin, "I myself would like to take up literature. It is boring, old man, to live this way; one wants at last some food for the soul [*pishcha dlia dushi*]. As I see it, exactly what I need is to take up something elevated." The connection between literature and gastronomy in *The Inspector General* is made clear not only through Khlestakov's words, but also through his gestures. By means of the stage directions provided for the hero in acts 2 and 4, the playwright further encourages the audience to make this connection between eating and writing. In act 2, scene 6, when Khlestakov reluctantly accepts the unappetizing meal brought him by the waiter at his hotel room, the stage direction "he eats" (*est*) is repeated several times, just as later, in act 4, scene 9, when the hero is composing his letter to Triapichkin, the stage direction "he writes" (*pishet*) is likewise several times repeated.

It is literature, curiously enough, that will ultimately bridge the gap of misunderstanding that separates Khlestakov from the Mayor in this play. For Khlestakov, who wishes he had the soul of a writer, literature, like food, serves as a source of pleasure (*goûter*). For the Mayor, on the other hand, both eating and literature signal instead the threat of power and violence (*manger*). If we were to invoke Horace's classic dictum for literature—that it brings pleasure as well as profit (*dulce et utile*)—then we could say that Khlestakov enjoys literature's capacity to entertain, while the Mayor fears its ability to instruct. It is, after all, fear of the potential for violence and aggression that could possibly be unleashed by an inspector general that leads the Mayor and his fellow townspeople to project an identity of power onto the hapless Khlestakov in the first place. They then seek to appease this imagined hunger by "feeding" him whatever pleasures he might like and thus avoiding the terrible *agression gastronomique* they anticipate with so much dread and apprehension. Throughout most of the play, therefore, the Mayor is concerned to fend off being "devoured" by the inspector general; he does so by attempting to appease what he perceives to be that official's formidable appetite for dominance. He tries to "bribe" both Khlestakov and his servant, offering them not only money, but also, significantly enough, food. Thus, the banquet that is arranged at the hospital as well as the wine ordered for the Mayor's table are both obvious attempts to placate the imagined inspector general by satisfying his "appetite." Likewise, the Mayor gives Osip money at first as a tip (*na chai,* literally, "for tea") and then later for sustenance on the road (*na baranki,* "for a bun"). Osip, who realizes very quickly that an instance of mistaken identity has occurred, cleverly exploits the Mayor's fear of being "eaten" to his own self-advantage. "My master is most pleased when other people feed me well," he informs the Mayor in act 3, scene 10. Osip further exploits this feeling of fear (which is harbored by the Mayor and townspeople) during the scene in act 4 when a crowd of angry merchants approaches Khlestakov in hopes that he will listen to their complaints about the Mayor. Khlestakov, who has come to realize at last that he has been mistaken for a person of consequence, refuses at first their offering of bread and salt—the ceremonial food items symbolic of hospitality in Russian culture—mistaking them as attempts to bribe him. "I do not accept any bribes," he tells them, "but if you were, for example, to loan me about three hundred rubles—well, then it would be a different matter entirely. I can accept loans." The clever and pragmatic Osip, on the other hand, does not hesitate for a moment to accept these culinary tokens of hospitality. "Your excellency! Why don't you accept them?" he asks Khlestakov. "Take them! On the road everything turns out handy. Hand over those loaves and baskets! Hand it all over! It will all come in handy. What's that over there? A bit of rope? Hand that over as well—the rope might come in handy on the road too." The most obvious attempts to bribe Khlestakov occurred earlier in act 4 when the local officials paraded up to this imagined inspector general, one after another, clumsily and nervously offering him various sums of money. Curiously enough, the verb used to describe these bribe attempts (*podsunut',* "to slip") is the same one Khlestakov uses to characterize the food and drink served him the day before at breakfast: "yesterday they slipped [*podsunuli*] me something at breakfast." In any event, it is clear that the

bribes, like the food, are attempts to satisfy the prodigious appetite for power and dominance of the inspector general—attempts to "feed" this monster before he devours the Mayor and his fellow town officials.

Once the Mayor is convinced that the inspector general's appetite has finally been satisfied, however, he then begins to exhibit quite openly his own carnivorism: that is, once he feels that Khlestakov has been sufficiently fed and bribed, the Mayor reveals his own propensity for violence and aggression toward others less powerful than himself. At the end of act 4, the newly engaged Khlestakov drives away (supposedly to visit his uncle), promising to return later to marry the Mayor's daughter. In act 5, therefore, the Mayor need no longer worry about satisfying the prodigious appetite of the inspector general. Instead, he can now indulge his own appetite for power and dominance over his subordinates, an appetite that manifests itself, once again, in gastronomical terms. When he threatens violent retribution upon those merchants who complained about him to Khlestakov, the Mayor claims that he will "feed" them sufficiently: "Before I fed you only up to your mustaches, but now I'll feed you [*nakormliu*] up to your beards." Indeed, he even refers to these merchants in gastronomical terms, calling them "fat-bellies" (*tolstobriukhi*): that is, tax farmers who have become rich ("fat") by controlling state monopolies on liquor. In threatening to settle scores with his constituents, the Mayor thus resorts to the same *agression gastronomique* that he had feared so much from the inspector general. Yet when he switches his thoughts from how he will reprimand those beneath him to how he will enjoy his newly acquired prestige and power in St. Petersburg (as father-in-law to a high-ranking inspector general), the Mayor dreams of glory, just as Khlestakov had earlier, largely in gastronomical terms. "To dream about power," Kott observes with regard to this play, "is to dream about food." Indeed, the Mayor's fantasies about what life will be like as a general in the capital seem to duplicate the picture of St. Petersburg as a gastronomical paradise that Khlestakov had helped to paint earlier when boasting about his life there in act 3. "Yes, they say that there are two kinds of fish there," the Mayor muses, "eels and smelts, both of which are so succulent that your mouth waters as soon as you begin to eat."

In the denouement of the play, when the postmaster and others read aloud Khlestakov's satiric letter to Triapichkin, the Mayor reverts back to his earlier fear of being "eaten" and "devoured." His fear, however, now expresses itself in literary rather than gastronomical terms; he is mostly afraid that such a writer as Triapichkin will hold him up to public ridicule:

> He will spread my story across the whole world. What is even worse than having fallen into ridicule is the fact that some scribbler, some hack will put me into a comedy. That's what is so insulting! . . . I'd fix all of these hacks! Oo! the scribblers, the damned liberals! devil's seed!

What frightens the Mayor most about literature is the way that its practitioners—the so-called "hacks" and "scribblers"—can devour him, a local government servant, by holding him up to public ridicule. Conversely, what attracts Khlestakov to the literary calling and makes him envy his journalist friend Triapichkin is the amusement and pleasure he can derive from ridiculing others. "I can just picture how Triapichkin will die laughing," Khlestakov notes while writing to his friend the letter in which he satirizes the various inhabitants of this provincial town. The desire for "spiritual food" which Khlestakov reveals in this letter—the desire to occupy oneself with something more elevated—has arisen in Khlestakov, however, just as have his other desires, only after his hunger for physical food has been satisfied. Thus, while Khlestakov, in act 2, scene 8, complains about the food he has been served at the hotel restaurant, he adds that the poor lighting in his room prevents him from reading a bit at night after dinner and from "composing something" when the inspiration strikes him.

Eating and writing are pleasures linked together not only for the hedonistic hero of *The Inspector General,* but also for his creator. Gogol', for his part, has been characterized as a "verbal glutton"—as a writer whose voracious appetite for words manifests itself in a highly exuberant prose style. Indeed, Gogol' himself employs gastronomy as a metaphor for literature when he writes to a friend for a critique of *Dead Souls,* phrasing his request in the following manner:

> Imagine that I am an innkeeper in some European hotel and I have a table for everyone or a *table d' hôte.* There are twenty dishes on my table and perhaps more. Naturally, not all these dishes are identically good or, at least, it goes without saying that everyone will choose for himself and eat only the dishes he likes. . . . So I am only asking you to say this: "This is what is more to my taste in your work, these places here."

During the last ten years of his life, when he was being pressed by his acquaintances about the status of the eagerly awaited part 2 of *Dead Souls,* Gogol' made use of the metaphor of "author-as-chef" several times, complaining in one instance that his masterpiece was not like *bliny,* "which can be prepared in an instant."

The ultimate irony, of course, is that whereas Khlestakov, the fictional alter ego of Gogol', capitalizes upon his situation in *The Inspector General* to his own gastronomical and literary advantage, his creator eventually fell under the deleterious influence of Father Matvei Konstantinovskii, who nurtured a growing religious fanaticism in Gogol', one that led him ultimately to forsake entirely both eating and writing. Gogol' would be encouraged by him not only to practice extreme abstinence, but also to renounce his literary mentor, the sinful, paganistic Pushkin. In his later years, Russia's most famous comic writer would produce only the preachy, moralizing, and distinctly unartistic *Selected Passages from Correspondence with Friends* (1847) and would eventually burn the troublesome second part of his greatest literary masterpiece, the epic poem *Dead Souls.* This enigmatic gourmand and gourmet, who once referred to meals as "sacrifices," restaurants as "cathedrals," and restaurateurs as "pagan priests," would also come more and more to fast rather than feast and to associate gourmandizing with sin. He would finally be driven to starve himself to death at the relatively tender age of forty-two, apparently in a case of what Rudolph Bell might now call "holy" anorexia. In this respect, the life of Gogol' may have unwittingly imitated his art, for the author of *The Inspector General* not only came to lose all "pleasure" in eating and writing but, as he became progressively devoured by religious fanaticism, he also came to fear with much dread the satanic "power" that could be wielded over him by both food and literature.

Source: Ronald D. LeBlanc, "Satisfying Khlestakov's Appetite: The Semiotics of Eating in the Inspector General," in *Slavic Review,* Vol. 47, No. 2, Fall 1988, pp. 483–498.

SOURCES

Adams, Amy Singleton. *Dictionary of Literary Biography, Volume 198: Russian Literature in the Age of Pushkin and Gogol: Prose,* edited by Cristine A. Rydel, The Gale Group, 1999, pp. 137–166.

Beresford, M., "Introduction," in *The Government Inspector: A Comedy in Five Acts,* by N. V. Gogol, Edwin Mellen Press, 1996, pp. V, 1–94.

Braun, Edward, ''Introduction,'' in *Nikolai Gogol: The Government Inspector,* edited by Edward O. Marsh and Jeremy Brooks, Methuen & Co., 1968, pp. 7–14.

Brown, Nigel, *Notes on Nikolai Gogol's The Government Inspector,* Heinemann, 1974, pp. 2, 4, 30, 36.

Campbell, D. J., ''Forward,'' in *The Government Inspector,* by Nikolai Gogol, Heinemann, 1947, pp. 15–22.

Erlich, Victor, *Gogol,* Yale University Press, 1969, pp. 100–101, 103, 105–109.

Lavrin, Janko, *Gogol,* Routledge, 1926, 13–15, 153–154, 156.

———, ''Introduction,'' in *The Government Inspector,* by Nikolai Gogol, Heinemann, 1947, pp. 8–14.

Lindstrom, Thais S., *Nikolay Gogol,* Twayne, 1974, pp. 1–7, 115–116, 119–121.

Peace, Richard, *The Enigma of Gogol,* Cambridge University Press, 1981, pp. 1, 181.

FURTHER READING

Dostoyevsky, Fyodor, *Notes from the Underground and the Gambler,* Oxford University Press, 1991.
> Originally published in 1864, the novella *Notes from the Underground* is the best-known work by one of Russia's greatest writers.

Erofeyev, Victor and Andrew Reynolds, eds., *The Penguin Book of New Russian Writing,* Penguin Books, 1995.
> This book is a collection of prose fiction by contemporary Russian authors.

Magocsi, Paul Robert, *A History of the Ukraine,* Washington University Press, 1996.
> This book includes a historical overview of the region of Russia in which Gogol grew up.

Maguire, Robert A., *Exploring Gogol,* Stanford University Press, 1994.
> This book includes criticism and interpretation of Gogol's major literary works.

Pushkin, Aleksandr, *Eugene Onegin,* Penguin, 1979.
> Originally published in 1833, this novel, by Gogol's friend and Russia's leading writer of the early nineteenth century, is a masterpiece. It provides a broad-based depiction of Russian life and culture.

The Green Pastures

MARC CONNELLY

1929

The Green Pastures, the Pulitzer Prize-winning play by Marc Connelly, is a reenactment of stories of the Old Testament in which all the characters (including God) are African American and speak in a black southern dialect. The play was first performed at the Mansfield Theatre in New York City in 1930. Connelly attributes his idea for the play to the retelling of Old Testament stories in Roark Bradford's book *Southern Sketches, "Ol' Man Adam an' His Chillun."*

The Green Pastures follows stories of the Bible, such as Adam and Eve, Noah and the flood, Moses and the exodus from Egypt, and the crucifixion of Christ, but places them in a rural black southern setting. Thus, one of the opening scenes takes place at a "fish fry" in "pre-Creation Heaven," during which God spontaneously decides to create Earth and man. God eats boiled pudding, smokes cigars, and runs Heaven out of a shabby "private office" assisted by Gabriel. The settings are roughly contemporary to the time period in which the play was first written and performed, so that, for instance, the city of Babylon is represented as a New Orleans jazz nightclub. The costumes are also contemporary: God wears a white suit and white tie, Adam is dressed in a farmer's clothes, Eve wears the gingham dress of a country girl, and so on. The play ends with God's decision, while back at the fish fry in Heaven, to send Jesus Christ down to Earth.

Connelly's play was unusual at the time of its initial production in that it featured a cast made up exclusively of African-American actors. Connelly's portrayal of African Americans as "simple" people, particularly as created by a white playwright, will likely strike today's reader as stereotyped.

AUTHOR BIOGRAPHY

Marcus Cook Connelly was born on December 13, 1890, in McKeesport, Pennsylvania. His father, Patrick Joseph Connelly, was an actor and hotel owner, while his mother, Mabel Louise (maiden name Cook), was an actress.

From 1902 until 1907, Connelly attended Trinity Hall, a private school in Washington, Pennsylvania. From 1908 until 1915, he was a reporter and drama critic for several Pittsburgh newspapers. He then moved to New York, working as a newspaper journalist and freelance writer from 1916 until 1920.

Connelly became a prominent member of the "Vicious Circle" of the Algonquin Round Table, an informal group of sharp-witted writers, editors, actors, and intellectuals who met regularly at the Algonquin Hotel. In 1925, he was named to the editorial board of *New Yorker* magazine. In 1929, he wrote *The Green Pastures,* his most celebrated work, for which he won a Pulitzer Prize for Drama in 1930. In the same year, *Collier's* magazine published his short story *"Coroner's Inquest,"* which won an O. Henry Award, and on the personal front, Connelly married screen actress Madeline Hurlock. She divorced him in 1935.

From 1933 until 1944, Connelly moved between New York and Hollywood, writing both stage plays and screenplays. He wrote and directed the screen adaptation of *The Green Pastures* in 1936. From 1946 until 1950, he was professor of playwriting at Yale University.

Connelly held several posts in cultural organizations, including United States Commissioner to the United Nations Educational, Scientific, and Cultural Organization (appointed in 1951); and President of the National Institute of Arts and Letters (in 1953). His autobiographical work, *Voices Off-Stage: A Book of Memoirs,* was published in 1968. Connelly died in New York City on December 21, 1980.

PLOT SUMMARY

Part I

In Part I, Scene I of *The Green Pastures,* Reverend Deshee teaches Sunday school to a group of children in a Louisiana town. He explains the first five chapters of Genesis, after which the children ask him questions.

Scene II takes place at a fish fry in pre-Creation Heaven. The fish fry is attended by angels of all ages. An Archangel arrives and hands out diplomas to all of the children. Then Gabriel arrives, followed by God. After tasting the boiled custard, God decides that the recipe needs more "firmament" to taste right. To produce more firmament for the custard, God performs a miracle. There is so much firmament, however, that it starts to rain down on the fish fry. God creates Earth to drain off the excess firmament. God then creates man to farm the earth.

Scene III takes place on the newly formed Earth, where Adam is alone. God tells Adam that he needs a family; he tells Adam to lie down while he creates Eve. Adam and Eve taste the fruit of the tree God has forbidden them to harvest and are kicked out of the Garden of Eden, after which they have two sons, Cain and Abel.

In Scene IV, God descends upon Earth to find that Cain has just killed Abel by hitting him with a stone, because, he says, Abel was making a "fool" of him while he worked in the field. God tells Cain that he has committed a "crime" and orders him to go as far away as possible.

In Scene V, Cain stops by the side of a country road, where he meets a young woman. She agrees to be Cain's Girl, and takes him home to find lodging at her father's house.

Scene VI takes place in "God's private office in Heaven." God comments to Gabriel that he hasn't walked the earth for several hundred years, and decides to see how things are going.

Scene VII takes place on Earth on a Sunday. God finds the people engaged in gambling and debauchery, few of them attending church. Noah, a country preacher, comes along, and God walks with him. Noah, thinking God is also a preacher, tells him of the general lack of faith among the people. Noah invites God home for dinner with his wife.

Scene VIII takes place in the home of Noah and his wife. While there, God draws up a plan for Noah to build an ark, warning him that He will be sending a flood to drown all the people, who are full of sin, except Noah and his family.

In Scene IX, Noah and his sons build the ark while their neighbors look on, jeering at Noah and calling him crazy. Cain the Sixth kills Flatfoot with a knife for flirting with his girlfriend. As the rain comes, Noah and his sons begin to load the animals onto the ark.

In Scene X, the ark finally finds dry land, where Noah and his family release the animals and plant seeds. God appears to admire the new world he has created and to congratulate Noah on his success. Gabriel, who accompanies God, is less enthusiastic.

Part II

Part II, Scene I takes place in God's office. God is once again unhappy with the abundance of sin among human beings. He calls Abraham, Isaac, and Jacob into his office and informs them that he has chosen one of their descendants, Moses, to lead his people to the Promised Land of Canaan, which God has set aside especially for them.

In Scene II, God speaks to Moses, explaining the task for which he has been chosen. Moses is not convinced that he is hearing the voice of God until God first sets a bush on fire and then turns a rod into a snake.

Scene III takes place in the throne room of the Pharaoh, who is being entertained by a magician. Moses and his brother Aaron arrive and demand that Pharaoh release their people from bondage in Egypt. The Pharaoh refuses, and Moses (with the help of God) causes a swarm of gnats, and then a swarm of flies, to descend upon the Pharaoh's court. He tells the Pharaoh he will not call off the pests unless the Pharaoh agrees to let his people go. Pharaoh tricks Moses several times, but does not truly agree to release the people until his dead son is brought in to him.

In Scene IV, Moses, Aaron, and their people have been wandering in the desert for forty years. They have come to the river Jordan, where Moses finds that he is too old and sick to enter the Promised Land of Canaan with the others. He appoints Joshua to lead them in battle for the city of Jericho. God

Marc Connelly

comes to Moses and shows him that his people have won the battle and entered Jericho. God then leads Moses to Heaven.

Scene V takes place in Babylon, where the people, who are full of sin and without faith, attend a wild party in what looks like a New Orleans jazz nightclub. Even the King and the High Priest are corrupt and sinful. A Prophet arrives, but is shot dead by the Master of Ceremonies. God is so angered by this that he renounces his people and vows to abandon them.

Scene VI takes place in God's office, where He decides to go down to Earth one more time.

Scene VII takes place at the Temple of Jerusalem, where a battle has been fought. God appears to Hezdrel and questions him about his faith and the faith of the people. Hezdrel says that they worship a ''new'' God, the ''God of Hosea,'' rather than the ''God of Moses.'' Hezdrel explains that the ''old'' God was full of ''wrath and vengeance,'' whereas the ''God of Hosea'' is full of ''mercy.''

Scene VIII takes place once again at the fish fry in Heaven, where God gets the idea to send a ''God who must suffer'' down to Earth in the form of Jesus Christ.

CHARACTERS

Adam

Adam is the first man created by God to inhabit the newly created Earth and to cultivate the land. Adam is at first puzzled by his existence. He is described as a man "of thirty, of medium height, dressed in the clothing of the average field hand." God decides that Adam needs a family because "in yo' heart you is a family man." After Adam and Eve have eaten the forbidden fruit, they are thrown out of the Garden of Eden.

Archangel

An Archangel appears at the "fish fry" in Heaven. He is described as older than the other angels and has a white beard. His clothes are "much darker . . . and his wings a trifle more imposing."

Cain

Cain is a son of Adam and Eve. When God comes down to Earth, he finds that Cain has just slain his brother, Abel, by hitting him on the head with a rock because, he claims, Abel had been making a "fool" of him. God tells Cain that he has committed a crime. He tells Cain to go as far away as possible. After traveling for a long time, Cain takes up with a country girl that he meets along the way.

Reverand Deshee

Mr. Deshee is the preacher who teaches Sunday school to the children in a Louisiana town. He tells them the story of the first five chapters of Genesis, then takes questions from the children. This opening scene frames the rest of the play, which is an enactment of biblical stories.

Eve

Eve is created by God so that Adam will have a family with whom he can live. Eve is described as "about twenty-six, and quite pretty." Her costume is that of "a country girl," with a gingham dress that is "quite new and clean." After they have eaten the forbidden fruit and are thrown out of the Garden of Eden, she and Adam have two sons, Cain and Abel.

Gabriel

Gabriel is God's right-hand man. He is described as "bigger and more elaborately winged than even the Archangel," but younger and without a beard. His costume is "less conventional than that of the other men" and is likened to the drawings of Gabriel by the artist Doré.

God

God is "the tallest and biggest" of all the inhabitants of Heaven. His costume includes "a white shirt with a white bow tie, a long Prince Albert coat of black alpaca, black trousers, and congress gaiters." His voice is described as "a rich bass," and he speaks in a southern black accent, as do all the characters. God created the Earth to drain off the excess "firmament" that resulted from a certain miracle. He runs Heaven from a desk in a shabby-looking office, with the help of Gabriel.

At the play's end, the Christian God turns out to be the same God as the Hebrew God, but seen from a different perspective by human beings. The difference between the old and the new perceptions of God is that the new is seen as more merciful. As the play ends, God, sitting in Heaven, decides to send down Jesus Christ to demonstrate to people a God who both suffers and is merciful.

Moses

Moses is chosen by God to lead his people out of bondage in Egypt and into the Promised Land of Canaan, which God has set aside for them. Moses goes with his brother Aaron to see the Pharaoh in his throne room. They demonstrate several "magic" tricks (with the help of God) in which they cause flies, and then gnats, to descend upon the Pharaoh's court. Each time, Moses vows that he will not call off the pests unless the Pharaoh promises to free the Jews from bondage in Egypt. Finally, the Pharaoh's son is brought to him dead, and the Pharaoh agrees to let the Jews go.

After leading his people out of Egypt, and leading them as they wander in the desert for forty years, Moses dies of old age just as they reach the Promised Land of Canaan. As God has foretold, Moses reaches the river Jordan, but is too old and sick to accompany his people into the city of Jericho. Moses appoints Joshua to succeed him. God then appears to Moses to show him that his people have won the battle over Jericho, and leads Moses to Heaven.

Noah

Noah, "a country preacher," meets God while walking along a road. He thinks that God is also a preacher, and tells him that the land is full of sinful, faithless people. Noah then invites God home to dinner with his wife. Over dinner, God reveals who he is, and draws up the plans for Noah to build an ark, warning him of the flood that he will send to wipe out all the sinful people who inhabit the Earth. Noah obeys God's wishes, building the ark and bringing his family, as well as two of every kind of animal, aboard the ark. After forty days and nights, Noah and his family find dry land where they release the animals and plant the seeds they have brought.

Pharaoh

The Pharaoh is visited in his throne room by Moses and his brother Aaron, who come to demand that he free the Jews from bondage. The Pharaoh refuses until his son is brought to him dead, after which he agrees to let them go.

Zeba

Zeba is the great-great granddaughter of Seth. She is one of the sinners whom God meets along the road. Zeba is entirely invented by Connelly and does not actually appear in the Bible.

THEMES

Sin

A central theme of Connelly's retelling of the stories of the Old Testament is sin. Ward W. Briggs, Jr., commented in *Dictionary of Literary Biography,* ''The theme throughout is that man sins and is either punished or renounced by God.'' The play presents the Earth and humans primarily from the perspective of God. Adam and Eve are the first sinners, and are punished by being thrown out of the Garden of Eden. After Cain has killed his brother Abel, God tells him, ''I'm yere to tell you dat's called a crime,'' and advises him to go as far away as possible, then ''git married an' settle down an' raise some chillun.''

When, several hundred years later, God returns to Earth on a Sunday, he finds a girl singing blues music, a group of men betting, and a family wracked with drunkenness and debauchery. Walking down a country road, God comes upon Noah, who confirms that the people are ''jest all lazy, and mean, and full of sin,'' and, ''Dey ain't got no moral sense.' God is so displeased that he decides to drown all of the humans, except Noah and his family, with a flood.

MEDIA ADAPTATIONS

- Connelly wrote and directed the 1936 film *The Green Pastures*, which was produced by Warner Brothers.

- Connelly wrote an adaptation of *The Green Pastures* for a television broadcast in 1959.

After the flood, when a prophet is killed in Babylon, God becomes so enraged that He renounces humanity. God tells the people

> Dat's about enough—I's stood all I kin from you. I tried to make dis a good Earth. I helped Adam, I helped Noah, I helped Moses, an' I helped David. What's de grain dat grew out of de seed? Sin! Nothin' but sin throughout de whole world. I've given you every chance. . . . Ev'ything I've given you, you've defiled. Ev'y time I've fo'given you, you've mocked me. . . . I repent of dese people dat I have made and I will deliver dem no more.

By the end of the play, however, God realizes that He needs to be a more ''merciful'' God, sympathetic to human ''suffering.''

Faith

While God finds mostly sinners upon the Earth, there are a few men who maintain their faith in him. Noah, for instance, appears as a country preacher, discouraged by the sinning of those all around him. Noah is rewarded for his faith when God gives him the plans and instructions to build an ark and save his family from the flood.

Moses is another who maintains his faith in God. When God first speaks to him, however, he is not convinced, until He performs several miracles, at which point Moses confirms his faith.

At the very end of the play, God conceives the idea to send Jesus Christ down to Earth, so that people may develop faith in a God who ''suffers.''

God's Relationship with Man

Connelly's play is notable for his everyday personification of God as a black man. Throughout

TOPICS FOR FURTHER STUDY

- Connelly's play is a retelling of stories from the Old Testament. In what ways does Connelly's rendition of these well-known stories differ from their traditional telling? To what extent does Connelly's message in this play comply with traditional interpretations of the Old Testament? To what extent does Connelly's play present a different message?

- Connelly was a prominent member of the Algonquin Round Table, an informal group of writers, editors, actors, and intellectuals who met regularly at the Algonquin Hotel in New York City. Learn more about the Algonquin Round Table. Who else was associated with this group?

What can you learn about some of the other writers? What aesthetic, literary, and cultural perspectives did the Algonquin Round Table generate?

- Throughout his career, Connelly worked as a screenwriter, and sometimes as an actor and director, for the Hollywood film industry. Learn more about the film industry during Connelly's career. What significant changes and developments took place in Hollywood during this period? Who were some of the prominent movie stars? What important films were made during this era?

---

the play, God's human qualities are emphasized, while his divine powers are also acknowledged. God is represented as a man who attends a fish fry in Heaven, tastes the boiled custard, and discusses the recipe with one of his angels. He also occasionally visits Earth as a human, walking side by side with various other characters. God's relationship to humanity is thus represented as very personal. Such a personification of God throughout the play makes way for the arrival of Jesus Christ, a God who suffers like a man, as the curtain goes down and the play ends.

STYLE

Setting

The Green Pastures takes place in several key settings, all of which interpret Old Testament Biblical stories in the context of Southern, rural, locations inhabited by African Americans. Connelly chose these settings as the context in which to retell biblical stories because he imagined that rural, Southern African Americans probably imagined the stories of the Bible to take place in the same type of locations with which they were familiar. (Today,

Connelly's representation of such African-American conceptions of the Bible can be seen as stereotyped and without basis.) Heaven, for instance, is represented as a giant fish fry picnic, attended by angels, cherubs, an archangel, and God Himself. The Garden of Eden is set in the rural South, and is described in the stage directions as filled with trees, plants, bushes, and flowers native to the South. Babylon is depicted as ''a Negro night club in New Orleans.'' God runs Heaven and earth from his ''private office,'' a shabby old space, where ''the general atmosphere is that of the office of a Negro lawyer in a Louisiana town.'' The throne room of the Pharaoh is described as resembling ''a Negro lodge room.''

Costumes

The costuming of the play combines and translates traditional conceptions of biblical characters into a rural southern African-American setting. Some of the stage notes describing the costumes, however, contain elements of the stereotyping Connelly employed in attempting to represent African-American culture. The angels in Heaven wear ''brightly colored robes and have wings protruding from their backs''; however, they otherwise ''look like happy negroes at a fish fry.'' God wears ''a white shirt with a white bow tie, a long Prince Albert coat of black alpaca, black trousers and congress gaiters.'' Adam wears ''the clothing of the average field hand,'' and Eve wears a ''gingham dress,'' which is ''quite new and clean.'' Noah is dressed as ''a country preacher.'' The Pharaoh of Egypt wears ''a crown and garments'' which ''might be those worn by a high officer in a Negro lodge during a ritual.''

Biblical References and ''Artistic License''

Almost all of the characters in *The Green Pastures* are drawn directly from the Old Testament: God, Gabriel, Adam and Eve, Cain and Abel, Noah, Moses, etc. Connelly, however, took ''artistic license'' in creating several supplemental fictional characters to tell his version of these traditional biblical stories. The term ''artistic license'' is used to describe a writer's claim to the right to bend or alter facts, events, or characters in an unrealistic way to better suit her or his narrative concerns. In the ''Author's Note'' of the published play, Connelly explains that, ''One need not blame a hazy memory of the Bible for the failure to recall the characters of Hezdrel, Zeba and others in the play. They are the author's apocrypha, but he believes persons much like them have figured in the meditations of some if the old Negro preachers, whose simple faith he has tried to translate into a play.'' One such ''apocryphal'' character is Zeba, the great-great granddaughter of Seth. In the play, God encounters her during a visit to earth on a Sunday. When God meets her on a country road, she is singing a blues song, accompanied by a ukulele. She represents one of the many sinners God encounters during his visit. He chides her for singing blues music when she should be in church, but she merely responds to him in a ''sassy'' manner. Zeba turns out to be the girlfriend of Cain the Sixth, who later stabs a character named Flatfoot after he flirts with Zeba. Through this device of integrating such characters as Zeba into biblical stories, Connelly was able to narrate scenarios which were suited to the themes he wished to stress in his play.

HISTORICAL CONTEXT

African-American History and Culture in the 1920s–1930s

The Green Pastures was first produced in 1929, the year of the stock market crash that brought on the Great Depression. One reason for the play's continued popularity throughout the 1930s may have been due to the massive migration of African Americans from the South seeking employment in Northern cities. Since Connelly's play was seen primarily by white audiences, his portrayal of rural, Southern African Americans as humble, pious, ''simple'' people may have held a particular appeal to white Northern populations in urban centers.

The Green Pastures, while written by a white man, includes an entirely African-American cast of characters. Although by today's standards these characters are mostly stereotypes, this play represented a breakthrough in the history of African-American theater because of the unique opportunity it provided for black actors to play in major roles that went beyond standard bit-parts playing servants. During the 1920s, when *The Green Pastures* was first written and produced, African-American writers were strongly influenced by the literary movement known as the Harlem Renaissance. Organizations such as the Krigwa Players in Washington, D.C., worked to promote African-American dramatic writing and theatrical production. Connelly, as a white man, was not involved in the Harlem Renaissance movement, although *The Green Pastures,* performed in New York City, would certainly have been noted by writers of the Harlem Renaissance. The Depression had a detrimental affect on the Harlem Renaissance, because many of the writers fell into economic hard times, which made it harder for them to pursue literary efforts.

The Green Pastures is set in an imaginary location in which biblical stories take place in settings that resemble the rural South, and are peopled exclusively by African-American characters. The historical era in which the play is set is referred to as biblical times. Connelly's representation of the rural Southern United States can be termed ''pastoral''—meaning that it is depicted in an idealized, nostalgic light, which ignores any historical or social conflict taking place in the actual American South. Connelly's South is a world without white people, without racism, without a legacy of slavery, without the legal and illegal practices of racial discrimination that have characterized the history of the South, and without the struggles of African Americans to achieve equality and civil rights. It is important, therefore, to be aware of the real social and historical conditions that characterized the South in the 1920s and 1930s, during the time in which *The Green Pastures* was first written

COMPARE & CONTRAST

- **1930s:** America is in the midst of the Great Depression, caused by the Stock Market Crash of 1929—the same year in which *The Green Pastures* was first produced. The Great Depression is characterized by the worst unemployment in U. S. history, with about twenty-five percent of eligible workers unable to find jobs.

  1990s: America enjoys a period of economic prosperity, characterized by low unemployment, and many middle-class Americans profiting from investments in the stock market.

- **1920s–1930s:** African-American theatrical production is strongly influenced by the Harlem Renaissance movement. Theaters devoted to the black productions are established across the U. S.

  1960s–1990s: African-American theatrical production is strongly influenced by the Black Arts Movement of the 1960s and '70s. The Black Arts Theater is established in Harlem in 1965.

- **1860s:** In the Post-Civil War era, white Southern resistance to the efforts of Reconstruction leads to the organization of the Ku Klux Klan (KKK) in 1866. The KKK reaches the height of its membership and activities in the period of 1868–70.

  1870s–1980s: Federal legislation becomes involved in efforts to both limit and defend the Ku Klux Klan. In 1869, the KKK is ordered disbanded. Congress attempts to curb KKK activities via the Force Act of 1870, and the Ku Klux Act of 1871. However, these efforts are partially reversed in 1882, when, in the case of the *United States vs. Harris*, the Supreme Court rules that the Ku Klux Act of 1871 is unconstitutional.

  1920s: Re-organized in 1915, the Ku Klux Klan enjoys renewed participation, with as many as five million members. The burning cross becomes the symbol of the KKK.

  1930s–1940s: During the Depression era, KKK membership sharply declines, and the organization is disbanded in 1944.

  1960s: In response to the efforts of the Civil Rights Movement to integrate the South, as well as new federal legislation such as the Civil Rights Act of 1964, the KKK is once again revitalized. In Alabama, after the murder of a civil rights worker and subsequent arrest of four Klan members, President Lyndon B. Johnson makes a television address denouncing the KKK.

  1980s–1990s: The Ku Klux Klan begins to form a coalition with other hate groups and white supremacist and anti-federalist organizations, such as the Neo-Nazis.

---

and produced—as well as during earlier periods in U.S. history which bear upon this era.

During the late 1920s, in which the play was first created, as well as the 1930s, during which it enjoyed enormous popularity among white Northern audiences, the legacy of racial discrimination in the United States, both in the South and elsewhere, involved a number of conflicts and struggles. The Ku Klux Klan, an organization formed in the Post-Civil War Era, with the aim of maintaining white supremacy through violence and intimidation tactics, experienced a revival in the teens and twenties.

In 1915, the Klan, which had essentially died out by the 1880s, was reorganized in Atlanta, Georgia—inspired in part by the 1905 novel *The Clansman*, by Thomas Dixon, which glorified the Klan, and the popular 1915 film adaptation of Dixon's novel, entitled *The Birth of a Nation* (directed by D. W. Griffith). This revived Ku Klux Klan flourished in the South and Midwest, boasting a membership of some four to five million during the 1920s. Membership in the Klan was at its highest of the twentieth century in 1928, when *The Green Pastures* was written. However, membership sharply dropped in the 1930s. Racist activities such as lynching, while not necessarily always organized by the Klan, also remained rampant from the early 1880s through the early 1950s, during which some 3,437 African Americans were lynched in a seventy-year period. In 1918, for example, sixty-three African Americans were lynched. By 1940, however, the number of lynchings had greatly declined. Great efforts to combat racial discrimination were also made throughout the 1920s and 1930s. Anti-lynching campaigns were waged by such African-American activists as Mary Elizabeth Church Terrell, and Walter White, and by white activists such as Jessie Daniel Ames, who founded the Association of Southern Women for the Prevention of Lynching in 1930. Efforts at improving the status of African Americans in the U.S. through legislation included the foundation of the National Association for the Advancement of Colored People (NAACP), in 1909, with the leadership of W. E. B. Du Bois.

The Prohibition Era

In *The Green Pastures,* drinking alcohol—particularly on Sunday—is one of the sinful activities that God observes among the people he has created. Reference to drinking in 1929 is especially significant because it was in the midst of the Prohibition era in the United States, during which the manufacture, transportation, and sale of alcohol was prohibited by federal law. Prohibition began in 1919, with the passage of the Eighteenth Amendment, and lasted until 1933, when it was rescinded by the twenty-first amendment. Prohibition was ultimately deemed unsuccessful because many law-abiding citizens continued to purchase and drink alcohol. That the entire liquor industry was run illegally by ''organized crime,'' which was characterized by violent warfare among competing producers and distributors of alcohol. Prohibition, largely supported by Protestant organizations, was a major issue in the presidential elections of 1928, during which *The Green Pastures* was written. Republication Herbert Hoover won the presidency that year in part due to the support of Protestant, Pro-Prohibition voters. A major incident in 1929 was the St. Valentine's Day Massacre in Chicago, in which the gang led by Al Capone shot and killed seven members of the gang led by ''Bugs'' Moran. *The Green Pastures* represents a Protestant practice of Christianity and depicts drinking as a sign of sin and human corruption. Audiences watching *The Green Pastures* in 1929 would have been aware of the national issues surrounding drinking.

The Algonquin Round Table

Connelly was a member of the ''Vicious Circle'' of the Algonquin Round Table, also called simply The Round Table, an informal group of writers, dramatists, editors, and intellectuals who met daily for lunch at the Algonquin Hotel in New York City, during the 1920s and 30s, although the first meeting of The Round Table took place in 1919, and the final meeting in 1943. The Algonquin Round Table became known for its members' capacity for witty repartee and acerbic comments. Paul T. Nolan describes the ''Vicious Circle,'' which they also called themselves, as ''a group of wits that included half of the quotable men and women in New York during the 1920's.'' Among its prominent members were: the drama critic, poet, and prize-winning short story writer, Dorothy Parker; the comic film actor Harpo Marx; the writer Edna Ferber; the author, critic, actor, and informal leader of the Round Table, Alexander Woollcott; colorful stage and screen actress Tallulah Bankhead; drama critic, playwright, and speechwriter for President Franklin D. Roosevelt, Robert E. Sherwood; and playwright and screenwriter George S. Kaufman. Connelly collaborated on a number of plays with George S. Kaufman, and with Edna Ferber. *The New Yorker,* a weekly magazine, was founded by Harold Ross, a regular member of the Algonquin Round Table, in 1925, and many of the members of The Round Table became regular contributors to the magazine. Connelly was among the first members of the editorial board of *The New Yorker,* which became popular for witty and urbane coverage of arts and culture in New York City. It was in the context of this milieu of screenwriters, actors, drama critics, and intellectual theatre-goers that Connelly created *The Green Pastures,* and one can only assume that the writing of the play was influenced by his association with The Round Table.

CRITICAL OVERVIEW

The Green Pastures is Connelly's most outstanding literary achievement, garnering him a Pulitzer Prize, and, according to Ward W. Briggs, Jr., ''theatrical immortality.'' Paul T. Nolan states, ''*The Green Pastures* is the finest single piece of writing that Mr. Connelly has ever done,'' adding, '''*The Green Pastures*' . . . is the one play by Connelly that has never, except for minor cavils, been criticized for artistic 'faults.''' Walter C. Daniel comments that, during its first year-and-a-half run in New York,

The Green Pastures ''had gained praise from practically every source. It had kept the legitimate theater alive, literally, and had brought thousands of Americans and many visiting foreign dignitaries to see the spectacle at the time the nation was reeling from the pangs of economic disaster.'' Daniel goes on to state, ''*The Green Pastures* presented night after night the dramatization of a shared religion and a vision through which both black and white Americans who realized their common bond in this experience could approach a social, moral, and philosophical coalition needed for the day. The artifacts of Hebrew folk stories, Negro spirituals, the dramaturgy of Marc Connelly with its superb stage sets, and the acting of the superb cast led by Richard B. Harrison combined to provide the crucial thought-piece for a frightened and desperate 1930 America.'' Nolan notes, ''*The Green Pastures* is, undoubtedly, among the half dozen or so most respected plays in American dramatic literature,'' adding, ''It gave Mr. Connelly an international reputation, a private fortune, and a great deal of personal satisfaction.''

The Green Pastures opened at the Mansfield Theater in New York City, where it ran for 640 performances in 1930 and 1931. The play then made a national tour. It returned for a second run in New York in 1935, running for seventy-three performances, and only closing upon the death of Richard B. Harrison, the actor who had starred as God (''De Lawd''). A revival performance of the play on Broadway was attempted in 1951, but closed after a short run. Connelly wrote and directed the screen adaptation of *The Green Pastures,* which was produced in 1936 by Warner Brothers. Nolan notes, ''The success of the film not only helped to make Connelly 'the highest paid' writer in Hollywood, but it also spread the fame of *The Green Pastures.*'' Connelly later wrote a television adaptation of the play, which aired in 1959.

The Green Pastures won immediate popularity and critical acclaim following its opening night on Broadway. According to Daniel, the *New York Times* drama critic J. Brooks Atkinson ''wrote that Connelly's play excelled as comedy, fantasy, folklore, and religion. He, who became the play's most continuous and most ardent supporter, wrote that it was a work of surpassing beauty from almost any point of view.'' Further, ''Atkinson believed Connelly created a miracle on the stage, which, after all, is what the theater is supposed to do.'' Nolan asserts that the play may be as famous a theatrical phenomenon as it is a literary and dramatic achieve-

ment: ''The popularity of *The Green Pastures* is such that the history of the play, from its composition through its long runs both here and in Europe, has become a part of the legend of American drama; it is not too much to argue, in fact, that the 'story' surrounding *The Green Pastures* is probably the best-known single piece of theatrical history in America.'' Nolan adds, ''*The Green Pastures* and all associated with it have become part of the general cultural history of the 1930s.''

Briggs, in *Dictionary of Literary Biography,* asserts that Connelly is ''a central but not pivotal figure of twentieth-century American theatre: a man of enormous popularity but little lasting influence, of considerable instinctive talent but scant genius, of grand ideas but slight thought.'' Briggs sums up Connelly's theatrical career as one in which he ''enjoyed the good fortune of early success, the advantages of a brilliant collaborator, and the services of the leading stars of his day.'' Briggs concludes, ''Regardless of how his plays appear today, Connelly remains one of the most important figures of the Broadway stage in the first half of this [the twentieth] century.''

CRITICISM

Liz Brent

Brent has a Ph.D. in American Culture, specializing in film studies, from the University of Michigan. She is a freelance writer and teaches courses in the history of American cinema. In the following essay, Brent discusses elements of legitimate African-American culture in Connelly's play.

In the ''Author's Note'' to the 1929 edition of *The Green Pastures,* Marc Connelly explains his intent in depicting stories from the Old Testament as peopled by everyday African Americans and set in rural Louisiana:

> *The Green Pastures* is an attempt to present certain aspects of a living religion in the terms of its believers. . . . Unburdened by the differences of more educated theologians, they accept the Old Testament as a chronicle of wonders which happened to people like themselves in vague but actual places, and of rules of conduct, true acceptance of which will lead them to a tangible, three-dimensional Heaven.

Connelly's commentary likely strikes today's reader as based on an offensive stereotype of African Americans as simple and childlike. Thus, while prominent black religious leaders and intellectuals

Ingram Rex in a scene from the 1936 film adaptation of the Pulitzer Prize-winning play The Green Pastures.

such as W. E. B. Du Bois praised the play upon its first run in the 1930s, later critics, influenced by the Civil Rights Movement and Black Nationalism, found it offensive in its stereotyping of African Americans. In the published script, stage directions describing ''happy negroes at a fish fry,'' are reminiscent of the Sambo figure, and the character of a ''Mammy angel'' recalls the Aunt Jemima or black Mammy stereotype—both prevalent images throughout American cultural history.

Nonetheless, Connelly's play includes a number of more or less authentic elements of African-American culture, including: a well-researched rendition of the speech patterns of African Americans in rural Louisiana; the use of an all-black cast; the singing of ''spirituals,'' or gospel songs, by a choir throughout the production; and reference to blues and jazz musical traditions.

While *The Green Pastures* does not necessarily reflect an accurate representation of African Americans or folk culture, it does use an authentic rendition of a Black Louisiana dialect. In the ''Author's Note,'' Connelly acknowledges the source that inspired him to write the play: ''The author is indebted to Mr. Roark Bradford, whose retelling of

several of the Old Testament stories in 'Ol' Man Adam an' His Chillun' first stimulated his interest in this point of view.'' Roark Bradford (1896–1948) grew up on a plantation in Tennessee, where he, a white child, heard many African-American folk stories from the black workers. In 1920, he began working as a reporter, and, according to *Encyclopaedia Britannica,* ''met the colorful characters of various southern cities, including the musicians, preachers, and storytellers on the riverfront of New Orleans.'' Based on these experiences, Bradford wrote down a series of African-American folk stories, which were published in the New York *World.* His first book, a collection of the retelling of biblical stories from among his published works, *Ol' Man Adam an' His Chillun,* was published in 1928. Bradford's work, however, cannot be considered an accurate or authentic representation of African-American folk culture. As is noted in the *Encyclopaedia Britannica,* ''A major weakness of Bradford's work is his reliance on stereotypes of his black subjects. Yet his writing accurately reflects their dialect, and his approach is gentle and humorous.''

Connelly prominently acknowledged this source for his play, subtitling it: *A Fable Suggested by*

WHAT DO I READ NEXT?

- *Voices Off-Stage: A Book of Memoirs* (1968), by Marc Connelly, is Connelly's autobiographical account of his life on Broadway and in Hollywood.

- *Marc Connelly* (1969) by Paul T. Nolan provides discussion of nearly all of Connelly's major works to the late 1960s.

- *"De Lawd": Richard B. Harrison and The Green Pastures* (1986) by Walter C. Daniel is an account of the history of Connelly's play, as produced in the early 1930s. The discussions focuses on actor

Richard B. Harrison, whose role as God ("De Lawd") in the play contributed in no small measure to its success on the stage.

- The short story "Coroner's Inquest" (1930) by Marc Connelly won an O. Henry Award.

- *Southern Sketches, "Ol' Man Adam an' His Chillun"* (1928) by Roark Bradford is the retelling of Bible stories through African-American folklore and inspired Connelly to write *The Green Pastures*.

Roark Bradford's Southern Sketches, "Ol' Man Adam An' His Chillun." However, Paul T. Nolan asserts in *Marc Connelly* that the influence of Bradford's work on *The Green Pastures* was minimal:

> Bradford's book, as [Connelly] acknowledged in the preface to the play, had 'suggested' the play to him; but, largely, beyond the fact that *Ol' Man Adam* gave Connelly the idea of a biblical play done in southern American Negro dialect, *The Green Pastures* owes its literary source to the Old Testament and its diction to Connelly's research on the scene.

Nolan praises Connelly for his extensive and accurate research into the dialects of African Americans in the South:

> Connelly spent considerable time in Louisiana, researching the subject . . . 'I went into the farm country of St. Francis Parish—near Baton Rouge,' he wrote of his experiences in Louisiana; ' . . . I read my play to sharecroppers.'

Nolan adds, "Connelly's ear for oral language, although given little attention in the discussion of his earlier plays, was always one of his great assets as a playwright." Nolan concludes, "Connelly was wonderfully trained and admirably suited by talent and interest to make the kind of careful language study that was necessary to give *The Green Pastures* its authenticity."

Although written, directed, and produced by white men, and attended by primarily white audi-

ences, *The Green Pastures* was a significant event in the world of black theater. The Harlem Renaissance, a literary movement that flourished in New York's black Harlem neighborhood, inspired the development of black theater in the 1920s and 1930s. Theaters devoted to black productions were established in major cities throughout the United States, the most prominent being the American Negro Theater and the Negro Playwrights' Company.

While not a black production, *The Green Pastures* represented a new development in the presence of African Americans on the mainstream stage. According to Walter C. Daniel in *"De Lawd": Richard B. Harrison and The Green Pastures, New York Times* drama critic Brooks Atkinson saw *The Green Pastures* as a milestone in the on-stage representation of black culture:

> Atkinson judged that audiences were rapt in attention because they realized they were in the presence of a new cultural artifact being performed before their eyes. That was the elevation of the folk art from riotous low comedy to something not yet named but essentially and demonstrably different from the ribald jokes and denigrating stereotypes of the black stage idiom.

Casting for the play created shock waves in the black drama world. Daniel observes, "Black actors hoped the play would bring them a new significance. Never before had so many black actors and singers been employed in a single stage endeavor.

A play about African-American culture and religion, written by a white author and featuring an all black cast, *The Green Pastures* was bound to raise racial issues at the time of its initial production. Connelly had had great trouble selling the play to a producer in the first place, for a variety of reasons, one being that, according to Nolan, "There were . . . fears that a play with a Negro actor playing God would offend the white, religious theatergoers." However, the casting of unknown sixty-five-year-old actor Richard B. Harrison as God ("De Lawd") turned out to be one of the production's finest attributes and a key factor in the long-running success of the play; upon Harrison's death in 1935, the play quickly lost its box-office appeal. Daniel observes, "The trick of putting a black God on the stage turned into fortune as Richard B. Harrison's talent at acting, dignity, rich voice, and gentle, endearing humor flooded over the auditorium and balcony." Furthermore, Harrison proved an important link between Broadway and African-American communities. According to Daniel, "Few of them could purchase tickets to see him [Harrison] perform at the Mansfield, but they related to him and clamored for his presence in their little theater groups, social gatherings, and churches."

Daniel observes that "equally important as the newspaper critics' comments on the play were indications of approval that came early from the clergy and from New York black intellectuals." W. E. B. Du Bois, for example, "praised *The Green Pastures* because in it Marc Connelly 'has made an extraordinarily appealing and beautiful play based on the folk religion of Negroes.'" Daniel adds that Du Bois "could not agree with those who considered the play sacrilegious." Furthermore, "Sermons preached in black and white local churches frequently included some reference to the play." In 1931, Harrison was awarded the National Association for the Advancement of Colored People's Spingarn Medal for making the most significant contribution to the advancement of African Americans in the country that year; the award speech was delivered by Du Bois.

The Green Pastures brought authentic African-American culture to the stage through the key role of music in the play's production. Stage directions call for a choir, which breaks into spirituals as accompaniment to the biblical narrative of the play. Daniel describes the effect of the first sounds of the choir on the play's opening night, when "from the darkness came the burst of the magnificent sounds

> " WHILE *THE GREEN PASTURES* DOES NOT NECESSARILY REFLECT AN ACCURATE REPRESENTATION OF AFRICAN AMERICANS OR FOLK CULTURE, IT DOES USE AN AUTHENTIC RENDITION OF A BLACK LOUISIANA DIALECT."

of the Hall Johnson Choir" singing "Rise, Shine, Give God the Glory."

The spiritual is a form of American folk music, characterized by the singing of hymns. Over time, black and white folk culture developed the spiritual along different lines, although sharing many hymns and tunes. Both are rooted in revival and camp meetings, a practice of Christian religious worship popular in the South. Important differences, however, developed between the two folk cultures. According to *Encyclopaedia Britannica*, "Black spirituals were sung not only in worship but also as work songs, and the text imagery often reflects concrete tasks." The spiritual thus developed as "a complex intermingling of African and white folk-music elements," in that "complementary traits of African music and white U.S. folksong reinforced each other." The musical style of spirituals in particular is derived from African culture, as imported by the slave trade. "Most authorities see clear African influence in vocal style and in the . . . clapped accompaniments."

Spirituals sung in the play include: "When the Saints Come Marching In"; "So High You Can't Get Over It"; "Hallelujah"; "A City Called Heaven"; "Go Down Moses"; "Mary Don't You Weep"; and "Hallelujah, King Jesus."

Jazz and blues music, both strongly rooted in African-American culture and history, play a small but important role in *The Green Pastures*. The roots of jazz in African culture are especially strong. As stated in *Encyclopaedia Britannica*,

> Had it not been for the traffic in slaves from West Africa to the United States, jazz would never have evolved, either in the United States or Africa, for jazz is the expression in music of the African native who is

FORTY-FOURTH STREET THEATRE

❀ ❀ ❀ THE ❀ ❀ ❀
PLAY
BILL

Playbill cover for the 1935 production of
The Green Pastures *at New York's
Forty-Fourth Street Theatre.*

isolated both socially and geographically from his natural environment.

In Connelly's play, both jazz and blues are contrasted with the spirituals sung by the heavenly choir, and represent the human descent into sin.

In act 2, scene 7, when God returns to Earth on a Sunday to see how the people he made are doing, he first encounters Zeba on a country road. Zeba, "a rouged and extremely flashily dressed chippy of about eighteen," is sitting on a stump, singing "a 'blues'" and playing a ukulele. God immediately disapproves, saying "Now, dat ain't so good." He tells Zeba to "Stop dat!" When Zeba responds with indifference and resumes singing, God tells her, "Don't you know dis is de Sabbath? Da's no kin' o' song to sing on de Lawd's day." This encounter represents the first of many in which God finds that man has descended into sin, paying no heed to the Sabbath.

Act 3, scene 5, takes place in "a room vaguely resembling a Negro night club in New Orleans," where "about a dozen couples are dancing in the foreground to the tune of a jazz orchestra." The costumes are meant to "represent the debauches of Babylon." Connelly thus chose to depict a city

which has descended into sin as a jazz club, and the sinners as flashily dressed young people dancing to jazz music.

Jazz music and, to a lesser extent, blues have long been associated with sin and debauchery. Flourishing in the red-light district of New Orleans, jazz became associated with moral depravity. According to *Encyclopaedia Britannica,* "jazz, linked to the black performer and the social events of black life in the city, retained a connotation of sin and dissipation for many years after the New Orleans pioneers were forgotten." The setting of Connelly's play in Louisiana, and the portrayal of Babylon as a New Orleans black Jazz club, is especially appropriate, as New Orleans is known to be the birthplace of jazz.

While today's reader will most likely balk at the stereotypical and condescending representation of African Americans in this play, it is important to acknowledge the significant impact it had on the black theater of the day, as well as the elements of legitimate African-American culture used within the play itself, such as black spirituals, references to jazz and blues music, and the use of an accurately rendered black Louisiana dialect throughout the dialogue.

Source: Liz Brent, in an essay for *Drama for Students,* Gale Group, 2001.

Paul T. Nolan

The following chapter essay discusses elements within and surrounding Marc Connelly's play, including the composition and history of the work, its critical and social status, and its thematic elements.

The Green Pastures is, undoubtedly, among the half dozen or so most respected plays in American dramatic literature. It gave Mr. Connelly an international reputation, a private fortune, and a great deal of personal satisfaction. Unfortunately for his other works, it also gave many theater critics and historians the general impression that Marc Connelly was a one-play author. Such an impression came not merely because *The Green Pastures* is the finest single piece of writing that Mr. Connelly has ever done, but also because, in various superficial ways, it appears to be utterly different from all his other works. It is his only play about Negroes; it is his only full-length play on a religious subject; it is his only play without a conventional happy ending.

I The Composition and History

The popularity of *The Green Pastures* is such that the history of the play, from its composition through its long runs both here and in Europe, has become a part of the legend of American drama; it is not too much to argue, in fact, that the story surrounding *The Green Pastures* is probably the best-known single piece of theatrical history in America. In 1928, Harper and Brothers published a collection of dialect stories by Roark Bradford, *Ol' Man Adam an' His Chillun,* which was popular immediately with the Broadway literary colony. F. P. Adams, for example, on December 28, 1928, reported to his readers that he had had lunch with Bradford, "the author of my favorite book . . . and so to dinner with M. Connelly. . . ." This linking of *Ol' Man Adam* and Connelly by Adams was, probably, not accidental. Sometime earlier that year, Rollin Kirby, three-time winner of the Pulitzer Prize for cartooning, had recommended the book to Connelly, who immediately saw dramatic possibilities in its materials; and in 1929, when he went to New Orleans to see Bradford, he wrote "the first act of *The Green Pastures* on the boat S. S. Dixie en route."

Connelly spent considerable time in Louisiana, researching the subject. Bradford's book, as he acknowledged in the preface to the play, had "suggested" the play to him; but, largely, beyond the fact that *Ol' Man Adam* gave Connelly the idea of a Biblical play done in Southern American Negro dialect, *The Green Pastures* owes its literary source to the Old Testament and its diction to Connelly's research on the scene. "I went into the farm country of St. Francis Parish—near Baton Rouge," he wrote of his experiences in Louisiana; ". . . I read my play to sharecroppers." Connelly's ear for oral language, although given little attention in the discussion of his earlier plays, was always one of his great assets as a playwright. Sometimes critics, like John Mason Brown, had complained that his ear for the idiom—"the half-written Algonquins"—led him to sacrifice plotting for tone, theme for "local color"; but, if his friends on Broadway had thought about the problem of research in terms of language, they would have agreed that Connelly was wonderfully trained and admirably suited by talent and interest to make the kind of careful language study that was necessary to give *The Green Pastures* its authenticity.

Mr. Connelley, moreover, had always had a great deal of sensitivity to intent. Charley Bemis in *The Wisdom Tooth,* J. Daniel Thompson in *The Wild Man of Borneo,* and Merton in *Merton of the Movies*

> "FEW RELIGIOUS PLAYS SUCCEEDED AT THE BOX OFFICE, AND, AT THE TIME, NO PLAY WITH AN ALL-NEGRO CAST HAD EVER BEEN A GOOD INVESTMENT. THERE WERE, MOREOVER, FEARS THAT A PLAY WITH A NEGRO ACTOR PLAYING GOD WOULD OFFEND THE WHITE, RELIGIOUS THEATER-GOERS."

are all treated as heroes, not because they perform heroic actions or make heroic speeches, but because, in spite of their doing the weak thing and saying the wrong thing, Connelly "intuits" their good intentions. This sensitivity to intent, as well as Connelly's eye and ear for accurate detail, has made *The Green Pastures* appealing to millions of viewers and readers who have been able to gain from the experiences of the characters some insight into their own lives.

Connelly spent over a year writing the play and then another six months looking for a producer. All of the established New York producers turned down the play, in spite of Connelly's reputation for commercial success, convinced that, for a variety of reasons, *The Green Pastures* would be "bad business." Few religious plays succeeded at the box office, and, at the time, no play with an all-Negro cast had ever been a good investment. There were, moreover, fears that a play with a Negro actor playing God would offend the white, religious theater-goers. Finally, Rowland Stebbins, a retired stockbroker, made himself a part of American theater history by risking his reputation for financial shrewdness by backing the play. Connelly's casting of the play—especially the selection of Richard B. Harrison to play the Lawd—is almost a separate story, certainly an important episode in the history of the Negro actor in American theater.

The play opened in the Mansfield Theatre in New York on February 26, 1930; and, although there were still a few doubts about the financial future of the play, there were none about its worth as drama. Burns Mantle summed up critical opinion when he wrote of the awarding of the Pulitzer Prize to *The Green Pastures* as the best play of the year: "In the awarding of the prize, not a single dissenting voice was heard, either in the committee or in the press. . . ." *Variety* approved of the play as "art theatre," but expressed doubts that the play would run long in a commercial theater.

Some critics, to be sure, had reservations about certain aspects of *The Green Pastures*. Mantle, for example, felt there was some injustice done to Bradford, who was given credit merely for "the suggestion," rather than as a collaborator. Francis Fergusson, in answering that charge, called *The Green Pastures* "a myth [belonging more to the Bible than to Bradford] which Mr. Connelly discovered nearly intact and devoted himself humbly to translating into stage terms." Fergusson argued that Connelly's discovery of the "truth" in Bradford's "farcical" tales deserved special credit. "Discovery of this kind," he wrote, ". . . is of course more creative than confecting something supposedly new." Fergusson, however, complained that the "sinful folk" were modeled on "smart Harlemites," rather than on the Louisiana Negro, perhaps unaware that the New Orleans native, of any race, is also metropolitan, "smart." In commenting upon Fergusson's complaint, Mr. Connelly told me, "The Harlem aspect mentioned was an actual attempt to create the atmosphere I found in the 'barrel-house' in New Orleans." Fergusson's complaint was, moreover, only a qualification; and he approved of Connelly's other characters. "He has managed," Fergusson wrote, "to avoid condescending. . . ."

The Green Pastures and all associated with it have become part of the general cultural history of the 1930s. Mantle, in writing of a new play that Rowland Stebbins produced a dozen years later, for example, identified Stebbins as the man "who will be known to the end of the century as the noble soul who had enough faith in Marc Connelly's 'Green Pastures' to bring it to production after so-called wiser heads of Broadway had neglected to do so." *The Green Pastures* was even given credit for "saving" the reputation of the Pulitzer Prize. In commenting upon other Pulitzer Prize selections for 1929–30, a reviewer for the *Literary Digest* argued that *The Green Pastures* was the only work awarded the prize that year that "No one questions. . . ." All the other Pulitzer choices were challenged, sometimes bitterly. Why should Oliver LaFarge have been selected rather than Hemingway, or Conrad

Aiken rather than Elinor Wylie? With obvious approval, the *Literary Digest* concluded its account with a statement from Woollcott's article in the *Morning Telegraph:* "'*The Green Pastures*' does not need the Pulitzer Prize, but, oh, how the Pulitzer Prize needs '*The Green Pastures*.'"

Perhaps longer than any other twentieth-century American play, *The Green Pastures* was important for its news value alone. In the 1930s, the production of the play, the awarding of the Pulitzer Prize, the suggestion that the play demonstrated an awakened social conscience, the various long-run records that the play established, all were reported with enthusiasm by the press. And then in June, 1935, while the play was still enjoying an unbroken run throughout the United States, Warner Brothers purchased the film rights to it on terms that "were all Connelly's." He directed it, staged it, cast it. The success of the film not only helped to make Connelly "the highest paid" writer in Hollywood, but it also spread the fame of *The Green Pastures*.

In 1951, Connelly again staged *The Green Pastures* in New York. It opened at the Broadway Theatre March 15 and closed April 21. "No amount of enthusiasm on the part of the individual critic, including this editor," John Chapman wrote of that production, "could make this American miracle play stick. Modern Broadway was just not interested in de Lawd, Gabriel, and the fish-loving angels." Although in one respect *The Green Pastures* on the professional stage is past history at the moment, the play still has its supporters by the thousands, men like John Mason Brown, who, as late as 1963, summed up his critical opinion with this statement: "Let's face it with proper gratitude. *The Green Pastures* is a masterpiece."

For the past two decades, however, there has been a general feeling that the play is too simple for complex academic criticism, too soft for an age of revolution, and perhaps too patronizing for the new role of the Negro in the United States, too much like *Uncle Tom's Cabin.* Just a few years ago, for example, the Bishop of the African Methodist Episcopal Church charged that the play was "irreligious" and "perpetuated outmoded stereo-types" of Negroes. As these various comments indicate, much of the existing criticism of the play has been concerned with its stage history rather than with its literary merit and ideational content. A recent edition of *The Green Pastures,* with sensible, religious essays by W. R. Matthews, John Macmurray, and

Henry Self, gives hope that a new interest in the play—a critical interest—is coming into being.

II Critical Status

The tremendous success of the play in the theater, strangely enough, seems to have discouraged serious dramatic criticism about the merits of the play as literature, to a large degree, perhaps, because its "literary merit" was never questioned. Most critics have been content merely to state a verdict. Joseph Wershba, for example, has said that for this play alone Connelly has "assured himself a lasting place in American drama . . . "; and this judgment has been rendered hundreds of times. *The Green Pastures,* which has been republished in at least thirty-three different anthologies in the past thirty-seven years, is the one play by Connelly that has never, except for minor cavils, been criticized for artistic "faults."

During the past twenty-five years, however, it has become the fashion to praise the play for what it was, not for what it is. John Gassner, for example, calls *The Green Pastures,* "a play that is inscribed in the permanent records of the American theatre." His critical discussion of the play, however, is limited to a short statement concerned with the difficulty of classifying it: "*The Green Pastures* is unique; it cannot be placed in any existing classification without some reservations. . . . Is there no discrepancy between the 'Harlem' scene and the spirit of the play? Is the play entirely free from a spirit of condescension toward primitive folk and their notions? Yet one cannot overlook the tremendous fascination the play exerted for years after it opened on Broadway. It seemed the culmination of everything we considered a movement toward folk drama for at least a decade, and it was also the only religious drama anyone succeeded in making tolerable to the American public since Charles Rann Kennedy's old-fashioned morality play, *The Servant in the House.*"

E. Bradlee Watson and Benfield Pressey also defend the play in historical terms: ". . . *The Green Pastures* . . . seems itself both miraculous and inevitable—miraculous because it arose out of such unpredictable comings-together; inevitable because by 1930 the theatre in America was overripe for a great Negro play and a great religious play. . . . Unconsciously . . . America needed *The Green Pastures.*" In judging the play as living dramatic literature, however, they are less certain: although ". . . it remains a monumental attainment in the American theatre," they write, ". . . it is not likely to be often available in revivals. . . . "

The Green Pastures, to be sure, is an expensive play to stage; but the modern reader still finds it an exciting experience, not merely an historical monument. In an interview with Ward Morehouse in 1951, following its last full-scale professional revival, Connelly said of the play: "I'm glad that the critics find it a simple play. I feel that it is offered as an honest inquiry into man's attempt to find dignity and virtue within himself, that it invites introspection and a search for old dignities."

III The Play

The Green Pastures is not a play utterly different from everything that Connelly had done before; *The Deep Tangled Wildwood, The Wisdom Tooth,* and *The Wild Man of Borneo,* for examples, are quite obviously searches for "old dignities." What distinguishes *The Green Pastures* from these earlier plays is its scope. In this play Connelly selected his materials, not from minor aspects of contemporary society, but from the central religious-philosophical myth of Western civilization, the Hebraic-Christian accounts in the Bible; and he then applied some of the implications of that myth to one group of suffering American humanity, the Southern Negro.

The play is divided into two parts: the first, in ten scenes; the second, in eight. The first part opens in a Negro Sunday School in New Orleans, where the kindly preacher, Mr. Deshee, is beginning a study of the Bible for his young charges. Although, seemingly, the selection of the Biblical episodes—life in Heaven before creation, the creation of Adam and Eve, the fall of Cain, and the Noah story—merely follow a chronological account, they have a thematic purpose: they deal with a theory of human reformation. They present, from the Lawd's point of view, a theory of crime and punishment. Man—especially starting with Cain—has sinned; and with the flood, he has been punished. The new world—that is "startin' all over again"—is founded only by the virtuous, the chosen few who survived the flood.

Many of Connelly's earlier plays stopped at this point, the moment of the new start; but quite obviously, in the context of *The Green Pastures,* a good life created by the "remaining virtuous" is too narrow a view of man to succeed. It is not merely that the first part ends with God saying softly, "I only hope it's goin' to work out all right"; it is, also, that Gabriel, while still respectful of the Lawd, has "no enthusiasm" for the success of the project.

In the second part of *The Green Pastures,* the materials are selected from episodes in the Bible from the story of Moses to the fall of Jerusalem; and, upon first observation, the second part seems merely to repeat the theme of the first: man, in spite of God's help, again proves incapable of reform. This time, God does not punish with a flood, but with a renunciation. Quite obviously, the history of man, from the Lawd's point of view, demonstrates that mankind is incapable of being "worthy of de breath I gave you."

Starting with the sixth scene of Part Two, however, *The Green Pastures* moves from a concern with the "reformation" of man to a concern with the "nature" of man. The question is no longer, "How can man be reformed?"; instead, it becomes, "What is man?" In the seventh scene, the Lawd gets a suggestion of an answer to that second question: man is a creature full of weaknesses, but he tries. He has hope in the midst of catastrophe, courage in the midst of despair, and compassion in the midst of suffering. And he learned to be so wise "Through sufferin'," as Hezdrel tells God.

God, when He comes to understand His own creation, learns the lesson: even a God must suffer, must be involved with mankind as man is. *The Green Pastures* ends in the spectacle of Christ on the cross; and the "Voice," man, learns not to behave differently, but to feel beyond himself. The play ends with the extension of human sympathy to a suffering God: "Oh, dat's a terrible burden [involvement with suffering mankind, as well as the cross] for one man to carry!" As Vincent Long comments in his "Introduction" to the play, however we start our association with *The Green Pastures*—with "amusement" or with "indulgent condescension"—"We soon find . . . that we are entering into an experience of real religion."

The "religious truth" of the play is not, however, concerned with a question of theology. It is, rather, concerned with man's relationship to man. If, the play seems to ask, even with a just God, man sins but is yet redeemed because he knows suffering and has learned mercy, how should men treat each other? Specifically, the question raised for an American audience centers around the attitude the fortunate white-American theater-goers should have toward "the least of these, thy brothers."

IV The Use of Sentimentality

Modern Negroes, weary of the "Uncle Tom" picture of the "Good Ol' Darky," may be offended at the opening scene of *The Green Pastures.* Although Mr. Deshee is shown as a good man, he is a kind of "Uncle Tom," a man who *seems* so simple that his goodness appears to be the result of simple-mindedness rather than of virtue. In the first Sunday School scene, for example, he is teaching a class of small Negro children. In his opening speech, he summarizes the first five chapters of Genesis; and the emphasis is entirely upon long life: "Adam lived a hundred an' thirty years an' begat a son in his own likeness . . . Seth. An de' days of Adam after he had begotten Seth were eight hundred years!" The only reference to contemporary life is that "ol' Mrs. Gurney's mammy" is called "ol' Mrs. Methusaleh caize she's so ol'." This summary, with its list of *begats* and *deaths,* Mr. Deshee calls "de meat and substance" of the first five books; and he concludes his lesson with the question, "Now, how you think you gonter like de Bible?"

All questions from the children are answered with a proper respect for conventional morality and a dependence upon the literal truth of the Bible as Mr. Deshee understands it. In the third scene, for example, one boy wants to be certain that Adam and Eve had been married a proper length of time before the birth of Cain. "My mammy say it was a hund'ed years," the boy says. Mr. Deshee admits that it is now difficult to be exact about the number of years, but his answer assures the boy that at least the proper number of months had passed.

This concern with age and with proper behavior seems to suggest a lack of understanding of the "central truths" of the religious story, at least from the view of modern, educated Americans in the 1930's. Mr. Deshee, however, is not ignorant of life. As the spiritual leader of a people who live hungry, die young, and face day-after-day indictments that they are "by nature" immoral, Mr. Deshee's concern with age and conventional behavior is part of an attempt to translate the abstract religion into a practical guide. A people who die young must be impressed by old age.

Connelly avoids making obvious social-protest associations. Mr. Deshee's life among the poor, the hungry, and the shamed—the Negro scene—is never mentioned. Rather a kindly, old preacher and a chorus of innocent children set the stage. No one, whatever his racial opinions, would deny the basic goodness of such people; but the audience's sympathy for this group must also be mixed with some mild, sophisticated contempt. Undoubtedly in such a state, the folk are good; but the suggestion is that "such a state" is, therefore, necessary for them.

The first scene in Heaven, the second scene of Part One, develops the same concept of the good, simple "Darky" and suggests the kind of state necessary for his goodness. This scene does show "adults"—Angels, God, Gabriel; but the notion of their "simple goodness" is strengthened by their childlike responses and by the fact that, in terms of the religious story used, they are naturally good. Connelly, moreover, surrounds them with children, Cherubs. The use of characters who conform to the stereotype of the "good Darky" and who are yet loosely drawn from the Biblical story makes a sentimental appeal to the audience. Showing the "naturally" good, simple Negro in his pursuit of "naturally" good, simple goals reinforces a sentimental view with a religious overtone. The normal audience response, it seems to me, is largely sentimental; but there must also be the slightly uncomfortable feeling that this sentiment has the support of powerful forces.

V The Harlem Evil

In the following scenes—with Cain, with the blues-singing Zeba, with the Children of Noah, with the Children of Israel, and in the "Harlem" scenes that Francis Fergusson and John Gassner did not like—the Lawd and the audience have another view of man, the Negro. To some degree, the desired response is also to a stereotype: the Negro as naturally violent and naturally brutal. The evidence offered is overwhelming. He is a "depraved being" capable of any crime: he kills his brother, he steals, he lies, he betrays. He does, in fact, everything that all the imperfect heroes and villains of the Old Testament did; and he does it all in a fashion that will allow those who view the Negro actors in the play to conclude that what is being shown is a Realistic portrayal of "Negro behavior."

The uneasiness of those who would like *The Green Pastures* to be a propaganda piece for the Negro—both white critics in the early 1930's and Negro leaders in the 1950's and 1960's—is a clear demonstration that Connelly did his work well. The audience is ready to join the Lawd in His weariness with sin. "Dat's about enough," the Lawd announces. "I's stood all I kin from you. I tried to make dis a good earth. I helped Adam, I helped Noah, I helped Moses, an' I helped David. What's de grain dat grew out of de seed? Sin! Nothin' but sin throughout de whole world. . . . So I renounce you. Listen to the words of yo' Lawd God Jehovah,

for dey is de last words yo' ever hear from me. I repent of dese people dat I have made and I will deliver dem no more."

Connelly's insight into the nature of the "Good Outsider," weary with the "transgressions of the folk," seems so fresh that this characterization might have been created in the 1960's, rather than in 1930, as the play relates to the race problem in the United States. White Americans still complain that the Negro drive for "equal rights" is moving too fast, some evidence perhaps of a repentance of past "deliverances."

The accumulative view of these central scenes of the play contrasts with the first three scenes and shows the Negro as violent and depraved. At first, a sentimental solution seems suggested; for, if the Negro could move back to the world of Mr. Deshee's Sunday School and the Heavenly fish fry, there would be no necessity to deal with the world of Cain and Harlem; however, the Lawd, like the audience, must contemplate punishment and desertion as the answer.

VI The Reconciliation

With the Lawd's renunciation scene, however, a pronounced change takes place in the tone of the play and in the response from the audience. Until the last few scenes, the white, sophisticated audience has been watching—with some amusement, some sympathy, and probably some impatience—the history of "the folk" from the point of view of the Lawd. In another place, I have argued that, in spite of the fact that the Lawd was played by a Negro actor, his character, in part, is based on a stereotype of the "Good White Man," as he sees himself in relationship to the folk. There may be some question as to the validity of that argument, but there is little to the assumption that the Lawd in his renunciation speech reflects the varied attitudes of well-meaning, sympathetic, tired outsiders to the problems and errors of the folk.

From the moment of renunciation, however, the Lawd, in dramatic terms, loses his superiority. In the sixth scene of Part Two the Lawd recognizes the righteousness of Hosea, now a resident of Heaven, although Hosea obviously disagrees with the Lawd's renunciation. He becomes the Lawd's superior, and in their conflict—an unspoken *agon*—Hosea overwhelms the Lawd. The Lawd's final speech in this scene shows his capitulation to a superior force. "You know I said I wouldn't come down," the Lawd shouts down to the voice of goodness on earth after Hosea's silence has weakened his resolve. "Why don't he answer me a little? Listen, I'll tell you what I'll do. I ain't goin' to promise you anythin', and I ain't goin' to do nothin' to help you. I'm just feelin' a little low, an' I'm only comin' down to make myself feel a little better, dat's all."

In the last dramatic scene of the play, the Lawd comes in conflict with Hezdrel, one of the characters Connelly created without Biblical authority. If the characters to this point in the play can be divided into "good, simple" and "bad, smartalecky Harlem" Negroes, Hezdrel is something new. He is good, courageous, faithful, but he is also a complicated human being, wiser in the matters of man than the Lawd himself. The Lawd, in fact, finally has to ask Hezdrel for the secret of knowledge—how does one (even God) discover mercy? Hezdrel's answer— "Through suffering"—leaves the Lawd confused, but full of admiration. The Lawd is now an "inferior being" who must be removed from the scene of the heroic action for his own safety. He can be only a supporting character as He leaves the heroic Hezdrel, giving the battle cry of man, "Give 'em eve'ything, Boys."

In these two scenes, the audience's sympathy must shift from the Lawd to Hosea and Hezdrel. They are, in terms of *The Green Pastures,* morally superior. They hold, in terms of their *agons* with the Lawd, the same position that Tiresias holds against Oedipus, Antigone against Creon: they are right. At this point, the audience must become aware that, although the actors are Negroes, the subject is man; and the Lawd's renunciation of "dese people" includes not merely the *folk* in the play, but the folk in the audience.

The identification of the audience with the Lawd has now ceased. The history of the play is no longer a Negro history, but the history of Hebraic-Christian man. If the white outsider continues in his sympathy with the Lawd's decision to withdraw from the Negro world, he must put himself in a world from which God has withdrawn, and he must approve of that withdrawal. The sophisticated audience has been sentenced by its own biases to a God-forsaken world.

The Lawd of *The Green Pastures* concludes that He cannot judge men fairly from without, and the play ends with the sacrifice of Jesus on the cross. Whether this is orthodox Christian doctrine or not is a matter for theologians, but from a dramatic point of view, Connelly's *The Green Pastures* offers a successful pattern for the writer of folk drama. He starts with the biases for and against the folk, and he forces his audience to examine these biases and their assumptions not only about the "folk" but about themselves. Once we are caught up in *The Green Pastures,* it is difficult to refuse Connelly's invitation to introspection.

Source: Paul T. Nolan, "The Green Pastures," in *Marc Connelly,* Twayne Publishers, 1969, pp. 79–91.

SOURCES

Briggs, Jr., Ward W., "Marc Connelly," in *Dictionary of Literary Biography, Vol. 7: Twentieth-Century American Dramatists,* edited by John MacNicholas, Gale Group, 1981, pp. 124–30.

Connelly, Marc, *The Green Pastures: A Fable,* Farrar & Rinehart, 1929, pp. XV–XVI.

———, *Voices Offstage: A Book of Memoirs,* Holt, Rinehart and Winston, 1968, p. 258.

Daniel, Walter C., *"De Lawd": Richard B. Harrison and The Green Pastures,* Greenwood, 1986, pp. 90–4, 99, 105–7.

Nolan, Paul T., *Marc Connelly,* Twayne, 1969, pp. 79–83.

FURTHER READING

Baker-Fletcher, Garth, ed., *Black Religion after the Million Man March: Voices on the Future,* Orbis Books, 1998.
    This book is a collection of articles discussing the role of religious life in African-American politics and thought after the 1995 Million Man March in Washington, D.C.

Bascom, William, *African Folktales in the New World,* Indiana University Press, 1992.
    Bascom's book is a collected discussion of African-American folktales derived from traditional African folktales. It serves as a useful counterpoint to Connelly's representation of African-American interpretations of the Bible in terms of folk narrative.

Bryan III, J., *Merry Gentlemen (and One Lady),* Atheneum, 1987.
    This work is a cultural history of the Algonquin Round Table, an informal affiliation of writers, artists, and intellectuals in New York City with whom Connelly was associated.

Filler, Louis, ed., *American Anxieties: A Collective Portrait of the 1930s,* Transaction, 1993.
    Filler provides a cultural history of the era in which Connelly wrote. The collections are from several historians.

Hurston, Zora Neale, *Dust Tracks on the Road,* Harper-Perennial, 1991.

This book has come to be considered a classic work of African-American folklore in the South, as collected by novelist and anthropologist of the Harlem Renaissance, Zora Neale Hurston. It includes a forward by celebrated African-American poet and novelist Maya Angelou.

Lincoln, C. Eric, and Lawrence H. Mamiya, *The Black Church in the African American Experience,* Duke University Press, 1990.

Lincoln and Mamiya present a history of the role of religion in African-American culture, thought, and politics.

A Life in the Theatre

DAVID MAMET

1977

A Life in the Theatre is one of American playwright David Mamet's early successes. The two-character drama/comedy has hallmarks of Mamet's later work: intense characters; taut, revealing dialogue; and a mentor/teacher relationship. Describing life in the footlights from an actor's point of view, *A Life in the Theatre* focuses on the relationship between two thespians: Robert, an older, experienced performer; and John, a relative newcomer. Though Robert's guidance is welcomed by John at first, as the play progresses Robert falters as an actor and mentor, and John emerges as a mature actor.

Mamet was inspired to write *A Life in the Theatre* by what he had observed backstage as well as by his own experiences in his short, unsuccessful career as an actor. *A Life in the Theatre* made its premiere at the Goodman Theatre in Chicago, Illinois, in February 1977. A slightly different, expanded version of the play debuted in an off-Broadway production in New York City's Theatre de Lys in October 1977.

A Life in the Theatre has been regularly performed around the world since these first productions, and though a few critics vehemently dismissed the play, it has received generally positive review. Many who praise the play share the opinion of Edith Oliver in the *New Yorker*. Writing about the original New York production, Oliver declared, "Mr. Mamet has written—in gentle ridicule; in jokes, broad and tiny; and in comedy, high and

low—a love letter to the theatre. It is quite a feat, and he has pulled it off.''

AUTHOR BIOGRAPHY

David Mamet was born on November 30, 1947, in Chicago, Illinois. He is the son of Bernard Mamet, a labor lawyer, and his wife, Leonore. Mamet's parents had high expectations for Mamet and his younger sister, Lynn. Mamet's father especially emphasized the importance and potency of language. The family spent hours arguing for the sake of argument, and Mamet learned the subtle nuances often found in well-spoken words. This experience had a direct bearing on Mamet's plays, for he is known as a master of subtle dialogue.

After his parents' divorce when he was eleven, Mamet lived with his mother for four years, then moved in with his father. At this time, Mamet got his first taste of theater, working backstage and doing bit parts at Chicago's Hull Theatre. At first, Mamet wanted to be an actor, and to this end he studied the craft in New York City's famous Neighborhood Playhouse with Sanford Meisner. When he was deemed not talented enough to succeed as an actor, Mamet returned to college and began writing. His first full-length play, *Camel,* was his senior thesis and was performed at his school, Goddard College.

After graduation, while Mamet wrote plays, he supported himself with some small acting roles and by teaching acting at Goddard College and Marlboro College in Vermont. During this period, he began writing what became his first hit when it was produced in 1974, *Sexual Perversity in Chicago.* The play won the Joseph Jefferson Award for the best new Chicago play before it moved to off-off-Broadway and off-Broadway productions in New York City. *Time* magazine said it was among the ten best plays of 1976.

Mamet's next play, *American Buffalo,* was regarded as an even bigger smash. Again, it opened in Chicago first, but this time when it moved to New York City, it was staged on Broadway in 1977. Around the same time, Mamet wrote his homage to those actors he observed in his brief acting career, *A Life in the Theatre.*

Several years later, in 1984, Mamet won the Pulitzer Prize for one of his most respected plays, *Glengarry Glenn Ross.* The story revolves around

David Mamet

survival in a dog-eat-dog business environment. Similarly, Mamet's *Speed-the-Plow* (1988) revolves around another cut-throat business world, that of Hollywood and the movie business. Throughout the 1980s and 1990s, Mamet wrote a number of screenplays, many of them adaptations of others' work, and was well-versed in the harsh business of getting movies made.

In 1992, Mamet produced one of his most controversial works, *Oleanna.* This play concerns unfounded allegations of sexual harassment surrounding a male college professor and a young female student. Mamet directed the original Broadway production of this and several other of his plays in the 1990s. He also directed the occasional film. Mamet's reputation is based primarily on his writing, however, and he is considered one of the best American playwrights of the twentieth century.

PLOT SUMMARY

Scene 1

A Life in the Theatre opens backstage after the end of an opening night performance. Two actors talk. They are Robert, an older actor, and John, a relative newcomer to the stage. Robert compliments John on his performance and asks about his plans after the show. John informs Robert that he is going out for dinner. He compliments Robert's performance in one scene, but tells him he was ''brittle'' in another. When Robert questions him on the latter, John backpedals, faulting the actress in the scene. Robert pontificates on being an actor. Robert asks about another scene, and John flatters him. Robert takes the opportunity to expound on his feelings about the scene, implicitly praising himself. John later invites Robert to join him for dinner. As they leave, John notices that Robert still has some makeup on. John fetches a tissue and wipes it off.

Scene 2

In the wardrobe area backstage, John worries about being in Robert's way. Robert soliloquizes a line, to which John is indifferent.

Scene 3

John and Robert are onstage in a play set in the trenches of World War I. John plays a character very upset over the killing of a fellow soldier by the enemy. Robert's character tries to calm him down. John's character decides to charge the enemy. He is shot after running offstage.

Scene 4

Backstage after a curtain call, Robert chides John for his swordplay in the Elizabethan piece they are in. Robert shows him how to do it right, and they practice a couple of times.

Scene 5

Robert pontificates to John on how actors, and others, work on their bodies but not their voices and accents. Offensive sounds are his pet peeve. He tells John about the importance of style and that they, as actors, must continue to grow. Robert admonishes John several times to keep his back straight. When John asks if his back is straight, Robert says no.

Scene 6

At the end of the day backstage, John is on the phone telling someone he cannot go out with him or her because he is obligated to go out with an actor, Robert. Robert appears, telling John that he must have a life outside of theater. John will not tell him who was on the phone.

Scene 7

The pair meet coming in for a morning rehearsal. Robert is more friendly than John.

Scene 8

At the backstage makeup table, John and Robert ready themselves for a performance. Robert believes the show will be special this night. Robert pesters John about a new brush he has. John is terse with him. Robert compliments John on how he takes care of his possessions, then asks him to do a little less during their scene together. John is offended by Robert's implications.

Robert becomes frustrated when the zipper on his fly breaks. John insists on helping him pin it, but has problems completing the task.

Scene 9

John and Robert are in a scene onstage in a lawyer's office. Robert plays the lawyer. John's character, David, enters, informing Robert's character that David's wife is pregnant with the lawyer's child. In the middle of the scene, Robert flubs a line, but corrects himself. The scene ends with Robert's character wondering if he will be harmed by David.

Scene 10

Robert and John are in the wardrobe area. Robert is angry at ''all of them,'' and though John inquires, he never finds out who ''they'' are.

Scene 11

The pair are appearing in a scene together. Robert forgets several words and whole lines. John has to prompt him.

Scene 12

Robert and John change clothes backstage. Robert complains that their costumes should be washed more often. He asks John if he is tired. John says only a bit.

Scene 13

John and Robert are reading a new script. Robert reads along, commenting on the author's intention. John reads his lines, though Robert interrupts him with his musings and directions related to his needs.

Scene 14

Robert and John are eating at the makeup table during a break. Robert inquires about an audition

John had that day. John tells him it went well, which prompts Robert to speak of how a person cannot control what others think of him. He assures John that if the people holding the auditions seemed not to like him, it does not mean he is not a good actor. John tells Robert that he knows this. Robert hopes that John gets the part.

Scene 15

John and Robert are dressing backstage for a performance. Robert is complaining that the play would be better if there were more experimentation.

Scene 16

Robert is onstage doing a scene with a monologue. He flubs his lines.

Scene 17

John and Robert are at the makeup table. When Robert begins musing aloud on the objects at hand, John asks him to be quiet. Robert is offended, telling John that he has breached theater etiquette. Robert says he is only trying to educate the younger generation. John is indifferent, but apologizes. Robert does not accept the apology, and the scene ends at an impasse.

Scene 18

Onstage, Robert and John are performing a lifeboat scene rehearsed in scene 13. Robert forgets some of his words. John has a monologue at the end of the scene in which he tells Robert's character that he does not know what he is talking about.

Scene 19

John and Robert stand in the wings waiting for the cue to go onstage. Robert is talking to himself. John asks Robert about a line of his that he has forgotten. Robert does not know what the line is, though he tries to remember it. His insistence that he will remember it leads to John missing his cue. John panics, but finally goes onstage.

Scene 20

Backstage, John is dressing in street clothes. Robert enters, talking to himself, when he notices and compliments John's new sweater.

Scene 21

John is on hold on the telephone backstage. Robert enters, complaining about everyone taking a piece of his paycheck. Robert wants John to go for a drink. The person John is waiting for comes on the line, and he makes an appointment. Robert leaves to go for a drink on his own.

Scene 22

John and Robert are taking off their makeup after a scene. Robert complains about critics, saying that they praised John's performance too much. John listens politely, but disagrees. Robert calls him a "twit," then uses one of John's towels. John tells him to use his own towels.

Scene 23

On a darkened stage, John rehearses some lines alone. Robert interrupts, informing John that he has been watching. Robert tells John that he has become a good actor. Robert goes on about the theater being part of life before leaving. John starts to rehearse again when he realizes that Robert is still watching him. John calls him out, and sees that Robert is crying. Robert pulls himself together and seems to leave again. John begins again, but Robert is still there.

Scene 24

In a play set in a hospital, John and Robert play doctors performing surgery. John and Robert disagree about what line they are on. John says his line, but Robert shakes his head, then forgets his next speech. Robert insists they are at a different part of the play. John walks offstage, leaving Robert alone. As Robert addresses the audience, the curtain is brought down on him.

Scene 25

Backstage, Robert has cut his left wrist deeply. John wants to take him to the hospital or doctor, but Robert insists that he is fine. Robert will not let John take him home either, but sits and rests for a moment after John leaves.

Scene 26

After a show, Robert and John exchange compliments on their scenes. Robert tells John that his father always wanted him to be an actor. John gets ready to leave. When Robert asks, John says that he is going to a party. Robert talks about life as an actor in the theater. John asks him for a loan. Robert gives him the money, and John exits. Robert addresses the empty house from the stage, thanking him for their attention. John reappears, telling him they are locking up the theater so he has to leave. John goes again, and Robert says good night.

CHARACTERS

John

John is a young actor, relatively new to the theater. At the beginning of *A Life in the Theatre,* he is nervous about performing, so much so that he has not eaten in several days. In scene 1, he looks forward to dinner as his appetite has returned now that opening night is over. In these early stages, John is respectful of Robert's opinions, knowledge, and pontificating about the theater. John compliments him on his performances and invites him to dinner.

John listens to Robert's directions on acting until scene 8, when Robert asks him to do less with his performance. John is insulted by this advice. Thereafter, John replies in terse phrases and monosyllables to Robert's musings and mentions his costar's faltering lines. John himself improves as an actor over the course of *A Life in the Theatre.*

Robert

Robert is an older actor in the theater. From the first scene, he plays mentor to John, reveling in long-winded speeches about aspects of the theater, acting, and life. Robert appreciates John's willingness to listen and the compliments he gives the elder performer. He is sensitive to every aspect of how life in the theater relates to life outside, though it seems for Robert that all of life is a performance.

THEMES

Reality and Fantasy

The lines between reality and fantasy are blurred by certain aspects of *A Life in the Theatre.* For Robert, life is the theater. He plays the role of a professional actor both onstage and off, insisting on indoctrinating John with his accumulated knowledge. Throughout *A Life in the Theatre,* Robert does not draw many definite boundaries between the fantasy world of the theater and the reality of life offstage. Though he tells John in scene 6 that an actor must have a life outside the theater, in scene 5, Robert goes on about how ugly sounds, like voices and accents, bother him on and offstage. The reality of being human breaks into Robert's fantasy life as an actor, however, when he begins to forget his lines onstage. Adding to this reality is John's regular rejection of Robert and his values in the second half of the play. Still, at the end of *A Life in the Theatre,*

Robert speaks his final words onstage to an empty house. At his core, he cannot accept the difference between theater and life.

Friendship, Growth, and Development

At the core of *A Life in the Theatre* is a tension between friendship and growth and development. In scene 1, the older actor Robert takes the younger actor John under his wing, befriending him. At first John welcomes the attention of the mentor, inviting him to dine with him after opening night and complimenting his performance. John takes Robert's cues and advice seriously, though he does keep much of life private. As John grows in confidence and experience as an actor, and Robert continues to treat him with the same, somewhat overbearing attitude, their friendship becomes more professional. Though John becomes frustrated with Robert's never-ending commentary and the decline in his ability to remember lines, he still can feel a friendly sympathy for the elder actor. In scene 8, for example, John insists on fixing the zipper in Robert's fly when it becomes stuck.

Though John is disturbed by the fact that Robert is watching him from the shadows as he rehearses in scene 23, he is concerned when he realizes that Robert is crying. When Robert cuts his wrist—something of a suicide attempt—John tries to take care of him, but Robert will not let him. Though John has probably learned something about the theater through their friendship, he has also developed as a person because of this bond.

Human Condition and the Cycle of Life

Though Robert and John are actors and *A Life in the Theatre* concerns existence on and offstage, the problems and concerns brought up are universal to humankind. Both John and Robert need attention, an audience. They have chosen the theater as their profession, their place in the universe. Humans want the attention of others; Robert and John have made their livelihood by it. Each also acknowledges the other throughout the play, positively as well as negatively, providing a more intimate audience of one. They form a relationship that is not without tension.

Related to the idea of the human condition in *A Life in the Theatre* is the cycle of life. The older teaches the younger, who replaces the older. Robert is the elder actor. He tries to impart his accumulated knowledge and wisdom to John as a mentor/friend. John, as the younger and less experienced actor, willingly accepts Robert's attention and respects his wisdom. But as John grows more confident as an actor, he becomes less interested in Robert's words. Soon, Robert's acting skills decline as John's continue to rise. Robert forgets lines during his scenes and cannot accept John's corrections. John no longer needs him and merely tolerates his mentor. Robert tries to hold on to John by watching from the wings as he rehearses alone in scene 23 and by making a suicide attempt in scene 25. By the end of the play, John pities the old man as he is forced to take his bow and exit the stage.

STYLE

Setting

A Life in the Theatre is a comedic drama set in a nonspecific, though contemporary, time. The action of the play is confined to places within a theater. While the scenes from ''real'' plays are set onstage, Robert and John's relationship develops in the backstage areas. These include the wardrobe area, the dance room, the makeup table, the wings, and other undefined backstage areas. By setting this play only in such places in the theater, Mamet constructs a version of the theater world for the audience. Most theatergoing audiences never see what goes into the making of actors and plays. By limiting the settings to the theater, Mamet gives *A Life in the Theatre* a concentrated authenticity. Yet because a majority of the scenes take place backstage, parallels to everyday life, people, and relationships also can be drawn.

Vignettes, Plotting, and Time

Because *A Life in the Theatre* comprises twenty-six scenes, it is not constructed in the same way as a two- or three-act play. Each scene is a vignette. A few are no more than a handful of lines, while the longest is about twelve and one-half pages. The latter is scene 1, which sets up the play and its tensions. The majority of scenes are only two to three pages. The brevity of the scenes affects their content and the way the plot is drawn. Action is limited. The evolution of Robert and John's relationship—the heart of the play—is constructed through their changing attitudes toward each other. Often this can be found in the nuances of the short scenes. Though it is obvious that over the course of the play a significant amount of time has passed, it is not specifically delineated. Time is measured by

MEDIA ADAPTATIONS

- *A Life in the Theatre* was filmed for television in 1979. Recreating the roles they created off-Broadway, Ellis Rabb plays Robert and Peter Evans plays John. The film was directed by Gerald Gutierrez and Kirk Browning, and produced by Peter Weinburg.

- Another made-for-television version was adapted by Mamet in 1993. It featured Jack Lemmon as Robert and Matthew Broderick as John. Produced by Patricia Wolff and Thomas A. Bliss, directed by Gregory Mosher.

these spoken and sometimes unspoken changes in the characters.

Plays within a Play

The scenes where Robert and John perform scenes from other plays serve several purposes. Mamet parodies several types of plays, providing some humor. Additionally, the playlets show how John and Robert do their job as actors in the theater. Over the course of the play, John becomes a more confident actor, while Robert's decline is highlighted by his flubbed lines. This aspect comes to head in scene 24, the surgery scene. Robert loses his place in the playlet and will not listen to John's cues about where they are. John finally walks offstage in frustration. Thus, the playlets also provide another forum that highlights the development of John and Robert's relationship.

In several cases, the playlets also implicitly reflect on the nature of that relationship as well as the characters themselves. In the first playlet, scene 3, Robert plays the experienced soldier trying to calm the younger, very distraught soldier. John's character charges the enemy from the trenches and is shot. In scene 9, the playlet in the lawyer's office, Robert plays a lawyer while John plays a wronged man. In the previous scene, one set backstage, Robert has insulted John by asking him to do less on stage. Then, in scene 9, John's character confronts

TOPICS FOR FURTHER STUDY

- Choose one of the playlets that John and Robert perform and analyze it. Discuss the style of the playlet and compare it to other, similar plays.

- Compare and contrast the relationship between Robert and John with that between the rival characters William Charles Macready and Edwin Forrest in Richard Nelson's *Two Shakespearean Actors* (1992).

- In what ways could Robert and John have better balanced their mentor-neophyte relationship? Research the psychological aspects of such a relationship.

- There were many backstage plays (a play that takes the audience behind the curtain) and musicals produced in the 1970s, including 1975's *A Chorus Line*. Choose one of these backstage plays and compare it to *A Life in the Theatre*. In your essay, consider the historical context in which such plays were produced. Why were they so popular?

Robert's lawyer character because he has impregnated John's character's wife. There is confrontation brewing: John could beat him up or they could talk about it. Robert also flubs one line, showing his decline as an actor. These playlets underscore much about *A Life in the Theatre*.

HISTORICAL CONTEXT

The 1970s were known as the "me" decade in the United States. Americans were generally passive and self-absorbed. There was much apathy about, if not backlash against, government and social issues (save the burgeoning environmental movement). The federal government was seen as untrustworthy because of the Watergate scandal of the early 1970s, which led to the resignation of President Richard M. Nixon in 1974. Nixon and his senior aides had

abused the powers of their offices for their political gain. Nixon was succeeded by his vice president, Gerald Ford, who could not win the presidency on his own in the 1976 general election. Instead, Jimmy Carter, a Democrat from Georgia, won, taking office with his vice president, Walter Mondale, in early 1977. Like Ford, Carter was seen as a weak president.

The United States was troubled in other ways as well. The country had not fully recovered from the energy crisis of 1973–74. At that time, the nations of OPEC imposed an oil embargo on the United States because of its support of Israel. In 1977, a Department of Energy was created. The end of the Vietnam War still affected Americans. The so-called living room war (so-called because it was televised) did not make the country look good. In 1977, ten thousand Indochinese boat people were admitted into the United States on an emergency basis. The American economy was not strong. Perhaps these problems explain why nostalgia was so popular in television (*Happy Days*) and movies (*American Graffiti*), among other entertainment and artistic genres.

The Theater

Like other aspects of American life, commercial theater struggled in the early 1970s. Fewer real taboos were left after the freewheeling 1960s. Few plays of quality were produced on Broadway, and much money was lost. Fringe theater and off-Broadway were places where dramatic innovation was taking place. Off-Broadway was where many new and developing writers were nurtured, including Mamet, Sam Shepard, and David Rabe. Many of their plays were introspective, trying to make sense of life in a broken society. Mamet was but one playwright encouraged by Joseph Papp and his Public Theater and New York Shakespeare Festival. Papp was a producer who developed the plays of Mamet and other playwrights off-Broadway, before bringing them to Broadway. By the late 1970s, these playwrights and their work were reaching Broadway. Mamet's *American Buffalo* was produced on Broadway in 1977. Broadway was very profitable in 1977, setting new revenue records.

Another reason for Broadway's newfound profitability was musicals like *A Chorus Line*. In the 1970s, there were several behind-the-scenes plays, but the dance musical *A Chorus Line* was arguably the biggest. The story focused on struggling dancers trying to make it. *A Chorus Line* was created in rehearsal based on stories from real dancers, and

COMPARE
&
CONTRAST

- **1977:** Studio 54, the first celebrity disco, opens in New York City. It attracts those luminaries and aspiring celebrities who want to see and be seen.

  Today: Somewhat nostalgic movies about places like Studio 54 and about the people who went there are made. The emptiness of the lifestyle is often highlighted.

- **1977:** *Annie* opens on Broadway, where it runs for 2,377 performances.

  Today: Though it no longer plays on Broadway, *Annie* is still regularly performed in repertory and has been made into a feature film and television movie.

- **1977:** In music, the burgeoning punk movement challenges the dominant rock bands, dismissing them as dinosaurs.

  Today: Many musical styles, like punk and classic rock, exist side by side.

- **1977:** There is general distrust of the American government because of the recent Watergate scandal involving President Richard M. Nixon.

  Today: There is a sense of distrust of the American government because of the Monica Lewinsky scandal involving President Bill Clinton.

---

opened in 1975. The dance musical won a Pulitzer Prize in 1976 and played on Broadway for more than a decade. The biggest musical in 1977 was another long-running hit, *Annie*. At the end of the 1970s, theater was on an upswing both creatively and financially because of these successes.

CRITICAL OVERVIEW

From the play's first productions in Chicago and New York City, most critics either found much to praise in *A Life in the Theatre* or dismissed it entirely. Mel Gussow of the *New York Times* wrote of the Chicago production, "It is slight, but it does not lack consequence. It has bite and it also has a heart." His opinion of the play improved when *A Life in the Theatre* was produced off-Broadway. He wrote, "Though the work has serious undertones, it is, first of all, a comedy—and Mr. Mamet's language glistens. His writing is a cross between the elegant and the vernacular, an ironic combination that is uniquely his own." Many critics who liked *A Life in the Theatre* praised the content of the playlets. T. E. Kalem of *Time* wrote, "With marvelous

mimicry, Mamet conjures up parodistic echoes of past play-writing titans together with melodramatic fustian [pompous] talk."

John Simon of *The Hudson Review* complimented certain aspects of *A Life in the Theatre* but wrote

> [U]ltimately, two problems weigh down *A Life in the Theatre*. One is that these are all anecdotes, quips, rivalries that can be hung on any theatrical stick figures, which is, in fact, what John and Robert are. Under the all too typical mockery, there are no human beings.

The *New York Times'* Walter Kerr did not like the play at all, sharing Simon's concerns. He argued,

> Mr. Mamet has not listened well himself; the loosely linked entertainment, intended as a charm bracelet, is skimpy, imprecise, too easy, and more than a little bit borrowed. Nonetheless, expectation continues to sit in the air. Mr. Mamet, attacking his trade as often and as assiduously as he does, will come along."

Harold Clurman of *The Nation* was one critic who could find no redeeming value in *A Life in the Theatre*. In addition to deriding the playlets as unreal, Clurman wrote, "What we see is not a life in the theatre (not even a reasonable caricature of it) but a cliché that exists for the most part in the minds of those 'out front' who know the theatre chiefly through anecdotal hearsay.''

After its initial runs, *A Life in the Theatre* was regularly produced in the United States and abroad. By the late 1980s and early 1990s, Mamet's reputation as a playwright had skyrocketed, with the success of *Glengarry Glen Ross* (1982) and other plays. Because *A Life in the Theatre* was written toward the beginning of Mamet's career, it was sometimes seen by later critics as a throwaway. Others saw it as a early indication of what was to come, especially in terms of his use of language. Of a 1989 production in London, Douglas Kennedy of *New Statesman & Society* wrote, ''It has its moments; especially in its spot-on observations of backstage paranoia—but it's ultimately too lightweight to be anything more than a series of interlinking sketches which don't amount to much.'' In contrast, Michael Billington of the *Manchester Guardian Weekly* declared, ''Mamet simultaneously satirises the fragility of theatre and celebrates its almost masonic rituals. But what motors the play (even in an early piece like this) is the dazzling economy of language.''

The way *A Life in the Theatre* was perceived by critics continued to evolve in the United States as well. Of a 1990 New York production, Alvin Klein of the *New York Times* wrote, ''[I]t now seems naïve to perceive the play as pure homage, since it isn't a particularly effective one. And many colored interpretations could be tantalizing in the view of Mr. Mamet's considerable later work.'' Yet Klein's colleague, Wilborn Hampton of the *New York Times,* believed the play retained its power. Writing about a 1992 production by the Jewish Repertory Company, Wilborn argued

> A Life in the Theatre stands up extremely well. It is infused with the playwright's obvious affection for the theater and the people who populate it. And like Mr. Mamet's other works, the play has hidden depths of real poignancy.

CRITICISM

Annette Petrusso

Petrusso is a freelance writer and editor living in Austin, Texas. In this essay, Petrusso interprets the relationship between John and Robert in Mamet's play and argues that, despite most critics' interpre-

tations, Robert depends on John from the beginning of the play.

Many critics who have written about David Mamet's *A Life in the Theatre* have maintained that Robert and John have a mentor-protégé relationship. Early on, they believe, Robert dominates the relationship, though the roles reverse as the play progresses. By the end, critics hold, John has matured and become the dominant person in the relationship. Catharine Hughes of *America* is one such critic. Writing about the original off-Broadway production in 1977, Hughes claims

> At first, the older Robert is the obvious mentor, and John merely the subservient apprentice. But John begins to enjoy some success, and there is a considerable role reversal, which finds the veteran becoming increasingly insecure and dependent.

However, a closer analysis of the play shows that it is John who controls the relationship from the beginning. Robert needs someone to listen to him, to validate his existence as an actor and a person. This is a role that John willingly fills, at least at first. While John gets something out of this at the very beginning, Robert becomes a pitiful annoyance midway through *A Life in the Theatre*. As Hughes and others have argued, by the end, Robert depends fully on John as a lifeline. Only John interacts with the outside world, in contrast with Robert, who is out of touch with it. Robert is truly the needy one, the protégé when it comes to real life.

In scene 1, the longest scene of *A Life in the Theatre,* the nature of John and Robert's relationship is established. From the first lines, Robert seeks out John, rather than vice versa. Robert delivers the first line of the play: ''Goodnight, John.'' John responds ''Goodnight,'' but does not use Robert's name. Robert wants to start the conversation, and John plays along. Robert proceeds to compliment a scene that John has apparently been in, the bedroom scene. John thanks him and leaves it at that. In turn, John does not compliment him, but rather the audience that saw their performance that evening. This slight shows that John does not feel the need to garner Robert's favor, but Robert has an interest in John's.

A bit later in the conversation, John does compliment Robert on his courtroom scene. Robert cannot take the accolade at face value, but insecurely dismisses it by saying, ''I felt it was off tonight.'' When John offers a bit of criticism as a follow-up, opining that the doctor scene was "brittle," Robert questions him in detail about what he means. Robert asks if it was really he who was at fault, or his female co-star. John backpedals from his obvious criticism of Robert, first changing what he said, then placing the blame on Robert's female co-star.

While these exchanges could be interpreted as John's establishing himself as Robert's lesser in the mentor-student relationship, they also show that John is learning how to feed Robert's ego. Throughout the rest of scene 1, John provides a forum for Robert to express his interpretation of his performance. John compliments Robert to satisfy the elder man's ego, giving John control of the relationship. John does not depend on Robert's compliments the way Robert depends on John's ear.

Another, more subtle aspect of John and Robert's relationship is established in scene 1. At one point in the scene, Robert inquires about John's plans for the evening. John tells him that he is going out to eat. The conversation drifts away from this topic, but, toward the end of the scene, Robert brings up the subject again. John is more specific about what he wants to eat. Robert again plays coy, telling John that he cannot eat at night because he has a weight problem. This elicits another compliment from John, who also asks about Robert's plans. Robert reveals that he will be going home to read or take a walk. It is John who goes out into the world, while Robert retreats to his private, insular domain. Because of the way Robert handles John's polite inquiries ("Why'd you ask?"), John is nearly coerced into asking Robert to join him. Without John, Robert would not be going into social situations.

The nature of the relationship between John and Robert is underscored by the final incident in the first scene. John notices that Robert has some makeup remaining behind his ear. It is John who gets the tissue, spits on it, and cleans the makeup off. Robert needs John more than John needs Robert.

The patterns of dependency established in scene 1 continue throughout the play. As John becomes less tolerant of Robert's ranting and declining acting skills, Robert wants John's attention even more. He gets desperate by the end, when he feels that John does not really care anymore. These changes are seen when John is somehow part of the world outside of the theater.

The next scene in which John is involved in the outside world is scene 6. In scenes 2 through 5, John

Samuel West and Denholm Elliott in a scene from a theatrical production of A Life in the Theatre.

listens and responds to Robert's theatrical musings with open-mindedness. In scene 6, a relatively short scene, Robert catches John on the phone. John is turning down a chance to go out with a close friend of unstated gender to go out with Robert. John sounds like he would rather be going out with this friend than Robert. When Robert maintains, "We all must have an outside life, John. This is an essential," it is an ironic statement. Robert does not practice what he preaches. When he asks John with whom he was speaking, John will only say, "A friend." John keeps much of his life and many of his feelings to himself.

After this exchange, John is a little less tolerant of Robert. The six lines of scene 7 are dominated by Robert, and John is merely polite. In scene 8, Robert tries to be the dominant person in the relationship, asking John to "do less" in their scene together. John does not take such an obvious criticism lightly. Robert then creates another situation in which he needs John to take care of him. He notices that the zipper on his trousers is broken. Instead of allowing John to bring in an outside person ("the woman," probably a wardrobe mistress), Robert allows John to fix it with a safety pin for him. Though John does

WHAT DO I READ NEXT?

- *Oleanna*, a play by Mamet first performed in 1992, focuses on a topsy-turvy mentoring relationship between a female student and her professor.

- *Six Characters in Search of an Author*, a play by Luigi Pirandello, written in 1921, is the story of a group of actors rehearsing a play, which is interrupted by six created characters.

- *Waiting for Lefty* is a play by Clifford Odets, written in 1935. Like *A Life in the Theatre*, the play is constructed of short scenes that contain realistic action.

- *Harlequinade* is a play by Terence Rattigan, published in 1948. The play focuses on a regional acting troupe.

- *It's Only a Play* is a comedic play by Terrence McNally, written in 1985. The plot focuses on people who have worked on a theatrical production, as well as critics and other hangers-on, as they await public reaction to their work.

---

it in part because of guilt, he also takes the opportunity to comment on Robert's weight, which he believes might be increasing. Robert's attempt to show real dominance—controlling how John acts on stage—totally backfires.

In scene 14, John has again interacted with someone other than Robert. He has recently auditioned for another role, and Robert asks him about it while they eat a meal between shows. By this point, Robert's boorishness has increased. He complains more about the powers that be, and he begins to forget lines and flub his acting. John goes along with Robert's demeanor to a certain point, but says nothing to encourage Robert to speak to him. John continues this attitude in scene 14, though he reveals nothing about what he thinks or feels about the audition or what Robert says. It is also worth noting that none of Robert's auditions is discussed or depicted to further emphasize that John is the only one who functions outside of the theater.

It is seven more scenes before John again connects to the outside world. He finally tells Robert to ''shut up'' in scene 17, a pivotal scene that shows John finally directly challenging Robert's attitude. Robert tries to leverage his position by reminding John, ''The Theatre's a closed society,'' among other things, but John continues to hold his own. Late in the scene, John apologizes for his transgression, if only because it might shut Robert

up about the rules of the theater. In scene 19, John's distrust of Robert is confirmed when the elder actor is unhelpful about a forgotten line and makes John miss his cue.

When John next interacts with an outside person, he cares little for Robert's feelings. In scene 21, as in scene 6, John is on the telephone, waiting for the person on the other end, Miss Bonnie Ernstein, to get back to him. It is obviously an important call related to his career. As John listens and waits for her, Robert continues to rant about the theater. Robert tries to get John to end his call and go out with him; John refuses. The caller gets on the line, and John talks to her, much to Robert's displeasure. Robert finally leaves to drink on his own as John makes an appointment with Miss Ernstein. Again, John has a life—human interaction outside the theater—while Robert does not.

In the next few scenes, Robert tries to hold onto his friendship with John but to no avail. Robert cannot make John listen any longer. John does not tolerate Robert's criticism of John's positive reviews in scene 22, or appreciate Robert's furtive watching of John's solo rehearsal in scene 23. In the last two scenes of *A Life in the Theatre,* John has both potential and real non-theater interactions. In scene 25, Robert has cut his wrist in what could be seen as a suicide attempt. John tries to get him to go to a hospital or doctor, and even offers to go home with him or take him home, but Robert refuses all help. Robert revels in John's attention, which is all he seems to want or need.

The last scene of *A Life in the Theatre* shows how little John and Robert's relationship has changed. John is still clearly in the driver's seat. Robert still compliments John in hopes of holding onto him, but John will only allow him a few moments. When Robert asks, John tells him that he is going to a party. He does make inquiries about Robert's plans, but when Robert says that he is hungry, John does not offer to go for a meal with him, as he did in the beginning. Instead John uses Robert's need for him for his own gain. He allows Robert to light his cigarette and goes on to borrow twenty dollars from him. Before this point, John has not taken anything from Robert. But because he is so in control of the relationship at this point, John can do as he pleases. Though Robert gets the last line in the play, ''Goodnight'' to an empty theater, it is John who tells him he must leave so they can lock up. As in scene 1 of *A Life in the Theatre,* John holds the keys to Robert's personal and professional happiness.

Source: Annette Petrusso, in an essay for *Drama for Students,* Gale Group, 2001.

Anne Dean

In the following essay on David Mamet's A Life in the Theatre, *author Anne Dean reviews the drama with special regard to the two central characters, and argues that, ultimately, the drama may be written as much about the theatre life as life itself.*

Without exception, all of Mamet's characters are storytellers or performers—or both. They are somewhat like O'Neill's gallery of misfits in *The Iceman Cometh*; rather than face the realities of an uncertain, often threatening world, they rely upon illusion and the performance of a comforting role to get by. Actors all, they prefer the relative security and coherence of their fictional ''pipe dreams'' to the incompleteness and ambiguousness of cold experience.

In Mamet's world, to act is also to exist, to make a mark in space. His characters take on their myriad roles to create meaning in their lives, and to give themselves importance and substance. That these roles are sometimes as unsatisfactory as the reality they are designed to conceal is one of the recurring ironies of his work. In *A Life in the Theatre,* Mamet's characters are literally actors, professional players who perform in public as a

> ROBERT NEEDS SOMEONE TO LISTEN TO HIM, TO VALIDATE HIS EXISTENCE AS AN ACTOR AND A PERSON. THIS IS A ROLE THAT JOHN WILLINGLY FILLS, AT LEAST AT FIRST.''

career. However, Robert and John do not restrict their acting abilities to the stage—they are actors both in and out of the theatre. They put on the costumes and makeup for the drama they must perform as actors, but Mamet makes it very clear that the roles they perform onstage are but a small part of their mimetic gifts. They never stop acting; from the moment they awake to the moment they go to sleep, Robert and John are each performing a role for the benefit of the other. They strive to reinforce their own self-images as they quibble, bicker, and generally try to upstage one another. Their ''real-life'' performances become hopelessly confused and merge with the characters they represent.

When Mel Gussow first saw the play, he described it as ''a comedy about the artifice of acting'' but when, some months later, he saw a revival, he felt that ''it was about the artifice of living.'' The very title of the work gives a clue to Mamet's intentions: it is at once a parody of Stanislavski's autobiography, *My Life in Art* and an indication of the analogy he intends to make between life and drama. It also points to the pastiche he will use affectionately throughout the play and subtly suggests the serious elements that both offset and contribute to its humor.

A Life in the Theatre is primarily a comedy, but one that is not without pathos. Mamet describes the work as a ''comedy about actors'' but goes on to say that

> as such it must be, and is, slightly sad. It is, I think, the essential and by no means unfortunate nature of the theater that it is always dying: and the great strength and beauty of actors is their bravery and generosity in this least stable of environments. They are generous and brave not through constraint of circumstances, but by choice. They give their time in training, in rehearsal, in constant thought about their instrument and their art and the characters which they portray.

IN THE IMAGE OF THE
SOLITARY ACTOR SPEAKING OUT
INTO AN EMPTY SPACE, HE CONVEYS
NOT MERELY THE EGOISTIC NEED
FOR POSTURING CENTER-STAGE BY
AN AFFECTED NARCISSIST, BUT THE
FUTILITY AND DESPERATION OF
MAN'S UNCERTAINTY OF HIS PLACE
IN THE UNIVERSE."

In an essay about the play, Mamet quotes Camus as saying that the actor's task "is a prime example of the Sisyphean nature of life." Even as that metaphorical rock begins to roll backward, the actor doggedly continues with the struggle. Further he notes how "a life in the theater need not be an analogue to 'life.' It *is* life." For example, Robert is terrified of losing his touch, of growing old and becoming obsolete in the modern world, hence his insistence upon the necessity for actors to grow and accept change—although change is, in fact, the last thing he can accept. At the beginning of the play, John is full of the insecurities of youth: he is naïve, eager to please, and most reverential of his older colleague. As the work progresses, however, his reverence turns to contempt and irritation as he comes to believe—perhaps erroneously—in his own star quality.

Mamet recalls Sanford Meisner humorously remembering a certain kind of actor, whom it is wise to avoid: "When you go into the professional world, at a stock theatre somewhere, backstage, you will meet an older actor—someone who has been around a while. . . . Ignore this man." Freddie Jones, who played Robert in the 1979 Open Space production agrees that this character can be exasperating, but also points out that he fulfills an important function in the work: "The play is an allegory about death and rebirth—Robert is on the wane and the young actor is on the way up."

Evanescence is a fundamental concern in *A Life in the Theatre;* an actor's life is, of necessity, evanescent; there is nothing fixed about a stage performance. At the end of the evening, the player's exploits live on only in the imagination of the audience. As a result, Mamet believes that "this is why theatrical still photographs are many times stiff and uninteresting—the player in them is not *acting* . . . but *posing—indicating feelings.*"

Actors constantly tell each other stories because "the only real history of the ephemeral art is an oral history; everything fades very quickly, and the only surety is the word of someone who was there, who *talked* to someone who was there, who vouches for the fact that someone told him she had spoken to a woman who knew someone who was there. It all goes very quickly, too." As Mamet notes, Robert relies upon ephemera and nostalgia to capture important memories, recall past glories, and reflect upon his career. In spite of his assertions that he is "modern" in outlook, Robert's speech is florid, hyperbolic—sometimes positively Victorian in nature. In an ecstasy of theatrical self-indulgence, he speaks of

> A life spent in the theatre. . . . Backstage. . . . The bars, the House, the drafty halls. The pencilled scripts . . . Stories. Ah, the stories that you hear. (scene 26)

This is not the speech of everyday conversation: it is studied, pretentious, and melodramatic. Robert is not acting a part here, but merely making random observations about his experience of theatrical life. It is clear that the often overripe diction of certain melodramas has influenced him to the extent that even the most ordinary discourse is imbued with theatricality and exaggeration. Thus, Robert clings to the past because it comforts him to do so. Old-fashioned diction lends him a specious sense of security as he battles to fend off fears of impending obsolescence—in and out of the theatre.

The main metaphor of the play is, as the title suggests, that all life is a kind of theatre. Here, as elsewhere in his drama, Mamet seems to be saying that the kind of life his characters are forced to endure is a second-hand affair, full of clichés and desperate pretensions. Not only this, but their metaphysical position is unclear. In *A Life in the Theatre,* perhaps more obviously than in his other works, Mamet depicts the absurdity of the human condition. In the image of the solitary actor speaking out into an empty space, he conveys not merely the egoistic need for posturing center-stage by an affected narcissist, but the futility and desperation of man's uncertainty of his place in the universe. The potency of the image is clearly intended to extend far beyond the theatre into a question concerning the very existence of God. In *Rosencrantz and Guildenstern are Dead,* Tom Stoppard touches upon a similar theme. The Player cries out in alarm that his one purpose in life as an actor has been seriously undermined—he suddenly realizes that he is performing without an audience:

> You don't understand the humiliation of it—to be tricked out of the single assumption which makes our existence viable—that somebody is *watching*.

Similarly, in Arthur Miller's *The Archbishop's Ceiling*, the characters' uncertainty as to whether the seraphically decorated ceiling is bugged or not is surely intended to carry resonances beyond their immediate situation. They conduct their lives as though unseen eyes are indeed watching, but neither they nor the audience are ever able to verify this fact.

The language used by Mamet to convey the ambiguities of life both in front of and away from the footlights seems once again to be effortless and completely authentic. It is, of course, far from effortless but as carefully wrought and constructed as that found in any of his plays. Nothing is included without a reason, every word forwards the plot or comments upon a previous action or emotion. It is true that the text resembles a number of conversations that have been faithfully captured and rendered verbatim. Mamet does indeed include all the ellipses and idiosyncrasies of ordinary conversation but, as John Ditsky has noted, although the dialogue may *appear* banal or merely naturalistic, it is "a deliberately bland language [that] is used to mask action of only apparent simplicity." Mamet allows us to cut through the excesses of Robert's hyperbole and see beneath the brevity of much of John's dialogue by his careful manipulation of every word they utter. He provides a fascinating glimpse into the personalities of men who do all they can to hide their true feelings. Emotions may often run riot in this play, but it would be difficult without Mamet's linguistic virtuosity to ascertain those that are genuine and those that constitute yet another aspect of an unceasing performance. Patrick Ryecart, who played John in the Open Space production considers that

> what Mamet achieves with so little is . . . quite incredible. With so few words, he can tell us all we need to know about Robert and John. He achieves amazing economy. He must write a great deal in the beginning and then set about bringing it right down, paring and paring, getting the words down to the narrative bone. The text of *A Life in the Theatre* is not only supremely funny, but also brilliant in its conciseness.

A Life in the Theatre is a kind of love letter to everything Mamet holds dear about the stage and its performers. The lines of the text are imbued with a sweetness and affection that are not wholly negated by the often critical stance adopted by the play-

wright. Like Chekhov, Mamet has the ability to like and even admire his characters at the same time as exposing their weaknesses and faults. Mamet's own summary of the play is that it is "an attempt to look with love at an institution we all love, The Theater, and at the only component of that institution (about whom our feelings are less simple), the men and women of the theater—the world's heartiest mayflies, whom we elect and appoint to live out our dreams upon the stage."

The work was first staged in 1975 at the Goodman Theatre, Chicago and was then produced in 1977 at the off-Broadway Theatre-de-Lys in New York City. Since then, it has enjoyed a number of revivals, the most recent of which was at the Open Space Theatre, London in 1979. The play has been described by Michael Coveney as being "rather like Terence Rattigan's *Harlequinade*, with a nod in the direction of Molnar [*Play at the Castle*] and Pirandello [*Six Characters in Search of an Author*]." Although Mamet has expressed his admiration for Rattigan's work, and there is certainly more than a hint of Molnar's verbal trickery in the play, the presiding genius of *A Life in the Theatre* is undoubtedly Luigi Pirandello. In both his dramas and his fiction, Pirandello, like Mamet, creates works that explore the many faces of reality. He examines the relationships between actor and character, self and persona, and face and mask, and was a precursor of the work of writers such as Anouilh (*Dear Antoine*), Giraudoux (*Intermezzo*), Genet (*The Balcony* and *The Maids*), and Stoppard (*Rosencrantz and Guildenstern are Dead*), all of which explore the possibilities inherent in such a concept. Pirandello wrote:

> Your reality is a mere transitory and fleeting illusion, taking this form today and that tomorrow, according to the conditions, according to your will, your sentiments, which in turn are controlled by an intellect that shows them to you today in one manner and tomorrow . . . who knows how? Illusions of reality, represented in this fatuous comedy of life that never ends, nor can ever end.

In *Six Characters in Search of an Author*, a company of actors rehearses a play, which is itself an illusion of reality. As the rehearsals progress, six created characters—other aspects of illusion—enter and interrupt the proceedings. Raymond Williams describes how "the resulting contrast between these various stages in the process of dramatic illusion, and the relation of the process to its context of reality, is the material of Pirandello's play." Michael Billington notes how Mamet demonstrates that "the theatre [is] a place that both imitates life and devours it. . . . where . . . actors begin to feel trapped inside their stage roles. . . . one gets so occupied with representing life one ceases to notice it passing one by.''

Certainly Robert's life has been ''spent'' in the theatre in every sense of the word. He explains to John how his life as an actor cannot be separated from that which he lives when not onstage—the time spent somehow merging and becoming one:

> *Robert:* . . . the theatre is of course, a *part* of life . . . I'm saying, as in a grocery store that you cannot separate the *time* one spends . . . that is it's all part of one's *life*. (*Pause.*) In addition to the fact that what's happening on *stage* is life . . . (scene 23)

Robert has become so much a creature of the theatre that his own identity is unclear. Robert, the man, puts on the mask of Robert, the actor; that Robert is himself a character played by a real actor merely adds to the metadramatic ironies. Where does reality end and fantasy begin? A mock-prayer spoken by Guildenstern in Stoppard's play accurately sums up the fantasy life into which it is all too easy for actors to retreat when he intones ''Give us this day our daily mask.''

In *A Life in the Theatre,* Mamet constantly blurs the boundaries between life and art, and the work has been described by Mel Gussow as ''a triple Pirandello.'' He observes how ''the actors play to [an] imaginary audience, while we, behind the scenes, see and hear the artifice—the asides, whispers and blunders.'' The real theatre audience watches two actors playing another two actors, who in turn perform to an unseen audience apparently located at the opposite end of the stage. We see Robert and John perform to their audience with their backs toward us, whereas when Mamet's play proper is in progress, they play facing outward into the stalls. This is the way in which the first American production was staged, and Mamet has called this staging ''a beautiful solution.'' He goes on to explain how it operates in practice:

> . . . Gregory Mosher and Michael Merritt, the play's first director and designer, respectively. . . . decided that it might be provocative if, a *second* curtain were installed—this one on the *upstage* portion of the stage. It is behind this curtain that the audience for the ''plays'' in which John and Robert play sits. This curtain is opened when John and Robert are onstage, which is to say, playing in a ''play.'' Thus we see the actors' backs during the *onstage* scenes, and we get a full-face view of them during their moments *backstage*.

The theatre audience therefore listens to the characters' backstage gossip, witnesses the ambigu-ity between the roles they inhabit onstage and their real selves, follows the inexorable shifts in power, and learns to detect the reality behind what looks artificial and the speciousness of what is presented as truth. Patrick Ryecart speaks about the metadrama-tic ironies within the work:

> The kind of play which constantly reminds the audi-ence that it *is* indeed a play can become very tedious and rather patronizing. However, Mamet is very good with this in *A Life in the Theatre.* In our production, we had a mirror at the back of the set which enclosed the audience even more within the piece, making them really feel a part of it . . . they were thus brought right into the action in a very unselfconscious way. Not only this, but Mamet brings them into the action in another, brilliant way: on the first page of the text you have a direct reference to them. John says, ''They were very bright'' and goes on to flatter them further. They were ''an intelligent house,'' he says, ''atten-tive,'' and so on. Mamet includes at least five in-stances of direct audience flattery within the first few moments of the play!

The playwright therefore incorporates the out-side world into the work, fusing theatre and reality in a memorable dramatic form. Robert's benedic-tion at the conclusion of the play, addressed to a supposedly absent audience but in fact spoken to the real stalls, similarly identifies a gesture of incorpo-ration. Robert stands alone center-stage as he deliv-ers his farewell speech:

> *Robert:* . . . The lights dim. Each to his own home. Goodnight. Goodnight. Goodnight. (scene 26)

Much of the humor in the play derives from Robert's pompous efforts to link life and drama. Whereas Mamet is in no doubt whatever that direct connections do exist, he invests Robert's linguistic forays on this topic with an undercutting irony and wit. Robert has a certain idea of himself as a consummate professional, what has been called ''a flamboyant actor of the old school,'' an ''old Wolfitian barnstormer,'' well as ''an ageing, histri-onic bombast.'' Patrick Ryecart comments upon Robert's self-importance and hilarious egotism, and marvels ''at his ability to be such a huge fish in such a tiny, insignificant building . . . such as the third-rate rep theatre in which he obviously works.'' Because of Robert's many years in the theatre, he feels perfectly justified to act as John's mentor and guide, endlessly pointing out the ambiguities of and the connections between life and art. He strives to maintain his sense of superiority and worldliness by prattling on incessantly about the importance of the theatre. He grandly avers:

> *Robert:* Our history goes back as far as Man's. Our aspirations in the Theatre are much the *same* as man's.

(*Pause*) Don't you think? . . . We are explorers of the *soul.*

and later

> *Robert:* About the theatre, and this is a wondrous thing about the theatre, and John, one of the ways in which it's most like life. . . . in the *theatre,* as in life— and the theatre is . . . a *part* of life. . . . of one's *life.* . . . what's happening on *stage* is life . . . of a sort . . . I mean, it's part of your *life.* (scene 23)

The way in which Robert emphatically underscores the words "theatre," "stage," and "life" suggests the urgency he feels in communicating some of what he believes to be his profound insight. Mamet breaks up his sentences, making him begin again and again without finishing and inserting phrases such as "of course," "of a sort," and "I mean." All this serves to undercut the portentousness—and pretentiousness—of the tone. Robert believes he has a truly important task to perform; however, he is constantly shown to be full of self-delusion and evasion and his hyperbolic remarks are therefore somewhat diminished in the light of our knowledge of his true state of mind. He struggles to find meaning in banality because to admit the frailty of his position as a third-rate actor struggling to make a living on the very fringe of the profession would be to invite terror and despair. Tennessee Williams once wrote that "fear and evasion are the two little beasts that chase each other's tails in the revolving wire cage of our nervous world. They distract us from feeling too much about things." Fear and evasion are certainly present behind Robert's false bluster and phony air of confidence. So long as he can keep on talking, inventing, and pontificating, he can convince himself—and, hopefully, others—of his importance as an actor.

Robert has become the kind of performer who gives his all to plays that do not warrant such devotion; nagging doubts about his worth force him to struggle to find depth where none exists and to give performances of almost Shakespearian profundity in scenes that are little more than badly-scripted soap operas. Certainly, none of the scenes we witness bear any scrutiny whatsoever: they are laughable because of their in-built pretentiousness. Watching Robert and John flinging themselves wholeheartedly into such poorly-crafted episodes is a source of much humor and reminds the audience that the two men are very far from the center of American theatrical excellence. Indeed, they spend their time playing to half-hearted provincial audiences who are probably among the "bloody boors,"

"bloody s—ts," and "boring lunatics" (scene 10) whom Robert decries in a fit of rage.

Although both players seem to be dedicated to the work they are given to perform, it is Robert who works doggedly to invest their dreadful scripts with some sort of artistic credibility and, amazingly, finds it! As he and John discuss the "Lifeboat" scene, Robert waxes lyrical about the script's 'profundity':

> *Robert;* . . . I'm just thinking. "Salt. Saltwater." Eh? The thought. He lets you see the thought there. . . . Salt! Sweat. His life flows out. . . . Then *saltwater!* Eh? . . . "Kid, we haven't got a chance in hell.". . . . "We're never getting out of this alive." (*Pause.*) Eh? He sets it on the sea, we are marooned, he tells us that the sea is life, and that we're never getting out of it alive. (*Pause.*) . . . . The man could write . . . . Alright. Alright. (scene 13)

Mamet invests a scene like this with just enough evidence of the sheer tawdriness of the material Robert and John are given, and then goes on to show the older actor in ecstasy at the quality of the text. All his pretensions fritter away before us while he remains gloriously unaware of the absurdity of his position. The heavy significance of his words act as a hilarious correlative to the tackiness of the script. He sounds like a particularly anxious—although naïve—undergraduate faced with his first essay in literary criticism—his frequent use of "Eh?" acts as an indication of a need for approbation and a shared opinion. Mamet ends the discussion of this particular slice of dialogue with Robert's assertion that "the man could write. . . . Alright. Alright." The repetition suggests a mind mulling over what it considers to be first-class literature, pondering on the brilliance of one who could garner so much meaning, so much *life* into a metaphor about the sea. Robert's previous experience as an actor has apparently taught him little about quality writing; it is quite absurd that he should admire that which is so blatantly hackneyed and risible.

Elsewhere, Robert talks about the trite legal drama in which he and John are about to perform. John asks him how he is feeling as they prepare to go onstage:

> *John:* . . . How do you feel this evening?
>
> *Robert:* Tight. I feel a little tight. It's going to be a vibrant show tonight. I feel coiled up.
>
> *John:* Mmm.
>
> *Robert:* But I don't feel tense. . . . Never feel tense. I almost never feel tense on stage. I feel ready to act. (scene 8)

The repetition of the words "tight" and "tense" indicate the extent of Robert's nervousness, despite his denials. The way he almost spits out his response to John's initial query suggests the reaction of one who is not merely "coiled up" but rather pitched on the edge of nervous collapse. The alliterative sound of the repeated *t* adds to the tension and demonstrates all too clearly Robert's deep-rooted anxiety. That he should refer to the show as "vibrant" and declaim in the manner of an Olivier or a Gielgud that he is "ready to act" is quickly shown to be an absurd pretension given the vacuity of the scene that follows in which stage props refuse to work properly, cues are missed, and both actors go completely to pieces with a script that would shame a troupe of amateur players.

Robert may elevate the theatre into a kind of holy shrine for the worship of moral values and all that is laudable and pure, but he is all too capable of indulging in spiteful and cruel denigrations of his fellow performers. Life in the theatre and life outside have merged for Robert and become hopelessly confused. When he speaks of an actress whom he despises for her unnecessary "mugging" and "mincing," he mixes up moral standards and theatrical technique. He avers that the woman has "No soul . . . no humanism. . . . No fellow-feeling. . . . No formal training. . . . No sense of right and wrong" (scene 1). Thus "soul" and "formal training" are inextricably linked in Robert's mind. What the actress *is* probably guilty of is daring to upstage him and what we are witnessing is little more than petulant jealousy.

In a mistaken effort to side with Robert against the woman, John comments that she relies on her looks to get by:

John: She capitalizes on her beauty. (*Pause.*)

Robert: What beauty?

John: Her attractiveness.

Robert: Yes.

John: It isn't really beauty.

Robert: No.

John: Beauty comes from within.

Robert: Yes, I feel it does. (scene 1)

Patrick Ryecart comments on this scene:

At this stage, John hangs onto every word Robert utters. He wants to establish a bond, a trust, a feeling that they are in league together and plunges ahead rather recklessly. He thinks he will be pleasing Robert but actually succeeds in rather annoying him. This sort of conversation is so true, so superbly caught . . .

people getting themselves into corners whilst trying to flatter or please and then having to eat their words.

Despite his irritation, Robert knows that John is trying to please him and feels smugly secure in the knowledge that he has the young man on his side. He even lets John lead the conversation, a rare event indeed. It is very infrequently that Robert responds to a remark with only a monosyllabic "yes" or "no," but on this occasion he feels confident enough to restrict his comments. His complacency is momentarily rattled, but John qualifies his statement about beauty by offering, by way of atonement, the assertion that the woman's charm "isn't really beauty." He is anxious not to upset what he currently sees as the fine sensibilities of his companion. Once Robert's responses have assured him that all is still well and that they are friends, John even chances a platitude: "Beauty comes from within." It could almost be Robert speaking here, clichès to the fore.

Robert may lecture John about the importance of good behavior, sensitivity, and the evolution of theatrical "etiquette," but such sentiments are easily jettisoned when his own security is threatened. Far from behaving in a gentlemanly fashion, he calls the actress a "c—t" and announces that he would willingly murder her if he thought he could get away with it (ibid). Later, he swears at John, calling him a "f—ing twit" (scene 22); Mamet utilizes the irony in John's overly polite reply, "I beg your pardon" to consolidate further our doubts about Robert's claims that he embodies all things fine and elevated in the theatre.

To make quite certain that the audience should not even momentarily take Robert a little too seriously, Mamet deflates his pomposity by having him use the most hackneyed clichés ("the show goes on", scene 1 and "good things for good folk," scene 14) or, more frequently, by setting his speeches in contexts that by their very nature undermine their seriousness. For example, he rambles on about the necessity to "*grow*" as artists while John is practicing at the barre: the latter is more concerned with looking at his own reflection in the rehearsal room mirror than with listening to Robert's platitudes yet again. Consequently, he responds infrequently and appears to practice selective deafness, not really taking in what is being said. The scene ends with his prosaic question, "Is my back straight?" to which Robert can only reply, "no" (scene 5). Elsewhere, John interrupts his colleague's speeches with such demotic remarks as, "Please pass the bread" (scene 14), "How's your duck?" (ibid.), and "May I use your brush?" (scene 17). He also frequently responds to Robert's speechifying with an ''mmm,'' a linguistic tic Robert himself adopts toward the end of the play, signifying the level of influence the younger man gradually exerts over him.

Mamet describes one of the play's intentions as a means of delineating a turning point in the acting careers of the two players. However, the actual moment of change is ambiguous. Mamet notes how ''the event we have decided on as the turning point . . . was, looking back, quite probably not it at all.'' Nevertheless, it is clear that Robert views *any* change with caution and trepidation. He tells John that the process of life is ''a little like a play'' (scene 5) in which ''you start from the beginning and go through the middle and wind up at the end'' (ibid.). As Robert speaks airily about his favorite analogy, Mamet imbues his words with fear. That acting, like life, has a beginning, a middle, and an end is a sobering thought for Robert. As he speaks, the logic of his narrative pulls him inexorably into dangerous and frightening areas. Like those of Emil and George in *The Duck Variations,* Robert's speeches have a habit of wandering into territory he would rather not explore.

Patrick Ryecart describes as ''those terrible scenes'' the episodes in which Robert pathetically lingers backstage to hear the voice of the new generation as it practices onstage and where, tragically, he attempts to cut his wrists. Robert is a genuinely tragic figure, but one who is drawn without sentimentality or condescension. Freddie Jones notes how ''The character of Robert is drawn with great powers of observation and is completely without sentimentality. The writing is witty, observant, but never sentimental. What's sentimental about getting old? . . . Mamet's writing is astute and compassionate, not sloppy.'' Patrick Ryecart believes the work is wholly without cloying sentimentality:

> I don't think it is at all sentimental. On the contrary, it is often very harsh. Even in those terrible scenes where Robert stays behind and the young actor catches him watching and listening with great sadness . . . and where he tries to slash his wrists . . . these are totally unsentimental. It would have been easy for Mamet to veer over the edge but he does not. . . . There is nothing remotely excessive or cloying in the play. Each situation arises quite naturally out of the text.

This is a view which is not shared by Milton Shulman who avers that ''there is a hollow and artificial ring to this sentimentalised portrayal of the life-style of actors.'' Mamet walks a fine line between genuine pathos and overt sentimentality, and mostly succeeds in avoiding the latter. Colin Stinton

has observed how the playwright is constantly— even pathologically—aware of and on the lookout for ''creeping sentimentality'' in his work and will go to great lengths to excise all traces of it. In *A Life in the Theatre,* Mamet wishes to demonstrate the generosity and bravery of actors but, in so doing, realizes that he must temper any potential sentimental incursions with irony. Perhaps he goes a little too far. He is at such pains to show up the pretentiousness of Robert and the rampant ambition of John that, although we still regard them with affection, we also see them diminished as representatives of their profession. However, in spite of his characters' inadequacies—perhaps even because of theme— we do enjoy Mamet's representation of their experiences and attitudes. There is also an often unstated but nonetheless tacit expression of friendship in the play; despite Mamet's ironic deflations, the bond that exists between Robert and John ensures that we regard them with warmth and empathy.

The depiction of character through language is wonderfully accurate in this play. Each actor's speech changes subtly throughout to indicate his present mood and John's move from gauche naïveté at the beginning of the work to unnerving self-reliance by the end is superbly controlled. John has less showy dialogue than Robert but this is no way detracts from the power of his presence. Of this aspect of Mamet's writing, Patrick Ryecart says:

> It all comes down to reaction to Robert's words . . . John ''speaks'' just as much as if he had three pages of dialogue—You can make or break an entire speech just by your reaction . . . If reaction is not catered for in the writing then it is a different thing . . . but in a good play with good writing (as this has) it doesn't matter if a character has ten minutes of silence—if its relevance is there, then it is fully justified.

There *is* a bond that unites Robert and John, but its strength is sometimes weakened, as in the latter's eventual move away from his colleague. John no longer feels he need tolerate Robert's endless rhetoric and this is shown through the almost monosyllabic quality of most of his lines, a brevity that demonstrates all too clearly his impatience and exasperation. However, Patrick Ryecart insists that John's behavior is perfectly understandable; he does not see him as a cold and callous individual, but merely one who is quite naturally trying to get on with his own career and avoid the proselytizing excesses of his garrulous friend. Ryecart suggests John does not mean to be cruel and his gradual rejection of Robert is entirely legitimate.

> You cannot have a relationship that goes beyond working with everyone. . . . Robert has been such a

bloody old bore that, frankly, you can't blame John for his coolness, if that is what it is. I *know* these types like Robert; they sit in their dressing rooms with a little tin of sardines and they drone on and on and they are so *boring*. . . . It isn't necessarily coldness or cruelty . . . I would argue that it is not callous for John to want to get away from such a person.

However, in spite of such assertions in defense of John's character, Mamet's play does hint at his dismissive nature and his brash, ambitious manner. His language is terse, even curt, and his responses to Robert's verbal forays take on a rather brutal impatience. He becomes patronizing and sarcastic, apparently absorbing the very worst aspects of Robert's personality. This is clearly *not* the kind of education that Robert had in mind! Where once John was eager to please, in the later stages of the play he becomes arrogant and rude. His actions may be understandable, given the often trying circumstances he has to endure, but Mamet ensures that he is, nonetheless, seen as rather cool and calculating.

A good example of the gradual change in the actors' relationship occurs when John tries to rehearse alone onstage. Suddenly Robert appears and launches into a long speech that is both dubiously flattering and coolly critical of the younger man's work. John is irritated enough to indulge in a little sarcasm; he decides to mock Robert by echoing one of his favorite theatrical terms, ''fitting'':

Robert: . . . It's good. It's *quite* good. I was watching you for a while. I hope you don't mind. Do you mind?

John: I've only been here a minute or so.

Robert: And I've watched you all that time. It seemed so long. It was so full. You're very good, John. Have I told you that lately? You are becoming a very fine actor. The flaws of youth are the perquisite of the young. It is the perquisite of the Young to possess the flaws of youth.

John: It's fitting, yes . . .

Robert: Ah, don't mock me, John. You shouldn't mock me. It's too easy. (scene 23)

John can perceive the edge to Robert's ''flattering'' remarks; Robert observes that he had watched John ''all that time''—a period that was apparently only a minute or two. The implication is surely not that John is mesmerizing in his ability to fit so much power and meaning into his acting but that he is laboring the point, spinning out what should be brief and succinct. To counteract this inference and to play it safe, Robert immediately states that John is becoming ''a very fine actor.'' However, he then deflates this by mentioning ''the flaws of youth'' and then, in another verbal swerve, reverts to complimentary remarks about John's abilities—although

he is almost certainly insincere. His use of the rather archaic word ''perquisite''—twice—is another indication of his fussy and pedantic nature; it is no doubt intended to demonstrate his learning and superior command over language, but probably only succeeds in irritating rather than impressing John. There is in this exchange a sour sense of the alienation that is gradually developing between the two men; they no longer speak to one another as they once did and now expend their energies trying to falsely flatter or deflate egos. Robert's habit of referring to the ''fitness'' of things has obviously rankled John to the extent that he now nastily throws a mocking echo of it into Robert's face.

Robert's last remark, ''You shouldn't mock me. It's too easy,'' can be interpreted in two contrasting ways. His plain and simple diction is in marked contrast to his usual verbose style and could be intended to indicate that this is indeed the real Robert. The mask of pretense has been momentarily cast aside and the true identity of the man is revealed. A bitter, self-deprecating irony can be detected in the words and, for the first time in the play, Robert is perhaps acknowledging his own absurdity and egotism. On the other hand, he may be simply admonishing John for using sarcasm to demonstrate his irritation; as a professional, John should be able to counter any attack by means more worthy than parody.

The reversal in dependence that occurs in Robert and John's relationship in fact begins much earlier. One of the most powerful aspects of the work is the peerlessly executed role delineation and subsequent role reversal that begins on the first page of the script and is concluded, neatly and succinctly, on the last. Patrick Ryecart observes how

there are two little instances of dialogue, right at the beginning and right at the end, which convey what the whole play is about. At the beginning, Robert says to John: ''I thought the bedroom scene tonight was brilliant''—or words to that effect—to which John eagerly replies, ''Did you?'' He is at this stage delighted to have the praise of a respected and revered colleague. In the last scene, Robert says: ''I loved the staircase scene tonight'' to which John now replies: ''You did?'' It's so subtle but the effect of the two is totally different. The nuance is entirely changed. John's new-found confidence and maturity just shines out . . . so Mamet, with those four little words, two at the start and two at the finish, conveys the essence of the piece. . . . The role reversal happens throughout the play but is set off by the opening words. . . . There are probably examples on every page in which you can see how Mamet builds up the sense of changing attitudes.

A further hint of irony is injected in that Robert's first compliment concerns the ''bedroom scene'' whereas at the end it is the ''execution scene'' that is discussed. Robert's professional ''death'' is thus carefully made ready by Mamet. It is tempting to read significance into the choice of bedroom scene—with its suggestions of intimacy and even regeneration—and the execution scene, which carries its own obvious implications.

Another good example of reversal in dependency occurs after an audition at which John believes he has done very well. He has received some good notices from the critics and these have, perhaps not surprisingly, made him a little conceited:

> *Robert:* They've praised you too much. I do not mean to detract from your reviews, you deserve praise, John, much praise. . . . Not, however, for those things which they have praised you for.
>
> *John:* In your opinion. (scene 22)

Robert continues to advise John not to take what the critics have to say too seriously, until John is moved to respond:

> *John:* I thought that they were rather to the point.
>
> *Robert:* You did.
>
> *John:* Yes.
>
> *Robert:* Your reviews.
>
> *John:* Yes.
>
> *Robert:* All false modesty aside.
>
> *John:* Yes.
>
> *Robert:* Oh, the Young, the Young, the Young, the Young.
>
> *John:* The Farmer in the Dell. (ibid.)

Mamet captures the slightly bitchy, though ostentatiously sincere diction of an actor like Robert. There is more than a touch of effeminate spite in his remarks and Mamet picks up on his linguistic slip in the line, ''Not, however, for those things which they have praised you for,'' undercutting the words of Robert, a man who believes he has a superior command over language. As John defends his position, Robert half-smilingly patronizes him with short statements intended to annoy him. In case John should somehow miss the subtle deflation of all this, Robert then flounces off into what he wishes to convey as an affectionate scoff at the charming pretensions of youth. John remains quite unamused, responding only with the sardonic: ''The Farmer in the Dell'' with its echoes of nursery rhymes and childhood, perhaps intended to suggest Robert's incipient senility and imbecilic childishness.

Rival recriminations notwithstanding, both men know that they are engaged in something of an uphill battle to survive and this knowledge unites them. There are a number of overtly affectionate scenes scattered throughout the work, but perhaps the most touching of these occurs when John removes a smear of grease-paint from behind Robert's ear:

> *John:* Here. I'll get it. . . . No. Wait, We'll get it off. . . . There.
>
> *Robert:* Did we get it off?
>
> *John:* Yes. (scene 1)

John's language is paternalistic, even down to the plurality of, ''We'll get it off.'' He changes from the singular pronoun to the plural in order to render the sentence more intimate, something that Robert immediately notices and to which he responds,—in fact, he then uses the same style of speech. Moments later, *he* takes on the parental role; John throws the crumpled tissue toward the wastebasket but misses. Robert picks it up ''*and deposits it in the appropriate receptacle*'' murmuring: ''Alright. All gone. Let's go. (*Pause*). Eh?'' (ibid.).

There is, in this scene—and elsewhere in the play—the suggestion that there may be some latent homosexual feelings between the two men, although neither Patrick Ryecart nor Freddie Jones agree that any such implication exists. It is difficult to completely reject this inference, particularly when considering the scene in which Robert's fly breaks and John tries to fix it. Robert's exhortations for John to hurry up surely suggest more than a mere plea for speed; the double entendres practically collide as they spill out. The scene begins innocently enough:

> *Robert:* My zipper's broken.
>
> *John:* Do you want a safety pin?
>
> *Robert:* I have one. (*Looking for safety pin.*)
>
> *John:* (*Rising, starting to leave.*) Do you want me to send the woman in?
>
> *Robert:* No. No. I'll manage. S—t. Oh, s—t. (scene 8)

Even here there are subliminal suggestions of what may follow. Having refused the attentions of the ''woman,'' Robert struggles with the pin until John is moved to offer his assistance:

> *John:* Oh, come on. I'll do it. Come on. (*Pulls out chair.*) Get up here. Come on. Get up. (*Robert gets up on the chair.*) Give me the pin. Come on . . . (ibid.)

They lose the safety pin, but John finally sees it and begins again:

> *John:* Stand still now.

Robert: Come on, come on. (*John puts his face up against Robert's crotch.*) Put it in.

John: Just hold still for a moment.

Robert: Come *on,* for God's sake.

John: Alright. Alright. You know I think you're gaining weight . . .

Robert: Oh, f—k you. Will you stick it in.

John: Hold still. There. (scene 8)

Apart from being hilariously ''naturalistic'' dialogue that conveys Robert's desperation as he tries to get ready in time for his cue, Mamet's dialogue imbues both actors' speech with a subtly suggestive harmony. The repetition of pseudosexual phrases, such as ''Come on'' and ''Hold still,'' deftly contributes to the flirtatious undercurrent of the scene. As it moves towards its conclusion, and John is placed with ''*his face up against Robert's crotch,*'' the scene provides John with a deliciously cheeky quip, which is at once an acknowledgment of the physical intimacy of the moment and a mildly sarcastic observation of the kind that might be frequently utilized by homosexual or effeminate men. The tone is quite different from that of the first scene, when Robert comments upon his weight problem and John replies: ''You're having trouble with your weight? . . . But you're trim enough'' (scene 1).

John may not be absolutely sincere in his flattery, but there is at this stage no trace in his tone of the impertinent and rather effeminate stance he later adopts. Robert's response to John's later saucy remark is itself suggestive and almost equally flirtatious; he responds with an obscenity (which may even be a half-conscious wish!) and an exhortation that it is difficult to ignore as yet another double entendre. Such a reading of certain scenes should not, however, be viewed as the mainspring of Mamet's intention in the play. Homosexuality may well be a subtext in specific instances, but *A Life in the Theatre* is not a work wholly concerned with the subject. To view it in this manner is to seriously diminish its impact and to lessen the subtlety of Mamet's characterization. It is enough to be aware that such an element probably exists and to leave it at that.

By the last scene in the play, the roles have reversed. It is Robert who is nervous and slightly uneasy in John's company; it is now Robert who accepts John's compliments about his performance with what seems to be excessive gratitude:

John: I thought the execution scene worked beautifully.

Robert: No. You *didn't* . . .

John: Yes. I did. (*Pause.*)

Robert: Thank you . . . (scene 26)

It is now Robert who is ''not eating too well these days'' because he is ''not hungry'' (ibid.), as opposed to John who, in the opening scene spoke of not having ''had an appetite for several days'' (scene 1), and it is now Robert who addresses the empty auditorium with a pathos that was not evident in John's earlier solitary speech.

In *A Life in the Theatre,* Mamet's dialogue is, once again, taut with invention. Milton Shulman notes how Mamet ''cleverly reproduces those exchanges of hesitant compliments and sly insults that actors use when they discuss each other's performances.'' Mel Gussow feels that the language in the play ''glistens. . . . [it] is a cross between the elegant and the vernacular. . . . [his] timing is as exact as Accutron. . . . he is an eloquent master of two-part harmony.'' As Robert and John's linguistic battle for supremacy gathers momentum, it is easy to see why Gussow feels that their language ''glistens'' and why he compares Mamet's timing to ''Accutron.'' In the following scene, the playwright's command over rhythm and subtle inflection reaches its zenith. Robert feels that John is unfairly upstaging him during one of their scenes together and suggests that he should ''do less'':

Robert: (Pause.) In our scene tonight . . .

John: Yes?

Robert: Mmmm . . .

John: What?

Robert: Could you . . . perhaps . . . *do* less.

John: Do less?

Robert: Yes.

John: Do less???

Robert: Yes . . . (*Pause.*)

John: Do less *what???*

Robert: You know.

John: You mean . . . what do you mean?

Robert: (Pause.) You know.

John: Do you mean I'm walking on your scene? (*Pause.*) What do you mean?

Robert: Nothing. It's a thought I had. An aesthetic consideration.

John: Mmm.

Robert: I thought may be if you *did* less . . .

John: Yes?

Robert: You know . . .

John: If I *did* less.

Robert: Yes.

John: Well, thank you for the thought.

Robert: I don't think you have to be like that. (scene 8)

Freddie Jones has observed that Mamet's writing in such scenes is "fluid, musical. We really do speak in an iambic pentameter and Mamet's work is never rhythmically erroneous." Patrick Ryecart believes that examples like this scene consolidate Mamet's position as "a superb dramatic poet. There is a strong and true rhythm in the lines which propel the actors along."

The timing here is as acute as that to be found in any music-hall patter; it is reminiscent of the verbal bantering that occurs between many of Beckett's aging burlesques as they bicker and prod one another into responsive action. Robert begins politely and even deferentially, delaying the moment by pauses and contemplative noises, until he feels he can safely make his request. His nervousness and uncertainty as to the exact moment to choose is cleverly conveyed; he is perhaps a little unnerved by the curtness of John's responses, and believes that it may be prudent to wait a moment before stating his case. In the exchange that follows, "Could you . . . perhaps . . . *do* less" to "Do less *what???*" Mamet uses rhyme as well as rhythm. The phrasing is as tight and measured as jazz. Indeed, Patrick Ryecart comments upon Mamet's use of rhythm and rhyme. "'Do less', 'do less,' 'do less what' . . . the words are so musical. It's like jazz. The rhymes have the rhythms of the purest forms of jazz. I am sure Mamet listens to his texts as music . . . counting the beats, working in the pauses."

John is both outraged and indignant that he should be asked to modify his acting technique. He becomes coldly angry and his tone takes on a hint of menace. Certainly Robert senses the potential danger and negates the request by pretending it was an "aesthetic consideration." When John merely responds with a less threatening "Mmmm," erroneously conveying to Robert a lull in his anger but probably intending contemptuous resignation, Robert decides to take on another tone. In an effort to buy back any lost sympathy, he tries to convey meek insecurity; the use of the uncertain "thought" and "maybe" are clearly intended to deflate the seriousness of his request and to show the unnecessarily ruffled John that it was merely a casual suggestion. When John counters his groveling with sarcasm, Robert again changes his tone, this time to indignation. He tries to impress upon John that his response to mild criticism is unprofessional and

childish, wholly improper for a man of his "calling." Thus, Robert tries to stabilize an inflammatory situation by reverting to familiar sentiments—the need for a mature approach to acting in which one eschews minor and selfish considerations and embraces criticism in an endless quest for perfection.

Such high-minded sentiments are obviously something that Robert himself cannot adopt since, later in the play, he responds with almost hysterical venom to what can only be seen as poor critical response to his work:

> *Robert:* The motherf—ing leeches. The sots. (*Pause.*) The bloody boors. All of them . . . All of them. . . . Why can they not leave us alone . . . (scene 10)

Elsewhere in the work, he describes critics as "F—ing leeches. . . . [who will] praise you for the things you never did and pan you for a split second of godliness. What do they know? They create nothing. . . . They don't even buy a ticket" (scene 22). To Robert, critics are ignorant philistines who lead a parasitic existence, living off professionals like him. Unlike actors, "they create nothing" and do not even contribute financially to the theatrical arts.

Critical response to *A Life in the Theatre* has been largely favorable, although some reviewers have criticized the lengthy pauses that exist between some scenes due to costume changes, positioning of props, and so on. However, as both Patrick Ryecart and Freddie Jones point out, these "longeurs" are crucial to the whole structure of the play. It is precisely *because* the audience is permitted a glimpse into a backstage world that is usually denied them that the play is so fascinating. Freddie Jones considers these moments as essential to the overall structure of the piece as the dialogue:

> The most important thing in a work like this is not to rush. Part of the fascination of it is the drama of watching people at work. The way they put sight-holes in hoardings so that you can watch people digging a hole sixty feet below suggests the spell of watching—it is almost voyeuristic. You see bowler-hatted businessmen in the city avidly watching the laborers. The psychology of *A Life in the Theatre* is identical to that. If you rush it, it makes it look like a bottleneck, a failure in the script. If you trust it, do it leisurely, the only way you really can, it works . . . by moving more slowly, you are smoothing the action, making it fluent. . . . But as actors, you are always sorely tempted to rush, the pressure is so great. This must be avoided!

Similarly, Ryecart believes that "for a member of the audience, the hold-ups would not be seen as hold-ups at all, but as an integral part of the action which, of course, they are . . . they are what Mamet wants and are deliberately written into the play.'' Although there is a degree of sadness in *A Life in the Theatre,* there is also a great deal of humor, the majority of which undoubtedly stems from the brief scenes from the ''plays'' within the work. Ryecart recalls how

> these scenes were very difficult to act because the writing is so deliberately bad, whereas the backstage scenes are easy due to the superb characterization . . . it is important to do the little scenes awfully well because if there are any areas in the play where one might lose the attention of an audience, it is there. They have to be *very* funny and the acting style quite different to the (most important) backstage scenes.

Freddie Jones stresses the importance of ''a judicious use of 'ham' in the playlet scenes,'' to get the very best theatrical effect.

The structure of *A Life in the Theatre* is quite similar to that of Clifford Odets' *Waiting for Lefty* in that realistic action is coupled with brief scenes within scenes, which both comment upon and forward the action of the whole. However, the playlet scenes in Mamet's work forward the action only insofar as they contribute to the sense of inexorable decay on Robert's part and the increase of confidence on John's. This becomes more evident in the later scenes when lines are fluffed, cues are missed, and off-stage irritations intrude.

The first of these scenes is set ''*in the trenches .''* John and Robert are dressed as Doughboys and sit in a trench, ''*smoking the last cigarette.''* Mamet has obviously seen a great many films that contain scenes of just this banal and clichéd type. The dialogue is appallingly—and hilariously—stilted and is redolent of B-films popular in the 1940s and 1950s in which actors like John Wayne and Audie Murphy conversed with a sincerity that only emphasized the dire quality of their scripts. Mamet captures perfectly the phony gritty dialogue spoken in such films—language only considered realistic by writers without any experience on which to base their fantasies and with ''tin'' ears for naturalistic cadences:

John: They left him up there on the wire.

Robert: Calm down.

John: Those bastards.

Robert: Yeah.

John: My God. They stuck him on the wire and left him there for target practice. . . . Those dirty, dirty bastards. (scene 3)

This is followed by a supposedly sophisticated scene in which two lawyers struggle to maintain their dignity. From the outset, Mamet ensures that the audience is unable to take this seriously since it has been preceded by the episode in which Robert's zipper breaks and must be held together by a safety pin. Robert plays an urbane attorney, a successful individual at the peak of his career; a broken fly zipper hardly goes along with this image. Consequently, Robert must try to conceal his embarrassment and adopt an air of sobriety and authority. John, playing a lawyer, confronts Robert's character with the news of his wife's pregnancy:

John: Gillian's going to have a baby.

Robert: Why, this is marvellous. How long have you known?

John: Since this morning.

Robert: How marvellous!

John: It isn't mine.

Robert: It's not.

John: No.

Robert: Oh. (*Pause.*) I always supposed there was something one said in these situations . . . but I find . . . Do you know, that is, have you been told who the father is?

John: Yes.

Robert: Really. Who is it, David?

John: It's you, John.

Robert: Me!

John: You!

Robert: No.

John: Yes.

Robert: How preposterous. (scene 9)

This is purely the language of soap opera, right down to the way in which both men pointedly call each other by name. There is also the additional joke of having John call Robert ''John''. This somehow adds to the idiocy of what the two men are doing in a play such as this. The short, almost monosyllabic sentences, quickly following one another add to the artificiality of the text, although the ''writer's'' intention is undoubtedly that it should be seen as realistic, serious dialogue.

The next playlet is written in a ''Chekhovian'' style. Here, Mamet manages to invoke aspects of several Chekhov plays while retaining a dialogue that is stultifying—even stupefying—in its boredom and banality. Robert is wheeled onstage in a bath chair by John—a sight that is in itself bound to cause tittering in the audience. Robert asks for his robe:

John: Oh, the autumn. . . . Oh, for the sun . . .

Robert: Will you pass me my robe, please?

John: Your laprobe. (scene 11)

In these lines, Mamet manages to suggest echoes of at least two of Chekhov's plays—*The Three Sisters* and *Uncle Vanya.* The specific, and rather clumsy, reference to a "laprobe" is no accident since Serebryakov's laprobe falls about his ankles while he sleeps in act 2 of *Uncle Vanya.* Not only does Robert and John's script suggest not even an inkling of Chekhovian subtext (although the references to seasonal and meteorological topics are clearly intended to suggest one), it is also quite useless as naturalistic dialogue:

John: Maman says just one more day, one more day, yet another week.

Robert: Mmm.

John: One more week.

Robert: Would you please close the window?

John: What? I'm sorry?

Robert: Do you feel a draft?

John: A slight draft, yes. (*Pause.*) Shall I close the window?

Robert: Would you mind?

John: No, not at all. I love this window . . . (ibid.)

The puerile repetitions and blatantly contrived questions render any hint of naturalism null and void. Mamet demonstrates how a poorly understood Chekhovian style can very easily turn into farcical absurdity. The script strains toward a Russian feel, but fails at every turn. John's assertion that he loves the window is a weak and clichéd reference to Gayev's affectionate speech to the bookcase in act 1 of *The Cherry Orchard.* Both are sentimental, but the difference is that Chekhov knew how to make sentimentality work as a means of character delineation whereas Mamet's imaginary dramatist does not. The scene drags on interminably; far from suggesting Chekhovian emotions such as apathy, frustration, and resignation, the fictional author achieves only a drawnout—and unintentionally hilarious—melodrama in which, literally, nothing happens. If the piece had genuine humor (apart from Mamet's wickedly ironic comedy), it could almost be Beckettian!

In the French Revolution scene, Robert's lengthy soliloquy reads a little like a scene from an inferior version of Büchner's *Danton's Death* or Sardou's *Robespierre,* the play commissioned by Irving to provide him with a truly "dramatic" role. There is definitely something of the Irving school of acting

about Robert's part here. The "dramatist" clearly believes he can display a linguistic flourish in bombastic rhetoric and overwhelm through the power of words alone. Alas, the rhetoric is fatuous and frequently downright silly:

Robert: . . . The heart cries out: the memory says man has always lived in chains . . . has always lived in chains . . . (*Pause.* Bread, bread, bread, the people scream . . . we drown their screaming with our head in cups, in books . . . in newspapers . . . between the breasts of women . . . in our work . . . enough. (scene 16)

Robert must relish the opportunity of playing such parts. He can strut about displaying his self-importance and enjoy the excitement of having the stage completely to himself. He has nothing to worry about, other than that he must give his best performance; the increasingly threatening presence of John is not even there to distract him. At this halfway stage of the play, Robert *is* still mostly in control, but there are already hints of John's lessening dependence upon him, and Robert's sad realization of this fact.

The vacuity of the piece Robert so lovingly performs bears little scrutiny. The "manliness" and robust nature of the speaker is meant to be conveyed in lines such as, "our head in cups . . . between the breasts of women," and similar bathetic exclamations. What is actually conveyed is the very limited imagination of the author. Whether the repetition of "has always lived in chains," in the first part of the speech is intentional or is an indication of Robert simply forgetting his lines is unclear. When, at the conclusion of the extract, he utters, "enough," it is difficult not to agree with him. Robert's character goes on to list the causes to which it is necessary to swear allegiance in the interests of the Revolution:

Robert: . . . Our heads between the breasts of women, plight our troth to that security far greater than protection of mere rank or fortune. Now: we must dedicate ourselves to spirit: to the spirit of humanity; to life: (*Pause.*) to the barricades. (*Pause.*) Bread, bread, bread. (ibid.)

This part of the soliloquy appears to lean toward Shakespearian rhythms, rhythms that are plainly ill-suited to the sheer vacancy of the words. Robert separates the "causes" by means of emphatic colons. Unfortunately for the grandeur of the speech, the final "cause" is "the barricades," which necessitates a change in tone and meaning. The call is surely to march *to* the barricades themselves, but the speech is so badly written that it could appear to be merely another in the speaker's list of worthy causes. The concluding, "Bread, bread, bread," serves to emphasize the true lack of passion in the writing, calling to mind, if anything, a musical moment from *Oliver*.

The scene about the barricades is not only noteworthy because of its accurate verbal humor, it also contains the visual debacle of Robert flinging back his head in a grandiose gesture and consequently losing his wig. The next time we see Robert's thespian skills is in the famous lifeboat scene. It should be recalled that this is the episode to which he had given so much thought in an earlier scene, finding meaning where little existed and lauding the author to the skies. The dialogue is, once again, trite and risible but is here rendered totally ludicrous by the actors' obligatory *"English accents"* (scene 18). This is one occasion when an American actor's voice is most definitely called for:

> *Robert:* Rain . . .? What do *you* know about it? (*Pause.* I've spent my whole life on the sea, and all that I know is the length of my ignorance. Which is *complete,* Sonny. (*Pause.*) My ignorance is complete.
>
> *John:* It's gotta rain.
>
> *Robert:* Tell it to the marines.
>
> *John:* It doesn't rain, I'm going off my nut.
>
> *Robert:* Just take it easy, kid . . . What you don't wanna do now is sweat. (*Pause.*) Believe me. (*Pause.*)
>
> *John:* We're never getting out of this alive. (*Pause.*) Are we?
>
> *Robert:* How do you want it?
>
> *John:* Give it to me straight.
>
> *Robert:* Kid, we haven't got a chance in hell . . . (scene 18)

The fictional dramatist is evidently attempting dialogue that is a hybrid of Steinbeck and Hemingway, the latter in his *The Old Man and the Sea* period. What he actually achieves is an inane and mannered version of such classic works. The ''author'' has a stab at metrical scansion: ''the length of my ignorance'' and so on. Such serious speculation is then mercilessly rejected in favor of phrases like, ''It's gotta rain'' and, even worse, ''Tell it to the marines.'' The so-called sea-dog experience of the elder man is suggested in a series of clichés that would probably seem overdone in a children's adventure serial but that, as we have seen, Robert considers inspired writing. This truly dreadful piece of work probably *is* the best the actors have to perform, which is saying very little.

The final playlet takes place in an operating room; it is here that Robert's professional expertise is seriously called into question and where he refuses to take notice of John's desperate attempts to prompt him. The scene begins well enough: Robert,

though in character, is momentarily back in his paternal role as an older surgeon doling out advice to his junior colleague. Offstage, his authority may be crumbling, but here it is he who teaches the novice the ropes and it is he who knows the tricks of the trade, just as Robert the actor knows well the tricks of his own profession. However, it soon becomes clear that Robert has mixed up his lines and is confusing the action here with that of another scene:

> *John:* (*Pointing.*) What's that!!!?
>
> *Robert:* What is what? Eh?
>
> *John:* What's that near his spleen? (*A pause.*) A curious growth near his spleen?
>
> *Robert:* What?
>
> *John:* A Curious Growth Near His Spleen? (*Pause.*) Is that one, there?
>
> *Robert:* No, I think not. I think you cannot see a growth near his spleen for some *time* yet. So would you, as this man's in shock . . . would you get me, please, give me a reading on his vital statements? Uh, *Functions* . . .? Would you do that one thing for me, please?
>
> *John:* (*Sotto.*) We've done that one, Robert.
>
> *Robert:* I fear I must disagree with you, Doctor. Would you give me a reading on his vital things, if you please? Would you? (*Pause*) For the love of God?
>
> *John:* (*Sotto.*) That's in the other part. (scene 24)

It is illuminating to look at this scene in some detail in order to glean how Mamet builds up the comedy. Robert is incensed that John should think he has forgotten what to do and persists with the wrong lines despite John's efforts to save the situation from disaster. Robert improvises frantically; he begins to flounder. Panicking, he fishes around in his mind for any medical-sounding terms that might cover up John's ''error.'' Eventually, he runs out of even remotely suitable ''medical'' words and requests ''a reading on [the patient's] vital things.'' Patrick Ryecart recalls how this particular section always induced near hysteria in the audience and often led to considerable ''corpsing'' between Freddie Jones and him: ''We often played the scene absolutely shaking with laughter,'' he says. Robert's intransigence unnerves John. He too begins to panic, and this is suggested by his pointed remark, highlighted by capital letters for full effect: ''A Curious Growth Near His Spleen.'' As the scene limps weakly to its conclusion, John seems deflated and completely devoid of energy. He mutters: ''We've done that one, Robert,'' calling his colleague by name to let him know that it is *he* who is at fault. Robert ignores this; he is adamant and carries on frantically like a man possessed, the professional to the end. To keep up the charade, he refers to John as ''Doctor'' even when all credibility has plainly been sacrificed.

A final mix of reality and artifice occurs in the next few lines when Robert berates John for a lack of feeling, which, it seems, is not only intended for his partner's onstage character:

> *Robert:* . . . He's in shock. He's in shock, and I'm becoming miffed with you. Now: if you desire to work in this business again will you give me a reading? If you wish to continue here inside the hospital? (*Pause.*) Must I call a *policeman!!?* Have you no feeling? This man's in deepest shock!!! (ibid.)

Is Robert telling John the actor that he must cooperate if he wishes to ''work in this business again''? Is it John the actor with whom Robert is ''miffed?'' Robert tries to make his ''lines'' sound as if they were written for him, while at the same time criticizing John for what he feels is his total incompetence and refusal to cover up his gaffe. However, when Robert mentions the ''*hospital*'' rather than the reality of the stage on which they both stand, he betrays his nervousness and fear of the younger man. He realizes that John is aware of his direct criticism and so, to be safe, once more moves into the relative security of fantasy. His final words, ''This man's in deepest shock!!!'' underlines the ambiguity. Which man is in shock? The imaginary patient or Robert himself?

Mamet prefixes his play with a short quotation from Rudyard Kipling's poem, *Actors:*

> We counterfeited once for your disport,
> Men's joy and sorrow; but our day has passed.
> We pray you pardon all where we fell short—
> Seeing we were your servants to this last.

This appears to be a comment on the decline of Robert but it could also be viewed as a worried reminder of the declining importance of theatre to the general public, a state of affairs Mamet is most anxious to prevent. *A Life in the Theatre* has been called ''a wary hymn to the theatre'' and so it is. It celebrates the fleeting joys of a satisfying performance and it dramatizes most touchingly the bond that exists between those who dedicate their lives to the stage. On the other hand, it offers a far from glamorous picture of theatrical life. For the audience, such a play is somewhat akin to watching a third-rate conjurer whose magic tricks all come to nought. We see behind the artifice into the sometimes painful areas that usually remain concealed; as Robert rather grandly avers of one of the fictional authors in the play, the writer ''lets you see the

thought there'' (scene 13). The work may be a play about two actors and their particularly specialized lives in the theatre, but it is universal in its theme. It may be about acting, but it is also about the conflicts of age and youth, rites of passage, and simple human nature. Mel Gussow believes that *A Life in the Theatre* is a play in which ''the author spoofs actors' insecurities, pretensions [and] illusions— the pretensions and ignominies of the profession.'' One might add to this that Mamet additionally deals with the ''insecurities, pretensions [and] illusions'' of life itself, the ''ignominies of the profession'' standing for the ignominies of human existence.

Source: Anne Dean, ''A Life in the Theatre,'' in *David Mamet: Language as Dramatic Action,* Associated University Presses, 1990, pp. 119–47.

William W. Demastes

In the following excerpt, author William Demastes discusses how the relationship between Life in the Theatre*'s two main characters reflects the theme of capturing the moment.*

Mamet does produce a more ''epic'' work in *The Water Engine* (1977) and later in *Glengarry Glen Ross* (1984). But before achieving these more ''audience-pleasing'' and epic designs, Mamet wrote *Reunion, The Woods, Dark Pony,* and other shorter works. As noted earlier, they are dramas that focus very specifically on select human relationships— between a father and daughter or man and woman, for example. Perhaps the most *popularly* successful of this type was *A Life in the Theatre* (1977). Several critics suggest that its popularity was due to its subject matter, the theatre, but it must be conceded that the dynamics illustrated in the relationship presented, between a veteran actor and a newcomer, plays a significant role in the play's gaining acclaim.

It is a play comprised of twenty-six scenes which, more than the other fragmented plays, works as an interesting experiment in manipulating conventional temporal considerations. The relationship moves from that of a student-teacher type, through various crises, into a secure and mature relationship based on understanding, once again despite language. Many themes are touched on—a variation on *theatrum mundi,* for example—but the key is less its traditional thematics than its structure. As Kerr congratulated Mamet on finding a working form for the material in *Sexual Perversity in Chicago,* so should he have congratulated Mamet for *A Life in the Theatre.* The play is chronologically ordered,

A scene from the 1989 production of A Life in the Theatre *at London's Theatre Royal.*

one must assume, but it freely dispenses with actual day/date considerations, and the episodic structure—as in *Sexual Perversity in Chicago*—does succeed at providing a framework for material while dispensing with the busy-ness of filling in or explaining away time lapses. One central theme, for example, is that life is fleeting and must be enjoyed for the moment—the *carpe diem* theme. Eliminating concrete time (to force life in the present) and choosing an episodic form enforce the theme and formally capture the essence of the elder actor's musings, ''Ephemera! Ephemera!'' Gussow suggests, ''Acting is for the moment, and Mr. Mamet has captured moments that add up to a lifetime.'' If there is a unifying thread that binds the scenes, it is finally up to the audience to produce it, as was required in *Sexual Perversity in Chicago*. Life is episodic, Mamet suggests, and it is human artifice that insists on linking them and even on fossilizing them for understanding and for posterity. Mamet comes very close in this play to producing a work of raw material, then asking we put it together.

There was of course criticism of the play, namely that the characters and actions were stereotypical and clichéd, but given the choice of form, the characters and events could never be as

developed as they would have been if given a more conventionally narrative approach. It is very likely that such was Mamet's intent, an argument that what we look at as ''personality,'' whole and consistent, is rarely if ever experienced in the real world.

Source: William W. Demastes, *Beyond Naturalism,* Greenwood Press, 1988.

SOURCES

Billington, Michael, ''Life in the Final Stages,'' in *Manchester Guardian Weekly,* November 12, 1989, p. 26.

Clurman, Harold, Review in *The Nation,* November 12, 1977, p. 504–05.

Gussow, Mel, ''Illusion within an Illusion,'' in *New York Times,* October 21, 1977, p. 12.

———, ''Mamet Wins with *Life in Theater,''* in *New York Times,* February 5, 1977, p. 10.

Hampton, Wilborn, ''Looking At Life As a Play,'' in *New York Times,* February 29, 1992, sec. 1, p. 18.

Hughes, Catharine, ''Great Expectations,'' in *America,* December 10, 1977, p. 423.

Kalem, T. E., ''Curtain Call,'' in *Time,* October 31, 1977, p. 94.

Kennedy, Douglas, ''Hey, Big Spender,'' in *New Statesman & Society,* December 8, 1989, pp. 44–5.

Kerr, Walter, ''Parody In and Out of Focus,'' in *New York Times,* October 30, 1977, p. D5.

Klein, Alvin, ''An Early Tribute to Performers from Mamet,'' in *New York Times,* November 4, 1990, sec. 12, p. 21.

Mamet, David, *A Life in the Theatre,* Grove Press, 1977.

Oliver, Edith, ''Actor Variations,'' in *New Yorker,* October 31, 1977, pp. 115–18.

Simon, John, Review in *The Hudson Review,* Spring 1978, pp, 154–55,

FURTHER READING

Dean, Anne, *David Mamet: Language as Dramatic Action,* Fairleigh Dickinson University Press, 1990, pp. 119–47.
> This chapter offers interpretation of and covers topics critical to *A Life in the Theatre.*

Kane, Leslie, ed., *David Mamet: A Casebook,* Garland Publishing, 1992.
> This collection of critical essays includes several that comment on aspects of *A Life in the Theatre.*

Lahr, John, ''Profile: Fortress Mamet,'' in the *New Yorker,* November 17, 1997, pp. 70–82.
> This biographical article covers the whole of Mamet's life and work.

Mamet, David, ''A 'Sad Comedy' About Actors,'' in the *New York Times,* October 16, 1977, p. D7.
> In this article, Mamet discusses the inspiration for and writing of *A Life in the Theatre.*

The River Niger

JOSEPH A. WALKER

1972

The River Niger, a loosely autobiographical play by Joseph A. Walker, was first performed by the Negro Ensemble Company in New York City in 1972. The play was first published in 1973, and was adapted to the screen by Walker in the 1976 production starring Cicely Tyson and James Earl Jones.

The River Niger is about Jeff Williams, a young African-American man returning home to his family in Harlem after several years in the Air Force. His mother, Mattie; father, John; and grandmother eagerly await his arrival. Ann Vanderguild, a nurse from South Africa who met Jeff at a hospital in Canada, unexpectedly arrives at the Williams' house with her suitcases, intending to convince Jeff to marry her. When Jeff finally arrives, he is greeted by his childhood friend Mo and Mo's men, a small group of revolutionaries who try to bully Jeff into joining their organization. But Jeff does not agree with their politics and is set on becoming a lawyer. Jeff, however, severely disappoints his father when he informs the family that he has flunked out of the Air Force and never liked it in the first place. Jeff's father, John, is so enraged by this that he leaves home and doesn't return until a week later, having gone on a drinking "bender." After Jeff reluctantly agrees to help Mo and his organization, they all find themselves in the Williams' house, surrounded by police who have discovered a violent plot planned by the young revolutionaries. Jeff's father sacrifices his life to save Jeff from being implicated in the crime.

The River Niger focuses on themes common to much of Walker's work: the struggles of black men in a racist society; the camaraderie between black men; the role of men in the black family; and efforts among African Americans to achieve greater equality.

AUTHOR BIOGRAPHY

Joseph A. Walker made a name for himself in the 1970s with his dramatic stage plays highlighting the struggles of African-American men in a white-dominated, racist society. Walker was born on February 23, 1935, in Washington, D.C., to Joseph (a house painter) and Florine Walker. In 1956, Walker graduated from Howard University, where he majored in philosophy and minored in drama. From 1956 to 1960, Walker was in the United States Air Force, reaching the rank of first lieutenant before being discharged.

While in the Air Force, the experience of being teased by a white fellow Air Force member for writing poetry inspired Walker to quit the armed forces and devote himself to the craft of writing. In the one-paragraph ''Joe Walker's Autobiography,'' which prefaces *The River Niger*, Walker explains, ''I started to become a professional philosopher, whatever that means, changed my mind on account of I got what you may stuffily call an artistic temperament and I like to do my thinking through plays and things.''

In 1963, Walker earned a Master of Fine Arts degree from Catholic University. He then turned to teaching, first in a Washington, D.C., high school and later at City College of New York. His first marriage, to Barbara Brown, ended in divorce in 1965, and was followed by his marriage to Dorothy A. Dinroe in 1970. From 1970 to 1971, Walker was playwright-in-residence at Yale University. He returned to Howard University, where he became a full professor of drama.

Walker's first play, *The Harangues*, was staged by the Negro Ensemble Company in 1970, and was followed by *Ododo* in 1971. Walker's most critically acclaimed work, *The River Niger* (1972), garnered numerous distinguished drama awards, including an Obie Award, an Antoinette Perry (Tony) Award, the Dramatist Guild's Elizabeth Hull-Kate Award, First Annual Audelco Award, John Gassner Award from Outer Circle, Drama Desk Award, and the Black Rose Award. Walker also wrote the screenplay adaptation of *The River Niger*, which was produced by Cine Arts in 1976, starring Cicely Tyson and James Earl Jones.

Walker has appeared as an actor in stage productions of *A Raisin in the Sun* and *Once in a Lifetime;* in the movies *April Fools* (1969), and *Bananas* (1971); and in an award-winning episode of the popular TV show *N.Y.P.D.*

Walker was also the co-founder and artistic director of the dance-music theater repertory company The Demi-Gods.

PLOT SUMMARY

Act 1

In act 1 of *The River Niger*, John and Mattie Williams prepare for the return home of their son Jeff, who has spent several years in the Air Force. As the play opens, Jeff's grandmother Wilhemina Brown, Mattie's mother, sneaks a drink from her hiding place in the kitchen. John and his friend Dr. Dudley Stanton share a drink and banter; their banter includes both crude insults and obvious expressions of loving camaraderie. Ann Vanderguild arrives at the Williams' house. She is a nurse in her twenties, from South Africa, who cared for Jeff in a hospital in Canada and has arrived without invitation or warning, hoping to get Jeff to marry her. Everyone perceives this right away, but the men are impressed by her physical attractiveness, and John reads aloud a poem he has written. When Jeff's mother and grandmother return home from shopping, Mattie is quickly won over by Ann's sincerity and charm, but Grandma immediately and openly disapproves of her.

John and Dudley leave for the Apple, the local bar. Ann explains to Mattie that her father has been in prison in South Africa for the past nine years because her two brothers had been carrying out anti-government activities; her father took the blame so that her brothers could flee the country.

Ann and Mattie begin preparing dinner. Chips, a childhood friend of Jeff's, shows up at the door looking for Jeff. Chips is sexually aggressive toward Ann. That night, as Ann is sleeping in the living room, Mo and his friends—Chips, Skeeter, Al, and Mo's girlfriend Gail—members of a local revolutionary group, barge in looking for Jeff. They attempt to intimidate Ann, until John and Dudley arrive home from the bar, drunk, and John threatens them with a gun. After they leave, John and Dudley share another drink in the kitchen, while Jeff sneaks in and awakens Ann, who is sleeping in the living room. The two have sex, then Jeff sneaks up to his bedroom.

Act 2

In act 2, the next morning, John pauses in the middle of mopping the kitchen floor to write a poem which begins, ''I am the River Niger.'' Dudley arrives, and the two men leave for the local bar. Mattie explains to Ann that John wanted to become a lawyer, but had to quit school to support various members of Mattie's family who had migrated from the South to Harlem. Mattie tells Ann that she allows John to drink because she feels responsible for his disappointments in life.

After Mattie and Grandma leave to go shopping, Mo, Gail, Skeeter, Al, and Chips show up and begin harassing Ann. Al follows Ann upstairs and attempts to rape her at gunpoint. Jeff, who has been in his bedroom, attacks Al, takes the gun away from him, and comes downstairs holding it to Al's head. Mo and his men try to bully Jeff into joining their organization, but Jeff does not agree with their politics and tells them he plans to become a lawyer. Mo, Gail, and Mo's men leave. Mattie and Grandma return from shopping and Jeff announces his arrival home. He tells them that he wants to marry Ann. John and Dudley arrive home drunk, and John insists that Jeff put on his military uniform. Jeff tells them that he has flunked out of the Air Force, and that he never liked it. John is so enraged that he walks out.

Act 3

In act 3, the following Friday evening, Mattie, Grandma, Jeff, Ann, and Dudley all sit at the dinner table. John has been gone for almost a week. Dudley informs them all that Mattie has cancer and is going to need radium treatment. Mo and Gail show up, and Mo tells Jeff and Ann that there is a ''stool pigeon''

in his organization and asks Jeff to help find out who it is. Jeff and Ann both agree to help. At this point, John arrives home, obviously having been on a week-long drinking ''bender,'' with a gash on his head from being beaten up by Mo's men. John reads aloud his poem ''The River Niger,'' which he has written for Mattie. Mo unexpectedly arrives with Skeeter, who has been injured during their botched attempt at a violent political action. Gail, Chips, and Al also arrive. The voice of Lieutenant Staples is heard announcing that the police have surrounded the house. Jeff figures out that Al is the one who betrayed them, by informing the police of the location of their attempted action. Al and John simultaneously shoot each other—Al dies immediately, while John is fatally wounded. As he is dying, John tells them to blame the entire incident on him, so that Jeff will not be implicated in the illegal activities of the organization. John then dies in Mattie's arms.

CHARACTERS

Al

Al is one of ''Mo's men,'' a black revolutionary organization. He is described as a ''closet homosexual, capable, determined, very young.'' In the end of the play, Al turns out to be the informer who has betrayed his fellow revolutionaries. In a scuffle that ensues, Al and John simultaneously shoot one another, and they both die.

Grandma Wilhemina Brown

Grandma Wilhemina Brown is Mattie's mother, Jeff's grandmother. She is described as ''a stately, fair-skinned black woman in her middle eighties'' and ''very alive.'' Grandma is drunk just about all the time, from the liquor bottles she hides in the kitchen. She often sings or hums ''Rock of Ages'' and other hymns. She also frequently mentions her deceased husband, whom she idealizes as a model man. Grandma immediately disapproves of Ann, whom she perceives to be roping Jeff into marriage.

Chips

Chips, in his early twenties, is one of ''Mo's Men,'' a local revolutionary organization. He is described as "a tall, rangy young man," a "sexually perverted young fool" who "has an air of 'I'm a bad nigger' about him." Chips is sexually aggressive towards Ann. When Jeff later catches Chips attempting to rape Ann at gunpoint, he wrestles Chips's gun out of his hands and threatens him with it.

Gail

Gail, twenty-one, is described as "sincere and very much in love with Mo." Gail pleads with Jeff to help straighten Mo out, as she feels his revolutionary organization has gotten out of hand. Jeff reluctantly promises her that he will.

Mo

Mo, twenty-four, is described as "athletic-looking." He is the head of a small group of black revolutionaries and is further described as a "young black leader of underlying beauty and integrity."

Skeeter

Skeeter is one of "Mo's Men," a black revolutionary organization. He is described as "basically good, but hung on dope."

Dr. Dudley Stanton

Dr. Dudley Stanton, in his late fifties, is a very close friend of John, with whom he shares sarcastic banter as well as heart-felt mutual love. Dudley informs John that his wife, Mattie, has been diagnosed with cancer, and will need radium treatment. Dudley is also John's drinking buddy, and often accompanies him to the local bar. He is described as "cynical, classic Jamaican, lover of poetry," and he speaks in "a thick and beautiful Jamaican accent." The content of Dudley's speech, however, is extremely crude. Dudley's thematic significance in the play is threefold: He is an example of the deep, loving camaraderie between men; a representative of the successful black middle class; and a cynic in regard to both the racial oppression of African Americans and to any efforts at political action.

Ann Vanderguild

Ann Vanderguild, twenty-two, a nurse, is described as a "strong black South African girl, lover of quality." She is also "very attractive" and

MEDIA ADAPTATIONS

- *The River Niger* was adapted by Walker as a film with the same title. It was produced by Cine Arts in 1976 and starred Cicely Tyson and James Earl Jones.

"sparkles on top of a deep brooding inner core." Ann's father has been in prison in South Africa for nine years, because he chose to take the blame for the anti-government activities of his two sons.

Ann, who fell in love with Jeff while caring for him at a hospital in Canada, unexpectedly shows up at the Williams' house the day before Jeff returns home. Everyone immediately perceives that she has arrived without Jeff's knowledge to get him to marry her. Grandma remains disdainful of her, but Mattie, Jeff's mother, is almost immediately won over and accepts her love of Jeff. Jeff proposes to Ann, and the two talk of marrying within the week.

Jeff Williams

Jeff Williams, twenty-five, is the son of Mattie and John. He is described as "thoughtful, wild, a credit to his father." There is also "a heavy seriousness about him, frosted over with the wildness he has inherited from his father." In addition, "His presence is strong and commanding." Jeff's childhood friend Mo, now the leader of a local revolutionary organization, and Mo's men attempt to bully Jeff into joining their organization. Jeff, however, does not agree with their politics and plans to become a lawyer.

John Williams

John Williams, in his fifties, is Jeff's father. He is described as "an alive poet," and his poem "The River Niger" is an important element of the play. John is a housepainter, as well as an alcoholic. He sneaks drinks, borrows money from his friend Dudley to pay the rent, and frequently takes off for the local bar, the Apple, when he is supposed to be at home. Mattie, his wife, is indulgent of his weaknesses because, she explains, he wanted to become a lawyer but had to quit school to support a number of Mattie's relatives who migrated to Harlem from the South. At the end of the play, John heroically takes responsibility for the illegal activities of the young black revolutionaries and is shot to death. Like Ann's father, who took the blame and went to prison for her brothers' illegal revolutionary activities, John sacrifices his life to save his son.

Mattie Williams

Mattie Williams, in her fifties, is Jeff's mother, John's wife, and Grandma's daughter. She is described as "an embittered but happy woman." Although she does not learn this until late in the play, Mattie is dying of cancer. Mattie adores both her son and her husband, and completely accepts them as they are. She secretly condones her husband's drinking, because she feels that his ambitions of becoming a lawyer were dashed by the need to support her extended family.

THEMES

African-American Identity Politics

Throughout the play, Walker explores a variety of approaches to black struggles for racial equality. Several of the different political philosophies and organizations active among African Americans during the early 1970s are mentioned, discussed, and debated by various characters. Mo, Al, Chips, and Skeeter have chosen to fight racism through belonging to a "revolutionary" organization resembling the Black Panthers. Their approach is to attempt to commit a violent act in the name of revolution. The early black nationalist and separatist leader Marcus Garvey is mentioned, as well as Muslim black nationalist leader Malcolm X.

Jeff chooses to struggle against racism within the law, by planning to become a lawyer. John's wish for his son is that Jeff will succeed in the "United States of America Air Force"—that is, in the white, mainstream world. John himself, however, is unsure of where to direct his energies in the struggle for racial equality; he calls himself a "fighter" but doesn't know where the "battlefield" is. Dudley, on the other hand, remains cynical about any prospect of either successfully assimilating into white America or effectively fighting racism. He refers to Jeff's position in the Air Force as that of "a powerless nub in a silly military grist mill" and has no faith in the power of black community, describing it as "Just a bunch of black crabs in a barrel, lying to each other, always lying and pulling each other back down."

Poetry

Poetry is an important theme of Walker's play. Although he is a housepainter by trade and a hopeless alcoholic, John is also a poet. Early in the play, John describes himself as a warrior without a battlefield, unsure of how to go about fighting for racial equality. In the end of act 2, he comes closer to defining his "battlefield" in asserting that his racial pride is expressed through his poetry. He tells Dudley, "I'm a poet, ya hear me, a poet! When this country—when this world, learns the meaning of poetry—" John then turns to his son, explaining to him, "Don't you see, Jeff, poetry is what the revolution's all about—never lose sight of the true purpose of the revolution, all revolutions—to restore poetry to the godhead!" John goes on to assert,

> Poetry is religion, the alpha and the omega, the cement of the universe. The supereye under which every other eye is scrutinized, and it stretches from one to infinity, from bulls—t to the beatific, the rocking horse of the human spirit—God himself. God himself is pure distilled poetry.

For John, poetry is both a spiritual and a political force. He concludes that, "Ain't none of us gonna be free until poetry rides a mercury-smooth silver stallion."

John, however, fails to appreciate that Jeff has left the military precisely because he values poetry—being teased by a fellow serviceman for writing a poem was the incident which caused him to reassess his values and choose to pursue his own will rather than that of his father or of white society.

The importance of poetry to Walker's concerns with African-American identity and racial equality is indicated by the fact that the title of the play is borrowed from the title of the poem John writes, a

TOPICS FOR FURTHER STUDY

- In the play, the character of Ann Vanderguild is from South Africa, and her father is in prison for political activities carried out by her brothers. Learn about the history of racial relations in South Africa in the twentieth century and beyond. In what ways have racial relations in South Africa changed since this play was written?

- African-American political leader Malcolm X is mentioned in the play. Learn more about his political philosophy and activities. In what ways did he influence racial politics in America in the twentieth century? What do *you* think of his political philosophy and activities?

- Walker's play was written and takes place during the era of the Civil Rights Movement. Learn more about the history of the Civil Rights Movement. What important events took place? What significant changes in American race relations resulted from the efforts of members of the Civil Rights Movement?

- Walker's play was first produced during the period of the Black Arts Movement. Learn more about the Black Arts Movement. Who were some of the influential people in formulating and defining the movement? What were the political and aesthetic values set forth by the movement? What important works emerged from the Black Arts Movement?

poem which celebrates African-American history, culture, and identity.

The Role of Women in the African-American Family

Walker's play is concerned with the role of women in the African-American family, particularly in terms of how they treat their men. All the women in the play—Grandma, Mattie, Ann, and Gail—are presented in a positive light because they are completely loving, supportive, and non-judgmental toward their men. Grandma seems to be a role model in her absolute idealization of her deceased husband, asserting, "my man was a king." Mattie is also presented as a model wife in terms of her acceptance and devotion to her husband and her praise of black men in general. Referring to John, she tells Ann, "A good man is a treasure." Mattie comments, "White folks proclaim that our men are no good and we go 'round like fools trying to prove them wrong," and asks, "If our men are no good, then why are all these little white girls trying to gobble 'em up faster than they can pee straight?"

Although John is an alcoholic, Mattie feels it is her fault; he gave up his educational ambitions in

order to support her extended family. The younger women, Ann and Gail, are equally supportive of their men.

STYLE

Music

The only musical accompaniment specified in the play is that of a bass. Interestingly, the Bass Player is listed as one of the characters, although not actually part of the story or seen on stage. The Bass Player, who "provides musical poetry for the play," is described as "highly skillful at creating a mood." The bass line fades in and out to create a particular mood at key points in the play, often associated with specific characters. Grandma's solo trips into the kitchen to sneak alcohol from her various hiding places are often accompanied by a bass line, sometimes as a backup to her frequent singing of hymns. A bass line also accompanies John when he is reading his poetry aloud, either to himself or others, sometimes specifically with a "jazz theme." A bass line often accompanies Ann during key moments of the play. When she first enters the Williams' home, "a bass line of beautiful melancholy comes in." Here, the musical accompaniment is meant to provide a sense of Ann's inner character and mood. Later, as she tells Mattie the tragic story of her father's nine years' imprisonment in South Africa, the "bass melancholy" enters again. When Jeff and Ann kiss at the close of act 1, the bass line "plays under" to accentuate the romantic mood of the two lovers reunited.

Poetry

Poetry is an important theme in the play, and John's poem "The River Niger" is clearly a key element of the story, as it lends the play its title. In act 1, John has only begun the poem, which he reads to himself from a scrap of paper in his pocket. Later, John reads a different, completed poem aloud to Ann and Dudley. In the beginning of act 2, John continues to work on "The River Niger," which he reads aloud to himself. Finally, in act 3, after John returns home from a week-long drinking spree, he reads the completed poem, which he has written to Mattie, aloud to an audience that includes the whole family as well as Dudley and Jeff's friends. The poem, which begins, "I am the River Niger—hear my waters!" evokes images of the African roots of African-American people and culture. It suggests that these cultural origins were transported to America with the slave trade, "to the cloudy Mississippi / Over keels of incomprehensible woe" and continue to flow in African-American culture, "Transplanted to Harlem / From the Harlem River Drive." The poem ends with a plea for African Americans not to "deny" their cultural roots: "I am the River Niger! Don't deny me!"

Setting

The play is set in Harlem, New York City, on "February 1, the Present: 4:30 p.m." In specifying the exact time and day of the year, but designating the year as "the Present," Walker makes the setting specific, yet relevant to the contemporary reader or theater spectator regardless of the year in which the play is actually read or a production attended. The setting is more specifically designated as a "brownstone on 133rd between Lenox and Seventh." The setting in a specific neighborhood of New York City is important because Harlem has long been associ-

ated with the African-American community. Harlem became occupied primarily by African Americans beginning in the early twentieth century, although, by the end of the twentieth century this demographic was no longer accurate. The setting on 133rd Street between Lenox and Seventh Avenue is further significant in that, according to *Encyclopaedia Britannica,* landlords in the area first began renting primarily to African Americans along Lenox Avenue, and, by World War I, "the chief artery of black Harlem is 125th Street, popularly called the 'main stem.'" In other words, Walker has set the Williams family brownstone in a neighborhood that has long been in the heart of black Harlem. This setting is significant to Walker's thematic focus on African-American identity as rooted in African-American history.

HISTORICAL CONTEXT

African-American Literary Movements

Twentieth-century African-American literature has been characterized by two important movements: the Harlem Renaissance and the Black Arts Movement. The Harlem Renaissance, also referred to as the New Negro Movement, designates a period during the 1920s in which African-American literature flourished among a group of writers concentrated in Harlem, New York City. The Black Arts Movement, also referred to as the Black Aesthetic Movement, which flourished during the 1960s and '70s, embodied values derived from black nationalism, promoting politically and socially significant works, often written in Black English vernacular. Important writers of the Black Arts Movement include Amiri Baraka, Eldridge Cleaver, Angela Davis, Alice Walker, and Toni Morrison.

African-American Theater

The development of African-American theater in the first half of the twentieth century was inspired by the Harlem Renaissance and included the establishment of theaters devoted to black productions in major cities throughout the United States. In the post-World War II era, black theater became more overtly political and more specifically focused on celebrating African-American culture. One of the

COMPARE
&
CONTRAST

- **1825:** Explorer Hugh Clapperton attempts to determine the course of the Niger River.

  1830: The British government commissions Richard and John Lander, English explorers of West Africa, to complete Clapperton's exploration of the river. The brother's explorations determined the Niger River flowed into the Atlantic Ocean, dispelling the previous belief that the Niger was a tributary of the Nile River.

  2000: The river Niger provides irrigation for agriculture and serves as a major means of transportation to the cities and villages it transgresses. Many visitors can travel the Niger River on large river boats, which takes them down the river and over half the country in one week's time. Tourists can also take more leisurely tours on the river by using a traditional pirogue (small canoe) or a pinasse (motor boat).

- **1950s:** Malcolm X becomes the primary spokesman for the Nation of Islam. The Nation's message, preaching self-help and personal responsibility, is particularly popular in Harlem, Chicago, Los Angeles, and Detroit. Malcolm's anti-white man speeches and calls for a separate country for blacks inspires Huey Newton and Bobby Seale to form The Black Panthers.

  1960s: Malcolm X breaks with the Nation of Islam, denouncing Elijah Muhammad as a fake. He no longer preaches a message of hatred and separatism. Malcolm X establishes Muslim Mosque, Inc., Elijah Muhammad appoints Minister Louis Farrakhan to Temple No. 7 in New York City. In 1964, Malcolm X is assassinated while delivering a speech to his followers.

  1970s–2000: Under the spiritual leadership of Minister Louis Farrakhan, The Nation of Islam gains new respect and more members, extending to mosques and study groups in over eighty cities in America. Farrakhan is active in lecturing throughout many countries, drawing crowds of 60,000, preaching the Nation's messages and promoting the issues of freedom, equality, and unity.

- **1920:** During the 1920s, many popular and critically successful African-American artists live in Harlem and produce important works during their time there. Some of the artists living in Harlem at this time include Langston Hughes, Jean Toomer, Billie Holiday, and Bessie Smith. This time period becomes known as the Harlem Renaissance.

  1970s: Although Harlem retains a predominantly African-American population and many artists continue to settle in this village of New York, it has lost much of its former glory. Harlem gains a reputation for being an area high in crime and poverty.

  2000: Much has been done to improve Harlem's reputation, and tourists to New York are encouraged to visit Harlem and see many of its historic sites and attractions, including Riverbank State Park, the Apollo Theater, Sugar Hill, which is the area where Count Basie and Sugar Ray Robinson lived, and the Schomberg Center, which was the home of the Harlem literary renaissance.

most prominent works to emerge from this period was the 1959 play *A Raisin in the Sun* by Lorraine Hansberry. The Black Arts Movement, which emerged in the 1960s, led to the establishment in 1965 of the Black Repertory Theater in Harlem, initiated by Amiri Baraka. Baraka's award-winning

1964 play *Dutchman* is among the most celebrated dramatic works of this period. Ntozake Shange's 1977 *for colored girls who have considered suicide/ when the rainbow is enuf* used an experimental dramatic format to address issues facing African-American women. In the 1980s, August Wilson emerged as one of the most important African-American playwrights with his play *Ma Rainey's Black Bottom* (1985), set in Chicago in the 1920s, about a blues singer and her band.

The Niger River

The title of Walker's play is taken from the poem "The River Niger," written and read aloud by the character John Williams. The Niger River runs through West Africa and is the third-longest river on the continent (after the Nile and the Congo). Until the abolishment of the British slave trade in 1807, the Niger River Basin was regularly used in the slave trade for transporting captured Africans. (After the slave trade was abolished, slave merchants changed their trade to that of palm oil, which was likewise shipped through the Niger River Basin.)

In John's poem, the River Niger represents the ancestral roots of African Americans in Africa, as well as the river's historical use in the slave trade, as expressed in the lines: "I came to the cloudy Mississippi / Over keels of incomprehensible woe." Reference to the River Niger in the poem also asserts the continuation of the "spirit" of African heritage; the poem begins, "I am the River Niger—hear my waters!" and includes the lines, "I sleep in your veins," and "I flow to the ends of your spirit."

The Black Panthers

Although the Black Panthers are never named in Walker's play, the small, local band of revolutionaries led by Mo is clearly meant to refer to the Black Panther Party and other such organizations. Originally called the Black Panther Party for Self-Defense, the Black Panther Party was organized in 1966 in Berkeley, California, by Bobby Seale and Huey Newton. Their primary focus was to arm African Americans and patrol the streets of black neighborhoods to protect the African-American community from police brutality. Their signature "uniform" was a black beret. (In act 3 of Walker's play, John tells Mo that being a revolutionary "takes more 'n wearing a goddamn beret." At its height, membership in the party was over 2,000. Although many more African Americans clearly sympathized with the Panthers' politics, others were critical of their violent approach to battling racism. The police in major cities of California, Illinois, and New York were suspected of inciting unnecessarily violent conflicts with members of the Panther Party. By the early 1980s, the Black Panther Party had essentially disbanded.

Marcus Garvey

In act 3, John Williams mentions "the great Marcus Garvey." As Marcus Garvey (1887–1940) was an early organizer in trying to empower African Americans, reference to him is significant to the play's theme of African-American struggles for racial equality. Garvey was born in Jamaica, where he and several friends founded the Universal Negro Improvement Association (UNIA) in 1914 to advocate the establishment of a black-governed nation in Africa. (Most African countries before World War II were still colonies of European empires.) Although not a successful leader in Jamaica, Garvey became highly influential in the United States after his move to Harlem in 1916. Within several years, Garvey, who was dubbed the "black Moses," had a following of some two million African Americans, and had established a newspaper, *Negro World*. Garvey used the term "new Negro" to advocate racial pride and a separatist philosophy. In 1920, he organized and led a parade through Harlem with a turnout of 50,000. Garvey, however, was criticized by other African-American leaders, such as W. E. B. Du Bois, for his advocacy of extreme racial separatism.

CRITICAL OVERVIEW

The River Niger is Walker's most widely recognized and most critically acclaimed work, garnering a host of awards, including the Obie Award in 1971, the Antoinette Perry (Tony) Award in 1973, the Elizabeth Hull-Kate Award from the Dramatists Guild, the First Annual Audelco Award, the John Gassner Award from Outer Circle, the Drama Desk Award, and the Black Rose. It was first performed by the Negro Ensemble Company at the St. Mark's Playhouse in New York City in 1972, and in 1973 opened at the Brooks Atkinson Theater in New York City. It was first published in book form by Hill and Wang in 1973. *The River Niger* was also adapted to the screen by Walker and produced as a film of the same title by Cine Artists in 1976, starring Cicely Tyson and James Earl Jones.

Grace Cooper, in the *Dictionary of Literary Biography,* praises *The River Niger*—Walker's fourth play to be produced—as an advancement in his writing. She asserts that it "shows his full growth as a playwright" in that, "[w]hile it expresses many of the same strong feelings of the earlier plays, *The River Niger* is more subtle, therefore allowing him to make his points acceptable to a larger audience."

Critics often mention the autobiographical element of Walker's play. In particular, the incident in which Jeff is teased by a fellow serviceman for writing poetry represents a similar incident in Walker's life that inspired him to quit the military and devote himself to writing. Cooper notes, ''The play has been widely recognized as a realistic depiction of black life,'' adding, ''The realism of the play is derived in part from Walker's reliance on his own experiences and on family members as models for many of the characters.''

Cooper also points out the use of a diverse range of characters within the African-American community, stating, ''The characters come from a variety of black cultural backgrounds, reflecting a cross-cultural interchange that whites often do not note.'' Cooper goes on to observe the skill with which Walker uses language to create a variety of characters: ''Walker manipulates language in all its nuances to create the proper tone for each character.'' Writing in 1985, Cooper concludes that, ''Walker continues to be a vital force in black theater'' and that he ''will remain a force to consider wherever black theater in America is discussed.''

Stanley Kauffmann, however, writing in *The New Republic* in 1973, is highly critical of the play: ''I haven't in a long time seen a realistic play so clumsily built, so naively motivated, so arbitrarily whipped to climaxes, and so ridiculously concluded . . .'' He sums up the play's weaknesses by describing it as

> laden with this erratic language, this dramaturgy so clumsily clever that it's not primitive but bad, torturously serpentine in its progress, devoid of any sense of emphasis as to which scenes should be long or short

Kauffmann does allow that, ''the play nevertheless has a certain insistent life.'' He also reserves praise for the play's ''veracity,'' and ''truth of affection.'' He explains that this veracity has a different significance for white and black audiences: ''For a white viewer, this veracity is informational—a peek behind closed doors. For black viewers, as I have seen twice with black audiences, there is warm recognition. Clearly, *The River Niger* is doing for many black people what hundreds of realistic plays have done for whites for a century: quite apart from its quality, the play certifies the audience's existence. This is not arbitrarily a negligible function, particularly for American blacks, who have so long been deprived of accurate theatrical vicars.'' Furthermore, the play's ''truth of affec-

tion'' is expressed by the ways in which ''people care for one another in this play in different alliances and affinities.'' Kauffmann concludes, ''Walker writes at his best when he's dealing with these feelings.''

In an overview of Walker's work in *Contemporary Authors,* his predominant theme of black masculinity is described: ''The focus of most of his works is on the psyche of black American males. Cut off from their ancestral home and exploited by whites, these disoriented men are portrayed as lacking a sense of identity, purpose, and self-worth.'' In light of this thematic focus, ''Walker's plays are still relevant because of their compelling depictions of those black males stagnated by feelings of impotence, frustration, and hopelessness.'' However, Walker is criticized for his poorly developed white and female characters: ''Walker's portraits of black women and whites rarely escape the limitations of stereotypes. Black women seldom have any personal goals, but instead function as either supporters or 'castrators' of their men. White women serve as sexual playmates and status symbols for their black lovers. White men exploit blacks and destroy those who pose a threat to their way of life. . . . some critics feel these characters weaken the credibility of Walker's plays.''

CRITICISM

Liz Brent

Brent has a Ph.D. in American Culture, specializing in film studies, from the University of Michigan. She is a freelance writer and teaches courses in the history of American cinema. In the following essay, Brent discusses references to cultural and historical figures in Walker's play.

The dialogue in Joseph A. Walker's play *The River Niger* makes reference to a wide array of historical and cultural figures, both real and fictional. These references include the Shakespearean character Shylock, the African folktale figure Brer Rabbit, the blues great Lightnin' Hopkins, the comic book superhero Superman, the biblical King Solomon, Hollywood movie star Gary Cooper, and the notorious French writer the Marquis de Sade. A brief explanation of who each of these figures is, and the significance of each one to the meaning of Walker's play, will enhance the reader's appreciation of this dramatic work.

**BROOKS ATKINSON
THEATRE**
Under the direction of James and Joseph Nederlander

The River Niger is being presented on Broadway because of an overwhelming demand for tickets which the Negro Ensemble was unable to fill during the play's recent four-month run at the St. Marks Playhouse.
For six seasons now, the NEC has been producing quality plays at our small 150-seat home base theatre. This unprecedented engagement on Broadway is noteworthy. However, it does not mean that we are departing from our well established activities as a non-profit producing institution and training program devoted to the continued growth and development of Black talents in every phase of theatre.

THE NEGRO ENSEMBLE COMPANY, INC.
presents
THE RIVER NIGER
by
JOSEPH A. WALKER

Directed by
DOUGLAS TURNER WARD

with
(Alphabetically)

TAUREAN BLACQUE	GRAHAM BROWN	BARBARA CLARKE
FRANCES FOSTER	ARTHUR FRENCH	DEAN IRBY
SAUNDRA McCLAIN	NEVILLE RICHEN	LES ROBERTS
LENNAL WAINWRIGHT		GRENNA WHITAKER

Lighting by	*Scenery by*	*Costumes by*
SHIRLEY PRENDERGAST	GARY JAMES WHEELER	EDNA WATSON

Incidental Music by
DOROTHY A. DINROE-WALKER

Scenery and Costumes Supervised by
EDWARD BURBRIDGE

PREMIERED DECEMBER 5, 1972 AT ST. MARKS PLAYHOUSE

This play is dedicated to my mother and father and to highly underrated Black daddies everywhere.
—JOSEPH A. WALKER

*Playbill title page from the 1972
production of* The River Niger.

In act 1, John Williams and Dr. Dudley return to the Williams's house, drunk from an evening spent at the local bar. As is characteristic of their friendship, the two banter rather ruthlessly. When Dudley asks John for a drink "for the road," he replies, "One for the road! Why didn't you buy one for the road before we hit the road? Shylock stingy bastard." This comment refers to the character Shylock from Shakespeare's play *The Merchant of Venice*. Shylock is a Jewish lender who insists on extracting "a pound of flesh" from a man who has not repaid his loan on time. "Shylock" has thus come into common usage to refer to a greedy, stingy creditor who uses extortion to collect his debts.

Shylock has become a controversial character among literary scholars, because, on one hand, he represents a common anti-Semitic stereotype of Jewish people as ruthlessly stingy and greedy, especially in matters of money-lending. Others, however, interpret Shylock as a spokesperson against society's unfair mistreatment of Jews; this interpretation is based on his famous speech to this effect, which begins, "Hath not a Jew eyes?"

In Walker's play, John calls Dudley "Shylock" to indicate that he was stingy in not buying his own last drink while still at the bar. Throughout their banter, John has referred to Dudley as a "Jew." It is not clear if his character may in fact be part Jewish; rather, it seems that John is referring to Dudley, a successful African-American doctor, as a "Jew" to insult him. To further the comparison to Shylock, Dudley has recently lent a large sum of money to John to pay his rent. John is thus implying that for Dudley to request a drink from him is equivalent to Shylock demanding "a pound of flesh" from the man to whom he has lent money.

Walker's repeated use of phrases such as "Godd—n black Jew doctor" in John's dialogue, and the reference to Shylock, seem to be anti-Semitic in their implications.

In the beginning of act 2, John stops mopping the kitchen floor to sit down and work on the poem he is writing. Dudley, his friend and drinking buddy, stops by, and John tells him he's "just in time" to take off for the local bar. John says jokingly, "Do you know that, I—me—Lightnin' John Williams—more powerful than a speeding locomotive—do you realize that I have mopped this entire house by myself?" This line includes references to two figures in American cultural history. The first is the great blues musician Lightnin' Hopkins. John is comparing himself to a great African-American blues artist because he has just been working on his own artistic creation—a poem—and is feeling proud of what he's written so far. At the same time, John is being silly by comparing the work of a great musician to the accomplishment of having mopped the floor of a house. Likewise, his use of the phrase "more powerful than a speeding locomotive" refers to the introductory lines of a Superman comic book story. Again, John is describing the accomplishment of his domestic chores, traditionally considered to be women's work, with a legendary image of pure, unchecked, masculine strength and power. This indirect reference is significant to a central theme of Walker's play, which is about African-American men feeling disempowered and emasculated by racial and economic oppression. By referring jokingly to the powers of Superman, John is expressing his feelings of comparative powerlessness and emasculation.

In the beginning of act 2, John plans to sneak out of the house without his wife's knowing in order to escape his housecleaning responsibilities and go out drinking with his friend Dudley. Dudley chides him for "always sneaking around like Brer Rabbit" instead of acting like an "African warrior" and asserting himself with his wife.

WHAT DO I READ NEXT?

- *Black Drama Anthology* (1972), edited by Woodie King and Ron Milner. This anthology is a collection of plays by African-American writers, including *Ododo* (1970) by Joseph A. Walker.

- *The Best Plays of 1967–1968* (1968), edited by Otis L. Guernsey. This collection includes *The Believers*, a play by Joseph A. Walker and Josephine Jackson.

- *The Slave Ship* (1964), by Amiri Baraka/LeRoi Jones. Baraka's play is an early experimental play about racial oppression in America, written by a leading writer in the Black Arts Movement. The play takes place during three periods of African-American history.

- *Black Drama in America: An Anthology* (1994),

edited and with an introduction by Darwin T. Turner. This collection of plays by African-American authors includes Langston Hughes, Imamu Amiri Baraka, and August Wilson.

- *They Had a Dream: The Civil Rights Struggle, from Frederick Douglass to Marcus Garvey to Martin Luther King and Malcolm X* (1993), by Jules Archer. This text provides a history of some of the most influential figures in the struggle for racial equality in America.

- *The Amen Corner*, by James Baldwin (1968). *The Amen Corner* is the first play by the leading African-American writer James Baldwin. Baldwin's play focuses on the theme of the struggles of black men in the African-American family.

Brer Rabbit is a figure from African folktales which were transported to African American and then American culture with the slave trade. Brer Rabbit appears in a cycle of tales which fall into the culturally widespread category of the "trickster" figure. The "trickster" is a character, often an animal, who is able to beat out more powerful opponents through his cleverness; Brer Rabbit, for instance, outsmarts characters such as Brer Bear, Brer Fox, and Brer Wolf.

Brer Rabbit became well-known throughout American culture with the publication of "Uncle Remus" stories by the white writer Joel Chandler Harris (1848–1908) in the book *Uncle Remus: His Songs and His Sayings* (1880). Harris collected tales of Brer Rabbit from the oral culture of African-American plantation slaves and published them as a series of stories told by his fictional character Uncle Remus, an elderly African-American slave.

In Walker's play, Dudley's mention of Brer Rabbit is first of all a reference to the survival of African cultural roots from the days of slavery to contemporary African-American culture. Second, Dudley is suggesting that John is like Brer Rabbit,

using cleverness to outsmart his wife, who is more powerful than he. Dudley contrasts such a trickster figure with the image of an "African warrior," thus making clear to John the extent to which he is disempowered and emasculated in his own home and family. One of Walker's primary concerns in this play is African-American men feeling disempowered and emasculated by white American society, as well as by the women in their own homes.

In act 2, two of the members of Mo's revolutionary organization, Skeeter and Al, argue to the point where they find themselves holding each other at gunpoint. The stage notes indicate that, "In furious desperation, Skeeter suddenly reaches inside his coat, but Al is too quick. At about the same time, they both produce their revolvers." As they face each other, Al says to Skeeter, "Don't make the mistake of thinking a sissy can't play that Gary Cooper s—t if he want to." This line refers to the extremely popular classic Hollywood movie star Gary Cooper (1901–1961), who played the leading man in many films throughout the 1930s, 1940s, and 1950s, often as the hero in Westerns. He is perhaps most famous for his Academy Award-

> THIS INDIRECT REFERENCE IS SIGNIFICANT TO A CENTRAL THEME OF WALKER'S PLAY, WHICH IS ABOUT AFRICAN-AMERICAN MEN FEELING DISEMPOWERED AND EMASCULATED BY RACIAL AND ECONOMIC OPPRESSION. BY REFERRING JOKINGLY TO THE POWERS OF SUPERMAN, JOHN IS EXPRESSING HIS FEELINGS OF COMPARATIVE POWERLESSNESS AND EMASCULATION."

winning role in the Western *High Noon* (1952), which ends with one of the most famous shoot-out scenes in movie history.

In Walker's play, Al is referring to the ability of Cooper's Western characters to be fast-on-the-draw, as he manages to outdraw Skeeter. Furthermore, Al refers to himself as a "sissy," because he is a homosexual; in referring to Gary Cooper, Al is indicating that, although homosexuals are stereotyped as un-masculine, or "sissies," he himself can be compared to an icon of American masculinity and heroism.

In act 2, during a confrontation with Mo and his fellow "revolutionary" men, Jeff angrily refers to Chips as "Marquis de Sade." The notorious Marquis de Sade (1740–1814) was a French writer and eccentric from whose name the term "sadism" was derived. Throughout his life, de Sade was repeatedly arrested and imprisoned for kidnapping prostitutes and subjecting them to sexual tortures. During the 1780s, de Sade wrote and published several novels describing such sexual transgressions, the most well-known of which are *Justine* and *One Hundred and Twenty Days of Sodom*. Although officially banned in France, de Sade's writings became popular among artists and intellectuals during the nineteenth century, and today he is considered by some to have made a significant contribution to French literature.

In Walker's play, Jeff refers to Al as the "Marquis de Sade," because Al has just threatened to rape Ann at gunpoint and has repeatedly boasted of having had sex with a corpse. Unlike the cultural references discussed above, this one is not clearly associated with central themes of the play. However, since Al turns out to be the villain who betrays his fellow "revolutionaries" to the police, this reference works to establish him as a moral degenerate lacking in human compassion.

In act 2, Mattie explains to Ann the extent to which her husband John, although now an alcoholic, was once extremely smart and studious. She tells Ann that his fellow college students "used to call him Solomon," and that "some of his bummified wino friends still call him that. . . . Solomon!" Mattie is referring to King Solomon, who is legendarily the greatest king of ancient Israel.

Almost all historical knowledge of King Solomon and his reign is derived from biblical sources. Among Solomon's most noteworthy accomplishments was the great Temple of Jerusalem. In addition, Solomon is legendary for his wisdom and for his poetry as recorded in the biblical "Song of Solomon."

In Walker's play, the association of John Williams with Solomon is due both to his wisdom and to his skills and accomplishments as a poet. John is a talented poet whose greatest accomplishment is his poem "The River Niger," which he recites to his wife shortly before his death.

Throughout the play, John's decline as a man is indicated by various actions, characterizations, and comments. His association with the astoundingly accomplished King Solomon suggests that John's potential as a poet and wise, learned man was never realized due to oppressive conditions of racism and poverty.

Walker's play includes a rich variety of references to cultural and historical figures, each of which adds depth and dimension to central themes of African-American cultural identity, black masculinity, and the effects of racism and poverty on the African-American family.

Source: Liz Brent, in an essay for *Drama for Students,* Gale Group, 2001.

Anthony Barthelemy

Author Anthony Barthelemy discusses the political nature of The River Niger *regarding its representations of women and men and their inter-racial and intersexual struggles.*

Perhaps no single work by a black American play-wright has reached so vast an audience as Lorraine Hansberry's *A Raisin in the Sun.* A success on Broadway in 1959, the play enjoys frequent revivals by professional and amateur theater groups alike. It remains in print twenty-five years later, and the 1960 movie version appears regularly on our televi-sions. Unknown to this immense audience is the fact that *A Raisin in the Sun* responds to an earlier play by black playwright Theodore Ward and constitutes the middle third of a larger literary debate—a debate that began in 1938 when Ward's play *Big White Fog* opened in Chicago under the auspices of the Federal Theater Project. Playwright Joseph Walker contrib-uted the final third in 1973 when he wrote his Obie winning play *The River Niger.* As the first of the three, Ward's play is innocent of any attempts "to correct" or to displace a precursor text. *Big White Fog* quite simply dramatizes the story of a long-suffering black family from Chicago's Southside during the ten years between 1922 and 1932. Hansberry in *A Raisin in the Sun* seeks to correct Ward's representation of black women and to place black political aspirations firmly within the tradi-tional American bourgeois context by countering the revolutionary Marxist politics of *Big White Fog.* Although *The River Niger* equivocally endorses/ condemns sixties militancy, Walker really sets for himself a conservative, traditionally male political and social agenda. Stated quite simply, *The River Niger* valorizes male dominance and female sub-mission. Together the three plays provide an inter-esting study of the influence black playwrights have on each other and reveal the power that dramatic representation possesses. The plays also demon-strate the influence of a playwright's personal po-litical agenda in shaping character and theme.

The feminist revision of *Big White Fog* by Hansberry served as a catalyst to playwright Joseph Walker who in his play *The River Niger* challenges and faults Hansberry's representation of black men and women. In his play, Walker places before us another image of black men and women, one that is as politically charged as Hansberry's. Like her, he identifies his agenda in the play's dedication: "This play is dedicated to my mother and father and to highly underrated black daddies everywhere." The question that the dedication raises is this: Will Walker in rehabilitating "highly underrated black daddies" adopt an antifeminist agenda? However,

> HE REPLIES: 'OH, THESE STRONG BLACK WOMEN!' 'I'M ONLY STRONG,' ANN RESPONDS, 'IF MY MAN NEEDS ME TO BE, SIR.'"

before we turn to the play to seek the answer to this question, it would be useful to look at Walker's personal reminiscences of his father and mother. As Hansberry's recollections of her mother inform her portrayal of women in *A Raisin in the Sun,* so too do Walker's. In a page-long sentence entitled "Joe Walker's Autobiography" that appears just after the dedication page in the text of the play, Walker writes:

> . . . [daddy] was a bad-loud-talking dude of five feet eight inches tall, whom I once saw beat up a man six foot five because he insulted my seven-year-old dig-nity by beating the daylights out of me on account of I and my buddies were on a hate-little-girls campaign, throwing bottle tops at the cutest little brown oak girl . . . whom I don't think I really hated in retrospect because of her almond-shaped eyes—anyway, my pop was some dude . . . my ma, man, was a scornful bittersweet lovable crazy lady who was not quite as sweet as Mattie in *The River Niger* but who was pretty goddamn sweet and giving anyway.

Of course, Walker's play is not wholly autobio-graphical; however, he publicly acknowledges a correspondence between his mother and Mattie, the principal female character, and no doubt intends for there to be an equally strong correspondence be-tween his father and the play's hero, John Williams.

Personal correspondence notwithstanding, *The River Niger* presents to us a family that obviously and purposely resembles the ones—or one—that we have seen in the two previous plays. There are three generations in the same household, the oldest per-son being a widow. There is a couple with children. The family struggles to survive financially. There is the question of Africa, and in this play a Jamaican cynic, a sort of anti-Garvey. And, of course, the play's denouement results from American racism and the efforts of this black family to resist and overcome this pervasive fact of life. A closer look at the family and the action of the play will reveal its important and self-conscious dissimilarities to *A Raisin in the Sun.*

The River Niger opens with the Brooks/Lena analogue, Wilhemina Brown, creeping into the kitchen to sneak herself a drink. After pouring herself a cup of coffee, she ''stealthily'' locates her hidden bottle of Bourbon from which she pours into her coffee ''an extremely generous portion.'' This comic scene indicates the kind of treatment the elderly black woman will receive in the play and, of course, instructs us how to view her. But everything about her is not humorous. Like Brooks in *Big White Fog,* Wilhemina, ''a fair skinned black woman,'' takes pride in her light complexion and never hesitates to boast of her bigotry. Although she describes her late husband as ''black as a night what ain't got no Moon,'' she happily disparages others who are black. To her daughter Mattie and son-in-law John, whom the playwright describes as ''brown,'' Wilhemina brags of her children: ''And ain't none of 'em black either. . . . Mattie's the only black child I ever spawned—my first and last, thank Jesus.''

Wilhemina continues to drink and meddle and pontificate throughout the play, and she is the source of much comedy. However, Walker does allow her to redeem herself; she achieves this redemption as she acknowledges that she has played an important role in hampering and ultimately ruining her son-in-law's chances for success. Warning her grandson of the dangers of an early marriage, she confesses: ''Look at your father. He wanted to be a lawyer, didn't he? Then I jumped on his back, then those two no good daughters of mine, then their two empty-headed husbands—then you. The load was so heavy till he couldn't move no more. He just had to stand there, holding it up.'' Conventionally in the drama, self-knowledge no matter how harsh, if honest, is never unwelcomed nor condemned. Yet when Wilhemina indulges in self-evaluation, the results go beyond individual follies and insensitivity. She warns Jeff because she believes that her behavior is typical of female behavior; she cautions her grandson against marriage and women. In the larger political debate on the image of black women Wilhemina's self-assessment produces even worse fruit; women become the real and present danger. Men must be cautious. The conventions of drama only increase the ambiguity of Wilhemina's self-revelation/self-deprecation.

Perhaps ambiguity describes best the nature of Walker's representation of female characters. As the play's hero proclaims: ''So we're contradictions—so what else is new?'' The principal female character, Mattie, described as ''an embittered but happy woman'' in the list of characters, is one such contradiction. Mattie always knows her place as a woman. In the midst of a heated family debate, her husband declares: ''I'm the head of this house.'' She quickly responds, ''Ain't nobody disputing that.'' Like her mother, Mattie too understands her part in ruining her husband's chances for success. In a history of her married life given to her son's soon-to-be fiancée, Ann Vanderguild, Mattie tells of all the burdens she placed on John's back and of his failed potential. Finally she says: ''I got nobody to blame but myself.'' Mattie's sense of self is defined by her relationship to John and her unshakable belief that she, his loving black wife, with the help of her mother and sisters and their selfish husbands, turned John into a failure and an alcoholic. Because of this she is willing to accept anything that John does, including his playfully obscene and derisive behavior. But Mattie counts all of this as a part of her ''treasure'' and offers a panegyric to John and presumably to the rest of the ''highly underrated black daddies'' in the world:

> A good man is a treasure. White folks proclaim that our men are no good and we go 'round like fools trying to prove them wrong. And I fell right into the same old trap myself. That's why I can't get angry with that man no more. Oh, I pretend to be, but I'm not. Johnny ran a powerful race with a jockey on his back who weighed a ton. So now he's tired. Do you hear me? Tired—and he's put himself out to pasture—with his fifth a day, and I say good for Johnny. I knew he was a smart man. Good for Johnny. If our men are no good, then why are all these little white girls trying to gobble 'em up faster than they can pee straight?

While one assumes that the referent of ''them'' in the sentence ''White folks proclaim that our men are no good . . .'' is ''White folks,'' it could also be ''our men.'' Consequently the meaning of this sentence is somewhat ambiguous. Whom are black women trying to prove wrong, white folks or their men? While it is clear that ''white folks'' are wrong, black women are fools because they do not ignore the mendacity of whites; instead they give heed to it. Note that the praise of black men seems to require self-deprecation from black women. Racism alone does not destroy black men according to Mattie and the play; racism aided by black women proves to be the real culprit.

Mattie's devotion to her husband receives its final test at the play's conclusion, a conclusion that is in many ways a reprise of the last scene of *Big White Fog.* Through a series of blunders, a group of black militants arrive seeking refuge at the Williams' house. John, who has searched for a battlefield on which he could fight for his people, finally finds one, but he receives a mortal wound in an exchange of gunfire with a police informant whom he kills. Dying, John contrives a plot in which he will be thought guilty of an earlier shooting. After John dies, Mattie, so unlike Ella, takes control of the situation, proclaiming: ''Shut up! And tell it like Johnny told you. He ain't gonna die for nothing, 'cause you ain't gonna let him! Jeff—open the door, son! Tell 'em to come on in here! And you better not f—k up!'' These are the last words of the play, and they are Mattie's. She, not her adult son, assumes control at her husband's death. Interestingly enough the play's end focuses attention on its own ambiguous treatment of black women. Mattie's strength is real and also a real asset at this time. For her to be less than strong would mock her husband's sacrifice. Yet the fact that she, rather than her son, assumes control promotes female dominance and matriarchy. Surely Walker intends us to view Mattie's powerful and unwavering response as good, but the situation that he sets up valorizes female strength. However, neither her son nor her husband, were he able, would object to this situation.

The ideological justification for Mattie's ascendancy can be found at least in part in the comments of Ann Vanderguild, the third female principal. Immediately after Ann arrives on the scene, she requests assistance in finding a job as a nurse from Dudley, the Jamaican doctor. He replies: ''Oh, these strong black women!'' ''I'm only strong,'' Ann responds, ''if my man needs me to be, sir.'' John enters the discussion with the proud observation: ''You hear that, Dudley, a warrior's woman! A fighter. . . .'' Clearly the play endorses this concept of womanhood, and Ann lives by her motto. She allows Jeff to protect her and to make decisions for her. Never does she exert her will. When she asks to participate in the plot to discover the police informant, Jeff adamantly refuses to grant her permission; he agrees only after another man assures him that it will be safe: ''It's safe, Jeff, I swear. You know I wouldn't have my woman doing anything that would put her in a trick. No jeopardy, man, I promise.'' The ''fighting lady Ann,'' like Mattie, knows when to make meat loaf and when to fight; decisions, however, are always made within the boundaries established by the head of the household.

It is impossible to ignore in the characterization of Ann a certain amount of correction of Beneatha. First and foremost, Ann is a nurse, a traditionally female profession, and nurses, we all know, take their orders from (male) doctors. Nursing actually

serves as an interesting metaphor for the role of women espoused by *The River Niger*. Women should be strong, but that strength should be circumscribed by male dominance. Beneatha accepts the authority of no one. Only when her brother demonstrates pride and dignity does she respect him as a man, but she never surrenders her ambition or assertiveness. Also, both Beneatha and Ann are central to their plays' discussion of black America's relationship to Africa. Beneatha longs to know her African past. From her African suitor she receives a proposal of marriage and an invitation to return to Africa to practice medicine. Beneatha is offered a future in Africa, a romantic, cultural and professional future: ''Three hundred years later the African Prince rose up out of the seas and swept the maiden back across the middle passage over which her ancestors had come. . .'' (*A Raisin in the Sun*). Ann, on the other hand, has come from South Africa; she comes to North America to escape the oppression in Africa. Her brothers have also had to flee South Africa for political reasons. Her father remains in jail nine years later because he, in a move that foreshadows John's, sacrifices himself for his sons' freedom and safety. There is neither romance nor a future in the Africa of *The River Niger*. The romance is in America and most significantly in the African-American male. The paradigm of *A Raisin in the Sun* is totally reversed in *The River Niger*. African-American men are the desired, the free and, as we shall later see, the new African.

What do we learn in *The River Niger* of this African-American man? The play's hero is a ''bad-loud-talking dude,'' the long-suffering John, the alcoholic poet who seeks a battlefield and finally dies for his people. He had the promise of a great future but because of American racism and four black women, he fails and puts himself out to pasture with a fifth a day. But all of this notwithstanding, he loves his wife Mattie, his mother-in-law Wilhemina, and his son Jeff. When he returns from a binge, having been gone six days, he explains to his wife: ''I wanted to write a love poem— to you, Mattie. Words are like precious jewels, did you know that? But I couldn't find any jewels precious enough to match you, Mattie.'' John's profession of love supposedly compensates for his disappearance and absence at a moment of great personal crisis for Mattie who earlier learns that she has inoperable breast cancer. But the play, like Mattie, truly loves John and indulges his every act.

While on his binge John writes a poem that he offers to Mattie as a token of his love. The poem, "The River Niger," as John admits, "ain't a love poem." It is, however, a panegyric to black manhood, and in it, the poet translates himself into Africa, transplanted to America, but Africa nonetheless.

> I am the River Niger!
> I came to the cloudy Mississippi
> Over heels of incomprehensible woe.
> I ran 'way to the Henry Hudson
> Under the sails of ragged hope.
> I am the River Niger,
> Transplanted to Harlem
> From the Harlem River Drive.

In this redaction of Langston Hughes's "The Negro Speaks of Rivers," John claims for himself and his black compatriots the heroic past as well as an exclusive right to the African future. The trope that he employs incorporates and transcends the African past. Black American men, as Ann recognizes, possess the power to engender a pan-African world:

> Holds hands, my children, and I will flow to the
>   ends of the earth
> And the whole world will hear my waters.
> I am the River Niger! Don't deny me!
> Do you hear me? Don't deny me

Africa's glorious future will come when Africa in its manifestation as the American male is no longer denied.

But as ambiguity defines the nature of female representation, so does it define male representation. John's disappearance (desertion?) at Mattie's moment of crisis clearly raises questions about his reliability. He may be tormented by Mattie's illness and impending death, but his response is not unproblematic. Similarly, John's death at the end of the play prompts questions; foremost among these is this: Is his death really meaningful? Does it achieve anything for blacks? John earlier tells Dudley that he seeks a battlefield on which to fight for his race. But John dies in a battle which produces a Pyrrhic victory at best and which wins only symbolic results. In fact, John falls victim to incompetent black revolutionaries as much as he does to white racism. After these revolutionaries fail to locate the police informant and to complete successfully a guerrilla action they arrive at the Williams' home in desperate need of assistance from competent black men. Finally the informant is discovered to be "the closet homosexual" Al. John attempts to subdue Al, but Al fires and mortally wounds John. In the meantime, the police close in. In the end, John and Al are dead; the revolutionaries have accomplished nothing meaningful, and some impotent,

entirely useless and, ironically, wasteful macho bravado has been displayed. John's death wins nothing. John believes that he will die for the cause he holds to be worth his life: "I found it, Dudley—I found it . . . my battlefield—my battlefield, man! I was a b—h too. . . ." Like so many other battlefields, this one too bears a waste of men. Painfully absent from this is any unequivocal, authorial comment on the waste of John's death. John himself proclaims it to be poetry and dies boasting of his prowess.

As in the earlier two plays the son learns something valuable from the father; machismo is the virtue John passes to his son Jeff. Walter Lee's son Travis learns from his father and grandmother a lesson in pride and dignity. Victor's son Les who converts his father to Marxist revolutionary politics also learns to be proud of his black heritage from his Garveyite father. Of course, Jeff learns things in addition to machismo from his father; foremost among these is a real sense of race pride. Like his father he seeks a battlefield, but Jeff intends to become a lawyer and to fight in the courts. He distrusts the revolution that the incompetent militants seek and presages the play's conclusion when he says: "The revolution ain't nothing but talk, talk, talk, and I ain't gonna waste my life on talk." He will marry the "fighting lady Ann" and presumably enjoy the status of *pater familias.* Jeff offers to assist his former gang in finding the informant, but wants no part of their urban guerrilla tactics. He wants to be his own man, free of the claustrophobic restrictions placed on him by others who have less than his best interest at heart. For *The River Niger,* Jeff is the future. He is black American manhood at its finest, self-assured, self-possessed. He is the heir of the River Niger.

As is often the case, in *The River Niger* machismo is accompanied by its near-cousin, misogyny; of course, the antifeminist agenda of the play does facilitate its descent into misogyny. We have noted earlier that there is some ambiguity in the representation of female characters, but that ambiguity is resolved when one considers the accumulated language of the play. Hostility, sometimes aggressive, sometimes subtle, characterizes the language of males about females in this play. One obviously must consider the play's idiom, a kind of streetwise, bad dude style; but coupled with the ideological goal of the play, this language cannot be dismissed as unintentionally hostile or as harmless. Examples abound, but none better than the clearly pornographic words of Dr. Dudley Stanton. Dudley, who earlier jokes of how his mother supported him through college and medical school by prostitution, tells of his medical examinations of women: ''I distribute sugar pills and run my fingers up the itchy vaginas of sex-starved old b—s. Women who're dried up, past menopause—but groping for life. They pretend to be unmoved, but I feel their wrigglings on my fingers. I see 'em swoon with ecstasy the deeper I probe.'' Although there is nothing else quite as excessive as this, the play finds ample opportunity to identify women as ''b—s'' and ''superb—s.'' Were this language restricted to a few individuals, it would be easier to see it as language that partakes in characterization and mimesis. But the language is used uncritically and in fact is a constituent part of the male behavior that the play valorizes. When John dedicates ''The River Niger'' to his ''superb—h,'' the play's pervasive hostility towards women, whether it is active or passive, becomes impossible to deny or overlook.

Although the misogyny articulated in *The River Niger* does have its unique roots in black American culture, this misogyny is no worse than that which permeates Western culture. What differentiates the manifestations of misogyny in black culture from its manifestations in the majority culture are the permutations that result from racism. The systematic sexual abuse that black women suffered in America during slavery and well into the twentieth century is widely documented. To consider this abuse to be only the libidinous excesses and license of white men is to misunderstand the political nature of that abuse. Black women had no real political control over their bodies, and their husbands, brothers, fathers and lovers were raped of their power to protect their women from the unsolicited sexual aggression of white males. Indeed, white males used their sexual power over black women as an emblem of the political power that as white men they held over black men. ''Sexually as well as in every other way,'' Winthrop Jordan writes in *White Over Black:* ''Negroes were utterly subordinated. White men extended their dominion over their Negroes to the bed, where the sex act itself served as ritualistic re-enactment of the daily pattern of social dominance.'' In effect, the bodies of black women became the battlefield on and over which men, black and white, fought to establish actual and symbolic political dominance and to demonstrate masculine prowess. Truly black men had more than wounded machismo at stake here: the lives and safety of their female relatives and friends were in real danger. Yet the passive role thrust upon black

women by this struggle in a very real way served to minimize their individuality and humanity and to objectify them as possessions and symbols. Also because the victimization of black women was intended to humiliate, to emasculate black men, female oppression paradoxically became a version of male oppression and consequently could be construed to be less significant than male oppression. The oppression of black women by white men when viewed only in its racist context, allows for the continuation of that oppression by black men. Nor should we forget that there was an obvious political reason for black men to establish their dominance over black women. Of course, black men would neither desire nor establish a system of oppression against their mothers, sisters, wives and lovers as ruthless and brutal as the one white men instituted against black women, but because the oppression of black women by white men was so politically charged and in part aimed directly at black men, the relationship between black men and black women necessarily reflects these facts. Additionally there exists the belief that the black mother in preparing her son to survive in a racist America ''must intuitively cut off and blunt [her son's] masculine assertiveness and aggression lest these put the boy's life in danger.'' Accordingly, Grier and Cobbs hypothesize in *Black Rage:* ''. . . black men develop considerable hostility toward black women as the inhibiting instruments of an oppressive system. The woman has more power, more accessibility into the system, and therefore she is more feared, while at the same time envied. And it is her lot in life to suppress masculine assertiveness in her sons.'' Grier's and Cobbs' failure to distinguish here between female lovers and mothers should not go unnoticed. The assertion made here is that all black women partake in this emasculating activity and that all black men respond with a general hostility toward women. Calvin C. Hernton in his book *Sex and Racism in America* offers yet other and somewhat contradictory reasons for alleged male hostility towards females: ''. . . there arose in me an incipient resentment . . . towards all black women—because I could not help but compare them with white women, and in all phases of public life it was the Negro female who bowed her head and tucked her tail between her legs like a little black puppy.'' The important common denominator here is racism, but its release becomes misogyny. Whether or not we agree with Grier's and Cobbs' assessment or Hernton's is irrelevant. These ideas, expressed as they are, go a long way to explain how racism informs sexism in

black America. And it is from this that *The River
Niger* takes shape. No matter what Hansberry's
intentions, to those who subscribe to this image of
black women, Lena, Ruth and Beneatha all seem to
participate in that emasculating tradition identified
by Grier and Cobbs.

Related to the problem of misogyny and
machismo in *The River Niger* is the question of
sexual identity. Who among the characters is trustworthy and a true heir of the River Niger? The
women who know their role in a male dominant
society become the play's "superb—s." Men who
demand and exercise male prerogative over women
and win for themselves hierarchical power over
their male colleagues are the play's real revolutionaries. Its counterrevolutionaries are those who do
not align themselves with this paradigm, most notably Al, the "closet homosexual," police informant.
However, Al's sexuality is really over-determined
in this play. His sexual passivity—and the play
makes it clear that he is passive—symbolizes his
separation from real black manhood and hence real
blackness. Al does not understand his blackness: he
denies Africa and the play's definition of manhood.
By not being true to his manhood, Al cannot be true
to his blackness. Perversely, he defends the majority
culture that oppresses black people, that dams the
River Niger. Al proves to be untrustworthy and the
"real men," Jeff, John and Dudley, must ferret the
Als out and destroy them.

It is, finally, the intraracial intersexual struggle
that seems to consume *The River Niger.* At the end
of *Big White Fog,* the Marxists are moving the
Masons' furniture back into the house. The hoped
for revolution—were it to come—would protect the
dispossessed. In *A Raisin in the Sun,* the furniture is
being moved out and the dispossessed move to take
possession of their dream deferred. At the end of
The River Niger there is no movement. Everything
including the furniture remains in place; the movables
are fixed. John dies not for a cause but to demonstrate a point: black men, black fathers are heroic
and heroically macho. The play calls on black
women to learn this lesson before it is too late,
before they are bereft of their men. Yet the real
irony of this conclusion is its unintended feminist
correction of *Big White Fog*; Mattie does exactly
what Ella ought to do. But Mattie is left to protect
the past, to insure that John's sacrifice does not turn
into an egregious waste. Nothing else stands to
be won. We move nowhere, out of nothing, towards nothing.

Source: Anthony Barthelemy, ''Mother, Sister, Wife: A
Dramatic Perspective,'' in *Southern Review,* Vol. 21, No. 3,
Summer 1985, pp. 770–89.

Chester J. Fontenot

*Author Chester Fontenot examines the dichot-
omy between mythic and linear conceptions of
history, focusing on how Walker's* The River Niger
seeks to resolve this conflict.

There are a number of ways one might approach
setting criteria for evaluating Afro-American drama.
We might say, for instance, that a significant number of these plays employ reversals of the American
minstrel tradition, and thus move from tragedy into
satire and farce (i.e., Douglas Turner Ward's *Day of
Absence*). Or we could say that some plays use the
mysticism of Black folk tradition as a basis for
building their character types (i.e., Jean Toomer's
Balo and Adrienne Kennedy's *The Owl Answers*).
We may argue that Black music (spirituals, blues,
jazz) provides the key, so to speak, which enables us
to decode a large number of Afro-American plays.
And, finally, we could trace the development of
Afro-American drama thematically by ascertaining
the point(s) where the playwrights seem to be concerned with freedom, social protest, theatre for a
Black audience, and so on.

Though each of these approaches is valid in
itself, in this essay I want to discuss another way of
criticizing Afro-American popular drama. In many
of these plays, there is a tension between the linear
and the mythic conceptions of history. These two
conceptions are diametrically opposed views, for
the linear consciousness advocates the annihilation
of the Black historical past, while the mythic consciousness threatens to keep the past alive through
the social conditions of the present. The former
attempts to substitute for the Black historical past a
version of progress which, by its very nature, implies that the conditions Black people have had to
live under are vestiges of a bygone age of disharmony. According to this theory, Black people are no
longer slaves, but have been integrated as full
participants in society. The extent to which Black
people have not become full participants in American society indicates their unwillingness to accept
the routes the larger society has created for them.
Within the linear conception of history, the events
which produced and continue to sustain the psychological enslavement of Black people are a set of
discontinuous events linked together chronologically. But these events have no real connection to
one another except that they happen along a particu-

lar part of the historical cycle. These events have no real connection to the present social conditions of Black people in the sense that Black people's present social predicament is simply the result of their lack of ability to take advantage of opportunities. The linear historical consciousness negates the past in favor of a distorted version of the present and an obscure vision of some distant future.

In contrast to the linear historical conception, the mythic view of history insists on the constant recreation of the Black historical past through the actions of white Americans against Black people. Within the mythic consciousness, slavery is not a vestige of a bygone age of disharmony but is alive in the segregation of Black people in the ghettos, in the lack of employment for Black youths, and in the aborted dreams of Black people in general and Black men in particular. This vantage point implies that there is no such thing as a distant past and obscure future, but that there is only a radical present which is constantly recreated through the suffrage of Black people. The mythic view threatens to destroy the linear conception, since the former is better able to substantiate its claims to truth than the latter. All one has to do to support the mythic view is to point toward the present conditions of Black people. To substantiate the linear conception, one must formulate a set of abstractions which gather strength from philosophical musings, and not from historical reality or from present social conditions. The oppression of Black people tends to create a mythic consciousness wherein ''progress'' is not seen as something achieved through the humanistic grace of Anglo-Americans, but is rather the product of sacrifice by Black Americans. Progress, in this sense, is not organic but is an imposed system on linear history. This is viewed within the mythic consciousness as not really progress, but as appeasement.

Since Black people, for the most part, live within the mythic consciousness, they are constantly put at odds with the linear system in their attempts to cope with American society. This conflict is presented in Afro-American popular drama not as vague abstractions of massive struggles of light and dark forces, of good and evil powers, but as real tensions between characters who represent either side of the dichotomy. The tension is seldom resolved, since it would take an herculean effort to synthesize moral turpitude with pragmatic choices to bring the conflict to an end. Instead, Afro-American playwrights seem to provide the reader

CAST
(in order of appearance)

Grandma Wilhelmina Brown	FRANCES FOSTER
Johnny Williams	ARTHUR FRENCH
Dr. Dudley Stanton	GRAHAM BROWN
Ann Vanderguild	GRENNA WHITAKER
Mattie Williams	BARBARA CLARKE
Chips	LENNAL WAINWRIGHT
Mo	NEVILLE RICHEN
Gail	SAUNDRA McCLAIN
Skeeter	TAUREAN BLACQUE
Al	DEAN IRBY
Jeff Williams	LES ROBERTS
Voice of Lt. Staples	WYATT DAVIS

Bass Player: Jothan Callins

Time: Early February. The Present
Place: New York City—Harlem
Setting: The Williams' Brownstone on 133rd Street,
between Lenox and Seventh Avenues.

ACT I
Scene 1: Friday: 4:30 p.m.
Scene 2: After Midnight
INTERMISSION

ACT II
Scene 1: Saturday
The Next Day: 10:45 a.m.
INTERMISSION

ACT III
Scene 1: Friday, Six Days Later: Early Evening
Scene 2: Later That Same Night

UNDERSTUDIES
Understudies never substitute for listed players unless a specific announcement for the appearance is made at the time of the performance.
Taurean Blacque, Barbara Clarke, Louise Heath, David Downing
Standby for the role of Mattie Williams: Roxie Roker
Understudying the role of Jeff: Dean Irby

THE AUTHOR
The Negro Ensemble Company opened its 1969 season with Joseph A. Walker's *Harangues*. NEC's 1970 season opened with *Ododo*, written, directed and co-choreographed by him. The December, 1972, premiere of *The River Niger* marked the third time Walker had opened an NEC season. Mr. Walker also co-authored, designed the set for and played the lead in the Off-Broad-

A 1972 playbill cast list of The River Niger *performed at New York's Brooks Atkinson Theatre.*

with an analysis of the problem and to suggest different strategies by which to resolve it. Two plays which illustrate this thesis are Joseph Walker's *River Niger* and Lonne Elder's *Ceremonies in Dark Old Men*; these show the tension between myth and history.

The *River Niger* centers on the struggle of John Williams, a fifty-year old Black man who is characterized as an ''alive poet.'' John is a poet both in the sense that he writes poems and in that he sees the Black experience not as something which is fixed and dictated by history, but as a massive unshaped potential which must be given form by human experience. John's struggle is against the role of manhood which has been created and sustained by American culture. Manhood in this specific context refers to John's ability or lack of ability to reach his goal, which was originally to be a lawyer, and to provide material goods for his family. John can realize neither potential, and thus is trapped within a conception of humanity from which he cannot escape. This continual battle creates a mythic consciousness for John in that each time he confronts his wife, Mattie, and her mother, his inability to realize his aborted goal is kept alive. The constant

IN HIS PRISON HOUSE, SO TO SPEAK, JOHN ATTEMPTS TO REALIZE HIS DREAM THROUGH HIS SON, JEFF, BY CONVINCING HIM TO BECOME A LIEUTENANT IN THE AIR FORCE. THE TENSION BETWEEN JOHN'S PAST AND JEFF'S PRESENT PRODUCES THE PLOT IN *THE RIVER NIGER*."

confrontation between his past and present leads John to frustration, and, finally, to alcohol. In his prison house, so to speak, John attempts to realize his dream through his son, Jeff, by convincing him to become a lieutenant in the Air Force. The tension between John's past and Jeff's present produces the plot in *The River Niger*.

The play begins with John struggling to write a poem he has been working on for some time. As the opening scene gets underway, John reads aloud three lines of his poem:

I am the River Niger—hear my waters.
I wriggle and stream and run.
I am totally flexible—

The tone of this poem suggests that John's plight in writing is the same as that of Black people who are struggling against oppression. Just as John is having difficulty moving the poem from passive to active voice, Black people experience hardships moving their experience from historically determined events to constitutive actions. John as poet is symbolic of the struggle of Black people in general and of Black men in particular—the fight against linear history as an enslaving force. In fact, linear history espouses the notion that Black men are worthless, shiftless, lazy, and so on. John's wife, Mattie, discusses this idea that Black men are no good. "A good man is a treasure," Mattie says. "White folk proclaim that our men are no good and we go 'round like fools trying to prove them wrong. . .If our men are no good, why are all these little white girls trying to gobble 'em up faster than they can pee straight?"

We find that John is fighting against this conception of Black men through poetry. For poetry is not something removed from reality, "art for art's sake." It is "what the revolution's all about—never lose sight of the true purpose of the revolutions, all revolutions—to restore poetry to the godhead!" John believes that Black poetry is experiential; he comments that the Empire State Building was built from over three hundred years of Black poetry. All accomplishments by Black people form the core of Black poetry. It is within this poetic philosophy that John wants to find his battlefield. But John's battlefield is not such that it will enable him to win himself a piece of the American dream. It is the kind of battlefield which will allow him to regain his dignity and to make a positive impact on humanity from his own cultural base. John's search for this battlefield engages the tension between the linear and the mythic conceptions; the former advocates no need for a battlefield since a measurable amount of progress has occurred in America, while the latter insists on the constant need for a battlefield, since social conditions have changed little since slavery for Black people.

The other characters in this play intensify this struggle. Mattie, an embittered Black woman, is referred to by her mother as "the only Black child I ever spawned—my first and last, thank Jesus." Mattie—locked within this foreshadowing statement—turns the burden of her heritage inward toward herself and John; she blames herself for his psychological castration. John wanted to go to law school, but Mattie let her relatives impose so heavily on their relationship that John was forced to give up his career goal and work odd jobs to support the family. Her guilt over John's turning to alcohol, combined with her own mastectomy, lead Mattie to self-destructiveness. She assumes the position of a martyr in her defense of the alcoholism of both John and her mother.

Much of Mattie's plight has been created for her by her mother, who is a very color conscious woman. Mattie's mother stands at the midpoint of the tension between John and Mattie, since she has been directly responsible for the abortion of John's career and for Mattie's failure to find fulfillment in womanhood. Joseph Walker conveys the tension symbolically through the grandmother's actions. On the one hand, she claims to be a Christian, while on the other hand, she hides whiskey in the house and sneaks a drink whenever the family is not around. She embodies both the problem of one struggling against the linear conception of history through the memory of her husband, whom she describes as a proud Black man, and the urge to accept the linear conception through her emphasis on color and proper social decorum.

The forces represented by Mattie and her mother threaten to return John to the Black historical past—to hopelessness and psychological slavery. In an effort to free himself, John turns to fulfilling his dreams through his son, Jeff. He wants Jeff to make an accomplishment which will serve as proof that Black men in particular can fulfill the role of manhood. Since the armed forces offer one of the clearest available avenues toward manhood, John pressures Jeff into enlisting in military school. As the plot begins to shape, we see the entire family anxiously awaiting Jeff's return from the Air Force as a commissioned lieutenant.

In John's struggle to have Jeff fulfill his hopes, he doesn't see that Jeff rejects his intervention in his life. The son views his father's attempts to push him to a goal as an imposition of progress on his version of history, which is mythic. Jeff does not think moving into the world dominated by White people is an accomplishment; he thinks it is "selling out." He would rather work from within the Black community to effect social change. But in his rejection of his father's route to manhood, Jeff finds that the Black community has its own pitfalls, in the form of gangs masquerading as revolutionary organizations.

The conflict between Jeff and his father is caused by different views regarding accomplishments. John sees Jeff's commission, not as an act of loyalty to his country, but as an accomplishment, as "another fist jammed through the wall." John wants to be able to participate in American society fully, for he regards such a participation as his birthright. He doesn't want American society torn down completely; he only wants it modified. Jeff, on the other hand, wants to annihilate linear history by totally destroying American civilization. An accomplishment which helps to perpetuate the American mythos is tantamount to nothing for Jeff.

But Jeff's view of history is altered drastically when he confronts the street gang of which he was once a member, which has now been transformed into a self-styled revolutionary group. The leader of the gang, Mo, has put together a band of street-level Blacks composed of his girl friend, a homosexual (Al), a dope addict (Skeeter), and a sexual degenerate (Chips), whom Mo calls Famaldehyde Dick for raping an embalmed corpse. Those Mo has recruited are bound together by their sordid past,

which does not provide the necessary bond for trust and devotion for one another needed for true revolutionary activity. The leader of the gang feels, like Fanon, that the call for revolution will cleanse the street level Blacks he has enlisted in his group. Yet, in his idyllic philosophy, Mo realizes that he needs leadership to complement him; therefore he attempts to enlist Jeff.

Jeff, however, initially rejects Mo's incessant demands that he become a member of the group, in the same way as he rejected his father's attempts to push him into the Air Force. He also finds that he must confront his grandmother, who pressures him to marry a "decent girl" and not the one to whom Jeff is presently engaged. In his selection of a viable path toward manhood, Jeff unintentionally paves the way for his father to find the battlefield for which he has been searching all his life. Finally, Jeff decides to join Mo's group on his own terms, not knowing that Mo's organization is being held responsible for the death of a local politician. Al, one of Mo's gang members, is also an undercover policeman; he informs the authorities of the group's intentions and brings about their downfall. At the end of the play, the police surround John's house. Al, the informer, pulls a gun on the gang and demands that they reveal the killer of the politician. John enters through the kitchen, hears the commotion, and shoots it out with Al. Al is killed instantly, while John is seriously injured. Here, John is given the chance to attain his final goal. He achieves manhood by taking the blame for the entire group and by insisting that they tell the police that he alone was responsible for the gang's activities. John finds his battlefield in death and breaks the cycle of linear history.

John's poem is completed as he moves from passivity to constitutive action. The forces which have threatened to destroy his mythic consciousness are held at bay, while John carves a realistic path for himself. John's death, then, is not tragic in the sense of his being ousted from society in order to return the moral world intact to the reader. The world is better in that he has been a part of it. His death is a conscious choice, a moral strategy. In a statement near the end of the play, John realizes what poetry actually is. He says while dying that he doesn't care about the poems he has been trying to write all of his life, but that "this is poetry, man—what I feel right down here and now." John finds that he has created his own path to realization of manhood, even though, for him, finding his own way means to contradict everything for which he has struggled all along. Yet the path he chooses acknowledges the mythic sense of history and thus annihilates the linear conception.

Ceremonies in Dark Old Men presents his conflict in a different way. The shadow of the deceased mother in this play looms as the manifestation of the linear consciousness. Mr. Parker's daughter, Adele, constantly reminds her father and two brothers of their failure to achieve manhood through employment. Adele, the sole supporter of the family, keeps her mother's memory alive by confronting the family with the reason for Mrs. Parker's untimely demise. In one scene Adele challenges her father's devotion to her mother: ''What about Mama? She died working for you! Did you ever stop to think about that! In fact, did you ever love her? No!!.'' The conflict between Adele and the castrated men produces the mythic consciousness in the play.

Adele, as the breadwinner in the family, is likewise the source of moral authority. For it is she who attempts to place limits on the illegal actions her father and brothers wish to undertake. But placing these restrictions does not resolve the source of conflict between moral turpitude and pragmatic action. Even though her father might try to keep Adele happy because she pays the rent, he still feels that his dreams have been aborted and are unreachable through the route dictated to him by history—getting a job. To Mr. Parker, a job is simply a way of aborting his dreams. In the opening scene of the play, his longtime friend, Mr. Jenkins, questions the validity of Mr. Parker's masquerading as a barber when he could ''count the heads of hair you done cut in this shop on one hand.'' Mr. Parker replies, ''This shop is gon' work yet; I know it can. Just give me one more year and you'll see. . .Going out to get a job ain't gon' solve nothing—all its gon' do is create a lot of bad feelings with everybody. I can't work! I don't know how to!''

The irony in this statement is not that Mr. Parker really doesn't know how to work, but that the kind of work he is accustomed to doing is obsolete. He was a minstrel man who has been outdated by the lack of historical consciousness of the new Black generation. He is part of a distinct age of slavery and oppression. For Mr. Parker to acknowledge this fact is tantamount to him accepting the linear view of history, which advocates the annihilation of the Black historical past. Adele intensifies this struggle by her incessant demands that her father and brothers get a job.

When faced with this dilemma, Mr. Parker, his two sons, Theopolis and Bobby, and his best friend, Mr. Jenkins, choose an alternate route to fulfillment of manhood; they accept an offer from ''Blue Haven,'' a Black gangster, to turn the barbershop into a front for manufacturing and selling bootleg liquor. But in doing this, Mr. Parker throws into chaos the moral world Adele has sought to keep intact. Bobby puts his talents at thievery to work for Blue Haven; Mr. Parker embezzles money from the enterprise to reclaim his lost youth; and Theopolis is left to do all the work.

Blue Haven symbolizes a path through which Black men can gain access to manhood, the ability to determine one's destiny. Such an ability has been stifled by segregating Blacks, by confining them to ghettos, and by prohibiting them from entering the labor force. Blue Haven—regardless of his moral code—represents an achievement for Black men, an achievement which, in its very essence, attests to the inhumanity Black people have experienced in America. Blue Haven is able to conceal his immoral actions from Mr. Parker, Theopolis, Bobby, and Mr. Jenkins, because of the attractiveness of the route he offers them. If they participate in Blue Haven's organization, they can regain the dignity they have lost in their confinement in the ghetto. After all, they have not sought jobs actively, not because there is little chance of them finding a suitable one, but because they do not wish to work for white people. To work for white people is tantamount to acknowledging the linear historical consciousness and to participating in the destruction of the mythic conception. Blue Haven's offer acknowledges the Black historical past and provides them with a route to fulfilling their role as men without ''selling out,'' so to speak.

Just as John Williams must die in *The River Niger* to unify the cosmos which has been thrown into chaos in his search for a battlefield, Mr. Parker's youngest son, Bobby, must die in order for the family to be shocked into reality. Bobby's death while participating in a robbery attempt for Blue Haven's gang returns Mr. Parker and the rest of the family to the moral world where they see that Blue Haven's offer was not a viable choice, but only the appearance of one. Blue Haven has simply inverted the world, overturned societal values, not for the good of Black people as a whole, but for his own selfish purposes. The route Mr. Parker and his son, Theopolis, must find to manhood cannot be defined in opposition to that dictated by history. It must be firmly grounded in the Black historical past and must contain a viable vision of the future.

Ceremonies in Dark Old Men attempts to resolve the tension between the linear and mythic conceptions, but falls short. At the end of the play, the family decides to stand on moral grounds and to reject Blue Haven's enterprise in their barber shop. They make a decision to throw the equipment Blue Haven has placed in the barber shop into the river and to confront him when he comes to collect his money. The strength the family acquires in the death of Bobby might lead one to think that they will triumph, as a family, over the efforts of Blue Haven to keep them in the business of making bootleg liquor. But this resolution is somewhat superficial. Blue Haven's character is drawn in such a way that his presence dominates the play. The tone of the play shifts when Blue Haven enters the scene—the entire moral world is overturned when he makes his offer to the family. A character with this type of appeal cannot be dispensed with in such a perfunctory manner. When the play ends, there is still the feeling that Blue Haven is going to come back to the barber shop to collect his money, only to find that the family has rejected his business and has destroyed his equipment. The family must still confront the gangster with more than moral philosophical rantings. All that is finally resolved in the play is that Blue Haven represents a facade, not the resolution to the conflict between the linear and mythic conceptions of history.

The problem that is presented in these two plays is common to a large number of Afro-American plays which are aimed at large audiences. These plays attempt to present the problem DuBois speaks of in *Souls of Black Folk.* Black people live within what DuBois called "the veil," that is, the realization that one is neither a part of American society nor a member of a distinct ethnic group which is tied to linear history. In other words, Black people experience a double-consciousness which manifests itself in the tension between the linear and mythic conceptions. In developing criteria to evaluate these plays, one must realize that drama, unlike other literary genres, is often construed as a direct manifestation of reality and not as something remote and suspended from historical reality. Afro-American playwrights have been required to make their plays directly responsive to the needs of oppressed peoples, and they have done so by presenting the conflict in the consciousness of Black people. This can serve as a basis for developing parameters within which one can operate when discussing the subject. And it can hopefully provide the dramaturgical enterprise with the perspective with which it can categorize Afro-American popular drama.

Source: Chester J. Fontenot, "Mythic Patterns In *River Niger* and *Ceremonies in Dark Old Men,*" in *Melus*, Vol. 7, No. 1, Spring 1980, pp. 41–49.

SOURCES

Cooper, Grace, "Joseph A. Walker," in *Dictionary of Literary Biography, Vol. 38,* Gale, 1985.

"Joseph A. Walker," in *Contemporary Authors Online,* The Gale Group, 1999.

Kauffmann, Stanley, "Theater: The River Niger," in the *New Republic*, Vol. 169, No. 12, September 29, 1973, pp. 22, 33.

FURTHER READING

Branch, William B., ed., *Black Thunder: An Anthology of Contemporary African American Drama,* Mentor Books.
    This collection of plays by contemporary African-American writers includes Amiri Baraka and August Wilson.

Sewell, Tony, *Garvey's Children: The Legacy of Marcus Garvey,* Africa World Press, 1990.
    Sewell's text provides an historical survey of the influence of Marcus Garvey on civil rights leaders.

Shange, Ntozake, *for colored girls who have considered suicide/when the rainbow is enuf: A Choreopoem,* Macmillan, 1997.
    Shange's experimental play focuses on the struggles of African-American women against racism and sexism.

Wilson, August, *Ma Rainey's Black Bottom,* New American Library, 1985.
    Black Bottom is a critically acclaimed play by the leading African-American dramatist of the 1980s. Wilson's play concerns a female blues singer and the members of her band.

X, Malcolm, as told to Alex Haley, *The Autobiography of Malcolm X,* Random House, 1975.
    This famous biography of the black nationalist leader Malcolm X provides a compelling description of Malcom X's life and the varied paths it took.

The Seagull

ANTON CHEKHOV

1896

Anton Chekhov's *Chayka* or *The Seagull* (variously translated in English as *The Sea Gull* and *The Sea-Gull*) is the first play in the author's second period of writing for the theater—that of the last few years of his life—in which he penned his widely acknowledged dramatic masterpieces. With it, after a hiatus of seven years, Chekhov again returned to writing plays, and he revealed his mastery of techniques that he would exploit in his other great plays of that final period: *Uncle Vanya, Three Sisters,* and *The Cherry Orchard.* In all of them, Chekhov employs a method of "indirect action," one in which characters confront changes that result from offstage occurrences, often in a period of the characters' lives that elapses between acts. The plays also share the unique Chekhovian mood, a pervasive melancholic tone that arises from the haplessness of the characters that seem destined either to wallow in self-pity or indifference or consume themselves in frustrated passion. It is in these plays, with his special brand of "slice of life" realism, that Chekhov journeys to the outer limits of comedy, to a point in which its distinctness from quasi-tragic *drame* is blurred and at some points all but lost.

In *The Seagull,* a work that the author himself claimed contained "five tons of love," is a play about a very human tendency to reject love that is freely given and seek it where it is withheld. Many of its characters are caught in a destructive, triangular relationship that evokes both pathos and humor. What the characters cannot successfully parry is the

destructive force of time, the passage of which robs some, like Madame Arkadina, of beauty, and others, like her son Konstantine, of hope.

When the play was first staged, in St. Petersburg in 1896, it was very badly received. The audience was unwilling to applaud or even abide a work that in technique and style countered the traditional kind of play built on comfortable conventions. Audiences were simply not ready to accept a work that seemed to violate almost all dramatic conventions, a play that, for example, had no clear protagonist or an easily identified moral conflict or characters who rigorously kept to points relevant to that conflict in their dialogue. For Chekhov, the response was devastating. There seemed to be no audience prepared to welcome the ''new forms'' championed by one of the play's characters, the young writer Konstantine Treplyov.

Had Chekhov's friend, Nemirovich-Danchenko, not taken an interest in the work despite its initial stage failure, the dramatist might well have given up writing for the theater. Nemirovich-Danchenko and his more famous codirector of the famous Moscow Art Theatre, Konstantin Stanislavsky, brought *The Seagull* to the stage again in 1898 and turned it into a remarkable success, the first Chekhov play that they produced in what soon became one of the most fortuitous associations in the history of modern drama. It was their staging of *The Seagull* and the other later plays of Chekhov that brought the writer his lasting acclaim as a dramatist.

Anton Chekhov

AUTHOR BIOGRAPHY

Anton Chekhov was born on January 17, 1860, in Taganrog, a dreary Russian seaport village on the Black Sea. His grandfather was an emancipated serf who had managed to buy his own freedom. His father, Pravel Yegorovitch Chekhov, a cruel and dictatorial taskmaster who made his children's lives miserable, ran a small grocery store. In 1876, that business failed, forcing the family to flee to the anonymity of Moscow to escape from creditors. Although Chekhov's fame as a dramatist rests largely on works he wrote during the last eight years of his life, his love of the theater extended back into his youth in Taganrog, where he frequented dramatic presentations at that city's provincial playhouses. Young Anton remained in Taganrog to complete his schooling before following the family to Moscow and entering that city's university to study medicine.

It was there that Chekhov began writing his sketches and stories, works that fairly quickly brought him financial independence and a moderate degree of fame. Between 1880, when the first of his pieces appeared, and 1887, Chekhov published about 600 pieces in periodicals. Quite literally, he wrote his humorous sketches as ''pot boilers,'' works providing money enough for his family to get back on its feet.

By 1884, when he graduated from the university and began practicing medicine, Chekhov already knew that he had contracted tuberculosis, a disease that would leave him but twenty additional years to write. His success and much improved financial situation soon allowed him to give up medicine to concentrate on his writing, though he sometimes worked as a physician to help the poor.

At first Chekhov did not take his writing very seriously, but starting in 1885, after he moved to St. Petersburg, his attitude began to change. He became a close friend of A. S. Suvorin, the editor of *Novoe vremja*, a fairly conservative journal. Recognizing Chekhov's genius, Suvorin encouraged the writer to take more pride in his work and to seek a greater critical reputation. It was there, too, that Chekhov fell under the influence of the great novelist, Leo Tolstoy, especially that writer's moral preachments, including his passive response to evil.

Chekov began to write plays at about the same time that he started writing fiction but did not immediately achieve the success and acclaim that he did in fiction. His work in drama falls into two distinct periods. The first, from 1881 until 1895, is predominately one in which he wrote adaptations of his prose sketches as curtain-raisers or "vaudevilles," single-act farces of the sort that were immensely popular in Russian theater at the time. Two of these pieces, *The Bear* (also known as *The Brute* and *The Boar*) and *The Marriage Proposal,* are extremely durable examples of this kind. Chekhov also experimented with longer pieces in his early years, but, except in the case of *Ivanov* (1887), he had little success with them. In fact, because one of them, *The Wood Demon* (1889), was so chillingly received by critics and was rejected for performance, Chekhov all but gave up writing drama for the next seven years. With *The Seagull* (1896), he entered his second period of dramatic writing and produced the world-renowned masterpieces on which his fame as playwright largely rests. In this second period, lasting to his death in 1904, he wrote his greatest plays, which, besides *The Seagull,* include *Uncle Vanya* (1899), *The Cherry Orchard* (1900), and *Three Sisters* (1901). It was also in this period that Chekhov commenced his fortuitous association with the Moscow Art Theater, then under the joint directorship of Constantin Stanislavsky and Chekhov's friend, Vladimir Nemirovich-Danchenko. In their stage interpretation of his work, these two men and their actors brought the author both great fame and fortune. His sickness soon took its toll, however, and after his marriage to the actress Olga Knipper in 1901 until his death in 1904, Chekhov's failing health depleted his energy and prevented him from adding new works to his limited dramatic canon.

However, by 1901 he had done enough to acquire an international reputation. In these latter plays, Chekhov perfected hallmark techniques and a style that earned him a lasting reputation as a seminal figure in modern drama—in the minds of many the coequal of the "father" of modern drama,

Henrik Ibsen. To this day, in manner and technique, he is still admired and imitated by aspiring playwrights.

PLOT SUMMARY

Act 1

The Seagull opens on an early summer evening in a park on the estate of Peter Nikolaevich Sorin, brother to Irina Arkadina, a celebrated actress. A small stage blocks a view of the lake that borders the park. Around it are some bushes, a few chairs, and a table. Behind the platform's curtain, Yakov and other laborers are finishing work on the makeshift structure.

Masha and Semyon Medvedenko are returning from a walk. She is the daughter of Sorin's steward, Ilya Shamreyeff. He is a poor schoolmaster, infatuated with her but perplexed by her sorrow, which is overtly revealed in her mournful world view and black clothing. He cannot understand why she is sad, for she is not poor. From their conversation, it is learned that a play written by Konstantine, Madame Treplyov's son, is about to be performed, and that he and Nina Zaryechny, who is to act in it, are in love.

As Masha tries to discourage Semyon's love, Sorin and Konstantine Treplyov enter. Sorin confides that the country does not really suit him. He complains to Masha about the dog that her father keeps chained up, but she curtly dismisses his request that she tell Shamreyeff that the dog's howling bothers Sorin. She and Medvedenko exit, followed by Yakov and the other workers who go off for a swim while Sorin and Treplyov await the appearance of Nina. Sorin, after remarking on his own frumpishness and inadequacies as a lover, asks the cause of Treplyov's mother's bad humor. Konstantine claims that she is jealous and launches into a diatribe about her inadequacies—her petulance, stinginess, volatile temperament, and, the greatest shortcoming of all, her shallow view of the theater. He then explains that with "new forms" he is helping to sweep away the old, worn-out tradition. He also reveals that he is in fact very jealous of her, of her fame and her lover, the novelist Boris Trigorin, who annoys him because of his success.

Konstantine's assessment of Trigorin is interrupted by the arrival of Nina, upon whom he clearly fawns. Nina, concerned that she might be late, explains that she has had to slip away from her father and stepmother, who do not approve of their "Bohemian" neighbors. She is obviously very nervous, and after Sorin goes off to collect his other guests for the play's performance, she explains that she is fearful of acting before such a literary luminary as Boris Trigorin, whose stories she admires. She then complains to Konstantine that his play has no "living characters in it," offending him.

The others begin arriving, starting with Pauline, wife of Ilya Shamreyeff, and Eugene Dorn, a doctor. They discuss Dorn's enchantment with Nina and his easy success with women, something that has prompted her jealousy and suggests that they are engaged in an illicit affair. Their talk is cut off by the arrival of the others—Madame Arkadina, Sorin, Trigorin, Shamreyeff, Medvedenko, and Masha. They are discussing the state of the Russian theater and its actors, the "mighty oaks" that in Shamreyeff's view are now nothing but "stumps." After Irina asks Konstantine about his play and exchanges lines with him from Shakespeare's *Hamlet,* the performance begins. It consists of a recitation by Nina, a prospective glance 200,000 years into the future, when most life forms of our era will long since have become extinct. It is more a threnody than a play. When the spirit represented by Nina is approached by the Devil, represented by two red "eyes" and the smell of sulphur, Irina begins laughing, greatly annoying her son, who orders the curtain closed, aborting Nina's performance, and storms off in disgust. His mother is upbraided by Sorin, who seems much more aware of her son's hurt pride than she is. She finds him simply "an unruly, conceited boy," one whose ideas about theater arise from his temperament, not from any artistic convictions. She soon relents, however, and expresses regrets for hurting his feelings.

When Nina appears from behind the stage, Madame Arkadina praises her for her voice and looks, and Nina confides that she has hopes of becoming an actress. Irina introduces her to Trigorin. They briefly discuss the play, the substance of which seems to have evaded them. He then talks of his joy in fishing, a pleasure that surprises Nina. The act winds down with some final revelations that help explain the character tensions in the play. Nina, afraid of her father, must run off, but it is clear that her regret at leaving arises from her infatuation with Trigorin. After she leaves, Madame Arkadina explains the girl's unfortunate situation as the daughter of a man who has taken a second wife. She then goes off with Sorin, who complains about the damp night air. Dorn is left alone, but is soon joined by Konstantine Treplyov, who complains of being pursued by Masha, an "unbearable creature." Dorn praises him for his play of "abstract ideas," of which he approves. Treplyov, almost frantic, is merely interested in finding Nina, and quickly runs off just after Masha enters. After his departure, treating Dorn like a surrogate father, she asks for his help. She is tortured by her love for Konstantine. Dorn remarks then on the nervousness of everyone and the "magic lake" that seems to have inspired the hapless love of all of them.

Act 2

The action continues on another part of Sorin's estate, a croquet lawn near the lake. It is noon on a hot day, perhaps a week later. Seated on a tree-shaded bench, Madame Arkadina and Masha engage in idle conversation while Dorn attempts to read a de Maupassant story. Rather vainly, Irina asks Dorn to say which of them, herself or Masha, looks the youngest, then carries on about her fine appearance and flawless grooming. She exclaims that she never looks frumpy, an obvious contrast to her brother, Sorin. She takes the book from Dorn and reads aloud, then, apropos of the author's words, comments on her relationship with Trigorin.

When Sorin enters, accompanied by Nina and Medvedenko, who bring in his wheel chair, the conversation turns to Trigorin and his persistent habit of fishing alone and then to Konstantine, who Madame Arkadina finds "sad and morose." While Sorin snores in his wheel chair, Masha effusively praises Konstantine's genius and poetic soul. Annoyed, Irina wakes her brother and complains about his failure to take medicine. Dorn, in turn, carps about Sorin's consumption of wine and his smoking. According to the doctor, these habits affect his character, but Sorin only laughs and defends his use of sherry and cigars as a defense against his boring life, which in turn prompts a discourse by his sister on the dullness of country living.

After Shamreyeff and Pauline enter, and Irina confirms that she had hoped to take a horse and carriage to town in the afternoon, the steward grows angry and abrasive over her request. She threatens to leave for Moscow, and he threatens to quit his post. Followed by Trigorin, she exits with a complaint about the insults she is subjected to at Sorin's estate, leaving her brother to rebuke his steward for his insolence. Thereafter all go off except Dorn and Pauline. The doctor claims that Sorin should fire her husband but says that it will not happen, that instead the steward will be pardoned for his rudeness. Pauline begins complaining about her husband's coarseness, then pleads with Dorn to requite her love. She grows contrite when rebuffed, admitting her jealousy of other women.

Nina, who has been picking flowers, joins them and explains that Irina is inside crying and that her brother is in the throes of an asthma attack. She gives Dorn the flowers, but as he goes in to tend to Sorin, Pauline demands them from him. She tears them to pieces and throws them away before following him into the house. Alone, Nina expostulates on the strangeness of seeing a famous actress grow so passionate over nothing at all. She is joined by Konstantine Treplyov who carries a gun and a dead seagull, which he lays at her feet. He claims that is the way that he will end his life. Irritated, she complains that he cannot speak except in symbols. He complains bitterly about her growing frigidity towards him. When Trigorin appears, Konstantine remarks that he will not stand in Nina's way and exits.

Alone with the novelist, Nina talks of her envy for his fame, something that he claims he is unresponsive towards. She argues that his life is beautiful, but he rejoins that his writing is an annoying obsession that is more punishing than rewarding. The act of writing may be pleasurable, he says, but he detests the result. As a writer, he exclaims, he hates himself, for other than as a ''landscape artist'' he is ''false'' to the very core of his being. Nina is not discouraged, however, and expresses her willingness to sacrifice anything for fame.

After Madame Arkadina calls him from the house, Trigorin is about to go in when he notices the dead seagull and asks Nina about it. He then asks her to try to persuade Irina to stay and makes a note in a book that he carries with him. He is jotting down ideas for a sad story about a girl much like Nina, who a man destroys like the seagull. Madame Arkadina, appearing at a window in the house, calls again, announcing that they are staying after all. After Trigorin goes in, the act ends with Nina's remark that ''it's all a dream!''

Act 3

The scene shifts now to the interior of Sorin's house, to the dining room. From the conversation, it is made clear that about a week has elapsed since Konstantine shot the seagull. From the trunk and hat boxes deposited on the floor, it is also clear that preparations for a departure are in progress.

Masha is alone with Trigorin, who sits at a table eating his lunch. She tells him that she is going to marry Medvedenko, even though she does not love him. The fact that she is drinking annoys the writer. He is also upset because Treplyov has been behaving badly. As Boris explains, during the elapsed period between the acts, Konstantine has bungled an attempt to kill himself with a pistol shot to the head. He is reportedly also planning to challenge the novelist to a duel and has been preaching about the need for new art forms, which Boris finds offensively inflexible. As Nina enters, Masha speaks of Medvedenko as a poor and not very clever man, but one who loves her. She plans to marry him from pity as much as anything else.

After she exits, Nina gives Boris a medal that she has had engraved to commemorate their meeting. He recalls the moment when he saw her in her white dress with the seagull lying at her feet. They are then interrupted by Madame Arkadina and Sorin, who enter followed by Yakov, who is packing for Trigorin and Irina. The novelist goes off to find one of his books, lines from which are referenced on the medal's inscription.

Madame Arkadina tells Sorin to look after Konstantine, whom she is leaving behind. She says that she will never understand her son's bungled suicide attempt but that she must take Trigorin away because of Treplyov's threats. Sorin says that her son's behavior springs from his wounded pride and that she could help him by giving him some money for clothes, making him feel less like a poor relation. At first, Irina insists that she has none to give Konstantine, but she finally confesses that she has some money but that, as an actress, she needs it for her costumes.

When Sorin begins to stagger, about to faint, Madame Arkadina cries out for help. Both Treplyov and Medvedenko enter to assist, but the spell quickly passes, and Sorin again insists that he will accompany Irina and Boris to town. He goes off with Medvedenko, who poses the riddle of the Sphinx to him as they leave.

Alone with his mother, Treplyov asks her to change the bandage on his head, after first suggesting that she should lend her brother, Sorin, some money. When she is done applying the fresh bandage, Konstantine asks why she continues to be influenced by Trigorin, who, he says, is a coward for running off to escape a duel with him. A heated argument ensues over the novelist, as Konstantine attacks both Boris and his writings, and Irina defends him. She accuses her son of envy, and he explodes, announcing that his talent is greater than that of both his mother and Trigorin put together. In angry recriminations, he calls her a miser, while she retorts that he is a beggar. A sudden, contrite reconciliation follows, as Konstantine confides that he has lost the love of Nina, leaving him spiritually impoverished.

Just as Irina exacts a promise from Konstantine to make up with Trigorin, the writer enters and Treplyov hastily retreats from the room. Thereafter, the writer confesses his feelings for Nina, asking that they stay a bit longer. He pleads with Irina to let him go, to free him from her influence. She grows angry, then weepy, and finally throws herself on her knees pleading with him to remain true to her. She grows very possessive, overbearing his weak will and exacting a promise from him not to leave her. Then, as if nothing had just happened, she says that he can stay on for another week if he wishes.

Sorin's steward, Shamreyeff, enters to announce that the horse and carriage are ready for the trip into town, a notice he embellishes with recollections of an unintended comic moment in a serious melodrama. The family retainers begin scurrying in and out with the luggage and clothes, as Sorin, Pauline, and Medvedenko enter. Gifts are given, after which Sorin goes off to get in the carriage, followed by the others. Nina then enters, encountering Trigorin, who has returned to find his walking stick. As the act closes, the pair have a passionate moment in which they promise to meet in Moscow and seal the promise with an ardent kiss.

Act 4

The action again occurs in Sorin's estate house, in one of his drawing rooms that has been put to use by Treplyov as a study. It is stormy night, a full two years later. At rise, Masha and Medvedenko, now her husband, enter, looking for Konstantine, who, it is soon learned, has become a moderately successful writer. For the moment or so that the couple are alone, they reveal that they have a child, on whom Medvedenko dotes but towards whom Masha seems completely indifferent. The baby and her husband seem merely to annoy her.

They are joined by Treplyov and Pauline, who come in carrying bedding for turning a sofa into a bed for Sorin's use. The old man, now ill, has insisted on being near Konstantine. Medvedenko then leaves, ignored by Masha and rather curtly dismissed by Pauline, who thereafter turns warmer

attention to Konstantine, affectionately running her hand through his hair as she discusses his unanticipated acclaim as an author and begs him to be kind to Masha. Without uttering a word, he rises from his desk and exits, leaving Pauline and Masha to discuss Masha's forlorn love for him. Masha's only hope is that her husband's imminent transfer will put her ache behind her.

After Konstantine begins playing a melancholy waltz in another room, Dorn and Medvedenko enter, pushing Sorin in his wheelchair and arguing about money, a constant problem for the school teacher. Dorn says that he has no money either, claiming that his life savings have been spent on a journey abroad. As the rest converse with Sorin, it is learned that Madame Arkadina has gone to town to meet Trigorin, prompting Sorin to remark on his own illness and Dorn's unwillingness to let him have any medicine. Sorin wishes to give Konstantine matter for a story, a thinly-veiled, abstract account of his own life, prompting Dorn to remark on the old man's self pity and the fear of death.

Treplyov returns and sits by his uncle just as Medvedenko begins asking Dorn about his travels. After identifying Genoa as his favorite foreign city, Dorn inquires after Nina. Treplyov gives an account of her poor fortune as both an actress and Trigorin's mistress. He notes that in letters that she exchanged with Konstantine, Nina always signed herself "the seagull," and that though she did not complain in them, he could sense the sadness behind her words. He also reveals that she is now in town, staying at an inn, and that her father and stepmother have disowned her.

When Madame Arkadina and Trigorin arrive, accompanied by Shamreyeff, and greetings are exchanged, Trigorin graciously remarks on Treplyov's newly acquired fame as a writer and announces his intention to return to Moscow the next day, after fishing on the lake in the morning. Masha asks Shamreyeff to lend a horse to her husband, a request that prompts the steward to mimic her and Medvedenko to insist that he can walk home. Most of the characters sit down to play lotto, but Treplyov leaves after looking through a magazine given to him by Trigorin and announcing that Boris had read his own but not Treplyov's story. He once again begins playing the sad waltz offstage. The ensuing conversation of those remaining is interspersed with exclamations relating to the game. During it, Irina talks of her ongoing successes as an actress, while Trigorin voices doubts about Konstantine's skills as a writer. Dorn in turn defends Treplyov's artistry, while Madame Arkadina confesses that she had not even read any of her son's work.

Treplyov stops playing and returns to the drawing room as Shamreyeff informs Boris Trigorin that he has had the seagull stuffed for him. When Trigorin wins the lotto game, all the characters except Treplyov go off for some supper. In a monologue, Treplyov remarks that, despite his preaching about new forms, his work is becoming as routine as that which he despises. Then, hearing a tap at the window, he opens the doors, goes out, and leads Nina into the room. After she talks morosely of her faltering career, and her disappointments, Treplyov reveals his ambivalent feelings towards her, his love-hate, from which she recoils and tries to distance herself. She starts to try to leave, but Konstantine pleads with her to stay. She verges on going when she overhears Madame Arkadina and Trigorin in another room, and she reveals that, despite Boris' wretched treatment of her, she still loves him. She embraces Treplyov, then runs out through the terrace door. Left behind, Konstantine tears up all his manuscripts, then exits through another door.

After Dorn enters and moves a chair that Treplyov had used to block a door, he is joined by Irina and Pauline, and then Masha, Shamreyeff and Trigorin, who have returned to resume their game. Yakov follows with a tray and bottles. Almost immediately, they hear a shot from offstage. Dorn goes out to see what has happened, then returns. He exclaims that a bottle of ether in his bag exploded but then leads Trigorin away from the rest and, in a lowered voice, tells him to take Irina away, explaining, at the curtain, that Konstantine has shot himself again and that this time, presumably, has killed himself, though Trigorin does not explicitly say so.

CHARACTERS

Pauline Andreevna

Ilya Shamreyeff's wife, Pauline is often found in the company of the physician, Eugene Dorn, with whom she may be carrying on an illicit love affair, though whether her passion for him is being requited or is merely expressed remains one of the play's mysteries. In any case, she is seeking fulfillment outside of her marriage. Dorn, who has always been popular with the opposite sex, seems noncommittal in their relationship, even bored by it. She,

meanwhile, is well aware of the deadening effect that time is likely to have on her hopes and tries to push him into running off with her. He seems completely disinterested, however, worn down by his weary life as a physician. He is virtually penniless and no longer feels the stirring of passion, thus nothing really ever comes of their relationship.

Madame Irina Nikolaevna Arkadina

See Madame Treplyov.

Eugene Sergeevich Dorn

Dorn is a doctor, like Chekhov himself, and as such is a familiar figure in the playwright's dramas. He is a rather world-weary man, seemingly indifferent to his calling. After years of practicing medicine, he is virtually penniless, having spent his life's earnings on foreign travel. As if resentful towards his profession, he seems almost unwilling any longer to attempt to help the sick, notably Sorin.

Like some men, Dorn in his life has had no trouble attracting the interest of the opposite sex, and in this fact he contrasts with Sorin who complains that he has had no luck at all with women. The doctor is ardently pursued by Pauline, Shamreyeff's wife, but he resists her efforts to get him to run off with her. He does not openly repel her love but instead waits for time to wear it away.

Curiously enough, only Dorn gets excited over Konstantine's work, first his play and then his fiction, about which he is most effusive in his praise. He shares Treplyov's belief that something like a literature of "new forms" is needed to sweep out the old.

Maria Ilyinishna

See Masha.

Kostya

See Konstantine Gavrilovich Treplyov.

Masha

Daughter of Ilya and Pauline Shamreyeff, Masha (also called Maria Ilyinishna) is a young woman who assumes a melancholic demeanor, though it may be more fashionable than real. She dresses in mourning black, the outward reflection of her inner sorrow—or at least that is what she tells Medvedenko, the schoolmaster who dotes on her. She seems to

MEDIA ADAPTATIONS

- In 1968, *The Seagull* was adapted to film by director Sidney Lumet. Its stellar casts includes James Mason as Trigorin, Alfred Lynch as Medvedenko, Ronald Radd as Shamraev, Vanessa Redgrave as Nina, Simone Signoret as Arkadina, David Warner as Konstantin, Harry Andrews as Sorin, Eileen Herlie as Polina (Pauline), Kathleen Widdoes as Masha, and Denholm Elliot as Dorn. It is available on video from Warner Brothers.

- A Russian film version of *The Seagull* was produced in 1971, directed by Yuri Karasik and featuring Alla Demidova, Vladimir Chetverikov, Nikolai Plotnikov, Lyudmila Savelyeva, Valentina Telichkina, Yuri Yakovlev, Yefim Kopelyan, Armen Dzhigarkhanyan, Sofiya Pavlova, Sergei Torkachevsky, S. Smirnov, and Genrikas Kurauskas. It is available from Facets Multimedia, Inc., with English subtitles.

- *The Seagull* was produced for television, both in the United States and in Europe. In 1968, the year Lumet's film was made, a British version of the work was produced as a ''Play of the Month'' selection, featuring Robert Stephens. In 1975, the play was produced on American television, and featured, among others, Blythe Danner as Nina, Olympia Dukakis as Polina, Lee Grant as Irina Arkadina, and Frank Langella as Treplev (Treplyov). Three years later, another British version was aired, with a cast headed by Michael Gambon. There is also an Italian version, directed by Marco Bellocchio, dating from 1977. Also aired in the United States, this version featured Laura Betti, Giulio Brogi, Remo Girone, and Pamela Villoresi. While these performances attest to the great resurgence of interest in the plays of Chekhov, tapes of them have never been released for commercial use.

---

luxuriate in his misery, however, and her posturing borders on the ridiculous.

Masha's problem is her unrequited love for Konstantine Treplyov, who seems utterly blind to her desire and considers her a pest. He is in love with Nina and has his own problems with unrequited love. Although Masha does not love Medvedenko, who is a rather bland and unimaginative fellow, she ends up marrying him. They have a child, towards whom she reveals not the slightest maternal interest. She is ill tempered and cold towards her well-meaning husband, as is her mother, Pauline, who has been privy to Masha's hopes for a love liaison with Treplyov. At the last, she can only hope that her dull husband will be assigned to a new district so that she might put her painful love for Konstantine behind her.

Semyon Semyonovich Medvedenko

A rather unassuming and placid schoolmaster, Medvedenko diligently woos Masha, a woman whose passionate nature and eccentric manner simply seem puzzling to him. Because his own needs are so mundane and simple, he is unable to understand why she is so sad. As he observes, unlike him, she is hardly lacking in creature comforts. That her sorrow might spring from a despised love or some other nonmaterial cause simply escapes his understanding or sympathy.

Though she does not love or admire Medvedenko, Masha marries him, then behaves badly towards both him and their child. Medvedenko suffers her abuse without complaint, unwilling, perhaps, to risk the loss of her.

Ilya Afanasevich Shamreyeff

Ilya Shamreyeff, a retired army lieutenant, is Peter Sorin's irascible and tyrannical steward. As the inept Sorin complains, Ilya runs the estate, which, in truth, Sorin permits because rural life bores him. Peter is content to let Shamreyeff take charge, though the man is rather insolent and moody.

At times he is also rude to Sorin's guests, especially when he feels put upon. He seems to resent the fact that he is a retainer and not their social equal.

Ilya is married to Pauline, and Masha is their daughter. He seldom seems to be in their company, busy as he is sorting out such matters as how the horses are to be used at any particular moment. He seems blissfully unaware of his wife's infatuation with the physician, Eugene Dorn, and indifferent towards his daughter, who complains that she is unable to talk to him. With her, he seems much more gruff and short-tempered than loving. He has, in fact, some of the insularity that is characteristic of many career military men, and he has clearly alienated both his wife and daughter.

In a few instances, Shamreyeff talks at length about the theater, recalling what he considers great moments in Russian stage history. His nostalgia for the low comedy that was part of the traditional theater offers a contrast with Treplyov's attack upon traditional works as cliche ridden and formulaic.

Peter Nikolaevich Sorin

Peter Sorin, brother to Madame Arkadina, is a retired magistrate in his early sixties. He is also the host and owner of the country estate that is the play's setting.

Although easy-going and genial, Sorin constantly complains about the tedium of country living. He thinks of himself as a man of the town, miscast in his retirement role as rural squire. There is about him the smell of mortality, and in the course of the play he seems to wither away as his sense of boredom saps his energy. Towards the end of the play, he is confined to a wheel chair where he dozes and snores as life continues around him. Once an important man and the embodiment of authority, he can no longer curb the insubordination of his estate steward, Shamreyeff, or even of ordinary workmen. He has trouble with others as well, the physician Dorn, for example, who seems unwilling to heed his request for medicine. Towards him and other guests, Sorin seem pathetically deferential.

However, as a critic of Madame Arkadina's treatment of her son Konstantine, Sorin points up important character flaws in his sister, confirming, for example, the selfishness of which Treplyov accuses his mother, but she does not change one iota as a result of his criticism. He does love his nephew and provides him with a home and place to work, revealing a greater sense of concern for his welfare than Konstantine's mother has. Yet Sorin's fatherly love for his nephew is not powerful enough to stay the suicidal impulses of the young writer.

Konstantine Gavrilovich Treplyov

Son to Madame Arkadina and nephew to Peter Sorin, Konstantine Treplyov (also known as Kostya) is an aspiring writer in his early twenties. Moody and often depressed, Treplyov has an antagonistic relationship with his mother. He is an unrelenting critic of the traditional theater, which he considers tired and moribund, while she, having made her successful career in that theater, defends it. It is she who interrupts the performance of his ''new forms'' play on Sorin's estate, mocking its special effects and enraging her son, a signal event that sets in motion the destructive recriminations that further erode the relationship of Konstantine and his mother.

Treplyov's play also manages to alienate Nina Zaryechny, who, although she acts in the play, neither likes it nor understands what it is all about. Although Treplyov loves her, she turns away from him, attracted to the novelist Boris Trigorin and sets out to become an actress. From jealousy and envy, Treplyov verbally attacks Trigorin as a coward and wants to challenge him to duel. He also tries to kill himself, though the effort is suspect because, although he is able to bring down a seagull with a rifle shot, he bungles at least one try at blowing his brains out with a pistol.

In the final part of the play, despite his growing success as a writer, Treplyov remains melancholy and alienated from the other characters. He becomes critical of his own work, observing that it is becoming as conventional as the literature he had attacked for being staid and worn out. At the last, realizing that Nina will never relinquish her love for Boris and profoundly depressed by his own sense of his inadequacies, he makes a second and probably successful attempt on his life.

Madame Treplyov

Madame Treplyov (also called Irina Nikolaevna Arkadina) is the sister of Peter Sorin and mother of Konstantine Treplyov. She is a very successful and once a strikingly beautiful actress, who, although in her mid forties, still looks much younger, a fact in which she takes great pride. Although a sentimental woman prone to effusive emotional moments, she is a poor parent, stingy with her money and totally disinclined to sacrifice anything for her son. She is, in fact, rather embarrassed around him, in large measure because his presence serves to remind her of her real age. Although she is capable of tender moments with him, there is a strong antagonism between them that may be interpreted as having Oedipal undercurrents. In some of their exchanges, recriminations fly back and forth between them, and from start to finish she remains more hostile than loving towards him. Her antagonism is a major reason for his attempts at suicide.

Madame Treplyov holds the writer Boris Trigorin, her lover, under her spell, and although he is drawn to Nina Zaryechny, he ends up treating her badly and returning to Irina, who at one point plays shamelessly with his emotions and loyalty. Irina's son despises Trigorin, both for his writing and his apparent lack of courage. Irina is not able to make peace between them, though she hardly seems to try very hard. Because she is so selfish and self-centered, she cannot understand her son, and is simply mystified by his attack on the theatrical tradition in which she has won her fame and fortune. More often than not, she finds her son to be gloomy and depressing, an unfit companion. Still, she is fond of her brother, Sorin, though her concern for his failing health hardly matches her concern with her own fading beauty.

Boris Alexeevich Trigorin

Boris Trigorin, a successful novelist, is the traveling companion and lover of Irina Arkadina. His relationship with her and the acclaim accorded his art gnaw at Konstantine's innards. He holds the older man in contempt, as much from envy and jealousy as any really contemptible character flaws in Boris. The conflict between the two provides a good part of the play's tension.

Trigorin is actually a rather easy-going fellow. His success has made him neither arrogant nor aloof; thus, despite his wretched treatment of Nina, he remains rather likable as a character. His favorite activity at Sorin's estate is fishing in the ''magical'' lake, something that gives him peace and contentment.

Trigorin's fiction, realistic in nature, also rankles Konstantine, who is preaching a new style and mode in literature. Trigorin is open to new styles, and sees no reason why Treplyov's writing cannot coexist with his own. Konstantine is not so obliging, however, and seems bent on destroying both the man and his work. A central irony of the play is that Trigorin, without even trying, wins the adoration of Nina with whom Treplyov is hopelessly in love.

Yakov

Other than the steward, Ilya Shamreyeff, Yakov is the only named employee on Sorin's estate. He is one of the workers who at the opening of the play are putting the finishing touches on the stage being built for Konstantine's play, but later he also appears as a household servant, helping with the visitors' luggage and serving drinks. Like the unnamed cook and housemaids, he is otherwise an anonymous character.

Nina Mikhailovna Zaryechny

Nina Zaryechny is the pretty daughter of a wealthy landowner living on an estate near Sorin's estate. Her tyrannical father and stepmother disapprove of the ''bohemian'' guests of Sorin and try to prevent her involvement with them, but she is too much a free spirit to bend to their will. At first she seems to be in love with Konstantine, but after her performance in his play is interrupted, her loyalty to him quickly wanes. She is rather star struck by Trigorin, a much older man emotionally attached to Irina Arkadina. However, in her he sees a story, drawing parallels to her and the seagull that Treplyov has shot and laid at her feet. When she sets out to make a career of acting, somewhat precipitously encouraged by Irina, she takes up with Trigorin and bears his child. Irina's encouragement is somewhat suspect, for in some ways, like Konstantine, Nina is Irina's nemesis, representing as she does the youth and beauty that in Irina is swiftly fading. In any case, Nina's relationship with Trigorin is ill fated. He abandons her and the baby soon dies. However, despite Trigorin's rather wretched treatment of her, Nina cannot abandon her love for him, even though she has no more realistic hopes as a result of disappointments in love, the loss of her child, and her faltering acting career. The fact that she will not renew her earlier love relationship with Konstantine takes its final emotional toll on the young man, who, at the end of play, again shoots himself.

THEMES

If there is an overriding theme in *The Seagull,* it is that humankind's greatest enemy is time, the relentless enemy of passion and hope. It is a play of hopelessly misplaced love or desire. Many of the characters want love from others who are either indifferent or have emotional commitments elsewhere and are frustrated in their own turn. There are no fortuitous liaisons in the play. Rather, except for

TOPICS FOR FURTHER STUDY

- Investigate Henrik Ibsen's use of symbolism in *The Wild Duck* and compare it to Chekhov's use of it in *The Seagull*.

- Investigate life expectancy and infant mortality rates in Russia at the time of Chekhov's play and relate your findings to two significant revelations of *The Seagull*, the death of Nina's child and Sorin's disclosed age.

- Research the state of medicine in Russia in the 1890s and relate your findings to Dorn, the physician in *The Seagull*, and to Chekhov's own medical career and struggle with tuberculosis.

- Study some of the artistic manifestos of the late nineteenth century, such as George B. Shaw's *The Quintessence of Ibsenism* (1891), and Leo Tolstoy's *What Is Art* (1898), that elucidate the principles of realism in literature, whether in drama or fiction, and relate them to Chekhov's practice in *The Seagull*.

- Research the structural principles of the "well made" play, that is, one that follows the form described by Aristotle in his discussion of tragedy in *The Poetics*. Compare those principles with Chekhov's practice in *The Seagull*.

- Research Count Leo Tolstoy's complaints about Chekhov's alleged failure to use his art to advance a moral cause. Explain whether or not you think that charge is validated by the playwright's thematic concerns in the play.

---

the residual and somewhat enigmatic passion that binds Irina Arkadina and Boris Trigorin, the passions of each of the needful characters make them miserable, albeit, at times, comically so.

Alienation and Loneliness

A theme developed and exploited in much of modern literature is the individual's susceptibility to a sense of isolation and alienation in an environment that is basically inimical to that individual's emotional or mental health. The most important isolated figure in Chekhov's play is Konstantine Treplyov, the uncompromising artist alienated from those around him because they are much too conventional to share his convictions about a need for "new forms." He is, of course, even isolated from his mother, a selfish woman who perceives her son as a rather unpleasant and distressingly gloomy young man who threatens both her pocketbook and those things held most dear to her—her career and her loyalty to Boris Trigorin.

Familial alienation is also found elsewhere in the play. For example, Masha and her mother, Pauline, are both unhappy with Shamreyeff. Masha finds him impossible to confide in and seeks a surrogate father in the person of Dorn, to whom she confesses her love for Konstantine. Her mother, meanwhile, also looks for love from Dorn, a man who seems constitutionally ill-suited to fulfill the needs of either of the two supplicants. Another example is Nina, who is alienated from her father and stepmother, background characters who have a disapproving, puritanical suspicion of their artistic neighbors.

Others, like Sorin, experience a different kind of isolation. Once a magistrate with the authority of law supporting him, he has lost control of his own estate, even of his life. He is estranged from the only life he valued, that of the town, and is simply bored by the country. Dorn and Shamreyeff, even Trigorin, offer parallel examples in their own peculiar way.

Apathy and Passivity

While some of the characters in *The Seagull* struggle with their frustrated desires, a few seem apathetically resigned to living their unfulfilled lives with only a token resistance to their fate. Examples in the play are Dorn and Sorin and to a lesser degree Trigorin. While to some extent these men protest against their fate, they do little or nothing to change it. Sorin is simply bored by his rural life, yet he evidences neither the ambition nor the gumption to alter it, even to take charge of his estate's affairs. Although the town life that he is so nostalgic about is but a short carriage ride away, he just listlessly slides along, unable to muster up the physical or mental energy to return to it. Dorn, despite Pauline's passion for him, seems oddly detached from those around him. He does little or nothing to encourage Pauline. He seems also to have given up the practice of medicine, perhaps because the profession has left him virtually penniless. He seems more a hesitant observer than a doer, even in such simple matters as medicating the ailing Sorin. Even Trigorin, a successful writer, is curiously apathetic about his fame. He would rather spend his time at the estate's lake fishing, away from the company of the other characters, engaging in his private reveries.

These characters help give the play its crepuscular feel, that unnerving sense of lassitude that marks Chekhov's greatest plays. As in the actual Russian society at the time, the people in these plays talk of necessary change but prove ineffectual when it comes to effecting it, drawn as they are into a morass of self-indulgence, languishing in memories of better moments in their lives while life simply slips away from them.

Artists and Society

To some extent, *The Seagull* is concerned with the artist's role in society. Chekhov, who throughout his career had been subjected to criticism for his unwillingness to use his pen for doctrinaire purposes, was profoundly interested in the matter of the writer's social or political responsibilities and obligations. He was also writing at a time when not just the content but also the form and technique of literary works were undergoing revolutionary change.

Through his various characters, Chekhov studies the conflict arising from the resistance of tradition to that change. Clearly, Madame Arkadina, a denizen of the existing theater, embodies the views of the establishment. Standing against her is her own son, Konstantine, who preaches the need for a new art, one of "new forms," an art of forward-looking ideas, not one that merely entertains with timeworn conventions and hackneyed ideas that no longer have any social relevance. As his play indicates, the new art should have prophetic insights into humankind's destiny. His would be a theater

light years away from the theater that, for example, Shamreyeff favors, a theater of brick bats and pratfalls.

The conflict in *The Seagull* is only studied, not resolved. Even though Trigorin argues that both the traditional theater and allied literary arts and new ones could coexist, the closemindedness of the adherents to the old and the new argue that such an accommodation can not be. Konstantine's art is dismissed by his unsympathetic mother as the ravings of his "bad temper," while he sees in hers a mindless art that merely continues to pander to the bumptious fools making up the traditional theater audience. Meanwhile, as members of the artistic community spar on these issues, the philistines try to isolate them, dismissing them, as Nina's father and stepmother do, as immoral bohemians.

Love and Passion

The melancholy that pervades *The Seagull* arises from pangs of despised or unrequited love. In Chekhov's intricate design, most characters are both victim and tormentor, loving one of the others while rejecting the love of another character. That is, in the various triangular liaisons, each character loves another who either totally rejects that love or abuses it while having his or her own desires spurned by a third character. Konstantine Treplyov, for example, loves Nina, but she pursues Boris Trigorin, who ends up treating her very badly. Meanwhile, Masha pines after Konstantine, who only views her as a pest. She in turn is loved by Medvedenko, and although she does not love the schoolmaster, marries him as a convenience and then treats him shamelessly. Those not caught up in this sort of triangular love intrigue seem no better off—particularly, of course, Irina Arkadina, a selfish narcissist who is unable to face aging gracefully or find any satisfaction in her maternal role.

Identity: The Search for Self

The principal searcher in *The Seagull* is Konstantine, although in one way or another each of the main characters is trying to find an identity in a relationship that is fated to disappoint them all. Konstantine's quest is artistic. He seeks "new forms," to break with a conventional theater epitomized by his mother, the highly successful actress. Although Konstantine's desire for Nina plays a part in his frustrations, his mother's scoffing dismissal of his work and the acclaim afforded Boris Trigorin, whom he deems unworthy, are also devastating influences. When he finds his own work growing conventional, Treplyov despairs and, rejected again by Nina, shoots himself for a second time.

Other characters are caught in situations that prevent an inner peace or self-fulfilling relationship with another figure. For example, both Masha and her mother, Pauline, look to Dorn to help them alleviate their disquietude, to provide something lacking in their lives. Masha treats him as a surrogate father, confiding her feelings in him, while Pauline, unhappy with her husband, tries to inflame a passion in him for her. Dorn remains too detached, growing passionate only in his approval of Konstantine's artistic efforts to produce his "new forms." Others are similarly frustrated—Sorin, for example, by country life, which he finds tedious, or Trigorin, who seems to find no satisfaction in his success as a writer.

Success and Failure

In *The Seagull,* those who succeed in one sense invariably fail in another. In material terms, the most successful characters are Irina Arkadina and her companion, Boris Trigorin. She is an acclaimed actress, he a renowned writer. Both seem to sacrifice much of their essential decency to their success, however. Fearful of what the loss of beauty might do for her career, Irina is much too self-centered to respond to the needs of her son Konstantine. As a reminder that she is growing old, something that she cannot face, he simply annoys and threatens her. Meanwhile, Trigorin is so jaded by his success that he has grown cynical and desultory. He treats the adoring Nina badly, abandoning her when she badly needs his support.

In the case of Konstantine, a growing success has as an ironic consequence, for the acclaim makes him feel that he has somehow sold out his ideals, that he has failed to bring about the revolutionary change needed to develop "new forms" in writing. His publication of a story in the same magazine that contains one by Boris Trigorin distresses him, and in the play's last act, along with Nina's final rejection, it leads to his depression and second attempt at suicide.

Time

Time is the main enemy in *The Seagull.* In fact, it may be viewed as the play's principal antagonist. It is relentless and erosive, never a healing influence, as it is, for example, in a play like Shakespeare's *Winter's Tale.* Its effect pervades the lives of all the characters, and, because that is basically true to life, it is a defining element of Chekhov's realism.

The most devastating impact of its passage is seen between the third and fourth acts, when two years elapse. Nothing works out for the better, or at least what the various characters believe is the better. Sorin grows older and weaker. Irina Arkadina's beauty continues to fade. Nina's acting career goes nowhere. Perhaps worse yet, other things remain the same. If it is not betrayed, love merely languishes in its hopelessness, molding like some buds that rot without ever bearing fruit. Masha marries her schoolmaster, Semyon Medvedenko, and bears him a child but is neither a loving wife nor mother, still suffering from a misguided passion for Konstantine, who, in turn, still pines for Nina. Time, merely implacable, works to no one's advantage in *The Seagull.*

Aestheticism

The Seagull reflects Chekhov's aesthetic concern with his art. Several of the characters in the play are to some degree interested in the nature and theory of literary and dramatic arts. Two of them, Boris Trigorin and Konstantine Treplyov, are writers, while two others, Irina Arkadina and Nina Zaryechny, are actresses. Others, like Dorn and Shamreyeff, offer critical judgments on these arts. In fact, Sorin's estate serves as a kind of retreat for artists and intellectuals, and much of the play's dialogue, rich with allusions and topical references, concerns artistic matters. From the vantage point of Nina's puritanical father and stepmother, who remain offstage, those who gather there are self-indulgent and immoral. Nina's parent's view reflects the traditional attitudes still dominant in Russia at the time.

STYLE

Allusion

The Seagull makes use of allusion to literary works that in their suggestiveness enrich the texture of Chekhov's play. Chief among these is Shakespeare's *Hamlet,* from which Konstantine and his mother quote lines that help define their own relationship. Konstantine is angry with his mother for her attachment to Boris Trigorin, a man whom he intensely dislikes, as Hamlet dislikes Claudius. Like Hamlet, too, Konstantine erupts into fury with his mother, though as much for her selfishness as for her attachment to Trigorin. Like *Hamlet, The Seagull* is open to a Freudian, Oedipal interpretation of the relationship between Treplyov and his mother, a view buoyed up by a similar and common reading of the relationship between Hamlet and his mother, Gertrude.

Another allusion in *The Seagull,* concerns a story by the French writer, Guy de Maupassant. De Maupassant one of the very successful exponents of realism in fiction—still a relatively ''new form'' in Chekhov's day, but one against which contemporary currents were already beginning to turn. There are also several allusions to the Russian theater of the day, some of which provide insights to the characters who make them, though these references are more topical and less memorable than those made to Shakespeare.

Comedy of Manners

The Seagull, though not in mood or theme, has some similarities to a comedy of manners, those amoral drawing-room pieces of the English stage in the eighteenth century. In them, love intrigues are the principal focus of both the dramatists and his characters, and adultery is at least condoned if not actually practiced. Some characters, often libertines, are caught in triangular relationships that impose dilemmas that must be resolved through wit and clever stratagems, even reformation of character. In them, clever young rakes manage to satisfy the heart while also replenishing an empty purse.

Chekhov's comedy is much heavier, of course, and its outcome very different. In *The Seagull,* love's quests are frustrated and triumph over financial adversity remains an unrealized dream. The potential for self-fulfillment of any kind simply erodes as time passes. However, in its way, and certainly compared to much nineteenth-century melodrama, *The Seagull* shares with the earlier comedy of manners a complex intrigue plot, a degree of amorality, a focal concern with social mores, and a setting—a country estate—offering an ideal locale for the various character encounters necessary to the intrigue. As with some of those earlier plays, there is also an apparent shapelessness to *The Seagull.*

Conflict

There is no central conflict in *The Seagull,* no struggle between a protagonist and some opposing character or force, but there are minor conflicts arising from a character's desire out of harmony with the needs or aspirations of another character.

Mostly these have to do with love, invariably misplaced in the play. The play chronicles the frustrations of most of the major characters, their fruitless efforts to achieve what they want, and in a few cases—like that of Konstantine—depicts their disillusionment when they manage to gain a measure of success, if not in love, then at least in fortune.

Some of the conflict is familial, pitting offspring against parent, as in the case of Konstantine and his mother, but more often it arises from unrequited love. It leads to unhappiness, to the misery that seems to afflict all but the more dispassionate characters, Dorn, for example, or the waspish Shamreyeff, both of whom are aloof from love. In any case, the conflicts remain unresolved, at best only dimmed or diluted by the passage of time.

Farce

There is a very limited use of the low comic in *The Seagull,* elements of which abound in some of Chekhov's earlier one-act curtain raisers. Still, there are some farcical moments that help remind the audience that the play is, after all, a comedy, and that some of the characters' behavior is a kind of posturing. For example, there is something insincere about Masha's unhappiness expressed in the play's opening dialogue. ''I am in mourning for my life,'' she says, and she wears Hamlet's ''inky cloak'' as an outward manifestation of her professed inner sorrow, which, at least to Medvedenko, she cannot explain.

How seriously and sympathetically is the audience to take Masha or, for that matter, other unhappy figures, even Konstantine and Nina? *The Seagull* can be interpreted for staging as rather gloomy melodrama, or, as Chekhov himself seems to have wanted, it can be interpreted more as comedy. At times it seems to jar back and forth between the two moods, as, for example, in Konstantine's blundered suicide attempt. Its serious import is comically punctured when, after failing to blow his brains out, he appears with a turban-sized bandage on his head. In reminding the audience that life is not shaped as either comedy or tragedy, Chekhov juxtaposes a mundane observation or event against a soulful outpouring or serious action, and at times uses a kind of comic bathos, pitting the ridiculous against the sublime.

Fin de siècle

In art, *fin de siècle* suggests both art for its own sake and, warranted or not, decadence. The term was used to refer to artists in various genres who were breaking with tradition, producing works that defied conventional morality and eschewed a didactic function. Many of the artists involved led scandalous lives, flaunting that morality in their public behavior, the free-spirited Oscar Wilde, for example. Konstantine, in his quest for ''new forms,'' is cast in that bohemian mold, full of scorn for tradition and ready to tear down Russia's old theatrical edifice with his revolutionary art.

Foil

A common method of illuminating character in drama is through the use of character foils. It is a technique particularly well suited to plays, which are brief and ephemeral experiences when staged. By using sharply contrasting characters, the playwright is able to present each in high relief, making them both more distinct and memorable. In *The Seagull,* Sorin's character, his ineffectualness, is not just a correlative of his age and increasing feebleness, it is highlighted by the insubordination and surliness of his steward, Ilya Shamreyeff. Similarly, Konstantine Treplyov's imaginative but volatile nature is brought into sharper focus because it is seen against the character of Semyon Medvedenko, who, far more stolid and reasonable, never flies into rages. So, too, Irina Arkadina—a woman who protests too much—has a foil in Nina, a younger reflection of herself, one who in her youthful beauty reminds the older actress that her own beauty is fading. Chekhov effectively reveals other characters through such contrasts.

Oedipus Complex

Much has been made of the relationship of Konstantine and his mother, Irina Arkadina. With loose parallels and even allusion to Shakespeare's *Hamlet,* Chekhov develops an angry young man whose dislike of his mother's companion and lover, Boris Trigorin, transcends an artistic jealousy enlivened by his rebellious contempt for the older man's talent. Konstantine simply hates the man, even wants to kill him, a response that suggests more than a mere disgust with Trigorin's success as a writer. Although controversial, the Freudian explanation—a subconscious sexual jealousy—certainly has merit. The Oedipus Complex involves a male's latent love for his mother and corresponding hatred for his father, his rival for his mother's love. That hatred can be displaced, directed at a surrogate figure, especially if, like both Boris Trigorin in Chekhov's play and King Claudius in *Hamlet,* that person takes the father's place in the mother's bed.

Soliloquy

Curiously enough, Chekhov uses the soliloquy, a device that on the face of it seems inimical to realism. The soliloquy had a traditional use in theater. A vocalized monologue, it was used to reveal the inner thoughts and feelings of a character who delivers the speech while alone on stage. Although the speech may be overheard by hidden auditors, as happens in *Hamlet* for example, generally it reveals the character's inner self only to the audience. The realist's objection to the device is based on the idea that people do not normally talk to themselves aloud, unless, perhaps, they are mentally unbalanced. Chekhov makes spare use of the soliloquy, and perhaps, given what happens in the play, deliberately suggests the character's mental and emotional instability in employing it. In act 4, it is Konstantine who, briefly alone, discontentedly mulls over the fact that he is ''slipping into routine.'' This happens just before Nina appears and again rejects his love, leading to the play's perplexing finale, when Konstantine once again shoots himself.

Symbol

The Seagull has, as is suggested by the play's title, a central symbol, the seagull that Konstantine shoots and lays at the feet of Nina in act 2. Although Nina adopts the seagull as a signatory emblem, with a special meaning for her, its import for the play remains both elusive and debatable. There is no simple equation explaining its purpose. In fact, Chekhov seems to include it offhandedly, almost whimsically, as if defying the reader or viewer to find any meaning to it at all. Even Nina at first says that the symbolic meaning of the gull is beyond her understanding. However, symbols are often elusive beasts, talking points with no definitive answers, in part because they can mean different things to different people. What is clear is that Konstantine is a crack shot, bringing down a bird on the wing, suggesting that his attempt at suicide is deliberately bungled, making the attempt seem a mere ploy for sympathy. In any case, Konstantine relates the killing of the bird, a thing of beauty, to his depressed emotional state. He speaks of earlier events, including the failure of his play—which, like the seagull's life—was aborted by an act of cruelty, that is, by his mother's dismissive scorn. He also tells Nina that he has burned the manuscript of his play, deliberately destroying what, in his view, was a thing of beauty.

Other symbols in the play include the estate's lake, which, like the gull, means different things to different characters. Dorn sees it as magical, able to evoke dreams, while Trigorin views it more practically, as a refuge, a place to fish, and Nina as a catalytic influence in her desire to become an actress. Flowers figure in the play, too. In their ephemeral beauty, they suggest the fragile dreams of various characters, which, like the flowers in the play, are deliberately destroyed or succumb to the ravages of time.

HISTORICAL CONTEXT

In the year in which Chekhov's *The Seagull* was first staged, 1896, Nicholas II, of the Romanov dynasty, became the last czar of Russia, a nation that at the time had a population of about 128 million people. Dominated by the Russian Orthodox Church, an inept bureaucracy, and an entrenched landed and hereditary aristocracy, the vast country had settled into a seemingly inert, twilight period, a sort of fitful hibernation resistant to political change and social amelioration. While many members of the educated class recognized a need for progress, they were largely ineffectual in achieving much of anything until violent revolution brought the Bolsheviks to power in 1917 and Russia, for good or ill, finally entered the modern world. Until then, despite some unrest, including a crushed rebellion in 1906, Russia was simply a sleeping giant that had barely started to respond to the industrial revolution that a century before had begun transforming many of its European neighbors to the west into emerging industrial powers. However, at the same time, despite its backwardness and cultural isolation, Russia produced some of the greatest writers, composers, and artists of the age, among whom Chekhov stands in the front rank. Russian cities, notably Moscow and St. Petersburg, were cultural centers of tremendous importance, and places, too, where new ideas were fomented by a growing number of disaffected intellectuals. But these cities also lacked adequate housing, health care, and transportation and communication facilities, and were plagued by poverty and disease—including tuberculosis, the consumptive sickness which, even as he wrote *The Seagull,* was slowly wasting Chekhov's own life.

Although the modern age in the United States—and such European countries as England, France, and Germany—was dawning more rapidly than in the future Soviet Union, a much accelerated rate of change awaited inventions and discoveries that in 1896 were, at best, still in their infancy. In that year, Henry Ford drove his first car through the streets of Detroit and the German scientist, Wilhelm Roentgen, discovered x-rays. Also, the dial telephone and electric lamp were patented in America, and the first movie was screened in the Netherlands. In that year, too, the first modern Olympic Games opened in Athens, a seminal event that presaged the breakdown in the isolation of nations and the advent of internationalism in the postindustrial age.

Besides changes wrought through science and technology, social and political changes were in the winds. The impact of two major thinkers—Karl Marx and Charles Darwin—continued to affect everything from politics and religion to art and letters. It was in the 1890s that a third major thinker, Sigmund Freud, had begun evolving his psychoanalytical method, providing new and sometimes distressing insights into human behavior. Freud would greatly impact both literature and art, which, in the same era, were already in search of new directions and the ''new forms'' of which Konstantine speaks in *The Seagull.* The fin de siècle artists of the 1890s, although a hydra-headed group, were united in their efforts to replace the traditional with the new and different, to experiment with form and technique. Although never given to the personal excesses of many of his contemporaries, Chekhov, particularly in his last few plays, reflects that need to make things new.

CRITICAL OVERVIEW

Anton Chekhov wrote *The Seagull* in 1895, at the demarcation point between his first and second periods of development as a dramatist. In the first stage, starting in 1881, the writer was chiefly recognized for his adaptations of his own short fiction into ''vaudevilles,'' one-act farces that were very popular curtain raisers in Russian theater. To a great extent, these are formulaic pieces, focusing on the absurdities of such eccentric character types as the hypochondriacal suitor and his man-desperate, bride-to-be counterpart in *The Marriage Proposal* (1888–1889) or the blustering male intruder and the reclusive, long-suffering widow in *The Bear* (1888).

COMPARE & CONTRAST

- **1890s:** Long travel is difficult, limited principally to rail and horseback or horse-drawn cart, carriage, or sleigh, often on roads that for half the year were impassable. Although the telephone has come into use in some cities in Europe and America, it has not yet reached the likes of Sorin's country estate. While such estates could be situated fairly close to towns providing railway connections to Moscow and other major cities, many people live their lives never venturing more than a few miles away from where they were born.

  Today: Modern technology makes it possible for even the most physically isolated communities to stay in touch, not just with the world's urban centers, but with each other. Today, even those geographically isolated in what few wilderness outposts remain, or in transit over the world's remote regions, can talk to relatives or friends with whom a reunion may be just a few hours or, at most, a day or two away.

- **1890s:** Medicine, though verging on important breakthroughs, is a dreadfully imperfect art. There is little understanding of the nature of most diseases, of the bacteria or viruses that caused them, thus treatment is largely limited to dealing with the symptoms rather than the causes. Medicine is also unregulated, and many doctors, some of them quacks, depend upon homeopathy and herbal-based, family elixirs, passed down from one generation to another. Alcohol and opium derivatives are standard painkillers, dispensed without much knowledge of their addictive nature. All too often, patients are sent to hospitals, not to be cured, but to die. By the end of the nineteenth century, average life-expectancy in the United States is in the mid-forties. In Russia it is even lower.

  Today: Medicine may still be an imperfect art, but scientific advances in the twentieth century have made it a much more exact and effective one. More medicinal practises are preventative in nature. Through immunization, doctors control diseases that used to be dreaded killers.

Physicians and medical scientists now attempt to discover the cause of a sickness, for if the cause can be isolated, a cure is deemed possible. That life expectancy will soon double that of a century ago is evidence of the great strides medicine has made in the last one hundred years.

- **1890s:** Aside from the entertainment provided by books and card and board games, most home entertainment has to be provided ''in-house'' by those dwelling or visiting there. The houses of the upper and middle classes usually have pianos and other musical instruments; some even have music rooms, where family members can gather to form small chamber-music ensembles. Plays and recitations were common, too. There is, in fact, a fairly active engagement of family members and guests in the production of entertainment.

  Today: Thanks to great technological advances, family members and guests can enjoy a tremendous array of entertainment experiences simply by ''channel surfing'' on television or the Internet, or by inserting different compact discs or tapes in home-entertainment components. In fact, the greatest audience for various arts is now found in the home, not at the live event. The home audience is more passive now, however, and often has no participatory role in providing entertainment.

- **1890s:** Class distinctions are still strongly etched in the consciousness of its citizens, even though the serfs have been liberated for several years and a middle class is rapidly emerging.

  Today: Although in many democratic societies there remains a vestigial sense of class distinctions, power associated with class and hereditary right has greatly diminished. Class distinctions today are usually based on wealth, education level, or professional standing, and they are reflected more in such things as country-club memberships and cultural tastes than in the size of one's estate and the number of servants in the household.

Also belonging to the first period are four full-length plays, two of which are no longer extant. In only one of these, *The Wood Demon* (1889), did the playwright begin experimenting with an "indirect action" technique in an attempt to more faithfully represent actual life, free of the many stage conventions that, because they in some way falsified it, had become anathema to realists. However, until entering his second period with *The Seagull,* Chekhov still continued to depend on traditional techniques and devices, including direct, on-stage action and plots contrived to heighten dramatic impact and force an artificial closure.

In the inner-action technique used in *The Seagull,* some of the most vital action occurs offstage, not just Konstantine's two attempts at suicide, but in events that transpire between acts, as, for example, the ill-fated liaison of Trigorin and Nina and the unfortunate marriage of Masha and Medvedenko. Most of these events occur between acts 3 and 4, when two years pass. Furthermore, on the surface, *The Seagull* totally lacks the causal arrangement of episodes that characterized the more traditional fare of the time. Since action is not locked together in a discernible pattern, the work seems almost shapeless, much like life itself.

These daring departures from the usual theatrical fare were simply too much for the St. Petersburg audience when the play premiered there on October 17, 1896. It was staged at the Alexandrinsky Theater, a house that was, as quoted in Lantz, "associated with popular, low-brow entertainment," and was turned into "a complete fiasco," in part because it was "an inadequate production that was unequal to the play's striking dramatic innovations." In fact, as quoted in Styan, the Alexandrinsky's own literary committee forewarned that the play's structure was too loose and carped about its "symbolism, or more correctly its Ibsenism." In any case, the play was hastily prepared for production under the direction of E. M. Karpov, a writer of popular melodramas who evidenced little sympathy for Chekhov's revolutionary technique, and when it went on the boards, it was openly mocked. The reaction devastated the playwright, who left the Alexandrinsky confused and deeply depressed. Although audiences for the remaining performances in the eight-day run were more receptive, the damage to the dramatist had already been done.

One of the harshest critics of the play was Leo Tolstoy, who, in 1897, voiced his wholly unfavorable opinions to Chekhov's close friend, Alezxy Suvorin. As David Magarshack notes, while admitting that *The Seagull* was "chock full of all sorts of things," Tolstoy complained that nobody had an inkling of what they were there for, and he dismissed the work as "a very bad play." That was a view shared by many, most of whom were blind-sided by Chekhov's innovative genius. As Magarshack notes, "apart from his purely moral objections to Chekhov's characters, Tolstoy's main criticisms of Chekhov's plays concern their structure and their apparent lack of purpose."

Fortunately, both for Chekhov and the modern theater, a complete reversal in the play's fortunes occurred in 1898, two years after the initial staging, when the newly formed Moscow Art Theatre revived it under the joint direction of that group's founders, Vladimir Nemirovich-Danchenko and Konstantin Stanislavsky. These two, brilliant advocates of ensemble theater, were dedicated to purging the Russian theater of its insidious star system, in which plays, often bad, were written as vehicles for popular actors. They were also dedicated to preserving the authority of the dramatist, to honoring a play's text and its creator's intentions.

Nemirovich-Danchenko, who knew Chekhov, convinced both the reluctant dramatist and Stanislavsky to attempt a revival of *The Seagull* at the Moscow Art Theatre. After a rigorous rehearsal schedule, it opened there on December 17, 1898, and was greeted with tremendous enthusiasm and deafening applause. Although the work was not the first play produced by the M.A.T., it was the one that brought it overnight fame, and it acknowledged its indebtedness to the play by adopting a seagull as its own symbol.

The play also brought critical acclaim for Chekhov, who thereafter was inspired to continue writing for the stage, producing three other masterpieces before his untimely death in 1904. Although some, like Irina Kirk, view the work as "the most innovative of his plays," the other three that came in its wake—*Uncle Vanya, Three Sisters,* and *The Cherry Orchard*—are generally more highly regarded, and in the history of theater have been more frequently revived. Some modern criticism views *The Seagull,* if not as a mediocre play, at least a flawed one. Echoes of the original complaints about the play's loose structure and blatant symbolism persist. Still, as the first of the four major plays, *The Seagull* enjoys a reputation both for being Chekhov's seminal work in his second and greatest period of writing for the stage and a fascinating play in its own right.

CRITICISM

John W. Fiero

Fiero holds a Ph.D. degree. He formerly taught drama and playwriting at the University of Louisiana at Lafayette and is now a freelance writer and consultant. In the following essay, he examines the ways in which Chekhov employs structural elements and characterization to achieve a sense of uncompromising realism.

Among the early modern playwrights associated with the advent of realism in drama, none seems more wholly committed to its principal mimetic tenant—of depicting life as it actually appears—than does Anton Chekhov. *The Seagull* (1896) clearly illustrates this dedication, as do the rest of the dramatist's later works: *Uncle Vanya* (1898), *The Cherry Orchard* (1900), and *Three Sisters* (1901). In all of them, Chekhov's signature forte is his ability to reveal character depth while maintaining an almost clinical detachment from his subjects, something he first achieved in his fiction and then successfully carried into his drama.

There is also a unique quality to these plays, a quality that recalls W. H. Auden's praise of "The Old Masters" in his well-known poem, "Musée des Beaux Arts." According to the poet, those painters unerringly placed suffering in its appropriate "human position" or perspective, one in which matters of great pith and moment unfolded before attendants or witnesses, who, absorbed by their more mundane pursuits, remain either unaware or uncaring. To exemplify his idea, Auden uses Pieter Brueghel's *Icarus,* a painting in which Icarus's mythic end is depicted in a background corner of the painting, as barely discernible legs plummeting into the sea, while the foreground focus is on a ploughman and his horse, seemingly oblivious or indifferent to Icarus' fate.

The painting could almost serve as a visual metaphor for Chekhov's perspective in *The Seagull* and the other three plays of his final period. In all of them, as a quintessential realist, Chekhov places individual suffering in a similar, sometimes disquieting position. In them he juxtaposes the comic

inflexibility of mundane and myopic attitudes of one or more characters against the pain and suffering of another, producing his highly original work that seems neither comic fish nor tragic fowl, but an odd sort of creature with its own taxonomy. These are his plays of "indirect action," in which the most significant events in the characters' lives occur either offstage or in entre-act crevices, in a rough equivalent to the background corner of Brueghel's painting. At times, what happens on the stage, in the foreground, is comically inappropriate to or heedless of what is happening just beyond a door or, at a further remove, in the larger world beyond. In *The Cherry Orchard,* for example, while at an offstage auction their world is collapsing, Chekhov's onstage characters mark its passing in dance and idle, if anxious, chatter, unable to do anything to prevent the inevitable. For Chekhov, such was the way of the world, and, as a realist, it was the way he chose to depict it.

Beginning with *The Seagull,* to meet the fairly rigorous demands of realism, Chekhov completely scrapped traditional stage conventions as well as the time-honored dramatic structure delineated, notably in Aristotle's *Poetics,* and served up as a guide to writing plays in countless handbooks on the craft. Central to this structure is a sense of completeness, of unity and wholeness, achieved through a succession of dramatic moments that move towards an anticipated climax, an obligatory "recognition" scene in which the central conflict of the work is resolved and its tension released. Though it is clearly a formulaic scheme, it has worked well for some of the greatest dramatic masterpieces in the world, especially in tragedy. However, because it is a "tendency" structure built on the principle of necessity or inevitability, it is highly selective in what it depicts, and therein it goes against the theoretical grain of unalloyed realism. Life is simply not packaged that neatly.

Compared with a play like Ibsen's *Hedda Gabler,* which has a tendency structure, Chekhov's *The Seagull* eschews any vivid sense of dramatic inevitability. There are no vital seeds sown in the first act, either in action or character recollections about the past, that set the major figures on an unalterable course to an anticipated fate. Nor, at the end, is there a sense of completeness, for the conflicts in the play are simply too diffuse and unresolved. Although the implication of Dorn's behavior is that Konstantine Treplyov's second attempt at suicide has been successful, even the young writer's fate remains in

A scene from act 3 of the theatrical production of The Seagull *at Moscow Art Theater.*

doubt, as do the affairs of most of the other characters. Thus, in its inconclusiveness, the play is open-plotted, and it leaves most of its characters in their own emotional and isolated limbos. That time will not improve their lot seems the only certainty.

In essence, much more so than Ibsen, Chekhov approaches a "slice of life" fidelity to real human existence. He provides no neat, ordered array of episodes, but rather a matrix of action that ultimately fails to take his characters very far down a path of self-realization or sense of personal fulfillment. That is not to say that Chekhov's last plays lack plots or significant action. According to David Magarshack, one of those who describes those masterpieces as "plays of indirect action," it is not a plot's "absence but its complexity that distinguishes them." The late plays teem with life and are almost overloaded with ideas. In *The Seagull,* however, there is no central problem that is the focal concern of all its characters, except, perhaps, such an intangible thing as the nature and purpose of art, an issue of vital concern to Chekhov, and one that resonates throughout the play and pervades its dialogue. It provides a thematic counterpoint to the frustration and unhappiness felt by most of the characters, especially Konstantine, Nina, Masha,

and Pauline, who are all disappointed in love. None of these characters finds happiness in some final comic triumph, for, simply put, no Jack gets his Jill, or at least not his proper Jill. In fact, there seems to be no end to the pain. Except perhaps for Treplyov, life will merely continue in its entropic vein, with a pervasive sense of ennui, of a melancholic world weariness that is erosive of the human spirit.

The Seagull has no principal character, no protagonist, nor even any plot driver whose need or desire is the engine of the action, as is, for example, Hedda's in Ibsen's *Hedda Gabler.* Even if one claims that Nina and Konstantine are the "leads," as J. L. Styan does, their dramatic potency is sapped because the critical events in their lives, her seduction and his suicide attempts, occur offstage. Chekhov's plot can in fact be seen as the sum of its minor plots, most of which have to do with love that is frustrated or abused. It simply lacks a cohesive, unifying symbol and an impending change that is of concern to all its characters, elements that Chekhov so brilliantly provides in *The Cherry Orchard,* generally acknowledged to be his finest work.

However, as Magarshack points out, the lack of a central protagonist was hardly a new phenomenon

WHAT DO I READ NEXT?

- August Strindberg's *Miss Julie* (1888) and its "Foreword," in which the dramatist reveals the Darwinian influence on his art, is worth contrasting with Chekhov's themes and technique in *The Seagull*.

- Henrik Ibsen's *Hedda Gabler* (1890) is also worth comparing with *The Seagull* for its themes and technique. One early complaint with Chekhov's play was that it evidenced too strong an influence of Ibsen.

- Maxim Gorky's play, *The Lower Depths* (1902), a more naturalistic play than any by Chekhov, focuses on lower-class Russians struggling for survival. Like Chekhov, Gorky came to prominence through productions at the Moscow Art Theatre.

- *Anna Karenina* (1875–1877), by Leo Tolstoy, is one of the greatest of all Russian novels. Tolstoy, though he wrote plays, is really only remembered for his fiction. He had a tremendous influence on Chekhov.

- *Heartbreak House* (1916), by George Bernard Shaw, has some interesting parallels to Chekhov's play. Its focal interest is the eroding of class distinctions, also of concern to Chekhov. Shaw's play also takes place in a country house, that of Hesione Hushabye. Like Sorin's estate, it provides a microcosmic setting for investigating a social hierarchy.

- *The Autumn Garden* (1951), by Lillian Hellman, reflects Chekhov's influence in its technique, structure, and theme. Generations of family and friends gather together, haplessly trying to reinvigorate their lives, which have settled into dull and listless routines.

---

in drama. He notes the absence of such a figure in many direct action plays, especially those of Chekhov's contemporary, Alexander Ostrovsky. More important, says Magarshack, are the changes in dialogue and Chekhov's use of invisible, off-stage characters in the dramatist's last four plays. Regarding the text, the critic argues that "the dialogue of the early plays is remarkable for the directness of its appeal to the audience," whereas in the mature works "its appeal is indirect and, mainly, evocative"—in brief, more lyrical. As for the unseen characters in the background, they provide "a motive force for the action, which is all the more powerful because the audience never sees them but is made to *imagine* them." By their offstage actions, the "invisible characters" in *The Seagull,* the disapproving parents of Nina, in fact reveal much about Irina Arkadina and her friends, their presumed moral laxity, for example, or their threat to traditional mores. In their final disowning of Nina, they have an important symbolic significance. They represent the traditionalism that blocked what Chekhov believed were necessary changes in both art and society.

Although the play is crammed with action, it is wrought small. There are no big events, not in the foreground at least. As noted, the two suicide attempts by Konstantine, certainly traumatic moments, occur offstage; the first attempt is made in the interval between acts 2 and 3, the other at the end of act 4, when Treplyov tears up all his manuscripts and walks out of the room and, in despair, shoots himself. Even as he storms off, other characters enter the vacated room to resume a game that was earlier interrupted and begin chatting about matters that argue that they are simply oblivious to Konstantine's self-destructive mood. When the shot is heard, they do not even question Dorn's assertion that something in his medicine case must have exploded. They simply go on with their parenthetical lives as if nothing of significance has happened.

Elsewhere, the focus of *The Seagull* is, as Styan suggests, "on several intense and potentially melodramatic relationships, which tend to distort the objective view by calling for an audience's empathy with exhibitions of individual emotion.'' Characters do at times vent a passion, especially Konstantine, but Chekhov never permits an emotion to explode into onstage, self-destructive violence. Reminders that life will go on in the face of individual suffering always seem to assert themselves, deflating passions and defusing the moment, even rudely so, as when, in act 1, with derisive scorn, Irina Arkadina abruptly intrudes on Konstantine's serious feelings—which hang out in his play within the play like so much emotional laundry—and compels him to abort Nina's performance and bring down the curtain.

That scene is part of a pattern of unsympathetic disengagement that characters evidence from the opening moments of *The Seagull*, when Medvedenko questions Masha about her unhappiness with his practical observations that she has little to be unhappy about. Throughout the play, in parallel fashion, characters seem unwilling or unable to cooperate when others make a plea for love or understanding. Some reactions are unintended, like Sorin's dozing off, but others seem singularly insensitive, especially in situations in act 2. When Konstantine lays the dead gull at Nina's feet, she is simply irritated with him and complains that she is ''too simple to understand'' him. In turn, she is given an emotional cold shoulder by Trigorin, with whom she is infatuated. He fumbles with her words most awkwardly, nervously laughing and consulting his watch while politely attempting to deflect her obvious hero worship.

Such are the Chekhovian moments on which *The Seagull* is built. They seem to come almost haphazardly, like a series of accidental encounters. They are, of course, very carefully placed beads on the playwright's structural string, asymmetrical perhaps, but dramatic nonetheless, and much closer to mirroring actual life than those more traditional plays in which episodes are placed in a progressive, logically-ordered arrangement. Chekhov's genius for making such a structure work explains why, despite the topicality of much of his matter, particularly in *The Seagull*, his final plays are still highly valued for their technique and are still imitated in method.

Source: John W. Fiero, in an essay for *Drama for Students*, Gale Group, 2001.

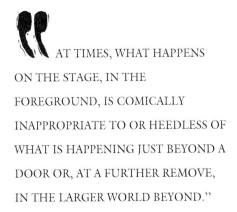

AT TIMES, WHAT HAPPENS ON THE STAGE, IN THE FOREGROUND, IS COMICALLY INAPPROPRIATE TO OR HEEDLESS OF WHAT IS HAPPENING JUST BEYOND A DOOR OR, AT A FURTHER REMOVE, IN THE LARGER WORLD BEYOND.''

Ryan D. Poquette

Poquette has a B.A. in English, and specializes in writing drama and film. In the following essay, Poquette analyzes Chekhov's play in light of both its historical context as a transitional example of modern drama and in Chekhov's character, Treplyov, regarding the state of a symbolist in a realist society.

At the end of the nineteenth century, the classical conventions of drama introduced largely by Aristotle more than two millennia ago were being replaced by a new, modern theatre. Modern drama emphasized realism in place of melodrama, fantasy, and romance. Whereas earlier writers had focused on elevating theatre and its characters to an imaginary level, often depicting fictional situations outside of the average playgoer's experience, modern playwrights attempted to approximate the reality of life as it is really lived.

In the modern play, the audience was asked to imagine that the curtain was a fourth wall that existed between them and the actors. The characters were seen as regular people going about their business, oblivious to the audience. When the curtain rose, these audience members were allowed to peek through this imaginary wall and into a certain time period and situation in the characters' lives.

Other conventions that changed were in the use of dialogue. Realistic drama featured dialogue that was not embellished or exaggerated. Modern actors did not play to the audience with grand, poetic solitary speeches, known as soliloquies, as Shakespearean actors did. There were no stars in the modern system. Instead, playwrights used well-rounded ensembles of people who discussed their

CHEKHOV'S MAJOR PLAYS PLACED MORE IMPORTANCE ON THE CHARACTERS THAN THE PLOT, LEADING MANY CRITICS TO SAY THAT NOTHING HAPPENS IN A CHEKHOV PLAY. BUT '. . . NONE, OR AT LEAST FEW, WOULD ARGUE THAT THEY ARE ABOUT NOTHING: SOMEHOW HE MAKES THE 'NOTHING' OF HIS ACTIONS A NOTHING THAT HAS TO DO WITH EVERYTHING.'"

situation using the same types of realistic dialogue that an audience member might use in his or her own life.

In the case of Anton Chekhov, realism also extended to include a focus on mood and emotion among the characters, as opposed to a unifying plot and a direct, easily recognizable dramatic action. Instead, Chekhov's major plays placed more importance on the characters than the plot, leading many critics to say that nothing happens in a Chekhov play. But, as Anthony Caputi stated in 1991 in his anthology, *Eight Modern Plays,* ". . . none, or at least few, would argue that they are about nothing: somehow he makes the 'nothing' of his actions a nothing that has to do with everything."

Chekhov was well aware of the conventions that he was breaking and the problems it might cause, particularly in the case of *The Seagull.*

The Seagull was the first of Chekhov's final four plays (referred to as his "major" plays) and is considered by many critics to be his most innovative dramatic work because it introduced new conventions that would serve as a transition to his and others' later modern plays. Simon Karlinsky and Michael Henry Heim noted this fact in 1973 in their anthology, *Letters of Anton Chekhov.* "It was in *The Seagull* that this liberation first occurred, the creative breakthrough that made Chekhov as much an

innovator in the field of drama as he already was in the art of prose narrative."

Even though *The Seagull* is widely regarded as a pivotal work for both Chekhov and modern drama, the wealth of criticism on the play is anything but unanimous in its treatment of the material. Even Chekhov was a little unsure at the time about what he had written. Donald Rayfield makes reference to a letter that Anton Chekhov wrote on October 21, 1895, to his longtime friend and editor, Alexis Suvorin, in which he remarked that his play was unstageable due to the radical departure from conventional stage rules.

With that fact in mind, one can nevertheless make the case that Chekhov intended *The Seagull* to be a statement on his literary ideas, specifically by using the character of Treplyov to show that a true symbolist could not survive in a modern society that was focused more and more on realism.

Symbolism was a movement that focused on mysticism as opposed to reality. It involved sacrificing realism for imagination and attempted to achieve a dramatic ideal.

David Magarshack explores Chekhov's views toward the symbolists in 1973 in *The Real Chekhov.* "Chekhov dismissed the 'decadents,' as the symbolists were called, as 'frauds.'" As Magarshack notes, Chekhov never engaged in public debates over his art but instead distributed his ideas about drama through his characters.

In *The Seagull,* these characters consist of a well-rounded group of people, all of whom are faced with the real despair of having wasted their lives or experienced unrequited love.

The most passionate of these characters is Konstantin Treplyov, the young writer who attempts to live his life and art completely through the idealistic views of symbolism.

Throughout the course of the play, Treplyov's attempt to achieve his ideal life is slowly beaten down by the reality of the situation surrounding him. In the beginning, he has pretensions of being a great writer of "a new form," and it is with this aim that he produces a short play that he attempts to show to his friends and relatives on his Uncle Sorin's country estate. The play includes no living characters and features only one performer, Nina Zarechny, a young woman who Treplyov loves. Nina, however, does not return his love, although she also aspires to live the ideal creative life, in this case as an actress.

Treplyov's play details a mystical struggle 200,000 years in the future on a barren earth, between the devil and a "world soul," which is composed of all of humanity's past souls. "The consciousness of all humanity, together with the instincts of animals, have united in me," Nina intones. Magarshack notes that this abstract idea of a world soul and a mystical struggle was based largely on the ideas of the leader of the Russian Symbolist movement.

Treplyov's play ends in failure when his mother, Irina Arkadina, an actress in the traditional theatre, criticizes the play during the performance, calling it "decadent." Treplyov angrily stops the show and stomps off, leaving his audience members to discuss the play. His mother dismisses the play as merely "decadent ravings. . . . what we have here are pretensions to new forms, to a brand-new era in art. There are no new forms available, as I see it, just a bad temper."

The failure of Treplyov's symbolist play is an attack by Chekhov on symbolism itself. The irony of Arkadina's statement is that Chekhov himself, with the writing of *The Seagull,* is helping to usher in a new era with his radical conventions and the new realism of modern drama.

Chekhov is not totally unsympathetic to the symbolist movement, however. In the play, the character of Dr. Dorn echoes Chekhov's ideas about abstract art such as symbolism. Says Dorn:

> There must be a clear and definite thought in a work of art. You must know what it is you're writing for. Otherwise, if you go along that picturesque road without a definite aim, you will lose your way and your talent will destroy you.

This idea of unrestrained art being destructive is a clear foreshadowing of Treplyov's suicidal fate, and is, as Magarshack notes, the central theme of the play. For Dorn and for Chekhov, an abstract idea is not bad in and of itself. Instead, it is art without structure that can destroy an artist, in this case the symbolist, Treplyov.

Treplyov's next appearance in the play, in act 2, signals even more his dismal fate. After witnessing Nina fawn over the established writer Trigorin, and realizing that his love for Nina will be forever unrequited, Treplyov kills a seagull and presents it to Nina, telling her that he will soon kill himself.

The seagull, which has been noted by critics as a heavy-handed use of symbolism to represent hopes betrayed, is also linked to the image of Nina herself, beginning with her statement back in the first act: "My father and his wife won't let me come here. They say this place is Bohemian . . . They're frightened I might become an actress . . . But I ache to return to this lake, as if I were a sea gull." Nina feels trapped in her house and her life, and she seeks the escape to Treplyov's stage, and eventually, to the acting life itself.

When Treplyov kills the seagull, he is trying to make a symbolic statement, by killing something that Nina has identified herself with, and by warning her that her love is driving him to kill himself— but it doesn't work.

Nina wounds Treplyov when she tells him that he has grown irritable. To make matters worse, she demonstrates that Treplyov's symbolism was wasted on her. "And I suppose this sea gull here is obviously a symbol, too, but—forgive me—I don't understand it . . ."

Treplyov leaves, crushed. Nina soon brightens up when Treplyov leaves, and she sees Trigorin approach. For Nina, Trigorin, an established writer, represents her dream of being an actress, and she hopes that by following him, she will be given access to this ideal dramatic world.

Trigorin sees the seagull that Treplyov has killed, and it gives him an idea for a story:

> A young girl has lived her whole life on the shores of a lake. A girl like you. She loves the lake, like a sea gull, and she's as happy and free as a sea gull, too. A man happens to come by, sees her, and, having nothing else to do, destroys her like that sea gull there.

This speech foretells how Trigorin will treat Nina later in the play.

The seagull, which gives the play its name, has a double meaning, standing for both hopes betrayed, an idea which many characters in the play can identify with, and also for Nina herself. This is not uncommon in Chekhov's later plays.

As Nicholas Moravcevich discussed in 1984 in his essay, "Chekhov and Naturalism: From Affinity to Divergence," Chekhov's major plays introduce a theme or governing idea early in the action, in this case, the theme of the self-destructive power of unrestrained art. Since Chekhov's later plays do not use direct plotting to move the action forward, they instead rely on a "symbolizing device" that keeps the theme alive throughout the play, in this case, the seagull.

At the beginning of act 3, after a week has gone by, the audience learns that Treplyov has shot himself in a ''moment of mad despair.'' Although the wound was not fatal, it has signified his intent to kill himself. For Treplyov, an extreme idealist, it would be better to take his own life than to suffer knowing that Nina loves another, and that he is a failure as an artist.

After his failed suicide attempt, Treplyov toys with another idealistic notion, by planning on challenging Trigorin to a duel, a highly romantic, unrealistic way to both win Nina's love from Trigorin and destroy his writing nemesis.

What Treplyov fails to acknowledge is the fact that even if he were to kill Trigorin in a duel, it would not win Nina's love. Nina is attracted to Trigorin's success as an artist, and Treplyov cannot offer her that. He tries to cling to his idea of a duel nonetheless.

But Treplyov is a lover, not a fighter in the realistic sense, and he is easily turned away from his intent. After an impassioned exchange with Arkadina, in which she further chips away at Treplyov's idealism by calling him a ''nonentity'' and telling him he can't even write a ''pitiful little skit,'' Treplyov breaks down, crying. ''If you only knew! I've lost everything. She doesn't love me, and now I can't write . . . All my hopes have gone down the drain . . .''

Nevertheless, Treplyov perseveres. He knows that he's lost Nina for now, but he also suspects that it will never last with Trigorin, and so he waits, with the romantic hope that he and Nina will someday be reunited. He gets his first opportunity between acts three and four, when he tries to visit her in her hotel room, after she has been used and discarded by Trigorin.

''I saw her, but she didn't want to see me,'' Treplyov tells some guests in the first part of act 4. ''The chambermaid refused me entrance into her hotel room. I understood the way she felt, so I didn't insist on a meeting.'' Treplyov understands what it is like to have a lover leave, and he hopes that Nina will realize that they are meant to be together, as they had discussed in their childhood dreams.

Nina keeps this hope alive by sending him letters. She signs the letters, ''The Sea Gull,'' which he takes as a sign of her shattered mental state,

ironically forgetting the very symbolism that he bestowed on her earlier, when he killed the gull.

During the between-acts time period, Treplyov has also experienced some success at his Symbolist writing, although not all of the attention has been good. As one character puts it, he has gotten a ''first-rate roasting in the newspapers.'' Even Trigorin patronizes him, when he tells everybody that Treplyov is a big mystery in Moscow and Petersburg, and that everybody wants to know what he's like.

There is no mention of Treplyov's writing skills, only his image in the major cities. Treplyov has become successful in the sense that his writing is getting noticed, but it is not happening in the idealistic way he had imagined it. The final insult comes when Trigorin gives Treplyov a journal that contains stories by both him and Treplyov, and Trigorin quite obviously has not even cut the pages to read Treplyov's story.

In the only lengthy monologue in the play, Treplyov calls into question his own writing ideals. ''I've talked and talked a lot about new forms, yet I feel now that I am slipping little by little into a conventional rut.'' After comparing his own work to Trigorin's, he comes to a final conclusion:

> Yes, I'm invariably coming more and more to the conviction that the issue is a question neither of old nor of new forms, but that a person simply writes, never thinking about the kind of forms, he writes because it pours freely out of his soul.

With this admission, Treplyov realizes that he is lost as a writer. As Maurice Valency discussed in 1966 in *The Breaking String: The Plays of Anton Chekhov,* ''. . . although he feels in himself a talent that dwarfs Trigorin, Trigorin writes better than he, and is able to succeed effortlessly where Treplyev fails.'' This contrast, Valency notes, ''is intolerable for Treplyev.''

At that moment, Nina enters. Treplyov, clinging to the last shred of his idealism, tries to take this as a sign that she is ready to be reunited with him. ''My warmhearted girl, my beloved, she's come here.''

But Nina still has no love for him. She has resolved her own issues with art and life and is in a much better state than Treplyov. As Valency notes, Nina has ''lost her youth, her child, her innocence, and her peace of mind; but she has discovered her vocation, and the joy of work, and therefore she is saved.''

She no longer thinks the theatre is the dream that she had anticipated:

> I've come to realize that in our work—it doesn't matter whether we play roles on stage or whether we write—the important thing is neither fame nor glamor nor what I used to dream about, but it's knowing how to endure.

Nina has accepted her fate, and will leave the next morning for a winter acting engagement in Yelets, a job that will fall somewhere between acting and prostitution, as "cultured businessmen will bedevil me with their little gallantries."

But Treplyov cannot accept his fate. Nina's rejection is more than he can take. She leaves, and he is distraught both by the fact that he cannot have her and that he can't accept his realizations about his art.

In a scene that Chekhov deliberately makes about two minutes long, Treplyov silently destroys all of his writings, then fulfills the prophecy that Dorn suggested in the beginning when talking about the self-destructive power of unrestrained art, by taking his own life.

Treplyov is the only character who reacts to his fate this way. His symbolist views in his work and love life have not served him well, and at the end, he can't cope with the realism of his situation, whereas the other characters, who all embody various aspects of realistic people, go on living and enduring.

Source: Ryan D. Poquette, in an essay for *Drama for Students,* Gale Group, 2001.

Wendy Perkins

Perkins, an Associate Professor of English at Prince George's Community College in Maryland, has published several articles on twentieth-century authors. In this essay, she examines Chekhov's play and his presentation of the artistic temperament.

In *Natural Supernaturalism: Tradition and Revolution in Romantic Literature*, M. H. Abrams characterizes a recurrent figure in romantic and modern literature—the suffering artist. He notes that the central character in many literary works of the nineteenth and twentieth centuries is "the alienated and anguished artist whose priestly vocation entails the renunciation of this life and of this contemptible world in favor of that other world which is the work of his art." In the nineteenth century, this figure first emerged in the romantic poetry of authors like Samuel Coleridge, William Wordsworth, Lord Byron, and Percy Shelley. At the turn of the century,

playwright Anton Chekhov employed this dominant image in *The Seagull* and so encouraged a new generation of writers to construct realistic portraits of this enigmatic character. Through the play's penetrating study of several people who gather together at a Russian country estate, Chekhov explores the complex relationship between art and personal identity.

The Seagull focuses on intimate moments shared by four artists with varying degrees of devotion to their calling. Arkadina and her lover Trigorin have both enjoyed successful careers—Arkadina as a celebrated actress and Trigorin as a best-selling novelist. Yet neither are true artists. In her analysis of the play, critic Emma Goldman argues that Arkadina "is the type of artist who lacks all conception of the relation between art and life."

Arkadina's shallow and self-centered nature emerges in her response to her son's play. Her negative reaction has little to do with the play's artistic merit. Treplyov understands that she will dismiss his play before she views it because she has not been included in the cast. He notes, "She's angry about my play because Nina's acting in it, and she's not. . . . She's angry in advance because, even though it's just on this little stage, it will be Nina's success and not hers." While he admits she has talent, he notes that her focus is on herself rather than her art:

> You may praise only Mother, write only about productions that Mother's in, rave only about Mother's performance in *Camille* or *The Fumes of Life.* And since she finds no intoxicating adulation in the country—Mother's bored.

Her jealousy prompts her to disrupt the performance of her son's play with questions and jeers, which causes Treplyov to bring the curtain down during the first act. Later, while discussing the theatre with her, Treplyov concludes, "you won't recognize or tolerate anything but your own superficial notions. You sit on and suppress everything else."

Unlike Arkadina, Trigorin admits to his artistic limitations. He tells Nina during a discussion about his work, "Yes, I enjoy writing, and reading proofs. But as soon as something's published, I hate it. I see it's not what I meant—and I feel angry, I feel bad." Trigorin acknowledges that his reading public appreciates the charm and cleverness of his works, but that they also consider them inferior to those of the truly great authors like Tolstoy and Turgenev. In an attempt to create classic works of art, he has focused on what he thinks are important themes, yet these "hurried" attempts received attacks "from all sides,"

A scene from the 1905 production of Anton Chekhov's The Seagull.

until he was forced to admit that he did not understand what he was writing about. As a result, he concludes, ''I think in the end all I can really write about are landscapes. About everything else, I'm false, false to the core,'' and so has given up his dream of creating true art.

Trigorin continues to write best-sellers but would rather spend his days fishing than hone his craft. Goldman argues that ''exhausted of ideas,'' Trigorin finds that ''all life and human relations serve him only as material for copy.'' While talking about his stories with Nina, he admits, ''I've forgotten what it is to be eighteen or nineteen. I can't picture it. That's why young women in my stories and novels are unconvincing.'' Chekhov suggests that Nina might be able to inspire him to write greater works when, after seeing the dead seagull Treplyov killed for Nina, he determines to write a story about the incident. However, Arkadina plays on his weakness, convincing him that only she truly appreciates him, and so pulls him away from the younger woman. As he leaves with Arkadina, Trigorin admits, ''I've never had a will of my own. . . . I'm flabby and weak. I always submit.''

When he was a young man, Trigorin insists that he had artistic sensibilities and suffered for his art, that his life then ''was a torture.'' He explains,

A beginning writer, especially an unlucky one, feels awkward and unwanted—the world doesn't need him. His nerves are frazzled, he's always on edge. But he can't resist being around people in the arts and literature. They, of course, are not interested in him. They ignore him, while he's too shy to even look at them.

After his works began to enjoy popular but not critical success, Trigorin drifted away from his early devotion to his craft.

As Trigorin gives up his pursuit of artistic excellence, he loses his connection with others. The shallow relationships he forms reflect his inability to actively engage with his world. He seems to stay with Arkadina not because he has strong feelings for her but because their relationship is convenient, especially since it affords him the opportunity to stay at a comfortable country estate. His detachment from experience becomes most noticeable in his callous treatment of Nina. After their brief love affair that resulted in a pregnancy, Trigorin ''tired of her'' and, according to Treplyov, ''went back to his old attachments . . . in his spineless way.''

Trigorin's portrait of a suffering artist reflects not only his experience, but also that of Nina and Treplyov. Unlike Trigorin, though, both of these young artists become consumed with their pursuit of the creative process and so devote their lives to it. In ''The Seagull: The Stage Mother, the Missing Father, and the Origins of Art,'' Carol Flath comments, ''in aesthetic terms, Treplyov renounces knowledge of the world and consequently self-destructs as a writer and as a man; Nina, on the other hand, embraces knowledge and suffering and becomes a mature artist.''

When Treplyov renounces the traditions of the theatre, he turns his back on his and his mother's world. Flath notes that Treplyov's '''decadent,' intangible, and inaccessible play represents a wholly spiritual or idealistic art.'' He answers Nina's complaints over the difficulties in his play insisting, ''I don't want to show life as it is, or tell people how things should be. I want to show life in dreams.'' He condemns the playwright who ''squeezes out a moral, a smug cozy little moral, fit for home consumption'' and who only ''repeats the same formula with tiny variations.'' Afraid that following this same path would ''cheapen his mind,'' he breaks with tradition as he strives for ''new forms.'' Yet his avant garde productions gain him little success and often alienate him from his audience and from other artists. While Dorn admits, ''I liked his play. There's something fresh and direct about it,'' his mother and Nina find it troublesome and ''decadent.'' As a result, Treplyov's sense of isolation increases.

His surroundings reinforce his isolation and despair. He notes to Sorin that life with his mother means a house full of famous actors and writers and complains, ''Can you imagine how I feel? The only nobody there is me.'' He claims that because he has neither money nor talent, her friends continually measure his ''insignificance.''

His mother, whose petty, shallow nature prompts her to play on her son's insecurities, compounds Treplyov's feelings of insignificance. He admits, ''My mother doesn't love me. . . . I'm twenty-five now. That reminds her she's no longer young. . . . She hates me for that.''

Commenting on their damaging relationship, Flath argues,

> Arkadina's view of herself as attractive and eternally youthful is directly threatened by the presence of her grown son. By willing Treplyev into nothingness (''nonentity'') she is attempting to stop the flow of time itself—time that ages her and allows this boy to outgrow her to find a younger, more beautiful woman of his own, one who will replace her as a woman and as an artist.

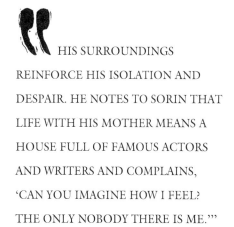

HIS SURROUNDINGS REINFORCE HIS ISOLATION AND DESPAIR. HE NOTES TO SORIN THAT LIFE WITH HIS MOTHER MEANS A HOUSE FULL OF FAMOUS ACTORS AND WRITERS AND COMPLAINS, 'CAN YOU IMAGINE HOW I FEEL? THE ONLY NOBODY THERE IS ME.'''

When Treplyov finally does earn a measure of success after his stories appear in magazines, Dorn tells him one afternoon, ''[your work] made an impression on me. You have talent. You must write more.'' Dorn commends his abstract subject matter that expresses ''great ideas'' for, he claims, ''Nothing can be beautiful if it's not serious.'' Trigorin also praises Treplyov's stories, but later notes to Dorn that the young playwright's work is often criticized, insisting ''he's had no luck. He can't find a style of his own. There's something vague and strange about his writing—almost like delirium. And never a single live character.''

When Treplyov learns that neither Trigorin nor his mother has read his work, he again begins to despair until Nina arrives. During the past two years Nina has been struggling to establish herself as an actress. Treplyov notes, however, that during this period, ''her acting was crude'' and ''lacked subtlety.'' He claims, ''at moments she showed some talent—she screamed well, and she died well. But that's all. They were only moments.'' When Nina appears at the house, Treplyov hopes that the two of them can ease each other's suffering. Yet while Nina initially looks back on their time together fondly, she decides to reject Treplyov's declarations of love and to continue to strive for artistic integrity. She tells him that the previous night she went into the garden to see if the stage was still there. When she finds it, she admits, ''I cried for the first time in two years. It was like a weight started to lift from me—I started to feel lighter.'' Yet she also notes the difficult nature of the pursuit of art when she tells him, ''We've been drawn into the maelstrom, both of us.''

She then recalls her affair with Trigorin who, she claims, ''laughed at my dreams, until finally I stopped believing in them.'' Nina, however, found the strength to endure Trigorin's waning affections and the loss of her child and becomes strong enough to pursue her artistic dreams. She tells Treplyov that now she is a true actress and that her work ''intoxicates'' her. She admits,

> I know now, Kostya, what matters in our work . . . is not fame, glory, or the things I dreamed about, but knowing how to endure—how to bear your cross and have faith. I have faith now, and it's not so painful anymore. When I think about my calling, I'm not afraid of life.

Treplyov, however, cannot find a similar source of strength in his art. He admits to Nina, ''you've found your way. You know where you're going. But I'm still living in dreams and images. I can't make sense of them. I don't know what or who it's all for. I have no faith, no calling.'' His inability to retain faith in his art, coupled with his unrequited love for Nina, fills him with an overwhelming sense of despair, and he kills himself.

Chekhov's compelling portrait of the suffering artist explores the problematic relationship between life and art. Flath suggests that in the play, Chekhov raises

> serious questions as to the ethics of artistic creativity; for art to be truly compelling and powerful, it must drain energy from real life; it must murder its object, be that object others or oneself. An art that does no harm is impossible, for it would be the same as life itself.

Some—like Arkadina and Trigorin—who do not have the strength of character to pursue artistic excellence focus instead on gaining popular success. Others, like Treplyov, are destroyed by their inability to retain their faith in their art. Nina alone survives, damaged by her pursuit of her craft, but unwavering in her devotion to it. In his study of these four artists, Chekhov illustrates the difficulties inherent in the struggle to achieve true art.

Source: Wendy Perkins, in an essay for *Drama for Students,* Gale Group, 2001.

Donald Rayfield

In this essay, Rayfield provides an overview of Chekhov's play.

Any comedy where the young hero destroys his life's work and then himself, where the heroine is abandoned pregnant and unhinged, while the survivors bask on in their own egotism, must be considered highly innovatory. Apart from its black comedy, however, Chekhov's *The Seagull* has many other modern features. It is full of ''intertextuality,'' incorporating or alluding to a great deal of *Hamlet,* to *Faust,* to Guy de Maupassant, and to Chekhov's own prose. It was also ''interactive'' theatre: many characters, incidents, props, and lines were taken from Chekhov's own life and his social circle, and he took some care to see that they experienced the full impact of this fictionalization by being invited to the first performance. It is ''deconstructive,'' since it is a play about the futility of the theatre, in which the old art (Trigorin) and the new art (Trepliov) fight out the battle of naturalism and symbolism, and the old theatre (Arkadina) and the new theatre (Nina Zarechnaya) fight out the conflict between histrionics and expressionist acting.

The Seagull is a total anomaly in Chekhov's work. Nowhere else does he have the writer as hero or blatantly exploit autobiographical material. Even the symbolic title—a parody of Ibsen's *Wild Duck*—is utterly out of keeping with his reluctance to advertise a play's intentions. Written in 1895, it was performed in 1896 in St. Petersburg with unscripted and catastrophic results that equalled the disasters of the drama itself. It must be seen as an attack on the conventional theatre, designed to embarrass and disable actors and audience. At the same time, so many lines of Chekhov's own fiction and letters, as well as his fishing rods, self-evaluation, and compulsions are attributed to Trigorin, that it appears to be a work of intense self-parody—a product of an inner crisis in which both old and new forms of writing and behaving seem trite.

The Seagull was written after six years of virtual abstention from writing plays. Apart from Ibsen, other Nordic reading seems to have suggested the new directions Chekhov's dramaturgy now took. As in Strindberg, a female oligarchy takes control of the action, the males—whether the writers, the old brother Sorin, or doctor Sorin, the objective bystander—being unable to resist their ruthless atavism. The eroticism of the play, however, is uniquely Chekhovian: the middle-aged Arkadina and Polina pursue their lovers, Trigorin and Dr. Dorn, with unrelenting passion; the male characters are locked into a ludicrous chain of unrequited love: Medvedenko loves Masha who loves Trepliov who loves Nina who loves Trigorin.

The experimental absurdity is deliberate, as Chekhov's letters show: ''I am writing it with some pleasure, although I do awful things to the laws of the stage ... not much action and two hundred-weight of love.'' Many of the preoccupations of his short stories surface here in dramatic form: the idea of Hamlet as a naturalized Russian citizen is reinforced in the semi-incestuous quarrelling between Trepliov and his mother and in the playlet he stages in Act I to provoke her anger; Nina Zarechnaya and Arkadina, both examples of womanhood destroyed by acting, are the culmination of the unhappy Katya of *A Dreary Story*. An adoration of Maupassant as the workmanlike writer's writer saturates Chekhov's prose: *The Seagull*'s opening lines, ''Why are you wearing black?—Because I am in mourning for my life''—are lifted straight from Maupassant's *Bel-Ami.* The futility of medicine and contemplation, which Chekhov expressed in his bitter *Ward No. 6,* reaches its climax in the cruel refusal of Dr. Dorn to treat ''old age.''

But Chekhov also incorporated farce and vaudeville techniques into *The Seagull.* When Arkadina successively rows with her brother, her son, and her lover, it is with all the speed of a music-hall sketch. Usually quoted by the ironic Dr. Dorn, popular song and snatches of operetta—though their import is lost on today's audience—only remind the other characters of how commonplace their predicament is.

The play functioned primarily as a purgative both for Chekhov's creativity and for the contemporary theatre—all the more surprising is its importance as the first of the truly Chekhovian later plays and as the emblem of Stanislavsky's Moscow Arts Theatre. As with *The Cherry Orchard*, the subtitle, ''Comedy,'' provides an insistent tempo-marking to override any temptation to dwell on the tragic possibilities; the setting, remote from Moscow or St. Petersburg, imbues a spirit of exile in those characters who will never leave; powerful forces off stage hold the cast in thrall and prevent them from acting on their motivation; phrases pass from character to character putting them under a disabling spell: Chekhov appears to have invented a new dramatic genre simply by demolishing the old.

Although Stanislavsky's theatre, with its totalitarian control over the actors, redeemed the play from the oblivion that otherwise threatened it, *The Seagull* remains the most ambiguous of all Chekhov's plays. Is Trepliov's playlet about the end of the world a parody of symbolist drama still to be written, or is it—as its echoes of Chekhov's narrative landscapes suggest—a serious attempt to convey what a new poetic drama might sound like? Is Nina, drenched and raving in Act IV, an Ophelia-

> CHEKHOV IS ONE OF THE FEW MALE WRITERS WHO CAN BE SEEN BOTH AS MISOGYNIST AND FEMINIST: HE KNEW WELL THAT THE SEAGULL IS AS PREDATORY AS IT IS VULNERABLE AND THE PLAY, FOR ALL ITS 'THROW-AWAY' SYMBOLISM, EXPLORES BOTH THE DANGER AND THE APPEAL OF LOVE FOR THE ARTIST.''

like victim of ruthless and self-obsessed males, or is she an example of female indestructibility, just an Arkadina at a more decorative phase? Perhaps the play's real intent is buried in the allusion it nearly makes: in Act II, Arkadina takes over from Dorn the reading of Maupassant's travelogue *Sur l'eau* and shuts the book in annoyance. The passage she cannot stomach reads: ''As soon as [a woman] sees [a writer] softened, moved, won over by constant flattery, she isolates him, cuts bit by bit all his links.'' Chekhov is one of the few male writers who can be seen both as misogynist and feminist: he knew well that the seagull is as predatory as it is vulnerable, and the play, for all its ''throw-away'' symbolism, explores both the danger and the appeal of love for the artist.

Source: Donald Rayfield, ''*The Seagull*,'' in *The International Dictionary of Theatre,* Vol. 1: *Plays,* edited by Mark Hawkins-Dady, St. James Press, 1992, pp. 720–21.

Harold Clurman

Calling The Seagull *''a play of infinite tenderness and compassionate understanding,'' Clurman reviews a 1954 production of Chekhov's play.*

The Sea Gull is a play of infinite tenderness and compassionate understanding. That is why it is humorous as well as touching. Contrary to the common cliché, it is also full of action: no moment passes which is not dense with the subtlest interplay of human conflict.

MONTGOMERY CLIFT—WHO IS WELL CAST—IS HANDSOME, TALENTED AND IN EVERY WAY SYMPATHETIC. BUT HIS TREPLEV IS TOO DEPRESSED IN FEELING, TOO RUNDOWN IN APPEARANCE. TREPLEV IS A YOUNG AND ARDENT SPIRIT. HIS TRAGEDY IS THAT THOUGH HE CONTAINS THE SEED OF THE FUTURE, AS COMPARED TO THE FACILE BUT ESSENTIALLY UNCREATIVE NOVELIST TRIGORIN, HE IS GROUND UNDER BY THE WEIGHT OF TEMPORAL CIRCUMSTANCES."

It is often said that Chekhov is the dramatist of futility and frustration. This is misleading. What Chekhov tells us is not that life is a frustration but that a particular kind of life, a particular environment and time, was frustrating. This makes him a social playwright. But he is also ''universal'': the inner music of his work extends beyond the particular moment he depicts.

The essence of Chekhov lies in the warmth of his feeling for people, his boundless sympathy, his love. What endears his characters to us whether they be simpletons or sophisticates—and there is something charmingly and childishly foolish about all of them—is the fact that we recognize in them deeply human traits with which Chekhov identifies himself with his whole being. Because they are seen in the context of his wonderfully sound sense of life, the wretched fate of his characters comes to seem unaccountably worthwhile to us. Chekhov's plays, therefore, are never dreary, for where life is affirmed, particularly in the face of adversity, we are in the presence of the noble and the heartening.

We do not live in czarist Russia; still, Chekhov is of our time. Our younger generation is not a hopeful one. For all their aches, Chekhov's people

remember, yearn for, desire and dream a good life. The key to their natures is in the cry, ''I want to live.'' This informs their sorrow with a pulsing substance of experience and meaning which enriches it beyond the muscular straining and jumpiness of our young people, unconscious of any pleasure in present difficulty because they have no vision or belief in a future to which they can look forward. Our young folk fail to have fun because their lives have been emptied of content for want of values that might give them an inspired view of their daily activity. The girls and boys of the Miller and Williams plays might well think of the sad people of *The Sea Gull* as the lucky ones!

What impression the Phoenix production makes on a person who has never before seen or read *The Sea Gull* I cannot tell. Perhaps its beauty is still apparent. For anyone who knows the play—I have seen four previous productions—the present one is signally miscast in several important parts. I refer not only to individual actors but to a lack of homogeneity and correlation in the ensemble. Midwest speech is echoed by Russian; mid-European accent alternates with Southern United States; New York genteel tones respond to New York Irish. It is also evident that even some of the actors who are suited to their roles have not been helped by the director in their interpretations.

Maureen Stapleton, for example, is thoroughly affecting here and there because of her fine emotional endowment, but she has no specific characterization. The part she plays—Masha—is that of a woman deprived of the normal attentions and affection due her; as a result she has become mannish, eccentric, a little grotesque. But Miss Stapleton is allowed to remain the most attractive person on the stage. This distorts the story by making Treplev, who never notices Masha but persists in his desperate love for Nina (impersonated by an actress who looks old enough to be his mother), seem peculiar.

Montgomery Clift—who is well cast—is handsome, talented and in every way sympathetic. But his Treplev is too depressed in feeling, too rundown in appearance. Treplev is a young and ardent spirit. His tragedy is that though he contains the seed of the future, as compared to the facile but essentially uncreative novelist Trigorin, he is ground under by the weight of temporal circumstances.

The real pathos of Clift's performance, I cannot refrain from saying, is not only that he makes Treplev more downcast than he need be—and thus more American than Russian—but that as an earnest actor he believes he can pay his debt to his ideals by attempting a challenging role for four weeks out of ten years. He needs ten years of work on the stage to act as well as he potentially can in the kind of parts he aspires to. It is not idealistic and it is certainly not healthy to reserve oneself for certain rare occasions to do what one wants to.

Source: Harold Clurman, ''Anton Chekhov,'' in *Lies like Truth,* Macmillan, 1958, pp. 131–33.

SOURCES

Auden, W. H., ''Musee des Beaux Arts,'' in *The Norton Anthology of English Literature,* Vol. 2, edited by M. H. Abrams, 5th ed., W. W. Norton & Company, 1985, p. 2298.

Caputi, Anthony, *Eight Modern Plays,* Norton, 1991, p. 133.

Chekhov, Anton, *Anton Chekhov: A Life,* by Donald Rayfield, Henry Holt, 1997, p. 353.

Karlinsky, Simon, ''The Seagull,'' in *Letters of Anton Chekhov,* translated by Michael Henry Heim, Harper & Row, 1973, p. 280.

Kirk, Irina, *Anton Chekhov,* Twayne Publishers, 1981, p. 133.

Lantz, K. A., *Anton Chekhov: A Reference Guide to Literature,* G. K. Hall & Co., 1985, p. xix.

Magarshack, David, *Chekhov the Dramatist,* Hill and Wang, 1960, pp. 17, 159–160, 163–164.

———, *The Seagull,* Barnes & Noble, 1972, pp. 21–23.

Moravcevich, Nicholas, ''Chekhov and Naturalism: From Affinity to Divergence,'' in *Anton Chekhov's Plays,* edited by Eugene K. Bristow, Norton, 1977, pp. 294–295.

Styan, J. L., *Chekhov in Performance: A Commentary on the Major Plays,* Cambridge University Press, 1971, pp. 10, 13.

Valency, Maurice, ''The Sea Gull,'' in *The Breaking String: The Plays of Anton Chekhov,* Oxford, 1966, p. 154.

FURTHER READING

Hahn, Beverly, *Chekhov: A Study of the Major Stories and Plays,* Cambridge University Press, 1977.
> Although in drama Hahn's principal focus is on *The Cherry Orchard,* her refutation of the dramatist's alleged deficiencies—for example his formlessness, insipidity, and negativism—is very helpful for understanding Chekhov's achievement in his late plays.

Kirk, Irina, *Anton Chekhov,* Twayne Publishers, 1981.
> This overview of Chekhov and his work offers a good starting point for further study. It offers brief but insightful interpretations of Chekhov's plays and the artistic principles underlying them.

Lantz, K. A., *Anton Chekhov: A Reference Guide to Literature,* G. K. Hall, 1985.
> For those needing to conduct further research on Chekhov, this is an indispensable aid. It includes a biography and checklist of the author's works with both English and Russian titles, with a helpful annotated bibliography of critical studies published before 1984.

Magarshack, David, *Chekhov the Dramatist,* Hill and Wang, 1960.
> In this introduction to Chekhov's plays, Magarshack divides the dramatist's canon into ''plays of direct action'' and ''plays of indirect action,'' with *The Wood Demon* serving as a transitional work between the two types. He relates *The Seagull* to Chekhov's life and his estate in Melikhovo.

———, *The Real Chekhov: An Introduction to Chekhov's Last Plays,* Allen & Unwin, 1972.
> This study offers a scene by scene analysis of each of Chekhov's four major plays and the dramatist's attitude towards matters addressed in them–which, in the case of *The Seagull,* Magarshack argues, is the nature of art.

Styan, J. L., *Chekhov in Performance: A Commentary on the Major Plays,* Cambridge University Press, 1971.
> Styan also provides a close analysis of Chekhov's four major plays. A principal focus is the ''submerged life'' of the playwright's text and Chekhov's stage technique. Styan also discusses the preparation and initial staging of each play.

Valency, Maurice, *The Breaking String: The Plays of Anton Chekhov,* Oxford University Press, 1966.
> This work relates Chekhov's major plays both to his own fiction and to the Russian theater of his day. Valency argues that Chekhov is essentially an ironist and comedist, although each play involves the breaking of a ''golden string'' that binds man both to his heavenly father and his own past.

Williams, Lee J., *Anton Chekhov, the Iconoclast,* University of Scranton Press, 1989.
> This study takes the view that Chekhov was a self-conscious agent of change in Russia, that he employed a scientific method to dispel old, class-biased myths about Russian peasants, and that in both method and philosophy he was, as the title indicates, a dedicated iconoclast.

Street Scene

ELMER RICE

1929

Since its debut on January 10, 1929, at The Play-house on Broadway in New York City, *Street Scene* has been considered one of Elmer Rice's most successful works and has cemented his reputation as a serious playwright. Rice himself directed the original production, which ran for 602 perform-ances. *Street Scene* won the 1929 Pulitzer Prize for drama. Rice had written the play over several years and saw it rejected by numerous Broadway produc-ers for what they perceived as a lack of content, too many characters, and too much plot. Nothing like *Street Scene* had been produced before, and many producers were not sure this kind of play would draw an audience. Yet when a producer was found, the success of *Street Scene* defied expectations.

Street Scene was one of the first plays to critique the negative effects of urban and industrial society on the average person. It was also praised for its innovative structure, including the same multiple plots and characters of which so many potential producers had been wary. Many believed *Street Scene* captured a mosaic of different kinds of lower-middle-class people living in New York City.

After its initial run, *Street Scene* was produced regularly throughout the world, though not always successfully. Surmounting the difficulties of trans-lating the plethora of types was not always easy in other countries. In 1947, Rice contributed the book to an operatic version of the play scored by Kurt

Weill. *Street Scene* is still produced today. While critics acknowledge its strong core and praise how it captured a moment in time, many regard its prejudices and situations as dated. When *Street Scene* won the Pulitzer Prize, J. Brooks Atkinson of the *New York Times* wrote, "It is saturated in the America that is New York. It is the finest wrought chiaroscuro of middle-class life that an American dramatist has drawn across the stage. It is complete. It is original by virtue of its simple integrity."

AUTHOR BIOGRAPHY

Rice was born Elmer Leopold Reizenstein in New York City on September 28, 1892. He was the son of Jacob Reizenstein and his wife Fanny (neé Lion), German-Jewish immigrants. Jacob Reizenstein worked as a traveling salesman and bookkeeper but suffered from epilepsy and had problems finding employment. This situation contributed to Rice leaving high school while he was still a sophomore to seek employment. He worked in several office jobs, which left him unhappy. After spending a year at a law firm, Rice decided to pursue a legal career to support himself, though he was not particularly interested in the law.

To that end, Rice passed a state exam that gave him the equivalent of a high school diploma, then entered New York Law School in 1910. During the long legal classes, Rice would read plays to relieve his boredom. He had been a fan of the theater since his youth. After graduating from law school and passing the New York State bar in 1912, Rice spent a year working as a lawyer. Still wearied by office work, Rice took night classes at Columbia University. He also began writing plays, poetry, and short stories. By 1913, Rice decided that he would become a professional playwright and left his legal career behind.

In 1914, Rice had his first play produced, *On Trial,* a success from the first. This success established Rice's reputation as a serious playwright whose plays were in demand. Rice used his position to promote his left-wing views and his concerns with social issues. He sympathized with socialists and often discussed issues from a socialist perspective in his plays. In addition to continuing to write plays, Rice also taught and worked with an acting troupe, Columbia University's Morningside Players. In 1918, Rice began writing for the movies. He

Elmer Rice

wrote for Samuel Goldwyn for two years but was not happy at the studio.

One of Rice's most important plays was *The Adding Machine* (1923). An expressionist drama about an oppressed office worker, it has become a classic of the American theater. Many of the plays that followed *The Adding Machine* in the 1920s were not as successful—until 1929, when he wrote *Street Scene*. The Pulitzer Prize-winning, realistic drama was one of Rice's major plays. Rice directed the production and many of his subsequent plays. Two works that followed *Street Scene—The Left Bank* (1931) and *Counsellor-at-Law* (1931)—were successful, but many subsequent plays in the 1930s met with mixed or little success.

In the mid-1930s, Rice worked briefly as the head of the Federal Theatre Project, before becoming one of the founders of the Playwrights' Company, which produced many of his plays. Rice continued to write plays throughout the 1940s and 1950s. Only a few were truly successful and well received, among them *Two on an Island* (1940) and the romantic comedy *Dream Girl* (1945). After retiring from playwriting, Rice published his memoir, *The Living Theatre,* which revealed much about the inner workings of the theater world. By the time of his death, twenty-four of his plays had been produced on Broadway. Rice died of a heart attack on May 8, 1967, in Southampton, England, survived by five children from three different marriages.

PLOT SUMMARY

Act 1

Street Scene opens outside a brownstone tenement (apartment building) in New York City in the evening. Dwellers are seen in their windows and meeting outside on the stoop. They exchange small talk about the hot weather and their neighbors. Several women gossip about Mrs. Maurrant whom they believe is having an affair with the milk company bill collector, Steve Sankey, right under her husband's nose. Their suspicions seem confirmed when Mr. Maurrant comes home and announces he will be working out of town the next day, which pleases his wife.

Sankey walks by, ostensibly on the way to the drug store to get a ginger ale for his wife. After he leaves, Mrs. Maurrant excuses herself to look for her young son Willie. As soon as she is gone, the gathered neighbors continue their gossip. One tenant enters, a Miss Cushing, who tells them that she has just seen Sankey and Mrs. Maurrant together outside a nearby warehouse. Mr. Maurrant comes out looking for his wife. They tell him that she is searching for their son.

Another tenant, Mr. Fiorentino, arrives with ice cream cones for everyone. A charity worker, Alice Simpson, looks for Mrs. Hildebrand and her children. Mrs. Hildebrand is about to be evicted because her husband abandoned their family, and she cannot pay her rent. Simpson is angry that Mrs. Hildebrand has spent money taking her children to the movies when they accept money from charity. Affected by Mrs. Hildebrand's plight, Mr. Fiorentino gives her some money. Miss Simpson disapproves, and asks to talk to Mrs. Hildebrand inside.

Mrs. Maurrant returns and tells her husband that she could not find Willie. The tension between them is broken as Miss Simpson returns and reiterates to Mr. Fiorentino that he should not give Mrs. Hildebrand money. Old Mr. Kaplan gets in an argument with her about charities. He believes they are part of a capitalist economic system, which exploits people. This leads to an argument between Kaplan and his daughter Shirley and their other

neighbors. Mr. Maurrant decries the influence of foreigners in the United States, much to the chagrin of his many immigrant neighbors. Mr. Maurrant wants law and order to rule. Maurrant and Kaplan nearly come to blows.

After the argument ends, Mrs. Maurrant declares that she would like to live in peace. Sam Kaplan, Mr. Kaplan's younger son, returns from law school. He gets into a discussion about music with Fiorentino. Mrs. Fiorentino plays piano in their apartment, and Mr. Fiorentino and Mrs. Maurrant dance. Their steps are interrupted by the reappearance of Sankey, who is on his way home. Willie Maurrant finally comes home, but Mr. Maurrant continues to be angry that his elder daughter, Rose, has not come home from work yet. All the Maurrants, save the missing Rose, retire to their apartment. The neighbors catch each other up on the relevant gossip, including the fact that Sam Kaplan is in love with Rose. Everyone soon goes inside for the night.

Rose Maurrant appears with her boss, Harry Easter. Closing her window, Mrs. Fiorentino wishes them a good evening. Easter wants to spend more time with her, to come up to her apartment. He tells her he will put her up in her own apartment and try to get her started in an acting career. Easter's wife does not have to know anything. Rose turns him down, but he only leaves when Mr. Maurrant comes down. There is a confrontation, which is interrupted by the appearance of Mr. Buchanan. His wife is in labor. Rose goes to make his calls for him so he can stay with his wife.

When Rose returns, another neighbor's son, Vincent Jones, tries to get her to go out with him. She refuses, and Sam Kaplan steps in. Vincent hits Sam, but the confrontation is interrupted by the appearance of Vincent's mother, Mrs. Jones, who makes him come upstairs. Sam still wants to kill Vincent, but Rose calms him down. Sam and Rose have a long conversation and share their ideas about life. It ends with the appearance of Mrs. Buchanan's doctor, Dr. Wilson. Rose goes upstairs to help.

Act 2

The next morning, the doctor is on his way out. Sam comes outside looking for Rose, but his sister makes him come in to eat breakfast. Mr. Buchanan tells Mrs. Fiorentino that his wife delivered a girl late last night, and that Mrs. Maurrant stayed with her nearly the whole time. Rose tells Mr. Fiorentino that she is not in love with Sam Kaplan. Mrs. Maurrant comes out for a bit and is chided by Mrs.

Jones for considering letting her daughter marry a Jewish man (Kaplan).

Mr. Maurrant leaves for work, angry that his wife seems more concerned with Mrs. Buchanan than their family. After an upset Mrs. Maurrant leaves to buy a chicken, Mr. Maurrant starts in on Rose. She tries to convince him to move to the suburbs, but he will not consider it. Mr. Kaplan talks with Rose, but is much kinder to her. Mrs. Maurrant returns with the chicken and tells Rose that she has tried to be a good wife to her husband, but that never seemed to matter. Rose tries to persuade her mother that Sankey should not come around as much but to no avail.

After her mother goes upstairs, Rose stays on the stoop. Shirley tells her to stay away from her brother. Rose becomes angry at what Shirley is implying about her. Sam comes outside, and they have another conversation about the meaning of life. Rose tells him that she is considering Easter's offer because it might mean a better life for her family. When Rose makes an offhand comment about wanting to run away, Sam eagerly chimes in that he would like to run away with her. Easter appears to take Rose to the funeral of an office mate. Easter continues to try and manipulate Rose, but she remains independent, even in the way she goes to the funeral.

Sankey comes by, on his collection rounds for the milk company. Mrs. Maurrant invites him upstairs. In the meantime, the marshals come to evict Mrs. Hildebrand and her children. Mr. Maurrant appears again, drunk. Sam tries to stop him from going inside, but Maurrant pushes him aside. Shots are fired: Mr. Maurrant shoots both Mrs. Maurrant and Sankey. Mr. Maurrant escapes through the gathered crowd. Sankey was killed instantly, but Mrs. Maurrant is still alive and taken out by ambulances. Rose Maurrant returns to the horrible scene of her mother being taken away.

Act 3

Later that afternoon, the marshals continue to put Mrs. Hildebrand's furniture on the sidewalk. Random people stop by to view the now famous crime scene. Mr. Maurrant is still at large. Easter appears looking for Rose. When she returns to the tenement, she tells him that she hopes her father gets away. Rose reports that her mother has died. She again turns down Easter's offer of a place to live. She intends to take Willie and live somewhere better on her own.

While Rose is in the apartment gathering some things, Mr. Buchanan informs everyone that the police have found Mr. Maurrant hiding nearby. Rose confronts her father as he is carried off, asking him why he did it. He says that he was insane at the time and tells her to take care of Willie. Sam offers to come away with her again, but Rose turns him down. Sam tells her that he loves her, but Rose points out the reality of the situation and declares that she does not want to belong to anyone. Still, he kisses her passionately before she leaves. As she goes, a couple sees a sign for rooms to rent. The gossip on the stoop continues.

CHARACTERS

Daniel Buchanan

Daniel Buchanan is a tenant in the apartment building. He is a nervous expectant father whose wife is in labor. Buchanan has Rose call the doctor and his wife's sister for him. In the morning at the beginning of act 2, he is the semi-proud father of a new baby girl.

Harry Easter

Harry Easter is the office manager who is Rose Maurrant's boss. Despite the fact that he is married, Easter is enamoured with his employee. He wants to be involved with her. Easter offers to get Rose her own apartment and start her on a new career as a stage actress. Rose turns him down, but Easter is persistent. In the morning, at the beginning of act 2, Easter shows up again, offering Rose a ride to the funeral. Again, she refuses him. At the beginning of act 3, Easter shows up at the tenement and wants to take care of Rose and her brother. Rose finally dismisses him without taking a thing. Easter finally accepts that Rose does not want him in her life at the moment, either as a friend or lover.

Filippo Fiorentino

Filippo Fiorentino (also known as Lippo) is the husband of Greta Fiorentino. He is an Italian immigrant. Mr. Fiorentino makes his living as an accordion player and musician. He belongs to the musician's union. Mr. Fiorentino is generous with his money. On this hot day, he brings home several ice cream cones for his neighbors and gives money to Mrs. Hildebrand and her children when Alice

MEDIA ADAPTATIONS

- *Street Scene* was adapted for film by Rice, who wrote the screenplay. The film was directed by King Vidor and starred Sylvia Sidney as Rose Maurrant. It was released by United Artists in 1931.

Simpson, the charity worker, is critical of their going to the movies. He also plays music for his neighbors and dances with Mrs. Maurrant. While Mr. Fiorentino is a lively, happy man, he also is a bit callous towards the feelings of others. He chides his wife for not yet having children, when the subject is touchy for her. He does the same thing to others who live in the tenement, but his happy-go-lucky demeanor makes up for it to some degree.

Greta Fiorentino

Greta Fiorentino is the rather large, loving wife of Filippo Fiorentino. She is a German immigrant and a musician. She makes her living giving children music lessons in her tenement apartment. Mrs. Fiorentino is frustrated by the fact that she has not been able to have children of her own. She gets slightly annoyed by her husband's generosity and his callousness towards her over her barrenness. She is one of the women who spends much time gossiping on the stoop of the tenement but is generally kind.

Charlie Hildebrand

Charlie is the child of Laura Hildebrand. He and his sister Mary are about to lose their apartment because of their destitute state. Still, they go to school in the morning at the beginning of act 2. They do not seem to be particularly affected by their imminent eviction.

Laura Hildebrand

Laura Hildebrand is the mother of Mary and Charlie Hildebrand. She has been abandoned by her husband and is destitute. Her family is about to be

evicted from the building. Though Mrs. Hildebrand is about to lose her place to live, she tries to keep her children's lives as normal as possible. She takes them to the movies as they did every Thursday night. When Miss Simpson admonishes her for such actions, Mrs. Hildebrand meekly agrees because she has no choice.

Mary Hildebrand

Mary is the child of Laura Hildebrand and the sister of Charlie. She and Charlie share an apartment, which they are going to be evicted from.

Emma Jones

Emma Jones is the middle-aged wife of George and the mother of Mae and Vincent. She also has a dog, Queenie, whom she takes on walks regularly. She is one of the more gossipy tenants in the apartment building, fond of judging the others, especially those who are immigrants. Mrs. Jones is also critical of Willie and Rose but does not see the problems with her own children.

George Jones

George is the husband of Emma Jones, and father of Mae and Vincent. Like his wife, George is a gossip and very judgmental of those who are not like himself. He is critical of foreigners, though not as much as his wife.

Mae Jones

Mae Jones, about twenty-one years old, is the daughter of George and Emma Jones and the sister of Vincent. She is not a ''nice girl'' but stays out all night with her boyfriend, Dick McGann. She works in a shop.

Vincent Jones

Vincent Jones is the son of George and Emma Jones and brother of Mae. He is a young adult and works as a taxicab driver. He is a large man, and likes to throw his weight around. Vincent is attracted to Rose and tries to get her to go out with him. When she refuses him, Sam tries to step in to get Vincent to leave her alone. Vincent pushes Sam aside. Like his parents, Vincent is not very tolerant of those who are different than him.

Abraham Kaplan

Abraham Kaplan is the old Jewish man who lives in the tenement apartment building with his daughter Shirley and son Sam. Kaplan is unpopular with most of his neighbors for several reasons, including his religion. Kaplan also spouts off his radical political and economic beliefs on a regular basis. He is critical of the capitalist economic system, preferring instead socialism. Kaplan generally means well, but his demeanor rubs most the wrong way.

Sam Kaplan

Sam Kaplan is the younger brother of Shirley Kaplan and son of Abraham Kaplan. He is a university student who is studying law and considered quite bright. Sam is fond of poetry, music, and, especially, Rose Maurrant. Sam is ready to abandon his father and sister and go anywhere with Rose. He tells her he loves her and intercedes when men like Vincent Jones try to take advantage of her. While Rose is fond of Sam, she ultimately rejects him, for both his own good and hers. Sam is essentially under his sister's thumb but has a promising future.

Shirley Kaplan

Shirley Kaplan is Abraham Kaplan's eldest child and primary caretaker. The unmarried woman works as a teacher to support her elderly father and to put her younger brother through law school. Like her father, Shirley is unpopular among the tenants of the tenement for her brusque ways and religion. Shirley is primarily concerned with her family, making sure her father and brother's needs are met. To this end, she tells Rose Maurrant to stay away from her brother Sam because he is their future breadwinner. Shirley does have a sympathetic side. When Rose has to go back into her apartment after her father murdered her mother and her mother's lover, Shirley accompanies her for support.

Lippo

See Filippo Fiorentino

Anna Maurrant

Anna Maurrant is the wife of Frank and mother of Rose and Willie. Mrs. Maurrant is unhappy in her marriage to Frank and is having an affair with the milk company's collector, Steve Sankey. This liaison provides much of the fodder for the tenement gossips. It also distracts Anna from the care of her son Willie. Though Rose Maurrant tries to dissuade her mother from being so obvious about the affair, it does no good. At the end of act 2, Mr. Maurrant

finds Sankey and his wife together, and he shoots both of them. Mrs. Maurrant later dies from the gunshot wounds.

Frank Maurrant

Frank Maurrant is the husband of Anna, and father of Rose and Willie. He works as a stagehand and is in the stagehands' union. Mr. Maurrant is a rather hard man to his wife and children. He does not approve of Rose's life choices and suspects something might be going on with his wife. Because of this situation, he is also the subject of much of the tenement's gossip. When Mr. Maurrant comes home unexpectedly at the end of act 2, he catches his wife together with Steve Sankey, the milk company collector. He shoots them, killing Sankey instantly while his wife dies later. After the shootings, he hides out in a nearby furnace room. The police catch him, and he is taken to prison. At the end of the play, it is implied that Mr. Maurrant will be put to death for his crime.

Rose Maurrant

Rose Maurrant is the twenty-year-old daughter of Frank and Anna Maurrant and older sister of Willie. She is a young woman who works in a real estate office and has many male admirers. They include her office manager, Harry Easter, who wants to set her up in an apartment of her own and get her started on a career in show business. Rose rejects all of his insistent advances. Vincent Jones also tries to get Rose to stay out all night with him, but she refuses him as well. Rose's most sincere suitor is Sam Kaplan. Kaplan pledges his love to her. While Rose connects with Sam in some ways, she also knows that he has a better future without her and that she has problems of her own. Rose tries to please her father, while influencing her mother's choices with Sankey. Rose's actions cannot change the outcome of the story, but at the end of the play, she is determined to make sure Willie has a better life in a better place. Rose is kind to many of her neighbors, including Mr. Buchanan.

Willie Maurrant

Willie Maurrant is the ten-year-old son of Frank and Anna Maurrant and younger brother of Rose. His mother cannot particularly control him. He runs rather freely on the streets, much to the chagrin of his father and sister. Willie is more interested in ice cream and being with his friends than being neat and tidy and hanging around at home. Rose tries to protect Willie as much as possible and keeps him in mind when she makes decisions.

Dick McGann

Dick McGann is Mae Jones' boyfriend. They stay out all night together at the end of act 1.

Carl Olsen

Carl Olsen is the husband of Olga Olsen and father of an infant child. Like his wife, he is an immigrant from Scandinavia. He lives in the basement apartment and is the building's janitor and maintenance man. Olsen is not above gossiping but is not particularly malicious. He helps the other tenants when he can. For example, at the end of the play when Rose wants to put up black crepe as a symbol of death, Olsen completes the task for her.

Olga Olsen

Olga Olsen is the wife of Carl Olsen and has an infant child. She is an immigrant from Scandinavia and lives in the basement apartment. She helps her husband with his janitorial duties in the building. Mrs. Olsen is one of the tenants who enjoys gossiping about her neighbors, though she is not as judgmental as some of the others. Mrs. Olsen helps others when needed.

Steve Sankey

Steve Sankey is the milk company collector who is having an affair with Mrs. Maurrant. Sankey is married and has two children. His rather open affair leads to his murder by Mrs. Maurrant's jealous husband.

Alice Simpson

Alice Simpson works for the charities and comes to the tenement to help Laura Hildebrand and her children. She is a spinster and rather cold and dismissive of the tenement's residents. Miss Simpson is especially hard towards Mrs. Hildebrand because she has taken her children to the movies, despite the fact that they are about to be evicted from their apartment. Still, she makes sure the Hildebrands have a place to go after their eviction.

Dr. John Wilson

Dr. John Wilson is the doctor who comes to the tenement to deliver Mrs. Buchanan's baby.

THEMES

Ethnic and Religious Intolerance

In *Street Scene,* many of the residents of the crowded tenement building express beliefs that are prejudiced and intolerant of their neighbors and others. Sitting on the brownstone's front stoop, they deride the way those different from themselves conduct their lives. For example, in the first moments of the play, Mrs. Jones, one of the non-immigrant residents of the building, says "What them foreigners don't know about bringin' up babies would fill a book" about Mrs. Olsen. Mrs. Olsen is an immigrant from Scandinavia. Mrs. Jones makes this statement to Mrs. Fiorentino, a German immigrant who is married to an Italian immigrant. Mrs. Fiorentino is slightly offended by the implication. Mrs. Jones also expresses intolerant beliefs about most everyone in the play.

One of the more unpopular resident families in the tenement is the Kaplans. Elderly father Abraham, his daughter Shirley and son Sam are disliked by many of their neighbors for being Jewish as well as for holding radical political beliefs. Abraham Kaplan is a socialist who believes the capitalist economic system exploits workers. Many residents are intolerant of Mr. Kaplan and his beliefs, and blame Jewish people for various problems in their world. Similarly, most residents do not approve of the potential relationship between Sam Kaplan and Rose Maurrant. They tell Rose and her parents that they would never let their daughter become involved with someone who is Jewish. By depicting these kinds of prejudices and situations, Rice depicts the diversity of New York City's populace and their beliefs. Not every aspect is positive.

Individual versus Machine

Throughout *Street Scene,* Rice underscores how oppressive the machine of modern urban life is. (The machines here are New York City, life in the tenement building, and the kind of jobs held by these lower middle class people.) The play is set on a hot day in June and many of the characters suffer from the heat. Because the characters reside in an unbearably close living situation, they are packed on top of one another, making the heat all the more oppressive. This situation also leaves them very little real privacy and, in many ways, limited opportunity. For example, everyone knows about Mrs. Maurrant's affair with Steve Sankey, the milk company's bill collection man. But she also might not be having the affair if the machine did not affect her husband, Mr. Maurrant, so deeply. Mr. Maurrant works as a stagehand and does not seem happy with his life. These tensions contribute to *Street Scene*'s tragic ending but do not end with the double murder. More tenants will move into the building, and those who live there will continue to be affected by these pressures.

Victim and Victimization; Choices and Consequences

The focal point—if there is one—of *Street Scene*'s diffuse plot is the affair Mrs. Maurrant is having with Steve Sankey, the milk company's bill collector, and its effect on the tenement. In many ways, Mrs. Maurrant is a victim of the city as well as an unhappy marriage. Mr. Maurrant is depicted as a rather loutish man who tries to control his family by the threat of violence. His marriage is not particularly happy, and he does not seem very concerned about his wife's emotional needs. To replace some of what her marriage lacks, Mrs. Maurrant has the affair. While her husband suspects that something is going on, her daughter, Rose, knows about the affair. To that end, Rose encourages her mother to be more discreet. Rose's warnings are not heeded, and Mrs. Maurrant and Sankey are murdered by Mr. Maurrant. Mr. Maurrant believes he will be put to death for the crime.

Though Mr. and Mrs. Maurrant are victims whose choices lead to serious consequences, Rose and her brother might benefit from their mistakes. She will not be a victim of the city or a bad marriage. Rose decides not to live her life for others (except her younger brother) and rejects the amorous offers of her boss, Harry Easter, and her young admirer, Sam Kaplan. She will move her brother to the suburbs or some place outside of New York City. In her family, at least, the cycle of victimization will not be repeated.

Cycle of Life

In *Street Scene*, Rice includes the entire cycle of life from a birth to two (untimely) deaths. By the beginning of act 2, the unseen Mrs. Buchanan has given birth to a daughter. At the end of the same act, Mr. Maurrant has shot both his wife and Sankey. As the play ends, it appears that a new couple is about to replace the recently evicted Hildebrand family. Rice has characters of every age in the play, from infants to old Mr. Kaplan and contrasting types of similar ages (Mae Jones contrasts with Rose Maurrant; Sam Kaplan to Vincent Jones). By depicting such a breadth of characters, Rice shows the

TOPICS FOR FURTHER STUDY

- Research paintings that are "street scenes," perhaps landscapes of Claude Lorrain, a French artist who influenced Rice when he wrote *Street Scene*. Pick one and compare it to the play.

- Discuss *Street Scene* in terms of "realism," the artistic and literary movement of the late nineteenth and early twentieth centuries.

- In what ways could the Maurrants avoid their sad situation by the end of the play? Would better communication have prevented the murder?

- Research trends in urbanization and suburbanization in this time period. Why does Rose believe that she and her family would have a better life outside of the city? Would their lives really be better in the suburbs?

diversity of New York City and how the city affects this cycle.

STYLE

Setting

Street Scene is a drama that takes place in New York City in contemporary time (the late 1920s). The date is a hot day in June. The action of the play is confined to one location: the exterior of a brownstone tenement that is about thirty years old. The building is somewhat shabby but features a stoop where many of the residents gather to escape the heat and socialize. Also visible are the front windows of several of the apartments, in which residents can be seen or heard. The building is located on a street that features warehouses as well as other housing. By limiting the play to one familiar setting, Rice underscores *Street Scene*'s themes. It emphasizes the characters' social circumstances and how dehumanizing life in New York City can be for those of the lower-middle classes.

Realism

Street Scene is a written as a realistic play. Realism is the faithful depiction of real life. Rice tries to capture what life was really like in New York City in the late 1920s for a certain class of society. To that end, he sets his play in a realistic setting: the tenement. Many of his characters are immigrants who speak English with an accent. Some, like Mr. Kaplan, maintain distinct ties to their past. Mr. Kaplan reads a newspaper written in Hebrew. Rice also shows how these people interact with those who consider themselves American, like the Joneses and the Maurrants. Their concerns are simple, related to everyday life: the affair that Mrs. Maurrant is having, how to stay cool on warm summer day, the young love of Rose Maurrant and Sam Kaplan.

Many minor characters add the play's realistic elements. Throughout the play, different kinds of people walk by the building, from children, to policeman, to those who want to gape at the murder scene in act 3. Many do not have lines, but those who do just talk about things like playing Red Rover or the like. To emphasize Rice's social message, he includes some better-developed minor characters as well. Miss Simpson, the spinster charity worker, looks down upon many of the tenement's residents. Though she is ostensibly helping Mrs. Hildebrand and her children (who have been left destitute after Mr. Hildebrand abandoned them), Miss Simpson cannot help but push her beliefs on others. Such characters add to the play's realism by including the kinds of people who would be found in such a place in real life.

Sound Effects

Rice goes to great lengths in the play's directions to emphasize the importance of sound to the realism of *Street Scene.* Throughout the play, Rice calls for steam whistles, traffic, and other street noise to be heard by the audience. In the original production, which Rice directed, he had the stage constructed so that audiences would hear footsteps as they are heard when walking down the street. He also made records with the kinds of street noise he believed was vital to the play's realism.

Multiple Plots

In *Street Scene,* Rice does not use a typical linear plot. Instead, he weaves many plots, both large and small, throughout the play. The primary plot focuses on the Maurrant family: Mrs. Maurrant's affair, her husband's knowledge of the affair or lack thereof, Rose's love life, and Willie's rambunctiousness. While many of *Street Scene*'s subplots are linked in one way or another to the Maurrants, there are a significant number that are not, including Mrs. Hildebrand's eviction. By depicting this kind of variety of stories, Rice adds to the realism and power of the play. There is not one primary story in life, but many that are linked and some that are not.

HISTORICAL CONTEXT

In 1929, the United States was on the verge of transition from the Jazz Age to the Great Depression. The 1920s were a complicated decade in American history. There was an illusion of economic prosperity. Big business got bigger in the economic boom as corporations grew. This boom made many rich and powerful and gave others the idea that they could become wealthy as well. The source for this wealth was perceived to be the stock market, which kept getting bigger throughout the 1920s. In 1929, stock market madness hit its peak, and those who ran the stock market could not keep up with the rapid changes. Warning signs were ignored about the artificially high bull market. On October 29, 1929, the stock market crashed on Black Tuesday and soon the Great Depression set in. Within a month, unemployment rates had quadrupled.

Before the crash, cities were seen as places of opportunity. Throughout the United States, there was an increase in urbanization. Office buildings, industrial complexes, hotels, and apartment buildings were constructed at a rapid rate. The Empire State Building was begun in 1929, and completed in 1931. New York City was regarded as the epitome of possibilities and drew many new immigrants and rural Americans to make their fortune. Yet in New York City there was widespread pollution and overcrowding. As people became successful, they moved to newly constructed suburbs. First the upper classes moved to the suburbs, then middle-class suburbs grew as well.

Not everyone benefited in the 1920s economic boom. Working- and lower-middle classes, which included teachers, did not, though they did have steady employment and relatively high wages. Unions were not really powerful or respected in the 1920s, though they did exist. Unskilled factory work was boring and their work situations were unstable. Many urban dwellers lived in crowded apartments.

COMPARE
&
CONTRAST

- **1929:** The primary entertainment in the home is the radio. Over ten million households (about half of the country) have radios in 1929, where few had them in 1921.

  Today: Television and computer-related technology have far surpassed radio as the primary forms of home entertainment.

- **1929:** After a period of unheralded prosperity, the stock market crashes in October. The American economy is soon in turmoil. Warning signs about the economy had been ignored.

  Today: There is unheralded prosperity in the United States, though there are some doubts about overvalued Internet-related stock. Procedures are in place to prevent a crash similar to that of 1929.

- **1929:** In general, unions are not particularly powerful or respected, though they are growing a bit in manufacturing. Public opinion towards them is generally negative. A strike in a Tennessee textile mill ends in defeat for labor.

  Today: After decades of power, unions are in decline. While some unions have power in certain industries, respect for them is generally declining.

- **1929:** Because there is often no refrigeration in the home, milk and ice are delivered to homes on a daily basis.

  Today: Refrigerators are commonly found in homes. Consumers buy dairy products in markets. The concept of daily delivery is alien.

Only seventy-one percent had running water and eighty percent had electricity. Rural America was even worse off. Rural America and small towns were already on the decline, and farmers were already suffering under tremendous economic pressure. Only ten percent of farm families had electricity, and only thirty-three percent had running water.

Throughout the 1920s, there was a conflict between rural and urban America and between the native-born and immigrants. There was concern over what to do with all the new Americans and their needs: more than a quarter who came to this country were illiterate. While many groups sprang to indoctrinate immigrants into American society, a nativism movement feared what immigrants brought to this country. People were afraid of communism, socialism, and other radical ideas. Many did not like Germans (because of World War I), Jews, or Catholics. Anti-Semitism was rampant. The Ku Klux Klan grew in power, though the actual number of lynchings declined in 1929. Such pressure led to the National Origins Act in 1924, which placed restrictions on the numbers and kinds of European immigrants. Still, immigrants came, even after the stock

market crash signaled the end of an optimistic decade and the beginning of a desperate decade.

CRITICAL OVERVIEW

When *Street Scene* was first produced, most critics praised the play for its realism and its characterizations. R. Dana Skinner of *Commonweal* called it ''a play of extraordinary sweep, power and intensity, which catches up with amazing simplicity and sincere feeling the ragged, glowing, humor and tragic life that pours in and out of one of those brownstone apartment houses hovering on the upper edge of the slum district of New York.'' *New York Times* critic J. Brooks Atkinson was also nearly unqualified in his praise. He wrote, ''He has transferred intact to the stage a segment of representative New York life, preserving not only its appearance but its character, relating it not only to the city but to humanity.''

Atkinson also approved of Rice's characterizations. In another review, he wrote, ''Mr. Rice has succeeded in relating it to life and enlisting your sympathies for the tatterdemalions who troop along his average street, hang out of the windows on a hot summer evening, gossip, quarrel, romance, and make the best of their stuffy lot. Mr. Rice does not sentimentalize about them. He does not blame them for their prejudices and blunders and short tempers.'' Later in the same review, Atkinson argued, ''Never did the phantasmagoria of street episodes seem so lacking in sketchy types and so packed with fully delineated character.''

Many critics of the original production commented on these ideas, though they were more mixed in their praise. The unnamed critic in *Catholic World* believed that Rice's characters alone redeemed the play. The critic wrote, ''[B]ecause all these insignificant bits of characterization are a legitimate and helpful part of the larger design, *Street Scene* is rescued from being merely photographic.'' Similarly, Joseph Wood Krutch of the *Nation* wrote, ''One may distrust the 'slice' or the 'cross-section' of life. One may doubt, as I certainly do, the ultimate importance of this particular kind of naturalism as a dramatic method. But one cannot doubt Mr. Rice's remarkable mastery of it.''

Stark Young of the *New Republic* was one of the few critics who had many problems with the play. *Street Scene,* he noted, ''on one plane of consideration is pleasantly entertaining. On another plane, where you take the play seriously and where you ask yourself whether for an instant you have believed in any single bit of it, either as art, with its sting of surprise and creation, or as life, with its reality. For me, who was not bored with it as an evening's theater, it is something less than rubbish, theatrical rubbish, in that curious baffling way that the stage provides.''

In writing about the original London production in 1930, Charles Morgan of the *New York Times* had some problems with Maurrant's love/murder plot and how it affected the story but found much to praise structurally. He wrote, ''Mr. Rice's method is an extremely interesting one which has its symbol in the fact that we see the apartment house always from the outside, never entering into it and being permitted only now and then to glance through its windows. The truth of its inhabitants must appear, Mr. Rice would seem to say, without admission of the audience into the position of all-seeing God with keys to individual hearts.''

Street Scene's power remained intact for at least one critic through the 1940s. Though writing about the musical version of the play written by

Rice with a score by Kurt Weill in 1947, Atkinson of the *New York Times* commented on the stage play. He believed its power as a drama made it a good choice for musical adaptation. Atkinson wrote, ''To him the characters are not specimens but human beings, grinding out what pleasure they can from the squalor, heat and grime of an ugly neighborhood. . . . Toward the characters his attitude is kindly without sentimentality, amused without condescension; it is realistic without bitterness or judgment. In the midst of a swirling and raucous city, he is observing life in tranquility.''

By 1996, when the play was revived by the Willow Cabin Theater Company at the Theater Row Theater in New York City, what had been seen as innovative and rich in 1929 was regarded as outdated. Calling the play ''a sprawling mess,'' D. J. R. Bruckner of the *New York Times* wrote, ''Its stock characters are poor immigrants from everywhere; its dialogue and ideas are clichéd, and its climax is a murder that seems pure camp by now.'' Donald Lyons of the *Wall Street Journal* thought better of the play, though he had similar problems. He argued that ''There is on parade a batter of working-class ethnic types . . . fresh maybe in 1929, but now merely stale. But Rice's focal stories still have power.''

CRITICISM

Annette Petrusso

In this essay, Petrusso shows how much Rice's play has in common with today's daytime television soap operas.

When Elmer Rice's *Street Scene* was first produced in 1929, it was unlike most other plays of the day. The play featured numerous, realistic characters, and many, sometimes intersecting, story lines, and neither of these aspects was developed in depth. Rice was discouraged from even producing *Street Scene* at all by his colleagues. Yet the drama was produced and was somewhat successful. To emphasize its realism, Rice insisted that the original production feature prerecorded street noise and other natural sounds to underscore that this tenement was really in the heart of New York City. Furthermore, Rice also added an element of contemporary social criticism to *Street Scene*. In one subplot, Mrs. Hildebrand and her two children are about to be removed from their home because they are with-

Janis Kelly and Kristine Ciesinski perform in a 1989 musical production of Street Scene.

out funds after Mr. Hildebrand abandoned them. They are "aided" by a social worker, Miss Alice Simpson, who seems only interested in controlling the poor family.

This kind of realism and social criticism is no longer so unusual in mainstream theater. *Street Scene* uses other techniques that are also common, not with socially oriented drama but with the daytime soap operas that have been found on television since the 1950s. The kind of events that occur in *Street Scene* are stock-in-trade of this kind of episodic television. More importantly, Rice's way of writing the play makes it seem like an episode in a longer drama. None of the stories in the tenement has a beginning that starts only after the curtain rises, and only a few story lines have a clear ending, though there is more to explore in these subplots. In other words, the interrelated stories of *Street Scene* could have had plays/episodes before them and continue after this point, not unlike a soap opera. This essay looks at two primary elements of *Street Scene*—themes and structure—and how they resemble a modern day soap opera.

In his essay "A Social Scientist's View of Daytime Serial Drama," George Comstock defines a soap opera as "the continuing saga of a group of people involved with each other through lineage, passion, ambition, hostility, and chance." This definition could well be applied to *Street Scene.* The characters in the play are grouped into small families who live in different apartments in the tenement. Their decision to live in this building is, at least in part, by chance. They may not have much money, but there are many other tenements in the city of New York. There is also hostility among them. Abraham Kaplan's constant stream of Marxist rhetoric, for example, is not appreciated by most of his neighbors. The Joneses are depicted as vicious bullies. The son, Vincent Jones, takes pleasure in harassing Sam Kaplan, who in turn is in love with Rose Maurrant. Sam is willing to give up his future to be with Rose, though his sister, Shirley, does everything in her power to discourage the romance. Ambition is hard to come by in the tenement: mostly characters hope to survive. Only the Kaplans seem to have much of a chance to escape, through education.

Admittedly, most modern day soaps do not focus on lower-middle to lower-class characters living in one tenement house. A majority of characters in soap operas are middle- to upper-class, with many professionals, both men and women. But

WHAT DO I READ NEXT?

- *The Adding Machine* is a play by Rice that was first produced in 1923. The story focuses on how a wage slave, Zero, is affected by oppressive modern day society.

- *Romeo and Juliet*, a play by William Shakespeare written in approximately 1597, concerns the effects of forbidden love.

- *Winterset*, a play Maxwell Anderson (1935), comments on how socioeconomic forces effect common people.

- The Subway, a play written by Rice in 1929, concerns how a woman reacts to an oppressive environment.

- *Bartholomew Fair*, a play by Ben Jonson written in approximately 1614, is a sprawling story with a large cast of characters.

---

almost every soap focuses on one community, and a number of families that live in it. James Thurber, in his essay "Ivorytown, Rinsoville, Anacinburg and Crisco Corners," provides another definition. He writes, "A soap opera deals with the plights and problems brought about in the lives of its permanent principal characters by the advent and interference of one group of individuals after another." This statement can be applied to *Street Scene.* If the families who live in the tenement are taken as the principal characters, then people like Miss Simpson, Steve Sankey (the milk company collector who has the affair with Mrs. Maurrant), or Happy Easter (Rose Maurrant's married boss, whose desire to have an affair with Rose and complicates Rose's life) can be seen as those who interfere.

No matter what class the principal characters are in, however, both soaps and *Street Scene* share thematic concerns. Mary Cassata and Thomas Skill in their essay "Television Soap Operas: What's Been Going on Anyway?—Revisited" define four kinds of stories in soap operas. They are "(1) Criminal and Undesirable Activity; (2) Social Problems; (3) Medical Developments; and (4) Romantic and Marital Affairs." All four of these elements can be found in *Street Scene.* The murder of Mrs. Maurrant and her lover falls under the category of criminal and undesirable activity. One medical development is the birth of Mrs. Buchanan's baby. There are at least two affairs in *Street Scene:* the illicit one between Mrs. Maurrant and Steve Sankey, and the more innocent, if one-sided, one between

Sam Kaplan and Rose Maurrant. (Social problems are discussed below.)

Other scholars add more specific situations to the list of soap opera themes. In the Comstock essay quoted earlier, the author argues that in soaps, "the kinds of tribulations are real enough for everyone—money, sex, health, mates, social competition, mental disorder, drugs, alcohol." Nearly all characteristics are also found in *Street Scene,* some of which already have been discussed. Money problems force the Hildebrands out of the tenement. Characters like Lippo try to be generous despite the general lack of funds, as when he buys a number of ice cream cones for his neighbor or when he gives the Hildebrand children a nickel each. His wife notes that this kind of behavior accounts for their economic problems. Marital problems have driven Mrs. Maurrant to have an affair. Indeed, many couples argue in *Street Scene.* There is much social competition, especially between the Jones and others. Alcohol plays a role in the murder of Mrs. Maurrant by her husband. These are but a few of the relevant situations in *Street Scene.*

Critical social elements are one of the most important themes of *Street Scene.* In the essay "The More Things Change, The More They Are the Same: An Analysis of Soap Operas from Radio to Television," Mary Cassata argues that "soap operas have dealt with issues and themes that have constituted the social concerns of their times." Among other things, *Street Scene* shows the diversity of people in New York City and how that creates some social squabbling. The different ethnicities get along but do not always live in harmony. Rice also touches on the problems of the working woman, as Rose tries to fend off Happy Easter.

The best example of a social theme, one that was extremely controversial in Rice's time, is the charity subplot involving the Hildebrands. In the way the story is depicted, Rice seems to question how helpful such charities really are. Miss Alice Simpson fails the Hildebrands in some ways because she tries to control them. She berates Mrs. Hildebrand for taking her children to the movies when they are about to lose their apartment. Simpson also becomes disgusted when Lippo gives the children money. While there may not be an outspoken Marxist like Abraham Kaplan on most soap operas, such shows, like this play, use the audience's sympathies, guiding them towards an emotional connection with what the creator considers wrong and right about societal attitudes.

Structural qualities are also common to both soap operas and *Street Scene*. In the play, the plot jumps between stories rather quickly and in short spurts. Though there is an overall flow, Rice weaves in bits about different story lines constantly. The plot is not linear but pieces of stories that develop over time. Soap operas use a similar technique in their use of multiple story lines. And as Laura Arliss, Mary Cassata, and Thomas Skill argue in their essay ''Dyadic Interaction on the Daytime Serials: How Men and Women Vie for Power,'' ''the action on daytime serial drama consists, for the most part, of talk.'' The same is basically true of *Street Scene:* a lot of talk and little actual action.

Though *Street Scene* has an ending, only a few of the stories are resolved with any finality: Mrs. Maurrant and her lover are murdered, Mrs. Buchanan has her baby, and the Hildebrands are removed. The rest of the story lines are left open-ended. Even those with endings are not particularly final. There is a baby to raise and different homes for both the Hildebrands and the Maurrant children. New families will be moving into the tenement, living different lives. As Horace Newcomb says in his essay ''A Humanist's View of Serial Drama,'' ''the triumph of the soap opera form is that it engages us in the sense of progressive unfolding, emergence, growth and change.'' None of the characters are static at the end of *Street Scene*. There is potential for yet more plays and episodes and more multiple crossing

> '' NEW FAMILIES WILL BE MOVING INTO THE TENEMENT, LIVING DIFFERENT LIVES. AS HORACE NEWCOMB SAYS IN HIS ESSAY 'A HUMANIST'S VIEW OF SERIAL DRAMA', 'THE TRIUMPH OF THE SOAP OPERA FORM IS THAT IT ENGAGES US IN THE SENSE OF PROGRESSIVE UNFOLDING, EMERGENCE, GROWTH AND CHANGE.'''

story lines. Rice was ahead of his time when he wrote *Street Scene,* anticipating the power of these innovations.

Source: Annette Petrusso, in an essay for *Drama for Students,* Gale Group, 2001.

Tara L. Mantel

Mantel is a freelance writer and editor based near Boston. In the following essay, Mantel contends that Rice's realistic play contains not-so-obvious expressionistic elements.

Elmer Rice's success and most-remembered works peaked during the second decade of the twentieth century. John Gassner claims in *Twenty-Five Best Plays of the Modern American Theatre,* ''So far as the theatre is concerned, the American century was born in 1919.'' American theater addressed the social conditions of the times via two main influences in dramatic style.

One influence arose out of the break from the idyllic and romantic plays of the late nineteenth century, with their moralizing and their admonitions of the less than morally pure audiences, to the desire to present the world in an authentic way. This style was known as realism. The second influence was the introduction, primarily through German plays, of the then-European technique called expressionism. Expressionism went beyond mere representation to exploring symbolically the inner life—

> THE EXPRESSIONISTIC PLAY
> USES SHORT DISCONNECTED
> SCENES, SOMETIMES OUT OF
> SEQUENCE, TO REFLECT THE
> DISORDER OF THE HUMAN MIND
> THAT IT SEEKS TO EXPOSE."

the psyche—of characters. It was a technique that, as Louis Broussard says in *American Drama: Contemporary Allegory from Eugene O'Neill to Tennessee Williams,* "abandoned the photography of realism, the dramatic sequence of events, for a stream of consciousness in terms of stage symbols whereby the surface of life becomes disjointed, scattered, as in a dream . . ."

On the surface, Rice's *Street Scene* (1929) seems like a play straight in the realism mode, but on further examination, it is filled with expressionistic elements. "It was not to be simply a realistic play," states C. W. E. Bigsby in *A Critical Introduction to Twentieth-Century American Drama.* It would be a stretch to say that the play is a type of expressionist realism, but one can still discern the experimental feel of the play and the themes that echo those found in expressionistic plays of the time.

The expressionistic play uses short disconnected scenes, sometimes out of sequence, to reflect the disorder of the human mind that it seeks to expose. It focuses on internal action. Because one cannot replicate these internal workings on the stage, symbols are used to represent emotional struggles and conflicts. Often characters exist as both individuals and types, which allows the playwright to tell a story involving individuals but also to allude to social or political trends via a type of dramatic shorthand. Expressionistic plays tend to address the theme of alienation. In stark contrast to the turn-of-the-century plays, which incorporated ills that fate or God willed on mankind, the experimental plays, as Jordan Miller and Winifred Frazer indicate in *American Drama Between the Wars: A Critical History,* addressed instead "what man has done to himself." The outsiders of the 1920s experienced rampant discrimination, and they as well as natives toiled away at repetitive, strenuous, and low-paying factory jobs—conditions that could be considered man-made. As a result, they began to experience a profound disconnection from each other.

In *Street Scene,* as in an expressionistic play, the characters are both individuals and types. Rice throws together a host of ethnic groups. These groups certainly represent the probable mix of a 1920s New York tenement building, but the divisions—an Italian man, a Russian-Jewish family, a Swedish couple, a German woman, and an Irish-American stagehand, among others—are almost forced. The mix is *too* accurate. The dialects and accents are so precisely reproduced that the individuals are types that border on being caricatures. Each character in *Street Scene* must embody the voice, culture, value systems, and expectations of his or her respective ethnic group, country, and religion. Of course, America, as a social experiment, is the great homogenizer, and being American is the common denominator of all these early twentieth-century ethnic groups. So we have a boisterous, happy-go-lucky Italian music instructor; a pondering Jewish student; and native New Yorkers who resent outsiders taking what rightly belongs to them and who believe that instilling "the fear of God" will somehow make the world and their lives better. Although each character is unique because of his or her ethnicity, this uniqueness ironically becomes the element that makes each character a representative type.

If being American is the common denominator of New York's inhabitants, then the tenement building is the common denominator of Rice's characters. *Street Scene,* like an expressionistic play, uses the gloomy brownstone as a symbol. The tenement building, the play's only backdrop, is an expressionistic symbol of urban life as a prison from which to escape. The oppressive heat, the characters lingering on the front steps, the cramped quarters—all reek of immobility and inertia. "Rice resisted the idea of simply copying an existing tenement building in order to create the set. It was a conscious effort to raise that setting to the level of symbol," Bigsby says. The characters' incessant climbing of the stairs can be viewed as another symbol—this time as the long economic climb of the middle class and its desire for material goods and a way of life that most of them agree is better.

Brief scenes and fragmented storylines characterize expressionism. Despite having a couple of traceable story lines, *Street Scene* mostly uses fragments and snippets of people's lives; these snippets, which all exist in real time rather than in an expressionistic heaven or hell or individual mind, are cleverly spliced together to form a cohesive whole. As Rice explains in *A Critical Introduction to Twentieth-Century American Drama,* "instead of unity of action, there was a multitude of varied and seemingly irrelevant incidents."

There are only two main storylines in *Street Scene:* the story of a woman and her jealous husband who shoots her and her lover in a jealous drunken rage; and the story of that woman's daughter, who now is the primary caretaker of the young son and who itches to escape the tenement and live on her own terms—even if that means rejecting several men. These storylines are not overly detailed or complicated but provide a hook on which to hang the rest if the action. For example, Mrs. Buchanan, whom we never see, endures a painful and complicated birth while Rose and Sam discuss their futures; Sam and Vincent Jones get into a couple of scuffles; and the Hildebrands get evicted. Bums shuffle by. Two schoolgirls discuss concavity. The Old-Clothes Man appears and disappears. Vendors hawk their wares. Crippled people hobble past. The central characters spend a good portion of stage time talking about the heat and gossiping.

But gossip is local color, and what Rice succeeds in doing is using expressionistic fragmentation as a tool for revelation. The seemingly insignificant drunken encounter between Mrs. Jones' daughter and her boyfriend reveal further the nature of Mrs. Jones' hypocrisy: her children's behavior is nowhere near the level she would have us believe. Her daughter is sexually easy, and her son is an obnoxious brute. Kaplan's rantings, particularly his hostility for Alice Simpson, reveals the contemporary collective fear of Socialism. Shirley's "Everybody has a right to his own opinion," spoken softly reveals the fragile democracy America espouses. How the characters react to seemingly unrelated and random occurrences—Mrs. Buchanan's labor cries, the Hildebrand eviction, and the affair everyone knows is going on between Mrs. Maurraut and Sankey, for example—allows Rice to address, through the expressionistic technique of story line fragmentation, the social mores of the times.

In addition, *Street Scene*'s themes are similar to those found in a typical expressionistic play. Mardi Valgemae, in *Accelerated Grimace,* writes that August Strindberg, the "father of German expressionism," addressed the "stifling effect of social conformity on personal happiness" in *Ghost Sonata.*

In that play, Strindberg's student asks, "What do we find that truly lives up to what it promises?" In *Street Scene,* Mrs. Maurraut, Rose, and Sam invoke similar questions. Sam says, "Everywhere you look, oppression and cruelty! . . . It's too high a price to pay for life—life isn't worth it!"

These seemingly innocuous complaints in *Street Scene* actually belie a Strindbergian/expressionistic concern with alienation. Bigsby discusses the importance of experimental theater in America, claiming that "it [took] as its primary subject the loss of an organic relationship with the natural world, with one's fellow man, and with oneself." In *Street Scene* the two most prominent forms of alienation are alienation from one's fellow man and alienation from oneself.

Mrs. Maurrant, always wondering why people can't be nicer to each other, is the spokeswoman for how people have lost touch with their fellow man. None of the characters in *Street Scene* really communicate with each other. It seems that they are either gossiping amongst themselves or arguing with each other. What passes for neighborly relations continues, but everyone seems to be watching and waiting, poised to criticize and pass judgement. Even an innocent round of ice cream leads to an argument about who discovered America—an argument that arouses nothing less than nationalist sentiments and quickly brings out the worst in everyone. Some of the characters lament the Hildebrands eviction, for example, but no one does anything about it. No one lends a hand or gives a kind word. The last few moments at the end of act 2 are telling: the shooting has just occurred, and a man, who is removing the personal items of the Hildebrands, pauses on the steps to look. How can the Hildebrands sympathize with the Maurrants and vice-versa? How can any of the characters, living in fear and distrust of each other, depending as they do on gossipy second-hand information and rumors, even begin to understand the real circumstances surrounding an event? Mrs. Maurrant is arguably the hero of this play: she is the only one who cares enough to actually lift a finger for another character—in this case making soup for a very ill Mrs. Buchanan—only to find herself bitterly rejected and criticized by her neighbors and severely wounded by a shot fired from her own husband's gun.

If Mrs. Maurrant embodies alienation with one's fellow man, then her daughter, Rose, is the voice for how people have lost touch with themselves. Rose says, "I don't think people ought to belong to anybody but themselves," and rightly supposes that the terrible shooting that serves as the dramatic underpinning of the play would never have happened if, say, her parents had been truer to themselves. The moment she learns this lesson she applies it to her own life: at the end of act 3 she shuns Sam's offer to take her away from the tenement, wisely doubting that his optimism and hope, his promise of living happily ever after, and his insistence that love can conquer all can be their salvation.

In *Street Scene,* we don't really enter the minds of the characters in a true expressionistic way, nor are the characters totally reduced to mechanical automatons as they typically are in a true expressionistic play. Nevertheless, the use of caricature and symbolism, as well as the theme of alienation due to social conformity, give this realistic play a distinct expressionistic feel.

Source: Tara L. Mantel, in an essay for *Drama for Students,* Gale Group, 2001.

Wendy Perkins

Perkins, an Associate Professor of English at Prince George's Community College in Maryland, has published several articles on several twentieth-century authors. In this essay, she explores how the structure of Rice's play emphasizes its focus on survival.

The positive public response to Rice's play was due to its authentic depiction of lower-class men and women struggling to survive the crushing reality of urban life. As Fred Behringer notes in his article on Rice for *The Dictionary of Literary Biography,* "the power of the play lies not in the surface reality, but rather in the intense struggles beneath." Rice illuminates these struggles through the play's creative structure. As he juxtaposes brief glimpses of his characters, he explores the various ways human beings find to cope with the harsh reality of everyday life.

In his stage directions, Rice sets the tone and establishes the fragmented structure characteristic of the entire play. He writes, "Throughout the act and, indeed, throughout the play, there is constant noise. . . . The noises are subdued and in the background, but they never wholly cease."

These noises represent a myriad of separate personal stories being played out simultaneously, creating a mosaic of lower middle class urban life. Behringer explains that in an interview, Rice claimed, "the intended total effect [of the play] was a panoramic impression of New York," one that included "shopkeepers, clerks, artisans, students, a schoolteacher, a taxi driver, a musician, janitors, policemen."

What all these characters have in common is their desire to overcome the hardships of their daily life. Rice's fragmented structure illustrates the various mechanisms humans employ during this difficult process.

In the first act, Rice introduces all the major characters and suggests some of the frustrations they face. As several of them sit on the front stoop of their "walk-up" apartment house "in a mean quarter of New York," their immediate concern is the oppressive and inescapable heat, which results in sweat-soaked clothes and crying babies. The audience soon discovers other problems caused by the urban environment. The play's cacophony of voices illustrates how life on these "mean" streets exacerbates family relationships. Parents fret about the negative influences on their children who stay out too late. Glimpses into their lives reveal how their marriages strain under the pressure of economic hardships coupled with concerns for the children. Some suffer as a result of prejudice while others must face the biological realities of childbirth and death.

Mrs. Jones never specifically identifies the problems her family experiences, but Rice suggests their source when he presents vignettes that focus on her daughter's and husband's alcoholism. Mrs. Jones illustrates the consequences of the tense relationship she has with her family when she insists, "Men are all alike. They're all easy to get along with so long as everythin's goin' the way they want it to. But once it don't—good night!" Mrs. Maurrant's more egalitarian response nevertheless confirms Mrs. Jones' point of view: "I guess it's just the same with the women. . . . People ought to be able to live together in peace and quiet, without making each other miserable."

Most of the characters cope with the stresses in their lives through affiliation. Sharing their problems helps alleviate them to a degree, especially when others offer sympathy. As each neighbor laments the consequences of the overwhelming heat and delineates their family problems, the others

A scene from United Artists' 1931 film adaptation of Street Scene.

respond with understanding nods and their own similar stories.

This camaraderie inevitably leads to another form of release for the characters—gossip, and in the opening scene, they feel that they have much to gossip about. As soon as Mrs. Maurrant comes into view, those on the stoop begin to chatter about her affair with Steve Sankey as they try to forget the heat and their own personal problems. All condemn the two for their actions, but some are more sympathetic than others to what they see as the couple's inevitable fate when Mr. Maurrant finds out.

Mrs. Jones shifts the focus of the conversation to the affair after Mrs. Fiorentino sympathizes with Willie Maurrant's treatment of his mother. Mrs. Jones notes, "I guess it don't bother her much. She's got her mind on other things." Her critical tone reveals another coping mechanism she employs—devaluation. Throughout the play, Mrs. Jones deals with stress by attributing exaggerated negative qualities to others. This becomes most evident in her racist remarks about her neighbors. For example, when Mrs. Olsen fails to comfort her baby, Mrs. Jones insists, "What them foreigners don't know about bringin' up babies would fill a book." After Mrs. Fiorentino takes offense at her words, Mrs. Jones makes a feeble attempt at tact:

"Well, I'm not sayin' anythin' about the Joimans. The Joimans is different—more like the Irish. What I'm talkin' about is all them squareheads an' Polacks—an' Jews."

Others take their minds off of their problems through altruism. As the neighbors gossip about the Maurrants, Filippo Fiorentino buys them ice cream cones to help ease the heat. He also shows his generosity when he gives money to a woman about to be dispossessed. When the worker from the charity office chastises him, insisting, "you'd be doing her a much more neighborly act, if you helped her to realize the value of money instead of encouraging her to throw it away, Filippo replies, "Ah, lady, no! I give 'er coupla dollar, make 'er feel good, maka me feel good—dat don' 'urt nobody."

Some of the other neighbors also reveal generous spirits. Filippo's wife Greta offers soup for Mrs. Buchanan who will soon deliver her baby. Mrs. Maurrant prepares food for Mrs. Buchanan and stays with her throughout her difficult labor. Mr. Buchanan tells the others that Mrs. Maurrant was up with his wife nearly all night and admits, "I don't know what we'd have done without her." Mrs. Maurrant, though, has found an additional way to ease her troubles, but this coping mechanism will result in her murder.

> GLIMPSES INTO THEIR LIVES REVEAL HOW THEIR MARRIAGES STRAIN UNDER THE PRESSURE OF ECONOMIC HARDSHIPS COUPLED WITH CONCERNS FOR THE CHILDREN. SOME SUFFER AS A RESULT OF PREJUDICE WHILE OTHERS MUST FACE THE BIOLOGICAL REALITIES OF CHILDBIRTH AND DEATH."

Pieces of dialogue from several of the characters reveal that Mr. Maurrant treats his wife harshly and continually complains about their children. Mrs. Maurrant expresses her need for comfort and suggests the reason why she enters into an affair with another man when she explains, "I think the trouble is people don't make allowances. They don't realize that everybody wants a kind word, now and then." In a moment of desperation, she tries to justify her actions when she insists to Rose, "What's the good of being alive, if you can't get a little something out of life? You might just as well be dead."

Kaplan deals with the stresses of his environment through intellectualization, the excessive use of generalizations to complain about a situation. He blames all the neighbors' problems on the country's economic system, insisting, "As long as de institution of private property exeests, de verkers will be at de moicy of de property owning klesses. . . ." Kaplan believes that if the country adopts a socialist system, poverty, along with their troubles, will be eliminated.

Mr. Maurrant also employs this tactic, which allows him to vent his frustrations over his suspicions about his wife. He decides, "what we need in this country is a little more respect for law an' order" and cites examples of what he sees to be the decline of the American family. Homes, he claims are being broken up by divorce and the relaxation of sexual taboos. As a result, he determines, "it's time somethin' was done to put the fear o' God into people!"

His intellectualism quickly turns threatening, however, as his humiliation over his wife's affair surfaces. When Kaplan suggests that if private property is abolished, "the femily will no longer hev eny reason to excest," Maurrant explodes. He insists the family will survive, with "children respectin' their parents an' doin' what they're told . . . An' husbands an' wives, lovin' and' honorin' each other, like they said they would, when they was spliced." He ends his tirade with a devaluation of Kaplan, warning him, "any dirty sheeny that says different is li'able to get his head busted open." Soon, his inability to cope with his wife's infidelity will push him over the edge, causing him to take her life and that of her lover when he finds them together.

Sam, Kaplan's extremely sensitive son, is another character who has not developed effective ways to cope with the reality of his life. He tries to escape into books, but they do not help him block out the cruelty and despair he finds everywhere. When he comes across the neighbors gossiping about Mrs. Maurrant, he tries to defend her, yelling "stop it! Stop it! Can't you let her alone? Have you no hearts? Why do you tear her to pieces, like a pack of wolves?" But he cannot face them and so escapes, dashing abruptly into the house, choking back a sob.

When he tries to defend Rose against Vincent Jones' advances, Vincent knocks him to the ground, where he remains, cowering in fear. After Vincent leaves, Sam crumbles. Rice notes, "he throws himself on the stoop and, burying his head in his arms, sobs hysterically." Rose tries to comfort him, but he resists, exclaiming

> That's all there is in life—nothing but pain. From before we're born, until we die! . . . The whole world is nothing but a blood stained arena, filled with misery and suffering. It's too high a price to pay for life. . . . life isn't worth it!

Rice's focus on short exchanges between Sam and Rose highlights diametrically opposed responses to the harsh reality of life. Sam suggests that he and Rose kill themselves and so end their suffering. Rose refuses, exclaiming that there is a lot to appreciate in life, "just being alive—breathing and walking around. Just looking at the faces of people you like and hearing them laugh. And . . . listening to a good band, and dancing." Out of all the characters in the play, Rose finds the most effective ways of coping with her life.

She refuses to adopt Sam's pessimistic attitude. While he sees nothing but cruelty and misery, she suppresses her problems during a walk through the park. There, she admits, "everything looked so green and fresh, that I got a kind of feeling of, well, maybe it's not so bad, after all." Her optimism later emerges in a discussion of religion with Sam. She asks him, "don't you think it's better to believe in something that makes you a little happy, than not to believe in anything and be miserable all the time?

At a moment of weakness, she accepts the attentions of Harry Easter, her married supervisor. Influenced by his offer to help her launch a career on the stage, she considers becoming his mistress. Eventually, though, after coming to terms with her family's tragedy, she finds the strength to survive through her determination to move out of the city and to live an independent life. Admitting that she does not love either Harry or Sam, and refusing to become dependent on either of them, she tells Sam, "I don't think people ought to belong to anybody but themselves."

Behringer concludes, "In spite of the violence, oppressiveness, and loss in the play, the central idea is one of affirmation. . . . Rice emphasizes the notion that not only is happiness possible, but that it is, in large part, a matter of personal choice." R. Dana Skinner, writing in *Commonweal,* suggests, "it is perhaps hard to believe that from incidents as varied and scattered as these, Mr. Rice could create an enthrallingly vivid sense of reality, poignancy, cowardice, despair and courage. But he has succeeded in an overflowing measure." He succeeds in large part because his arrangement of the short glimpses into the lives of his characters underscores the play's theme. As *Street Scene* catalogues the various ways we cope with the often harsh reality of existence, it ultimately affirms the resilience of the human spirit.

Source: Wendy Perkins, in an essay for *Drama for Students,* Gale Group, 2001.

Robert Hogan

Hogan examines the themes present in Street Scene *through the series of events that happen to the characters.*

Street Scene was produced in 1929, ran for 602 performances, won the Pulitzer Prize, and is one of the great plays of the American theatre. It had the longest Broadway run of any of Rice's plays, and, with the exception of the London production of *Judgment Day,* it gave him probably the greatest satisfaction. The tragicomic history of the play is fascinatingly told in Chapter XIX of *The Living Theatre* and Chapter XIII of *Minority Report.* Of special interest is the difficulty that Rice had in marketing the script.

> The responses of the producers were emphatically and unanimously negative. I remember some of them. The Theatre Guild, which had produced my play *The Adding Machine,* said that *Street Scene* had "no content." Winthrop Ames, a man for whose judgment I had great respect, said that it was not a play. Arthur Hopkins, who had scored a great success with my first play, *On Trial,* told me that he found *Street Scene* unreadable. Others found it dull, depressing, sordid, confusing, undramatic. One producer opened the script, looked at the list of characters and read no further.

It seems astonishing that so many astute authorities could have been so wrong; still, a book could be filled with similar cases. If any generalization is to be drawn from such facts, it might be that the commercial theatre imposes its own standards upon those who work in it. When money is the first consideration, safety is the second and quality is the last. Of the play itself, Rice once wrote:

> The background and subject matter had been in my mind for many years: a multiple dwelling, housing numerous families of varying origins; and a melodramatic story arising partly from the interrelationships of the characters and partly from their environmental conditioning. The setting was the façade of a "brownstone front"—a type of dwelling of which there are still thousands of examples in New York—and the sidewalk before it. . . . The house was conceived as the central fact of the play: a dominant structural element that unified the sprawling and diversified lives of the inhabitants. This concept was derived partly from the Greek drama, which is almost always set against the face of a palace or a temple. But mainly I was influenced, I think, by the paintings of Claude Lorrain, a French artist of the seventeenth century. In his landscapes, which I had gazed at admiringly in the Louvre and other galleries, there is nearly always a group of figures in the foreground, which is composed and made significant by an impressive architectural pile of some sort in the background. In fact, the original title of my play was *Landscape with Figures;* but I felt that this was a little too special, so I borrowed again from the terminology of painting and called the play *Street Scene* . . .

> There is a central love story: a sort of Romeo and Juliet romance between the stagehand's daughter and the radical's son; and a main dramatic thread of murder, committed by the girl's father when he comes home unexpectedly and finds his wife with her lover. But there are numerous subplots and an intricate pattern of crisscrossing and interweaving relationships. The house is ever present and ever dominant, and the entire action of the play takes place on the sidewalk, on the stoop or in the windows. I give these details in order to make it clear that, whatever the play's merits or defects, it is an unconventional drama, in setting, in technique and in size of cast.

THE EFFECT IS AS IF A SLAB
OF REALITY HAD BEEN HURLED
AT THE AUDIENCE, AS IF REALISM
ITSELF WERE ABRUPTLY
REVITALIZED AND ITS TRUE
POSSIBILITIES BEGINNING AT LAST
TO BE EXPLORED."

The problem of discussing this large and un-conventional play is that, in one sense, it is too large to discuss. So much happens and there are so many characters, that one scarcely knows where or how to begin. On the other hand, if one stands further back for a broader view, there seems curiously little to discuss. From the welter of incidents, ultimately emerges one simple story, and the rest is scene painting. So viewed, the whole conception seems simplicity itself.

Although the play is realistic, its realism has seldom been seen on the stage since the days of such sprawling Elizabethan plays as *Bartholomew Fair.* It is a realism that suddenly makes one understand with a sort of shock that experiments in realism are still possible. The realism bequeathed by Ibsen was the portrayal of a middle-class drawing room, a front parlor inhabited by half a dozen people. A play like Rice's takes the theatre out of that parlor and sets it down in the middle of a busy metropolitan street. The effect is as if a slab of reality had been hurled at the audience, as if realism itself were abruptly revitalized and its true possibilities begin-ning at last to be explored.

Compared with *Street Scene,* the front parlor drama seems unreal, contrived, and artificial. It is as if the front parlor dramatists had been using the delicately honed scalpel of realism to extract the meat from nuts rather than the pith from life. Per-haps it is wrong to forget a lesson from Ibsen's own front parlor drama, *A Doll's House.* At the end of that play, its heroine stormed from the house and into the street. And, indeed, most of Ibsen's later plays—*Rosmersholm, John Gabriel Borkman, The Master Builder, The Lady From the Sea* and *When We Dead Awaken*—all finally escape from the parlor, into the sea, the mountains, and the air. The

man who wrote *Brand* and *Peer Gynt* did not regard realism as a confinement, but as the quickest way to freedom. The free realism of *Street Scene* seems to prove the vitality of that realistic form from which so many lesser playwrights have found "No Exit."

I am not suggesting a return to the mere specta-cle for spectacle's sake so dear to the heart of Boucicault, but merely suggesting that the modern stage rarely uses its full resources, and that the large cast and the small spectacle performed by real people may be one realization of the theatre at its most vital. *Street Scene* is as pertinent a reminder as *Endgame* or *The Chairs* of what the theatre can do if it will but extend itself. Really, *Street Scene,* with its cast of eighty, may even beat the movies at their own game of spectacle. The eighty-odd characters of *Street Scene* are there, immediate, palpable, tangible; and the elect of real people over colored shadows (no matter how clearly one can see the cleavages in their Brobdingnagian bosoms) is so much more vivid, that eighty real people may dwarf thousands of celluloid shadows.

In the nineteenth-century theatre, actors were accustomed to play types, character types and na-tional types. In our post-Stanislavskian stress upon individual characterization, we may have forgotten a value of the older practice which was, after all, effective, economical, and based upon legitimate observation. *Street Scene* has many national types in its cast—Jews, Italians, Scandinavians, Irish, and so on, and much of the play's effect comes from the delineation and juxtaposition of these types. The jangling cacophony of their dialects, fusing with the diverse street noises, creates a convincing harmony of reality. Such roles not only provide valuable exercises for actors caught in a morass of subtlety, but also allow individual characters to be built up with an economy of effort. Consider, for instance, the effect that Rice gets from a mere stage move-ment in this exchange between the extroverted Italian Lippo and his German wife.

> MRS. FIORENTINO: Lippo, what do you think? Mr. Buchanan has a little girl.
>
> LIPPO: Ah, dotsa fine! Margherita, why you don' have da baby, ha?
>
> MRS. FIORENTINO: [*abruptly*] I must go and make the coffee.

With similar economy, Rice builds up the char-acterizations of his large cast, so that his play requires both considerable excellence from each actor and an ensemble playing difficult to achieve.

One character who benefits greatly from this economy and rings particularly true is the Irish father, Maurrant. His black savagery is clearly caught by the simple repetitions which Rice allows him.

> Who's been sayin' things to you?
>
> Shut up your swearin', do you hear?—or I'll give you somethin' to bawl for. What did he say to you, huh?
>
> What did he say to you?
>
> Nobody's askin' you? . . . What did he say? . . .
>
> G'wan up to bed now, an' don't let me hear no more out o' you. [*Raising his hand*] G'wan now. Beat it.

The theme is expressed with similar economy in several dialogues between Rose Maurrant and Sam Kaplan, the young Jewish student. It is probably, however, the part of the play that suffers most by blunt and economical statement. Most bluntly, it is stated in this interchange from Act I.

> SAM: That's all there is in life—nothing but pain. From before we're born, until we die! Everywhere you look, oppression and cruelty! If it doesn't come from Nature, it comes from humanity—humanity trampling on itself and tearing at its own throat. The whole world is nothing but a blood-stained arena, filled with misery and suffering. It's too high a price to pay for life—life isn't worth it!
>
> ROSE: Oh, I don't know, Sam. I feel blue and discouraged sometimes, too. And I get a sort of feeling of, oh, what's the use. Like last night. I hardly slept all night, on account of the heat and on account of thinking about—well, all sorts of things. And this morning, when I got up, I felt so miserable. Well, all of a sudden, I decided I'd walk to the office. And when I got to the Park, everything looked so green and fresh, that I got a feeling of, well, maybe it's not so bad, after all.

The events of the whole play can be seen in these terms, as examples of unfeeling brutality or of sympathy and compassion. Or, to put it another way, as examples of worthlessness and worth, or even of comedy and tragedy. The inhabitants of the tenement help each other, but they also tear at each other. For example, here are the last two speeches of the play, the first compassionate and the second callous.

> MISS CUSHING: The poor little thing!
>
> MRS. JONES: Well, you never can tell with them quiet ones. It wouldn't surprise me a bit if she turned out the same way as her mother. She's got a gentleman friend that I guess ain't hangin' around for nothin'. I seen him, late last night, and this afternoon, when I come home from the police.

This dramatization of compassion and brutality is more effective than the overt statement in the interchange between Sam and Rose. Further, just as Mrs. Jones's speech is much longer than Miss Cushing's, so do the brutal events come to outweigh the compassionate ones. There is more of geniality and humor in the first act than in the second, and the last act is relieved only sporadically from grimness. In this increasing darkness of tone, the play resembles the tragicomedies of Gorky and O'Casey and perhaps of Chekhov.

The compassion in the play establishes the worth and humanity of the characters. The brutality does not erase that worth, but makes the plight of these people even more poignant. Rice is not laying the blame on a narrow social basis. He is not condemning a particular society or a certain system of economics for the lives of his people. One of his characters, Abraham Kaplan, does make such a condemnation, but Rice makes it clear that Kaplan is not his *raisonneur*. Rice is not expounding socialism, but human nature; and his play seems to prove that people inevitably destroy themselves, that they carry in themselves the seeds of their own brutality. Without wishing to, they cannot avoid hurting each other. Even Maurrant, who is driven to kill his wife, cries out in agony that he had not meant to. There is no character, except perhaps one outsider, the social worker, who is basically unsympathetic—not even the bullying Irishman Vincent Jones, not even Rose's boss Harry Easter, who is trying to seduce her. Even the savage Maurrant is a basically sympathetic man driven by his own human nature. He is a mixture of brutality and compassion, and the brutality overwhelms the good. This triumph of brutality over compassion is probably the basic theme of the play—a generalization about the human condition, about the nature of man.

Many critics called the play, or at least the story of Maurrant, a melodrama. In the usual sense of the term, melodrama seems inappropriate. One way in which tragedy is usually distinguished from melodrama is by the thickness of characterization. While Maurrant is not a memorable character, as are Hamlet and Othello, he is certainly more valid than the Scarlet Pimpernel or even Sydney Carton. Further, one may plausibly argue that the thinness of his character is filled out by the other characterizations in the play. None is fully drawn, but none is false, and the group to which Maurrant belongs is memorable in the same way that the hero of a tragedy is memorable. Also, the theme of Maurrant's story is acted out in other forms by most of the other characters. Ultimately we get a group as hero, rather as we do in Hauptmann's *The Weavers* or Toller's *Man and the Masses*. The greatest difference is that

Rice's group hero is considerably more individualized than Toller's and even more than Hauptmann's.

The importance of the theme, however, is the strongest reason why one may not dismiss *Street Scene* as melodrama. The essence of melodrama is that the theme be unimportant, or at least stated in such heroic or sentimental or platitudinous terms that we do not have to take it seriously, and may therefore concentrate upon an exciting series of events. The theme of *Street Scene* is emphasized by its plot, and is in itself valid and moving. Really, the theme is the same as that of great tragedy and tragicomedy, and this fact seems established by the extent to which the play deeply moved its audiences.

If this notion is true, then the play is one further refutation of Krutch's theory that tragedy is impossible in the modern world. All that is necessary for tragedy is the affirmation of human value. By the compassion of its statement, *Street Scene* establishes that value. Actually, one might take this argument further without unduly stretching it: if one were to judge the play by the classic values of tragedy, it would stand up well. If we take the story of the Maurrant family to be the main story of the play, then the other characters provide an enormous chorus. If we apply the scale of beauty of language, we could even make a case, although some of the dialogue may at first seem flat and bald. The quotations above from Sam and Rose seem naïve and awkward, if compared to any purple passage from Sophocles or Shakespeare. Rice is admittedly not a poet, but the flatness of the Sam-Rose dialogue arises not so much from a limitation of Rice's talent, as from a limitation of realistic dialogue. Of this fact, he himself is quite conscious, as we shall see in *Not for Children,* where he satirizes the attempt of the realistic writer to rise above flat statement to beauty or poetry.

We must consider also that speech in a play is more than words and their meanings and overtones; it is also the sound of words. One of Shaw's most valid criticisms of the Shakespearean productions of the 1890's was that they extracted the meaning from Shakespeare while butchering the "word music." Even the Sam-Rose dialogue, when spoken with the right tone, expression, and dialects, provides beauty as well as realism. There is no way to prove this on paper. It can only be proved by speech, by actual production, but that fact is no reason for the assertion not to be made.

I have been emphasizing the tragic value of the play, but it has much comic value also. I do not merely refer to the many laughs which Rice's accurate observation will evoke, but also to the audience's satisfying realization that this observation truly reveals man's state with its faults, foibles, and poignance. *Street Scene* may not have the deft ironies of Chekhov's tragicomedies or the lyrical language of O'Casey's, but Rice's combination of tragedy and comedy, of brutality and compassion, does provide an effect of ineffable poignance at the tragicomic waste of humanity. It is a large play and a great play. The technical brilliance of putting so much together—so much action, so many characters—in a coherent and moving manner, I have scarcely touched upon, but the theme could never have emerged so lucidly and movingly had the play not been so superlatively wrought. *Street Scene* is one of those plays which affirm that the value of drama is that it asserts the value of man. Indeed, the way in which *Street Scene* pushes back the boundaries of the drama may almost itself negate the triumphant brutality of the play's theme. There can be no higher praise, I think, than that.

Source: Robert Hogan, "The Realist," in *The Independence of Elmer Rice,* Southern Illinois University Press, 1965, pp. 46–54.

Alan S. Downer

Street Scene is described as "selective realism at its best." In the following excerpt, Downer outlines the problems he notices with the play.

Rice presented his audience, not with a single family living under carefully controlled conditions, but with a cross section of city life as experienced by a large group of people who live in or are somehow connected with a huge brownstone tenement. They are varied in racial background, in philosophy, in occupation, in social status and intellectual stature: Italians, Jews, Swedes, Irish, musicians, electricians, milkmen, teachers, radicals, conservatives, poets and peasants. Yet the audience is not conscious that a cross section has been selected and presented to it; what is more natural in the melting pot of New York than that such a mixture occupy one tenement and animate one plot?

The plot, what there is of it, is hackneyed. *Street Scene* is really a conversation piece centering on a love triangle. But adultery and murder are not the exclusive interests of the play. More important is the play's attempt to present a generalized picture of middle-class urban living, an attempt so successful on the whole that the playwright was called a "mere journalist,'' and other terms suggesting critical disapproval.

Street Scene is anything but journalism. It is actually a kind of domestic symphony, taking the details of life, each as accurately rendered as possible, and arranging them within a frame (or perhaps better, against a background) that is itself a familiar commonplace, to yield an interpretation of what this crowded communal life means in terms of the individual and the group. Unlike *Awake and Sing!* the play seems to have no propagandistic purpose, unless it is expressed by Mrs. Maurant:

> I often think it's a shame that people don't get along better, together. People ought to be able to live together in peace and quiet; without making each other miserable.

Feeble as the sentiment is, it is characteristic of the speaker and pertains to every situation in the play. *Street Scene* is selective realism at its best.

Source: Alan S. Downer, ''From Romance to Reality,'' in *Fifty Years of American Drama,* Henry Regnery Company, 1951, pp. 63–65.

SOURCES

Arliss, Laurie, Mary Cassata, and Thomas Skill, ''Dyadic Interaction on the Daytime Serials: ''How Men and Women Vie for Power,'' in *Life on Daytime Television: Tuning-In American Serial Drama*, Ablex Publishing Corporation, 1983, p. 147.

Atkinson, J. Brooks, Review in *New York Times,* January 19, 1947, Sect. 2, p. 1.

———, ''Affairs on the West Side,'' *New York Times,* January 20, 1929, Sect. 8, p. 1.

———, ''Honor Where Honor Is Due,'' *New York Times,* May 19, 1929, Sect. 9, p. 1.

———, Review in *New York Times,* January 11, 1929, p. 20.

Behringer, Fred, ''Elmer Rice,'' in *Dictionary of Literary Biography, Volume 7: Twentieth-Century American Dramatists,* Gale, 1981, pp. 179–92.

Bigsby, C. W. E., *A Critical Introduction to Twentieth-Century American Drama,* Vol. 1, 1900–1940, Cambridge University Press, 1982, pp. vi, vii, 126,130.

Broussard, Louis, *American Drama: Contemporary Allegory from Eugene O'Neill to Tennessee Williams,* University of Oklahoma Press, 1962, pp. 3, 7.

Bruckner, D. J. R., Review in *New York Times,* November 6, 1996, p. C14.

Cassata, Mary, ''The More Things Change, the More They Stay the Same: An Analysis of Soap Operas Radio to

Television'' in *Life on Daytime Television: Tuning-In American Serial Drama,* Ablex Publishing Corp., 1983, p. 85.

———, and Thomas Skill, ''''Television Soap Operas: What's Been Going On Anyway:'—Revisited'' in *Life on Daytime Television: Tuning-In American Serial Drama,* Ablex Publishing Corp., 1983, p. 157.

Review in *Catholic World,* March 1929, pp. 720–22.

Comstock, George, ''A Social Scientist's View of Daytime Serial Drama,'' in *Life on Daytime Television: Tuning-In American Serial Drama,* Ablex Publishing Corp., 1983, p. xxiii.

Gassner, John, *Twenty-Five Best Plays of the Modern American Theatre,* Crown Publishers, 1949, pp. xvi, xxviii.

Krutch, Joseph Wood, ''Cross Section,'' in *Nation,* January 30, 1929, p. 142.

Lyons, Donald, Review in *Wall Street Journal,* November 4, 1996, p. A20.

Miller, Jordan Y., and Winifred L. Frazer, *American Drama between the Wars: A Critical History,* in *Twayne's Critical History of American Drama,* G. K. Hall & Co., 1991, pp. vii, xii, 158, 168.

Morgan, Charles, Review in *New York Times,* September 28, 1930, Sect. 8, p. 2.

Newcomb, Horace, ''A Humanist's View of Daytime Serial Drama,'' in *Life on Daytime Television: Tuning-In American Serial Drama,* Ablex Publishing Corp., 1983, p. xxix.

Rice, Elmer L., *Street Scene,* Samuel French, 1928, 1956.

———, *Street Scene,* in *Seven Plays by Elmer Rice,* Viking Press, 1950, pp. 111–90.

Skinner, R. Dana, Review in *Commonweal,* Vol. IX, No. 12, January 23, 1929, pp. 48–49.

Thurber, James, ''Ivorytown, Rinsoville, Anacinburg, and Crisco Corners,'' in *Worlds Without End: The Art and History of the Soap Operas,* Harry N. Abrams, Inc., 1997, p. 51.

Valgemae, Mardi, *Accelerated Grimace: Expressionism in American Drama of the 1920s,* in *Crosscurrents/Modern Critiques* series, edited by Harry Moore, Southern Illinois University Press, 1972, pp. xi, xiv, 14.

Young, Stark, Review in *New Republic,* January 30, 1929, p. 296–98.

FURTHER READING

Dunham, Frank, *Elmer Rice,* Twayne, 1970.
    This critical study of Rice's life and work includes commentary on *Street Scene.*

Hogan, Robert, *The Independence of Elmer Rice,* Southern Illinois University Press, 1965.
    This book discusses Rice's plays, including *Street Scene,* in social and cultural context.

Palmieri, Anthony F. R., *Elmer Rice: A Playwright's Vision of America,* Farleigh Dickinson, 1980.

> This book considers *Street Scene* and other Rice plays in terms of his development as a playwright and his reaction to the world around him.

Rice, Elmer, *Minority Report: An Autobiography,* Simon and Schuster, 1963.

> This autobiography considers the whole of Rice's life and theatrical career, including *Street Scene.*

Sweet Bird of Youth

TENNESSEE WILLIAMS

1959

Though Tennessee Williams's *Sweet Bird of Youth* (1959) was his biggest box office success since *Cat on a Hot Tin Roof* (1955), the play came to be regarded as an example of the playwright in decline. It was his second-to-last big success. Even before it opened on March 10, 1959, at the Martin Beck Theatre on Broadway, *Sweet Bird of Youth* had $390,000 in advance sales. The original production closed January 30, 1960, after 375 performances.

When the play opened, the frank depictions of various corruptions were considered somewhat shocking. Touching on familiar themes for Williams (including lost youth and aging, loneliness, sex, and pretending to be what one is not), *Sweet Bird of Youth* was inspired in part by his own life, though not autobiographical. Williams had written at least eight versions of the play. One version was published in *Esquire* and another, with only two characters (Chance and the Princess), was performed in Miami, Florida, in 1956.

From the earliest Broadway production of *Sweet Bird of Youth,* critics disagreed about the play. While some saw it as another example of Williams's prowess with language and character, others found it disjointed, disorganized, and distasteful. Critical opinion generally declined over time, though scholars were interested in how the play fit in with the rest of Williams's career.

Writing about a 1975 revival of the play, Edwin Wilson of the *Wall Street Journal* wrote

Sweet Bird of Youth is not considered on a par with Mr. Williams's best work, but it has its share of his power and magic both in the characters he has created and in the music of his words. No other writer of the American theater offers the lyricism Mr. Williams does, and it can be heard here. . . .

AUTHOR BIOGRAPHY

Williams was born Thomas Lanier Williams on March 26, 1911, in Columbus, Mississippi. He was the son of Cornelius Coffin and Edwina (maiden name, Dakin) Williams. Williams's father, a traveling salesman, was rarely home. The children and their mother lived with her parents in Tennessee until 1918. That year, Cornelius Williams moved the family to St. Louis when he was hired as the sales manager for a shoe company. Though Cornelius Williams was abusive to his family, his son found solace in writing, an interest of his since childhood. By the time he was in high school, Thomas was publishing short stories in national magazines.

After graduating from high school in 1929, Williams entered the University of Missouri at Columbia. He considered becoming a journalist, but was forced to leave school after two years because the Great Depression had limited his funds. Williams went to work for his father's employer, the International Shoe Company, and was miserable. He returned to college for a year at St. Louis's Washington University before being forced to drop out again. Williams finally finished his degree at the University of Iowa in 1938. He dubbed himself Tennessee Williams in 1939, based on a nickname he acquired at Iowa because of his southern accent.

Williams had written plays as early as 1935, some of which were produced locally. He won the Group Theatre prize in 1939 based on a sampling of his plays. This prize led to wider recognition, as well as to a Rockefeller Fellowship in 1940. Williams was able to make his living writing, including a half-year stint as a screenwriter for Metro-Goldwyn-Mayer in 1943. The experience and form did not suit him, and Williams turned to plays full-time by 1944.

In 1944, Williams had a massive hit with the play *The Glass Menagerie,* which made his career. He won numerous accolades for the work, which

had some basis in Williams's own life. Between 1944 and 1972, Williams produced more than a play every two years, many of which were extremely successful. He won the Pulitzer Prize for drama twice. The first to win was what many critics consider his best play, 1947's *A Street Car Named Desire,* followed by *Cat on a Hot Tin Roof* (1955). One of Williams's last big box office hits was 1959's *Sweet Bird of Youth.*

After *Night of the Iguana* (1962), Williams's plays differed in form and content from earlier ones, and many were not critically acclaimed or commercially successful. Many were seen as derivative of his earlier work. Williams suffered a mental collapse in the late 1960s, spending several weeks in a psychiatric hospital. His last minor success was in 1972 with *Small Craft Warnings.* Williams continued to write plays as well as novels and short stories until he choked to death on February 24, 1983, in his New York hotel suite.

PLOT SUMMARY

Act 1, scene 1

Sweet Bird of Youth opens in a hotel room in St. Cloud, Florida. In bed are Princess Kosmonopolis (the alias of aging actress Alexandra del Lago) and Chance Wayne, who has come back to his hometown. While the actress sleeps, Chance drinks coffee. George Scudder appears at the door, wanting to know why Chance has returned. When Chance informs him he wants to see his mother and his girlfriend, Heavenly Finley, Scudder tells Chance that his mother recently died and was buried, and that something has happened to Heavenly. Scudder had tried and failed to contact Chance about these matters. Scudder also warns Chance that he had better leave town before Heavenly's father and brother come after him. Before leaving, Scudder reveals that he will be marrying Heavenly soon.

Chance awakens the Princess. The Princess struggles to remember who he is and where they are. It becomes apparent that Chance is her gigolo. She has been drinking heavily and using hashish, which has contributed to her memory lapse. The Princess talks about being a middle-aged actress who does not want to retire. She has recently made a movie, and when she went to the premiere, she was horrified by herself on screen. The Princess is still on the run from this experience. As her memory returns, the Princess remembers how she became involved with Chance.

The Princess wants to know what Chance wants from her. While she was in her stupor, Chance had her put him under contract with a Hollywood studio of which she owns a part. The Princess tells him that the contract has loopholes and can be invalidated. When the Princess tries to seduce him, Chance pulls out a tape-recording he made of her discussing how she smuggled hashish into the United States. Chance attempts to blackmail her into signing traveler's checks to him. The Princess is offended, but she tells him that if they make love right now, she will give him some money.

Act 1, scene 2

The Princess signs traveler's checks for Chance, but insists that she will go with him to cash them. She is afraid to be left alone. As she puts on makeup, Chance tells her his life story. He was popular here. Instead of going to college, he went to New York and was in the choruses of Broadway shows. Chance also made love to many rich women in New York, giving affection to the lonely. During the Korean War, Chance joined the Navy because the uniform looked good on him. He felt he was wasting his youth, and had a nervous breakdown. After his honorable discharge, he returned home and again become involved with Heavenly. Though they were in love, Heavenly's father, Boss Finley, would not let them marry.

Chance asks the Princess to help him by staging a phony talent contest, which he and Heavenly will win. Chance will then take Heavenly to Hollywood. The Princess does not want the publicity. Instead, she sends him down to cash the checks. Chance wants to show the town he is not washed up, and promises to return with most of the money and the car. The Princess allows him to go, hoping he will come back.

Act 2, scene 1

At Boss Finley's house, Heavenly's father is angry that Chance has returned. He calls in his son, Tom Junior. Finley wants his son to throw Chance out of town because the last time he was here he gave Heavenly a sexually transmitted disease that required her to have a hysterectomy. As they talk, Tom Junior informs him that Chance Wayne has stopped outside and is talking with Aunt Nonnie. Tom Junior calls for Aunt Nonnie, who runs into the house. The Finleys question Nonnie. Though she

Tennessee Williams

says she will get Chance to leave town, she also defends him, telling Finley that he was a nice boy before Finley destroyed him.

After Nonnie leaves, Tom Junior becomes upset with his father. Finley is running for re-election with Tom Junior on the ticket. When Finley points out Junior's failings, he strikes back with a reminder that Finley keeps a mistress, Miss Lucy, at the hotel. Tom Junior reports that Miss Lucy has said that Finley is too old to have sex. Finley becomes upset by these words.

Heavenly finally appears. Finley compliments her on her beauty. When Finley tries to suggest how she should behave, Heavenly becomes angry. She reminds him that he drove Chance away and tried to marry her off to a succession of old men. She blames him for Chance's corruption. Finley tries to buy her off with a shopping spree. He also insists that she will be at the televised rally that night at the hotel. When Heavenly refuses to go, he informs her that Chance is back in town, and that if she does not appear, Chance will be harmed.

Act 2, scene 2

At the hotel's cocktail lounge, Miss Lucy tells the bartender that Boss Finley smashed her fingers with a jewelry box for her comments about his sexual performance. The Heckler enters. When Miss Lucy learns of his intentions to bring up Heavenly's unfortunate past, she offers to help The Heckler get into the Finleys' rally.

Chance comes into the bar. Aunt Nonnie soon follows. She informs him that he must leave town. Chance shows her the contract with the Princess's studio and tells her about the talent contest. When Nonnie emphasizes the danger he is in, Chance informs her that life is not worth living without Heavenly.

Chance runs into old acquaintances at the bar. They do not treat him well, but Chance does not understand what has changed. Miss Lucy enters and talks to him. She knows the truth about Chance's life. One of the old acquaintances tells Chance about the Finley rally that night and what it is about. When the old acquaintances leave, Miss Lucy offers to take Chance to the airport.

The Princess appears, disheveled and incoherent. She chides him for leaving her alone. As Hatcher, the hotel manager, approaches them, Chance insists on taking the Princess upstairs. Boss Finley and Heavenly enter the hotel. Chance and Heavenly come face to face. Before they can say anything, Finley drags Heavenly away.

Though the Princess wants to leave, Chance has to deal with Hatcher and Tom Junior about what happened to Heavenly. Chance demands an explanation from Tom Junior. Tom Junior informs Chance that Chance gave Heavenly a disease and that it will affect the rest of her life. He tells Chance to leave town before midnight or he will be castrated. Chance gets the Princess to go to her room.

Miss Lucy and Chance watch Finley speak on television in the lounge. The Heckler asks his awkward question about Heavenly's operation. Afterwards, he is beaten. Heavenly is horrified by his question, and collapses.

Act 3

In the hotel room, the Princess is on the phone demanding a driver. Hatcher and his cronies force their way inside, insisting that she leave. She tears into them. Tom Junior enters, demanding to know where Chance is. She says she does not know, and Tom promises to get her a driver. After the men leave, Chance returns. Chance assures her that he is still her driver, though he is in no state to drive.

The Princess tells Chance that she wants him to accept his life with her. Chance calls a Hollywood gossip columnist. The Princess speaks to her and learns that her movie has done very well, which will allow her to make a great comeback. Chance intended for her to tell the columnist about two rising future stars, meaning him and Heavenly, but the Princess does not. The Princess makes plans for her return. As the Princess prepares to leave, she wants Chance to come with her. He will not leave. They both realize how time has affected them. The Princess leaves, and Tom Junior enters with other men to deal with Chance.

CHARACTERS

Bud

Bud is a St. Cloud local who used to be friendly with Chance. When Bud and friends see Chance in the hotel cocktail lounge, Bud is rather mean. Like others, he doubts much of what Chance says about himself. At the end of the play, Bud helps Tom Junior with Chance's implied castration.

Charles

Charles is a servant in the Finley household.

Alexandra del Lago

See Princess Kosmonopolis.

Heavenly Finley

Heavenly Finley is the daughter of Boss Finley and sister of Tom Junior. She is also the object of Chance Wayne's obsession. She and Chance were lovers until she contracted a sexually transmitted disease from him. Left unchecked, it led to her having a hysterectomy at a young age. Heavenly still resents the fact that her father would not let her marry Chance before he became corrupted. Despite her problems, Chance still looks at Heavenly as the symbol of his lost youth—one that he desperately wants to recapture but never does.

Tom Finley, Junior

Tom Junior is the son of Boss Finley and brother of Heavenly Finley. Like his father, he is a politician. Tom Junior does not have the power of his father, but has organized the Youth for Boss Finley club. He also acts in his father's interests in other ways. Tom Junior leads the activities to get Chance Wayne out of town. When Boss Finley gives him free reign, Tom Junior intends to castrate Chance as revenge if Chance will not leave town. At the end of the play, it seems likely this event will occur, as Chance refuses to leave.

Boss Tom J. Finley

Boss Finley is a leading political figure in St. Cloud and the father of Tom Junior and Heavenly. Finley is a harsh, domineering man, and he is incensed that Chance has returned to town. Finley would not let Chance and Heavenly marry several years ago, which contributed to Chance's life choices and indirectly led to Heavenly's disease. Though Finley is protective of his daughter, he has also tried to marry her off to many older men. Finley enjoys having power over others.

Fly

Fly is an African-American hotel waiter who serves coffee and Bromo to Chance at the beginning of Sweet Bird of Youth. Chance promises him a big tip because Fly remembers Chance from happier times. In act 2, scene 2, Fly delivers a message to Chance, who only gives it a cursory glance.

Dan Hatcher

Hatcher is the assistant manager of the Royal Palms Hotel in St. Cloud, Florida, where Princess Kosmonopolis and Chance Wayne are staying and where Boss Finley's political rally is held. Hatcher is the one who informs George Scudder that Chance has checked into the hotel. Hatcher works with the Finley family to get Chance to leave the hotel and the town.

The Heckler

The Heckler is a hillbilly who attends Boss Finley's political rallies and asks questions to expose his hypocrisy. Miss Lucy facilitates his admission into the rally at the Royal Palms Hotel. He asks his question, which concerns the operation that Heavenly Finley underwent. After he asks it, he is beaten up.

Princess Kosmonopolis

Princess Kosmonopolis is the alias of middle-aged actress Alexandra del Lago, a central character of the play. She is ashamed of her life as an aging starlet and embarrassed by her latest work. At the beginning of the play, the Princess does not know who Chance is or where they are.

MEDIA ADAPTATIONS

- *Sweet Bird of Youth* was adapted as a film in 1962. This version was directed and written by Richard Brooks. It stars Paul Newman as Chance Wayne, Geraldine Page as Alexandra del Lago, and Ed Begley as Boss Finley.

- Another film version was made in 1987. It was directed by Zeinabu Irene Davis.

- A made-for-television version was filmed in 1989. It stars Mark Harmon as Chance Wayne, Elizabeth Taylor as Alexandra del Lago, and Cheryl Paris as Heavenly Finley.

The Princess slowly remembers that Chance is her driver/gigolo. She does not want to be left alone but knows that while Chance has been taking care of her, he wants something in return. Chance wants her to get him a studio contract; a means for getting Heavenly out of town; and material symbols of success to show off to the locals. Though the Princess gives him the first and last temporarily, this does not change Chance's destiny.

The Princess tries to help Chance get out of town, but he will not leave. Like Chance, the Princess is afraid of aging and the effects of time, but she is more realistic about her situation than Chance is about his.

Miss Lucy

Miss Lucy is the mistress of Boss Finley. She lives in the hotel in a room paid for by him. Finley's power over her is important to him. When he learns that she has said he is too old to have sex, he hurts her fingers by snapping a jewelry box on them. For this, Miss Lucy takes revenge by enabling The Heckler to get inside the rally. While she wants him to hurt Boss Finley, she is not fully comfortable with The Heckler's implied attack on Heavenly. Miss Lucy is one of the many people who tell Chance that he should not be in town, and she offers to take him to the airport.

Aunt Nonnie

Aunt Nonnie is the sister of Chance Wayne's dead mother, though she now seems to work and/or live with the Finleys. It was she who encouraged and facilitated the previous relationship between Heavenly and Chance, a fact that Boss Finley resents. Nonnie tries to get Chance to leave town. She also begs Boss Finley and Tom Junior not to resort to violence against Chance. It is Nonnie who realizes that Chance's obsessions with Heavenly and with acting are symptoms of a futile desire to return to his pure youthful state.

Scotty

Scotty is a St. Cloud local who used to be friendly with Chance. When Scotty and friends run into Chance in the hotel cocktail lounge, Scotty is rather cold. He doubts much of what Chance says about himself. At the end of the play, Scotty helps Tom Junior with Chance's implied castration.

George Scudder

George Scudder is a doctor in St. Cloud and the chief of staff at the local hospital. He performed the operation on Heavenly after her sexually transmitted disease ran rampant. Scudder also is allegedly Heavenly Finley's future husband. Though Scudder owes much to the Finley family, it is he who comes to Chance at the beginning of the play to learn his intentions and warn him of the trouble he faces. Scudder informs Chance that his mother has died and that Heavenly has had troubles since Chance last saw her. Scudder had tried previously to notify Chance about both matters, but Chance was impossible to track down. When Tom Junior wants Scudder to be part of his plans to take revenge on Chance, Scudder declines because it might jeopardize his career.

Stuff

Stuff is the bartender in the Royal Palms Hotel's cocktail lounge. He has held this job for only a short time, having previously worked as a soda jerk at a drugstore. Though Stuff once admired Chance, he is now a member of the Youth for Boss Finley club. It is he who tells Tom Junior what Miss Lucy says about Boss Finley's inability to have sex. This gets Finley's mistress in trouble and leads to revenge by Finley.

Chance Wayne

Chance Wayne is one of the central characters in the play. He has returned to his hometown of St. Cloud to see his mother and to take his girlfriend, Heavenly, away to Hollywood. Chance has arrived under difficult circumstances. He is now twenty-nine years old, and his primary occupation is gigolo. When Chance originally left St. Cloud, it was to be an actor. While he has had some opportunities, he has been unable to capitalize on them. Chance had better luck making love to rich New York socialites, a life to which he returned after a stint in the Navy and recovery from a breakdown.

Because Chance's lifestyle made it hard to find him, he does not know that his mother has died and that Heavenly has suffered a devastating loss because of a sexually transmitted disease that he gave her on one of his previous visits. Though Chance still loves Heavenly, he is clueless about the effects his actions have had on her and on the town.

Chance has also come to St. Cloud to prove to everyone that he is a success. While Chance is obsessed with recapturing his fading youth, he also has some compassion for the Princess. At the end, Chance will not leave town despite repeated warnings that he will be harmed (castrated) if he remains.

THEMES

Sex

Throughout *Sweet Bird of Youth,* the idea of sex and its consequences affects nearly every character's life. Having failed to make it as an actor, Chance's ''career'' consists of working as a gigolo, selling sex and/or companionship to rich, lonely, often older ladies. He met Princess Kosmonopolis while employed at a Palm Beach resort. Because of Chance's liaisons with many women, he gave his girlfriend, Heavenly Finley, a venereal disease the last time they were together. The innocent Heavenly unknowingly let the disease progress unchecked and eventually had to have a hysterectomy. Sex robbed her of her youth and her ability to have children. Because of this incident, everyone wants Chance to leave town, either for his own safety or to punish him. He does not leave, and it is implied at the end of the play that he will be castrated.

For some characters, sex is related to power and money. Princess Kosmonopolis forces Chance to have sex with her at the end of act 1, scene 1. Because she is in a fog about him during the scene, he tries to take advantage of the situation, demanding that she sign some traveler's checks for him. She only does this after the act is consummated. Along similar lines, Boss Finley keeps a mistress, Miss Lucy, at the hotel. When he learns that she has claimed he is too old to have sex, he takes his revenge. He brings her a diamond clip in a jewelry box, but snaps it closed on her fingers, injuring her, when she opens it. He then leaves her, taking the gift with him. The theme of sex drives much of the action of the play, directly or indirectly.

Time, Youth, and Aging

Many characters in *Sweet Bird of Youth* are obsessed with aging and the ravages of time. Though Chance is twenty-nine years old with thinning hair, he is still handsome enough to attract women like the Princess. Yet the only woman Chance truly wants is Heavenly, who shared a romance with him beginning when she was fifteen years old. Several characters point out to him that she has changed. Because of the sexually transmitted disease Chance gave her, she has had a hysterectomy. Heavenly tells her father at one point, ''Scudder's knife cut the youth out of my body, made me an old childless woman. Dry, cold, empty, like an old woman.''

But Chance believes that if he can take Heavenly away, nothing will have changed; they will move to Hollywood, and Chance will finally be successful as an actor. Heavenly is a symbol of his youth and his promise that he has lost along the way. When Chance and Heavenly meet face to face, they can say nothing to each other. Still Chance cannot give up on his last vestige of hope and submits to what is implied to be castration at the end of the play.

Princess Kosmonopolis shares Chance's fear of aging. She is really Alexandra del Lago, a middle-aged movie actress who knows that Hollywood favors the young. She does not want to retire, but ran out of the premiere of her latest movie when she saw herself on screen. The Princess is hiding out from her identity, drinking and smoking hashish in hopes of dulling the pain. Chance is a sympathetic distraction, though she is under no illusions about his intentions.

At the end of the play, when Chance tries one last time to get her to help him and Heavenly escape by telling a Hollywood gossip columnist about them as actors, the Princess learns that all is not lost. Her movie is a hit and she is praised as having made a comeback. She never mentions Chance and Heavenly. Though the Princess realizes that her victory over time is only temporary, and that eventually she

TOPICS FOR FURTHER STUDY

- Compare and contrast the character and motivations of Chance Wayne in *Sweet Bird of Youth* with Val Xavier in *Orpheus Descending* (1956). What kinds of pressures are the young men under and how do they handle them?

- Research racial politics in the South in this time period. Was the castration of an innocent African American in the play realistic? Would such a crime have been prosecuted? How has the political situation in the South changed since this time period?

- Compare and contrast *Sweet Bird of Youth* with the film *Sunset Boulevard* (1950). Consider how both the play and the film focus on movie starlets dealing with issues of aging. How do the different artistic forms affect content?

- Research the psychology of people who heckle politicians, entertainers, and other public figures. Why do they heckle? Is heckling an effective means of getting a point across?

will be tossed aside by Hollywood because of her age, she relishes her short-term victory. Aging and time are parts of life that cannot be avoided, but only Chance cannot accept that by the end of the play.

Politics and Hypocrisy

While many characters have their hypocritical moments and attitudes, Boss Finley is the biggest example of hypocrisy in the play. Much of this hypocrisy is linked to political ambitions, though some of it is personal as well. An upcoming political election is an important part of the play. Finley is having a televised rally to address voters about the recent brutal castration of an innocent African American. Those who castrated the man wanted to make sure it was known that white women would be protected in Florida. While Boss Finley wants to keep white blood ''pure,'' he condemns the crime in his speech and calls himself a friend to men both black and white.

When The Heckler asks a question related to Boss's hypocrisy, he is beaten. He is the only character who directly challenges the Boss. Chance only does so indirectly. Because Chance will not leave town, he, too, is castrated, with the implicit consent of Boss Finley. Heavenly points out another hypocrisy of her father's. While he married her mother for love, he will not allow his daughter the same privilege. He uses her, and others, to show how powerful he is, though this power is invariably linked to politics and/or hypocrisy.

STYLE

Setting

Sweet Bird of Youth is a drama set at the time the play was written in the late 1950s. All the action takes place in two settings over the course of one day, an Easter Sunday, in the Gulf Coast city of St. Cloud, Florida. A majority of the action occurs in the Royal Palms Hotel. All of acts 1 and 3 take place in one room in the hotel. The Princess and Chance Wayne occupy this room. Act 2, scene 2 occurs in the cocktail lounge and palm garden of the hotel. The other setting is the home of Boss Finley, specifically the terrace. These settings emphasize a specific time and place—the South during the 1950s, when racial and class tensions were still high. Chance has chosen to return to St. Cloud to reclaim his girlfriend Heavenly and his youth. Yet much of the play takes place in a hotel where he is really not welcome, not where Chance lived as a youth or other places where he might have more fond memories of the past (though he did work in the hotel at one time). This impersonal setting underscores the kind of life Chance now leads and its problems. A hotel is also a central place where the community meets, creating opportunities for Chance to run into people that he used to know.

Special Effects and Images

Throughout *Sweet Bird of Youth*, Williams calls for a cyclorama (a large wall placed at the back of a room or stage) on which to project images onto the stage behind the action. The images are not supposed to be realistic, but are intended to help set the mood of the play and underscore the setting. For most of the play, the image is a grove of palm trees blowing in the wind. The wind goes from soft to loud, depending on the action of the scene. When the wind is loud, it blends with the musical score in a specific sound/song called "The Lament." This is

used in act 1, scene 1, for example, when the Princess' memory finally returns and she first mentions that she is in hiding after what she believes has been a disastrous career move. Other images include a daytime image of the calm sea and sky, and a nighttime scene of a palm garden with branches and stars.

A significant use of the cyclorama occurs in act 2, scene 2, during Boss Finley's speech. An effect is created so that Miss Lucy, Chance, Stuff, and others are watching the televised rally in the hotel bar while it is occurring on the same stage. Because the rally takes place in another part of the hotel, Boss Finley, Heavenly, Tom Junior, and the Heckler, among others, walk by the bar and off stage into the ballroom. Those in the bar view the rally by "turning on" the television, which is actually a projection of a big television screen against a fourth wall on the set.

The volume of the television is very loud at first, making it seem as if Boss Finley is yelling. Stuff, a Finley supporter, is happy with the volume. Miss Lucy complains about the noise and turns the sound down, only to have Stuff turn it up again. When Stuff turns it up, Boss Finley is saying that he does not condone the castration of the innocent black man. Moments later, the Heckler appears on screen. Projecting the television in this matter emphasizes the kind of power Boss Finley thinks he has. He believes he is bigger and louder than anyone else. Because of their tense relationship with Boss, both Miss Lucy and Chance want to turn him down, hearing his message but limiting his impact.

Symbolism

Sweet Bird of Youth is replete with symbolism. All the action takes place on Easter Sunday. The use of this symbolic day of rebirth has been interpreted in several different ways. Boss Finley claims he has been reborn during the rally. On Good Friday, his effigy was burned at a local university, yet he is still alive and in charge on Sunday, preaching on television. By his side is his daughter, Heavenly, who has just been publicly humiliated by the Heckler. The Heckler is severely beaten. But Boss Finley rises above it all. Some critics believe that Chance Wayne has undergone a compacted reversal of the Easter cycle, beginning with Chance's resurrection in the morning and castration (crucifixion) at night.

Another use of symbolism in the play is found in some of the characters' names. Chance Wayne's chances in life are indeed on the wane. Heavenly

Finley's first name brings up a number of contradictions. She may still be beautiful, and heavenly to Chance and her father, but she is dead on the inside because her love has been denied and she has had her childbearing abilities taken away at an early age. Though Princess Kosmonopolis is only the alias of the actress Alexandra del Lago, she acts like royalty. She does not accept being condescended to and is always in charge. Kosmonopolis suggests Greek words that mean worldly and city. She is above the petty world of St. Cloud, merely using it for cover as she hides from her real world. These kinds of symbols enrich the text and add some definition to the characters.

HISTORICAL CONTEXT

In 1959, the United States was on the verge of major transitions, primarily on the home front, though the ever-escalating Cold War between America and the U.S.S.R. was also a constant threat. The country was expanding. Two new states were admitted in 1959: Alaska and Hawaii. Republican President Dwight D. Eisenhower was near the end of his second term. In 1960, Democrat John F. Kennedy would be elected to the presidency, defeating Eisenhower's vice president, Richard M. Nixon.

Many observers believed that Nixon lost at least partly because of his image and attitudes expressed during televised debates with Kennedy. In the 1950s, politicians were televised for the first time. Senator Joseph McCarthy's anti-Communist hearings were televised. Conventions were aired for the first time in 1952. In 1959, the Federal Communications Commission upheld an equal time rule for political candidates. The power of television was soon realized, then exploited, by politicians.

Eisenhower's United States was relatively economically strong in 1959. The country was recovering from a recession in 1957–1958, but generally sound. His government spending bill was scaled down, putting fiscal responsibility before both military and domestic concerns. Credit cards had only recently been introduced; they would have a great effect on the American economy in the coming decades. American Express issued its first credit cards in 1958.

One big issue in the late 1950s was civil rights. The civil rights movement that exploded in the 1960s was based in part on events of the 1950s. In 1954, the Supreme Court handed down a landmark decision in *Brown v. Board of Education*. This case focused on education, addressing the legality of separate schools for whites and blacks. The court ruled that separate was not equal, and that most schools for blacks were far inferior to those attended primarily by whites. Court-ordered desegregation of schools became a public tug-of-war. The actual process of integration was very slow, and many southern states, especially Virginia, fought integration, even as late as 1959 and beyond. True integration was not completed until the 1960s.

In 1959, Eisenhower tried to convince Congress to enact a seven-point civil rights program in a special session. Despite such measures, states like Tennessee continued to hold white primaries in which blacks could not vote. Racism was still rampant in the South. In 1956, Emmett Till was murdered for allegedly whistling at and/or assaulting a white woman. His killers were acquitted, though they were obviously, and later admittedly, guilty. Events like the castration of an innocent African American mentioned in *Sweet Bird of Youth* were not unheard of.

Despite such crimes, moral standards were changing in the United States. In 1959, the Supreme Court ruled that the postmaster general could not decide what was too obscene to be sent through the mail. The case concerned a book by D. H. Lawrence, *Lady Chatterly's Lover*. While single men were seen as swinging bachelors, women were supposed to be desirable, but untouchable until marriage. Yet the Kinsey Report on sexual activities of Americans in the early 1950s showed that Americans regularly had extramarital sex and that homosexuality was common. Depictions and discussions of sex became more common in movies, novels, and music. Though the government had organized public health officials to diagnose and treat venereal diseases in the post-World War II period, there was a slight rise in rates of syphilis and gonorrhea at the end of the 1950s as complacency set in.

Women's roles were also changing in this time period. More women were working outside of the home, but most were limited to jobs in the service industry or to clerical and assembly line positions. Fewer women attended college than in the 1940s. Only about thirty-five percent of college students were women at the end of the decade, and thirty-seven percent of those left before graduation, most to get married. Career options were limited. There was only one woman in the United States Senate in

COMPARE & CONTRAST

- **1959:** Political use of television is still in its infancy, though it soon becomes a major force in elections.

  Today: The power of the internet is still limited for politicians, but is expected to become a big factor in the coming years.

- **1959:** There are limited roles for older actresses in Hollywood movies, primarily mother and grandmother-type roles.

  Today: While there is a still an emphasis on youth in Hollywood, there is a greater variety of roles for older women in movies, reflecting the many roles women play in society.

- **1959:** Images of sex and violence are limited in the movies, in part because of a code that restricts such images.

  Today: While there is a movie ratings system in place, there are only tenuous limits on how sex and violence are depicted.

- **1959:** Sexually transmitted diseases are diagnosed and treated in both men and women, though many, especially young women, are not taught how to avoid getting them.

  Today: Because of the AIDS epidemic in the 1980s and better sexual education, many young women (and men) are aware of the possibilities of sexually transmitted diseases and know how to avoid getting them.

1959, Margaret Chase Smith. In the 1960s, women's roles would change and career options would start to expand. By the 1970s, there would be a burgeoning feminist movement. Big changes in American life were on the horizon in 1959.

CRITICAL OVERVIEW

When *Sweet Bird of Youth* made its debut in 1959, it received a mixed reception. While some critics thought it was another example of Williams's genius, others saw it as lesser Williams. Both sides, however, generally agreed that Williams's command of language had not diminished, and the play was a box office success. Over time, *Sweet Bird of Youth* came to be regarded as an example of Williams on the decline.

Walter Kerr of *New York Herald Tribune* was one critic who praised the play, though like most critics he had some problems with it. He wrote, ''There isn't a moment during *Sweet Bird of Youth* that it isn't seething to explode in the theater's face.

Mr. Williams's newest play is a succession of fuses, deliberately—and for the most part magnificently—lighted.''

Several critics who liked *Sweet Bird of Youth,* and even some who did not, believed that Act 2 did not fit well within the play's structure. For example, Richard Watts, Jr., of the *New York Post* praised the power of Williams's writing but added, ''What worried me were a number of loose ends, the lack of complete fulfillment of several characters, and the hinting at themes that were not developed.''

Among those critics who praised the play, some were disturbed by the play's content and themes, which were rather shocking for their day. Brooks Atkinson of the *New York Times* wrote, ''It is a play that ranges wide through the lower depths, touching on political violence as well as diseases of mind and body. But it has the spontaneity of an improvisation.'' John Chapman of the *Daily News* wrote, ''I don't see how it can be liked, in the sense that one might like the simple joys of *The Music Man,* but it cannot be ignored. . . .'' He added, ''Seeing . . . *Sweet Bird of Youth* . . . is something like finding oneself, unexpectedly and without premeditation, in a place one wouldn't be caught dead in.''

Other critics were more distressed by the content of *Sweet Bird of Youth.* Marya Mannes of *The Reporter* wrote

> The laughter at the Martin Beck Theatre in New York these nights is made, I think, of . . . a fascination with and amusement in depravity, sickness, and degradation which makes me equally disturbed at the public, the playwright, and those critics who have hailed *Sweet Bird of Youth* as one of Tennessee Williams's 'finest dramas' and 'a play of overwhelming force.'

Along similar lines, Kenneth Tynan of the *New Yorker* argued

> For my part, I recognized nothing but a special, rarefied situation that had been carried to extremes of cruelty with a total disregard for probability, human relevance, and the laws of dramatic structure. My brain was buzzing with questions. . . . I suspect that *Sweet Bird of Youth* will be of more interest to Mr. Williams's biographers than to lovers of the theatre.

Other critics also dismissed the play as only interesting to those who are fans of Williams. Robert Brustein of *Encounter* argued

> the play is interesting primarily if you are interested in its author. As dramatic art, it is disturbingly bad—aimless, dishonest, and crudely melodramatic—in a way that Williams's writing has not been bad since his early play, *Battle of Angels.* But if the latter failed because its author did not sufficiently understand his characters, *Sweet Bird of Youth* suffers both from his ignorance of, and obsession with, himself.

Harold Clurman of *The Nation* concurred. He wrote, ''Its place in the author's development and its fascination for the audience strike me as more significant than its value as drama.''

Several other critics disliked the play because of dramatic failings. Brustein, writing this time in *Hudson Review,* judged

> Williams seems less concerned with dramatic verisimilitude than with communicating some hazy notions about such disparate items as Sex, Youth, Time, Corruption, Purity, Castration, Politics, and The South. As a result, the action of the play is patently untrue, the language is flat and circumlocutory, the form disjointed and rambling, and the characters—possessing little coherence of their own—function only as a thin dressing for these bare thematic bones.

In short, Henry Hewes of *Saturday Review* concluded, ''the total play . . . adds up to a good deal less than the sum of its parts.''

Sweet Bird of Youth was revived several times over the years, and the critics remained divided, with most having serious problems with the play. Of a 1975 revival at the Brooklyn Academy of Music, Gina Mallet of *Time* wrote

Age has not refined *Sweet Bird*'s effulgent bathos. The reduction of personality to sex organs is the dynamic of skin flicks and soap operas. . . . Today it seems fatally misconceived, a sentimental melodrama instead of a savage, black comedy on southern mores.

A few critics were still impressed by Williams's creation, including Howard Kissel of *Women's Wear Daily.* He wrote

> In its time, *Sweet Bird of Youth* was a powerful emotional experience; now it impresses one mainly because of the deliciousness of the language. The characters may not be as tragic as they once seemed, but they still have credibility as American archetypes.

CRITICISM

Annette Petrusso

Petrusso is a freelance writer and editor living in Austin, Texas. In this essay, Petrusso argues that the character of Chance Wayne is focused on one thing—denying the reality of his life—and analyzes his futile quest.

Reviewing the original Broadway production of Tennessee Williams's *Sweet Bird of Youth,* Frank Aston of *New York World-Telegram and The Sun* pointed out, ''He [Chance Wayne] is racing toward something he can never gain, while she [Princess Kosmonopolis] is fleeing the ruins of something she never had.'' Implicit in Aston's observation is that both of these characters—the primary ones in the play—are living in denial of their current realities. *Sweet Bird of Youth* explores the desperation and panic of Chance Wayne. This essay looks at Chance, his reality, how he handles it, and its evolution to a tragic end.

Chance Wayne is a twenty-nine-year-old man who cannot accept what his life has become. He has come home to St. Cloud, Florida, to try to make himself and everyone else believe that his life is what it is not. When Chance was a young man growing up, he was popular and good-looking. He attracted numerous women and was friends with the sons of community leaders. Instead of going to college, Chance left home to pursue a career as an actor. He had numerous chances to make a success of it, but felt blocked by something. He only got as far as the chorus of a Broadway production of *Oklahoma.* He learned a profitable way of life along the way: Chance began sleeping with rich women as a means of supporting himself. Over time, this has become his career. Indeed, the only reason he is

Robert Knepper and Clare Higgins in a scene from a production of Sweet Bird of Youth *at London's Royal National Theatre.*

in St. Cloud is because he is with an aging actress, Alexandra del Lago (a. k. a. The Princess Kosmonopolis). He met her when he was working as a gigolo in Palm Beach, Florida.

It is Chance's secondary career that has created problems in his life. For many years he has been in love with Heavenly Finley, the daughter of local political bigwig Boss Tom Finley. Chance and Heavenly began a sexual relationship when she was 15 years old. They would have married if Boss Finley had not intervened and refused to allow it. Despite Boss Finley's directive, Chance and Heavenly have seen each other periodically when Chance has visited St. Cloud. One of the last times Chance was there, Heavenly contracted an unnamed venereal disease from him. He got it from one of the rich women with whom he was having a sexual relationship. Because of Heavenly's naiveté about what was wrong with her, the disease ran out of control and she was forced to have a hysterectomy at a very young age.

At the beginning of *Sweet Bird of Youth,* Chance is unaware of the harm he has caused Heavenly, or even that his own mother has died. Because Chance's "work" requires him to move often, no one was able to find him to tell him what has happened. This situation is telling. While Chance claims to still love Heavenly and is saddened by his mother's death when he learns of it, he apparently has made no effort to get in touch with them, even through an intermediary. This implies that Chance believes nothing has changed in St. Cloud. He has idealized his hometown to a great degree. The town once praised him for his small acting triumphs. While some things have changed, Boss Finley's intense disliking for Chance has not.

Because Chance believes that no one in St. Cloud knows that he has failed to have a solid acting career, he tries to use this ignorance to build himself up in their eyes as well as his own. Though the Princess purchased his clothes, the wad of money he flashes in act 2 is hers, and the Cadillac he drives is hers, Chance thinks he can fool everyone in St. Cloud into believing that he is a successful actor. Chance denies the reality of his situation over and over again. As the play progresses, these fantasies about his life grow deeper, and he grows more out of touch.

In act 1, it is revealed that Chance has tricked the Princess into giving him a movie contract at a studio she owns a stake in. Though the Princess tells him the contract is full of loopholes, Chance conveniently forgets such statements. In the same act, Chance also tries to force her to pretend to host a talent contest for two young future stars. The outcome would be rigged, of course, so that Chance and Heavenly would win and be able to leave for Hollywood together. These kinds of fantasies reveal much about Chance and his desperation. If nothing else, he is extremely self-absorbed and self-centered. He has not asked Heavenly if she wants to go with him, but assumes she does, even after Dr. Scudder has told Chance that Scudder will be marrying her the following month. It also shows that he believes he can control the Princess in her depressed state. He is wrong on both counts.

By act 2, scene 2, which takes place in the hotel lounge, Chance has grown more desperate. He laid out his plans in act 1, and is now acting on them, but this scene shows just how out of touch with reality Chance is. He acts as if he is still the most popular man in town. He shows Aunt Nonnie, Miss Lucy, and just about everyone who will look his contract with Princess's studio. When Chance describes the contest to Aunt Nonnie, he describes it as a beauty contest just for Heavenly so that she can win and then leave with him. Chance changes his stories as needed.

Also in this scene, Chance has the piano player play ''his song,'' but none of the former friends who have come in will sing with him. Chance denies that he has worked as a beach boy in Palm Beach, but makes up a movie called *Youth* that he will allegedly be starring in. This is to impress two men in his old group as well as Boss Finley's mistress, Miss Lucy. They know the truth, however. Scotty, one of the men, reveals that he knows the Cadillac is not Chance's. When the Princess comes down to the lounge to find him, she also knows the truth about him, though he cannot accept it yet. She tells him, ''Chance, when I saw you driving under the window with your head held high, with that terrible stiff-necked pride of the defeated which I know so well; I knew that your come-back had been a failure like mine.''

Despite such insights, Chance clings to his vain hopes, even after he comes face to face with Heavenly in the hotel lounge. Though Chance is doing all of this for Heavenly—or, more correctly, for his idealization of her—when he is looking her in the eye, he cannot say anything. He allows her to be taken off by her father and brother after a few moments. Chance never fights directly for what he wants. He knows by this point that he cannot have

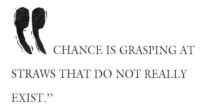

CHANCE IS GRASPING AT STRAWS THAT DO NOT REALLY EXIST.''

Heavenly and cannot be what he wants to be. Still, he denies the truth of the situation. As Chance watches Heavenly on television next to her father as he gives his speech, Chance tells Miss Lucy, ''Tonight, God help me, somehow, I don't know how, but somehow I'll take her out of St. Cloud. I'll wake up in her arms, and I'll give her life back to her.''

Chance has not given up at the beginning of act 3. He again tries to force the Princess into helping him. Though the Princess is prepared to continue to use him as her employee, he will not let go of the idealized life he wants. Chance calls Sally Powers, a famous Hollywood gossip columnist, and forces the Princess to talk to her. His idea is that the Princess will tell Powers about him and Heavenly, two future movie stars. The plan backfires when Powers informs the Princess that her latest movie is anything but the disaster the actress thought it was. She is back on top, at least temporarily. The Princess never mentions Chance and Heavenly. The flaws of Chance's desperate plan are obvious. Even if the Princess had gotten Powers to mention them as future stars, how would the situation have changed? Chance is grasping at straws that do not really exist.

Chance is told numerous times to leave town and is given several opportunities to do so. He refuses to leave with either Miss Lucy or the Princess in act 2, scene 2, and they are just two of several characters that warn him. But Chance cannot do it. This wanna-be actor is performing the role of his life. He cannot let go of the idea that Heavenly is his, and that he is more than a gigolo. He has set himself up in a losing situation, which he realizes by the end. He says in the last pages of the play, ''Something's got to mean something, don't it, Princess? I mean like your life means nothing, except that you never could make it, always almost, never quite?'' Chance has never outgrown St. Cloud and the role he played there. The world may have been Chance's stage, but the folks back at home in St. Cloud were the only audience he cared about. When that is gone, there is nothing left for Chance.

Source: Annette Petrusso, in an essay for *Drama for Students,* Gale Group, 2001.

Alice Griffin

In the following review, Griffin examines Sweet Bird of Youth *as a 'forceful' and 'compassionate' drama that highlights Williams' theme of 'time as the enemy.'*

Sweet Bird of Youth is Williams's most eloquent expression of his recurrent theme that time is "the enemy." In the face of time's relentless advance, transient youth takes flight, deserting those who trusted it. In one of the finest examples of Williams's plastic theater the theme pervades not only the characterization but also the words and action, as well as the setting and sound. It is a forceful and compassionate drama of one decisive day in the lives of a man and a woman played out against a background of sleazy politics and impending violence in a small Southern town.

The female lead is a Hollywood star who reluctantly retired when her youth and beauty faded. While traveling incognito, she changes her name from Alexandra Del Lago to Princess Kosmonopolis, from Williams's recurring symbolic rural lake to the city and Cinderella's ultimate title. Her twenty-nine-year-old male escort is to suffer shock after shock as he comes to realize that appearance and youth, on which he has staked his life so far, must inevitably go down to defeat by "the enemy, time." Gambling on his good looks, he expected to achieve fame and fortune in the movies and so far has gone from bit parts to beach boy, encouraged by what Williams sees as "the Cinderella story . . . our favorite national myth, the cornerstone of the film industry, if not of the Democracy itself." Appropriately, his name is Chance.

The play, like others by Williams, takes the form of a visit. The action begins with the couple's arrival on Easter Day, implying hope. But by the end only despair is left for Chance. As the play opens, they have checked in at "a fashionable hotel somewhere along the Gulf Coast, in a town called in St. Cloud," Chance's hometown, where in high school he was a "star."

Act 1 takes place in their hotel suite, where literally and figuratively circling each other, Chance and the Princess reveal the immediate and distant past, which brought them to the present instant. She is traveling in style, fleeing from failure. So shocked was she at her appearance in close-up at her come-back film's premiere that she ran up the aisle and out of the theater, in "interminable retreat from the city of flames." She seeks refuge in drink, drugs, and sex. Chance has made this detour on his trip with the Princess to show off in his hometown the expensive clothes, the Cadillac, and the acting contract the Princess has signed with him during their journey, "notarized and witnessed by three strangers found in a bar." Besides Hollywood stardom Chance has another impossible dream, to marry his hometown sweetheart, Heavenly, his "one true love," whose father has other ideas for her future.

In some ways the Princess represents Chance's dream of fame, although even he can see that she is far from happy, but she has one thing Chance lacks—talent. Chance brags that he had won an acting contest; the truth is that he received only honorable mention. Yet his illusions of stardom may be realized by means of the contract, which he will attempt to enforce by blackmailing the Princess after he has secretly tape-recorded her using drugs. But age and experience will be on her side. She is a survivor. Chance, who has only his youth and good looks, is destined to be a victim of time.

As the Princess lies asleep, a mask over her eyes blotting out the reality she cannot face, the first caller at their suite is young Doctor Scudder. He warns Chance to leave town; as a "criminal degenerate," he is threatened with castration for infecting "a certain girl," who is now engaged to the doctor. Although Chance and Heavenly have been lovers since high school, her father will allow her to marry only if the man is wealthy. This has led to Chance's pursuit of easy money as a gigolo to rich women, but he has gained nothing but a venereal disease. Unknowingly, he has transmitted it to Heavenly. The events of the day and the relationship with the Princess destroy Chance's dreams and teach him the bitter lesson that his youth will desert him as he reaches the noon of his life.

The Princess and Chance are among Williams's best character creations. She recognizes that she is a "monster," but she has confidence in her talent. She also is realistic about the ravages of time, recognizing the transience of her comeback (which she is to learn later has been successful). She is imperious, tough, self-indulgent, vulnerable, and alone. She tries to reach out when she feels some stirring in her heart for Chance, and there is the hope of caring companionship, if not love, between them. But when he rejects her she realizes that she is, and always will be, a loner. She knows she has to make it alone; she is not dependent on "the kindness of strangers." (Although one commentator classifies her with "women who have known happiness but who have lost their mates and who try to overcome the loss," there seems to be little justification for this in the text.)

The Princess is aware, as Williams points out in his stage directions, that "the clock is equally relentless to them both." Her long aria in act 1 explains that she retired from films because her looks were fading and her youth was gone, but she was still "unsatisfied and raging":

> PRINCESS: . . . If I had just been old but you see, I wasn't old. . . .
>
> I just wasn't young, not young, young.
>
> I just wasn't young anymore. . . .
>
> CHANCE: Nobody's young anymore. . . .
>
> (all Williams's ellipses)

The play's change of setting and shift of emphasis between acts 1 and 2 had its critics and its defenders. As Walter Kerr wryly observes, "*Sweet Bird of Youth* was. . . . quickly popular, and quickly attacked. Many things were said: that the political second act was the *real* play and should have been developed, that the personal story of the first and third acts constituted the *real* play and that the second should have been omitted." While Benjamin Nelson criticizes the play's "blatant lack of unity" and claims that "act one has almost nothing to do with act two," careful observation indicates that act 2 dramatizes conflicts established in act 1, namely between Chance and Boss Finley, Chance and the peers he left behind, and Chance and the Princess.

The act is a merciless mirror of small-town prejudice and its antagonism, rooted in envy, toward Chance. Scene 1 takes place on Boss Finley's plantation, always inaccessible to Chance because he was born on the wrong side of the tracks, and scene 2 is set in the hotel cocktail lounge where Chance's former pals, now his enemies, congregate. Not that Chance's condescending attitude endears him to these men. A reminder of his high school dreams of Hollywood stardom is his confiding to the bartender, whose job Chance formerly held, that he designed the uniform, based on a costume Victor Mature wore in a foreign legion film, and, he says, "I looked better in it than he did."

In scene 2 Williams creates in the cocktail lounge, almost entirely through offstage effects, all the hoopla and hype of a political rally. Car sirens,

WHAT DO I READ NEXT?

- *Suddenly Last Summer*, a play written by Williams in 1958, shares thematic and dramatic concerns with *Sweet Bird of Youth*.

- *The Little Foxes*, a play written by Lillian Hellman in 1939, concerns rivalries and disloyalties in a southern family.

- *Orpheus Descending*, a play written by Williams in 1956, has themes and characters similar to *Sweet Bird*.

- *Midnight in the Garden of Good and Evil: A Savannah Story*, a novel by John Berendt published in 1994, also concerns sexual mores and eccentrics in the South.

- *The Enemy Time* is a play by Williams published in *Theatre* in March 1959. This one-act play was an early version of *Sweet Bird of Youth*.

band music, headlights, and flashbulbs herald Boss Finley's arrival with Tom Junior and Heavenly, as they march through on their way to the platform in the ballroom, where Boss will deliver on "all-South-wide TV" his "Voice of God" speech. (A Cinderella figure himself, Boss rose from obscurity to prominence when, he claims, God spoke to him.) He says God told him to take violent action against "all of them that want to adulterate the pure white blood of the South." At the bar Miss Lucy, Boss's mistress, whom he has treated cruelly, protects the Heckler from discovery. When she comments that Boss "honestly believes" God has spoken to him, the Heckler counters: "I believe that the silence of God, the absolute speechlessness of Him is a long, long and awful thing that the whole world is lost because of. I think it's yet to be broken to any man, living or any yet lived on earth,—no exceptions, and least of all Boss Finley."

Then the back wall of the set becomes a huge television screen, with Boss's head filling the screen as he warns of the threat of "blood pollution" from the black race. In counterpoint to the speech Miss

"CONSTANT REMINDERS OF
THE PASSING OF TIME AND OF
YOUTH ARE WILLIAMS'S SYMBOLS OF
THE CLOCK AND THE MIRROR."

Lucy is warning Chance to leave: as punishment for infecting Heavenly, he has been threatened with the same fate as that suffered by a black man apprehended at random—castration.

On the TV screen the camera swings to the Heckler interrupting Boss Finley with a question about Heavenly's operation, then we see Boss trying to quell the outbreak of disturbance, and then, offscreen, the Heckler comes tumbling down the lounge stairs, beaten by Finley's henchmen. In eight minutes of sheer theatricality Williams has left no doubt of the threat to the state and the threat to Chance by the sanctimonious preacher of hate. Although Williams states "social consciousness . . . has marked most of my writing," and the truth of his remark can be seen in the wider implications of his works, this is the only specific intrusion of politics in the major plays. It dramatizes the dangers inherent in the Boss Finleys who claim God has spoken to them and directs their actions. This climactic scene closes act 2 with political conflict, while act 3 brings to a head the personal conflict between Chance and the Princess.

Williams's seventh sense of theatrical instinct is no-where so evident as in his reaching a note of high drama as the end approaches. He creates a magic that is so memorable it is forever associated with this play. Chance phones an influential gossip columnist to have the Princess announce him as a "discovery" to star with Heavenly in a new film called *Youth*. Instead, the Princess learns that her movie is not a flop but a hit, "the greatest comeback in the history of the industry." Her transformation from fugitive back into movie queen, in the course of a brief telephone conversation, is pure theater and pure Williams—humorous, lyric, compassionate, and true. It concludes:

> CHANCE: Here, get her back on this phone. . . . Talk about me and talk about Heavenly to her.
>
> PRINCESS: Talk about a beach-boy I picked up for pleasure, distraction from panic? Now? When the

nightmare is over? . . . You've just been using me. . . . When I needed you downstairs you shouted, 'Get her a wheel chair!' Well, I didn't need a wheel chair, I came up alone, as always. . . . Chance, you've gone past something you couldn't afford to go past; your time, your youth, you've passed it. It's all you had, and you've had it.

Chance reacts furiously, forcing her to look at herself in the mirror, to see that her youth and beauty have gone. Instead, she says she sees "Alexandra Del Lago, artist and star!" The difference between her and Chance, she tells him, is that "out of the passion and torment of my existence I have created a thing that I can unveil, a sculpture, almost heroic, that I can unveil, which is true."

But Chance can only wonder why he never got the chance to make it: "Something's got to mean something, don't it, Princess? I mean like your life means nothing, except that you never could make it, always almost, never quite?"

Chance in some ways resembles Val in *Orpheus Descending*. Both are young men who have chosen the easy path of "corruption" in life but who, at the ages of twenty-nine and thirty, feel the pressure of time. Both have a true love for a woman but are defeated by outside forces—the small town and its denizens who gang up on Val for a mistaken breach of conduct and, in *Sweet Bird*, the political force of Boss Finley, which punishes Chance for a personal reason, being a "criminal degenerate" whose venereal disease, transmitted to Heavenly, has resulted in her hysterectomy. The Heckler, of course, believes the operation to have been an abortion, illegal at that time. Chance is the more complex and human of the two, for, while both young men have fallen prey to corruption, Chance's own misguided ideals bring about his downfall. Unlike a true tragic hero, he never attains a significant recognition—that the fame and fortune he seeks are not inevitably the reward of good looks (especially as Hollywood demonstrates otherwise). The personal truth he does realize at the end, that his youth and attractiveness are fleeting, makes him a pathetic rather than a tragic figure.

Finley's forces are even more deadly than the towns-people in *Orpheus Descending*, for Finley stirs up state-wide racial hatred. Because of his political prominence and ambitions, Boss, who never could accept Chance as a son-in-law, is as ruthless in his family relations as in his political aims. Chance's former schoolmates, whose clothes and jobs he derides, form a chorus of men who join forces against him with the sinister Youth for Finley, a kind of junior Ku Klux Klan. They also demonstrate another facet of youth, its group violence. Their brutality is first seen against the Heckler, who is ''systematically beaten.'' Even though the final moments are quiet, their menacing members surround Chance at the end, and we assume he will be castrated, the fate with which he has been threatened.

Williams in his Sunday *New York Times* article of 8 March 1959 (often used as the play's ''Foreword''), prior to the opening of *Sweet Bird of Youth*, answers the charge that his plays are violent: ''I write about violence in American life only because I am not so well acquainted with the society of other countries. . . . If there is any truth in the Aristotelian idea that violence is purged by its poetic representation on a stage, then it may be that my cycle of violent plays have had a moral justification after all.''

In *Sweet Bird of Youth* Williams perfectly achieves his ideal of plastic theater, in which characterization, action, language, setting, and sound create an artistic unity expressing the theme. As always, the dialogue characterizes the speakers. In Williams's large cast of memorable women the Princess has her unique idiom—tough, resilient, decisive, knowing. In act 1, scene 1, she sizes up Chance after he tries to blackmail her: ''I hate to think of what kind of desperation has made you try to intimidate me, ME?. . . . You were well born, weren't you? . . . with just one disadvantage, a laurel wreath on your forehead, given too early, without enough effort to earn it.'' Then she sets forth her terms of employment for Chance in a passage that reminds us that time is even more of an enemy to her, being older than Chance:

> Forget the legend that I was and the ruin of that legend. . . . No mention of death, never, never a word on that odious subject. I've been accused of having a death wish but I think it's life that I wish for, terribly, shamelessly, on any terms whatsoever. When I say now, the answer must not be later. I have only one way to forget these things I don't want to remember and that's through the act of love-making.

She can be lyric as well. In act 2, scene 2, after Tom Junior has threatened Chance, she hears a strain of thematic music, which Williams calls ''The Lament.'' She describes time's loss in a passage that creates its own music through assonance, alliteration, onomatopoeia, repetition, and rhythm:

> All day I've kept hearing a sort of lament that drifts through the air of this place. It says, 'Lost, lost, never to be found again.' Palm gardens by the sea and olive groves on Mediterranean islands all have that lament drifting through them. 'Lost, lost.'. . . [Williams's ellipsis] The isle of Cyprus, Monte Carlo, San Remo, Torremolenas, Tangiers. They're all places of exile from whatever we loved. . . . Chance, believe me, after failure comes flight. . . . Face it. Call the car.

Unlike Chance, however, she at least has the assurance of her talent as she faces her faded looks in the mirror. Although she is clear-eyed about time, the defeater, she will still go on; as she says monosyllabically to Chance at the end, ''Chance, we've got to go on.'' This motif of going on despite obstacles will be repeated by Hannah, almost verbatim, in *The Night of the Iguana*.

Chance's idiom is less distinctive, but Williams's artistry heightens what could be the banalities of the less educated. Almost entirely monosyllabic, his speeches are nevertheless sharp, so that the give-and-take with the Princess, which occupies the entire first act, reveals the characters of both. When in scene 1 the Princess asks if he has any acting talent, Chance replies: ''I'm not as positive of it as I once was. I've had more chances than I could count on my fingers, and made the grade almost, but not quite, every time. Something always blocks me.''

Because Chance and the Princess are on the stage so much of the time, and the portraits of them are so detailed, the other characters are less well developed. Heavenly has very little to say; she is acted upon instead of active, a direct contrast to the Princess. Nonnie, Heavenly's ineffectual but kindly maiden aunt, who is sympathetic to Chance, resembles her counterpart in Williams's film *Baby Doll* and his one-act play *The Unsatisfactory Supper*.

Like Jabe in *Orpheus Descending*., Boss Finley is one of Williams's few characters without redeeming qualities, unless it be his (misguided) love for his daughter. In his one encounter alone with Heavenly, in scene 1 of act 2, there is, ''in her father,'' Williams points out, ''a sudden dignity'': ''It's important not to think of his attitude toward her in the terms of crudely conscious incestuous feeling, but just in the natural terms of almost any aging father's feeling for a beautiful young daughter who reminds him of a dead wife that he desired intensely when she was the age of his daughter.'' Boss's idiom resembles Big Daddy's, in that it is gruff, colorful, and proudly uneducated. In addition, because Boss is not sympathetic, his speeches reflect his sense of power; he is used to giving orders and seeing them obeyed.

When Heavenly suggests that he has "an illusion of power," he replies, "I have power, which is not an illusion." She informs him that, if she is accepted, she is "going into a convent." Boss shouts: "You ain't going into no convent. This state is a Protestant region and a daughter in a convent would politically ruin me."

With great economy but deadly aim and sure theatricalism Williams portrays in Boss Finley the danger of a corrupt, power-hungry politician who will destroy anything that stands in his way and anyone who threatens his public image. The symbol of this image and the danger it implies is the stunning stage effect in scene 2 of act 2, in which the entire back wall of the stage becomes an enormous TV screen, on which appears "the image of Boss Finley."

George Brandt believes Williams's cinematic style is illustrated by this scene, which is an attempt "to turn the playhouse into a picture theater." But it should be remembered that Williams had studied theater at the New School with Erwin Piscator, a proponent of the use of back-projected film to achieve stage effects. Piscator's wife, Maria Ley-Piscator, presents a strong argument for Williams's use of the latter technique.

The epigraph for the play is by Hart Crane, whose work Williams greatly admired: "Relentless caper for all those who step / The legend of their youth into the noon."

It is a warning to "all those" whose hopes depend on the legend of their youth that it will not survive the bright light of the sun when they reach the noon of life. Entitled "Legend," Crane's poem begins: "As silent as a mirror is believed / Realities plunge in silence by."

Constant reminders of the passing of time and of youth are Williams's symbols of the clock and the mirror. At the climax of the play, in act 3, Chance forces the Princess to confront in the mirror the reality of her aging face, a sight she confesses was so terrifying to her when it filled the screen at the preview of her comeback film that she fled: "The screen's a very clear mirror. There's a thing called a close-up. . . . Your head, your face, is caught in the frame of the picture with a light blazing on it and all your terrible history screams while you smile". But she is not defeated, for she tells Chance that in the mirror she sees herself as "artist and star," while his mirror image discloses

"a face that tomorrow's sun will touch without mercy."

In a rhythmic, onomatopoeic elegy Heavenly also laments the loss of her youth. The operation, she says in scene 1 of act 2, "cut the youth out of my body, made me an old childless woman": "Dry, cold, empty, like an old woman. I feel as if I ought to rattle like a dead dried-up vine when the Gulf Wind blows." And Aunt Nonnie, Chance's only confidant in St. Cloud tells him the truth about his return: "What you want to go back to is your clean, unashamed youth. And you can't."

Despite its lyric dialogue, Williams thought of the action of this play as realistic, yet sudddenly, just before the play ends, it shifts gears. The closing moments are nonrealistic and poetic. In the hotel room—and what can be more transient to reflect time passing?—Chance and the Princess sit side by side on the bed, directly facing the audience, "like two passengers on a train sharing a bench." The metaphor is that of a train trip, a journey through life. The Princess points out sights along the way:

> PRINCESS: . . . Look [Williams's ellipsis]. That little donkey's marching around and around to draw water out of a well. . . .—What an old country, timeless—Look—(*The sound of a clock ticking is heard, louder and louder.*)
>
> CHANCE: No, listen. I didn't know there was a clock in this room.
>
> PRINCESS: I guess there's a clock in every room people live in.

A trooper enters, and Tom Junior is at the door. The Princess pleads, "Come on, Chance, we're going to change trains at this station. . . . So, come on, we've got to go on. . . . Chance, please. . . ." (both Williams's ellipses). But Chance shakes his head, and she departs, as he at last realizes that life is a journey in time and that he is approaching the end of the line.

Yet at the end, with everything gone and violence imminent, defeated Chance retains his dignity, as he asks: "Time—who could beat it, who could defeat it ever? Maybe some saints and heroes, but not Chance Wayne." Williams points out in his stage direction that "Chance's attitude should be self-recognition but not self-pity—a sort of deathbed dignity and honesty apparent in it." As Tom Junior and three other men hover in the doorway, ready to strike, Chance advances to the front of the stage and addresses the closing lines directly to the audience: "I don't ask for your pity, but just for your understanding—not even that—no. Just for your recognition of me in you, and the enemy, time, in us all.''

In the 1959 Broadway premiere Geraldine Page as the Princess and Paul Newman as Chance were outstanding in evoking the poetry of the play and in preserving the magic of the final scene. In a 1945 interview Williams had asserted that ''the poetic theater needs . . . more fine, intuitive actors. . . . We've gotten into the habit, actors in the Broadway theater, of talking like parrots. And poetry dies through that form of delivery.

Although director Elia Kazan did well with the realistic scenes, Page's and Newman's own considerable talents were responsible for realizing the poetry and the magic that made the production memorable. Their familiarity with Williams's characters no doubt helped, as they had already achieved outstanding interpretations as Alma in *Summer and Smoke* and as Brick in the movie version of *Cat on a Hot Tin Roof.* In a role allegedly based on actress Tallulah Bankhead, Page brought out every facet of the part, quick-silver in her changes from imperious to pathetic, from brittle and determined to resigned and caring. Newman was equally impressive as Chance, his underlying desperation perceptible beneath the bravado.

Good newspaper reviews the following morning of 11 March led to long lines at the box office, with Brooks Atkinson of the *Times* pronouncing the play one of Williams's ''finest dramas.'' ''Williams Drama Attracts Throngs'' was the *Times* headline. Magazine reviewers were somewhat more critical. Harold Clurman, commenting on the curtain speech, asked: ''What is it we were asked to recognize in ourselves? That we are corrupted by our appetite for the flesh and clamor of success? That we are driven to live debased existences by the constrictions and brutality which surround us? That the sound instincts of our youth are thus frustrated and turned to gall? And that we have an inordinate fear of age, for the passing of time makes us old before we mature?'' Marya Mannes deplored the ''violence of corruption and decay. . . in which a poet's imagination must feed on carrion.'' In a more reasoned consideration of the play Robert Heilman feels there is insufficient sympathetic development of the character of Chance, which resembles that of Brick, in that both men experience a ''premature glory,'' which then fades. Interpreting Chance's actions as ''so shallow and preposterous that the self-recognition is hardly plausible in terms of character,'' Heilman wonders how the ending can work,

when Chance addresses the audience ''like the Doctor in the morality play.'' But for the audience in the theater the ending *does* work.

The 1962 film, written and directed by Richard Brooks, at least preserves the performances of Geraldine Page and Paul Newman as well as some of Williams's dialogue in their scenes together. Yet the banal new dialogue and the flashback scenes detailing the love affair between Chance and Heavenly (Shirley Knight) reduce the work to an average movie, with an ending that negates the premise. Williams complained that the happy ending was ''a total contradiction to the meaning of the play.''

Sweet Bird of Youth represents Williams at his best in combining realism, lyricism, and theatricalism. The characters are so realistically drawn, down to the last detail, that their names have become tags for real-life types—a Southern politician who wins votes by appealing to fears of racial discord is a ''Boss Finley,'' a good-looking young man who expects to succeed without talent, a ''Chance Wayne.'' At the same time, Williams's universal theme, expressed in symbolism, stage effects, and heightened speech, unites with his sure sense of theatricality to produce a work that enriched both his reputation and that of the American theater.

Source: Alice Griffin ''Sweet Bird of Youth,'' in *Understanding Tenessee Williams,* Matthew J. Bruccoli, General Editor, University of South Carolina Press, 1995, pp., 197–215.

John Lahr

In the following critique, reviewer John Lahr discusses how Williams' Sweet Bird of Youth *displays the subtleties between achievement and destruction and expresses Williams' fascination with America's competitive drive.*

Sweet Bird of Youth (1959), currently being revived at the Royal National Theatre, in London, picks up Williams' story at the panicky moment of the hardening of his spiritual arteries. In *Sweet Bird of Youth,* the most underrated of his great plays, two self-confessed monsters, Chance Wayne and the Princess Kosmonopolis, a.k.a. Alexandra Del Lago, act out the division in Williams' warped heart between being big and being good. The sense that time is running out on the Princess's career and, as his name implies, on Chance's opportunity is what gives the play its peculiar giddy climate of frenzy. Richard Eyre's vivid but unsubtle production— what might be considered an acrylic version—

Paul Newman as Chance Wayne and Geraldine Page as Princess Kosmonopolis in the 1962 film adaptation of Sweet Bird of Youth.

nonetheless allows us to see the grandeur of Williams' writing and to appreciate how much of America's competitive ethos he explores in his idiosyncratic meditation on the monstrous. "I'm a peculiar blend of the pragmatist and the Romanticist and the crocodile," Williams said in 1973. "The Monster." The notion of monsters crops up first in *Cat on a Hot Tin Roof* (1955), when Maggie admits that in her struggle to survive she has mutated, "gone through this—*hideous!—transformation,* become—*hard! Frantic!—cruel!!*" And in *The Night of the Iguana,* the last great play in the Williams canon, the monster—the eponymous iguana—is literally at the end of its tether under the veranda of Maxine's Costa Verde Hotel, trying "to go on past the end of its goddam rope," Shannon says. "Like *you*! Like *me*!" The iguana is eventually freed; but Williams never was. *Sweet Bird of Youth,* set on Easter morning, is a kind of resurrection play—a day-dream of atonement, in which Williams faces up to the sin of his separation from others and the dilemma of lost goodness.

The word "monster" has its root in the contrary notions of marvels and warnings; and *Sweet Bird of Youth* probes the ambiguities between achievement and destruction. "We are two mon-

sters, but with this difference between us," the Princess, a movie star on the run from the imagined failure of her Hollywood comeback film, says to Chance, her young "pitiful monster," who is attempting a comeback of his own, by blackmailing her into being his ticket to theatrical fame and fortune. "Out of the passion and torment of my existence I have created a thing that I can unveil, a sculpture, almost heroic, that I can unveil, which is true." Here Clare Higgins' husky voice and ravaged face invest the Princess's panic and vanity with a compelling ferocity. Dazed and demented, the Princess sprawls on the silk sheets of the hotel double bed, squinting at her gigolo through cracked eyeglasses. "Well," she says, in a line resounding with a lived sense of rapacity and loneliness, "I may have done better, but God knows I've done worse." Higgins isn't always so successful at finding the humor in the Princess's knowing detachment— partly because she lacks a star's deadly imperialism, and partly because there's no chemistry between her and Robert Knepper, who, as Chance, hasn't a whiff of sex or loss about him. This results in some strange readings. "Monsters don't die early," the Princess says, hectoring Chance. "They hang on long. Awfully long. Their vanity's infinite, almost as infinite as their disgust with themselves." Higgins punctuates these cauterizing lines with a wiggle of her hips.

Sweet Bird of Youth, which dramatizes Chance's twenty-four-hour return to the Gulf Coast town where the legend of his youth began and where it will end, is full of mordant commentary on the soul's decay. ''The age of some people can only be calculated by the level of . . . rot in them,'' Chance says to the Princess. ''And by that measure I'm ancient.'' The cavernous darkness that fills the stage at curtain rise is the perfect ambience for the immensity of shame they're in retreat from. Anthony Ward's monumental louvred bedroom shutters, which reach from floor to ceiling, make the point as spectacularly as Williams' poetry. The characters long to be redeemed from their dead hearts. ''Once I wasn't this monster,'' the Princess says to Chance, surprised to find herself feeling ''something for someone besides myself'' and momentarily looking to him for salvation. ''Chance, you've got to help me stop being the monster that I was this morning, and you can do it.'' She is a big winner in the American sweepstakes who is terrified of losing; he is a big loser who is terrified that he'll never win. She is trying to hide from the memory of achievement; he is trying to manufacture achievements to hide in. Together, they are a kind of psychological composite of Williams. ''Somehow we Americans have never stopped fighting,'' Williams said, in 1958, of the corruption brought on by the fever to win. ''The very pressure we live under, the terrific competitive urge of our society brings out violence in the individual. We need to be taught how to love. Already we know only too well how to hate.''

Sweet Bird of Youth is really Chance's story, but the play's flawed structure skews the focus. In an attempt to give a larger dimension to Chance's relationship with his beloved childhood sweetheart, Heavenly (who has to be sterilized because of his betrayal), and to give more coherence to Chance's ultimate fate—his castration by the henchmen of Heavenly's draconian father, Boss Finley—Eyre has boldly assembled his production script from seven drafts of the play. The retooling is generally effective (although giving the role of Heavenly to Emma Amos, who is neither delicate nor believable, cancels out much of the narrative gain). Eyre deserves enormous credit for having mounted three major Williams revivals since he took over as director of the Royal National Theatre, in 1988. ''I think the neglect of Williams by the British theatre, let alone the American theatre, has been absolutely

''AT THE FINALE, THE PRINCESS, FORCED BY CHANCE TO CALL A HOLLYWOOD GOSSIP COLUMNIST ON HIS BEHALF, LEARNS THAT HER FILM IS A HIT. IN THAT INSTANT, SHE IS REBORN ALEXANDRA DEL LAGO, 'REDEEMED' BY FAME TO HER FORMER INVULNERABILITY. SHE IMMEDIATELY FORGETS ABOUT CHANCE.''

shameless,'' he told me. ''I deeply underrated Williams. I didn't see him in the way that I do now, as a moralist and the best writer of English prose in the theatre of this century.'' The prose *is* wonderful; but, having tampered with the script, Eyre is oddly timorous about adapting Williams' stage directions, and, as Williams instructed, allows Chance and the Princess to speak their long arias to the audience, and not to each other. This may be Williams' scenic way of indicating the isolation of two major-league narcissists, but it bogs down the play's momentum. As if to recoup it, the production mistakes agitation for desperation.

But there is no mistaking Williams' dream of salvation. At the finale, the Princess, forced by Chance to call a Hollywood gossip columnist on his behalf, learns that her film is a hit. In that instant, she is reborn Alexandra Del Lago, ''redeemed'' by fame to her former invulnerability. She immediately forgets about Chance. Her vainglorious volte-face is hilarious and lethal. The kingdom of self is reasserted, and the monstrous invoked once again. ''I climbed back alone up the beanstalk to the ogre's country where I live, now, alone,'' she says to Chance, who refuses to be part of her entourage and to leave with her, despite Boss Finley's threats on his life. The parade has passed Chance by, as the Princess reminds him. ''Chance,'' she says, ''you've gone past something you couldn't afford to go past; your time, your youth, you've passed it. It's all you had, and you've had it.'' Chance, who has been notoriously irresponsible—he arrives in town unaware of his mother's death or Heavenly's operation—now owns up to his dereliction. He stops running, and chooses not "the spurious glory" of the Princess—the kind of fame he first glimpsed as a Broadway chores boy in "Oklahoma!"—but the Christian glory of self-sacrifice. In Eyre's production, Chance's pill-popping and manic behavior make his decision to stay and face down his tormentors more resigned than heroic. "Something's got to mean something," Chance says, in a line unfortunately cut from Eyre's production. The castration—what Williams referred to in a letter to Kazan as "the quixotic, almost ridiculous choice, to stay and atone"—is a kind of leap of faith: an expression of Williams' own longing to reclaim his belief. Eyre's production emphasizes the sacrificial nature of the act by having the Boss's men advance on Chance with torches. While Chance's back is to us, his arms shoot out from his body as if he were crucified; and as the lights fade he falls backward with his pelvis thrust upstage at the approaching mob.

Salvation was easier for Williams to create in his plays than in his life. Drugs, drink, and dementia eroded much of his power of penetration and organization in the particularly chaotic period between 1964 and 1969, which he called his "Stoned Age." After that, what remained to him was his "left-over life," a gradual attenuation of friendships and of energy. "I feel like a sinking ship," he wrote his new agent, Bill Barnes, in 1973, "but things have a habit of going on." When his plays could no longer find a receptive audience, Williams put himself and his moral drama directly before the public. Asked to explain his conversion to Catholicism, he said, "I wanted to have my goodness back." But he never really regained it. "To the world I give suspicion and resentment mostly," he wrote in 1980, in the introduction to his collected short stories. "I am never deliberately cruel. But after my morning's work, I have little to give but indifference to people. I try to excuse myself with the pretense that my work justifies this lack of caring for almost everything else. Sometimes I crack through the emotional block. I touch. I hold tight to a necessary companion. But that breakthrough is not long lasting. Morning returns, and only work matters again." Williams' particular poignancy is that he saw the light but didn't want it enough.

Source: John Lahr, "The Fugitive Mind," in *New Yorker,* Vol. 70, No. 21, July 1994, pp. 68–71.

Foster Hirsch

In the following review of Tennessee Williams's play Sweet Bird of Youth, *author Foster Hirsch gives an overview of the work and writes that while it is sloppily constructed, it remains "absorbing on a superficial level."*

Sweet Bird of Youth is a Southern Gothic horror story in which a sexually errant male is both punished and deified. Chance Wayne is a gigolo who sells his body in exchange for promises of stardom. As his name blatantly indicates, though, his chances are waning; and at the awkward transitional age of thirty, he grasps with increasing desperation for the movie star fame that eludes him. When we first see him, he is in the middle of his most fevered scheme, playing the male nurse to a fading actress, and prepared to blackmail her (for possession of hashish) into pushing him and his girlfriend into the movies.

Chance is one of Williams's desperate dreamers, a good-looking small town boy whose ambitions exceed his talent. Like many Williams characters, he is trying to hold on to the fleeting "sweet bird of youth." Traveling with aging prima donna Alexandra del Logo, Chance returns to his home town of Saint Cloud expecting to find it exactly as he left it. He soon learns that the memory of his former glories has dimmed. His mother has died, his girl's father won't let him see her; Chance returns home a fallen hero, and like Val Xavier in *Battle of Angels,* he is pursued and finally destroyed by the town rednecks. Chance's emphatic sexual presence is a threat to the men of the town, and like Val, Chance is regarded as a diseased intruder who must be expelled in order to insure the health of the community.

The character is so beleaguered that he himself comes to think that he deserves his awful fate, offering himself to his pursuers as a kind of sacrificial victim. Immediately before he is castrated by them, he speaks directly to the audience: "I don't ask for your pity, but just for your understanding—not even that—no. Just for your recognition of me in you, and the enemy, time, in us all." Many critics were puzzled by the character's request, for Chance is not convincing as an Everyman. Robert Brustein charged:

> Since Chance has had about as much universality as a character in an animated cartoon, to regard his experience as an illuminating reflection of the human condition is a notion which borders on the grotesque. For *Sweet Bird of Youth* is a highly private neurotic

fantasy which takes place in a Terra Incognita quite remote from the terrain of the waking world.

Williams treats his Adonis as both the purest and the most depraved character in the play. Chance is both childlike innocent and tortured self-flagellant, both pagan sensualist and Christian sinner. He laments the loss of the innocence he had when he and his girl Heavenly were young, unashamed lovers; and yet he celebrates his vocation (''maybe the only one I was truly meant for'') as a professional lover: ''I gave people more than I took. Middle-aged people I gave back a feeling of youth. Lonely girls? Understanding, appreciation! An absolutely convincing show of affection. Sad people, lost people? Something light and uplifting! Eccentrics? Tolerance, even odd things they long for.'' Though he is self-loathing at times, Chance nonetheless feels he is superior to Heavenly's dictatorial father Boss Finley: ''He was just called down from the hills to preach hate. I was born here to make love.''

Chance, then, is both healer and destroyer; his body soothes the lonely and the no longer young just as it has infected Heavenly, for Chance is an Adonis who spreads venereal disease. (As Kenneth Tynan noted: ''None of Mr. Williams's other plays has contained so much rot. It is as if the author were hypnotized by his subject, like a rabbit by a snake, or a Puritan by sin.'')

Chance is guilty because he has robbed Heavenly of her innocence and her womanhood (she has had to have a hysterectomy as a result of the disease Chance passed on to her) and because he has squandered his own youth on a succession of one-night stands with strangers. He regards his punishment as only just, and the courage he shows in the face of catastrophe is clearly meant to vindicate him. As John Hays has written, he ''ironically gains in manliness at the moment he faces the loss of his manhood.'' Chance is cleansed by willfully surrendering himself to castration. The play thus equates castration with resurrection—''a very personal and psychological resurrection,'' as Hays notes, rather than ''the spring-time renewal of fortune Adonis was credited with.''

Typically for Williams, as Arthur Ganz has suggested, it is only after the character ''has been punished and destroyed [that he can] be revered.'' The punishment, though, is not consistent with Williams's celebration of Chance as a healer and restorer. Robert Brustein pointed out the contradiction: ''The bird not only represents purity but. . . the male sexual organ. If the bird is a phallic image,

> AS KENNETH TYNAN NOTED: 'NONE OF MR. WILLIAMS'S OTHER PLAYS HAS CONTAINED SO MUCH ROT. IT IS AS IF THE AUTHOR WERE HYPNOTIZED BY HIS SUBJECT, LIKE A RABBIT BY A SNAKE, OR A PURITAN BY SIN.'

then Chance's sweetness and youth are associated with sexuality. . . and his purity is terminated only when he is castrated, not when he turns to more perverse pleasures.''

Chance is both Christ crucified for our sins (as the final speech makes clear) and Adonis, the unashamed, joy-creating god of fertility. Williams's play is both Christian fable and pagan myth. The play's unresolved conflicts are derived from the author's private neuroses, but he is showman enough to convert his personal obsessions into exciting melodrama. Although Williams tries to give the story religious significance, at heart *Sweet Bird of Youth* is a glossy shocker about sex and politics.

The hero may be the protagonist of both a popular romance and a symbolic religious pageant, but the play's two supporting characters, Alexandra del Lago and Boss Finley, are rooted firmly on the level of garish melodrama. Alexandra is such a rich character part that it is possible to overlook the fact that she is incidental to both the story and theme. Her try for a comeback, we learn, was disastrous because Alexandra del Lago at forty-seven has too many wrinkles to attempt the kinds of parts that made her a star when she was young. As she enters the play, she's on the run from her unsuccessful new career, and she's determined to forget failure through hashish and Chance. But improbably, Alexandra finds out that her comeback was not the fiasco she has imagined it was, and she is once again a star. In a flash, she forgets her promises to Chance, and she is on her way back to Hollywood. Williams elaborates the actress's role in the play much more than he needs to. Aside from eliciting his life story from Chance, Alexandra is necessary only as a thematic reinforcement of Chance's lust for success and his fear of growing older. Both characters regard time as the enemy; the actress ''knew in her heart that the legend of Alexandra del Lago couldn't be separated from an appearance of youth.'' Aware of the corruption of these two characters, Williams nevertheless sympathizes with them; typically, he wants both to punish them and to save them.

His feelings about Boss Finley are much less complicated. Williams claims he was unsuccessful with Finley because he hated him so much: ''I have to understand the characters in my play. . . . If I just hate them I can't write about them. That's why Boss Finley wasn't right. . . because I just didn't like the guy, and I just had to make a tour de force of his part in the play.'' But like Alexandra, Boss Finley is a wonderfully outgoing character. He is a backwoods politician who savors his power; and he is a fraud who is used to having his own way. He forces his defiled daughter Heavenly to stand before his constituents as a symbol of virginal Southern maidenhood. The old man resembles Chance in thinking of himself as a healer: ''I have told you before, but I will tell you again. I got a mission that I hold sacred to perform in the Southland. . . . When I was fifteen I came down barefooted out of the red clay hills. . . . And what is this mission? . . . To shield from pollution a blood that I think is not only sacred to me, but sacred to Him.'' Williams uses Hollywood glamor and Southern bigotry as tokens of universal corruption, but his treatment of movies and politics as tainted pursuits is too sketchy to serve a serious symbolic function.

Sweet Bird of Youth is tawdry and carelessly constructed. The first two acts have little connection to each other as the action moves disjointedly from Chance and Alexandra to Boss Finley; act 2 ends with a chaotically dramatized political rally; and in act 3, the destinies of Chance and Alexandra are uneasily integrated. But the play has vitality, and this gaudy story of movie stars and Southern demagogues is absorbing on a superficial level.

Source: Foster Hirsch, ''Three Dark Plays,'' in *A Portrait of an Artist: The Plays of Tennessee Williams,* 1979 Kennikat Press, pp. 58–62.

SOURCES

Aston, Frank, ''*Bird of Youth* Stormy Drama,'' in *New York World Telegram and The Sun,* March 11, 1959.

Atkinson, Brooks, ''The Theatre: Portrait of Corruption,'' in *New York Times,* March 11, 1959.

Brustein, Robert, ''Sweet Bird of Success,'' in *Encounter,* June 1959, pp. 59–60.

———, ''Williams's Nebulous Nightmare,'' in *Hudson Review,* Summer 1959, pp. 255–60.

Chapman, John, ''Williams's *Sweet Bird of Youth* Weird, Sordid and Fascinating,'' in the *Daily News,* March 11, 1959.

Clurman, Harold, Review in *The Nation,* March 28, 1959, pp. 281–83.

Hewes, Henry, ''Tennessee's Easter Message,'' in *Saturday Review,* March 28, 1959, p. 26.

Kerr, Walter, Review in the *New York Herald Tribune,* March 11, 1959.

Kissel, Howard, Review in *Women's Wear Daily,* December 31, 1975.

Mallet, Gina, ''Petit Guignol,'' in *Time,* December 15, 1975.

Mannes, Marya, ''Sour Bird, Sweet Raisin,'' in *The Reporter,* April 16, 1959, pp. 34–5.

Tynan, Kenneth, Review in *New Yorker,* March 21, 1959, pp. 98–100.

Watts, Jr., Richard, ''Tennessee Williams Does It Again,'' in *New York Post,* March 11, 1959.

Williams, Tennessee, *Sweet Bird of Youth,* New Directions, 1959.

Wilson, Edwin, ''The Desperate Time When Youth Departs,'' in the *Wall Street Journal,* December 8, 1975.

FURTHER READING

Griffin, Alice, *Understanding Tennessee Williams,* University of South Carolina Press, 1995.
    This critical study offers in-depth discussion and analysis of a number of Williams's plays, including *Sweet Bird of Youth.*

Nelson, Benjamin, *Tennessee Williams: The Man and His Work,* Ivan Obolensky, Inc., 1961.
    This critical biography includes a discussion of Williams's plays through the beginning of the 1960s, including *Sweet Bird of Youth .*

Williams, Tennessee, *Memoirs,* Doubleday & Company, Inc., 1975.
    This autobiography encompasses Williams's life and career.

Talley's Folly

LANFORD WILSON

1979

Lanford Wilson's romantic comedy *Talley's Folly* is the second of three plays in what came to be known as Wilson's Talley Family series. The first play in the saga, *5th of July* (later renamed *Fifth of July*), takes place in 1977, as members of the Talley family struggle with capitalism and the Vietnam War. Among the characters is the recently widowed Aunt Sally, who values the family home more than she values money. When the actress playing Sally in the original production of *Fifth of July* asked Wilson for help in understanding her character, he wrote *Talley's Folly* to show how Sally and her husband Matt became a couple in 1944. Two years later Wilson added a third episode to the story, *Talley & Son,* first produced in 1981.

Talley's Folly shows one evening in the courtship of two unlikely lovers, Sally Talley and Matt Friedman. Sally is from a conservative, small-town, wealthy family of bigoted Protestants, and Matt is a Jewish accountant twelve years older than Sally. The story of how they become brave enough to reveal their most painful secrets touched audiences and critics, and the play's Broadway run was a great success. First produced in 1979, the play was nominated for several Tony Awards and won the Pulitzer Prize and other awards in 1980. More than two decades after its first production, *Talley's Folly* is frequently staged and is considered one of Wilson's most hopeful and affirming plays.

AUTHOR BIOGRAPHY

Lanford Wilson was born on April 13, 1937, in Lebanon, Missouri, the town in which he set *Talley's Folly* and two other plays. His parents divorced when he was five years old, and he moved from place to place within Missouri with his mother and grandmother until he was a teenager. Although he has described his youth as a happy time, he never had what he created for the Talley family: a permanent home with a stable extended family.

At an early age, Wilson discovered a love for films, and then for the theater. He went to the movies as often as he could, and began acting in high school plays. As he became more involved with theater, he came to feel that plays had more potential than films to create magic and to touch an audience deeply. He attended Southwest Missouri State College for a few years, exploring his interests in art, but left without a degree and without a plan for his life. Finally he moved to Chicago, and experienced city life for the first time.

In Chicago, Wilson worked for a time as a prostitute, immersed himself in the city's night life, and met people who were unlike those back in Lebanon, Missouri. Later, he would turn many of these experiences into material for his urban plays. Wilson became a graphic designer and continued to write short stories, finally turning one story into a play and finding his true calling.

He moved in 1962 to Greenwich Village in New York, determined to make his way in the theater. Joseph Cino, an important figure in the Off-Off Broadway movement, became Wilson's mentor, critiquing his scripts and eventually staging the first production of a Wilson play, *So Long at the Fair.* The one-act play, about a young man from the Midwest struggling to become an artist, was well-received, and was soon followed by other successes.

By 1967, Wilson had seen several of his plays reach the stage in New York and London and throughout Europe. Then Cino committed suicide, and Wilson suffered a depression that lasted more than a year. When he emerged in 1969, he joined three other artists in founding the Circle Repertory Company, dedicated to building a collaborative community of actors, directors, writers, and designers. Over the next three decades, Circle Repertory produced many of Wilson's most important works. The company earned an international reputation for excellence, and Wilson won several national awards for his work.

In 1978, "Circle Rep" produced Wilson's *Fifth of July,* the first in what has come to be known as the Talley Series. The second play in the series was *Talley's Folly,* which won the Pulitzer Prize in 1980. Wilson continued to write plays for Circle Rep and to work closely with promising new playwrights.

PLOT SUMMARY

Talley's Folly opens with the frank revelation that this is a play: the set, which under the proper lighting represents a boathouse surrounded by weeds and trees, is here illuminated by work lights and the house lights, so that the artificiality of the set is obvious. Matt speaks directly to the audience, announcing that the play will run for ninety-seven minutes with no intermission, and that the story will unfold as a waltz, a valentine. If all goes well, he says, the play will end with a romance. He is somewhat nervous as he reveals that one year earlier he met Sally at a dance and the two were together in this same boathouse; he has returned to ask for her hand. Matt points up the hill to the Talley family home and explains that, even in this remote small town, world events including the Great Depression and the Second World War have their influence. He also describes Sally, whom he calls a "terrible embarrassment to her family." As Sally approaches the boathouse and calls Matt's name, the lights dim, the stage takes on its conventional theatrical appearance, and Matt steps into his character. For nearly the rest of the play, Sally and Matt will speak only to each other.

From their first moment on stage together, there is tension between Matt and Sally. She has just come home from work to find her family upset about the "communist traitor infidel" Matt—who came to the door asking for Sally. Although Sally's brother believes he has run Matt off with his shotgun, Sally has guessed that Matt is waiting for her in the boathouse. Matt has come to claim Sally for his own, but she insists she has no intention of encouraging his courtship. As the two squabble and Sally demands that Matt leave, several things are revealed: Matt has written Sally a letter every day since he last saw her a year ago; Sally has responded only once, asking him to stop writing. Matt tried to visit Sally at the hospital where she is a nurse's aide, but she refused to see him. Matt mocks the Talley family for their accent, their narrow-mindedness, and their bigotry, and although Sally tries to defend them she is clearly disgusted with them herself.

Matt is determined to keep the conversation going so Sally will not leave or send him back to St. Louis, where he works as an accountant. He senses, as the audience does, that beneath her scolding she does truly love him. He admires the beauty of the Talley land, and Sally also expresses appreciation for its beauty. He coaxes from Sally the story of Uncle Whistler, who built the whimsical boathouse in 1870. Like Sally, he was odd, a misfit, and Sally calls him ''the healthiest member of the family.''

Finding an old pair of ice skates in the boathouse, Matt tries them on. He and Sally share a brief moment of intimacy as they hold hands and pretend to skate across the floor, but Matt spoils it by referring to Sally as his ''girl,'' and she backs off again. She almost leaves the boathouse and ends the encounter, but Matt falls through the rotting floor and Sally comes back to be sure that he is not hurt. Now Matt urges Sally to remember their ''affair'' of last summer, when they were together every day for a week. Sally remembers, but claims to attach no importance to their time together. Matt begs her not to let fear keep them apart. He knows that the fact that he is Jewish and older is a scandal for her family, but he is sure she loves him in spite of their differences. He points out that although she claims to have come to send him away, she has put on a pretty new dress to do it. Why won't she admit that she loves him?

Now Matt reveals that he has learned quite a bit about Sally's past by talking with her patients in the hospital and with her Aunt Charlotte. Matt knows that Sally is not in sympathy with her capitalist family, and that they consider her an ''old maid.'' Charlotte is apparently the only spirited member of the family, and she has encouraged Matt to pursue Sally. Charlotte's approval intrigues Sally, who tries to turn the conversation to Matt's past, which he has refused to talk about. In the play's most wrenching episode, Matt hesitatingly, through a series of jokes and indirections, tells the story of his family's torture and murder in Europe when he was a child, before World War I. He was smuggled into the United States by an uncle, and has never recovered from the trauma of his childhood. Although he

Lanford Wilson

is forty-two years old, he has never dared love a woman before, because he has vowed never to bring children into this cruel world, and he has not thought any woman would want to marry him under those conditions. Sally, he is sure, is a woman who thinks and feels as he does, and he is confident of her love for him.

When Sally hears Matt's story, she is not swept away with passion, but instead becomes angry with him. She believes that he has made up his horrible story only to trick her into loving him, and that Aunt Charlotte has told Matt Sally's secret: an illness has left her unable to bear children. Sally was engaged to be married after high school to the handsome son in the town's other leading family, which would have created a merger of the town's richest empires. Her infertility made the marriage—and Sally—no longer useful to the families, and the engagement was broken.

Matt convinces Sally that he did not know her secret, that his story is true. They are a perfect couple, he says, because they love each other, they think alike, and they want the same things. At last, Sally agrees. Matt and Sally kiss and agree to leave for St. Louis right away. Matt speaks directly to the audience once more, pointing out that the waltz of love has ended exactly as he promised.

CHARACTERS

Matt Friedman

Matt is an accountant from St. Louis who met and fell in love with Sally a year before the play opens, when he came to Lebanon, Missouri, on vacation. He has been writing to her every day for a year, but her only reply has been to tell him to stop writing. Now Matt has come to Lebanon to propose to Sally in person. Jewish and forty-two years old, Matt seems all wrong for Sally, who is part of a wealthy Methodist family in a conservative, small Midwest town. Still, he is sure that he and Sally share true love, and that together they will have a chance at the happiness that has eluded them both. As the two talk in the old Talley boathouse, Sally denies that she loves Matt, but he refuses to leave. Finally, haltingly, he tells her the story of his family's persecution and murder in Europe, and of his decision never to father children, never to bring another soul into this world. He has never before dared to believe that any woman could love him enough to marry a man who will not father children, but he is sure enough of Sally to declare himself. His admission frees Sally to reveal her own secret, and the two discover a common ground. They agree to elope.

Sally Talley

Sally Talley is a lonely thirty-one-year-old woman who lives with her extended family in Lebanon, Missouri. The Talley family is wealthy and dedicated to conservative capitalism. Sally has let down the family by embracing socialist beliefs and by not marrying into another wealthy family and thereby increasing the family fortune. She works as a nurse's aide in a hospital in Springfield, Missouri, and dreams of getting away from her family. Still, when she meets Matt and falls in love with him, she spends a year denying her feelings. When Matt comes back to Lebanon and meets with her in the old boathouse, she reveals her affection for him but refuses to consider his proposal. She shows herself to be intelligent and quick-witted, but surprisingly lacking in self-confidence. When Matt declares his unwillingness to father children, she reveals her own secret: an illness in her late teens has left her infertile. Sure that no man would ever want to marry her, she has grown content as a single woman, but she learns that Matt will not resent her inability to bear children. Knowing that her family will not accept Matt, she agrees to elope that night and goes up to the house to pack.

THEMES

Prejudice and Tolerance

One of the hurdles Sally and Matt have to overcome if they are to be a couple is the intolerance of those around them. Sally, although she is white, Methodist, wealthy, and reasonably attractive, does not fit in with her family or community because she does not embrace the capitalism that has secured her family's fortune. She has been fired as a Sunday school teacher for encouraging her students to think positively about labor unions. Perhaps most scandalous to her family, Sally is still unmarried at thirty-one, and rather than being disgraced by this she has grown content to be alone. Because of the unwillingness of her family to embrace different ways of thinking, Sally's only pleasures come outside her home, when she is at work or with friends. At home, she is lonely, an outcast.

But in the minds of Sally's relatives, Matt's eccentricities are far worse. He is older, he has a beard, he believes in socialism, he is an immigrant, and he is Jewish. While marriage between people of different religions is not uncommon today, during the 1940s it was practically unheard of, and Jews were excluded from many social interactions with Christians. When Matt comes to the door to ask Sally's father for permission to marry her, it is only the second time he has met the family. A year ago he had dinner with them, and they immediately disliked him for his religion, his socialist ideas, and his beard. Without even asking what Matt wants on the night of *Talley's Folly,* Buddy gets a shotgun and runs Matt off the property.

Matt has allowed himself to fall in love with Sally because she does not share the prejudices of her community. She loves Matt for himself and does not fear his religion, his accent, or his political beliefs. But if Sally is going to be with Matt, she will have to cut herself off from her family, for they will not consider permitting her to marry a Jew. To them the shame of her marrying a Jew would be greater than the shame of her remaining an "old maid."

Gender Roles

While Matt's struggles have come from a political system that rejects him for his religion and his ideas, Sally's greatest suffering is the result of her not fulfilling the narrowly defined role demanded of a woman. As the daughter of a successful capitalist

TOPICS FOR FURTHER STUDY

- Research Lithuania, Latvia, Prussia, and the Ukraine, particularly their political status during and just after World War I. Why does Matt, speaking in 1944, feel so bitter about his family's homelands?

- Who was Emma Goldman? In what ways would Sally's family think Sally and Emma Goldman are alike?

- Matt makes a casual reference to a "Negro private" with whom he played checkers. Trace the history of the word "Negro" through the late nineteenth century and the twentieth century in the United States. What emotional and political weight did the term carry when Matt used it in 1944, and when Lanford Wilson wrote the play in 1979?

- How important is religious heritage in the community in which you live? How would parents in your community feel about Sally and Matt, or any other two people of different religions, getting married?

- Why does Lanford Wilson set this play on the Fourth of July? What difference does the date make in your understanding of what he is trying to convey?

family, she was expected to marry Harley Campbell, the son of another successful family. They did not love each other; Sally says, "It was more of a financial arrangement than anything." Sally did not object to the role she was to play, but enjoyed being the "Golden Girl," the head cheerleader engaged to the basketball star. It was not until she became ill and then infertile that she learned the truth: even her family did not love her for herself, but only for the gender role she could no longer play. Once she was "no longer of value to the merger," even her father rejected her, looking at her in the hospital "like I was a broken swing."

In the decade since her broken engagement, Sally has tried to define a new role for herself. It is an uphill battle: even though she is an adult of thirty-one, her brother still feels he has a right and duty to approve of Sally's choice of a man. But she has a job she enjoys, she knows how to change a tire, and she has worked to be content as a single woman. She smokes cigarettes and does not cook. She encourages socialist ideas, even though she knows that "unmarried daughters are supposed to help the menfolks keep the social status quo." By the time she meets Matt, he can see that she "actually thinks of herself as a human being rather than a feather-bed." Married to Matt, Sally will not have pressure to become a mother or to fit into any other traditional female role.

Family

More than anything else, Matt and Sally are longing for a family, although it will be a new kind of family. Matt's parents and sister were tortured and killed in Europe for political reasons. He escaped to America with the help of an uncle, but does not seem to have a relationship with that uncle now. He is alone. Ironically, Sally, who shares a house with three generations of Talleys, is also alone. She draws no comfort from her family, who have rejected her because of her political beliefs and because she has let them all down by not marrying Harley Campbell.

For both characters, the loss of family is their deepest sorrow, and both Matt and Sally have resigned themselves to never being part of a family again. Matt's experiences have convinced him that it would be wrong to father a child, and he is sure no woman would marry a man who has made that decision. Sally is physically unable to bear children, and she is sure no man would want to marry an infertile woman. What the two realize at the end of the play is that they are perfectly suited to each other, and that two people can be a family.

Capitalism and Socialism

An important theme in much of Lanford Wilson's work is the nature of work and profit. The Talley family has acquired its wealth by owning a large portion of a garment factory that now has a large contract to make army uniforms. For Wilson, the money they have accumulated is twice tainted: they are profiting from a war in which many thousands are dying, and they are profiting from the hard work of the laborers who do not earn decent wages and whom they will not permit to unionize. The Talleys do not produce anything of value with their own hands, and for Matt and Sally and Wilson this is an ignoble way to earn money.

Sally's Uncle Whistler did make things with his own hands, including the boathouse where the play takes place. "He made toys. Tap-dancing babies and whirligigs. He got pleasure out of making things for people." According to Sally, "He was the healthiest member of the family." Sally has chosen to follow Uncle Whistler's example. Although she could live off her family's wealth, she works as a nurse's aide in a hospital, providing a real service for wounded soldiers. Sally disapproves of her family's way of earning money and even encourages the students in her Sunday School class to push for labor unions in her family's factory. The fact that Sally and Matt share a disdain for capitalism makes them, in Wilson's eye, not only well-suited for each other, but also morally superior to the others.

STYLE

Setting

Talley's Folly takes place on the evening of July 4, 1944, in the old boathouse on the Talley property just outside the small Ozark town of Lebanon, Missouri. The boathouse, dripping with Victorian curlicues and gingerbread, was built in 1870 by Sally's eccentric uncle, Everett "Whistler" Talley, who also built the town bandstand and other fanciful structures, or "follies," all over town. By 1944, the boathouse has fallen out of use. It is surrounded by waist-high weeds and full of old fishing equipment, skates, and boats. The floor is so rotten that Matt falls through it. Sally sometimes comes here to get away from her family—or to be alone with Matt, as she did a year before.

The set is important to Wilson, and he describes it clearly in the text. The boathouse is meant to be lacy and ornamental as a valentine, the perfect setting for a romantic story. But Wilson also wants the audience to remember that it is a set, not a real boathouse. As the audience enters, the work lights and house lights are turned up so that the "artificiality of the theatrical set" is "quite apparent." Matt shows the audience the set and describes how the lighting will work. The audience, he points out, is sitting where the river would be. He acknowledges that there will not be much action, and says, "We could do it on a couple of folding chairs, but it isn't bare, it isn't bombed out, it's run-down, and the difference is all the difference."

The date, July 4, 1944, is also significant. The United States is heavily involved in World War II, and D-Day was just a month earlier. Matt has not enlisted in the Army, though he could, and Sally's family is profiting from the war, though Sally disapproves. In Europe, Jews are dying by the millions, and though Sally and Matt may not yet know that, the reader does. The backdrop of the war helps raise issues of patriotism, capitalism, and anti-Semitism.

The Fourth Wall

A convention of the theater is that there is an invisible wall at the front of the stage through which the audience watches the action. The audience is supposed to suspend disbelief, to go along with the notion that the world on stage is a complete world. In the "real world," the boathouse in which Matt and Sally meet would not be open along the river side. It would have four walls, not three, and the audience would not be sitting—as Matt points out—in the river. In a traditional theater experience, the audience would understand all of this without being told, and they would become thoroughly engaged in watching and believing the action on stage.

Wilson, however, makes it a point to break down the "fourth wall" of the theater, to call attention to the fact that this is a play, not reality. Matt opens and closes the play by speaking directly to the audience about the play. He tells them how long the play will run ("we have ninety-seven minutes here tonight—without intermission"), how the lighting will work, and how he hopes the story will turn out. He invites the audience to get a drink before the play starts. At one point he stops and delivers "this first part all over again for the late-comers." Matt addresses the audience again in the last line of the play, when he turns again to the seats to show the audience his watch, and assure them that the play is finished "right on the button."

Irony

Irony is a term used to describe a disjunction between what appears to be true and what actually is true. Often, in drama, the disjunction occurs when the audience has information that a character does not have, and the irony is in the character's not realizing the full meaning of what they say. *Talley's Folly,* however, is a textbook example of irony coming from the situation, from things that have happened before the play begins. Matt has decided not to father children, and he believes that no woman will have him because of this decision. Sally cannot bear children, and believes that no man will have her because of it. The irony is in the wonderful coincidence, in the way that Sally and Matt are both wrong in what they have believed. The reader has no special knowledge, but discovers the irony along with the characters.

Prior Knowledge

Although the play can stand on its own, many readers of *Talley's Folly* begin with some knowledge of Sally and Matt and the Talley family. When *Talley's Folly* opened, many in the audience had already seen the popular *Fifth of July,* which Wilson wrote before *Talley's Folly* but which takes place thirty-three years later. Many readers today have also encountered the third Talley play, *Talley & Son,* which takes place up at the Talley house on the same evening that Matt and Sally are in the boathouse.

A reader approaching *Talley's Folly* hopes and perhaps expects that Matt and Sally will come together in the end, but those who have experienced the other plays know it will happen. During *Talley & Son,* Sally comes up to the house to pack before eloping. Aunt Charlotte speaks with Sally, and persuades her to try to leave without telling anyone, but Sally and her father, Eldon Talley, do see each other before she leaves. Eldon, surprisingly, allows Sally to leave with Matt, telling her that he hopes she is not making a mistake. Years later, Sally reappears in *Fifth of July,* preparing to bury Matt's ashes. She and Matt were married and were happy together until death parted them.

Those coming to *Talley's Folly* without the benefit of the other Talley plays enjoy watching two fragile "eggs" find strength in each other. For those who have met the Talleys before, the pleasure is of a different kind: it is the pleasure of hearing old stories about old friends.

HISTORICAL CONTEXT

Examining Vietnam

Although the United States had withdrawn its last troops from Southeast Asia seven years before *Talley's Folly* opened in 1979, America was still trying to come to terms with the war. In 1979, Vietnam invaded Cambodia, and the mass graves of as many as three million Cambodians killed by the U.S.-supported Khmer Rouge were found, raising new questions about U.S. involvement in other countries.

Many American artists, including Lanford Wilson, explored the conflict in their work. The year 1978 saw the first production of Wilson's *Fifth of July,* about a man who has lost both legs in Vietnam, and the release of two Academy Award-winning movies about the war, *Coming Home* and *The Deer Hunter.* In 1979, as thousands of Americans were flocking to movie theaters to see another Vietnam film, *Apocalypse Now,* Wilson turned his attention to Sally Talley, one of the characters in *Fifth of July,* to show how she came to be who she was. Significantly, he placed his play about the younger Sally, *Talley's Folly,* in 1944, just as the United States was nearing the end of World War II.

Although he set *Talley's Folly* many years before the war in Vietnam, Wilson uses the play to examine issues raised by that war—and by all wars. During the late 1970s, some people questioned the role of the United States in Southeast Asia, asking whether Cold War fear of communism had caused the United States to make a dishonorable pact with the Khmer Rouge and unwise military decisions in Vietnam. Similarly, the character of Matt, who seems to speak for Wilson on political matters, raises questions about the things the Talleys fear. The Talley's have a narrow range of beliefs and behaviors that they consider patriotic, and they are suspicious of socialists, Jews, Emma Goldman, even Franklin Delano Roosevelt. Wilson believes that war is harmful to the psyches of individuals and of nations. In *Fifth of July* he shows how the Vietnam War eroded the humanity of the Talleys. In

COMPARE
&
CONTRAST

- **1940:** Laclede County, Missouri, which includes the town of Lebanon, is a mostly rural area in the wooded Ozark Mountains. Although the fictional Talley family owns an important garment factory, only about one-seventh of the work force is in manufacturing. A much larger portion, almost half, works in agriculture, forestry, and fisheries. About one-tenth work in retail.

  1980: Factories are more important to the economy of Laclede County. More than one-fourth of the county's workers are in manufacturing, while less than one-tenth work in agriculture, forestry, and fisheries. About one-fifth work in retail.

  1990: The trend away from agriculture and toward manufacturing and retail jobs continues in Laclede County. Agriculture, forestry, and fisheries account for only one-twentieth of the jobs, while manufacturing accounts for one-third and retail for one-fifth.

- **1940s:** Anti-communism is one of the most important issues in United States domestic politics. Although the American Communist Party attracted some middle-class support in the 1930s, especially among those who favored labor unions, by the 1940s most of the appeal had waned. Although the United States and Russia were allies in World War II, communism was seen by most Americans as a ''menace.''

  1970s: In large part due to the influence of the Civil Rights Movement and opposition to the Vietnam War, liberal thought is widely, but not universally, respected in the United States. Communism is associated in most people's minds with the political structures of the U.S.S.R., not with a social theory, and it is still suspect. At the end of the decade, Ronald Reagan mounts a successful run for the presidency by promising to stamp out communism.

  Today: With the fall of the Berlin Wall and the dissolution of the U.S.S.R., communism has come to be seen by the general American population as an outdated and failed political philosophy. Those who call themselves communists are met more with amusement than with anger.

- **1944:** Vietnam, under the leadership of Ho Chi Minh, declares its independence from France.

  1961 to 1975: The United States sends troops to Vietnam to help South Vietnam defeat communists in North Vietnam, in America's most unpopular military action. More than 55,000 Americans are killed, and many thousands more are wounded.

  Today: The Vietnam War is considered a humiliating defeat for the United States. Politicians look to the legacy of the war whenever they consider sending U.S. troops abroad; among their greatest fears is creating ''another Vietnam.''

Talley's Folly, Matt's horrible experiences in Europe and the immoral profit the Talleys realize from World War II demonstrate the same erosion.

Feminism

Equality for women was another major social issue in the United States during the 1970s. Fifty years after the U.S. Congress passed the Nineteenth Amendment to the Constitution, giving women the right to vote, the National Women's Strike for Equality in 1970 began a decade of publicity over the rights of women. In 1972, the never-ratified Equal Rights Amendment to the Constitution was passed by both houses of Congress, the first issue of *Ms.* magazine was published, and Title IX of the Higher Education Act banned gender bias in athletics and other activities in all institutions receiving federal funds.

The rest of the decade saw the Supreme Court protecting abortion rights with the *Roe v. Wade* decision (1973), the U.S. Tennis Association deciding to award equal prize money to men and women (1973), Little League Baseball being opened to girls (1974), and Margaret Thatcher becoming the Prime Minister of Great Britain (1979).

Not everyone welcomed changes in gender roles and attitudes. For example, Phyllis Schlafly, one of *Good Housekeeping* magazine's ten most admired women in the world for 1977, campaigned vigorously against the Equal Rights Amendment and is credited with stopping its ratification.

Against this backdrop, Wilson examined the expectations for women and for male-female relationships in many of his plays. In *Talley's Folly*, he creates two feminists in Matt and Sally, who each expect that a woman will work and be productive and that she will think of herself ''as a human being rather than a featherbed.''

CRITICAL OVERVIEW

Talley's Folly has been well-received by critics and by audiences since its first performance at the Circle Repertory Theatre on May 3, 1979. Tickets to the production sold unusually well, and the play would have run longer but for the fact that Judd Hirsch, the actor playing Matt, had another commitment. The play won several important awards, including the Pulitzer Prize, the New York Drama Critics' Circle Award for Best Play, and the Brandeis University Creative Arts Award. After moving to Broadway on February 20, 1980, the play ran for 227 performances and was nominated for several Tony Awards. In 1983 the text was included in the volume *Best American Plays: New York*. The text has remained in print since its first publication in 1980, and the play is often performed on college campuses and in community theaters.

When *Talley's Folly* opened on Broadway, it was reviewed in important New York and national publications, and early reviewers were almost unanimous in praising the play. The performances of actors Judd Hirsch and Trish Hawkins were much admired, as were the direction, the set, the lighting, and the costumes; but Wilson's script and vision also received great credit. Several reviewers noted that *Talley's Folly* was refreshingly optimistic about humans' capabilities for love and happiness, in contrast with many gloomy plays of the day. Veteran *New Yorker* reviewer John Simon called the play ''enchanting: a small, elegantly composed study of two interesting people.'' Jack Kroll, writing for *Newsweek,* called it a ''sweet, tender, funny, life-embracing play.''

A few reviewers, however, were troubled by the play's lack of plot. For these critics, two characters talking and doing little else was simply not enough. A tepid review was written by Catharine Hughes in the magazine *America.* Although she respected the actors' performances, she found the play ''too fragile for Broadway even in this dismal season.'' She believed the play had been ''much more at home at the Circle Repertory, where it originated.'' Harold Clurman, writing for *The Nation,* also had reservations. While he declared the play ''charming and gay,'' and ''a breath of fresh air on Broadway,'' he also felt that at times ''a touch of cuteness, a kind of decorative archness, threatens to mar the fundamental humanity of what is being said.'' He concluded that *Talley's Folly* ''may not be Wilson's best play, though it is his most engaging.''

The print version of *Talley's Folly* was published in April 1980, shortly after the Broadway opening. In a brief review for *Library Journal,* Gerard M. Molyneaux commented, ''It is not the plot that holds the reader's interest, but Wilson's craftsmanship, his sense of timing and humor, his sensitive use of language. The result is a charming theater piece whose strengths are retained on the printed page.'' Molyneaux recommended the text for ''all libraries with drama collections.''

Wilson himself was surprised by the success of his play. In a 1981 article by Scott Haller in the *Saturday Review* Wilson commented, ''I thought it was going to be the most unpopular thing I'd ever written. There was nothing compromised in the writing. I knew exactly what I wanted to do. I couldn't believe it when people liked it.''

The play was popular enough in the United States to be produced in other countries, but the reception abroad was not as positive. *New Statesman* reviewer Benedict Nightingale, who saw the play at its London opening at the Lyric Theatre in 1982, was not captivated by the play's charms. He found it ''not hard to nod off'' during the play, because Wilson ''is so in love with naturalistic detail that nothing can actually happen—nothing, that is, except these two people going on and on and on.'' By the end of the play, however, he found it ''increasingly easy to stay awake.''

The academic community has accepted Lanford Wilson as one of the most important American playwrights of the twentieth century, and *Talley's Folly* as one of his most important plays. More critical attention has been given to Wilson's so-called urban plays, which are somewhat edgier and less optimistic. Additionally, most formal criticism of the Talley plays deals with all three of them together and explores relationships and dynamics that carry over from one play to another. An example is Robert Cooperman's essay ''The Talley Plays and the Evolution of the American Family.'' Cooperman discusses *Talley's Folly* as the story of Sally and Matt, ''victims of a corrupt and dying institution''—that is, the traditional American family—who make an ''active decision to repair the damage that has already been done to themselves in particular, and to the family in general.'' His analysis is best understood if one sees *Talley's Folly,* as Cooperman does, as an answer to Wilson's later play *Talley & Son.*

Mark Busby, author of a small book on Wilson for the Boise State University Western Writers Series, also draws on information learned in the other Talley plays when he discusses Matt and Sally. Unlike most reviewers of performances of *Talley's Folly,* Busby emphasizes the play's treatment of the theme of ''the nature of work and prosperity,'' which he finds in several other Wilson plays. The fact that the Talley family is making a profit from World War II is troubling to Matt and Sally and to Wilson, and Busby points out that ''work dedicated singly to profit, although it has often been glorified in American experience, does not belong in Wilson's pastoral Midwest.''

In the only book-length study of Wilson, Gene A. Barnett's *Lanford Wilson, Talley's Folly* is given a brief chapter of its own. Barnett examines the simple plot and the effective ''impressionist structure, in which the plot seems to flow naturally, very much like 'real life.''' He also calls attention to Matt's direct address to the audience and suggests, ''Wilson deliberately calls attention to the contrivance and artificiality of his play to force the audience to recognize the unreality of some things that it might recognize the intense reality of others.'' Barnett considers *Talley's Folly* ''a major achievement.''

CRITICISM

Cynthia A. Bily

Bily teaches English at Adrian College in Adrian, Michigan. In the following essay she examines the character of Sally in Talley's Folly, *celebrating her oddness and drawing on insights gained from Lanford Wilson's other Talley family plays.*

Talley's Folly was first staged in 1979, a year after audiences had come to know one of its characters, Sally Talley Friedman, from her appearance in Lanford Wilson's *Fifth of July.* In *Fifth of July,* Sally is the family matriarch, the oldest and wittiest member of the extended family that shares the Talley home. Though she is not the most important character in the play, she is easily the most likeable. Sally has just been widowed, losing her husband, Matt, with whom she shared three decades of happiness; and she recently attended the funeral of an old friend, Harley Campbell, with whom she went to high school. Through a series of family conflicts and sorrows, Sally draws on her inner strength and her sense of humor to support herself and her family.

In some ways, *Talley's Folly* is the story of how Sally gained her strength and humor. Though the main character of *Talley's Folly* may appear to be Matt—after all, he has most of the best lines—it is actually Sally who most grows and develops during the encounter in the boathouse. Though he does not know exactly what he will say, Matt has already decided before he drives to Lebanon that he will ''once in [his] life *risk* something'' and declare himself to Sally. Sally, on the other hand, gathers her courage as the play goes on, through a series of starts and stops.

Set in 1944, the play begins with Sally an eccentric outcast in her own home, an unconventional woman in a conventional, male-centered household. She is a ''terrible embarrassment to her family,'' who see her as a ''crazy old-maid Emma Goldman.'' Her mother, Netta, reveals herself in *Talley & Son* to be neurotic and weak, no real support for her oddball daughter. Eldon, Sally's father, is unscrupulous and unfaithful. Also sharing the home are Sally's senile grandfather, Calvin Stuart Talley; her brother Buddy and his wife Olive; her other brother Timmy, who is off fighting in World War II; and Aunt Charlotte ''Lottie'' Talley. Buddy and Olive meet Matt at the door when he comes to ask for Sally's hand. All Olive can do when she sees Matt is stand with her mouth open,

George Sperdakos and Kerrie Keane in a scene from a theatrical production of
Talley's Folly.

"doing her imitation of a fish." Buddy is more direct: He asks Matt, "You're Sally's Jewish friend, ain't ya? What do you think you want here? Did you ever hear that trespassing was against the law?"

Sally's only support comes from Aunt Lottie, who is also Matt's only ally in the Talley home. When Buddy tries to run Matt off the property, Lottie steps in, yelling, "This man came to see me." She is lying to protect Matt, of course, but the truth is that Lottie and Matt have formed a friendship over the past year, talking on the phone "every few weeks during the winter." Sally at first speaks as though she has no respect for Lottie's judgment about people ("Aunt Lottie would invite the devil into the parlor for hot cocoa"), but as she begins to consider Matt more seriously she also comes to realize that Lottie is one member of her family who can be trusted, saying, "She doesn't gossip about me. She didn't tell you anything." Although *Talley's Folly* shows Lottie to be physically weak, lacking in confidence, and not respected by the others, she is the one of Sally's clan who is not anti-Semitic, and who gives Matt a chance to prove himself a good man.

WHAT DO I READ NEXT?

- *Talley & Son*, written by Wilson in 1981, shows what the rest of the Talley family is doing up at the house while Matt and Sally are talking in the boathouse on July 4, 1944. As the family copes with the death of a relative in World War II and with the probable dissolution of the family business, Sally returns to the house to pack for her elopement.

- *Fifth of July* (1978) was the first of Wilson's Talley family plays to be produced, but it is set in 1977, the most recent in terms of the family's history. It focuses on Ken Talley, Jr., a Vietnam veteran who has lost both legs in the war, and on his decision to sell the Talley property where Aunt Sally—after a long and happy marriage to Matt—has recently scattered her dead husband's ashes.

- *Beast on the Moon* (1998) is a play by Richard Kalinoski. Like Matt Friedman, this play's Aram Tomasian is a refugee from persecution in Europe. Determined to keep his past hidden, he learns that an important part of opening himself up to the love of another person is revealing his secret past.

- *A Doll's House* (1879), by Norwegian playwright Henrik Ibsen, is another play about a woman who, like Sally Talley, must ultimately leave her home to claim her individuality and personhood.

- American economist and sociologist Thorstein Veblen's *Theory of the Leisure Class* (1899) describes how social relations are transformed by the influences of industrialization. Veblen believed that the leisure class is a class of parasites whose conspicuous consumption increases demand for goods, thereby increasing production.

- *A People Apart: The Jews in Europe, 1789–1939* (1999), by David Vital, traces the history of European Jews like Matt Friedman's family up until the beginning of the Holocaust.

Both Matt and Sally seem to enjoy their own madness and comment frequently on it. Matt admits, ''It was crazy to come down here,'' but says he could not help himself. ''You've got a wire crossed or something,'' Sally says, and Matt agrees, ''A screw loose.'' ''You are one total, living loose screw,'' Sally repeats. Later, Matt tells Sally, ''Sally has decided she is an eccentric old maid, and she is going to be one.'' Sally replies, ''I'm looking forward to it.'' She calls him ''goofy,'' and he calls her ''a crazy woman.'' Matt is right when he comments, ''We are a lot alike, you know?''

Sally, Lottie, and Matt are all alienated from the others, but the reader's fondness for them does not grow out of sympathy. Instead, their oddness has taught them a kind of inner strength and an engaging, humorous detachment. We like them because they are not like everyone else—and because everyone else is boring, selfish, and cruel.

There is another relative from whom Sally draws courage: Uncle Everett ''Whistler'' Talley, the creator of the folly. Uncle Whistler is really the brother of Calvin, Sally's now-senile grandfather. While Calvin was building up the family business, Whistler was building follies, or elaborate, fanciful buildings, ''all over town.'' Like Matt, Sally, and Lottie, Whistler was misunderstood by those around him. He built the boathouse because his brother would not let him build a gazebo, a ''frivolity,'' near the house, and when he wanted to build the bandstand in the park, ''The town didn't want it, but he'd seen it in a picture somewhere so he went right over and built it.'' Sally seems to be the only one who understands Uncle Whistler, as she says:

He was not in the least frustrated. He was a happily married man with seven kids. He made toys. Tap-dancing babies and whirligigs. He got pleasure out of making things for people. He did exactly what he wanted to do. He was the healthiest member of the family. Everybody in town knew him.

It was another one of Everett Talley's oddities that earned him the nickname "Whistler": "he sang and whistled" everywhere he went. "He used to go stomping through the woods singing '*Una furtiva lagrima*' [a secret sorrow] at the top of his lungs; nobody knew what he was singing, so they all said he was crazy." If Sally could only see it, an appreciation for music is another quality that Uncle Everett shares with Sally and Matt, and another clue that Sally and Matt are suited for each other.

Music plays a symbolic role in *Talley's Folly* from the beginning, when Matt repeats insistently to the audience, "This is a waltz, remember, one-two-three, one-two-three." Matt is "not a romantic type," but he needs the play to turn out as "a no-holds-barred romantic story," and the music is an essential ingredient for him. It was, after all, at a dance that Matt and Sally first met, and they went back to the Shriners' mosque every night for seven nights to dance and be together. This evening in the boathouse, Matt tries several humorous approaches to break down Sally's resistance, but at first has little success. As he tries to skate, Sally is impatient with him, until he "has taken hold of her and let go of the wall" and at the same time has begun to sing "'Over the Waves,' waltz-tempo, low at first, gaining in confidence." The music makes him more confident, and also draws her closer; it is their first moment of real intimacy, and it lasts until Matt stops singing to say, "I'm having an old-fashioned skate with my girl."

A bit later, when Matt has fallen through the floor and Sally has coldly wiped away the blood, Matt draws her in again by recalling the memory of "Poor Uncle Whistler. He should see what is happening to his boathouse. He'd sing '*Una furtiva lagrima*.'" Matt's appreciation of Whistler, the boathouse, and the music turn Sally toward him again. She tells Matt how much she has loved the place, and how "nobody else would come here and discover the magic of the place except me." The fact that Sally has brought Matt here, and that he has passed the test by admiring the folly, should tell her, as it tells the reader, that he is meant for her.

Matt sings to Sally again after he has told the story of his past and she has pushed him away. This time he sings "Lindy Lou," a song the Lebanon band played as they danced the year before. Again the music weakens Sally's resistance, and again Matt spoils the moment by mentioning marriage.

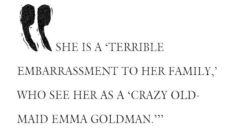

SHE IS A 'TERRIBLE EMBARRASSMENT TO HER FAMILY,' WHO SEE HER AS A 'CRAZY OLD-MAID EMMA GOLDMAN.'"

But finally she gives in, and agrees to elope. The two people who fit nowhere else are going to start a life together. As they sit in eccentric Uncle Whistler's boathouse, they can hear the band playing "Lindy Lou" in Uncle Whistler's bandstand across the river. As Matt says, it is just like a Valentine.

Sally has been resisting marriage, because her inability to bear children makes her feel unsuitable or inadequate for her conventional role. What she only begins to understand by the end of *Talley's Folly* is that there are different ways to be a family. Sally's parents have primarily thought of her more as a bargaining chip than a daughter worthy of love, and withdrew from her when she was "no longer of value to the merger." The fact of her oddness makes her less appealing to her family, even as it makes her more appealing to Matt and to the reader. In her own life, Sally has looked up to and drawn love from the odd ones—her grandfather's brother Whistler and her father's sister Lottie—not from her immediate family.

Thirty-three years later, the Sally of *Fifth of July* knows what it takes to make a family. Matt is gone, but they lived together happily until the day he died. In many ways, Sally has followed in her Aunt Lottie's footsteps. Lottie did not share the politics or the anti-Semitism of the rest of the Talleys, and was able to bless the love between Sally and Matt. Now Sally blesses the love between her nephew Ken and his partner Jed—an attitude which puts her in a small minority in 1979. Just as the childless Aunt Lottie supplied Sally with the love that the ineffectual Netta could not, Sally loves and guides her own niece's daughter Shirley, whose parents are not up to the task.

In an article entitled "The Talley Plays and the Evolution of the American Family," Robert Cooperman describes two sociological models of the American family, the "family of security" and the "family of freedom," and he concludes that in pairing Matt and Sally, Wilson rejects both models in favor of something newer. Matt and Sally are both unconventional, and, ''Their dissimilar backgrounds and decision not to have children to impose a hierarchy on . . . leaves them in a non-traditional, but ultimately workable, family situation.'' I have more hope for these two than Cooperman does. To me, the union of these unconventional people looks not just ''workable,'' but delightful, ''constructed of louvers, and lattice and geegaws.''

Source: Cynthia A. Bily, in an essay for *Drama for Students,* Gale Group, 2001.

Rena Korb

Korb has a Master's degree in English literature and creative writing and has written for a wide variety of educational publishers. In the following essay, she discusses the theme of identity in Talley's Folly.

In his critical study *Lanford Wilson,* Gene Barnett writes of *Talley's Folly,* ''The familiar motif of the impact of the past on the present underlies the . . . theme of spiritual isolation making real communication difficult.'' *Talley's Folly,* one of a trilogy about the Talley family, focuses on the union of two people, both of whom must break free from their solitude in order to join their lives.

On the surface, Matt and Sally seem to have little in common. He is a forty-two-year-old European Jew who works as an accountant in St. Louis. She is a thirty-one-year-old self-described spinster who still lives in her family home in the small town of Lebanon, Missouri. However, both are harboring past traumas and what they consider to be their own inadequacies—Matt's refusal to father children and Sally's inability to bear children. They have developed into adults cut off from all other people. That they have found each other in the first place is almost miraculous, the work of a ''mischievous angel [who] has looked down and saw us.'' However, on the evening of July 4, 1944, a challenge still remains, and it is what drives forward *Talley's Folly:* How will these two people open up to each other?

Indeed, at the heart of *Talley's Folly* is the issue of identity: how people are imprisoned by it as well as how they must actively work to change the way they see themselves. Throughout the play, Matt and Sally are invited to break free from their long-held roles. The story takes place a year after Matt and Sally's first meeting at a dance. At that time, they

were able to step beyond their boundaries because of the short nature of their love affair. Sally, for instance, daringly brought Matt home for dinner. After Matt's vacation ended, however, their individual progress took very different turns. Sally returned to her closed self, ignoring Matt's many letters, refusing to see him when he came down for a visit, and denying her feelings for him. Matt, however, chose to reject the man he once was. As he recalls, ''I said, Matt, go down, tell Sally who you are. Once in your life *risk* something. At least you will know that you did what you could. What do you think she is going to do, bite you?'' Matt gives up his identity in order to gain a better one—that of Sally's husband.

The importance of identity drives the play. It is referenced consistently up until the moment when Matt proposes marriage to Sally.

> SALLY: Don't sing to me, it's ridiculous. And my name is not Lindy Lou. It's Sally Talley. *(They both smile.)*
>
> MATT: I know, I came down to talk to you about that.

Through the eyes of others, as a European immigrant Matt's identity derives from being an outsider in the United States. Physically, he is different from those people who surround him. Unlike Sally, described as ''light,'' Matt is ''dark'' and wears a beard. He speaks with ''a trace of a German-Jewish accent, of which he is probably unaware.'' In Sally's provincial town of Lebanon, he is viewed primarily in light of his religious background. Sally's brother Buddy meets him with the words, ''You're Sally's Jewish friend, ain't ya? What do you think you want here? Did you ever hear that trespassing was against the law?'' On the whole, Sally's family, with the exception of Aunt Charlotte, wants Matt to have nothing to do with Sally. When Matt comes to the Talley house, Sally's mother and sister-in-law ''stayed up there on the screened-in porch, protected from the mosquitoes and Communists and infidels.'' He is a man whom Sally's father even calls ''more dangerous than Roosevelt himself.''

Matt, however, does not place much emphasis on his foreignness. Tellingly, he is blindingly unaware of certain truths about himself, such as his ''pronounced accent,'' which he does not believe exists. His claims that ''I have no accent. I worked very hard and have completely lost any trace of accent'' could be interpreted in two different ways: either he truly is unaware of his accent or he subconsciously denies it, realizing that it will set him apart.

Matt's own perception of his identity derives from his lack of interest in taking on the typical role of the adult male in American society. He sees himself as inherently unmarriageable because of his unwillingness to have children. Sally gives voice to the opinions society holds on such an anomaly: "Only something is wrong. Something is goofy, isn't it? A single man, forty-two years old. It doesn't make sense that a good man hasn't made a fool of himself at least once by your age."

By contrast, Sally comes from a traditional small-town family. Before the Great Depression, her family was one of the richest in Lebanon. Her brother, Buddy, has managed to hold on to the family factory despite the economic troubles of the mid-1900s. Sally, however, is the black sheep of the family. According to Sally, "Everyone is always saying what a crazy old maid Emma Goldman I'm becoming." Her words, immediately contradicted by Matt, show her negative self-perception. Although she demonstrates her independence and financial capability by working as a nurse and accumulating significant savings, she only dreams of escaping the confines of her family home. As Aunt Charlotte tells Matt, Sally "didn't have much courage [to do it]."

Even the play's minor characters—none of whom ever appears on stage—are presented through the narrow lens of how they are perceived by others and what they represent. The insignificant sister-in-law Olive is something "on a relish tray." Brother Buddy's real name is Kenny; according to Matt, both of these names are "absurd," not proper names "for a grown man." Sally's aunt, Charlotte, is the most important of this supporting cast. She helps engineer and actively encourages the reunion between Matt and Sally. Matt also learns about Sally's past from Charlotte; her age, for example, and her firing from Sunday school. As he tells Sally, "I've become great friends with your Aunt Charlotte. There's a counterspy in your home. You're infiltrated. I didn't tell you. You're ambushed. I've come up on you from behind." His words show that Charlotte's role is greater than that of a mere conduit of information. Sally would never anticipate Charlotte's spy-like actions. Thus Charlotte also functions symbolically to remind Matt and Sally, along with the audience, that people have multiple layers to their personalities and their identities.

As the play begins, Matt is attempting to step outside of his self-constructed identity. However,

> INDEED, AT THE HEART OF *TALLEY'S FOLLY* IS THE ISSUE OF IDENTITY: HOW PEOPLE ARE IMPRISONED BY IT AS WELL AS HOW THEY MUST ACTIVELY WORK TO CHANGE THE WAY THEY SEE THEMSELVES."

he finds it difficult to share the real Matt with Sally. He continuously relies on other personalities and voices to share his concerns. To find out the answer to the Sally "puzzle"—why she is avoiding him— he speaks in different accents. He even declares that he will become one of the Ozark "hillbillies": "I won't be Matt Friedman anymore. I'll join the throng. Call myself . . . August Hedgepeth. Sip moonshine over the back of my elbow. Wheat straw in the gap in my teeth." Matt's easy assumption of other personalities shows his unwillingness to let Sally see his true personality—he thinks she won't like the real him. This creates an interesting duality, as Matt hides behind the personae of others even while he is readying himself to share his biggest secret with Sally.

The importance of a person's speech patterns is further emphasized when Sally questions Matt about his background. "English wasn't your first language. What was?" she asks, as opposed to the more standard question, "Where were you born?" At first, Matt tries to avoid answering. When he finally does, he refers to himself in the third person, showing his need to distance himself from the past.

> What was Matthew's first language? It doesn't come out funny. What does it matter; he can't talk to the old man at the cafeteria in Lithuanian any more. Not the way he would like to . . .

When Sally insists on learning his family history, Matt submits by refusing to draw the characters of his father, mother, sister, and himself, and instead dubs them with nondescript labels: "A Prussian and a Uke and a Lat and a Probable Lit." The ensuing story of the death of his family, his parents (the Prussian and the Ukrainian) "indefinitely detained" by the Germans, after his older sister (born in Latvia) was murdered by the French, is also told from the third-person point of view. Only at its very end, after Matt has revealed his secret—that he has resolved ''never to be responsible for bringing into such a world another living soul. . . . not bring into this world another child to be killed for political purpose''—does he revert back to the first person. He asks Sally,

> And what woman would be interested in such a grown Probable Lit with such a resolve? . . . Anyway, he doesn't think about it. The day is over in a second. I spend my life adding figures. It breaks my head.
>
> SALLY: *(Very level)* He does. The Lit.
>
> MATT: Does what?
>
> SALLY: You said ''I.'' You mean the Lit. The Lit spends his life adding figures.
>
> MATT: Yes, well, I do too. We are much alike. We work together.

Although Matt and ''the Lit'' are alike, unlike the Lit, Matt decides to step out of the world of logic, as represented by numbers, and risk being hurt. Sally, however, resists such a change. Indeed, Matt almost constantly urges her to get her to rethink her situation. Her tenacity and her reticence is represented physically as well as verbally. Matt is wearing skates, but Sally turns to leave the folly.

> MATT: Sally? Hey, I can't run after you in these.
>
> SALLY: Good. I'm good and sick of you running after me, Matt. *(She is gone.)*
>
> MATT: Come on. *(He tries to run after her.)* Where do you think you are going—

Sally's personality is best symbolized by her actions the previous February. Matt drove down from St. Louis to visit her at the hospital where she works. Matt claims that she hid from him in the closet; Sally claims that she was working in the kitchen, where visitors were not allowed. Whoever is more correct, the essential point remains the same: Sally kept herself from Matt, as she keeps herself hidden from the world. After being rejected by her fiancé and her father because of her inability to have children, Sally has come to believe that the rest of the world will reject her for this supposed defect as well. She has constructed her life around this physical disorder; it has become her most important characteristic. After Matt tells her that he will not have children, she does not even believe the sincerity of his story. ''You've been talking to Aunt Lotttie?'' she says. ''Who else have you talked to? People in town? Have you looked in the Lebanon newspaper? The old files? I don't know how detectives work.'' Her choice of words, particularly her likening of Matt to a detective, shows just how

much a secret she views her infertility. In her mind, her inability to bear a child defines her and renders her valueless. She has some valid reasons for feeling this way. Not only did her fiance replace her, ''Dad was looking at me like I was a broken swing.'' These men, members of the two most important families in Lebanon, surely voice the feelings of many in their community. The stigma they visit upon Sally results in her having lived the past ten years of her life under the assumption that no one would want to marry her because she cannot have children.

Although neither Matt nor Sally can give birth to new life, there still could be ''a life for the two of us.'' Keeping this in mind, it seems hardly coincidental that one of the primary images in the play is eggs. Matt shares with Sally the belief of a man he knows.

> ''He said people are eggs. Said we had to be careful not to bang up against each other too hard. Crack our shells, never be any use again. Said we were eggs. Individuals. We had to keep separate, private. He was very protective of his shell. He said nobody ever knows what the other guy is thinking. We all got about ten tracks going at once, nobody ever knows what's going down any given track at any given moment. So we never can really communicate.''

At the time, Matt told the man ''he ought not to [be] too afraid of gettin' his yolk broke.'' Now he stands before Sally, despite the ''Humpty Dumpty complex,'' to ''take a big chance'' and tell her he loves her. For Matt has learned that in order to have any chance at forging a fulfilling life with another, he must learn to reveal his secrets. After Sally follows his lead and reveals her own secret, they both come to understand that their perceptions about the world are wrong. Even worse, these perceptions have developed into misapprehensions about their own self-worth.

After Sally becomes convinced of Matt's sincerity, she accepts his proposal. However, although Sally no longer sees herself as valueless to a man, she does not completely drop her habit of judging herself through the eyes of others. Matt wants to drive to St. Louis that evening, but she responds, ''Oh, Matt, it's absurd to be talking like that; we're practically middle-aged.'' Matt's answer—''So''—demonstrates that he is reaching beyond himself. Yet, the play ends on a high note of optimism. Both Matt and Sally have demonstrated their willingness to try something new—he in his new tie and she in her new dress. Sally quickly agrees to go with him that night, and the two take the first steps of what will begin a long, successful marriage.

Source: Rena Korb, in an essay for *Drama for Students,* Gale Group, 2001.

Gene A. Barnett

In the following study of Wilson's Talley's Folly, *Gene Barnett presents reasons for its critical success and popular appeal.*

When Wilson began to draft the Talley family history in preparation for work on *Fifth of July,* he became fascinated with a Talley daughter named Sally. So reversing the order of creation, he made her a mate and began to imagine their middle-age romance. ''I liked the two characters,'' he says simply, ''and I wanted to see the play.'' Remembering the wounds, both physical and emotional, that lacerated his fictional family, he decided that, for this love story, he ''should go all the way and make it the sweet valentine it should be.''

When *Fifth of July* was completed and in rehearsal, Wilson made up a biography of Aunt Sally Friedman in order to help the actress playing the role to understand her, ''a history for her to draw on.'' He also devised a biography for Matt Friedman, finding in the process that the character was assuming the form of Circle Repertory Company actor Judd Hirsch. The playwright told Helen Stenborg (Aunt Sally) that if she found it helpful, she could think of Hirsch as her deceased husband whose ashes she had brought back to Lebanon. Wilson remembers that when Hirsch came to see a rehearsal of *Fifth,* he told the actor, ''You're in the box'' (i.e., the urn), and so the central role of the second Talley play had been cast before the first play was even in previews.

Talley's Folly opened in May 1979 and received almost unanimous critical raves. Harold Clurman thought it the playwright's ''most engaging play,'' and the two reviewers for the *New York Times* called it ''a treasure,'' ''a lovely play,'' ''a charmer,'' and ''a play to savour and to cheer.'' The playwright himself, normally modest and objective about his own work, admits it is a ''personal favorite'' and ''more perfect than anything I've ever written.'' It was awarded the Pulitzer Prize for drama in the spring of 1980.

Plot: ''A Very Simple Story.''

In discussing his approach to the play, Wilson continually returns to the word ''simple.'' (''I wanted to write a simple story.'') The word is apt. Matt Friedman, a forty-two-year-old Jewish accountant from Saint Louis, has driven down to the central-

A scene from a 1982 production of Talley's Folly *at Toronto's Theatre Plus.*

southern Missouri town of Lebanon for the Fourth of July weekend in 1944 intent on resolving his romance with Sally Talley, thirty-one (she says) and turning spinsterish, whom he had met the previous year. After an unpleasant showdown with her family that afternoon, he woos her and wins her that night in the folly, the decaying boathouse down on the river from the Talley family home. That is the action of the play, hence the label ''simple.''

But as with other Wilson plays, the present action depends to a great extent on the past. Matt Friedman had come to the Lebanon area on vacation in the summer of 1943, met Sally Talley at a dance at the Shrine Mosque in Springfield (a landmark still there), and had driven her home to Lebanon that night and the other six nights of his vacation. At her urging, he met her family over dinner; they disliked him for his Jewishness, his lack of patriotism, and his beard. Sally's father denounced him as ''more dangerous than Roosevelt himself.''

Since then, he has written her almost daily from Saint Louis, but she has responded only once and has not seen him since the preceding summer. He has, however, spoken by phone to Charlotte Talley (Aunt Lottie), who has encouraged his suit. As the play opens, he means to propose to Sally, the first

THIS IS GOING TO BE AN EASY, COMFORTABLE LOVE STORY WITH A HAPPY ENDING, HE SEEMS TO BE WARNING US, SO BEWARE OF SENTIMENTALITY. THEN AS THOUGH TO SHOW HIS MANIPULATIVE POWERS, HE WARMS US WITH HIS CHARACTERS AND DRAWS US INTO THEIR PROBLEMS SO THAT OUR BELIEF IS WON."

proposal he has risked in his forty-two years. While waiting for her in the boathouse, he turns master of ceremonies and stage director, welcoming the audience and explaining the setting, lighting, sound effects, and the mood of a nation at the end of a world war.

The Folly

A "folly" in the architectural sense of the term is an elaborate structure, unusual and unique in design, quite expensive, and often built out of whim rather than purpose. As they pass the ninety-seven minutes of the play in the structure that gives the work its title, Matt elicits from Sally a bit of family history: that the builder was called "Whistler" because he whistled and sang a lot. (His signature piece was "Una furtiva lagrima" from Donizetti's *L'elisir d'amore,* but since none of the locals knew much about Italian opera, they merely thought him daft.) Uncle Whistler had built the boathouse and, in addition, the bandstand from which music drifts across the river on this Fourth of July evening.

The title of the play also refers to Sally's choice of a husband. Matt, a good ten years older than she and rather alien with his faint German-Jewish accent and Semitic background, was not considered a suitable husband by her provincial and bigoted family. Yet, she and Matt go on to have a very happy marriage, and Matt does so well financially that his brother-in-law, Buddy, envies him. Since we know from information given in *Fifth of July* how well the marriage turned out, reference in this play to the

union as "Sally Talley's folly" is ironic and meant to be.

But in 1944, the boathouse is rotting and decrepit and in need of restoration—like the family. At the same time its ruined state is a part of the romance of the place. Wilson describes it as Victorian in style, with "louvers, lattice in decorative panels, and a good deal of Gothic Revival gingerbread." The wood has weathered to a pale gray, and the boathouse is overhung with maples and a weeping willow.

The lighting and sound are to be very romantic, with watery reflections of sunset and moonlight on the boathouse walls. ("The water runs right through here," Matt tells the audience, "so you're all out in the river—sorry about that.") In addition, there are the sounds of the land and the river at dusk: water, frogs, bees, dogs, and crickets. The band, playing across the river in Whistler's bandstand, strikes up a fanfare just as Sally explains why she has not married, and a lightly swinging rendition of "Lindy Lou" concludes the play. To complete a nearly perfect romantic scene, Wilson conjures up the sweet odor of honeysuckle.

"You live in such a beautiful country," Matt tells Sally, and he promises that he will bring her back every year. The Talleys may live in a Garden, even though the race has fallen, but it is people like Sally and Matt who will bring restoration through love. The sense of evil, never strong in a Wilson play, is embodied by some of those in the house on the hill. Greed and bigotry lurk there, and evil is latent in the landscape, for snakes may be nesting under the boathouse. But the only serpents who materialize are some of the Talleys, for this is Eden after the Fall.

The folly has all the romantic atmosphere of a setting for opera or operetta. Was there a real model? No, Wilson says, "I've never seen the folly in Missouri or anywhere else until John Lee [Beatty, the principal designer for the Circle Repertory Company] built it for me." Wilson has implied that it was partly owing to the inspired stage design that he decided to write a play about Whistler Talley.

Structure

The playwright is aware that his work is often not strongly plotted. It may be that he is most comfortable with an impressionistic structure in which the plot seems to flow naturally, very much like "real life." This method proved effective for *Talley's Folly,* which seems indeed very natural yet demonstrates on inspection a structural rhythm. Generally, it might be said that the conversation of Sally and Matt goes back and forth between the past, always important to Wilson's characters, and the present, interrupted by several tangential episodes and observations. "The past" covers her family history, his early family background in Europe, and the beginning of their courtship the preceding summer. "The present" dramatizes the final stage of their courtship and their plans to elope that same evening. "Tangential episodes" include, for example, a scene in which Matt "ice skates" on the bare floor of the folly. Also woven into the play are Matt's observations on American labor, the greed of business, and the dangers of prosperity in the postwar era. These references set the love story against the larger, darker background of social, political, and cultural issues of the mid-1940s.

Structurally, the notable feature of the play is Wilson's use of Matt as chorus in the manner both of Wilder's Stage Manager (*Our Town*) or Williams's Tom (*The Glass Menagerie*). Matt addresses the audience in a three-page monologue as the play begins and briefly at its conclusion, in this way "framing" the evening. He immediately tells the audience that he has only ninety-seven minutes ("without intermission") for the story and points out "some of the facilities." About halfway through his long introduction, he replays very rapidly much of what he has already said for the benefit of latecomers. He comments on the "rotating gismo in the footlights," which provides the effect of moonlight on water ("valentines need frou-frou"). He calls attention to the night sounds to be heard throughout the evening. He describes post-Depression America, comparing it to 1944 when the country, like the Talleys, is "in grave danger of prosperity." And he tells the audience that the play they are about to see "should be a waltz, one-two-three, one-two-three; a no-holds-barred romantic story."

Yet, the play begins with the houselights up, and the set is seen in the hard, white glare of the "worklight" that intensifies the artificiality of stage scenery. Perhaps Wilson deliberately calls attention to the contrivance and artificiality of his play to force the audience to acknowledge the unreality of some things that it might recognize the intense reality of others. Much more to the point is the suggestion that this alienation of the audience from stage "reality" is to cause it to be "intellectually on its guard against the snares of romantic love, and then, in spite of ourselves to force us into believing in its truth." This is going to be an easy, comfort-able love story with a happy ending, he seems to be warning us, so beware of sentimentality. Then as though to show his manipulative powers, he warms us with his characters and draws us into their problems so that our belief is won.

Matt

Of the two roles, Matt's is the more complex, for he is a many-sided character. Basically, his is a tragic conception of life because of the personal horrors attendant on his youth in prewar Europe. Yet, he can encourage Sally to take a risk and "live for today." He believes in reason and communication. "I have great powers of ratiocination", he tells her, and this helps him to see not only that she is in love with him, but that there is "something to tell" that only she can tell. He can take "no" for an answer but not evasions.

Matt knows he is not a "romantic type," but his mathematical mind (he knows the multiplication table up to seventy-five times seventy-five) tells him his own worth, and hers. He is a mimic, attempting a comic German accent with the same confidence as he "does" Humphrey Bogart or a Missouri farmer. Although he makes fun of Sally's Ozark accent, he denies his own English is accented. He is also very witty and droll ("Olive! Olive! I could not think of your sister-in-law's darn name! . . . I knew she was on a relish tray."

Matt's most important scene comes when Sally asks him if he has ever been married. In answering, he tells the story of his life, almost as a fable, in the third person, perhaps to distance himself from the wounds of his youth. Briefly he explains how his parents, one Prussian and the other Ukrainian, were "indefinitely detained" by the Germans, after his older sister, born in Latvia, was murdered by the French. He himself, born in Lithuania, came via Norway and Caracas to America. Because of the loss of his family through war, no allegiances or causes can make any claims on him. He resolved "never to be responsible for bringing into such a world another living soul . . . to be killed for a political purpose." He has grown to middle age, thinking no woman would be interested in marrying a man who would never sire children, not because he could not but because he would not. Thus, Matt's resolution has kept him in a shell.

The most important image associated with Matt is found in a story he tells Sally: "This guy told me we were eggs," he begins, and we must not knock against each other or we will crack our shells and be of no use. Since we are isolated in our shells, we never really communicate. ''I told him he ought not to be too afraid of gettin' his yolk broke.''

Matt returns to the egg metaphor in his proposal to Sally: ''We all have a Humpty Dumpty complex.'' When he takes the risk and proposes, Sally puts him off. With only two or three of his ninety-seven minutes to go, he looks to the sky exclaiming, ''Eggs! Eggs! Eggs!'' He is annoyed at their terror of cracking the shell but hoping they both will find courage to do just that. In the minutes that follow, both of these curious ''eggs'' crack, and their marriage lasts thirty-two years, ending with Matt's death in 1976.

Sally

In his courtship of Sally, Matt has one factor very much in his favor: she does not like living at home, for she considers most of her family to be ''hypocrites and fools.'' But she would never consider marrying Matt just to get away and has given him no encouragement. She answered only one of his many letters and then only to tell him not to write. Apparently she accepts what people are saying about her, that she is turning into ''a crazy old-maid Emma Goldman.''

Nevertheless, Sally manages to escape the stereotype of the lonely, frigid spinster who secretly yearns for romance and sexual fulfillment by genuinely trying to put off Matt, while, at the same time, revealing in unintentional and subtle ways that she is attracted to him. Second, there is the pathos, even tragedy, of a revelation made approximately a decade before that she must face again in order to give Matt the explanation he insists on and deserves: that she is barren and therefore cannot imagine that Matt or anyone else would want to marry her. This most painful moment is the emotional climax of the play. We are touched by her personal tragedy, but we also know that paradoxically her sterility is the key to a long and loving relationship with Matt. Because she is inadequate in a way that is unimportant to him, they seem indeed made for each other. When she realizes he has not deliberately tailored his story to conform to hers, she is ready to accept him.

Talley's Folly is a notable achievement for Wilson. The dramatic structure is compact although the plot is not very strong. The characters are two of his best, one coming from the playwright's Missouri background and the other created from an entirely different social and cultural context. The setting is functional to the story. The familiar motif

of the impact of the past on the present underlies the deeper theme of spiritual isolation making real communication difficult. *Talley's Folly* has been truthfully described as Wilson's ''best crafted work,'' and with its wide audience appeal, it has been his most popular play. It is a major achievement and falls short of matching *Fifth of July* only in the modesty of its aims.

Source: Gene A. Barnett, ''Talley's Folly,'' in *Lanford Wilson,* edited by Warren French, Twayne Publishers, 1987, pp. 118–24.

Steven H. Gale

Steven Gale's critique of Talley's Folly *praises the production's cast and staging for presenting a unique insight into Wilson's view of human nature.*

As part of its fifteenth annual tour, the Missouri Repertory Theatre's staging of Lanford Wilson's *Talley's Folly* was crisply directed by James Assad, a former MRT member who returned from a teaching stint in New York City, and starred Jeannine Hutchings as Sally Talley and David Schuster as Matt Friedman. The high quality of the cast did full credit to Wilson's 1980 Pulitzer Prize winning play. Set in the Talley family's Victorian boathouse in Lebanon, Missouri on July 4, 1944, the romance begins with Matt walking into the auditorium while the house lights are still up, as though to make an announcement. He sits on the pit apron and conversationally begins filling in the drama's background in a casual, neighborly tone. Soon his dialogue becomes tinged with a Yiddish accent (later we learn that he was born in Lithuania) and suddenly we find ourselves in the middle of the action of the play.

The plot is simple. On a trip to St. Louis Sally met Matt and they were attracted to one another. Now Matt, a forty-two-year-old Jewish accountant from the big city, has come to a small, reactionary rural community to ask the thirty-one-year-old spinster to marry him. There are problems, the least of which is the resistance by Sally's family. More important is what is expressed as the eggs metaphor—the ''Humpty Dumpty Complex''—they are both ''afraid to be cracked.'' Matt's family has been destroyed in European warfare and in the world that he sees around he finds no place for children. Sally has had a bad experience in love and is unable to bring herself to take another chance.

Matt and Sally attempt to communicate, but both are fearful of the pain that might result from a relationship and, therefore, are hesitant to divulge information that might pinpoint their areas of vulnerability. Ultimately Sally reveals the details of her unhappy love affair, culminating in the exposure of her vital secret: her fiance broke their engagement when it was determined that a disease had left her unable to bear children. She had been unwilling to admit this to Matt, at least in part because she did not want to disappoint his desire for children. Since he does not want children, their needs and desires can mesh, and the play ends with them running off to get married.

Interestingly, *5th of July,* which takes place during the Vietnam War era, was written before *Talley's Folly.* In telling the story of Sally as a sixty-seven-year-old widow, Wilson became interested in the character to whom she had been married, and Matt (patterned after actor Judd Hirsh) and *Talley's Folly* resulted. It is only natural, then, that the stronger character is Matt, and Schuster's portrayal was just right. His accent conveyed a sense of foreignness, but it was not intrusive; his timing and his subtle combination of intelligence and emotion made Matt an attractive character. As Sally, Hutchings had a less demanding role, but she played it adroitly, never overshadowing Matt, yet letting the sensuality, humor, and intellect of her character show through her plainness.

The set, which arrived in a truck on the afternoon of the performance, was excellent. The boathouse, supposedly built by Sally's uncle in 1870, was typically Victorian in construction, with lattice and gables, but now fallen into disrepair. Capturing the freedom and independence of the two lovers who meet there to work out their lives, it also reflected their fragility and strangeness in a world of conservative, prejudiced rednecks whose off-stage presence is constantly felt.

Talley's Folly is particularly attractive to a southwest Missouri audience, and those who walked out of a production of Tom Stoppard's *Rosencrantz and Guildenstern Are Dead* last year raved over this play, the second of a projected series of works tracing the Talley family history. Two other plays in *The War in Lebanon* series, *5th of July* (the first segment) and *A Tale Told,* have already been mounted, but audience reaction to *Talley's Folly* indicates that for midwesterners Wilson has successfully returned to his Missouri roots to ''tell . . . what this country is really all about.'' Wilson once claimed that he ''set out to write a valentine,'' and this love story appeals to the kind of people about

> WILSON ONCE CLAIMED THAT HE 'SET OUT TO WRITE A VALENTINE,' AND THIS LOVE STORY APPEALS TO THE KIND OF PEOPLE ABOUT WHOM IT WAS WRITTEN— INDIVIDUALS WITH GREAT STRENGTH AND INTEGRITY WHO ARE INVOLVED IN DAY-TO-DAY HUMAN RELATIONSHIPS, NOT IN SOLVING ABSTRACT, INTELLECTUAL PROBLEMS.''

whom it was written—individuals with great strength and integrity who are involved in day-to-day human relationships, not in solving abstract, intellectual problems. The questioning of Rosencrantz and Guildenstern makes no sense to an audience secure in their beliefs and established in their world, while the familiarity of Wilson's characters and situation makes his play appealing.

Talley's Folly is a good theatrical vehicle, not great drama. In many ways it illustrates the typical strengths and weaknesses present in the rest of Wilson's canon: it reveals insight into human nature, yet it is not meant to be anything other than entertaining. Unlike Harold Pinter or David Mamet, Wilson rarely goes below the surface to determine what meanings underlie his characters' actions; he is satisfied with presenting predictable, emotional, character-based melodramas.

Recent criticism has claimed that plays such as *Talley's Folly, Crimes of the Heart, The Great Grandson of Jedediah Kohler,* and *The Dining Room* fail because they are nothing more than ''regional romanticism.'' In the long history of the theatre there is no doubt that this is an accurate assessment. However, it is also a shortsighted one, for the history of the theatre contains more plays like *Talley's Folly* than it does plays like *Old Times.* And this is as it should be. We savor the great plays when they appear, but in middle America it is perhaps the lesser works that keep the theatre alive.

On aesthetic grounds Pinter may be preferable to Wilson, but Wilson is better than no theatre at all.

Source: Steven H. Gale, Review in *Theatre Journal,* Vol. 35, No. 1, March 1983, pp. 124–6.

SOURCES

Barnett, Gene A., *Lanford Wilson,* Twayne, 1987, pp. 121–22.

Busby, Mark, *Lanford Wilson,* Boise State University, 1987, pp. 38–39.

Clurman, Harold, Review in *The Nation,* March 15, 1980, p. 316.

Cooperman, Robert, ''The Talley Plays and the Evolution of the American Family,'' in *Lanford Wilson: A Casebook,* edited by Jackson R. Bryer, Garland, 1994, pp. 67, 72, 75.

Haller, Scott, ''The Dramatic Rise of Lanford Wilson,'' in *Saturday Review,* August 1981, p. 26.

Hughes, Catharine, ''Four Uppers,'' in *America,* March 22, 1980, p. 247.

Kroll, Jack, ''Love in a Folly,'' in *Newsweek,* March 3, 1980, p. 53.

Molyneaux, Gerard M., Review in *Library Journal,* April 1, 1980, p. 874.

Nightingale, Benedict, ''Wound Up,'' in *New Statesman,* June 11, 1982, p. 34.

Simon, John, Review in *The New Yorker,* March 3, 1980, p. 62.

FURTHER READING

Dean, Anne M., *Discovery and Invention: The Urban Plays of Lanford Wilson,* Fairleigh Dickinson University Press, pp. 15–29.

> As the title indicates, this book-length study focuses on Wilson's plays that take place in cities, not on the Talley plays set in Lebanon, Missouri. However, Dean's first chapter is a brief biography of the playwright, written with his cooperation and the help of several of his close colleagues. This chapter is the best source for insight into Wilson's reliance on mentors and colleagues in his creative process.

Ryzuk, Mary S., *The Circle Repertory Company: The First Fifteen Years,* Iowa State University Press.

> A straightforward history of the theater company founded in New York by Lanford Wilson and the director Marshall W. Mason. The ''Circle Rep'' was the site of the first production of *Talley's Folly* and the other Talley plays.

Savran, David, ''Lanford Wilson,'' in *In Their Own Words: Contemporary American Playwrights,* Theatre Communications Group, pp. 306–20.

> In this interview Wilson discusses the years he studied the ''well-made play,'' a tightly constructed form of drama first produced in nineteenth-century France. Wilson used the structure of the well-made play in the writing of several of his own plays, including *Talley's Folley.*

Williams, Philip Middleton, *The Comfortable House: Lanford Wilson, Marshall W. Mason and the Circle Repertory Theatre,* McFarland.

> Examines the collaboration between Wilson and Mason, who directed almost forty productions of Wilson's plays. Through interviews, drama reviews, and analysis of scripts in various stages of revision, this book demonstrates how playwright and director working together can enrich a production beyond the capabilities of either alone.

That Championship Season

JASON MILLER

1972

Jason Miller's *That Championship Season* was regarded as one of the more important plays of its time. In addition to reflecting the emptiness of America's emphasis on winning and other suspect values, the play was also regarded as the kind of quintessential American drama Broadway should have been producing, but was not. *That Championship Season* made its debut off-Broadway at the Estelle Newman/Public Theatre on May 2, 1972, where it ran for 144 performances. The production was then moved to the Booth Theatre on Broadway, where it ran for an additional 844 performances. The play ran for a total of 988 performances before it closed on April 21, 1974.

That Championship Season was only the second full-length play Miller had written, and it was by far his most successful. Miller was primarily an actor, who wrote plays on the side. For this play, which lifted him out of obscurity, Miller won numerous awards, including the New York Drama Critics Award for Best Play, Drama Desk Award for Most Promising Playwright, and Outer Critics Circle John Gassner Playwriting Award, all in 1972. Miller also won the Antoinette Perry Award (the Tony) for best play and the Pulitzer Prize for Drama in 1973. In the early 1980s, he later adapted the play into a movie, which he directed.

From its earliest productions, *That Championship Season* was widely praised by critics, though a few dissenters had problems with certain aspects of

the play. Those who like the play compliment its humor, dialogue, and characters. Reviewing the Broadway production, Clive Barnes of the *New York Times* writes, ''Mr. Miller has a perfect ear and instinct for the rough and tumble profanity of locker-room humor. The coarsely elegant gibes go along with Mr. Miller's indictment of a society, which opens with an ironic playing of the National Anthem and then lacerates the sickness of small-town America full of bigotry, double-dealing, racism and hate.''

AUTHOR BIOGRAPHY

Jason Miller was born on April 22, 1939, in Long Island City, New York. He was the only child of John and Mary Claire Miller, an electrician and a teacher respectively. The family moved to Pennsylvania when Miller was very young and he spent the rest of his childhood there. As a child, Miller was unfocused. He loved to play sports but often got into trouble at the Catholic schools he attended. A nun encouraged him to learn to use his powerful voice. She got him involved in elocution (public speaking) competitions, which soon compelled Miller to pursue a career in acting.

After graduating from Saint Patrick's High School in Scranton, Pennsylvania, he enrolled at the University of Scranton. He studied theater and playwriting, earning his B. A. in 1961. In 1962, Miller entered the Catholic University of America for a year of graduate training in acting. There he met and married Linda Gleason, the daughter of actor/comedian Jackie Gleason. The couple eventually had three children (including Jason Patric Miller who became an accomplished actor in his own right as Jason Patric). Both Miller and his wife became professional actors, traveling to wherever they could find work on the stage.

By the mid-1960s, Miller and his family settled in New York City. Though he appeared in soap operas and regional productions, he also held jobs as a truck driver and a welfare caseworker when necessary to support his family. Miller made his New York acting debut in 1969 in *Pequod,* an off-Broadway play. He also dabbled in playwriting. One of his plays was *Nobody Hears a Broken Drum* (1970).

In the early 1970s, he began writing the play that became *That Championship Season.* Though producers initially rejected the play, it attracted the attention of Joseph Papp. With Papp's help, the play was produced off-Broadway in the spring of 1972. By fall, it had moved to Broadway.

Miller did not write another play that was produced for many years. Instead, he went to Hollywood and focused primarily on acting. In 1973, he played the role of Father Karras in the horror film *The Exorcist.* The role earned him an Academy Award nomination. Miller also appeared in television roles including *F. Scott Fitzgerald in Hollywood* (1976). Miller did not leave writing entirely behind. He wrote for television and films, beginning in the early 1980s.

Since the initial productions of *That Championship Season,* Miller spent many years trying to get the play made into a feature film. In 1982, his dream was finally realized. Miller wrote the adaptation, and when there were problems finding a director, he directed the production as well. The resulting film was not a commercial success.

By the mid-1980s, Miller left Hollywood to return home to Scranton. While taking care of his ill parents, Miller became the artistic director of the Scranton Public Theatre. In 1997, Miller returned to playwriting with *Barrymore's Ghost,* which was first produced in Seattle. Miller played the lead in its first production when the star dropped out. However, most of Miller's professional energies remain focused on acting and writing for television.

PLOT SUMMARY

Act 1

That Championship Season opens in Coach's decaying living room. He is hosting a reunion of the high school basketball team he coached to a championship about twenty years ago. Tom Daley and George Sikowski are in the room, catching up. Tom has come from out of town for the reunion, while George is now the hometown mayor. Tom drinks heavily.

George worries about his upcoming reelection campaign, and derides his opponent, Norman Sharmen. They talk about the Coach, who recently had an operation. George believes that he owes his mayorship to the Coach's influence. The pair wishes that Martin would have come to the reunion. Martin was the best player among them, but he has never returned.

George tells Tom that Phil Romano, one of their teammates and a rich businessman, will be contributing a big sum to his campaign in return for a favorable land lease. James Daley (Tom's elder brother), Phil, and Coach finally return with food and drink. Coach is happy to see all of them.

The Coach equates their team effort to get George elected with their winning the championship. The Coach tells all of them how proud he is of their accomplishments. James tells the Coach that he helped them succeed. The conversation turns to the current lack of respect in the country. When Tom leaves to use the bathroom, those who remain discuss his alcoholic state. While the Coach wants to put Tom to work on George's campaign, James informs them that his brother is leaving town.

Phil tells George that he might not be easily reelected. Among other things, George has raised taxes, and some local plants will be closing soon. James defends George. George cannot see that he has failed in some areas, including the purchase of an elephant for the local zoo that died ten days later, and that he might not be able to win again. George is defensive.

Coach finds it hard to tolerate the dissension in the room. He derides it as well as the dissension that has been growing in the United States. As Coach grows more agitated, he suffers severe pain related to his recent surgery. George helps him upstairs.

When the pair is gone, Phil tells James and Tom that George has no chance to be reelected. James asks Phil if he does not support George because Phil is having an affair with George's wife, Marion. James threatens to reveal this, reminding Phil that his business will be destroyed if George is not reelected. Phil tells James that he might contribute to the campaign of George's opponent, Sharmen. Because Phil does not believe George has what it takes to become mayor, James offers himself up as an alternate candidate. James has political aspirations of his own. Phil belittles James's idea.

James informs George that Phil might not support his campaign. George has an important piece of information on Sharmen. Sharmen's uncle was a communist in the 1950s. Phil does not believe it will change anything. Phil reminds them that his money got George elected in the first place. James insists that his campaign work was just as important as the money, and he tells George that Phil has been sleeping with his wife. Phil admits that they had a

Jason Miller

fling. George takes a rifle from the wall and points it at Phil.

Act 2

Coach gets George to give him the gun and calms him down. He learns about the affair and yells at Phil. When pressed by Coach, Phil tells the story of the incident. Coach is stunned, but tells the men that they must stick together. George does not want anything to do with Phil. He believes that Phil took advantage of his wife when she was vulnerable.

While the Coach admits that he had his liaisons, he believes his boys, these men, are the real trophies from his life. He tries to inspire them to stick together. Phil tells him that he cannot support George.

George exits to use the bathroom. Coach goes on about how Sharmen's uncle was a communist. Tom questions why he must use the communism aspect at all. Coach believes that one must exploit an opponent's weakness to win whether it's a game or an election. Tom leaves to use the bathroom when George returns. James dares Phil to call Sharmen and offer him a campaign contribution now. Phil does, but Sharmen turns him down.

Phil becomes angry with them for using him. As Coach continues to try to convince him to support George, Tom returns, but drunkenly falls down the stairs. He is unhurt. Phil asks Coach to talk outside for a moment. George is worried about their conversation. He becomes upset about his wife's infidelity and other family matters. James tries to convince George to accept Phil's money, if Coach can change Phil's mind. George asks James if he would take the money, if Phil was having an affair with James's wife. James says yes.

Tom and James begin to argue. George feels sorry for himself. James tries to convince George that Marion might have had the affair for his benefit. James becomes upset about his life, and the sacrifices he made to support his father, his alcoholic brother, and his family.

Phil comes back in, and tells George that Coach wants to see him on the porch. Phil talks about how bored he is in his life and how his crowning moment was the championship they won. He talks about the affair, telling Tom that George's wife has been sleeping with other men for several years. Phil also reveals that his wife sleeps around with his consent.

Phil tells them that he wants to hire professional outside people to run George's campaign. This means James will step down as his manager. James is upset because of his own political aspirations. Phil slugs James, breaking his dentures. James vows revenge—by defaming George—if they dump him. George becomes sick and throws up in their championship trophy.

Act 3

Coach takes George upstairs to clean up, while James leaves to wipe out the trophy. Phil tells Tom more details about the affair. James returns, still angry about their betrayal. James wants his turn now. Coach comes back. He is still upset by the dissension. James tells him that he wants to be respected, but Coach calls him a whiner.

George returns. He has talked to his wife, and she admitted that she had the affair in return for the campaign money. Coach tells George to go home and beat up his wife for her infidelity. He believes George has no pride. Though the men have talent, Coach believes they are wasting it. James still wants to be campaign manager, but no one will listen.

When Tom speaks up, Coach calls him useless. Tom tells him why Martin has not come back in twenty years. Martin had wanted him to refuse the championship trophy because Coach had told him to seriously hurt the best player on the opposing

team during the game. Martin complied, breaking the boy's ribs. Coach denies the whole matter, though Tom tries to needle him into admitting it. Coach hits Tom. Tom leaves.

Coach talks about his past, his mother and father, and how he made those present winners. He puts on a recording of the last moments of the championship game. Tom returns. The men make up. James agrees to do what George wants, though he will still work on the campaign. They take a picture of the four men and an individual one of the Coach.

CHARACTERS

Coach

That Championship Season's moral center, Coach, is an older man who coached the other four characters to a high school state basketball championship twenty years earlier. He considers that championship the crowning achievement of his career, if not his life. The victory made him and the other characters local legends. He still receives special treatment in the town because of this long ago victory.

In many ways, Coach lives in the past. He proudly proclaims that he has not changed in sixty years. His living room is nearly a museum to past decades, and he dresses in a suit with a 1940s cut. Coach's values are also out of the 1950s. He is anti-Semitic and pro-Joseph McCarthy and Father Coughlin, a controversial conservative Catholic radio preacher. Victory is to be had at any cost for Coach.

Coach dislikes dissension, especially among his boys. He wants them to succeed in life as they did in the game, and he uses their loyalty to him to influence their decisions.

James Daley

James is one of the players on the 1952 championship team, and the elder brother of Tom Daley. He is married to Helen and has five children. James has remained in his hometown and is currently the principal of the local junior high school. He was also George's campaign manager in the last election, and, at the beginning of the play, holds the position in this election as well. He hopes to run for school superintendent the following year, but when Phil hints that he might not back George for mayor,

James offers himself up as an alternative. Phil does not take him up on the offer.

James is resentful of his life and feels betrayed by it. He took care of his alcoholic, dying father and contributes to the support of his alcoholic brother, Tom. James deals with unmanageable students every day of his life. Now he wants his share of the spoils and believes George is the way to get it. By the end of the play, Phil forces George to fire James as campaign manager in favor of outside professionals. Though the group makes up, and James remains on George's staff, James's needs are again regarded as lesser than the whole group's.

Tom Daley

Tom is one of the players on the 1952 championship team, and the younger brother of James Daley. Tom is an alcoholic and drinks heavily throughout the play. He has not attended the past three reunions, and he plans to leave town soon after this one. He is unemployed and has lived in and been kicked out of many places. Tom spends much of the play pointing out the absurdities of the other character's positions on both life and the issues at hand. He irritates everyone, especially Coach, at some point. James is especially resentful of Tom's life because James is forced to help support him. Tom believes James only acts out of obedience, not love. Tom tells them all why Martin, the fifth player on the team, is not present, though they do not want to believe him. Coach tries to bully Tom into improving his life, but he will not submit. At the end of the play, Tom remains part of the group but still dissenting. Only he can see that they are living in a mythical world.

Phil Romano

Phil is one of the players on the 1952 championship team. He has remained in his hometown, running the successful business he inherited from his father. Phil is very rich and very bored. He finds pleasure in owning material possessions and in sexual relationships. Though he is married to Claire and has two children, Phil and his wife agree to have other relationships, and they both have had numerous affairs. Phil had a liaison with George's wife, Marion, which becomes a point of contention in the play.

With his money, Phil essentially bought George the mayorship in the last election. Phil received a favorable lease on local land in return for his support. Phil has his doubts about George's ability

MEDIA ADAPTATIONS

- *That Championship Season* was adapted as a film in 1982. This version was written and directed by Jason Miller. It starred Bruce Dern as George, Stacy Keach as James, Robert Mitchum as Coach, Martin Sheen as Tom, and Paul Sorvino as Phil.

- A made-for-television version of *That Championship Season* was aired in 1999. This version was directed by Paul Sorvino. It featured Vincent D'Onofrio as Phil, Terry Kinney as James, Tony Shaloub, as George, Gary Sinise as Tom, and Paul Sorvino as Coach.

to win this election, and he does not want to put his money behind him again. After deciding to support George's opponent, Norman Sharmen, then being rebuffed by him, Phil decides to fund George's reelection only if he can bring in professional people from outside their group. Phil agrees to support George with Coach's influence. Phil is a team player, but one with more influence than the others in the group.

George Sikowski

George is one of the players on the 1952 championship team. He has remained in his hometown and is currently serving as mayor. George ran for this position because Coach convinced him to. Though in his mind, he has been an ideal mayor, the other characters have pointed out his many shortcomings as a public official.

In many ways, George is the focal point of the reunion. He is running for reelection and is counting on Phil's financial support to help him win again. But George feels betrayed by those around him. His wife recently had an affair with Phil, which wounded him deeply. George accepts her explanation that she did it for his campaign, though this is not exactly true. He is also still upset that he and his wife had a child with Down's syndrome, whom they institutionalized under advisement from Coach.

Like Coach, George believes that winning the championship was the high point of his life. He also adheres to Coach's philosophy of victory at any cost and shares many of his prejudices. Because George wants Phil's money, he is willing to fire his loyal friend and campaign manager James, at Phil's behest, to get it. George does what he is told; he is a follower, not a leader as he believes himself to be.

THEMES

Loyalty versus Betrayal

At the center of *That Championship Season* is a tension between loyalty and betrayal among the five characters. Coach both wants and believes he has the absolute loyalty of the four members of his former team. Coach acts as if he is still their coach, the coach of their life. The loyalty comes from their shared experience as the 1952 state champion basketball team. Only George is truly blindly loyal to the Coach and thinks he (George) has the loyalty of the others. The other three are loyal only to a certain degree, to each other and the Coach. They acknowledge the ties of the past, but they have their own life agendas.

These agendas are what create betrayals between them. George and Coach are the ones who feel most betrayed by the others. Phil has an affair with George's wife, Marion, an act that George regards as a betrayal. Phil believes that George does not want to understand his wife, and what she needs. Their affair was just one of many for Phil. The only way George can rationalize the act is by accepting his wife's word that she did it so Phil would give George money for his reelection campaign. James also feels betrayed by George and the others at the end of the play. James has supported George's campaign and served as his manager. James believes that he will eventually be repaid when he runs for school superintendent with George's support the following year. Yet Phil, Coach, and George decide that James will no longer be campaign manager so George can win, effectively ending James's political aspirations. James accepts the decision out of loyalty, but he does not like it.

Coach feels betrayed when there is dissension among his four players. He wants them to do what he believes is right. He thinks highly of them and their skills (ignoring certain truths), but when they act independently, Coach regards it as a betrayal. Coach is very offended by Tom, a drunken loser

with no prospects. He feels Tom has wasted his life. But Coach also feels betrayed by time and American society. America has changed politically and socially much more than he has. Demanding loyalty from the men he coached twenty years ago is one way he can counteract the betrayal he feels from life.

Success and Failure

The definitions of success and failure are important components of *That Championship Season*. Coach, and most of the other characters, believe that success is winning. For Coach, the fact that he and these men won a state high school basketball championship means that they will be successes in life. Because this is not necessarily true, Coach goes to extremes to manipulate the men to make it true, no matter who gets hurt. Failure—that is, losing—is unacceptable.

George was elected mayor, making him the epitome of success. However, he only won the post because of the influence of Coach, and Phil's financial support. Phil got some valuable land leases out of the deal; he is a success because of his wealth. Continued success, that is reelection, might be harder, but winning at all costs is the only way. George wants to smear his opponent, Norman Sharmen, by revealing that his uncle was a communist in the 1950s yet does not want anything negative to be said about him by Sharmen. Later, it is revealed that Phil had an affair with George's wife. With her input, George rationalizes it as something she did to secure Phil's campaign contribution. In this case, success is more important than personal failings.

Yet Coach's definition of success at all costs does alienate people. Martin, the best player on the 1952 team, has not spoken to Coach since that time. As Tom tells it, during the championship game, Coach told Martin to take out the other team's best player. Martin broke the ribs of the player, but after the team won, he asked Coach to refuse the trophy because of what he did. Coach ignored Martin's request because to him winning is everything. Though Martin is still respected as a basketball player by them all, they consider him a failure for being disloyal. Tom is also a failure because he is an alcoholic with no prospects. Tom also points out the absurdity of many of their beliefs. Coach tries to get him on the path to success by working for George's campaign, but Tom will have no part of it. Tom is one of the only characters able to see the hollowness of their definition of success, even though their moral failings seem to be so obvious.

Nostalgia, Memory, and Reminiscence

Coach is generally uncomfortable with the present. He believes that the United States is mired in dissension and disloyalty. Coach lives in the past, nostalgic for what used to be. *That Championship Season* is set in his living room, which is cluttered with furnishings and decorations from the past, including pictures of people like Teddy Roosevelt. He dresses in a suit with a 1940s cut. For Coach, as well as George and Phil, winning that championship in 1952 was the highlight of their lives. This meeting is a reunion to celebrate their twenty-year-old victory. Throughout the play, memories from the game and that period in their life are discussed. Coach even plays a recording with the last ten seconds of the game. Coach uses the power of these memories and his obsession with them to influence his former players and their choices. While the men embrace the memories as well, they live in the present day much more than Coach.

STYLE

Setting

That Championship Season is a drama set in time contemporary with when it was written, 1972. The action is confined to one place, the living room of Coach's house. The living room is practically a museum to the past. The furnishings are frayed, torn, and of an old style. The curtains are made of lace and are dirty. The walls are decorated with pictures of political figures—like Senator Joe McCarthy and John F. Kennedy—and loaded shotguns. The television set is from the 1950s. The silver trophy the team won in 1952 seems to be the best-kept item in the room. The never-married Coach used to share this home with his mother before she died. He apparently never redecorated. This room emphasizes how much Coach lives in the past, how important the championship is in his life, and how big a role nostalgia plays in *That Championship Season.*

Dialogue

The realism of *That Championship Season* is underscored by the dialogue. Miller's characters speak in blunt terms, using the vernacular (common, everyday language). The text is full of slang, vulgarities, and racist and sexist words. The characters also speak in pauses, incomplete thoughts, and sentence constructions used in spoken, not written, language. The realistic dialogue under-

TOPICS FOR FURTHER STUDY

- Compare and contrast Biff Loman in Arthur Miller's *Death of a Salesman* with James Daley or one of the other former athletes in *That Championship Season.* How have their past athletic achievements affected their lives?

- Research one of the historical figures mentioned by Coach (such as Joseph McCarthy) in *That Championship Season.* What kind of values does this figure hold? How do these values contrast them with the values of the 1970s? Why does Coach regard this person so highly?

- Research the psychological techniques used by coaches to mold and inspire their teams. What do you think makes Coach successful? Is Coach a good coach in these terms?

- Compare and contrast the stage play and film versions of *That Championship Season.* How do the different forms affect the story and characters? Is one better than the other? Why?

scores the time, place, and fraternity these men have together. They are familiar with each other and speak uninhibitedly. The realistic dialogue makes *That Championship Season* all the more believable to audiences. The situations depicted become more credible.

Monologue

Two characters in *That Championship Season* deliver revealing monologues at key points in the play. Though these monologues are ostensibly spoken to the other characters in the room, in most cases, those who deliver these speeches are really talking to themselves in an attempt to understand their own lives. Coach has most of the monologues in the play, revealing much about who he is. Because the other characters are peers, while the Coach was their teacher, they do not have the same familiarity with him as they do with each other. Miller uses monologues to flesh out Coach's character, giving him more depth and background. In his monologues,

Coach talks about an affair he had with a Protestant woman, and why they never married; his parents and how the Great Depression contributed to his father's death; his memories of the town; and how important these players were to his life. He also emphasizes how important winning is to him, and how they must win together for him again.

Phil is the only other character that uses monologues in this way in the play. Though his monologues are shorter than Coach's, Phil also reveals something of himself. While George, James, and Coach regard him as basically a source of money, these monologues show Phil's problems with being rich. He talks about how bored he is with his life, how he drives his fast cars at full speed—which might lead to his death, and how he enjoys his affairs with married women. In other revealing speeches, Phil talks about how he never knew his father, and how he really loved only his mother. Phil may be the winner Coach so admires, but he is unhappy. The use of monologue in this way also draws a parallel between the two characters.

HISTORICAL CONTEXT

In 1972, the United States was in serious trouble on several fronts. Though incumbent president Richard M. Nixon was overwhelmingly reelected for a second term, it was later revealed that he used dirty tricks, as he had in previous campaigns. Within a short time, this victory was overshadowed by revelations related to the Watergate scandal. In the spring of 1972, during Nixon's campaign, five supporters broke into the offices of the Democratic National Committee located in the Watergate office building. The five were trying to fix electronic eavesdropping equipment that had previously been placed there. Though the break-in was reported, its importance was downplayed, and Nixon used the presidency to cover-up the crime. When the crime was prosecuted in court, and two *Washington Post* reporters published a series of investigative reports, more details were revealed. Nixon was facing impeachment over the matter when he resigned in 1974. Like George and Coach in *That Championship Season,* Nixon was willing to win at any price.

When Nixon was first elected in 1968, one of his campaign promises was to end the war in Vietnam. The United States had been involved in the conflict for many years, and by 1972, their involvement was deeper than ever. In 1972, Nixon pursued means both diplomatic and military to end the war. He bombed land and sea routes to North Vietnam and mined North Vietnamese ports. The United States thought a settlement was near, but they were unable to come to terms with the North Vietnamese. Public and institutional opposition to American involvement had been going on for many years. People were opposed to both the cost and the seemingly endless nature of the war. The war would continue for many more months and would eventually end with the United States on the losing side.

In part because of the enormous cost of the war in Vietnam, the American economy was faltering. Though the Dow Jones Industrial Average hit 1,000 for the first time in 1972, the economy was in a recession and had runaway inflation. The federal deficit continued to grow, which also negatively affected the economy. In 1972, the national debt was $436 billion. Economic concerns would worsen within the year as the price of crude oil increased, and the nations of OPEC declared an oil embargo on the United States for its support of Israel. Throughout the 1970s, there was a growing disparity between the wealthiest and the poorest Americans.

Many Americans were unconcerned about such economic disparities. Society was generally regarded as selfish and passive. Many Americans found solace in nostalgia as a reaction to the problems at hand. Many entertainment and artistic genres, including theater, film, and television, featured nostalgic products. *Grease* (1972), a musical about high school in the 1950s was in the theaters. *American Graffiti,* also about high school aged characters in the 1950s, was released in 1973. One of the most popular shows on television in the 1970s was *M*A*S*H,* a war comedy set during the Korean War (1950–53). Movies were also more violent and realistic than in previous decades, reflecting the coarser nature of American society in the 1970s.

CRITICAL OVERVIEW

When *That Championship Season* was first produced, the play was generally praised by critics who had found the quality of plays in New York on the decline. Though there were those who had various problems with the play, they were a distinct minority. Clive Barnes of the *The New York Times* is one

COMPARE
&
CONTRAST

- **1972:** The musical *Grease* opens on Broadway. It is a nostalgic look at the 1950s, and a prime example of the 1970s obsession with nostalgia in entertainment.

   Today: Grease has been revived for several years on Broadway. There is now nostalgia for past nostalgias.

- **1972:** There is an enrollment decline in Catholic schools in favor of public institutions. Numerous parochial schools close, in part because of funding problems. Those that remained have problems finding staff. Many believe that a Catholic school does not offer as good an education as a public school.

   Today: Public schools are under fire for not providing a solid education for students. Many parents turn to parochial schools, charter schools, and other private institutions, believing they offer a better education and better discipline.

- **1972:** The Watergate break-in occurs. Five men break into the Democratic National Committee's offices to spy on the committee, an event covered-up by President Richard M. Nixon. This scandal eventually brings down Nixon and his government, creating a distrust of government. In 1974, Nixon resigns office before he can be impeached.

   Today: President Bill Clinton's affair with Monica Lewinsky, and his subsequent attempts to cover-up the relationship, leads to the impeachment of the president. Though Clinton is impeached, he is not voted out of office.

- **1972:** Broadway theater is seen as in decline. All taboos have been broken, and plays like *That Championship Season* are seen as the hope for the near future. Soon, Broadway emerges stronger than ever with reality-based musicals like *A Chorus Line*.

   Today: While Broadway's box office is not strong, the emphasis is on family entertainment with musical productions based on Disney movies. There are fewer dramas being produced.

---

critic who believes *That Championship Season* struck a deep chord. He writes

> This is an enormously rich play. It is one of those strip-all, tell-everything plays in the tradition of *Virginia Wolf* or *Boys in the Band*. These are hollow men, bereft of purpose, clinging to the empty ambition of power. . . . They are morally and intellectually bankrupt. And yet they are human, recognizable and even, in a way, likable.

The way Miller drew these characters, and what these characters represent, appeals to many critics. Barnes' colleague at the *The New York Times* Walter Kerr believes it "is a play that commands, and seems to possess, a second sight. Its people are not just stand-ins for the rest of us, handy pegs to make a pattern or point a moral. They are people who don't want to get their shirts wet." Douglas Watt of *Daily News* concurs, believing "The play . . . is brimming with vitality. Miller writes with strength and insight.

His people are vivid and their situation becomes vital to us." Catharine Hughes of *America* also agrees. She argues

> *That Championship Season* is a good play, one of the very best—'conventional' or otherwise—American dramas of recent years. It is good for a quite simple reason: its characters are good, ring true, throughout. Equally important, it uses the recent past to illuminate the present, personal concerns to develop public insights, yet manages to be unobtrusive about it.

Several critics point out the power of Miller's writing, especially his use of the vernacular, for these men. *The New Yorker*'s Edith Oliver writes, "As the evening progresses and the men get drunker and drunker, everything is revealed about them and about the way they live and have lived and how they have been damaged and disappointed—and revealed in conversation, rather than in synthetic soliloquies." While Jack Kroll of *Newsweek* agrees with

Oliver and others about Miller's dialogue, he finds the play wanting. Kroll argues

> the men are shown to be a microcosm of America in decay: moral emptiness, fear, venality, bullying impotence. Miller writes with great theatrical effect; his dialogue is sharp and funny. The play works as a machine . . . but . . . it is thin underneath and its thesis, that the winner-take-all ethic explains everything bad about America, is much too simple-minded.

While several other critics have similar reservations about *That Championship Season,* a few could find very little to like about the play. Richard Watts of the *New York Post* writes, "They are, in fact, a group of deadly bores, and herein lies the weakness of Mr. Miller's drama. When they get in their cups, which is quickly, they may reveal the truth about themselves and their hatreds, but, in the midst of their self-revelations, they grow occasionally tiresome." *Saturday Review*'s Henry Hewes believes, "*That Championship Season* 's theatrical effectiveness depends less on thesis than on its free-swinging delineation of a very recognizable kind of nitty-gritty vulgarity." Along similar lines, Stanley Kauffmann of *The New Republic* argues, "The play brings out different degrees of rattiness and deception and venality and disintegration in each, together with glib revelations of race and religious prejudice that are all small reverse pats on the back for the superior audience."

After the first run of *That Championship Season,* the play was occasionally produced in the United States and other countries. While most critics of these productions found some value in Miller's writing, the play and its prejudices did not age well. Of a production in Boston in 2000, Karen Campbell of *The Boston Globe* who generally praises *That Championship Season* remarks, "this is compelling and provocative theater, if somewhat dated as social commentary."

CRITICISM

Annette Petrusso

In this essay, Petrusso explores the overriding role that the past plays in That Championship Season.

In Jason Miller's seminal 1972 play, *That Championship Season,* four members of a high school basketball team gather at the home of their coach for a reunion marking the twentieth anniversary of their state championship victory. (The fifth member of the team has never come to a reunion. It is revealed

why he has chosen not to remember the victory over the course of the play.) This party is not merely a reunion. It is also an opportunity for Coach to use his team motivating and managing techniques on his former team.

George Sikowski, one of the teammates, is currently the town's mayor and is running for reelection. His advisor/campaign manager is another teammate, James Daley. George's first campaign was funded by a third teammate, the wealthy Phil Romano. Phil is hesitant about funding George's campaign again, for George has not been a great mayor. The fourth teammate, Tom Daley (James's younger brother), no longer lives in town and has a problem with alcohol. Each of these characters, as well as their actions in *That Championship Season,* are defined and ruled by the past. The past includes not only their victory but the values, relationships and motivations from their high school era. This essay looks at how the past affects each aspect of the play.

More than any other character or part of the play, Coach lives only in the past, not in the present. Though Coach was forced to retire after thirty years of teaching for breaking a student's jaw when a boy made an obscene gesture to his face, he still goes by Coach. The audience never learns his real name. Coach is nothing but a coach and has no desire to be anything else.

The reunion takes place in Coach's living room, which itself is a monument to the past. At the beginning of act 1, Miller describes the setting. Nearly everything in the room is old or old-fashioned. The furniture is frayed, the wallpaper is faded and stained, and the lace curtains are dirty. The television set is from the 1950s, while the pictures on the wall include Teddy Roosevelt, Senator Joseph McCarthy, and John Kennedy. The only things that seem neatly kept are his shotguns (which are prominently displayed on gun racks) and the championship trophy from that victory.

Coach is the driving force in *That Championship Season.* Because he lives so deeply in the past, both literally and figuratively, it is also one of the most compelling motivators in the play. Physically, Coach wears a suit with a 1940s cut. Socially, Coach believes in the values of a bygone era.

Though somewhat conservative forces were in power in the United States in 1972 (President Richard M. Nixon and his supporters), Coach worships the anticommunist values of men like McCarthy. In the 1950s, the senator held anticommunist hearings in which he outed supposed communists and their sympathizers. McCarthy often had little or no evidence for his allegations, but they ruined many lives. Coach is also a fan of Father Coughlin, a Catholic priest who had a popular radio show in the 1930s and early 1940s. Like McCarthy, Coughlin revealed what he called the "truth" about minority groups, and those of other religions and political persuasions, before his activities were curbed. Coach believes such men were wrongfully muzzled, and that American society currently allows too much dissension and too much questioning of authority in its ranks.

More immediately, what Coach values above all else is winning, and he will win at any price. He is convinced it is the American way. His motto is "Never take less than success." To keep his "team" together, Coach reminds them of the importance of "Pride. Loyalty. Teamwork. No other way." Coach also believes that one has to pay the price of pain for victory. He says in act 2, "You endure pain to win, a law of life, no other way, none." While Coach says he believes in playing by the rules, in act 2 he also says, "Exploiting a man's weakness is the name of the game. He can't move to the left, you left him to death. . . . Find his weak spot and go after it. Punish him with it."

Coach knows these beliefs are true because he has won with them before. He got the men in the room to win a high school state basketball championship in 1952 using such tenets. This victory, which defined his and several of the other characters' lives, is the primary reason why Coach can live in the past. The trophy and his team are the concrete examples that Coach is right. Coach uses the past victory to influence, if not control, the present lives of George, Phil, and James. Tom can clearly see the problems in Coach's philosophies and is relatively immune to Coach's pressure. Still Coach tries to get them to work together to achieve more victories by reminding them, among other things, that "You turn on each other, and you don't have a chance alone, not a solitary chance."

The man who buys into Coach's philosophies the most, who is thus living in the past the most, is George. George believes that the high school basketball team's victory is the highlight of his life, more than even being the town's mayor. However, that post comes a close second and makes George a winner in present time. George believes he is a great mayor and deserves to run "his town." George is

A 1972 playbill cover featuring an illustration of the cast of That Championship Season.

even mayor because of Coach. George follows nearly everything Coach says to the letter. It was Coach who convinced him to run for mayor in the first place. Coach has a strong grip on George's whole life. He also convinced George to place his infant with Down's syndrome in an institution, though George resisted such a move for a long time. Though Coach acknowledges some of George's shortcomings as mayor, he has much invested in his former player. Coach wants him to win again, so that he can continue to coach him.

Coach is adamant that the values of the group are above individual values. Because Coach so wants George to be reelected, he and James convince George to overlook the fact that Phil had an affair with George's wife. Morals can be conveniently overlooked and/or rationalized when fighting the good fight. For his part, George has also taken to heart Coach's belief that victory is had by those who exploit their opponent's weaknesses. His opponent in the mayoral race, Norman Sherman, has two weaknesses that George wants to exploit; one weakness is that he is Jewish and two is that he has a communist for an uncle (later revealed to be a cousin). George does not see how these supposed

WHAT DO I READ NEXT?

- *No Exit*, a play by Jean-Paul Sartre written in 1944, also takes place in one room and focuses on the personal revelations of a group of people.

- *Glengarry Glenn Ross* is a play by David Mamet written in 1984. It features tight, realistic dialogue, all male characters, and a "need to succeed" theme.

- *Appointment in Samarra*, a novel by John O'Hara published in 1934, concerns life in Pennsylvania. The novel focuses on the class system and the

idea of success. It features strong use of the vernacular.

- *Nobody Hears a Broken Drum* is a play written by Miller in 1970. It focuses on a group of Catholic characters in Pennsylvania and shares similar thematic concerns.

- *Rabbit, Run* is a novel by John Updike published in 1960. Like many of the characters in *That Championship Season*, Harry Angstrom feels trapped by life.

---

weaknesses are mostly past prejudices, out of sync with the times and the voters. At one point, George calls Sharmen "an ecology nut," yet the ecology movement was becoming more and more important in this time period. In act 2, Phil dismisses George by saying, "George isn't a modern man."

Phil is controlled by the past in two ways. The first is the source of his wealth. Phil's father worked night and day to build a successful business before dying at an early age. Though Phil worked with his father, he did not really know him. Phil inherited the business and the money and is now a rich man. This wealth makes Phil unhappy. He is bored with life and believes that many of his friends use him just for his money.

But Phil has one memory that keeps him going: the championship game. He says in act 2 that it is "my best memory to date, yeah, nothing matched it, nothing." Because of the power of that memory and his loyalty to Coach, Phil ends up agreeing to financially support George's campaign for reelection by the end of the play. The decision is not an easy one. Though Sharmen's election would not be good for Phil's business (with George in office, Phil has favorable leases on land for strip mining), Phil does not believe that George can win or is even a good mayor. Phil regards George as incompetent and as having an image problem. When challenged by James, Phil calls Sharmen and offers a contribu-

tion in exchange for political favors. Though Phil is turned down, it takes Coach using the past (in the form of a Fillmore High jacket) to convince him. Unlike George, however, Phil sees the hold the past has on them and their town. Though he is referring to his "arrangement" with his wife, Phil could be speaking about the group at hand when he says in act 2, "everybody around here lives in the Dark Ages, pitch black."

Like Phil and George, James also believes that he owes much to Coach and that the victory was an important moment in his life. James is another character who is trapped in the past. James is a team player in Coach's current project, as the campaign manager and adviser to George. Unlike the others, James feels he is years behind everyone else because he always has responsibilities that limit his ability to succeed. In addition to taking care of George politically, James had to care for his abusive, alcoholic father before his death. He currently supports his alcoholic brother, Tom. James's job is as a junior high principal, which involves taking care of the student body.

James tries to live in the future, even if past relationships and family keep holding him back. He wants to run for school superintendent the following year, after George has been elected. He offers himself up as an alternate candidate to George when Phil does not want to support him. James is turned down. Someday, James hopes to run for congress. But his dreams seem dashed by the pull of past loyalties. Phil will not fund George's campaign with James as manager. He insists on bringing in outside professionals to run the campaign and improve George's image. While James eventually agrees to a more limited role in the campaign, these events clearly demonstrate how oppressive the past can be in these men's lives.

The one man in *That Championship Season* who sees problems with Coach's outlook and the power of the past is Tom. He never says this victory was his shining moment, and he resists all efforts to become deeply entangled in this codependent campaign. It is not clear why Tom is present at all. He has serious problems with alcohol and has missed three previous reunions. Tom is leaving the next day for another city. Miller uses Tom as the play's conscience. He points out the absurdities in everything that is said.

Tom also remembers the truth about their hollow victory twenty years ago. In act 3, Tom reveals the reason why Martin, the best player on the team and the one who had the winning basket, has never come to a reunion. During the game, Coach told Martin to injure the other team's best player so their team would win. Martin broke the player's ribs, and later asked Coach to return the trophy and renounce the victory because of his action. Coach would not give up his moment of glory, which has defined him to this day. Because of this, Tom says, "We are a myth." Though only Tom believes Martin, Tom knows that the past they cling to and that defines them is tenuous at best and does not really exist.

At several points in *That Championship Season,* moments from that championship game are relived. They are used by Coach to keep them together so that his hold remains as firm as possible on his team. In act 2, Coach says, "You can't make it alone, George, not anymore. Gone forever, those days, gone." Only Tom does not believe this. Deep down, even George knows the score. He admits late in act 2, "Everything is in the past tense. I'm in the past tense." For the men in *That Championship Season,* the past is only inescapable if you let it be.

Source: Annette Petrusso, in an essay for *Drama for Students,* Gale Group, 2001.

Rena Korb

Korb has a master's degree in English literature and creative writing and has written for a wide variety of educational publishers. In the following

> NEARLY EVERYTHING IN THE ROOM IS OLD OR OLD-FASHIONED. THE FURNITURE IS FRAYED, THE WALLPAPER IS FADED AND STAINED, AND THE LACE CURTAINS ARE DIRTY. THE TELEVISION SET IS FROM THE 1950S, WHILE THE PICTURES ON THE WALL INCLUDE TEDDY ROOSEVELT, SENATOR JOSEPH MCCARTHY, AND JOHN KENNEDY. THE ONLY THINGS THAT SEEM NEATLY KEPT ARE HIS SHOTGUNS (WHICH ARE PROMINENTLY DISPLAYED ON GUN RACKS) AND THE CHAMPIONSHIP TROPHY FROM THAT VICTORY."

essay, she discusses the way the Coach and his boys function as a team.

When *That Championship Season* first opened off Broadway in 1972, it immediately won a host of critical acclaim. In his introduction to the published script, the play's producer, Joseph Papp, explained why he believed the play was a "winner." According to Papp, "The work evokes a feeling of tradition, but in the real sense, the play is a modern work with its basic roots in America. Its simplicity is deceptive—but it is this simplicity translated into recognizable human form that gives the work its extraordinary power." This drama, which Papp called, "a play for the people of America," explores the frailty of humanity through a group of friends gathered for an annual reunion that celebrates the highlight of their lives, winning a state championship in high school basketball. In his discussion on Miller in the *Dictionary of Literary Biography,* Jonathan Hershey calls *That Championship Season* a "character study of men who refuse to examine the moral bankruptcy of their lives and their perverted values of competition."

"LIKE COACH, HIS 'BOYS' CANNOT ESCAPE THE PAST, BOTH THE GOOD MEMORIES AND THE BAD. THE CHAMPIONSHIP GAME, HOWEVER, HAS HELD THE MEN IN ITS THRALL ALL THESE YEARS."

The men at the reunion are George, the town's mayor; Phil, a wealthy businessman; James, a junior high school principal who also works as George's campaign manager; Tom, James's brother who is an unemployed alcoholic; and Coach, the men's former basketball coach. Collectively, the men exhibit a host of undesirable traits. They are prejudiced and bigoted. George tells racial and ethnic jokes, some directed at his so-called friends. George's mayoral opponent, Sharmen, is alternately referred to as "the Jew" or "Sharmawitz." The men privately denigrate each other, such as when George asserts to Tom that "Phil's not bright, really." They are selfish and self-involved. One statement of Phil's best typifies their lack of caring about others: "I like being rich, okay. I need money. I want two of everything. Cars, boats, women, etc., etc. Around expensive things I get a hard on, turned on, I want them."

Like Phil, the men all exhibit moral degradation of some sort. George is the most obvious representation of corruption. He vocally revels in the power he holds over other people through his position as mayor. His exploitation of the office ranges from the mundane, such as fixing parking tickets for his friends, to the extreme, such as awarding Phil lucrative land-mining contracts in return for campaign support. George also reveals his intention to back James for school superintendent after the election. "That's patronage," Tom points out, to which George complacently replies, "I know. Is there any other way?"

An ugly glimpse into the men's shared past is revealed early on through an exchange between Tom and George:

> TOM Hey, I remembered somebody. I saw her standing by the library yesterday. Mary . . . what's-her-name.
>
> GEORGE Who?

TOM The epileptic. Mary . . . you know, the one we banged in your garage. . . . We were freshmen or something.

GEORGE I don't remember.

GEORGE Don't ever breathe a word. . . . She wasn't an epileptic. She was only retarded not a word. It could ruin me. She was raped here about two years ago. . . .

The passage shows how the friends treat and feel about people who have less power. People become, for this group of friends, only objects to use for their own purposes. As young men, they sexually abused a girl but feel no shame; the only true emotion that George has about this event is fear—fear that it could adversely affect his political career.

The corruption depicted in the play extends to the group's family members. George's wife, Marion, lacks a moral center. Early in act 1, George tells Tom that Marion is his conscience. The irony of his statement is revealed later, when George—and his friends—learn about Marion's affair with Phil. Phil's collection of stag films apparently comes from George's brother-in-law, the chief of police. George sees no reason to defend his brother-in-law's actions; instead, he seems to admire his brother-in-law's ingenuity: "He sells what he's confiscated. Isn't free enterprise something else?"

Coach, however, is the most crude and regressive of all the men. Derogatory epithets such as "nigger" constantly pepper his speech. He calls George's wife Marion a "hot-pantsed b—h" and tells George to "Go home and kick her ass all over the kitchen." He despises "liberal bulls—t" and idealizes Joseph McCarthy, the senator who in the early 1950s led the nation on a communist witch hunt that ruined the careers and lives of many innocent people.

Coach is caught up in the days of what he considers to be his past glory. From his first appearance on the stage, his ties to the past are readily apparent: he wears a suit that is cut in the style of the 1940s. Although he relives the championship season, he claims the boys are what are most important to him. They are his "real trophies." He tells them at the beginning of the reunion, "Oh, Christ, boys, Christ, it's so good . . . the joy in my heart to feel you around me again." In speaking of their ball playing, he calls them, "a thing of rare . . . beauty."

Like Coach, his "boys" cannot escape the past, both the good memories and the bad. The championship game, however, has held the men in its thrall all these years. Within the opening moments of the play, the audience is keenly attuned to this reality through George's assertion that "I am sincerely more proud of winning that championship than I am of being mayor of this town." The other men reinforce George's attitude. Phil later comments, "Sometimes I think that's the only thing I can still feel, you know, still feel in my gut, still feel that championship season, feel the crowds . . . my best memory to date, yeah, nothing matched it, nothing."

The former teammates, all grown men almost forty, still rely on their coach for advice and validation. It was Coach's idea for George to run for mayor. "I owe my whole life, success to that man," George declares, thereby negating any other influences, his own included, on his political victory. It is Coach who advises George to place his son, born with Down's syndrome, in an institution. The child would impair George's political career, so George agrees to this plan, though it goes against his own wishes.

Coach maintains control through his constant emphasis on teamwork. This method works on the boys because none of them feel their accomplishments have measured up to their championship game. Coach takes whatever steps he feels necessary to make the men act like a team when their cooperation threatens to break down. For instance, when George demands that Phil relate Marion's sexual prowess, Coach snaps, "What's wrong with you, it's none of your business!" Clearly, he is trying to defuse an understandably volatile situation that could pit George and Phil against each other. Coach understands that "You turn on each other, and you don't have a chance alone, not a solitary chance." Indeed, the histories of the men bear out the truth of Coach's words. George would not have been elected without Phil's generous campaign contribution. Phil admits that without George's support, he faces "a complete business disaster." James's job, and more importantly, his political aspirations, come from his association with George. Without each other, these men would be outward failures as well as personal failures.

To further promote a sense of team spirit, Coach reminds the men, "We were one flesh twenty years ago; never forget that as long as you live!" Indeed, the men need plenty of urging to reconnect to their past closeness. Tom snidely questions any statement that George makes. Phil has carried on an affair with George's wife and has secretly planned to take his support from George and give it to his formidable opponent. James reveals the affair and

also proposes that he run for mayor in place of George. Ironically, the men all feel that they have done nothing wrong but that the others have wronged them. This attitude is best typified through James's reaction upon learning of his demotion from campaign manager; he declares that Phil and Coach have "knife[d] me in the back." By the end of the play, however, Coach's words are borne out; the men are intrinsically joined together. Even though their dislike and distrust of each other is readily apparent—in Hershey's phrasing, "They betray each other while claiming to be friends"—they return to each other.

The men maintain this connection because only when they band together are they able to accomplish some of their goals. They won the state championship twenty years ago, and they have since continued to work as a team, albeit a dysfunctional one. When the men discuss the challenge George's opponent Sharmen poses, James reminds them, "But it we can coordinate ourselves—" Phil shares that his best moments in life these days are "replay[ing] the good games in my head." They "[C]ould call each other's moves . . . every time."

Only Tom negates this ideal of teamwork. An inherent irony the play presents is that although Tom and James are brothers, of all the men, Tom is the odd man out. He has physically distanced himself from the group for three years in a row, skipping the annual reunions and missing out on the social machinations. He resists all efforts to draw him into the group via George's upcoming election. He also is the only person who openly mocks the hypocritical team mentality. Objecting to the proposed smear campaign against Sharmen, he pretends not to understand that Sharmen's "on the other side now." He even declares that he is "ready to campaign for Sharmen." In act 3, after Coach has gotten everyone to agree to his plans for the election by invoking memories of their championship game, Tom alone dissents. "Stop lying to us," he says, "Stop telling us how good we were."

There is also one other missing element, the fifth member of the winning team, Martin. When Martin's name is first introduced, in act 1, the men treat his memory with an emotion akin to reverence. "Let's say a little prayer for him, boys," extols Coach, "a prayer that he's safe and happy and still a champion." At the end of the play, however, the audience learns why Martin has chosen to renounce the team: following Coach's orders to "get that nigger center, the kangaroo," Martin went after the player and ended up breaking his opponent's ribs. He wanted Coach to refuse to accept the trophy, but Coach would not. ''He came babbling something about the truth,'' Coach recalls. ''What truth, I said, we won. That trophy is the truth the only truth.'' At the time when Martin shared this story, they did not stand by him against the Coach. Now Tom reminds the others that they ''stole that trophy, [the] championship season is a lie.'' When faced with Tom's defection, the other men suddenly change their opinions about Martin. Suddenly, he transforms from the ''perfect ballplayer'' whom they think about often and love into ''a real sonofab—h'' and someone who ''didn't have a brain.''

The discord among the men at this reunion threatens their team, and thus, their sense of self. Before reaching general consensus again, the men reveal their vulnerability. George tells the others, ''I can't find . . . myself. . . . I lose myself behind all the smiles, handshakes, speeches. I don't think I'm the man I wanted to be, I seem to myself to be somebody else.'' In this speech, George shows his dissatisfaction with a life empty except for the political role he inhabits, which is far from assured. For his part, James is ''beginning to see myself'' as a mediocre person and is upset that his gifted son recognizes him as such. Phil is ''so bored half the time it's killing me.'' Their personal dissatisfaction and their dissatisfaction with each other is mutually parasitic; one feeds the other.

It is Coach who brings the men back together in act 3. Several verbal tactics remind the boys that they are a winning team. Coach uses negative reinforcement, at one point mocking the men's vulnerabilities. He also attacks their loss of camaraderie. ''Never did I think I'd live to see you turn savagely . . . savagely turn on each other. You're not the same people who played for me.'' He draws on his own memories of past failures and successes: the Great Depression, idyllic town picnics, and the loss of American leadership. He invokes the ideals of patriotism, telling the men that ''Somebody has to lead the country back again.'' His final rally of his team of ''winners'' whom he ''won't let lose'' ends with his replaying a recording of the final ten seconds of the championship game.

Coach's reliance on the championship season, and the trophy that represents it, overcomes any dissent. When Tom drunkenly mumbles to himself, ''We are a myth.'' Coach overhears this denigrating comment and responds with great vigor: ''Is that trophy a myth! See the names engraved on it!'' This exchange underscores the truth: that the teammates are winners only in terms of winning the state championship—not in any personal way. They became ''champions'' by unscrupulous means, and they have followed this pattern of deceit throughout their lives. Although Coach attempts to hold on to the moment of glory by ''carving [the boy's] names in silver'' to make the moment ''last forever,'' his action is in vain. The trophy becomes a hollow symbol for the their so-called life successes.

By the end of the play, the men, with the exception of Tom, have all made up. They have asked each other's forgiveness and declared their fraternal devotion. They also agree to work as a team to secure George's reelection. The play culminates in their gathering around the trophy, taking pictures, reasserting their supremacy in a world where white men such as themselves own the basketball courts—a world that no longer exists.

Source: Rena Korb, in an essay for *Drama for Students,* Gale Group, 2001.

Frank W. Shelton

In his essay, Frank Shelton compares two plays, including Jason Miller's That Championship Season, *written a decade apart to show how America's ideas regarding competition and success has changed within that time.*

''We are the country, boys, never forget that, never,'' asserts the Coach to his returning players in Jason Miller's play, *That Championship Season.* A horrifying thought, yet characteristic of a number of American plays of the 1970's, which attempt to portray through a limited number of characters the corruption of America and the American dream. *That Championship Season,* a multiple award-winning drama, seemed to revive the realistic well-made play as a viable vehicle for such purposes, and a comparison with *Death of a Salesman,* of a generation earlier but with similar thematic and structural elements, will illustrate how our view of ourselves has changed under the influence of the Cold War and the Nixon years. In fact, the overlay of specific political content in Jason Miller's play suggests that politics has strongly affected his view of contemporary America.

In comparing the plays, a worthwhile starting point is the motif of sports—central to *That Championship Season* and seemingly only peripheral to *Death of a Salesman.* Yet the myth and ethic of sports in truth undergird both plays. Ideally the world of sports is a world set apart, independent and clearly structured, in which the game is played according to rules accepted by all participants. It is a world where one can succeed through sacrifice, hard work, and courage, a world of simple order offering the potential for heroic action. Biff Loman played football, while the characters in *That Championship Season* played basketball, in itself a suggestive comparison. For paradoxically, though Biff grew up in the city, it is basketball which is a particularly urban game. The centrality of the sport of basketball to our progressively more urban society may be one reason for Jason Miller's use of that sport. America's increasing urbanization is important to *Death of a Salesman,* but the presence of the game of football suggests that green spaces and pastoral areas still exist, an important theme in the play as a whole.

It may seem a long leap from sports to salesmanship in *Death of a Salesman,* but actually both endeavors are based on competition, on winning through striving to be number one. Seeing his sons as Adonises on the playing field, Willy is sure that they will have no trouble attaining equal success in the adult world, a feeling the Coach shares. Success in athletics is thus equated with success in life, a common enough attitude in our present sports-oriented culture, but one which the plays show to be fallacious, for the younger men in both are anything but successful.

The central structural device of the two plays is the homecoming—Biff returning on the one hand and the four players having their yearly reunion on the other. Perhaps the most striking parallel between the plays is the similarity between Willy and the Coach, the older adults to whom the younger characters keep returning. Almost against his will, Biff is periodically drawn back to his father, who continues to have a strong hold over his life. Jason Miller has said that his characters are all searching for a father, and the Coach is actually the nearest thing to a father they have. He has made them what they are, as Willy has formed his sons, with devastating results.

Both Willy and the Coach are out of place in the modern world—a fact first indicated by the settings of the plays. The Coach's living room is described as *A large and expansive living room in a Gothic-Victorian tradition. The dominant mood of the room is nostalgia.* Of Willy's single family dwelling, threatened by looming apartment houses, Arthur Miller suggests that *An air of the dream clings to the*

> FOR THESE CHARACTERS TRUTH IS IDENTICAL WITH A MATERIAL OBJECT. THE COACH, BECAUSE OF HIS POWERFUL DEVOTION TO HIS BELIEFS AND BECAUSE HIS BOYS HAVE A COMMITMENT TO NOTHING TO PUT IN THEIR PLACE, IS ABLE TO MAKE HIS VISION PREVAIL."

place, a dream rising out of reality. Choosing to live in such surroundings, both characters declare their allegiance to the past. Their pasts are very different, however. The Coach's loaded guns and the picture of Joseph McCarthy on his wall evoke the reactionary violence lurking beneath the surface of his character, while Willy's past is embodied by the recurring flute music, *small and fine, telling of grass and trees and the horizon.* Both characters too are present failures; Willy is fired during the course of the play and the Coach has already been fired for striking a boy.

In their current situations, they look to their boys for fulfillment and the justification of their own ideals. The Coach's "You were a thing of rare . . . beauty, boys," his more desperate "You're all still immensely talented" echo Willy's "You got a greatness in you, Biff, remember that. You got all kinds of greatness." In both cases the boys' present failure clashes sharply with their remembered success, but the Coach and Willy, through force of personality, and their power is considerable, attempt to impose success on them.

"Never settle for less than success," a well-worn slogan of the Coach's, could also be Willy's motto. In fact they measure success in the same ways, with Willy's emphasis on contacts and being well-liked corresponding to the Coach's pride when the policeman remembers him and tears up the speeding ticket. Even more important both characters exhibit a deep division of self. The Coach is described upon his first entrance as a *Huge man. Old Testament temperament. A superb actor. A man of immense and powerful contradictions.* His con-traditions are gradually revealed in the course of the play. He begins by emphasizing teamwork, love, pride, and loyalty as the keys to success. Gradually this modulates into: ''Exploiting a man's weakness is the name of the game,'' until finally he says, ''you have to hate to win, it takes hate to win.''

Though possessing a volatile temper, basically Willy is not a violent man. Much kinder than the Coach, he does, however, reveal some of the same kinds of contradictions. Consider, for example, the two men who embody his ideals. On the one hand is Dave Singleman, the perfect salesman who made his living through contacts, never even having to leave his hotel room to finalize a sale. If Willy is to be believed, he was universally loved. Yet there is also brother Ben, equally Willy's ideal, who went into the jungle and came out rich. His greatest lesson, which Willy does not seem to comprehend, is: ''Never fight fair with a stranger, boy. You'll never get out of the jungle that way.''

Describing Willy Loman's tragic stature, Arthur Miller wrote:

> It matters not at all whether a modern play concerns itself with a grocer or a president if the intensity of the hero's commitment to his course is less than the maximum possible . . . if the intensity, the human passion to surpass his given bounds, the fanatic insistence upon his serf-conceived role—if these are not present there can only be an outline of tragedy but no living thing.

I do not want to revive the tired debate over Willy Loman's tragic stature, and even less to suggest that the Coach is a tragic hero; yet perhaps the most significant similarity between Willy and the Coach is the powerful intensity of their commitment to their ideals. The Coach shows a strain of bigotry and hate absent in Willy, but both attempt to transmit a vision of heroism and wholeness to future generations. Both visions are corrupt, but a quality more emphasized in Willy, his love for his sons, is also present in the Coach. Devoting his life to moulding young men, he has been concerned deeply and sincerely for them, as Willy's life was lived for his boys.

Certainly neither realizes that he is responsible for the frustration and failure of the younger men, but the sons in both plays are paralyzed by the influence of the father figures on them. Jason Miller's comment on his basketball players—that they are men facing middle age with a sense of terror and defeat—is also applicable to Biff Loman, a thirty-four year old man who has yet to find himself. In fact, all the younger men are immature and unable to grow up. Biff's asking his mother to dye her hair again so she will still be his pal is but one instance. A closer parallel to *That Championship Season* is the dream of Happy and Biff to sell sporting goods by organizing two teams, the Loman Brothers, to travel around the country giving sporting exhibitions. To Happy, ''the beauty of it is, Biff, it wouldn't be like a business. We'd be out playin' ball again. . . . There'd be the old honor, and comradeship.'' Such a dream takes literally the Coach's concept of life as a game and shows how adolescent such an idea is. Only one side of Biff's divided nature can respond to such an appeal. Unlike the characters in *That Championship Season,* he has experienced a fulfilling life out West.

Pathetically the characters in *That Championship Season* have no such ideal with which to counter the Coach's emphasis on success. The gradual unfolding of the play reveals that they are all failures; James consumed with a sense of his own mediocrity and a determination to get his rightful share of the spoils; Paul monetarily successful but so bored that he can be stirred from his lethargy only by fast cars and fast women; George, the mayor of the town, blurting in a moment of painful candor, ''I can't find . . . myself. . . . I lose myself behind all the smiles, handshakes, speeches''; Tom the chronic alcoholic, seemingly the most complete failure of all.

Even though the Coach has preached love and teamwork, and apparently the players have believed him, they are constantly at one another's throats. Both James and Paul are ready to replace George as candidate for mayor, Paul is willing to support the opposing candidate, and George wants to dump James as his campaign manager. They have no love for one another; each is out simply for himself. In a strange way this very situation is the fulfillment of the Coach's ethos of competition. Love and competition are in truth opposites, mutually exclusive. Willy too devoted himself to a life based on love, personal regard, and contacts, but when he is fired, the business world, centered as it is around competition, is shown to have no room for love, fellow feeling, the human element. Thus the world of sports, theoretically based on such human feelings, is no different from the ''real'' world.

Tom, in a sense the most lost of the former basketball players, forces the truth to come out—that in effect they stole that championship game. The world of sports, apparently an ideal world governed by rules of conduct, is a fraud, for competition leads to the subversion of those very rules in the sacred name of success. Tom and Biff become the vehicles for the revelation of the truth about the Coach and Willy. Though the ideals both held are based on lies, they do not lie to their boys so much as to themselves, and they show a similar resistance to the truth. Tom tells the Coach, "Stop lying to us. Stop telling us how good we were," and proceeds to reveal how Martin was instructed to injure the opposing team's top player. However, the Coach and the others will not listen or admit that Tom's story is the truth. As the Coach says, "That trophy is the truth, the only truth." For these characters truth is identical with a material object. The Coach, because of his powerful devotion to his beliefs and because his boys have a commitment to nothing to put in their place, is able to make his vision prevail. All are reunited again by the end; the hard truths which have come out during the play are papered over. They come together in the face of a common enemy, Sharmen, against whom they can unite in competition.

Biff plays a role in *Death of a Salesman* similar to Tom's. In his climactic confrontation with his father, he is determined to tell the truth about himself and Willy. "No, you're going to hear the truth—what you are and what I am. . . . We never told the truth for ten minutes in this house!" Yet truth, the falsity and emptiness of his dreams, has no effect on Willy. Like the Coach in his refusal to listen, he carries out his suicide, a plan predicated on the same materialistic values as the Coach's.

The failure of the truth in *Death of a Salesman,* however, is not as complete as in *That Championship Season.* Ultimately Willy does realize that Biff loves him, and we see that all Biff's confusion arises from his frustrated love for Willy. The basic failure of the characters in *That Championship Season* is a failure of the heart, while in a sense the triumph in *Death of a Salesman* is one of love. Unlike the characters in *That Championship Season* who end just as they began, having faced their own emptiness but out of sheer terror denying it, Biff is able to say at the end, "I know who I am." His brother, Happy, like Phil, George and James, resists the truth and remains committed to the ethos of competition and success. Like Tom, Biff turns his back on that dream. Unlike Tom, who has nothing but alcoholic numbness to replace it, Biff gains self-knowledge.

His sense of himself is in fact a legacy from his father, who had really only been happy working with his hands. In a profound sense the American agrarian dream undergirds both plays. Even though

Death of a Salesman takes place in a city, where the population is a constant menace, Biff feels that he can be himself out West, which remains an arena for individual and independent action. Individuality is still possible in the world of *Death of a Salesman,* though it involves a rejection of contemporary American values. By contrast *That Championship Season* suggests the opposite, for its action bears out the Coach's statement that you can't do it alone anymore. The characters simply have no sense of themselves as worthwhile individuals. The play also provides one explanation for America's fall. While it is set in a much smaller city than New York, the main industry of the town is strip mining, with Phil the main beneficiary. Nature is being destroyed by industrial America, and no great good place remains for the man who wants to find himself. Tom, the vehicle for truth in the play, is directionless. The only character for whom one can hope is Martin, the absent player who rejected wholly the Coach's values. However, he never appears, and the characters who do appear refuse to recognize the significance of his absence.

Thus a comparison of the two plays measures America's fall in the two and a half decades between them. The ethos of competition and success has a much stronger hold on the characters of *That Championship Season,* and they are unable to cope with their emptiness. Although there was no hope for Willy Loman, at least Biff could take the best of his father's legacy and build a meaningful life around it. The agrarian dream, based on concepts other than material success, had a force and a possibility for Biff lost to the Americans of *That Championship Season.*

Source: Frank W. Shelton, "Sports and the Competitive Ethic: *Death of a Salesman and That Championship Season,*" in *Ball State University Forum,* Vol. 20, No. 2, Spring 1979, pp. 17–21.

John Simon

In the following review, author John Simon discusses the play's parallels of life and the game in Jason Miller's That Championship Season.

It was a good feeling, last spring when the New York Drama Critics' Circle was voting for the best play of the season, to find myself in a quandary: whether to vote for David Rabe's *Sticks and Bones* or Jason Miller's *That Championship Season.* Two good plays do not exactly constitute an embarrassment of riches. But they were both American plays; had both, thanks to Joseph Papp, made it to Broadway; and two good dramas on Broadway in one calendar year was more than we had had in some time. I have written here about Rabe's play before; now for Jason Miller's.

That Championship Season is a necessary play. In a naturalistic way it does more or less the same thing that *Sticks and Bones* does in its absurdist-symbolist fashion: it tells grass-roots America that it stinks. For even in this Vietnam-war-waging, Nixon-favoring, culture-despising year of 1972, when Neil Simon's *The Prisoner of Second Avenue* is the hottest ticket on Broadway, when *The Godfather* is the biggest cinematic money-maker, when Herman Wouk, Taylor Caldwell and Irving Wallace are perching on top of the best-seller list, there remains considerable faith in the solid backbone of America, the good and simple folk back in the small towns, the America that the two Walts, Whitman and Disney, could hear singing, the unspoiled, sweet salt of the earth. And it is these people that Miller reveals to be weak, cowardly, prejudiced, corrupt and sustained, if at all, by self-delusion. And what makes the indictment stick is, first, that it is made from an evident position of intimate knowledge and understanding of the people portrayed, and, secondly, that the judgment is made regretfully, without rancor, almost with love.

Understanding is clearly necessary for an intelligent verdict. The locale of the play, as we gather from both internal and external evidence, is Scranton, Pennsylvania, where Miller was raised. It is an unprepossessing milieu, this small, cultureless, coal-mining town, and treated without close knowledge (as in Barbara Loden's film, *Wanda*), it can strike us as completely dehumanized. But because the author was truly of that world, and now no longer is, he is able to give us both the inside-out and the outside-in view of it, the latter chiefly from the mouth of Tom, whose nomadic life has taken him largely out of the town. But more important even than knowledge is sympathy: a recognition of the humanity of these beings—of that bit of depth even in shallowness of the stirrings of awareness even in ignorance—which makes the five dramatis personae persons as well as dramatic, worthy of our concern because we cannot quite hide from ourselves that, under the superego, we are their brothers.

Who are the players in this quintet? There is, first, the old coach, known only as Coach, who twenty years ago guided the other four (along with another boy, Martin) to victory in the Interstate High-School Basketball Championship. The big

silver trophy, with all their names engraved on it, stands proudly displayed on a table in the coach's living room, the scene of the action. The coach was subsequently retired, pensioned off, for having broken the jaw of a disrespectful student. But he and his boys—always accepting Martin—have annually come together to celebrate a victory that "gave this defeated town something to be proud of," as the coach put it, a victory on account of which a local cop will still tear up the coach's traffic tickets. The coach became the moral, social and political mentor of his boys for life, and that role is now his only *raison d'être*. It is his values that have governed their lives in one way or another—and why not, since he has abundantly drilled it into them that life and basketball are essentially identical. When one of the boys, Phil, says, "Politics is not basketball," the coach retorts, "Hell, yes. You get the crowd behind you and you can't lose. Everybody votes for a winner." And again: "Life is a game and I'm proud to say I played it with the best." And yet again: "You quit on the field, you'll quit in life. It's on the playing fields the wars are won." The pathos of this is that it is, in a sense, true; or, at least, widely believed to be so. Between the playing fields of Eton and the basketball court of Scranton there may not be that much difference, and no less a sage than Sir Walter Scott has assured us that "life is itself but a game of football." But between believing it and living it, there is a world of difference.

The boys are now in their late thirties and the coach warns them that this is the age of heart disease. (The irony is that they are not so much weak as faint of heart.) He wants them, as he always wanted them, "lean and mean." (Well, they are getting less and less lean, but they are not wanting in meanness.) There is, first, George, the mayor, who, with the coach's help, won his election by a margin of 32 votes against an old drunk. Now, however, he is up against an appealing, intelligent, honest man, Sharmen the high school principal. George is worried, but he covers it up with bravado: Sharmen is a Jew, and a relative of his, as the coach has ferreted out, was a Communist; that and Phil's money should get George re-elected.

Phil Romano is the "dumb dago" who inherited his father's strip-mining business and is the town's rich man. Ever since school days, the boys depended on Phil's car to get laid in; now he will provide the required campaign funds. But Phil has lost confidence in George, as has most of the rest of the town, and would gladly support Sharmen, if it were not for the latter's opposition to him as an ecological menace. Then there is James Daley, the junior-high-school principal, who first had to look after his long-dying father, then after his numerous brood, and now even after Tom, his dipsomaniac younger brother, whom he has had to fish out of the alcoholic wards of several cities. James is embittered by having been a constant, dutiful grind, sacrificing himself for others; he hopes for a belated recompense: success in politics. He is George's campaign manager, for which he is to be rewarded with the post of school superintendent. His ultimate ambition is Congress; but James, like George, is a loser, identifiable by the sweatiness under his collar.

More obviously a loser is Tom, the drunkard. Yet alcohol has turned him into one of those privileged jesters whom the coxcomb allows to utter sardonic truths intolerable from a sober, responsible person. Tom is a ''happy'' drinker who finds the truth in wine; but he is too weak to be set free by it, except to go off to other cities for his binges. And then James has to bring him back home. Tom uses the truth merely as sarcastic witticisms to be hurled at his fellows, or as innocent-sounding questions that lead them into self-incrimination. But revealing the mud around him does not elevate Tom: a morass can't be used as a springboard; a morass sucks one in. Phil, too, with all his money, is a loser. ''I like being rich, okay,'' he boasts. ''I need money. I want two of everything. Cars, boats, women, etc., etc. Around expensive things I get a hard-on, turned on. I want them.'' But having two of everything is divisive and can be almost as frustrating and depleting as having none. Another time, Phil admits: ''I'm so bored half the time, it's killing me.'' The two things that console him are driving his sports car at suicidal speeds, and girls, mostly very young ones. And something else: ''Sit and replay the old games in my head . . . Sometimes I think that's the only thing I can still feel . . . that championship season . . . nothing matched it, nothing.''

What Miller does is to let his characters interact and gradually reveal themselves. This is, of course, a time-honored basic technique of realistic drama, but Miller handles it with admirable assurance. The two pegs on which he hangs the action are the basketball reunion and the mayoral race, which permits the conversations to oscillate between the blissfully nostalgic retrospect of victory and the somewhat parlous prospect of collaborating on George's re-election. The coach looms as chief strategist in both contests, and the parallel between the game and life is thus forcefully posited. But now things begin to emerge. George is unmasked as an

> IS IT, THEN, A CASE OF THE WONDERFUL OLD BASKETBALL DAYS VERSUS THE MEASLY, BICKERING, UNFULFILLED DAYS OF ADULT LIFE? NO; MILLER EVENTUALLY BRINGS LIFE AND THE GAME TOGETHER AGAIN IN PAINFUL HARMONY.''

incompetent politically and even humanly: Marion, his wife, has been carrying on with Phil and, indeed, a good many others in town. It comes out, too, that Phil would rather support the Jew, Sharmen; that James, whom his own young son considers mediocre, would as soon run himself for mayor; that the boys are about to bring in outside experts to run George's campaign and so cut out James; that Tom is not a hopeful but a hopeless alcoholic; that the coach, who claims to have fully recovered from his operation, is actually in precarious health; and that Phil, with all his money, has very little to look forward to.

The game-life parallel begins to fall apart. In the game they were all one harmonious team; now they are squabbling, undermining, insulting, betraying, hitting and even threatening to shoot one another as the evening and the flow of liquor progresses. In this respect, *That Championship Season* is reminiscent of *Who's Afraid of Virginia Woolf?*, where a friendly get-together deteriorates into a drunken orgy of hate and self-hate; but Albee, despite some attempts at making his play transcendent through references to the decline of western culture, is still dealing essentially with private, personal problems. Miller's play, however, takes on a genuinely social character by capturing both the private and the public lives of a town as they intermingle and uneasily fuse. Thus, for example, although Miller ostensibly writes a play about men only, he deftly intimates what the town's women are like. There is George's wife, Marion, with her joyless promiscuity; Phil's Claire, who, in collaboration with her mother, lives the gay life of the rich bitch with continual travel and sex abroad; and James's Helen, who mass-produces babies and sacrifices her talent for painting to her monomaniacal motherhood. Then there was the more sophisticated Miss Morris, the music teacher, with whom the coach had a long-lasting relationship but whom he could not marry because she would not convert to Catholicism and because he had to take care of his old mother. There is even Mary, epileptic and retarded, with whom the boys used to have gang bangs, and who was recently brutally raped. As the feminine side of town comes gradually to life, it too seems to be populated with losers.

Is it, then, a case of the wonderful old basketball days versus the measly, bickering, unfulfilled days of adult life? No; Miller eventually brings life and the game together again in painful harmony. Tom reveals why Martin left town and never came back to these reunions: because the championship was won crookedly. There had been a superb Negro center on the opposing team, and Martin, on instructions from the coach, broke his ribs (''I told him to get tough under the boards'' is how the coach euphemizes it), and that is how the trophy was captured. Now it all fits together: both life and basketball are a fraud, the one merely extending and perpetuating the other. Yet Miller does not allow things to become quite that simplistic, either. He makes the coach himself phrase his philosophy differently at different moments. There is the noble version, when the coach explains why he did not marry: ''I never had the time. Teaching the game was not just a profession, it was a vocation. Like a priest. Devoted my life to excellence . . . superiority. . . . You, boys, are my real trophies, never forget that, never.'' Soon after, there comes a more equivocal version, a stoic-masochistic one: ''Pain. The price is pain. Endurance. You endure pain to win, a law of life, no other way, none. The pain in my gut. It's been there all my life. It's good to hurt. The mind overcomes pain. You keep your marriage, George. Hold on to it.'' (It is, be it noted, in such incomplete sentences that much of the play's dialogue unfolds—the syntactic incompleteness becoming the objective correlative of the primitiveness and untidiness of these lives.) Finally, we get the third and ungarnished version: ''Exploiting a man's weakness is the name of the game. He can't move to the left, you left him to death. Can't stop a hook, you hook away on him. Find his weak spot and go after it. Punish him with it. I drilled that into you a thousand times!'' This is the coach's reply to Tom's accusation that they are smearing Sharmen with his long-dead Communist relative; forthwith, we see the application of this sports philosophy to the game of life. It is to be stated even more bluntly by the

coach at the very last: ''You have to hate to win, it takes hate to win.'' Dedication, pain, hate; it isn't any one of them but all three together. Two parts bad to one part good—that, alas, is the final truth about the games of basketball and life as they are played in Scranton, Pa., and just possibly elsewhere, too.

The game theory of life is, above all, immature, as the play copiously illustrates. For in stressing the team, the in-group, development is stunted in two directions: toward the single self, leading to self-reliance, self-cultivation, individualism; and toward public-spiritedness, ecumenism, world-citizenship. The coach and at least three of his boys are arrested at the level of parent and child servicing each other's physical and emotional needs—which the sports family, the coach-father and player-children, reiterates and prolongs into life. Miller lets us feel the weakness of unhappy families as paralleling the weakness of the in-group's morals and morale in contrast to those of Sharmen. Tom, as we have seen, does not really emancipate himself; only Martin has done that, but we do not know at what price.

This immaturity is neatly epitomized in various small but telling ways. I have mentioned the coach's need to look after his mother as his pretext for not marrying; more revealingly, Phil bursts out at one point: ''You know the only woman I ever loved? . . . my mother, f—k the psychiatrists . . . my mother is the only . . . woman I ever knew. The rest are all c—ts.'' (Ellipses the author's. This line, by the way, was loudly applauded by the opening-night audience on Broadway.) These men are inveterate mother's boys. Even more infantile is the unwillingness to accept as true what one doesn't want to believe. When Tom, mocking the coach's semiliterate eulogy of the Greek ideal, observes that the Greeks were homosexual, the coach explodes: ''The Greeks homos? Not the Greeks, maybe the Romans but not the Greeks! Don't come around me with that liberal bulls—t. I won't listen.'' ''I won't listen'' is arguably the motto of the play: the boys will be boys and hear and believe only what they want to hear and believe. George lets himself be convinced that Marion did it with Phil only to raise money for her dear husband, James is convinced that he spilled the beans to George just so that the truth would bring them all together again, Phil is readily persuaded that James would never hurt him intentionally. And the play ends with the coach and his boys pulling together against Sharmen, against good government, progress and truth, against anyone who isn't one of them.

Miller is skillful with some important devices. He knows how to make a character or a situation gradually take on a different complexion through a casual remark here, a small revelation there. Thus Marion appears at first as a woman who committed a single indiscretion; but, by accretion of information and the change of the coach's way of talking about her, she ends up as a slut. James's dedication to his slowly dying father is spoken of in Act One as a great personal sacrifice, such as, the coach declares, not many would have made. In the second act, this sacrifice, which James uses as an excuse for his underachieving, earns only a hollow, rote approbation from George: ''We all have great respect for you, James, you sacrificed, well, you know.'' By the third act, however, when James complains that his father never showed him the slightest respect in return for his sacrifice, the Coach lets him have it: ''Whine. . . . Bitch and whine and blame your life on everybody. You got the eyes of a beggar.'' Meanwhile we also heard from Tom that ''James never did anything out of . . . love. The word embarrasses him.'' For James is ''just obedient. An obedient man. Press a button . . .''. There it is again: obedience, a child's virtue; another great manly sacrifice was, like the coach's devotion to his mother, just infantile doing what one is told to do.

Feeling is immature in the boys. When George learns of his wife's infidelity, he cries out uncomprehendingly, ''Marion. Unfaithful. I'm the Mayor, for Chrissakes!'' This is pathetic—but for the shallowness, not the depth, of its feeling. What are feelings to George, anyway? When he wants to prove to the others that he has them, he exclaims: ''I can understand . . . understand what makes a man take a gun, go up a tower, and start blowing people apart. I know the feeling. All smiles, huh? I have rage in me . . . I hate like everybody, hate . . . things.'' This is the horrible confirmation of the coach's ''it takes hate to win''; yet it is also pathetic. Beautifully, Miller makes genuine pathos out of such inferior feelings, especially of that lame, evasive last word, ''things'': George does not even have the courage of his hates.

Another device Miller uses unobtrusively but compellingly is the parallel. The key revelation of the breaking of the black center's ribs is prefigured by an incident the coach recalls: ''A communist came through here, 1930 maybe. Bad times. Poverty like a plague. . . . He came to organize. We broke his legs . . . with a two-by-four and sent him packing.'' So, too, Phil makes a semi-pitying, semi-contemptuous statement about his father, an igno-

rant immigrant who had only hard work and premature death out of the fortune he amassed—and Phil doesn't realize how this parallels his own boring himself to death with his fast women, fast cars, and the fast demise he is courting.

What emerges is the picture of a society that makes a fetish out of success, but does not know what to do with it or even what it really is. It recognizes success, ultimately, only in material terms. However proudly the coach may talk about the Bach and Shakespeare he heard in his father's house, when he wants to prove the incontestability and value of that championship season he must reach for that prominently displayed trophy and exclaim: ''I carved your names in silver, last forever, forever . . .'' This echoes his earlier tribute to Teddy Roosevelt: ''They carved that man's face in a mountain,'' which is typical also of the misinformation he frequently spreads. Concrete proof is what is wanted, and Miller deftly brings on a set of concrete, pragmatic evidences of championship with which to cement anew these perennial basketballers' unholy alliance.

First is a recording of the last few seconds of a broadcast of that championship game. The coach plays this record that is cracked with age and scratchy from constant replay, but it is evidence, concrete evidence. The boys listen to it raptly, then burst into the school song, and Phil and George even end up crying in each other's arms. Tangible or, at any rate, audible success. And sloppy sentimentality, with grass-roots America singing ''Another victory for Fillmore''—a school named for a president whose face could at best be carved in a molehill.

After the aural, the ocular evidence. As the coach admonishes them, ''No way a man can do it alone. Got to belong to something more than yourself,'' the boys proceed to arrange themselves around that twenty-year-old, ill-gotten trophy for the annual photograph. Even the unconverted Tom smiles for the coach's camera. Then the boys insist on taking a picture of the coach holding the cup. To make him smile, Tom, recalling the coach's earlier puzzlement by that word, encourages him ironically, ''Say cunnilingus,'' but what dent can Thersites make in Achilles? The lights fade, and only a spotlight is left enshrining the coach. James, the photographer, announces, ''I got you, Coach,'' and the remark is rich in subliminal meanings. The coach responds with the curtain line: ''Yeah.'' The complacency of grass-roots America is engraved on that silver monosyllable.

Did the coach speak true when, early in the play, he declared, ''We are the country, boys''? I think the characters are truly representative, created with sympathy, authentic. While Miller reprehends their outlook and behavior, he allows them, nevertheless, a fleeting self-cognizance, a bit of misdirected decency, some juvenile affection. Even as he makes us aware of their racism, crudeness, jejuneness, he also makes us feel the pity of this entrapment by the pettiness, barrenness, monotony of small-town existence. An author who can be both surgically probing and charitable, both muck-raking and forgiving, performs that marriage of incisiveness and generosity from which truths are born. Miller's accuracy as a reported is mirrored in the persuasive shabbiness of the language. The incomplete sentences, lacunas and aposiopeses, awkward repetitions, omnipresent cliches, all that invincible prosaism that can nevertheless stumble onto some sort of clumsy dignity—these and other traits of speech are instinct with authenticity. Most interesting, perhaps, is Miller's avoidance of that folksy poetry with which writers tend to redeem the speech of plain people. That method is no more wrong than plain folk are incapable of unconscious poetry, yet I admire Miller's refusal to make use of it and still succeeding in making his characters fascinate us. He charges his dialogue with deliberate or inadvertent humor, self-revelation, conscious or unconscious, and the ominous ring of human hollowness. But, for all that, he does not encourage glib feelings of superiority in the audience: they recognize too much of themselves in these characters.

To one of them, however, Miller does grant a spurious poetry. Some of the coach's lines have a certain afflatus, a grandiose rhythm, obsessive refrains, and some fairly conventional but charismatic metaphors. This is true especially at the play's end, where the coach is given what amounts to a virtually two-page monologue. But the poetic heightening is undercut by a mixture of nostalgia for a past that was even more reactionary then the present and a grandiloquence that is more than faintly self-serving. The speech begins with a glowing evocation of the coach's father and the town as it was in his time; it ends with this prognostication about the mayoral race:

> You won't lose, boys—because I won't let you lose. I'll whip your ass to the bone, drive you into the ground. Your soul belongs to God but your ass belongs to me, remember that one, yes sir, we can do it, we are going to win because we can't lose, dare not lose, won't lose, lose is not in our vocabulary! I shaped you, boys, never forget that. I ran you till the blisters busted, ran you right into perfection, bloody socks and all; you couldn't put on your jocks, awkward, all legs, afraid, a mistake a second. I made you winners. I made you winners.

There is a horrible beauty in that, after all.

But in general, along with the purposive leanness of the dialogue, there is even an almost complete absence of stage directions and instructions about how a line is to be read (e.g., anxiously, softly, etc.). Though there is nothing wrong with such hints to actors, directors and readers, there is also something fine and fastidious about refraining from them. It allows the director, actor or reader to come to his own conclusions and fill in his own details; yet the movement of a speech is always so clearly plotted that this leeway will not alter basic meanings or imperil communication.

In Joseph Papp's production, first mounted at the Public Theatre, then transferred to the Booth on Broadway, the production values are all of the utmost artistry. A. J. Antoon's staging is as meticulous as it is resourceful, creating an elaborate choreography of movements that first delight us by their unexpectedness, then delight us again by their absolute rightness. A drunk falls down a flight of stairs almost too spectacularly; an angry man goes out on the porch to simmer down, and repeatedly sticks his head back in through the window to hurl further invective at his offender; a bit of violence erupts so swiftly that it is over before it is really fathomed; all these events have an uncanny aroma of credibility, of really happening and happening for the first time. The rhythms of speech are cogently orchestrated, motion flows freely across the entire stage, and each entrance and exit has its particular shape and flavor.

The set, by Santo Loquasto, is right to the last detail. The tacky curtains and doilies, the Persian rugs and flowered wallpaper, the framed photographs of teams, the Grand Rapids mahogany furniture, the archetypal dowel post and balusters of the staircase spiraling to the second floor—all share in a fadedness and mustiness that no amount of cleaning or polishing could assuage. It is bourgeois respectability going to seed, but gallantly hanging on to every graspable vestige. The very layout of the room, with its unequal spaces to which further nooks and crannies adhere like pockmarks and warts, generates an aura of mixed coziness and embarrassment. It all exudes an uncertain yellowness, which it seems to have absorbed from bygone lives and is now breathing back into the current ones. Ian Calderon's lighting cannily contributes to this impression.

But the ultimate triumph of *That Championship Season* is in its performances. The five actors could scarcely be surpassed individually, but are even more astounding together. One might perhaps object that some look a little younger or older than their prescribed ages, but that is as nothing to their perfection in every other respect. As the mayor, Charles Durning gives off exaggerated self-assurance with every paper-thin smile and briskly tossed-off conviviality. Durning has a jerkiness of speech and angularity of motion that jut out incriminatingly from under the assumed fluidity. Even crushed with pain or maddened with wrath, he retains that puppetlike pettiness that makes him in equal measure ludicrous and pitiful. As James, the junior-high-school principal, Michael McGuire conveys magisterially that ingrained mediocrity sweatily straining to please. Even his pomposity has a thin, brittle tinkle in it, and his slightly squeaky voice seems to curl upward as it slowly gathers courage. At bay, he fights back with the inept but desperately serious anger of an aging tenor with a second-rate opera company in a grand, dramatic moment. As Tom, his younger, alcoholic brother—the softly sardonic voice of defeated reasonableness—Walter McGinn gives a magnificently balanced performance, not allowing the justness of his perceptions to blind us to his hopeless decay, and infusing his genuine likableness with a chilling sense of the sodden impotence beneath. His drunkard's titubations are flawless in their underlying somnambulistic agility, and his cascading down the stairs is splendid and alarming.

Richard A. Dysart's Coach is no less superb. Dysart conveys the maniacal aspects of the man without losing any of his equally relevant joviality. Though he can, at times, sound and look like a lesser Old Testament prophet, at other times, as when he pries esuriently into the details of Phil's intercourse with Marion, he becomes childlike, almost Puckish. Dysart wisely eschews the extremes of distastefulness or cuteness that the part could seduce one into, and makes a marvelously kaleidoscopic jumble out of probity and mean prejudice. He declines Phil's invitation to watch basketball on color TV: "They all shoot down at the basket. Not my game," and sees to it that the line sounds too funny to be moving; then continues with "it's not the white man's game," in tones of such disarmingly serio-comic distaste that the underlying nastiness hits us only a second or two later.

But the most dazzling presence on stage—*primus inter pares*—is Paul Sarvino as Phil. He makes the "dumb dago" shrewd, warm-hearted, ruthless, amiably oafish and coldly cynical all at once. I cannot begin to describe how the actor can convey that many conflicting and contradictory characteristics with a single slow expression, one quick remark, or a solitary dismissing gesture—but he does. He makes you feel that everything comes from very deep in him, but also that he is just a huge, overgrown baby whose innermost core is right under the skin. He is so simple, so obvious, and then, suddenly, we don't know where this weeping has come from, or whether that inflection derives from silliness or great subtlety. And his comic timing is always exemplary. From all five actors we get ensemble acting of the highest order, which could hold its own against the finest acting aggregations of the world.

Jason Miller has written a first-rate commercial theatre piece. It is not quite profound or venturesome or novel enough to make it a work of art, but it is the very best example of the sort of play that keeps a commercial theatre meaningfully and honorably alive. If it cannot have a long life on Broadway, Broadway itself no longer deserves to live.

Source: John Simon, "That Championship Season," in *Hudson Review,* Vol. 25, No. 4, Winter, 1972–73, pp. 616–25.

SOURCES

Barnes, Clive, "Stage: That Championship Season," in *The New York Times,* September 15, 1972, p. 43.

———, "Theater: That Championship Season Is a Winner," in *The New York Times,* May 3, 1972, p. 34.

Campbell, Karen, "Compelling, if Dated Championship Season," in *The Boston Globe,* April 5, 2000, p. F16.

Hershey, Jonathan, in *Dictionary of Literary Biography: Vol. 7: Twentieth-Century American Dramatists,* Gale, 1981, pp. 112–115.

Hewes, Henry, "That Gentile Good Night," in *Saturday Review,* June 3, 1972, p. 66.

Hughes, Catharine, "Oh! Broadway!," in *America,* October 7, 1972, p. 264.

Kauffmann, Stanley, review, in *The New Republic,* June 3, 1972, pp. 22, 33–34.

Kerr, Walter, "Suddenly, There's a 'Champion' in the Ring," in *The New York Times,* May 14, 1972, section 2, p. 1.

Kroll, Jack, "Winner Take All," in *Newsweek,* May 15, 1972.

Miller, Jason, *That Championship Season,* Atheneum, 1972.

Oliver, Edith, ''Mr. Jason Miller (& Co.),'' in *The New Yorker,* May 13, 1972, p. 99–101.

Papp, Joseph, ''Introduction,'' in *That Championship Season* by Jason Miller, Atheneum, 1972.

Watt, Douglas, ''That Championship Season A Fine, Tight-Fisted Drama,'' in *Daily News,* May 3, 1972.

Watts, Richard, ''Basketball and Bigots,'' in *New York Post,* May 3, 1972.

FURTHER READING

Amdur, Neil, ''That Championship Season,'' in *Sporting News,* February 28, 1983, pp. 26–27, 29.
This article describes a championship basketball team from the same era and place (Scranton, Pennsylvania) featured in *That Championship Season.* The team may have inspired the play, or at least it shares many parallels with the fictional team.

''On the Set,'' in *The New Yorker,* May 20, 1972, pp. 32–33.
This article provides biographical information about Miller and background on the inspiration for and original productions of *That Championship Season.*

Peck, Ira, ''From Unemployment Insurance to Championship,'' in *The New York Times,* May 21, 1972, section 2, pp. 1, 10.
This piece discusses Miller's background and describes the inspiration for *That Championship Season.*

Warren, William E., *Coaching and Winning,* Parker, 1988.
This book is a guide for coaches on how to motivate athletic teams to win.

Top Girls

CARYL CHURCHILL

1982

Since its earliest productions, Caryl Churchill's *Top Girls* was regarded as a unique, if difficult, play about the challenges working women face in the contemporary business world and society at large. Premiering on August 28, 1982, in the Royal Court Theatre in London before making its New York debut on December 28, 1982, in the Public Theatre, *Top Girls* won an Obie Award in 1983 and was the runner-up for the Susan Smith Blackburn Prize. The play is regularly performed around the world and has quickly become part of the canon of women's theater. *Top Girls* helped solidify Churchill's reputation as an important playwright.

Critics praise *Top Girls* for a number of reasons. Churchill explores the price of success paid for by the central character, Marlene, while using unusual techniques including a nonlinear construction, an overlapping dialogue, and a mix of fantasy and reality. The last occurs at a dinner party celebrating Marlene's promotion, which is attended by five women from different times in history, literature, and art. The dinner party is the first scene of the play and, to many critics, the highlight of *Top Girls.* Churchill brings up many tough questions over the course of the play, including what success is and if women's progress in the workplace has been a good or bad thing. While many critics compliment the play on its handling of such big ideas in such a singular fashion, some thought *Top Girls* was disjointed and its message muddled. As John Russell Taylor of *Plays & Players* wrote, ''Like most of

Churchill's work, it is about nothing simple and easily capsulated.''

AUTHOR BIOGRAPHY

Churchill was born on September 3, 1938, in London, England, the daughter and only child of Robert Churchill and his wife. Churchill's father was a political cartoonist; her mother worked as a model, secretary, and actress. Churchill began writing stories and doing shows for her parents as a child. After spending her early childhood in London, the family moved to Montreal, Quebec, Canada, in about 1949, where Churchill spent most of her formative years.

In 1956, Churchill returned to England to enter Oxford University. While studying literature at Lady Margaret Hall, she began writing plays for student productions. Her first play was written as a favor for a friend. One of Churchill's student plays, *Downstairs,* won first prize at the National Student Drama Festival. Churchill graduated with her B.A. in 1960, intending to become a serious writer.

Family matters stymied her plans. In 1961, Churchill married David Harter, a lawyer, and had three sons over the next decade. Still, she managed to write about thirty radio dramas, usually one act, throughout the 1960s and early 1970s, as well as some television plays in the early 1970s. Many of these early plays were related to her life experiences and were somewhat depressing, but they did garner Churchill some notice for her writing abilities.

In the early 1970s, Churchill turned to theater, initially writing for fringe theater groups. *Owners,* a tragic farce, was her first major play, produced by a fringe group in London in 1972. This production led to her position as a resident playwright at the Royal Court Theatre from 1974 to 1975. Churchill began exploring feminist ideas with her first play for the Royal Court, *Objections to Sex and Violence* (1974).

Churchill continued to explore feminism with *Vinegar Tom* (1976). She wrote the play both with the help of and for Monstrous Regiment, a feminist touring-theater company. *Vinegar Tom* and *Light Shining in Buckinghamshire* (1976) use historical settings to discuss repression. These plays garnered Churchill more attention and critical praise.

In 1979, Churchill's *Cloud Nine* had its first production. This was her first big hit, and had a long run on both sides of the Atlantic. The Obie Award-winning play was set in the Victorian era, with the roles played by their physical opposites. For example, a man played an unhappy and unfulfilled wife. Critics enthusiastically praised Churchill's originality. Churchill followed this success with *Top Girls* (1982), a play about feminism and the price of success for women. Though some did not regard it as highly as *Cloud Nine,* the play cemented her reputation and won her another Obie.

Churchill wrote plays on a variety of topics throughout the 1980s and 1990s. *Fen* (1983), which focused on female tenant farmers, won her the Susan Smith Blackburn Prize. In 1986, she wrote *Serious Money* about the London stock exchange. Churchill used music and dialogue that rhymed in the play, which also won the Blackburn Prize and many other awards. She continued to experiment with technique in *Mad Forest* (1990) and *The Skriker* (1994), which incorporated music and dance. Though Churchill's output decreased in the late 1990s, she continues to push the limits of traditional dramatic forms using dance and music, and other unexpected constructions.

PLOT SUMMARY

Act 1, Scene 1

Top Girls opens in a restaurant where Marlene is hosting a dinner party for five friends. She has recently been promoted at work. The five guests are all women that are either long-dead or are fictional characters from literature or paintings.

The first to come are Isabella Bird and Lady Nijo. Nijo and Isabella discuss their lives, including their families. Dull Gret and Pope Joan, who was elected to the papacy in the ninth century, appear. The conversation wanders between subjects, including religion and the love lives of Nijo and Isabella. Isabella goes on about her travel experiences. Joan talks about dressing and living as a male from the age of twelve so that she could further her education. Marlene proposes a toast to her guests. They, in turn, insist on toasting Marlene and her success.

Joan relates her disturbing story. While she enjoyed being the pope, she also had a discreet affair with a chamberlain and became pregnant. In denial about her state, she gave birth to her child during a papal procession. Joan was stoned to death, and her child, she believes, was also killed. While

Joan relates her story, Nijo talks about her four children being born, and only being able to see one of them after having given birth. Isabella talks about how she never had children. Marlene wonders why they are all so miserable.

The final guest arrives. She is Patient Griselda, a character in Geoffrey Chaucer's *The Canterbury Tales.* Griselda tells her story. Though she was a peasant girl, she was asked to be the wife of a local prince, but only if she obeyed him without question. Griselda agreed, though it later meant losing the two children she bore him—they were taken from her as infants. Then Griselda was sent back to her father with nothing but a slip to wear. Her husband called her back to help him prepare for his next wedding to a girl from France. The girl was her daughter—all this was a test of her loyalty. He took Griselda back, and the family was reunited.

Marlene is upset by Griselda's tale. Nijo is also perturbed because her children were never returned to her. Gret finally speaks up about her journey through hell, and how she beat the devils. The scene ends with Isabella talking about the last trip she took.

Act 1, Scene 2

The scene opens in the Top Girls employment agency in London. Marlene is interviewing Jeanine for possible placement. Marlene tells Jeanine that if she is to be sent on a job with prospects, she must not tell them that she is getting married or might have children. Marlene evaluates Jeanine and suggests jobs based on her perception of Jeanine's future.

Act 2, Scene 3

This scene takes place at night in Joyce's backyard in Suffolk. Joyce is Marlene's elder sister. Joyce's sixteen-year-old daughter Angie and her twelve-year-old friend Kit are playing in a shelter they built in the backyard. Joyce calls for Angie, but Angie and Kit ignore her until she goes back into the house. Angie says she wants to kill her mother.

Angie and Kit discuss going to the movies. Kit gets mad at Angie when she talks about dumb stuff. Angie desperately wants to leave home. Kit believes they should move to New Zealand in case of a war. Angie is indifferent because she has a big secret. She tells Kit she is going to London to see her aunt. Angie believes that Marlene is really her mother.

Joyce sneaks up on them. Joyce will not let them go to the movies until Angie cleans her room. Angie leaves, and Kit informs Joyce that she wants

Caryl Churchill

to be a nuclear physicist. When Angie returns, she is wearing a nice dress that is a little too small for her. Joyce becomes angry because Angie has not cleaned her room. It starts to rain. Joyce and Kit go inside. Angie stays outside. When Kit returns to get her, Angie threatens to kill her mother again.

Act 2, Scene 1

It is Monday morning at Top Girls. Win and Nell, who work at the agency, are talking. Win tells Nell about her weekend that she spent at her married boyfriend's house while his wife was out of town. The conversation turns to office gossip. They consider changing jobs as Marlene has been promoted over them, limiting their prospects. Still, Nell and Win are glad Marlene got the job over another coworker, Howard. Marlene enters late. Win and Nell tell her that they are glad she got the promotion rather than Howard.

Win interviews Louise, a forty-six-year-old woman who has been in the same job for twenty-one years. Louise has done everything for her company, but has spent twenty years in middle management with no opportunities to go higher. Win believes there will be only limited openings for her.

In the main office, Angie walks up to Marlene. Marlene does not recognize her at first. Angie has come to London on her own to see her aunt, and she intends to stay for a while. It is not clear if Joyce knows where Angie is. Angie becomes upset when Marlene does not seem like she wants her to stay.

Their conversation is interrupted by the appearance of Mrs. Kidd, Howard's wife. Mrs. Kidd is upset because Howard cannot accept that Marlene got the promotion to managing director over him. In part, he is disturbed because she is a woman. Mrs. Kidd wants Marlene to turn down the promotion so that he can have it. Mrs. Kidd leaves in a huff when Marlene is rude to her. Angie is proud of her aunt's saucy attitude.

In another interview, Nell talks to Shona, who claims to be twenty-nine and to have worked in sales on the road. As the interview progresses, it becomes clear that Shona has been lying. She is only twenty-one and has no real work experience.

In the main office, Win sits down and talks to Angie, who was left there by Marlene while she is working. Angie tells Win that she wants to work at Top Girls. Win begins to tell Angie her life story, but Angie falls asleep. Nell comes in and informs her that Howard has had a heart attack. When Marlene returns, Win tells her about Angie wanting to work at Top Girls. Marlene does not think Angie has much of a future there.

Act 2, Scene 2

This scene takes place a year earlier in Joyce's kitchen. Marlene is passing out presents for Joyce and Angie. One of the gifts is the nice dress that Angie wore in act 1, scene 2. While Angie goes to her room to try it on, Joyce and Marlene are talking. Joyce had no idea that Marlene was coming. Marlene believed Joyce had invited her there. Angie made the arrangements, lying to both of them.

Angie returns to show off the dress. They chide her for her deception. Angie reminds her that the last time she visited was for her ninth birthday. Marlene learns that Joyce's husband left her three years ago. It is getting late, and Angie is sent to bed. Marlene will sleep on the couch.

After Angie leaves to get ready for bed, Joyce and Marlene continue their discussion about their lives. The sisters' conversation turns into an argument. Marlene believes that Joyce is jealous of her success. Joyce criticizes the decisions Marlene has made, including leaving her home and giving up her

child, Angie. Marlene offers to send her money, but Joyce refuses.

Marlene is excited about a future under the new prime minister, Margaret Thatcher, while Joyce cannot stand the prime minister. They talk about the horrid life their mother led with their alcoholic father. It becomes clear the sisters have very different views of the world. As Marlene nears sleep on the couch, Angie walks in, having had a bad dream. ''Frightening,'' is all she says.

CHARACTERS

Angie

Angie is the sixteen-year-old adopted daughter of Joyce. Angie is the biological daughter of Marlene, but was given up by her birth mother, who was only seventeen at the time and had career ambitions. In act 1 of *Top Girls*, Angie realizes that Marlene is her mother, though she has not been told directly. Both Marlene and Joyce do not think highly of Angie and believe her future is limited. She has already left high school with no qualifications. She was in remedial classes, and her best friend is Kit, who is four years younger. Angie is frustrated and wants to murder her mother. Instead, she runs away to visit her aunt in London and hopes to live with her. Previously, Angie tricked Marlene into visiting her and Joyce. Angie is Marlene's embarrassment, but she is also one of the things that links her to the women at the dinner party.

Isabella Bird

Isabella is one of Marlene's dinner party guests in act 1, scene 1. She is a Scottish woman who lived in the late nineteenth and early twentieth centuries and who traveled extensively later in life. In *Top Girls,* Isabella is the first to arrive at the party and dominates the conversation in a self-absorbed manner. She talks on and on about her travels; her complex relationship with her sister, Hennie; her clergyman father, and husband; her illnesses; religion; and her lack of children. While Isabella does listen and respond to the others, she mostly tries to figure out her own life and what it meant. She could never be as good as her sister, but her adventures made her happy. Isabella is one of the characters who helps Marlene define herself.

Dull Gret

Dull Gret is one of Marlene's dinner guests in act 1, scene 1, and the third to arrive. Gret is the subject of a painting by Brueghel entitled ''Dulle Griet.'' In the painting, she wears an apron and armor and leads a group of women into hell to fight with devils. Gret is generally quiet through most of the dinner, answering questions only when directly asked and making a few comments on the side. Near the end of the scene, Gret makes a speech about her trip to hell and the fight with the devils. Like all the dinner guests, Gret's story reflects something about Marlene's life.

Jeanine

Marlene interviews Jeanine for placement by Top Girls in act 1. She is engaged and is saving money to get married. Marlene is not supportive of Jeanine's ambitions to work in advertising or in a job that might have some travel, but she categorizes her according to what Marlene believes she will be able to accomplish.

Pope Joan

Pope Joan is one of Marlene's dinner party guests in act 1, scene 1, and the fourth to arrive. She is a woman from the ninth century who allegedly served as the pope from 854 to 856. Pope Joan is somewhat aloof, making relevant, intelligent declarations throughout the conversation. When the topic turns to religion, she cannot help but point out heresies—herself included—though she does not attempt to convert the others to her religion. Joan reveals some of her life. She began dressing as a boy at age twelve so she could continue to study; she lived the rest of her life as a man, though she had male lovers. Joan was eventually elected pope. She became pregnant by her chamberlain lover and delivered her baby during a papal procession. For this, Joan was stoned to death. At the end of the scene, Joan recites a passage in Latin. Like all the dinner guests, Joan's life and attitude reflects something about Marlene.

Joyce

Joyce is Marlene's elder sister and mother to Angie. Unlike her younger sister, Joyce stayed in the same area and social class she grew up in. Joyce is unambitious and unhappy. She was married to Frank, but she told him to leave three years previously because he was having affairs with other women. She supports herself and Angie by cleaning houses.

Because Joyce seemed to be unable to have children, she adopted Angie as an infant when Marlene decided to give her up. But Joyce soon got pregnant and miscarried the child because of the demands of raising Angie. Joyce resents both Angie and Marlene, in part because of her miscarriage. She calls Angie a lump and useless. Marlene is too ambitious and clever for Joyce.

Yet Joyce has pride. She will not take Marlene's money, and she does not cater to her crying. Joyce maintains her working class loyalty and stands her ground when Marlene starts to sing the praises of Margaret Thatcher. Despite such differences, Marlene and Joyce are very much alike. They both believe they are right and do what they must to survive in their different worlds.

Mrs. Kidd

Mrs. Kidd is the wife of Howard, the man who got passed over in favor of Marlene for the managing director position at Top Girls. In act 2, Mrs. Kidd comes to the office and tries to get Marlene to turn down the position. Mrs. Kidd hopes Marlene will understand how much it would hurt Howard's pride and livelihood. Marlene is not impressed by her pleas, and Mrs. Kidd leaves after insulting Marlene for being a hard, working woman.

Kit

Kit is the twelve-year-old best friend of Angie. Unlike Angie, Kit is clever and plans on being a nuclear physicist. The girls have been friends for years, though Kit gets annoyed by Angie's limitations. In some ways, Kit is a younger version of Marlene.

Louise

Louise is interviewed by Win for placement by Top Girls in act 2. Louise is a forty-six-year-old woman stuck in middle management who believes she has been overlooked for promotion and underappreciated by her present firm. Win is not particularly supportive of Louise's desires to use her experience elsewhere and does not offer much hope for a better position. Like Marlene, Win categorizes Louise according to what she believes Louise will be able to accomplish.

Marlene

Marlene is the central character in *Top Girls.* She is a successful businesswoman who has recently been promoted to managing director of Top

Girls, an employment agency. To celebrate, she has a dinner party at a restaurant with five guests, all of whom are women who are either dead or fictional characters from literature and paintings. Marlene's own life shares some parallels with these women.

Marlene's adult life has been focused on her career, to the exclusion of nearly everything else. She previously worked in the United States and has done well for herself. Marlene has little to no contact with her family. Her alcoholic father is dead, and her long-suffering mother is in some sort of home. Marlene does not get along with her sister Joyce, who has remained part of the working class and lives in the same neighborhood where they grew up.

Marlene let Joyce raise her daughter, Angie. Marlene became pregnant at age seventeen, and because the then-married Joyce did not have a child, she allowed her to adopt the baby. Marlene has as little respect and interest in Angie as Joyce does. Like the women she interviews at Top Girls, Marlene believes Angie's future is limited. Yet Marlene's own life is just as circumscribed, but in different ways. Her success has come at a high price, costing her both her empathy and her relationships.

Nell

Nell is one of the employees at the Top Girls employment agency. She is happy that Marlene got the promotion over Howard, but she has her own career ambitions and might want to find a job with better prospects. In the meantime, her boyfriend, Derek, has asked her to marry him, but she does not know if she will accept. Her career seems more important to her than the marriage. During the play, Nell conducts an interview with Shona, whom Nell believes might be good for Top Girls. Nell is disappointed to learn that Shona has lied about everything on her application.

Lady Nijo

Lady Nijo is one of Marlene's dinner party guests in act 1, scene 1, and the second to arrive. She is a thirteenth-century Japanese courtesan to the Emperor of Japan. She later became a Buddhist monk. Like Isabella, Nijo is somewhat self-absorbed, though not to the same degree. Nijo tells the others about her life, including information about her father, her lovers, her four children (only one of

whom she ever saw), symbolic clothing, and her time as a traveling monk. But she also listens respectfully to the stories of others and acknowledges her limitations. Nijo liked her silk clothing and easy life with the Emperor. By the end of the scene, Nijo is in tears. Like all the dinner guests, Nijo's life reflects something about Marlene's.

Patient Griselda

Patient Griselda is one of Marlene's dinner guests in act 1, scene 1, and the last to arrive. She is a fictional character, appearing in ''The Clerk's Tale'' in Geoffrey Chaucer's *The Canterbury Tales,* among other stories. As soon as she arrives, Marlene has Griselda tell her story. Griselda was a peasant girl who was asked to marry a local prince, but only if she would obey him without question. She agreed and bore him two children who were taken away from her while they were still infants. She did not question the decision. Her husband sent Griselda back home with nothing more than a slip to wear. She went without question. He sent for her to help him plan his second marriage to a young French girl. Griselda came back. At a pre-wedding feast, he revealed that the girl and her page/brother were their children and all these incidents were tests of her loyalty. Like all the dinner guests, Griselda's story reflects an aspect of Marlene's life.

Shona

Shona is interviewed by Nell for placement by the Top Girls agency in the second act. Shona tries to pass herself off as a twenty-nine-year-old woman with sales experience, which Nell believes at first. As the interview progresses, it becomes clear that Shona has been making up a story. She is really twenty-one and has no job experience. Shona is certain that she could handle high-profile jobs, but Nell does not believe her.

Win

Win is one of the employees at the Top Girls employment agency. Like Nell, she is glad that Marlene got the promotion over Howard, but she has her own career ambitions and might move on. She is relatively well educated and has previously lived in several different countries. Win spent the previous weekend with her married boyfriend at his house, while his wife was out of town. During the course of the play, Win interviews Louise for a job; she shares Marlene's callous attitude toward Louise.

THEMES

Choices and Consequences

Nearly every character in *Top Girls* has made or is in the process of making life-changing decisions with important consequences. The dinner party in act 1, scene 1 exemplifies this. Each of the historical figures has made a hard choice. For example, Pope Joan chose to live like a boy, and then a man, in public. When she became pregnant by her secret lover, the stoning death of her and her baby were consequences of her chosen life. Joyce chose to adopt Angie, which lead to a certain life path. Joyce believes that she miscarried her own child because of the demands of raising Angie.

Marlene also made several hard choices. She became a career woman who spent some time working in the States. Marlene is estranged from her family, including her biological daughter, Angie, and does not seem to have many close friends, female or male. Her dinner party in celebration of her promotion consists of women who are dead or do not really exist, not with friends or family. She has no love relationship. Marlene is very much alone because of her life choices. While her daughter Angie has already made two life choices—dropping out of school at the age of sixteen with no qualifications, and running away to London to live with her aunt/mother—the consequences of these actions in her life are unclear.

Success and Failure

Success is an important part of Marlene's life in *Top Girls,* defining who she is and whose company she enjoys. The dinner party is meant to celebrate her promotion to managing director as well as the successes of her guests. Joan became the pope. Isabella traveled the world. Gret fought the devils in hell. Griselda survived her husband's extraordinary tests of loyalty. Marlene sees these women as successful, though they are not in her real, everyday life. Marlene's personal life is a failure because of her success in business. She has no real friends in the play, and she has not seen her sister or biological daughter in seven years. At the dinner party, she moans at one point, ''Oh God, why are we all so miserable?''

Yet, Marlene believes that Joyce is mostly a failure because she did not grow beyond her neighborhood; instead, she got married and raised a child. Joyce cleans houses for a living, and she is not

TOPICS FOR FURTHER STUDY

- Research one of the five guests from history, literature, and art that come to Marlene's dinner party in act 1, scene 1 of *Top Girls*. Compare and contrast their lives to Marlene's life, focusing on issues of gender and success.

- Explore the psychological aspects of the complex relationship between Marlene, Joyce, and Angie. How could Marlene, Joyce, and Angie have avoided their sad situation?

- Research the state of the women's movement in Great Britain in the 1980s. Should Marlene be considered a feminist? Why or why not?

- Compare and contrast the public perception of Great Britain's prime minister in 1982, Margaret Thatcher, with Marlene. How were successful women viewed by society in this time period?

impressed by Marlene's life. Joyce does not really see her world in the same terms of success or failure. She does what is necessary to survive and to rear Angie. However, both sisters agree that Angie has no chance of being a success in life. Angie has no education, no ambition, and is regarded as dumb. The best she might do is menial work and marry. While this describes Joyce's life, both Joyce and Marlene perceive that Angie might not be able to take care of herself. This would be the ultimate failure in their eyes. They agree that one should support oneself.

Class Conflict

Marlene and Joyce's differing definitions of success stem in part from a class conflict. Marlene has moved beyond her working-class roots to a middle-class life by education and persistence. She holds a management position in a demanding field, an employment agency. She even lived and worked in the United States for several years. Marlene supports the political agenda of Great Britain's female prime minister, Margaret Thatcher, even though she is perceived as anti-workingclass.

Joyce remains firmly working class, leading a life only slightly better than her parents. She works as a cleaning lady to support Angie. Unlike Joyce and Marlene's mother, who stayed with her alcoholic husband and had nothing, Joyce told her husband to leave when she could no longer take his controlling nature and numerous affairs. Joyce regards Thatcher as evil, comparing her to Adolf Hitler, for her attitudes towards working-class people. Joyce believes that Marlene thinks she is too good for her. Marlene says she does not like working-class people, but she does not really include her sister as one of them. The pair never come to an understanding on class.

Sex Roles and Sexism

Throughout the text of *Top Girls* is an implicit discussion on what society expects women to be. Each of the guests at the dinner party defines womanhood in a particular era, either by what they are or by what they are not. Isabella, for example, could not live up to the standards of femininity defined by her sister, Hennie. Yet Isabella was a traveler who saw more of the world than most men. Marlene also breaks out of the traditional roles for women, by virtue of her career.

While Marlene has benefited economically from her career, her disregard for sex roles has its problems. She is not married, and it does not seem like she is in a long-term relationship. Joyce does not really like her. Mrs. Kidd, the wife of the man who was passed over for the promotion that Marlene got, begs her to not take it. Mrs. Kidd believes that the upset Howard should not have to work for a woman. Further, Mrs. Kidd hopes that Marlene will give up the promotion because Howard has to support his family. Mrs. Kidd calls Marlene ''unnatural'' for her uncompromising stand on the promotion and her attachment to her job. Marlene does not give in, but such sexism does not make her life and choices any easier.

STYLE

Setting

Top Girls is a feminist drama/fantasy set in contemporary times. The action is confined to two places in England, London and Suffolk. The realistic action takes place in two settings. One is the Top Girls employment agency, where Marlene works. There, potential clients are interviewed, and Angie shows up, hoping to stay with Marlene. The other is Joyce's home and backyard, where Marlene visits and Angie and Kit scheme. The fantasy dinner party that opens *Top Girls* also takes place in London. (In many productions, the restaurant is called La Prima Donna.) Though the dinner is clearly a fantasy because all the guests are dead or fictional, the setting is very real.

Fantasy versus Reality

In act 1, scene 1, Marlene hosts a dinner party with guests both long dead (Pope Joan, Lady Nijo, and Isabella Bird) and fictional (Dull Gret and Patient Griselda). While Marlene listens to and guides the conversation—injecting only bits about herself—these five women share their stories. The party is ostensibly to celebrate Marlene's promotion at work, but she intends it to be a celebration of all their successes. Though these women have each achieved something they are proud of, success has come at a large price in their lives. The dinner party itself shows the tensions between fantasy and reality because the guests are not ''real'' to the rest of the characters in *Top Girls,* only to Marlene. Yet the ideas and problems brought up by the fantasy women are very real. These issues echo in the plot and dialogue of the rest of the text, adding another dimension to the tension between fantasy and reality.

Time

Top Girls is not a linear play, but one in which time is used in an unusual fashion. The last scene of the play, act 2, scene 2, is the only part that takes place at a specific time in the story, about a year earlier than the other events. This flashback ties up some of the loose ends created by the story. The rest of the scenes, even the action within act 2, scene 1, do not have to take place in the order presented, though all are set in the present. The events are linked thematically, but not by a specific sequence of time. In addition, the idea of time is toyed with at the dinner party in act 1, scene 1. None of the guests can really exist at the same time, yet they share many of the same concerns.

Multiple Casting

Often when *Top Girls* is performed—including its premieres in England and the United States—several parts are played by the same actresses. Only the actress who plays Marlene, the central character in the play, has only one role. Thus guests at the dinner party are played by actresses who also play contemporary characters. Such casting decisions create visual links between seemingly disparate women. In the original production, for example, the same actress played Dull Gret and Angie, implying that these characters might have something in common. Similarly, another actress took on the roles of Pope Joan and Louise, drawing another parallel. This casting technique further emphasizes how alike the concerns of the historical characters and contemporary characters really are.

HISTORICAL CONTEXT

In the early 1980s, Great Britain was ruled by women. Though Queen Elizabeth II was only a royal figurehead, real political power was held by Prime Minister Margaret Thatcher. A member of the Conservative Party, Thatcher had been elected on May 3, 1979, and proceeded to put her own stamp on British life over the next decade or so. She was reelected in 1983 and 1987, and held office until late 1990, when she received a vote of no confidence and was replaced by fellow Conservative John Major. Thatcher had been the longest serving prime minister in Great Britain since the nineteenth century.

To improve the British economy, Thatcher dismantled the socialist practices that were put in place in the post-World War II era. She privatized major industries, like coal mining and telecommunications, which had been run by the British government, and she cut down on the power of trade unions. Because Thatcher's revolution benefited the middle- and upper-classes and seemed to hurt the working- and lower-classes, she was very unpopular among the latter groups. Unemployment continued to rise, and by 1982, over three and a quarter million people were unemployed. With cuts in both welfare and other social programs, such people's lives were becoming much harder. Though the economy was strong and interest rates and inflation were down, real living standards had been falling slightly for several years; international trade was also down.

In 1982, Thatcher and the Conservative party had some popularity problems among the general population. National morale was not particularly high until the Falklands War broke out. The Falkland Islands were a British possession in the Atlantic Ocean off the coast of Argentina. The group of islands are small and only about 1,800 people were living there. The territory was at the center of a dispute between Argentina and Great Britain for a number of years, and the two countries were in negotiations over them. In the spring of 1982, Argentina became impatient and invaded the Falklands. Great Britain responded and reclaimed the islands before Argentina quickly surrendered. Though there were approximately 243 British casualties, the victory improved national moral and the repute of Thatcher and the Conservatives. The popularity of the Labour party went down.

Thatcher was but one symbol in the 1980s of powerful women. There was a concrete change in the position of working women. In Great Britain in the early 1980s, women made up forty percent of the labor force, and over sixty percent of women aged twenty to sixty-four were working. Marriage rates fell in the 1980s, after having remained stable for many years. Before that decade nearly every adult woman was married at some point. Those that did marry gave up working after having a child, although sometimes they went back to work after their children went to school or reached adulthood. Most women who worked were employed in poorly paid white collar, service, and industrial occupations. Approximately seventy-five percent of women did personal services work, clerical work, retail work, or health, education, or welfare work. The number of professional women was still small, but more women were becoming lawyers than ever before. These professional women often had equal pay for equal work, but working class women did not. Despite the success of Thatcher, many British women were anti-Conservative, though they did not necessarily support Labour either. To these women, Thatcher may have shared their gender, but her political prominence did not necessarily make her their heroine.

CRITICAL OVERVIEW

Most critics agree that *Top Girls* is an intricate play; generally, they find much to praise in its themes, attitudes, and text. The play's depiction of women and feminism is particularly interesting to critics.

COMPARE
&
CONTRAST

- **1982:** Great Britain is led by a female Conservative prime minister, Margaret Thatcher, who was regarded as harsh.

  Today: Great Britain is ruled by a male Labour prime minister, Tony Blair, who is regarded as personable.

- **1982:** Great Britain goes to war with Argentina over possession of the Falkland Islands and wins.

  Today: The Falkland Islands are still a British protectorate, but self-governing. The citizens have been under constant British military protection ever since the war.

- **1982:** A ''have-it-all'' concept of life is common for women in the United States and Great Britain. Many strive for wealth, a successful career, and a perfect family.

  Today: While material and personal success are still important, a more realistic tone predominates as the difficulties of trying to balance it all are realized.

- **1982:** The feminist movement is floundering in Great Britain and the United States. The agenda of many feminist organizations has little to do with the reality of the lives of ordinary women. In the United States, this trend is symbolized by the failure to ratify the Equal Rights Amendment to the Constitution.

  Today: In a post-feminist society, women's organizations regroup to address concerns of women of different classes. In 1998 in the United States, the National Council of Women's Organizations (representing six million women) drafts potential legislation for the National Women's Equality Act, which calls for the end of sex discrimination.

Writing about the original London production, Bryan Robertson of *The Spectator* argued, ''her play is brilliantly conceived with considerable wit to illuminate the underlying deep human seriousness of her theme. The play is feminist, all right, but it is an entertaining, sometimes painful and often funny play and not a mere tract.'' Expanding on this idea, Benedict Nightingale of the *New Statesman* wrote, ''What use is female emancipation, Churchill asks, if it transforms the clever women into predators and does nothing for the stupid, weak and helpless? Does freedom, and feminism, consist of aggressively adopting the very values that have for centuries oppressed your sex?''

Writing about the same production, John Russell Taylor of *Plays & Players* is one of several critics over the years who believed that the rest of *Top Girls* did not live up to the promise of the dinner party scene. He found the play disjointed, arguing that ''the pieces in the puzzle remain determinedly separate, never quite adding up to more than, well, so many fascinating pieces in a fascinating puzzle.''

When *Top Girls* opened in the United States a short time later, a few critics were dismissive of the play and Churchill's potential appeal to American audiences. Calling the play ''confused,'' Douglas Watt of the *Daily News* proclaimed, ''Churchill can write touchingly and with a good ear for everyday speech about middle-class Londoners today. But while concern for ugly ducklings may be universal . . . *Top Girls* is a genre piece likely to arouse even less interest here than Alan Ayckbourn's equally tricky, but infinitely more amusing, works about the English middle class.''

Edith Oliver of the *New Yorker* was perplexed by certain aspects of the play. She wrote ''*Top Girls* . . . is witty and original, with considerable dramatized feeling, yet somehow never got to me, and I was never certain whether she was making one point with the whole play or a lot of points in its separate segments.'' Later in her review, Oliver emphasized that ''[d]espite my admiration of Miss Churchill's ingenuity, I was disappointed and at times puzzled—never quite certain, for example, whether the historical characters of the first scene were meant to be the prototypes of modern characters. . . .''

A majority of American critics commented on the uniqueness of certain aspects of *Top Girls,* but they were most concerned with its feminist theme and social meanings. For example, John Beaufort of the *Christian Science Monitor* called *Top Girls* ''a theatrical oddity in which the long view of what has been happening to womankind's 'top girls' combines with a sharp look at contemporary women achievers and a compassionate glance at the plight of an underclass underachiever who will never know the meaning of room at the top. Apart from one cheap shock effect, Miss Churchill has written a thoughtful and imaginative theater piece.''

Along similar lines, T. E. Kalem of *Time* asks in his review, ''Is the future to be divided between a smart, scrambling upper class of no-holds-barred individualists and a permanent underclass of poor souls who are unfit for the survival of the fittest?'' An unnamed reviewer in *Variety* added, ''If it's about male manipulation, *Top Girls* also pointedly involves the conditioned mentality of the sisterhood itself, with its inherited sense of role in a masculine or at least male-dominated world. The play seems to be saying that women historically have had themselves as well as sexist pigs for enemies.'' John Simon of *New York* believes the ideas in *Top Girls* have universal applicability. ''This is not easy theater, but funny, fiercely serious, and greatly worth thinking about. Its aporias [insoluble contradictions] are not only pertinent to women, they also concern the entire, always incomplete, human condition.''

Top Girls has continued to be performed regularly over the years. Most critics believe the play has withstood the test of time, despite specific references to British prime minster Margaret Thatcher and attitudes specific to the early 1980s. Of a 1991 revival in London, Paul Taylor in *The Independent* argued, ''What continues to distinguish *Top Girls* is its cool, objective manner. The scenes in the job agency are almost too cleverly efficient in the way they expose the heartlessness the women have had to assume along with their crisp power-outfits. Churchill permits you to identify with the tricky plight of these characters but she does not ask you to like them.'' Similarly, Alastair Macaulay of the *Financial Times* believes, ''Both as theatre and as politics, *Top Girls* is exciting and irritating. The

dialectic of its final scene, between the Thatcherite Marlene and her socialist sister Joyce rings true as you listen. The terms in which the sisters argue about Thatcherite politics have not dated.''

CRITICISM

Annette Petrusso

In this essay, Petrusso discusses the importance of the character of Angie in Top Girls, *and her role in the construction and development of the central character in the play, Marlene.*

Many critics who have commented on Caryl Churchill's *Top Girls* have focused their praise on the interesting characters and complexities of the scene that opens the play, act 1, scene 1's dinner party. The party is hosted by *Top Girl*'s central character, Marlene, and is attended by five guests, all obscure figures from history, literature, and art. Ostensibly, the party is to celebrate the success of Marlene, who has recently been promoted to managing director of Top Girls employment agency. The scene also defines many of the play's themes and dramatic tensions. There are a number of critics who share the opinion of Lianne Stevens of the *Los Angeles Times.* Reviewing a 1986 production of *Top Girls* in San Diego, California, Stevens writes, ''outstanding performances . . . cannot rectify the main defect in Churchill's play: Nothing that comes after is as interesting as having dinner with Pope Joan, Dull Gret, Lady Nijo, Patient Griselda and Isabella Bird.''

There are, in fact, several aspects of the rest of *Top Girls* that are as interesting, mostly because of what has been laid out in the dinner party scene. One is the character of Angie, Marlene's sixteen-year-old daughter, whom she allowed her sister Joyce to adopt at birth. Angie plays as pivotal a role in the play as any of the dinner party guests. While there is no doubt that Marlene is at the center of *Top Girls,* and that her character presents hard and conflicted ideas about women, success, power, and employment in the early 1980s, Angie and the dinner guests help to define Marlene as much as Marlene's own actions and comments do. However, the dinner guests were chosen by Marlene, while Angie was an accident Marlene has chosen to have very little contact with and is dismissive of.

Each of the dinner guests is an adult woman, though they are fantastic characters who do not

A scene from the 1991 production of Top Girls *at London's Royal Court Theatre.*

really exist in the modern world inhabited by Marlene and the rest of the characters in the play. Marlene turns to them, not to any of the "real" people depicted in the play, when she wants to celebrate her promotion. While the guests are successful in their own, though not always obvious, ways, their success has come at a price. Lady Nijo suffered many degradations including not being allowed to raise her own children. Marlene is deeply troubled by the story of Patient Griselda, who was humiliated by her husband as a test of her loyalty to him, mostly because she was of a lower class. To get an education, Pope Joan led a life of deception as a male. Though she later became pope, it was her womanhood—her ability to get pregnant and give birth to a child at an inopportune moment—that led to the murder which ended her life.

Marlene's choice of guests reveals much about her. First, she does not have anyone in her real life to share her promotion with, suggesting an alienation from real women. Second, the loss of her child still weighs on her, either in her conscious, subconscious, or both. Lady Nijo, Pope Joan, and Patient Griselda all suffer the loss of children. Only Joan is rather indifferent to the death of her infant. Marlene inquires about Dull Gret's children, clearly expressing her interest in the subject. Marlene's question

after the one to Gret is rhetorical: "Oh God, why are we all so miserable?" There is a link between unhappiness and the idea of children and loss. Third, Marlene has no real interest in her own daughter, Angie, though they have more in common than Marlene does with her chosen guests.

To understand the importance of Angie, Marlene's character must be better understood. Marlene grew up in an unstable home. Her father worked in the fields, and had a problem with alcohol. Her mother suffered at the hands of her husband, often going hungry and being beaten. Her sister Joyce was older, and did not share either Marlene's need to escape or her intelligence. Despite her background, Marlene managed to create a good life for herself by working hard and apparently acquiring a decent education. She even lived in the United States for several years. The only flaw, the only thing that could have held her back, was when Marlene got pregnant at the age of seventeen. The situation was stressful, and Marlene was in denial for part of the pregnancy. Rather than allow Marlene to give the baby up to strangers, Joyce insisted on adopting Angie, in part because she had no children of her own. This is a long-standing point of contention between the sisters, though Joyce makes it clear that she would not have approved of any

WHAT DO I READ NEXT?

- *Cloud 9* is a play by Churchill written in 1979. Like *Top Girls*, this play is experimental in form and characterizations and includes feminist themes.

- *Skirmishes*, a drama written by Catherine Hayes in 1982, also concerns two sisters conflicted over family matters.

- *Steaming* is a feminist play by Nell Dunn written in 1981. It is from the same era as *Top Girls*, and has themes similar to *Top Girls*.

- *Ugly Rumors*, a drama about Margaret Thatcher and other British prime ministers, was written by Tariq Ali and Howard Bronton in 1998. The play concerns the differences in the interactions between Thatcher and male prime ministers.

- *Objections to Sex and Violence* is a play by Churchill first produced in 1975. At the center of the drama is a tense relationship between two very different sisters.

- *The Feminine Mystique*, written by Betty Friedan and originally published in 1963, was one of the first important books addressing the issues of equality for women. Since its first printing, Friedan's book has inspired and encouraged women as they have sought to establish careers, widen their presence in the business world, and create a fulfilling home life. The reissued edition, published in 1984, features a new introduction and speaks to topics that are of particular interest to women today, including health insurance, welfare reform, sexual harassment and discrimination, the growing presence of women in sports, and the decreasing wage gap between men and women.

---

choice Marlene made in the situation except to have had an abortion early on or raise the child herself and not have tried to have a better life. Angie and related petty jealousies are at the heart of their conflict and thus at the center of *Top Girls*.

Yet, Angie is a reviled character. Everyone around Angie dismisses her and believes she has no future. Joyce, her adopted mother, calls her "a big lump." She believes Angie will have a hard time getting a job and her best bet in life is to get married, though she cannot imagine who would marry her. Joyce does admit at one point, "She's clever in her own way." Labeling her "thick," Marlene, Angie's birth mother, tells one of her coworkers, "She's not going to make it." She believes Angie's future career will be as a "Packer in Tesco," nothing as accomplished as working at the employment agency run by Marlene. Kit, her only friend and a twelve-year-old, says to Angie at one point, "Stupid f—ing cow, I hate you." She later tells Angie that she is not sure she even likes her. Kit amends that attitude by telling Joyce "I love Angie." The way those around

Angie talk about her, it seems like she is useless and incompetent. Joyce especially seems to hammer this idea home directly to Angie. Angie is definitely immature. She talks about being able to move objects with her thoughts, hearing a long-dead kitten in the backyard, and has only one friend, Kit, who is four years younger than her. She has ended her education in remedial classes at the age of sixteen.

Yet Angie accomplishes much over the course of *Top Girls,* more than expected considering how she is talked about. Angie has her own equivalent of the dinner party in act 1, scene 3. She and Kit hide in a shelter that they probably made in Joyce's backyard. Kit, however, is a real person, unlike the unreal guests at Marlene's. Angie and Kit have a real, if tense, friendship. They make tentative plans to go to the movies. Angie expresses her frustrations to Kit, saying she wants to kill her mother. She tells Kit about her secret, that she believes Marlene is her mother. Angie also says that she will go to London to see her aunt. Kit does not really believe her,

> EVERYONE AROUND ANGIE DISMISSES HER AND BELIEVES SHE HAS NO FUTURE. JOYCE, HER ADOPTED MOTHER, CALLS HER 'A BIG LUMP.' SHE BELIEVES ANGIE WILL HAVE A HARD TIME GETTING A JOB AND HER BEST BET IN LIFE IS TO GET MARRIED, THOUGH SHE CANNOT IMAGINE WHO WOULD MARRY HER."

though, underscoring that Angie is constantly underestimated by those around her.

Another success of Angie's is going to London from Suffolk on the bus, and finding her way to Marlene's work place in act 2, scene 1. Joyce and Kit do not think Angie could do such a thing on her own. But Angie wants to escape her life with Joyce and become a success. To that end, she goes to her aunt/mother and hopes to stay with her. Angie has the gumption to ask her aunt for help. She will even sleep on the floor of Marlene's home to have this different, better life, like her aunt/mother. It also creates a situation where Marlene gets her child back, a key point brought up in the dinner party. Angie wants to be with Marlene, to be Marlene, and does what she can to make that happen. Angie wants to be a top girl.

Angie's first success, though the last in the play since it takes place in act 2, scene 2, is getting Marlene to visit her in the first place. The last scene takes place a year before the rest of the *Top Girls*. Angie lied to Marlene to get her to visit her and Joyce in Suffolk. She has not seen her aunt/mother since her ninth birthday party. Angie knows that Marlene has had good jobs and has lived in America, and she admires her tremendously. Angie appreciates that Marlene has escaped their neighborhood and become successful, just as Marlene admired that about her fantasy dinner guests. Angie may not have the education or the intelligence that Marlene has, but she wants to do something like what Marlene has done. In this scene, Marlene reveals the key

to her success. She proclaims, "I'm not clever, just pushy." Angie has shown that she can be pushy as well over the course of the play, implying that she might have a better future than anyone imagined.

In writing about a 1998 production of *Top Girls* in Los Angeles, California, Don Shirley of the *Los Angeles Times* argues, "Churchill painted a stark picture of Margaret Thatcher's Britain as a place where women could end up in either a cushy but heartless career or a dreary life in domestic servitude. This may sound broadly feminist, but the play finally emerges as a more specific attack on Thatcherite insensitivities towards the girls who aren't on 'top.'" Shirley includes Angie as one who is not on top, but does not see that she could be. Angie is a younger—perhaps dumber but no less ambitious—Marlene.

Source: Annette Petrusso, in an essay for *Drama for Students,* Gale Group, 2001.

Jasbir Jain

In the following essay on Caryl Churchill's Top Girls, *author Jasbir Jain discusses how Churchill writes a feminist world to create an emotional space which develops a "collective description" of the characters' experience as women.*

Caryl Churchill's *Top Girls* (1983) and Charlotte Keatley's *My Mother Said I Never Should* (1987) are plays with an all women cast. Men, though present in the stories, are absent from the stage. They occupy emotional space but not physical space. At the very outset there is a defining of space, a creation of a feminist world. Keatley deliberately kept the men offstage to provide a space for the women to interact among themselves, "to show the way women use language, silence and subtext when alone together"; Churchill apparently does it for the purposes of sharing, for as Adrienne Rich has pointed out that unless women are prepared to share their "private and sometimes painful personal experience" it may not be possible to create a "collective description" of what is truly a woman's world. In both plays women from different generations and backgrounds meet together to share and to interact but with two major differences. Keatley's characters in the child-scenes are child characters and represent the same lineage whereas Churchill's characters represent several centuries, from the ninth to the present and have altogether different backgrounds.

The moment women are placed centre-stage they begin to interact and introspect, to analyze and to criticize; they cease to look at themselves through the male gaze, instead they begin to problematize their conflicts and the involuntary processes of their bodies. By defining space in female terms, women are transformed from objects into subjects and their passive acceptance of gendered roles is turned into an analysis of socially imposed codes of behaviour.

Plays by women need not be feminist, just as plays about women are not always so. But plays which concern themselves with women as subjects and explore their emotional realities acquire a feminist perspective. The sixties and the seventies witnessed the rise of women's theatre groups and collectives and a consciousness about women's roles. This was the beginning of a feminist theatre with, as already stated, overtly political aims. Women through exploring and talking about their experiences opened out their role confines, created female traditions and entered areas hitherto forbidden to them. Several all-women plays were also written. Megan Terry's *Calm Down, Mother* (1965) was a transformation exercise for women and hailed by Helene Keyssar as the first real feminist play, while her later *Babes in the Bighouse* (1974) was about women prisoners and closed spaces where violence became a natural inhabitant. Eve Merriam's *Out of Our Fathers' House* (1975) was a projection of the struggles of exceptional women, while Wendy Wasserstein's *Uncommon Women and Others* (1977) examined the role conflicts in a lighter vein. Maria Irene Fornes's *Fefu and Her Friends* (1977) is located in the thirties and is a powerful statement about the violence implicit in heterosexual relationships; it is as Schuler has pointed out "impossible to ignore that explicit critique of patriarchy" (226) present in the play. Marsha Norman's *'night, Mother,* coming out the same year as *Top Girls* (1983), is a tense kitchen drama about a mother and a daughter with the daughter at the end committing suicide behind a locked door.

Plays with an all-women cast make a specific statement even before they put this female space to different and individual use. They discard supportive roles for women and provide them with the freedom to relate directly to each other rather than through sons and husbands, "Language, space and the body are loci for the woman playwright to dramatically challenge the images of women determined in dominant discourse" (Hart), Memory, history, the past are evoked for different reasons.

> "BY DEFINING SPACE IN FEMALE TERMS, WOMEN ARE TRANSFORMED FROM OBJECTS INTO SUBJECTS AND THEIR PASSIVE ACCEPTANCE OF GENDERED ROLES IS TURNED INTO AN ANALYSIS OF SOCIALLY IMPOSED CODES OF BEHAVIOUR."

Time too becomes an important factor, often being projected non-chronologically.

Both *Top Girls* and *My Mother* create hypothetical situations which are historically not possible but are rendered so spatially and proceed to become emotional questionings. Both are 3-act plays but while Churchill after an initial juxtaposition of the past and the present moves on, Keatley keeps on coming back to the childhood scene which is a conjunction of 1905, 1941, 1961 and 1979.

Top Girls in the first act evokes the past, somewhat like Eve Merriam's *Out of Our Fathers' House* where six women are presented together in a "hypothetical conversation". They act out both for themselves and each other the stories of their lives. It is a journey into selfhood, and at each step they need reassurance from their own selves. They belong to the 18th, 19th and 20th centuries, Caryl Churchill, however, builds on a wider canvas and the dramatic purpose of the bringing together of six women from different backgrounds and periods is very different. The first act of *Top Girls* is in the nature of a prologue where Marlene, a top executive in an employment agency is hosting a dinner for five other women, three of whom are from the pages of history, and two from the world of male imagination. Pope Joan, a ninth century Pope who achieved this through cross-gendering, Lady Nijo an emperor's concubine and later a Buddhist nun, and Isabella Bird, a nineteenth century explorer are the three 'real' women. Dull Gret, a woman from Breughel's 16th century painting and Patient Griselda from the pages of Petrarch, Boccaccio and Chaucer are the two others (Note the words "dull" and "patient").

Each one of them—except Griselda—has in some way violated the social code as imposed upon them. Joan learnt Latin, ran away from home disguised as a boy and later became a pope. But yielding to passion, she conceives and is detected during childbirth. Male priests have fathered children, but she has never learnt to understand or live with her body, thus alienated from this most fundamental space she might own, she pays for it with death. Lady Nijo on the other hand accepts the code but renders it hollow by creating space for herself. Handed over to the Emperor as his concubine, she takes lovers to fulfill her emotional needs. Out of favour with the Emperor she takes holy orders as directed by her father, but instead of being confined in a convent, she walks the breadth and length of Japan. But she does this at the price of motherhood. Isabella Bird also has to sacrifice marriage and family life in search of adventure. Because she is a woman, she finds it difficult to accept the idea of living for herself alone and therefore occupies herself with good causes.

As contrasted with these women from real life, who have individually made space for themselves, questioned patriarchal structures like religion, ownership, love and motherhood, the two women from the world of imagination are limited in their projections. Griselda's life reads like a fairytale—a peasant woman married into the aristocracy, and children whom she had given up for dead restored to her later. The price of her marriage is unquestioning obedience to her husband's command which is first the taking away of her son and her daughter and later being turned out of her house. Griselda does not question her husband's right over her, nor does she resist his orders. Her case, like Nijo's, is one where motherhood has been reduced to an ''institution'' under male control (Rich). Dull Gret is also single minded like Griselda. If for Griselda it is surrender, for Gret it is anger.

These five women have got together to celebrate Marlene's success and as they share experiences they question patriarchal structures either directly like Joan and Isabelle, or obliquely like Nijo, or silently through victimization like Griselda. Travel is a major theme for Joan, Nijo and Isabelle. They travel in their different dresses, Joan in her papal robes, Nijo in her silkgowns and later her nun's habit, and Isabella in her full blue trousers and great brass spurs. (Dress also specifies space. Masculine dress does not constrain the women's private space, though, in the long run, there is no social recognition of that space.) Travel opens out new worlds and spaces. Their coming together in the first act provides ''a dramatic genealogy of Marlene's historical community'' (Keyssar).

The second act is the in-between act with 3 scenes. The first and the third are located in Marlene's office, the second in Joyce, her sister's, backyard. The office scenes have two interviews inbuilt into them, one with Jeanine and the other with Louise, Marlene's two clients; a competitive scene between Nell and Win and Marlene's interactions with Angie and with Mrs. Kidd. The themes of these two scenes are a replay of the themes introduced in Act One—Jeanine who is torn between marriage and a career, Louise who at the end of twenty years finds herself sidetracked by younger men, Nell and Win who wish to go places both literally and figuratively but Marlene has occupied the place at the top and Mrs. Kidd who has come to plead for her husband who has been superseded by Marlene. Mrs. Kidd tells Marlene:

> ''What's it going to do to him working for a woman? I think if it was a man he'd get over it as something normal. . . . It's me that bears the brunt. . . . I put him first every inch of the way. . . . It had crossed my mind if you were unavailable after all for some reason, he would be the natural second choice I think, don't you?'' (58–59)

In her view Marlene is abnormal in her determination to be at the top and she'll end up lonely and miserable.

The backdrop of the office room is confined and provides limited space where competition and aggression and violation of territorial rights go hand in hand. The middle scene sandwiched between these two office scenes is in a backyard in a ''shelter made of junk'' by children. It is a hiding place, away from the taboos and restrictions of the adult world. Kit and Angie talk about running away from home, they talk about travel, about the reality of their menstrual blood which flows from hidden spaces and their love-hate relationship to the adult world. Later Kit seeks shelter from rain within the precincts of her friend's house while Angie herself is left outside with a feeling of rejection.

The third act moves backwards in time. It takes place a year earlier than the second act. It is a confrontation scene between Marlene and her sister Joyce. They open out their past, the suppressed, sibling rivalry, Marlene's need to escape from her background, Joyce's support, the birth of Marlene's daughter Angie, and her adoption by Joyce, Joyce's miscarriage, and her separation from her husband Frank. Women sacrifice their motherhood for a career; but at times they also have to sacrifice their marriage for their motherhood. Joyce is denied space within her marriage while Marlene is aware that men want her to turn into "the little woman" which she is not prepared to do. In all this it is Angie who feels confused and dispossessed.

Keatley's play is also a three-act play with the first act having ten scenes and moving between 1905 and 1979. The second act is one uninterrupted scene located in 1982, and the third act is placed in 1987 diving back, towards the end, to 1923. There are five child-scenes spread over the play-Act I sc. 1, sc. 3 and sc. 8, Act III sc.3 and sc.6 which act like a conjunction of events, like a voice from the past, like an abandonment of the chronological process. The movement of the play can be seen from the graph. The conjunction scene is shown as a circle with four different time streams flowing together.

Covering four generations, it covers several sets of relationships. Space is used very consciously, and scene shifts are indicated not by sets but with the help of lights as Keatley has stated in her "Introduction" to the Methuen edition of her play. her stage directions specifically mention "no sofas" primarily because it is so easy to slip into comfortable positions once the sofas are there. It is so important to render the women vulnerable, to make them appear "awkward" or uncomfortable." Interestingly enough, it was also a conscious decision not to locate any of the scenes in a kitchen which is considered domestic space; instead the locales are houses, living rooms, gardens, backyards, a hospital room and Margaret's office, places which are gender-neutral or strongly affected by male environment. The recurring child scenes where Doris aged 5, Margaret and Jackie both aged 9, and Rosie aged 8 meet are located in a wasteground, "an uncompromisingly real place", beyond the reach of adults and beyond male vision. The wasteground is unpatterned and uncontrolled, closer to nature and reflective of the unconscious; it goes to show that girls are not "born good" and that little girls are not made of sugar and spice and all things nice. They experience rivalry and hatred and harbour murderous intentions, eager to get rid of the goodness of the female tradition.

The five child scenes are played by adult characters dressed up in childhood clothes emphasizing the use of body language. This also underlines the continuity of the unconscious well into adult life. Their attitudes are an indication of the direction their adult lives will take. The child scenes intro-duce the main themes of the play—"sex, death, gender, courtship, destiny and loneliness", they also contrast with the world of masks, lies and fibs of the adult world.

Keatley views her play as structured along emotional chronology—the past (Act I), the present (Act II) and the future (Act III). It is possible to view the structure somewhat differently—anxieties of growing up (Act I) widowhood and loss (Act II) loneliness, separation and death (Act III). The lives of the women are narratives of female growth and loss; the men—Jack, Ken, Graham, Simon—remain outside, mowing the lawn, honking the horn, or present at the death bed. Yet the choices women face are centred around men—marriage, family, motherhood. Doris gives up working when she gets married, Margaret decides not to have children because she wants to work. When she wants to better her qualifications, her marriage breaks up. Jackie goes ahead and has a child without marriage, but finding it difficult to cope with the child single-handedly passes her on to her mother. Margaret who has never acknowledged her body dies of stomach cancer and Jackie who takes to art, finds herself trapped in masculine roles and her grandfather's inheritance while Doris who had given her all in marriage ends up with a feeling of having been betrayed. Even the piano she had bought with her own earning is bequeathed to her by her dead husband. Life is a game of solitaire, but one doesn't find the solution to it all by oneself. There are no solutions. There is no space for meeting the conflicting claims.

The central act, Act II, is in many ways a very stark act. The house with its sense of closure, the furniture covered with sheets, the presence of the past in this house of death—they are indicative of Doris's unfulfilled sexuality and Jackie's lost female inheritance which bypasses her to be given to Rosie.

Space is used yet in another way. Suky, the doll which resurfaces as a comforter for three generations is mutilated, rejected, discarded and hidden in dustbins and urns. The background song "Suky Take It Off Again" has sexual implications, the rejection of the doll is the rejection of roles which may appear to be soft. Another song "All You Need is Love" a song escapist in intention contrasts with real life choices where the accent is on facing reality, the hard, cruel choices, and playing solitaire by oneself. Keatley uses the earth as a concrete sense of space:

Earth is the base element of the play. I think the stage floor the key to the design—grass—a worn rug, a stone backyard. It is only when characters touch earth that they make contact with their true feelings and powers. All child scenes take place on bare earth. On her birthday, Rosie buries Margaret's doll in the soil. When Doris and Margaret finally kneel together with their hands in the soil, planting geranium seedlings, they speak their real feelings. There are key moments of contact with the earth throughout the play.

Standing barefeet is a literal enactment of "earthing" one self. Characters in both the plays stress the act of running or walking barefoot whether it be Nijo or Patient Griselda.

Both Churchill and Keatley use an all-women cast to problematize the gender issues, and to project the realistic aspirations of women. Through the use of space, through juxtapositions, closing-ins and opening-outs they also project a need for a new understanding of space, a shifting and loosening of boundaries, of creating more space and moving out of territorial claims. In fact their use of space challenges the very structures of 'reality' that have kept women behind scenes (Hart). They move away from naturalistic structures and spaces towards magic and fantasy, mixing history and fiction, in order to fathom the unconscious and realize a woman's self.

Source: Jasbir Jain, "Feminist Drama: The Politics of the Self: Churchill and Keatley," in *Women's Writing: Text and Context,* edited by Jasbir Jain, Rawat Publications, 1996 pp. 274–87.

Joseph Marohl

In the following essay on Caryl Churchill's Top Girls, *author Joseph Marohl discusses how Churchill creates her characters and dramas with "deliberate confusion . . . and playfulness" to examine difficult social and emotional concepts of gender and history, effectively de-centering gender as the primary dramatic focal point.*

For a decade now, deliberate confusion of dramatic roles and playfulness about otherwise serious concepts of gender and history have distinguished Caryl Churchill's plays from the work of mainstream playwrights in Great Britain and the United States. For instance, six performers in *Light Shining in Buckinghamshire* play twenty-four different *dramatis personae* with individual role assignments which vary from scene to scene and are unrelated to the performers' actual sexes. In the finale of *Vinegar Tom,* her "sequel" to *Light Shining,* two female performers portray two seventeenth-century theolo-gians in the top hat and tails of music hall entertainers, singing with great irony the song "Evil Women." In a prefatory note to *Traps,* Churchill describes the play as an "impossible object," like an Escher drawing: "In the play, the time, the place, the characters' motives and relationships cannot all be reconciled—they can happen on stage, but there is no other reality for them. . . . The characters can be thought of as living many of their possibilities at once." The cast of seven performers in *Cloud Nine,* Churchill's first *bona-fide* commercial hit, play thirteen roles of varying age, gender, and race. In Act One, a white performer plays a black servant, a male performer plays the role of a woman, a female performer plays a boy, and a small dummy represents an infant girl. Act Two brings a degree of naturalism as women play women and men play men, with the exception of Cathy, a five-year-old girl played by a man. A stage note explains that "Act One takes place in a British colony in Africa in Victorian times. Act Two takes place in London in 1979. But for the characters it is twenty-five years later." Only three characters appear in both acts, and in all three instances the actors portraying them in the second act are not the same persons portraying them in the first. In *Top Girls,* an all-female cast of seven play a total of sixteen different characters, five of whom do not exist in the present. Even more recently, in *Fen,* five women and one man play twenty-two characters in an ambiguous setting which is simultaneously interior and exterior: in Annie Smart's 1983 stage design, "a field in a room."

Multiple casting and transvestite role-playing, which modern directors of the 1940s and 1950s practiced deliberately in several experimental productions of Shakespeare and other standard dramatists, reflect the many possibilities inherent in the real world and subvert conventional ideas about the individuality or integrity of character. The theatrical inventiveness of Churchill's comedies suggests, in particular, that the individual self, as the audience recognizes it, is an ideological construct and the "real world," the world as it is recast by the performers, klieg lights, and chicken wire on the stage, consists of people and events which are individual only in so far as they are rhetorically defined in contrast to others. Her plays conceive character and event as paradoxes. People in her plays are not whole, though sometimes they are ignorant of their own fragmentation; they exist only in tension with their environment (time and space), the other people in the environment, and with the "others" who they themselves used to be at an

Beth Goddard as Kit and Lesley Sharp as Angie in a scene from a theatrical production of Top Girls.

earlier age (their former ''selves''). Churchill describes the condition more vividly in dramatic terms in the closing image of *Cloud Nine,* when a character in Act Two confronts the version of herself from Act One: ''Betty *and* Betty *embrace.''*

In performance, the plays assume obvious political importance, espousing the social concerns of contemporary feminism: gender stereotyping, the division of labor according to sex, the proprietary family, the oppression of sexual variety through compulsory heterosexuality, class struggle, ageism, and ethnocentrism. The dramatic events raise the audience's consciousness about social principles through the actions depicted and, more importantly, through the actual events of the performance: woman playing man, man playing woman, one person playing two (or more) persons, two persons playing one, the deconstruction of history and geography (and the related unities of time, place, and action) in order to dramatize the cyclical progress of political and social events in history. What the audience experiences during the performance, then, is defamiliarization of the ordinary (alienation effect) and the subversion of positive ideologues about gender, social hierarchies, and chronology. The comedies are parodic enactments and satires of

prevalent, middle-class belief-systems and values, i.e., mythologies.

In *Top Girls,* the one continuous character, Marlene, embodies the characteristics of the popular myth of career woman as castrating female and barren mother. The play uses the myth in order to undermine it, to supplant radical and bourgeois feminist styles with a socially conscious feminism, to ''trick'' the audience into condemning the ''feminist hero'' for, in the end, practicing a too-conventional role in the existing power structure. In this, the play succeeds brilliantly and unconsciously. The purpose of the present reading is to discover the political practice of the play as it works through the performance, particularly of the first scene, but a summary of the play's successive parts is necessary first.

Top Girls begins at a restaurant, with a dinner party celebrating the protagonist Marlene's promotion to managing director of the ''Top Girls'' Employment Agency. Joining her at the party are five ghost characters drawn from history, painting, and fiction: the nineteenth-century Scottish lady-traveler Isabella Bird; the thirteenth-century Japanese courtesan-turned-nun Lady Nijo; Dull Gret, whom Bruegel pictured storming hell in apron and armor; the

WHAT THE AUDIENCE EXPERIENCES DURING THE PERFORMANCE, THEN, IS DEFAMILIARIZATION OF THE ORDINARY (ALIENATION EFFECT) AND THE SUBVERSION OF POSITIVE IDEOLOGUES ABOUT GENDER, SOCIAL HIERARCHIES, AND CHRONOLOGY."

legendary Pope Joan, who, disguised as a man, headed the Church in the ninth century; and Patient Griselda, ironically arriving late and last, the incredibly long-suffering hero of Chaucer's Clerk's Tale. The group ostensibly represents women of outstanding courage and achievement, but the dialogue, often cast as a series of overlapping narrative monologues, reveals pointed differences in ideology and practice. The scene is unique in that it is the only scene in which the play's seven actors appear together and the only scene which does not portray a naturalistic event. It is also the longest scene of the play. The women playing the ghost characters and the waitress appear in subsequent scenes as Marlene's clients, fellow workers, sister, and daughter.

Immediately following the dinner party scene is a brief scene at the employment agency, where Marlene interviews a secretary who aspires to a better position with a new company. There follows a long scene at Marlene's sister Joyce's back yard, where Marlene's sixteen-year-old daughter Angie, whom Joyce has raised as her own daughter, and Angie's younger friend Kit discuss violence on television, money, matricide, death in general, and menstruation, with Angie announcing at the end her intent to visit Marlene in London. The scene sets up the argument for the play's final scene, in which Marlene and Joyce quarrel about politics and family. More important, the scene reveals the complex disturbed psychology of the slow-witted Angie, whose sex, class, appearance, and low intelligence present a multiple threat to her eventual employability and welfare. The girl's resolution to travel to London to her successful ''aunt'' hints of Sophoclean

tragedy. But her threats of matricide and her Oedipal attachment to Marlene do not effect catastrophe or catharsis in the end; Churchill's play is neither tragic nor obvious. The tragic implications of the scene are not, however, wasted, for, as subsequent events prove, Angie, like Oedipus or Antigone, is a victim of history and fate.

Act Two opens at an office of the ''Top Girls'' Employment Agency. In the first scene, Win and Nell, two employment agents with the firm, arrive for work and discuss Marlene's promotion, aware that now, as one of them remarks, ''There's not a lot of room upward.'' To which the other one responds, ''Marlene's filled it up.'' Both women agree, nevertheless, that they had rather see a woman promoted than Howard Kidd, a male employee at the agency. Between interviews conducted by Win and Nell, Marlene receives two unexpected visitors at work: Angie, whose surprise visit is treated less than enthusiastically by her mother, and Mrs Kidd, Howard's wife, who asks Marlene to turn down the promotion so that her husband will not be reduced to ''working for a woman.'' The scene ends with news that Howard is in the hospital after a heart attack. The women in the office greet the news with deadpan irony, remarking, ''Lucky he didn't get the job if that's what his health's like.'' Marlene then turns towards her daughter, who has fallen asleep at Win's desk, and prophesies: ''She's not going to make it.'' The line is the end of the story but not the end of the play.

The last scene occurs one year before the scenes preceding it in the play. Once again, the scene is Joyce's house, the kitchen this time. The use of flashback allows the audience to observe a number of changes that will occur over the year in Marlene's character. In the last scene, Marlene, drunk and guiltily maudlin, argues that Angie will ''be all right'' someday. She regards her career advancement as beneficial to women everywhere and herself as an independent, self-made person, in the same mold as Margaret Thatcher, much to the annoyance of her sister, who reminds her that she could have accomplished nothing had not Joyce been willing years before to take the burden of Angie off her hands. Marlene asserts her belief in middle-class individualism; she is, she says, ''an original,'' a supporter of Ronald Reagan and a ''free world.'' Joyce, whose politics are Marxist and pro-Labour, criticizes her successful sister's priggishness and egotism. She reminds Marlene about her parents, common workers who lived wasted lives and died without happiness or meaningful employment, and about their daughter Angie, who will also be a victim of monetarism and class prejudice. Nevertheless, Marlene persists blindly to endorse a system that values profits over the needs of people, and in the end she seems to accept that Angie, Joyce, and her mother are reasonable sacrifices to make in order to realize her own success in the business world. Abandoned by Joyce, Marlene sits alone in the kitchen until Angie stumbles in, half-awake after a nightmare, and utters the last line of the play, the single word ''Frightening,'' an unknowing indictment of her mother's self-interested individualism or perhaps an apprehension of her own miserable future.

Taken as a whole, the play demonstrates several larger formal devices which appear immediately to be significant. The central image of the story related to Marlene is the employment agency, a company which locates meaningful and profitable work for its clients. Employment is likewise the central action of the play. All the characters are involved in the assessment of their own work and the division of labor in general: Marlene's promotion to managing director, Angie's unsuitability for the work force, Joyce's unpaid labor as wife and mother, and, of course, the employees and clients of the agency. Work, promotion, money, and success are topics of conversation among the characters throughout the play. The three interviews conducted in turn by Marlene, Win, and Nell in the course of the performance do not, however, indicate that much real change is possible for the status of women in the existing labor system. For Jeanine, the secretary looking for ''better prospects'' in Act One, Marlene is able to suggest only other secretarial positions. Jeanine wants more money and prestige, a job like Marlene's, for instance, but Marlene urges her to lower her sights. In the end, Marlene convinces Jeanine to interview for a secretarial position with a lampshade company, which pays no better than the job she already has. Marlene attempts to make the new job more enticing by assuring the client that ''the job's going to grow with the concern and then you'll be in at the top with new girls coming in underneath you.'' In a small firm operated by a man and his two sons, Jeanine's chances for a real promotion to the ''top'' are practically non-existent; her best bets are longevity and the chance someday to manage new girls in even more subordinate positions. Louise, an older client looking for a change from her middle-management position of twenty years, succeeds

only in stirring up the ire of Win, her interviewer. Louise complains that newer male employees move up the ranks much more speedily than her, but admits that she has difficulty with other female employees. Win develops an instant dislike for the client, who in some respects represents her own limitations in advancing at ''Top Girls.'' She tells Louise that in most situations she will be forced into competition with younger men and encourages her to accept a position with a cosmetics company, a field that is ''easier for a woman,'' but probably with a reduction in salary. The most pathetic case of all, however, is Shona, whom Nell interviews. She aspires to employment in a ''top field'' such as computers but seems willing to settle for a lesser position at the ''Top Girls'' agency. For all her ambition and energy, Shona cannot conceal the disadvantages of her class: poor education, an unrealistic and naive concept of the business world, and lack of connections or experience. She fails in her attempt to bluff Nell into placing her in a position with management status. Together, the three interviews challenge the idea of individual achievement, so important in Marlene's ideology and in the ideology of the English middle-classes who deny the existence of class. The three interviews depict the world of business as a vertical progress from bottom to top, hence ''Top Girls,'' which, intentionally or not, affirms the class distinctions which Marlene ignores: ''I don't believe in class. Anyone can do anything if they've got what it takes.'' The changes Jeanine, Louise, and Shona attempt to make in their social situations, in which the ''Top Girls'' agency professes to give assistance, prove to be impossible within the establishment. Despite all the talk of advancement, *Top Girls* dramatizes the economic stasis of women in business and, more important, the impossibility of genuine social reform of any kind within a system maintaining vertical class distinctions.

The same circular, self-consuming logic can be traced in other parts of the play. The audience's attention is drawn towards a particular line of discourse only to see it totter and collapse anticlimactically later on, its premises shattered. The play moves backwards, negating its ''arguments'' as it proceeds. It begins in a place of consumption (a restaurant) and ends in a place of production (a kitchen). It begins with a celebration for a promotion and ends anti-chronologically with a drunken reunion which occurred one year before the promotion. The progress of the principal character Marlene proves to be illusory, and, in the end, she is no more morally advanced than the other characters and seems unusually dependent upon the sacrifices of others. Marlene's solicitousness about Angie in Act Two, Scene Two, which initially resembles ''womb envy'' (before the audience is aware that Angie is Marlene's daughter), ends up being little more than feelings of guilt for having abandoned her, years before. Contrary to one's usual sense of dramatic cause and effect, Marlene's guilty conscience is not redemptive; she repeats the abandonment of her daughter at the end of the scene and resumes her original course. The first scene, moreover, celebrates a promotion which the audience comes to realize was achieved at the high cost of the displacement of a number of other women of equal worth. In the end, Marlene lacks the transcendent quality of heroism the audience had come to expect of her at the beginning. Neither is she as reprehensible as her antagonists Mrs Kidd and Joyce (both played by the same actor) would have the audience believe. Marlene, too, is a victim of the hierarchy in which she operates. Even though *Top Girls* lacks faith in individualism as a vehicle for social reform, it is not entirely pessimistic in its outlook. Its faith resides in the revolutionary processes of history, which a theatrical performance can duplicate.

The most obvious device of the play, that the performers are all women, allows the drama to take a number of directions which would otherwise have been impossible. Playwright and theater analyst Micheline Wandor says that the ''single-gendered play may be 'unrealistic' in the sense that we all inhabit a world which consists of men and women, but it does provide an imaginative opportunity to explore the nature of the gendered perspective (male or female) without the complexities and displacements of the 'mixed' play.'' Ironically, by the exclusion of active male characters, *Top Girls* manages to escape the pitfall of sexism, that is, allowing the audience to mistake the class struggle which is the basis of the dramatic plot for a ''battle of the sexes,'' which is exactly the mistake Marlene, Win, Nell, Mrs Kidd, and Angie make, Joyce being exceptional. The action of the play indicates that the female perspective is capable, too, of drawing class distinctions and enforcing a patriarch-like matriarchy based on tyranny and division. The issue of plural feminisms as opposed to homogeneous (i.e., authoritarian) Feminism emerges in the play through the demonstration of differences of class and history among members of the same sex, a demonstration which begins in the opening scene.

Before moving to a more particular reading of the play, it is important to recognize the multiple natures of the women in the play. They are first of all, obviously, real women—actors performing roles. They are also female characters—fictions and *dramatis personae*. On yet another level, they enact roles of gender—cultural codes by which ''female/feminine'' defines itself as different from ''male/masculine'' codes. The absence of male characters on stage diminishes the obvious importance of this third level of significance, even though it plays a major part in the discourse of some of the characters. The play in performance de-realizes the women in two ways: one, by being ''framed'' or abstracted by the theatrical event, their sex becomes a signifier within the dramatic discourse; and two, by performing assigned roles in the drama, their characters contribute to the dramatic discourse through action and dialogue. Thus, one can call *Top Girls* a ''women's play'' because all of its actors and characters are women, and, at least initially, gender appears to be the dramatic focal point. Gender, however, is de-centered as the real subject of the play almost as soon as the performance begins. The first scene, in which women of different historical periods and different cultures convene to celebrate Marlene's promotion, dramatizes the lack of unity among persons of the same sex, effected by the lack of ideological unity. The six women at the dinner party represent diverse cultural attitudes towards class, religion, family, ethics, and gender; gender is given only an equal footing with other matters of cultural identity. Apart from its definition in the context of a specific culture, male or female gender does not exist. Only by the reformation of entire social systems, then, can gender roles be changed (or dispensed with) and authentic liberation of the sexes occur. Marlene's bourgeois style of feminism is proved in the course of the play to be culturally conditioned, for her success does not really challenge patriarchal authority but appropriates it, conforming, as it does, to the existing hierarchy. Joyce's argument with Marlene in the last scene makes this criticism explicit:

> Marlene: And for the country, come to that. Get the economy back on its feet and whoosh. She's a tough lady, Maggie. I'd give her a job. / She just needs to hang in there. This country
> Joyce: You voted for them, did you?
> Marlene: needs to stop whining. / Monetarism is not stupid.
> Joyce: Drink your tea and shut up, pet.
> Marlene: It takes time, determination. No more slop. / And

Joyce: Well I think they're filthy bastards.
Marlene: who's got to drive it on? First woman
        prime minister. Terrifico. Aces.
Right on. / You must admit. Certainly
        gets my vote.
Joyce: What good's first woman if it's her? I
        suppose you'd have liked Hitler if
he was a woman. Ms Hitler. Got a lot done,
        Hitlerina. / Great adventures.
Marlene: Bosses still walking on the workers'
        faces? Still Dadda's little parrot?
Haven't you learned to think for yourself? I
        believe in the individual. Look at me.
Joyce: I am looking at you.

It is our cultural prejudice, perhaps, that women should be political only about "women's issues," and *Top Girls* uses the prejudice against its audience by deceptively foregrounding gender in order to displace it with Joyce's class-conscious politics in the last scene. Marlene's mistaken concept of female homogeneity in the first scenes, then, parallels the mistake the audience makes about the play's message: to overestimate the importance of sex in feminist politics.

The writing of the French semiotician Julia Kristeva has done much to demonstrate how the opposition of male and female, upon which much of Western thought rides, is constructed by the social hierarchy which it supports. It is ideologically circular; patriarchy invents a myth to justify and perpetuate its own existence. A concept of feminism, like Marlene's, which defines itself in the context of a polarity of the sexes (i.e., female *versus* male/male *versus* female) cannot transcend the inherently man-centered or phallocentric assumptions of the ruling power system. (The problem is portrayed imaginatively in the "Top Girls" Employment Agency, which cannot place women into high levels of corporations which are designed especially to exclude women.) *Top Girls* circumvents the cultural polarity with its single sex cast. The dramatic conflict arises not out of a battle of the sexes but out of class struggle as it persists through many generations of history. The first scene functions as the medium whereby certain lines are drawn so that the subsequent political discourse will be clear and understandable.

The play opens with a simple and familiar theatrical image, a table set for six. Marlene and the waitress enter or are discovered as the lights go up. They are costumed in familiar contemporary dress befitting their status and occupation. Enter Isabella Bird in Victorian blouse and skirt. Immediately,

Isabella's appearance estranges the setting. As each successive character enters in costume (Lady Nijo in kimono and geta, Dull Gret in apron and armor, Pope Joan in cassock and cope, and later Patient Griselda in medieval dress), the audience becomes aware, perhaps only dimly, of the process of history the costumes represents. Given the new context, what Marlene and the waitress wear is peculiarly historical and cultural, too. Modern dress is another form of period costume. The visual lesson of the opening scene, if taken, is to recognize the cultural relativity of certain norms.

Little is learned about Marlene in the first scene except that she has received a promotion at the employment agency where she works. Her function at the beginning is to serve as interviewer and interlocutor for the five ghost characters. Each of the characters delivers a personal narrative which, like her costume, distinguishes her from the others in the group by identifying her with the ideology of her culture. Each woman, moreover, has a distinctive manner of speaking appropriate to her class, the more extreme examples being Isabella's chatty and anecdotal monologues and Gret's monosyllabic grunts. Despite Marlene's frequent affirmation of a unity based on gender, the ghost characters do not discover much common ground among themselves. For Isabella, the others seem to lack civilization and education. Nijo perceives the others as barbarians, and Joan sees them as heretics and pagans. In fact, the common denominator of the group, besides sex, is zealous regard for their distinct cultural identities. Only Marlene perceives herself primarily as an individual apart and as a woman; the others view themselves as members of other collective enterprises: for Gret, it is a battle with her townspeople against the devils; for Griselda, it is her marriage to the Marquis; for Joan, it is the Church of Rome; for Nijo, it is her father's household and the Emperor's court; and for Isabella, it is the British Empire. Only Marlene feels a bond with the others based on sexual identity. Only she senses an allegiance to a subculture contradistinctive to the dominant culture in which she lives.

Parallels of situation do exist between the ghost characters' narratives, but the differences are more significant. Most of the women have survived tragic love affairs with weaker men. At one point, Joan asks rather unemotionally, "Have we all got dead lovers?" Nijo lost her lover, the poet-priest Ariake, before she bore their son. Isabella's American lover, the mountain man Jim Nugent, died of a gun-shot wound to the head. In later life, Isabella married John Bishop, because of his resemblance and devotion to her beloved sister Hennie, but he died shortly after the marriage. Joan's lover died in the midst of a debate with her over the theology of John the Scot.

Their narratives reveal also that many of them have borne children. Gret had ten children, whom either war or pestilence killed. Nijo gave birth to children by the Emperor and her lovers Akebono and Ariake. Griselda bore the Marquis a daughter and a son, which he removed from her in order to test her allegiance to him. Pope Joan narrates the grotesque nativity of her baby in the middle of a papal procession and their joint executions at the hands of the Roman cardinals. Only Isabella is childless, which she compensated for, she claims, by a fondness for horses. Marlene does not mention her daughter.

All the women left home, several at an early age, but for different purposes. Isabella traveled the world in search of adventure and a variety of experiences. Nijo wandered as a vagabond nun in Japan in obedience to her father's wishes and in penance for losing the Emperor's favor. At age twelve, Joan went with her comrade and lover to Athens to study theology. Gret made an epic descent into hell to avenge the death of her family and to rob the devil's storehouses. And Griselda was carried away, in fairytale fashion, to marry the Marquis, Walter.

Although, as Marlene says of them, the ghost characters are women distinguished by their courage and accomplishments, they have made obvious and often extreme concessions to their various patriarchies, against which they utter no word of condemnation or complaint. In order to study science and philosophy in the library, Joan disguised herself as a boy and continued to pass for male for the rest of her life. She moved to Italy because Italian men were beardless and became Pope after Pope Leo died. So strong was her identification with the male sex that she was unable to interpret obvious signs that she was pregnant, which failure led to her downfall and death. By way of explanation, she says she "wasn't used to having a woman's body." There is a hint of irony, perhaps, when later in the play Louise (whom the same actor plays) remarks during her interview with Win, "I don't care greatly for working with women, I think I pass as a man at work." What is more remarkable is Joan's lack of outrage against the vicious hegemony of the man-centered government of the Church. She even joins in the condemnation of herself and her sex, saying, "I'm a heresy myself" and "I shouldn't have been a woman. Women, children and lunatics can't be Pope."

Griselda submitted to paternal oppression in a different fashion. As part of a marriage contract, she agreed to obey her husband unconditionally. She then "patiently" allowed her husband to separate her from her own daughter and son and later to send her back barefoot to her father's house so that he could marry another woman. At the end of the story, the Marquis revealed that all this was only a test of her love and loyalty towards him, welcomed her back to his house, and reunited her with their children. All the women, except Nijo, seem shocked at the Marquis's tyrannical treatment of her, but like Joan, Griselda defends the hand that oppresses her. Explaining her own reluctance to interfere when the daughter was taken from her, ostensibly to be killed, she says, "It was Walter's child to do what he liked with."

Nijo's accomplishments in life were the result of strict adherence to the wishes first of her father and then of the Emperor of Japan. In every respect, she judges herself and the other women at the dinner party according to man-imposed standards, especially those of her father, even her decision to wander Japan as a penitent nun:

> Nijo: Oh, my father was a very religious man. Just before he died he said to me,
> 'Serve His Majesty, be respectful, if you lose his favour enter holy orders.'
> Marlene: But he meant stay in a convent, not go wandering round the country.
> Nijo: Priests were often vagrants, so why not a nun? You think I shouldn't? / I still did what my father wanted.

Isabella Bird's concern to be known as a "lady," despite her wanderlust and sense of adventure, is a milder, less obvious form of submission to male authority. Only Gret, who remains silent for most of the scene, gives less evidence of paternal domination. Isabella is less successful in her acquiescence to the standards nineteenth-century English society had set down for women, but her spirit was nevertheless willing. "I tried to do what my father wanted," she laments shortly after Nijo's speech above. And later in response to Griselda's strange tale of marital perseverance, she says, "I swore to obey dear John, of course, but it didn't seem to arise. Naturally I wouldn't have wanted to go abroad while I was married.'' Of all the characters present at the party, Isabella most closely resembles Marlene, an effect, no doubt, of their relative closeness in history and culture.

All the women at the dinner party are able to detect areas of intolerance and sexual tyranny in the cultures of the other women present; their blind spots are the inequities of their own cultures. Joan expresses shock and disgust at Griselda's servile obedience of the Marquis: ''I never obeyed anyone. They all obeyed me''; but she does not comprehend how her own denial of her sex was also a concession to anti-feminist hegemony. Isabella decries the ''superstition'' of the Church during Joan's lifetime, but she is ignorant that the Victorian woman's obsession with being a proper lady was another form of female subjugation. Marlene does not approve of Nijo's acquiescence to her rape in the Emperor's palace, but later in the play she encourages a client to adapt herself to a certain professional image to please male employers. Only near the end of the scene, after the women have begun to be drunkenly boisterous, do some of them guardedly criticize their cultures. ''How can people live in this dim pale island and wear our hideous clothes?'' Isabella wonders. ''I cannot and will not live the life of a lady.'' Nijo complains about the Emperor's granting permission to his attendants to flog his concubines. Patient Griselda ventures to comment aloud, ''I do think—I do wonder—it would have been nicer if Walter hadn't had to.'' Marlene's awakening comes much later, when she sees her daughter sleeping in the office and acknowledges, after everything, very little has really changed in the world: ''She's not going to make it.''

The first scene prepares the audience to perceive the play's subsequent scenes in the light of culturally-conditioned ideology. Like the ghost characters, Marlene has accomplished much in her life, and like them too, she has done so by making concessions to a phallocentric system oppressive to women. Although she expresses disapproval of the extreme, vicious acts of Griselda's Marquis, for instance, or the more intolerant doctrines of the medieval Church, she often praises the ghost characters for their pragmatic manipulation of the patriarchy to further their own ends, a compliment which, needless to say, baffles its recipients. Unwilling to be tyrannized herself, Marlene has joined the powers-that-be and, like Pope Joan, seeks to be obeyed rather than to obey. Nijo perceptively uncovers the secret significance of the promotion to

managing director when she adds the phrase ''Over all the women you work with. And the men,'' to Marlene's new title. Marlene's advancement helps no one but herself, however much she would like to believe in a right-wing feminism, and, as the following scenes reveal, she endorses a hierarchical system oppressive to the less fortunate women and men in her society.

Gender fails to be a rallying point in Act One, Scene One, because it is a signifier distinctive to the ideologies which encode it. The conceptions of gender differ culturally and historically as do the costumes. When Marlene proposes a toast ''to you all,'' Isabella responds, ''To yourself surely, we're here to celebrate your success.'' Pleased at the compliment to her promotion, Marlene nevertheless attempts to turn around Isabella's toast, ''To Marlene,'' by adding, ''And all of us.'' She says, ''*We've all* come a long way. To *our* courage and the way *we* changed *our* lives and *our* extraordinary achievements'' (italics mine). Marlene wants her promotion to be a sign of progress for women collectively, but the others perceive her success as peculiarly Marlene's own. Because of her blindness to class and ideology, Marlene persists in her naive belief that what she individually accomplishes for herself will automatically redound to the common good. Her separation from her sister Joyce in the last scene duplicates her separation from the five ghost characters in the first. In the quarrel which marks the end of the drama, the use of pronouns to demarcate the characters' opposing points of view becomes an explicit element of the discourse:

> Marlene: *Them, them. / Us* and *them*?
> Joyce: And *you're one of them.*
> Marlene: And *you're us,* wonderful *us,* and
>   Angie's *us /* and Mum and Dad's *us.*
> Joyce: Yes, that's right, and *you're them.* (italics mine)

Whereas the cultural divisions of the dinner party scene are somewhat blurred by the amicable situation, the bluntness of the sibling quarrel at the end of the play effectively splits Marlene and Joyce into separate classes, in spite of apparent shared features such as sex, family, and a common interest in the well-being of their daughter Angie. Gender fails to be a rallying point in Act Two, Scene Two, because Joyce, unlike Marlene, does not see the perpetuation of class differences within a hegemonic patriarchy (or matriarchy) as an acceptable feminist model for society. Joyce's argumentative point, which in effect is the political statement of the play, is that Marlene has misperceived the lines of conflict. Inadvertently, Marlene has become "them," the tyrants, even as she endeavors, on the basis of gender, to identify herself with "us" (a sisterhood of all women) in the first and last scenes.

The play in performance moves the audience from the apparent dichotomy of "female/male," which Marlene's discourse asserts, to the underlying dichotomy of "oppressor/oppressed" which is the effect of phallocentric hierarchism and which operates outside of the classifications of sex and gender. Within the society of the play, which includes only women, hegemony continues to exist even as women gain token power within the system. Given the context of the whole play, the expression "top girls" becomes, of course, ironic in as much as it implies a middle and a bottom, that is, hierarchy and class tyranny. The drama which the process of scenes enacts is the decentering of Marlene as "top girl" and the deconstruction of the ideology encoding the expression.

Churchill's comedy is disloyal to the historical process of civilization it chronicles in the opening scene. The apparent feminist front at the dinner party proves to be neither unified nor really feminist in any social or political sense. The five women present are as unconscious of Marlene's concept of sisterhood as they are of her concept of the individual. In their own ways, they endorse the several tyrannies under which they lived: Joan, Isabella, and Marlene by emulating the oppressor; Nijo and Griselda by conceding to him. Dull Gret's naive assault upon hell and its he-devils in an attempt to steal infernal wealth parodies radical and bourgeois forms of feminism, which either reverse or capitalize on existing inequalities rather than remove them. In Gret's army, the women-invaders stop to gather the money that the "big devil" sh—s upon their heads and bludgeon the "little devils, our size," an action which offers the satisfaction of victimization to those who themselves once suffered as victims. The ideology of these actions is not explicitly challenged until Joyce pronounces her judgment on it in the final scene: "Nothing's changed for most people / has it?" Marlene's feminism, defined by paternal models for dominating the weak, fails to envision "alternative, non-oppressive ways of living." It is the presence of "stupid, lazy, and frightened" Angie, however, who disturbs Marlene's ideology from the beginning. Angie, whose presence once posed a threat to Marlene's career, threatens at the end her sense of moral equilibrium— Marlene's world cannot account for or accommo-

date her. The world continuing to be what it is, Angie, like most women, can never be a "top girl."

Source: Joseph Marohl, "De-realised Women: Performance and Identity in *Top Girls,*" in *Modern Drama,* Vol. 30, No. 3, September 1987, pp. 376–88.

SOURCES

Barnes, Clive, "Wry *Top Girls* is Hard to Top," in *New York Post,* December 29, 1982.

Beaufort, John, "Innovative Guests from the Royal Court: *Top Girls,*" in the *Christian Science Monitor,* January 3, 1983, p. 15.

Churchill, Caryl, *Top Girls,* Methuen, 1982.

Kalem, T. E., Review in *Time,* January 17, 1983, p. 71.

Macaulay, Alastair, Review in The *Financial Times,* April 17, 1991, section 1, p. 13.

Nightingale, Benedict, "Women's Playtime," in *New Statesman,* September 10, 1982, p. 27.

Oliver, Edith, "Women's Affairs," in The *New Yorker,* January 10, 1983, p. 80.

Review in *Variety,* September 8, 1982, p. 116.

Robertson, Bryan, "Top-Notch Churchill," in The *Spectator,* September 11, 1982, p. 25.

Shirley, Don, "*Top Girls* Wins Sympathy for Britain's Lower Echelons," in *Los Angeles Times,* January 30, 1998, p. 6.

Simon, John, "Tops and Bottoms," in *New York,* January 10, 1983, p. 62.

Stevens, Lianne, "*Top Girls* Gets Lost in Shuffle," in *Los Angeles Times,* August 12, 1986, part 6, p. 1.

Taylor, John Russell, Review in *Plays & Players,* No. 350, November 1982, pp. 22–3.

Taylor, Paul, "Presciently Tough at the Top," in *The Independent,* April 16, 1991, p. 14.

Watt, Douglas, "British *Top Girls* Not for U.S.," in *Daily News,* December 29, 1982.

FURTHER READING

Ashton, Elaine, *Caryl Churchill,* Northcote House, 1997.
   This is a critical study of the whole of Churchill's catalog, including *Top Girls.*

Bruley, Sue, *Women in Britain Since 1900,* Macmillan, 1999.

This social history of British women includes information about the 1980s.

Gilmour, Ian, *Dancing with Dogma: Britain Under Thatcherism,* Simon & Schuster, 1992.
This is an economic and political history of the Great Britain that *Top Girls* is set in.

Kritzer, Amelia Howe, *The Plays of Caryl Churchill: Theatre of Empowerment,* Macmillan, 1991.

This book is a critical overview of and commentary on Churchill's work, including *Top Girls,* radio plays, and television plays.

Thompson, Juliet S. and Wayne C. Thompson, eds., *Margaret Thatcher: Prime Minister Indomitable,* Westview Press, 1994.
This collection of essays considers the whole of Thatcher's life and political career.

The Tower

HUGO VON
HOFMANNSTHAL

1925

Hugo von Hofmannsthal's five-act play *Der turm* (*The Tower*) was first published in book form in 1925. A revised version of *The Tower* was first performed on stage in 1927. Von Hofmannsthal adapted the story, set in seventeenth century Poland, from the play *La vida es sueno* (*Life Is a Dream;* 1635), by Pedro Calderon de la Barca, the great playwright of the Golden Age in Spanish literature.

The Tower concerns the fate of Sigismund, a young prince whose father, King Basilius, has kept him locked in the tower because of a prophecy that claimed he would rise up against his father in rebellion. As the play opens, Sigismund, now twenty-one years of age, has been locked in a cage like an animal, unaware of his royal heritage. A physician who has examined Sigismund convinces Julian, the tower governor, to persuade the king to restore his son as heir to the throne. But, as soon as the king grants Sigismund this power, the son rises up and attacks his father. After the king's attendants overpower him, Sigismund is sentenced to death. On the day of his execution, however, a planned rebellion among the noblemen dethrones the king and Sigismund ascends the throne as the new king. A peasant rebellion, however, lead by Oliver, results in the assassination of Sigismund.

As stated in *Contemporary Authors,* ''*The Tower* expresses the hopeless fate of human existence ravaged by the brutal forces of a modern world devoid of a Christian mission.''

AUTHOR BIOGRAPHY

Hugo Laurenz August von Hofmannsthal was born on February 1, 1874, in Vienna, Austria, the only child of Ann Maria Josefa Fohleutner and Hugo August Peter, the director of an investment bank. Von Hofmannsthal was raised in a prominent bourgeois family, which enjoyed both inherited wealth and professional success. His mother's father, originally Jewish, converted to Roman Catholicism to marry the daughter of an Austrian court official, and von Hofmannsthal's parents considered themselves fully assimilated into Austrian culture. Although they lost considerable assets in the stock market crash of 1873, his parents maintained a high standard of living, and von Hofmannsthal grew up with all the privileges of an elite education, cultural experiences such as regular opera and theater attendance, leisure activities such as fencing and riding lessons, and international travel.

Von Hofmannsthal attended Akademisches Gymnasium from 1884 to 1892. From 1892 to 1894, he attended law schools at the University of Vienna, but he left before earning a degree. From 1894 to 1895, he served in the Austrian army. In 1899, Von Hofmannsthal received a Ph.D. in philology, with a specialization in French literature, from the University of Vienna. However, he turned down the opportunity to pursue an academic career in favor of devoting himself to writing essays and plays. In 1901, he married Gertrud Schlesinger, with whom he had three children. During World War I, von Hofmannsthal served as a courier and translator. He died of a stroke on July 15, 1929, just before he was to attend the funeral of his eldest son.

Von Hofmannsthal was a noteworthy figure in the world of Viennese theater and letters. His first publication, a lyric drama, came when he was only seventeen, earning him the attention of such notable literary figures as the German Stefan George and the Austrian Arthur Schnitzler. After a period of mentorship under George, during which he published works in George's literary journal, von Hofmannsthal broke away from what he felt was an elitist literary philosophy. He formed the *Jung Wien* ("Young Vienna"), a literary circle concerned with the aesthetic principles of the French Symbolist Movement. Von Hofmannsthal became known internationally for his collaboration with the famous opera composer Richard Strauss. He was also one of

Hugo von Hofmannsthal

the founders of the Salzburg theater festival, which continues to perform some of his works.

PLOT SUMMARY

Act 1

Act 1, scene 1, of *The Tower* takes place in front of the tower. The son of King Basilius, Sigismund, who was condemned to be locked in the tower for life because of a prophesy warning the king that his son would one day rise up against him in rebellion, is now twenty-one-years old. Sigismund, unaware of his royal heritage, lives and acts like an animal, locked in a cage and taunted by his keepers. Julian, the tower governor, has called in a physician to examine Sigismund; the physician makes note of his royal bearing. Act 1, scene 2, takes place in a room in the tower. Julian explains to the physician that Sigismund had been accused of murder and without a trial was condemned to death at the age of twelve. Julian had put him in the care of a peasant family until age sixteen, when he locked him in the tower to protect him from being murdered. Julian conspires with the physician to obtain a potion that they can give Sigismund, which will put him to sleep so they can transport him to a monastery for his own safety. Julian pays the physician with a purse of money and a valuable ring for this service.

Act 2

Act 2, scene 1, takes place in the cloisters of a monastery. King Basilius arrives with his attendants, and speaks with Brother Ignatius, the grand almoner, a very old and wise priest. The king explains to Brother Ignatius the prophecy that his son would one day rise against him in rebellion. Brother Ignatius chides the king for his behavior, and the king, in anger, has him taken away. Julian arrives and convinces the king to allow Sigismund a retrial to determine if he is fit to be restored to his proper place as heir to the throne. The king agrees and praises Julian for twenty-two years of loyal service. Act 2, scene 2, takes place in a room in the Tower. The peasant woman who raised Sigismund as a child is brought in, informs him that his stepfather has died, and prays with him. Julian then administers the potion that renders Sigismund unconscious.

Act 3

Act 3 takes place inside the queen's death chamber. Sigismund, restored to his humanity, rides up on a horse. The king grants him the power to succeed as the royal heir to the throne. But Sigismund immediately attacks the king and continues until attendants stop him. The king states that the prophesy has come true, as his son has risen up against him in rebellion. The king then sentences Sigismund and Julian to death for treason.

Act 4

Act 4 takes place in a hall in the castle. It is the day scheduled for the execution of Sigismund and Julian. On the way to his death, Sigismund is paraded through the streets. A planned rebellion breaks out, the king is ousted, and Sigismund ascends the throne in his place. He is informed, however, that the peasants have not accepted his rule, and, under the leadership of a man named Oliver, are in revolt.

Act 5

Act 5 takes place in an antechamber of the castle. Julian, who has been attacked by the rebels, is brought in to Sigismund, before dying. Oliver, who has taken control of the rebels, enters and challenges Sigismund's authority. Several of Oliver's attendants confirm that they have assassinated King Basilius. Oliver announces to Sigismund that

he has taken control of the people. Sigismund is shot by Oliver's men and dies in the arms of Anton and the physician.

CHARACTERS

King Basilius

King Basilius is the father of Sigismund. Because he heard a prophesy that predicted his son would rise up against him in rebellion, the king had Sigismund locked away in a tower until he was twenty-one years old. After Julian, the governor of the tower, convinces him to take Sigismund back into his good graces, the king arranges for his son to become his successor. However, as soon as he does, Sigismund attacks his father—but he is overpowered by the king's attendants before he injures the king. The king then sentences his son to death, but, on the day of the execution, a rebellion breaks out. The king is dethroned, and Sigismund is made the new king. Sigismund then sentences the king to be locked in the tower. The king is later assassinated by the rebels who follow Oliver.

Julian

Julian is the governor of the tower in which Sigismund has been locked until the age of twenty-one. Julian is influenced by the physician to convince the king that Sigismund be restored to his rightful place as heir to the throne. When the king sentences Sigismund to death for attempting to rise up against him, Julian plots a rebellion on Sigismund's behalf. The rebellion succeeds, and Sigismund replaces his father as king. But Julian is killed by the rebels who have risen against Sigismund under the leadership of Oliver.

Oliver

Oliver takes command of the peasant rebellion that rises up after King Basilius is ousted by supporters of Sigismund. Oliver has King Basilius killed and then has Sigismund killed.

Physician

The physician is first brought to the tower to examine Sigismund, the prince who has been locked up like an animal until the age of twenty-one. The physician immediately perceives that Sigismund is of royal descent. He provides Julian, the governor of the tower, with a potion to put Sigismund to sleep while he is transported to a monastery for protection. After Sigismund is brought to the castle and sentenced to death for attempting to rise up against his father, the physician aids Julian in planning a rebellion. With the help of the physician, the rebellion succeeds, and Sigismund replaces his father as king. The physician remains loyal to Sigismund, even after Oliver has taken command of the rebellion. After Sigismund is assassinated by Oliver's men, he dies in the arms of the physician.

Sigismund

Sigismund is the son of King Basilius. King Basilius was warned by a prophecy that one day his son would rise up against him in rebellion, and so he had the child locked up in a tower. At the age of twelve, Sigismund was accused of murder, and without a trial he was sentenced to death. Julian, the governor of the tower, however, placed him in the care of a peasant family until the age of sixteen, when he brought him to the tower to protect him from attempts on his life. As the play opens, Sigismund is twenty-one years old, and has been kept in a cage like an animal throughout his life. Julian convinces the king to take Sigismund back as his successor. As soon as the king grants Sigismund royal power, Sigismund attacks him—but is soon overpowered by the king's attendants. The king then sentences Sigismund to death. On the day of the execution, a planned rebellion succeeds in dethroning the king, and placing Sigismund in power. Sigismund gains the loyalty of the peasants, as well as the nobility, but he is assassinated by Oliver, who has taken control of the rebellion.

THEMES

Christian Faith

Critics agree that the character of Sigismund in von Hofmannsthal's play represents the figure of a Christian martyr. Various characters, particularly the physician, directly refer to him in such terms. Upon his initial examination of Sigismund, the physician declares that he is the essence of "the highest earthly virtues." When he is asked to look upon an image of Christ on the cross, Sigismund "looks at it for a long time, mimics the posture, with spread-out arms." When Julian is attempting to convince Sigismund to take the elixir that will make him sleep so that he may awaken to a new life, Julian tells him, "the chosen one is born twice," thus comparing Sigismund to "the chosen one," Jesus Christ. Once Sigismund has taken the elixir,

Anton cries out, "he has a halo above his face!" and he refers to him as "my saintly blessed martyrized—" before he is interrupted by Julian. When the impoverished rebels face Sigismund, declaring their loyalty to him, a man "almost naked," calls him a "Lamb of God." Aron claims that images of Sigismund have been spread throughout the country, "and they light candles before it as before an ikon." In other words, Sigismund's image is worshipped as an icon, an image of God.

The physician further describes Sigismund as a Christian martyr, demanding, "Look over the whole world: it has nothing nobler than what confronts us in this human being." Alfred Schwarz explains that the character of Sigismund "imposes the role of savior on a time-bound creature"; furthermore, "his name and figure have stirred messianic hopes in the hearts of the poor and the oppressed. He is the nameless beggar king who comes in chains to deliver them." According to Schwarz, von Hofmannsthal's characterization of Sigismund provides a vision of "the salvation of humanity."

Politics and Power

A central theme of this play is the nature of power in the role of world politics. The struggles between the various key characters are essentially political struggles over who has the power to rule over the people of a nation. The king has imprisoned his son for fear that Sigismund will rise up and usurp him in a rebellion. As the play opens, rebellion is growing throughout the land, despite the fact that Sigismund is locked away in the tower and unaware of his royal heritage. The named successor to the king has died in a hunting accident, thus leaving the throne in question. Julian hopes to seat the twenty-one-year-old Sigismund as the rightful heir. Julian sends out other men to stir up rebellion in support of Sigismund. However, Oliver, one of Julian's men, takes charge of the rebellion, ultimately killing both Julian and Sigismund.

Critics have referred to Oliver as a "demagogue," a false leader of the people because he usurps Sigismund's power while maintaining the loyalty of the rebels who support Sigismund. Toward the end of the play, Oliver plans to find a man who looks like Sigismund and parade him through the streets so no one will know that he has actually killed the young prince.

Although Sigismund has been raised in imprisonment, without knowledge of his royal heritage, he both fears and strives to obtain power. Sigismund's

TOPICS FOR FURTHER STUDY

- Von Hofmannsthal's play takes place in seventeenth century Poland. Learn more about the history of Poland. What significant events and changes took place in Poland in the seventeenth century? What about the eighteenth to twentieth centuries? What recent events have occurred in Polish history?

- Von Hofmannsthal was born and lived in the city of Vienna, the capital and cultural center of Austria, around the turn of the century. Learn more about Viennese culture in the *fin-de-siecle* era. What changes have taken place in Vienna over the course of the twentieth century?

- Von Hofmannsthal lived and worked in Vienna over the same time period in which Sigmund Freud became prominent as the father of modern psychology. Learn more about the life and work of Freud. What were some of his major theories about human psychology and childhood development? What impact has Freud had on Western thought?

- Von Hofmannsthal's maternal grandfather converted from Judaism to Roman Catholicism in order to marry a Catholic. While von Hofmann-

sthal grew up in a family fully assimilated into mainstream Viennese culture, the Jewish population of Austria was subjected to virulent forms of racism. Learn more about the history and status of Jews in Austria during the nineteenth and twentieth centuries. What is the status of Jews in Austria today?

- Von Hofmannsthal gained an international reputation for his collaboration with Richard Strauss writing librettos for the opera. Learn more about the history of German opera. Who are some of the significant figures in German opera? What were some of the key German operatic productions during the turn of the century?

- Von Hofmannsthal was known as a leading figure in the German symbolist movement. The symbolist movement originated among artists and writers in France around the turn of the century. Learn more about symbolism in art. Who are some of the most significant artists of the symbolist movement? What are some of the central artistic works of the symbolist movement? What basic aesthetic principles were practiced by the symbolists?

urge to exert his power over others is expressed even within his cage as he strives to overcome and dominate the beasts and insects that plague him: "Beasts are of many kinds, all rushing at me. I cry: Not too close! Wood lice, worms, toads, goblins, vipers! All want to fall upon me. I beat them to death." When he is brought before the king for the first time, Sigismund is overwhelmed by the great power he represents. In wonder, Sigismund asks the king, "From where—so much power?" The king replies, "Only the fullness of power profit. . . . Such is the power of the king." The king perceives that Sigismund strives for power and tells him, "The desire for power consumes you. I can read it in your features." And, indeed, Sigismund soon seizes the opportunity to rise up against his father, de-

claring his own claim to power in the statement, "My power will reach as far as my will." Von Hofmannsthal's play explores the morality of absolute political power.

STYLE

Setting

The play, written in twentieth-century Austria, is set in seventeenth-century Poland. The historical setting of the play, as well as the historical and cultural context of its initial production, are significant in several ways. Von Hofmannsthal wrote *The*

Tower in the aftermath of World War I, as a commentary on political and cultural changes in Europe that resulted from the Great War. Von Hofmannsthal set the play in a distant century and location to remove it from the immediate experiences of his audience. By setting his play in this context, von Hofmannsthal creates a distancing effect on the audience, allowing them to view the political struggles represented in the play from the perspective of an observer. Writers often use such distancing techniques to present strong social and political commentary on current or recent events in a manner that is easier for the reader to accept because it does not immediately strike so close to home.

Choral Music

The play calls for a choir that can be heard singing religious hymns in Latin in the background during several scenes. Act 2, scene 1, takes place in the cloisters where the king converses with Brother Ignatius regarding the fate of Sigismund. As soon as a young monk informs the king that Brother Ignatius will be there shortly, "a muffled sound of singing voices becomes audible." The introduction of religious music at this point indicates the spiritual power of Brother Ignatius, as if the choir were announcing his imminent arrival and spiritual force. Once Brother Ignatius, the "Grand Almoner," enters the room, the sounds of the choir are amplified, as "The singing becomes distinctly audible." But, when the king asserts his royal power over the room, the singing of the choir stops, as if the king's power were in opposition to the religious power of Ignatius.

Act 3 takes place in the death chamber of the queen. As the scene opens, "the sound of the organ and the singing voices of nuns become audible." This chamber is presented as a very spiritual place, which none but two nuns have entered in twenty-one years, and the sound of nuns singing confirms the holiness of this death chamber. The king enters with his confessor, sprinkles holy water, and both kneel to pray. Once the king rises from prayer, the music stops. This implies once again that, however much he goes through the motions of religious faith, the king's will is at odds with that of the divine spirit. However, when Sigismund enters to face his father, "the organ sounds for a moment a little louder." Thus, while the king's presence seems to cause the religious music to stop, the presence of Sigismund, like that of Brother Ignatius, causes the religious music to increase in volume and force.

Latin

In addition to the Latin used in the choral singing at key points during the play, Latin is also occasionally used in the dialogue by certain characters. When the physician is first brought to see Sigismund, Anton assures him that "He [Sigismund] knows Latin and runs through a stout book as if it were a flitch o'bacon." This statement immediately establishes the fact that, though Sigismund appears to be little more than an animal in his behavior, he has been taught to read the Bible in Latin and is therefore a staunchly religious person. The only other character in the play who speaks Latin is the physician. The physician is one of the few characters who remains faithful to Sigismund, convinced that he is a sort of religious martyr to the cause of the people. The physician's association with Latin, and therefore with the Bible, confirms the righteousness of his religious conviction and his unfailing faith in Sigismund.

HISTORICAL CONTEXT

Austria

Von Hofmannsthal was born in Vienna, Austria, in 1874. Vienna is the capital of Austria, which was part of the Austro-Hungarian Empire, ruled by the Hapsburg dynasty, from the thirteenth into the twentieth centuries. The Hapsburg Empire included areas that are now parts of Poland, Czechoslovakia, and Austria. A revolution in 1848 lead to the emancipation of the serfs in Austria. Francis Joseph ruled the empire from 1848 to 1916, when Charles succeeded him. The Hapsburg Empire was formally dissolved in 1918, in the wake of World War I, when Poland, Czechoslovakia, and Austria each became independent nations.

Seventeenth-Century Poland

Poland in the seventeenth century was much different than it is today. Geographically, the Kingdom of Poland included what are now Lithuania, Belarus, and half of what is now the Ukraine. Also, half of contemporary Poland used to belong to Prussia. This century was a period of great upheaval for the Republic. Poland was trying to expand while defending its borders against other countries, mainly against Russia, which planned on inhabiting all lands of the Orthodox faith. Poland engaged in a war with Russia in 1610 and a war with Turkey in the years 1620–1621. In 1648, the Cossacks, joined by Ukrainian peasants, raised a mutiny against

Polish rule. King John Casimir tried to negotiate with the mutinous parties but failed. The Cossacks accepted protection from Moscow, and in 1655, two Russian armies invaded the Republic. The Swedes invaded in 1655, taking Warsaw and Krakow. King John Casimir fled the Republic. The Swedes were eventually driven from Poland, and a peace treaty was signed between the two countries in 1660. The last years of the seventeenth century saw many wars also being fought on Polish territory. They left much of the country in devastation. The wars had left the Republic largely depopulated from over ten million citizens to merely six million. Plague, famine, and economic difficulties also increased during these years.

Despite all these difficulties, the seventeenth century was a great time for artists in Poland. Baroque was in its heyday, and many Baroque art pieces were crafted here. The royal residence at Wilanow and the magnate residences at Lancut, Wisnicz, and Zolkiew are all wonderful examples of the Baroque style. The Vasa's court in Warsaw was the center of painting, opera, theater, and science. Poetry and literature also bloomed in these years. Unfortunately, the poor economy and the political and social chaos of this century hindered schooling and education, limiting people in reaching their full potential and expression.

Pedro Calderon de la Barca

Von Hofmannsthal's play, *The Tower,* is a loose adaptation of the play *Life Is a Dream* (1635) by Pedro Calderon (1600–1681). Calderon de la Barca was one of the greatest playwrights of the "Golden Age" of seventeenth-century Spain. *La hija del aire* (1653; *The Daughter of the Air*) is considered by some to be his masterpiece. In 1651, he was ordained into the priesthood, thereafter writing mostly religious plays. Although he still wrote plays for the court of King Philip IV, he renounced his involvement in public theater. Calderon wrote his first opera in 1660. Calderon succeeded Lope de Vega as Spain's leading playwright; Calderon, however, remained unchallenged as Spain's leading playwright for two centuries after his death. According to *Encyclopedia Britannica,* "Strained family relations apparently had a profound effect on the youthful Calderon, for several of his plays show a preoccupation with the psychological and moral effects of unnatural family life, presenting anarchical behavior directly traced to the abuse of paternal authority." In regards to the play on which *The Tower* is based, "Philosophical prob-

lems of determinism and free will are vividly dramatized in [*Life Is a Dream*], in which the escape route from the confusion of life is shown to lie in an awareness of reality and self-knowledge."

Richard Strauss

Von Hofmannsthal is known for his operatic collaborations, for both the German and Austrian stage, with the great German romantic composer Richard Strauss (1864–1949). The two collaborated on a total of six operas, for which Strauss wrote the music and von Hofmannsthal the libretti (which is the text of the opera). Their collaborative works include: *Elektra* (1903), *Der Rosenkavlier* (1911), *Ariadne auf Naxos* (1912; *Ariadne on Naxos*), *Die Frau ohne Schatten* (1919; *The Woman Without a Shadow*), and *Die agyptische Helena* (1928; *The Egyptian Helen*). The two were working on *Arabella* at the time of von Hofmannsthal's death in 1929.

CRITICAL OVERVIEW

Writing in 1966, Alfred Schwarz asserts that *The Tower* is "one of the masterpieces of contemporary drama." Michael Hamburger refers to it as von Hofmannsthal's "most personally committed play." Von Hofmannsthal first began the effort of adapting a play from *La vida es sueno* (*Life Is a Dream;* 1635), by the great Spanish playwright Pedro Calderon de la Barca, in 1902, but he did not produce the first completed version until 1925. According to Schwarz, von Hofmannsthal's early acquaintance with Calderon's play "arrested his attention," and it's central allegory "exercised a fascination on him which lasted for the rest of his life." In reconceptualizing and revising his adaptation, von Hofmannsthal "radically reshaped the play in the course of many years during which he pondered the subject."

It was only the debacle of World War I that provided von Hofmannsthal with a meaningful context for his adaptation: "The experience of the first world war and its aftermath in central Europe, the vision of a world in dissolution, a tradition demolished, at last rendered the full possibilities of the subject conceivable." Michael Hamburger concurs that *The Tower* "was his reckoning with the postwar world, a last attempt to embody the substance of his own life in a myth, and a kind of moral and spiritual testament." T. S. Eliot comments that "Calderon's play is for Hofmannsthal hardly more than a point of departure; two plays could hardly be more different in spirit and intention than those of the Spaniard and the Austrian.'' Schwarz elaborates upon von Hofmannsthal's central ideas in adapting Calderon's play to express his own thematic concerns:

> As the material of *The Tower* takes shape in his mind, Hofmannsthal sees it as the tragedy of a time-bound world gone astray, a world which needs deliverance in the person of a savior; for it is altogether deprived of the sound of God's voice and suffers the torments of guilt. But the potential savior of a forsaken humanity is himself human. Drawn into a world which is torn by rebellion and suppression, he suffers the tragic fate of all humanity betrayed in the life-and-death struggle of contending powers. In the figure of Sigismund, Hofmannsthal represents first the allegory of the Fall, man's tragic attempt to capture the world into which he is thrust, and the individual's tragic subjection to time, conceived as history.

Von Hofmannsthal's 1925 version of *The Tower* was published as a book, but not produced on the stage. At the suggestion of Max Reinhardt, von Hofmannsthal then revised it significantly for a 1927 stage production. Schwarz notes that, after extensive revision, ''A more austere dramatic economy informs the revised version, and the action moves relentlessly to its stark conclusion.''

Schwarz notes that ''Since its publication, *The Tower* appears to have become the poetic chronicle of our time. It is that rare instance in our time of a tragedy which touches at so many points the human situation essentially and the politics of human action historically that it belongs with the best traditional examples of great theater.'' Schwarz concludes that, in *The Tower,* ''Hofmannsthal succeeded in recreating an ample and representative theater in which to mirror the tragedy of a century of totalitarian ways of life.'' Describing *The Tower* as ''difficult,'' T. S. Eliot observes that, ''I doubt whether this play can be called a 'success,' but if not, it is at least a failure grander and more impressive than many successes.'' Eliot goes on to comment that, ''if *The Tower* is unplayable, we must attribute this not to failure of skill but to the fact that what the author wished here to express exceeded the limits within which the man of the theater must work.'' Hamburger observes that ''The distinction of *The Tower,* both in absolute sense and in the context of Hofmannsthal's work as a whole,'' is that ''It is the one completed work of Hofmannsthal that fully engaged all his disparate faculties and energies— the mystical and the worldly, the visionary and the analytical, the adventurous and the conservative— and coordinated his many-sided experience within a single imaginative structure.''

Describing the evolution of von Hofmannsthal's ''tragic theater,'' Schwarz explains: ''Chronologically, there are first the lyric playlets of the last decade before the turn of the century; then, in the years preceding the first world war, a period of search and experimentation, a wrestling with larger dramatic structures, the attempt to discover a theater of significant action for the times; and after the major catastrophe of the war until his death in 1929, years of personal restlessness and significant achievement, the poet's last works which revolve around the idea of universal world theater.''

Schwarz notes: ''Hofmannsthal's career as a playwright is the record of his effort to revitalize the great tradition of European drama on the modern stage. He tried in several ways to reestablish the authority of a truly representative theatre.'' Furthermore, ''He viewed the theater in terms of its intermittent and ideal function in society. Therefore, ignoring the modern renascence of the drama since Hebbel and Ibsen, he turned deliberately to the past for his idea of a theater.'' Schwarz adds, ''In comparison with the starkly realistic social and psychological dramas of his day, Hofmannsthal's work appears to have an old-fashioned, strongly literary flavor. He revived the figures of the ancient Greek drama and the Christian allegories, and brought them back on the modern stage. . . . Hofmannsthal re-dramatized ancient subjects and asserted his orthodox Christian reading of the human condition in traditional theatrical forms.''

CRITICISM

Liz Brent

Brent has a Ph.D. in American Culture, specializing in film studies, from the University of Michigan. She is a freelance writer and teaches courses in the history of American cinema. In the following essay, Brent discusses the father-son relationship in von Hofmannsthal's play.

The Tower explores the theme of fathers and sons in terms of Sigismund's relationship to two central father figures: King Basilius, his biological father, and Julian, his lifelong jailer and caretaker.

The relationship of King Basilius to his only son, the Prince Sigismund, fluctuates dramatically several times throughout the play. The king is torn between his fear of being usurped by his son, as stated in a prophesy and the natural love of a father

WHAT DO I READ NEXT?

- *The Correspondence between Richard Strauss and Hugo von Hofmannsthal* (1961), by Richard Strauss, is a collection of letters between von Hofmannsthal and the famous opera composer Richard Strauss, with whom he collaborated on six operas.

- *Drawings and Watercolours by Vincent van Gogh* (1955), with notes by Douglas Cooper, has color images by the Dutch painter van Gogh, accompanied by von Hofmannsthal's essay, ''Colors.''

- *Selected Prose* (1952), translated by Mary Hottinger and Tania and James Stern, is a selection of prose works by von Hofmannsthal, with an introduction by Hermann Broch.

- *Selected Essays* (1955), edited by Mary E. Gilbert, is a collection of essays by von Hofmannsthal.

- *Schnitzler, Hofmannsthal, and the Austrian Theatre* (1992), by W. E. Yates, includes discussion of von Hofmannsthal's theatrical productions in the context of the history of theater in Austria.

---

for his offspring. Throughout the play, the king alternates between these two impulses. The desire to maintain his sovereign power, however, always wins out over his paternal affections for Sigismund.

Because of a prophesy that stated that the king's son would one day rise up against him in rebellion, King Basilius sentenced his only son, Sigismund, to be imprisoned for life in the tower. The king justified this act by accusing his son, at the age of twelve, of ''high treason.'' Julian, the governor of the tower, however, had pity on the young prince and placed him in the care of a peasant family for four years. At this point, Julian reasoned that Sigismund, now sixteen, was too vulnerable to assassination and thereafter kept him locked in a cage in the tower like an animal.

With the encouragement of the physician, Julian decides to make a plea to the king to retry Sigismund, now twenty-one, thus giving the young prince a second chance to demonstrate his innocence. In making his decision, the king seeks council with Brother Ignatius, the grand almoner of the monastery. He asks Brother Ignatius if the prophesy is in fact true, to which the grand almoner responds ambiguously. He chides the king, however, for mistreating his own son, ''your child, got in holy matrimony!'' The king nonetheless declares that, if Sigismund is found to be ''a demon and a rebel,''

then ''his head shall fall and roll before your feet,'' but if he is found to be innocent, ''I shall take my child into my arms, and the crown, a triple crown wrought into one, will not be without an heir.'' Brother Ignatius replies that, in effect, the king has already been condemned for his sins against his son, telling him that God ''knows you and means to punish you.'' Upon hearing this, the king becomes angry, and has the grand almoner carried out. The king is, in effect, pronounced guilty for mistreating his own son but refuses to accept responsibility for his guilt, justifying it by his own fear of rebellion.

Yet, while he fears his own son, whom he has imprisoned for life and has never seen, the king also expresses deep sentiments in regard to Sigismund. When he meets with Julian at the monastery, the king states that he is ''moved ... deeply,'' by Julian's loyalty to him as the guardian of Sigismund, sentimentally embracing him with the words, ''It is your arms that shield our kin.''

Fearing his first meeting with Sigismund, the king turns to prayer and religious council in the hopes that his son will remain loyal to him. The king consoles himself regarding his mistreatment of his child by asking his confessor if he may be absolved, should he once again condemn ''my own son'' to life imprisonment in the tower. Under this current of morbid fear of his own son, the king is deeply moved by the thought of restoring Sigismund to his rightful role as heir to the throne. The king even muses that, were he to allow Sigismund to succeed him, he might retire peacefully. He imagines that "Perhaps I too will retire into a monastery for the remainder of my days," and that his son will regard him with "gratitude." The king nonetheless asks his confessor if he may be justified in inflicting "the extremest harshness" upon the prince, "if he were to raise his hand against me." The confessor has clearly been appointed for the purpose of justifying any action, no matter how immoral, the king undertakes and relieves the king's every fear of being accused of wrongdoing against his son.

Before the king lays eyes upon his son for the first time, Julian attempts to impress upon Sigismund the importance of obeying his father, without questioning his ill treatment up to this point. Julian equates Sigismund's conception of a Christian God as the Father with the figure of his biological father, the king. He tells Sigismund, "You have said to yourself that it is your father who thus governs over you. You comprehend that your father's ways had to be inscrutable to you. . . . You would not wish to live unless someone higher were above you, that is the sense of your thinking—You do not ask: What has happened to me?"

Upon seeing Sigismund for the first time, the king, impressed by his son's instinctively regal manner, is so moved that he must support himself on Julian's arm, as if he were weak in the knees with emotion. His impulse to fatherly affection toward his son is expressed when he sees in Sigismund, "The very image of my wife!" The king is literally moved to tears as he gazes upon his son and rightful successor. The king's feeling for the son, whom he has feared and imprisoned for twenty-one years, is sincere and heartfelt. He tells Sigismund, "You have returned home. Our arms are open." The king continues this emotional plea, "will you come to our heart, into its undivided warmth?"

Yet, while this "warmth" on the part of the king for his son may be heartfelt, the king maintains a sly, manipulative, and distrustful stance toward Sigismund, whom he will tolerate only if he can maintain his position of power over his son. He tells the young prince, "I look for child-like devotion in your eyes, and I do not find it." The king then tries to convince Sigismund that it was Julian who had deceived him, the king, into believing that his son was wild and harbored rebellious intentions against his father.

> HE TELLS THE YOUNG PRINCE, 'I LOOK FOR CHILD-LIKE DEVOTION IN YOUR EYES, AND I DO NOT FIND IT.'"

Despite the king's mighty efforts, however, Sigismund does, the minute he gets the chance, rise up against his father in rebellion. The king, dropping all notions of paternal affection, immediately sentences both Sigismund and his keeper, Julian, to execution for treason. The king declares Sigismund a "parricide"—a would-be murderer of his own father—thereby justifying his sentence of death upon his own son. The king's fear of being usurped outweighs any natural fatherly love or affection for his offspring. The king thus proves himself to be a sinner by valuing power over love.

Julian, the governor of the tower, serves as a second father figure to Prince Sigismund. The king has entrusted Julian for almost twenty-two years with watching over Sigismund. Julian at first appears to be an ambivalent figure in Sigismund's life, but he soon proves himself to be the young prince's most faithful caretaker. As Sigismund's guardian and jailer throughout the prince's life, Julian's relationship to him is fraught with ambiguity.

The physician, upon examining the imprisoned prince, quickly perceives the warring sympathies within Julian's heart over the proper action to take in regards to Sigismund. The physician tells Julian, "Your lordship is created of heroic stuff," but qualifies the statement by elaborating that "the source itself is troubled, the deepest root is cankered. In this your imperious countenance Good and Evil wage a fearful coiling battle like serpents." In other words, Julian has the potential to do heroic deeds in regard to Sigismund, but he is "troubled" at heart, hesitating between taking action against Sigismund, which the physician regards as Evil, and taking action to empower Sigismund, which the physician regards as Good. The physician goes on to describe the nature of Julian's troubles, stating that "you deny your heart—Heart and head must be one. But you have consented to the satanic split; you have suppressed the noble inner organ." The physician tells Julian, "I see heroic ambition in your carriage and gait, checked in the hips by an impotent will, gigantically warring with itself.'' The physician accurately perceives the desire within Julian to do right by Sigismund, also perceiving the extent to which his ''will'' is ''warring with itself'' over what to do. The physician concludes that Julian's ''soul's wings'' are ''shackled in chains.'' Thus, the physician, regarding the cause of Sigismund as a higher moral Good, sees Julian's ''soul'' as a slave to the Evil impulse that causes him to keep Sigismund imprisoned like an animal. The physician tells Julian that his conscience in the matter is troubled: ''The wrong done to this youth, the enormity of the crime, the complicity, the partial consent: all this stands written on your face.''

Julian, however, protests that he has ''saved his life, more than once,'' and that ''Without me he would have been murdered.'' He explains that he has placed Sigismund under such base conditions, locked in the tower, to hide him from the world and protect him from assassins. But the physician's words inspire Julian to conceive of a plan whereby the prince may be restored to the good favor of his father, King Basilius. The conviction with which Julian undertakes this effort is indicated when he tells the physician, ''I am risking my head'' to do right by Sigismund. When he pleads directly to the king to give Sigismund a retrial, an opportunity to prove his innocence, Julian offers the king his own head in execution if Sigismund proves disloyal to his father. At this point, the king acknowledges Julian's role as Sigismund's caretaker, telling him, ''It is your arms that shield our kin.''

At this point, however, Sigismund both fears Julian as his jailer and reveres him as the life giver and father figure who has taught him everything he knows—in particular, Julian has taught him the Christian Bible. Sigismund cowers in fear when Julian enters the room, telling him, ''You have supreme power over me. I tremble before you. I know that I cannot escape you.'' But Julian reminds him that ''I was your rescuer. Secretly, I poured oil into the lamp of your life; because of me alone there is still light in you. Remember that. . . . Did I not let you sit next to me at a wooden table and open before you the great book and pointed in it figure after figure to the things of the world and called them by name for you?''

When Sigismund does indeed rise up against his father, the king, he sentences Julian to death with the young prince. After the prince and Julian are both saved from execution by the rebellion, which

deposes the king and places Sigismund on the throne, Sigismund directly acknowledges Julian's role as his father and teacher. He addresses Julian as ''my teacher,'' and appoints him his ''minister,'' his closest confident. Julian likewise passionately declares himself to be Sigismund's father in spirit, although the king and queen are his biological parents: ''O my king! My son!—for you come from me who molded you, not from him who furnished merely the clump of earth, nor from her who gave birth to you.''

When the rebellion, taken over by Oliver, turns against Sigismund, Julian is fatally wounded. In the moments before Julian dies, Sigismund directly acknowledges his importance as father, teacher, and caretaker. He tells Julian, ''You have put the right word under my tongue, the word of comfort in the desert of this life.'' After Julian dies, Oliver, who has entered, notices Julian's dead body and tells Sigismund, ''I know him. He was your jailer. He kept you worse than a dog.'' But Sigismund defends Julian as the man whose actions were always in the service of Sigismund's own good, asserting that ''You are mistaken. He did not keep me as he was commanded to, but he kept me as he had planned in the fulfillment of his mind's work.''

Thus, the true nature of Julian's relationship to Sigismund becomes increasingly apparent over the course of the play. Outwardly his jailer, Julian emerges as the one truly nurturing father figure in the prince's life. By the time of Julian's death, Sigismund has acknowledged him as a teacher, father, caretaker, and guide.

Sigismund's two father figures throughout the play, the king and Julian, ultimately show their true moral colors in terms of their relationship to the young prince. Julian at first appears to be the prince's oppressor and jailer, but he shows himself to be his most ardent caretaker and supporter. The king waivers between fear of the son who is destined to rise up against him and a natural fatherly love for his offspring. In the figure of the king, however, the love of his power ultimately overrides the love of his child.

Source: Liz Brent, in an essay for *Drama for Students,* Gale Group, 2001.

David Kelly

Kelly is an instructor of Creative Writing and Literature at Oakton Community College and College of Lake County. In this essay, he examines the ways in which Hofmannsthal's version of this story differs from the play that it was based upon.

There is only a tenuous relationship between Hugo von Hofmannsthal's 1925 play *The Tower* and its inspiration, the 1635 romantic comedy *Life Is a Dream* by the Spanish playwright Pedro Calderon de la Barca y Henao. Both plays concern a king, Basilius of Poland, who has determined that his son is destined to one day overthrow him and take his place, and who has, therefore, taken the measure of having the child raised in captivity. Both plays follow the prince, Sigismund, as he gains his freedom, misuses it, and is sent back into captivity, only to be rescued later when a political uprising unseats Basilius and requires a royal heir to take his place. Beyond these similarities in their plots, though, there is a world of difference in the way the two authors develop the basic idea. For Calderon, the true story is a metaphysical one about the nature of human knowledge, which, as he presents it, is as ''real'' for one whose life is confined to a tower as it is for a monarch who reigns supreme. Hofmannsthal's take on the material stresses the opposite effect, presenting the king, in the end, as a convict in his own right. That the same story can bend to accommodate two such different viewpoints is a tribute to romanticism, to fatalism, and ultimately to every unified world view that helps humans interpret the world surrounding them.

In Calderon's version of the story, life really *is* a dream, just as the title says: a lively jumble of coincidence, intuition, and masquerade. The basic story that both plays follow, about a prince locked up in a tower, has been handed down through the ages, like many of the most potent fairy tales. As Calderon envisions it, the king's fear of his son began when the boy's mother died during childbirth and then continues with his own scholarly work. King Basilius explains that, in his extensive reading, he found it fore-written ''that Sigismund would be the most cruel of all princes, the most audacious of all humans, the most wicked of all monarchs;'' that he would split up the kingdom; and that he would take physical action against his own father. The play gives a vivid, lasting image of the cruelty he anticipates from Sigismund: ''I saw myself down-stricken, lying on the ground before him (What deep shame this utterance gives me!) while his feet on my white hairs were imprinted as a carpet.'' Readers can notice a similarity between the way that Calderon

> THAT THE SAME STORY CAN BEND TO ACCOMMODATE TWO SUCH DIFFERENT VIEWPOINTS IS A TRIBUTE TO ROMANTICISM, TO FATALISM, AND ULTIMATELY TO EVERY UNIFIED WORLD VIEW THAT HELPS HUMANS INTERPRET THE WORLD SURROUNDING THEM.''

lets a premonition drive the plot and some of the later romantic tragicomedies of Shakespeare, particularly between this version of Basilius and Shakespeare's Prospero, the wizard king of *The Tempest.* The two plays were, after all, written a mere twenty-five years apart.

After establishing that Basilius' motivation for imprisoning the infant boy was rooted in his own predictions, *Life Is a Dream* goes on to raise questions about the source of that prediction. Sigismund does, in fact, proceed once he is free to strike out violently, killing a guard and threatening Basilius in a manner that seems to be a fulfillment of the prophecy. As this scene unfolds, though, questions arise about whether his long imprisonment held back his naturally violent impulses or if it might have actually caused them. Sigismund's bitterness and horror boil over once he is told that he is actually a prince and that he was locked up by his own father before growing old enough to do anything to actually deserve it. Audiences are led to wonder whether Basilius might have created what we recognize today as a self-fulfilling prophesy.

Much is made in Calderon's version of the method of Sigismund's temporary release from custody. Unsure of how the prisoner will react to finding out that he is actually the royal heir, Basilius arranges for him to take a sleeping potion in his cell, so that, if his introduction to his rightful place in court goes as badly as predicted, he can be put back in his cell, with the whole incident explained away as a dream. While Hofmannsthal's version of the story does make use of the ''sleeping powder'' twist, it is not the king who devises this scheme, but rather Julian, who is sympathetic to Sigismund.

Julian uses the idea of knocking Sigismund out to help him retain some innocence and vulnerability, so that he would not have to automatically be put to death if the experiment of telling the truth should fail. Sigismund in *The Tower* does not confuse levels of reality, the way that his counterpart from *Life Is a Dream* does—he does not think that dream life is real life and vice versa; he merely notes the similarity between the two.

As if this blurring of the line between life and dream did not give his play enough lighthearted fantasy, Calderon includes a romantic twist of mistaken identity that is only glancingly related to the play's main idea. The following section is very confusing. None of the readers will be familiar with these characters, nor do they need to be. The point can be made quite well without naming them all. [Rosaura has come to Poland disguised as a man, to avenge being dishonored earlier by Astolfo; she is aided by Clotaldo, the jailer who has been sympathetic to the prince, although she does not realize that Clotaldo is really her father; and Astolfo intends to be named Basilius' heir to the throne because his mother was Basilius' sister and he is poised to strengthen that birthright by marrying Estrella, the daughter of Basilius' other sister.] Little about these complications involves Sigismund finding himself a prisoner one day, a prince the next, and then a prisoner again, other than pointing out the uncertainty of the political system, a point that Hofmannsthal would later make much of. These subplots do, however, establish a lighthearted tone, where chance and fate bounce off each other in no controllable pattern. In the end of *Life Is a Dream,* when Sigismund is given his true place on the throne (affirming the Elizabethan faith in the natural rightness of succession), he shows royal wisdom by telling Astolfo to make good on his broken promise and marry Rosaura, and he shows compassion for Estrella, who has just lost her fiancée, by offering to marry her himself. Basilius, whose studious nature led to his reading false prophesies in the first place, is left to spend his retirement reading.

Sigismund thus ends up a hero in Calderon's version of this story, a man who overcomes social disadvantage and a natural propensity toward resentment, showing that royal blood does (or at least can) overcome adversity. He takes to heart the lesson he learned when his first release ends in failure, always questioning whether what he believes to be real is in fact reality or a dream. Modern audiences might summarize his lesson as, ''Don't take everything so seriously.'' This version of the story shows, in a fashion as central to romantic comedy four hundred years ago as it is today, that anger and adversity are just the unfortunate by-products of misunderstanding. It is Basilius' misunderstanding of the prophesy that makes him lock his child away, and it is Sigismund's misunderstanding of power that makes him abuse it when he awakens one day to find himself a prince. Peace takes a bighearted gesture, such as Sigismund's willingness to end the cycle of revenge by conceding that the indignities that he suffered are no more important than a dream.

Hofmannsthal does not find humor or forgiveness in this situation, but instead he uses it to illuminate an entirely different view of the human condition. In his version of the story, King Basilius is not the primary mover who takes Sigismund's freedom, gives it back, takes it again, and eventually loses it to him. He is a loud, egotistical, obnoxious fool, whose people are tired of his unfair rules and his socially destructive proclamations. When Sigismund is brought from his jail in the tower, Basilius tries to use him as a tool to stop the popular revolution that he senses around him, but Sigismund rejects him and tries to steal the royal power for himself; when his power is restored, Basilius behaves all the worse, demanding for himself the virgin nieces of an innocent courtier and increasing taxes throughout the kingdom as a sort of victory celebration. If he understood the nature of his own power, Basilius would not be as likely to flaunt it in the faces of his subordinates, practically driving them to rebel against his rule.

The nature of political power in *The Tower* is such that it does not stem from the wisdom or intuition of those who have it, as it does in *Life Is a Dream,* but that it is a balance between opposing forces that will often settle upon one person to rule. Hofmannsthal's Basilius is as clueless about the source of his power as Sigismund is, when he finds himself suddenly wearing the royal seal on his finger. They both fail to acknowledge the fact that their power depends on the consent of the common people. The practical reason why Sigismund is brought out of his cell to take the throne is not because he has royal blood or natural intelligence, but because the rebel forces feel that it is necessary to have some justification that could support the legitimacy of their rule. They want him to stay quiet, to be seen but not heard. In act 5, Oliver, a rebel leader, explains that Sigismund is to be driven through the streets on a cart, to show that it is Basilius's son who has overthrown him. "In this way, the ignorant, tongue-tied people will be taught by us to read emblems with their eyes, and the lords will plunge head over heels into the earth." When Sigismund turns out to have ideas of his own, Oliver sends him back to prison and orders an aid to bring him another man who looks like Sigismund, who the crowds will think is him when he rides through the streets. Basilius is executed offstage, a deed mentioned in passing, and Sigismund is assassinated; neither member of the royal lineage is really necessary for running the kingdom in Hofmannsthal's view.

While the secondary characters in *Life Is a Dream* serve to loosen up viewers' expectations, the characters who surround the royal family in *The Tower* are there to inhibit any romantic hopes about the people who make governments run. For the most part, they are more craven, manipulative, and ruthless than is generally expected even if their goal to overthrow an unjust tyrant is noble. A notable exception is the character identified as "the Physician," a name clearly intended to put him outside of the circle of political machinations that decides many people's fates throughout the work. Because his job is to care for the flesh, the physician is outraged at the way he sees Sigismund treated, and he is willing to provide sleeping powders to control the wild Sigismund, supporting a dangerous scheme to present him before his father. Aside from the physician's natural concern for human suffering, the key motivation for human behavior in *The Tower* is power. There is no draw of love, as in the subplots of the Calderon version, nor a drive to avenge the honor of a woman scorned. Hofmannsthal's view is completely modern, a twentieth century tale of political expediency, with no need for traditional dramatic concerns to be added to fulfill a dramatic code.

Students comparing the two plays would be right to wonder what was gained over the course of the three centuries that separated them. The Calderon version seems more lighthearted, and more imaginative; by comparison, Hofmannsthal's play is leaden, and thumps along the ground with a sense of pervading doom that seems more concerned with the harshness of political life than with shedding intellectual light on the dynamics of power. It is true that Hofmannsthal is something of a political insider, fascinated with the subtleties of politics, often at the expense of his play's dramatic interest. He does, however, avoid the trap of presenting his string of events entirely raw, too much like life to be of interest to viewers watching them on the stage.

The most interesting thing about Hofmannsthal's casting of these characters is the layer of symbolism that he gives to the story. While, in the Calderon version, the significance of all that happens to Sigismund has to do with how much life and the dream world sometimes seem similar—an interesting but somewhat lightweight observation—Hofmannsthal's play is built around beliefs about sin and rebirth that are at the root of the Christian tradition. It is, without a doubt, interesting to hear about a prince who is locked away so that he cannot overthrow his father, and in the post-Freudian era, the story has taken on an even more significant air, but neither its interest value nor its psychological value is worth much after audiences leave the theater. Hofmannsthal's approach, on the other hand, gives the story a deeper meaning. Sigismund may have thought that he was awakened, and then awakened again from that awakening, in *Life Is a Dream,* but in *The Tower* he is born anew, and he has to experience life with a new awareness of the guilt that has been hung upon him since childhood. Viewers who can forget about the scheming of Julian, Oliver, and Basilius himself, and who can put the excitement of Sigismund's assault against Basilius into perspective can understand the prince to be a man who received a second chance, had it taken from him, and learned to live a noble life even when nobility did him no good. He could have riches and comfort, and had every reason to believe that the world owed him them, but he decided, after being mistreated, to become less, not more, cynical. That is the value of *The Tower,* and it is more significant than the sense of contentment that Calderon made sure to leave at his play's end.

Neither version of the story of Prince Sigismund is better, but they both certainly reflect the literary tastes of their times. Calderon's is a complex tale of interwoven coincidences and brushes with fate. Hofmannsthal gives his viewers a darker piece, but one focused more closely on how we understand what it is to be human and live with the guilt of those who came before. The same incident—Sigismund's return to captivity—is seen as the driving force in a comic mix-up and a catalyst that starts an inquiry into humanity's most pressing concerns. The differences in these two versions only serves to prove that genius will always see old stories anew.

Source: David Kelly, in an essay for *Drama for Students,* Gale Group, 2001.

SOURCES

Calderon de la Barca, Pedro, ''Life Is a Dream,'' in *Six Plays,* Las Americas Publishing Co., 1961, pp. 13–96.

Eliot, T. S., ''A Note on The Tower,'' in *Hugo von Hofmannsthal: Selected Plays and Libretti,* edited by Michael Hamburger, Pantheon Books, 1963, pp. lxxiii–lxxiv.

Hamburger, Michael, ''Introduction,'' in *Hugo von Hofmannsthal: Selected Plays and Libretti,* Pantheon Books, 1963, pp. ix–lxxii.

Hofmannsthal, Hugo von, ''The Tower (1927),'' in *Three Plays,* Wayne State University Press, 1966, pp. 141–241.

''Hugo von Hofmannsthal,'' in *Contemporary Authors Online,* The Gale Group, 1999.

Schwarz, Alfred, ''Introduction,'' in *Hugo von Hofmannsthal: Three Plays,* Wayne State University Press, 1966, pp. 13–42.

FURTHER READING

Bangerter, Lowell A., *Hugo von Hofmannsthal,* Ungar, 1977.
    Bangerter's book is a biography of von Hofmannsthal, which discusses his important works in drama and poetry. It includes a chronology of his life.

Bottenberg, Joanna, *Shared Creation: Words and Music in the Hofmannsthal-Strauss Operas,* P. Lang, 1996.
    This work is a discussion of the collaborative operatic works of Hofmannsthal and Strauss.

Del Caro, Adrian, *Hugo von Hofmannsthal: Poets and the Language of Life*, Louisiana State University Press, 1993.
    This book is a discussion of von Hofmannsthal's poetic works.

Gray, Ronald, *The German Tradition in Literature, 1871–1945,* Cambridge University Press, 1965.
    Gray's text is a literary history of German letters that covers the time period of von Hofmannsthal's life span.

Glossary of Literary Terms

A

Abstract: Used as a noun, the term refers to a short summary or outline of a longer work. As an adjective applied to writing or literary works, abstract refers to words or phrases that name things not knowable through the five senses. Examples of abstracts include the *Cliffs Notes* summaries of major literary works. Examples of abstract terms or concepts include "idea," "guilt" "honesty," and "loyalty."

Absurd, Theater of the: See *Theater of the Absurd*

Absurdism: See *Theater of the Absurd*

Act: A major section of a play. Acts are divided into varying numbers of shorter scenes. From ancient times to the nineteenth century plays were generally constructed of five acts, but modern works typically consist of one, two, or three acts. Examples of five-act plays include the works of Sophocles and Shakespeare, while the plays of Arthur Miller commonly have a three-act structure.

Acto: A one-act Chicano theater piece developed out of collective improvisation. *Actos* were performed by members of Luis Valdez's Teatro Campesino in California during the mid-1960s.

Aestheticism: A literary and artistic movement of the nineteenth century. Followers of the movement believed that art should not be mixed with social, political, or moral teaching. The statement "art for

art's sake" is a good summary of aestheticism. The movement had its roots in France, but it gained widespread importance in England in the last half of the nineteenth century, where it helped change the Victorian practice of including moral lessons in literature. Oscar Wilde is one of the best-known "aesthetes" of the late nineteenth century.

Age of Johnson: The period in English literature between 1750 and 1798, named after the most prominent literary figure of the age, Samuel Johnson. Works written during this time are noted for their emphasis on "sensibility," or emotional quality. These works formed a transition between the rational works of the Age of Reason, or Neoclassical period, and the emphasis on individual feelings and responses of the Romantic period. Significant writers during the Age of Johnson included the novelists Ann Radcliffe and Henry Mackenzie, dramatists Richard Sheridan and Oliver Goldsmith, and poets William Collins and Thomas Gray. Also known as Age of Sensibility

Age of Reason: See *Neoclassicism*

Age of Sensibility: See *Age of Johnson*

Alexandrine Meter: See *Meter*

Allegory: A narrative technique in which characters representing things or abstract ideas are used to convey a message or teach a lesson. Allegory is typically used to teach moral, ethical, or religious lessons but is sometimes used for satiric or political purposes. Examples of allegorical works include Edmund Spenser's *The Faerie Queene* and John Bunyan's *The Pilgrim's Progress.*

Allusion: A reference to a familiar literary or historical person or event, used to make an idea more easily understood. For example, describing someone as a ''Romeo'' makes an allusion to William Shakespeare's famous young lover in *Romeo and Juliet.*

Amerind Literature: The writing and oral traditions of Native Americans. Native American literature was originally passed on by word of mouth, so it consisted largely of stories and events that were easily memorized. Amerind prose is often rhythmic like poetry because it was recited to the beat of a ceremonial drum. Examples of Amerind literature include the autobiographical *Black Elk Speaks,* the works of N. Scott Momaday, James Welch, and Craig Lee Strete, and the poetry of Luci Tapahonso.

Analogy: A comparison of two things made to explain something unfamiliar through its similarities to something familiar, or to prove one point based on the acceptedness of another. Similes and metaphors are types of analogies. Analogies often take the form of an extended simile, as in William Blake's aphorism: ''As the caterpillar chooses the fairest leaves to lay her eggs on, so the priest lays his curse on the fairest joys.''

Angry Young Men: A group of British writers of the 1950s whose work expressed bitterness and disillusionment with society. Common to their work is an anti-hero who rebels against a corrupt social order and strives for personal integrity. The term has been used to describe Kingsley Amis, John Osborne, Colin Wilson, John Wain, and others.

Antagonist: The major character in a narrative or drama who works against the hero or protagonist. An example of an evil antagonist is Richard Lovelace in Samuel Richardson's *Clarissa,* while a virtuous antagonist is Macduff in William Shakespeare's *Macbeth.*

Anthropomorphism: The presentation of animals or objects in human shape or with human characteristics. The term is derived from the Greek word for ''human form.'' The fables of Aesop, the animated films of Walt Disney, and Richard Adams's *Watership Down* feature anthropomorphic characters.

Anti-hero: A central character in a work of literature who lacks traditional heroic qualities such as courage, physical prowess, and fortitude. Anti-heros typically distrust conventional values and are unable to commit themselves to any ideals. They generally feel helpless in a world over which they have no control. Anti-heroes usually accept, and often celebrate, their positions as social outcasts. A well-known anti-hero is Yossarian in Joseph Heller's novel *Catch-22.*

Antimasque: See *Masque*

Antithesis: The antithesis of something is its direct opposite. In literature, the use of antithesis as a figure of speech results in two statements that show a contrast through the balancing of two opposite ideas. Technically, it is the second portion of the statement that is defined as the ''antithesis''; the first portion is the ''thesis.'' An example of antithesis is found in the following portion of Abraham Lincoln's ''Gettysburg Address''; notice the opposition between the verbs ''remember'' and ''forget'' and the phrases ''what we say'' and ''what they did'': ''The world will little note nor long remember what we say here, but it can never forget what they did here.''

Apocrypha: Writings tentatively attributed to an author but not proven or universally accepted to be their works. The term was originally applied to certain books of the Bible that were not considered inspired and so were not included in the ''sacred canon.'' Geoffrey Chaucer, William Shakespeare, Thomas Kyd, Thomas Middleton, and John Marston all have apocrypha. Apocryphal books of the Bible include the Old Testament's Book of Enoch and New Testament's Gospel of Peter.

Apollonian and Dionysian: The two impulses believed to guide authors of dramatic tragedy. The Apollonian impulse is named after Apollo, the Greek god of light and beauty and the symbol of intellectual order. The Dionysian impulse is named after Dionysus, the Greek god of wine and the symbol of the unrestrained forces of nature. The Apollonian impulse is to create a rational, harmonious world, while the Dionysian is to express the irrational forces of personality. Friedrich Nietzche uses these terms in *The Birth of Tragedy* to designate contrasting elements in Greek tragedy.

Apostrophe: A statement, question, or request addressed to an inanimate object or concept or to a nonexistent or absent person. Requests for inspiration from the muses in poetry are examples of apostrophe, as is Marc Antony's address to Caesar's corpse in William Shakespeare's *Julius Caesar:* ''O, pardon me, thou bleeding piece of earth, That I am meek and gentle with these butchers!. . . Woe to the hand that shed this costly blood!. . .''

Archetype: The word archetype is commonly used to describe an original pattern or model from which all other things of the same kind are made. This term was introduced to literary criticism from the psychology of Carl Jung. It expresses Jung's theory that behind every person's ''unconscious,'' or repressed memories of the past, lies the ''collective unconscious'' of the human race: memories of the countless typical experiences of our ancestors. These memories are said to prompt illogical associations that trigger powerful emotions in the reader. Often, the emotional process is primitive, even primordial. Archetypes are the literary images that grow out of the ''collective unconscious.'' They appear in literature as incidents and plots that repeat basic patterns of life. They may also appear as stereotyped characters. Examples of literary archetypes include themes such as birth and death and characters such as the Earth Mother.

Argument: The argument of a work is the author's subject matter or principal idea. Examples of defined ''argument'' portions of works include John Milton's *Arguments* to each of the books of *Paradise Lost* and the ''Argument'' to Robert Herrick's *Hesperides.*

Aristotelian Criticism: Specifically, the method of evaluating and analyzing tragedy formulated by the Greek philosopher Aristotle in his *Poetics.* More generally, the term indicates any form of criticism that follows Aristotle's views. Aristotelian criticism focuses on the form and logical structure of a work, apart from its historical or social context, in contrast to ''Platonic Criticism,'' which stresses the usefulness of art. Adherents of New Criticism including John Crowe Ransom and Cleanth Brooks utilize and value the basic ideas of Aristotelian criticism for textual analysis.

Art for Art's Sake: See *Aestheticism*

Aside: A comment made by a stage performer that is intended to be heard by the audience but supposedly not by other characters. Eugene O'Neill's *Strange Interlude* is an extended use of the aside in modern theater.

Audience: The people for whom a piece of literature is written. Authors usually write with a certain audience in mind, for example, children, members of a religious or ethnic group, or colleagues in a professional field. The term ''audience'' also applies to the people who gather to see or hear any performance, including plays, poetry readings, speeches, and concerts. Jane Austen's parody of the gothic novel, *Northanger Abbey,* was originally intended for (and also pokes fun at) an audience of young and avid female gothic novel readers.

Avant-garde: A French term meaning ''vanguard.'' It is used in literary criticism to describe new writing that rejects traditional approaches to literature in favor of innovations in style or content. Twentieth-century examples of the literary *avant-garde* include the Black Mountain School of poets, the Bloomsbury Group, and the Beat Movement.

B

Ballad: A short poem that tells a simple story and has a repeated refrain. Ballads were originally intended to be sung. Early ballads, known as folk ballads, were passed down through generations, so their authors are often unknown. Later ballads composed by known authors are called literary ballads. An example of an anonymous folk ballad is ''Edward,'' which dates from the Middle Ages. Samuel Taylor Coleridge's ''The Rime of the Ancient Mariner'' and John Keats's ''La Belle Dame sans Merci'' are examples of literary ballads.

Baroque: A term used in literary criticism to describe literature that is complex or ornate in style or diction. Baroque works typically express tension, anxiety, and violent emotion. The term ''Baroque Age'' designates a period in Western European literature beginning in the late sixteenth century and ending about one hundred years later. Works of this period often mirror the qualities of works more generally associated with the label ''baroque'' and sometimes feature elaborate conceits. Examples of Baroque works include John Lyly's *Euphues: The Anatomy of Wit,* Luis de Gongora's *Soledads,* and William Shakespeare's *As You Like It.*

Baroque Age: See *Baroque*

Baroque Period: See *Baroque*

Beat Generation: See *Beat Movement*

Beat Movement: A period featuring a group of American poets and novelists of the 1950s and 1960s—including Jack Kerouac, Allen Ginsberg, Gregory Corso, William S. Burroughs, and Lawrence Ferlinghetti—who rejected established social and literary values. Using such techniques as stream of consciousness writing and jazz-influenced free verse and focusing on unusual or abnormal states of mind—generated by religious ecstasy or the use of drugs—the Beat writers aimed to create works that were unconventional in both form and subject matter. Kerouac's *On the Road* is perhaps the best-known example of a Beat Generation novel, and Ginsberg's *Howl* is a famous collection of Beat poetry.

Black Aesthetic Movement: A period of artistic and literary development among African Americans in the 1960s and early 1970s. This was the first major African-American artistic movement since the Harlem Renaissance and was closely paralleled by the civil rights and black power movements. The black aesthetic writers attempted to produce works of art that would be meaningful to the black masses. Key figures in black aesthetics included one of its founders, poet and playwright Amiri Baraka, formerly known as LeRoi Jones; poet and essayist Haki R. Madhubuti, formerly Don L. Lee; poet and playwright Sonia Sanchez; and dramatist Ed Bullins. Works representative of the Black Aesthetic Movement include Amiri Baraka's play *Dutchman,* a 1964 Obie award-winner; *Black Fire: An Anthology of Afro-American Writing,* edited by Baraka and playwright Larry Neal and published in 1968; and Sonia Sanchez's poetry collection *We a BaddDDD People,* published in 1970. Also known as Black Arts Movement.

Black Arts Movement: See *Black Aesthetic Movement*

Black Comedy: See *Black Humor*

Black Humor: Writing that places grotesque elements side by side with humorous ones in an attempt to shock the reader, forcing him or her to laugh at the horrifying reality of a disordered world. Joseph Heller's novel *Catch-22* is considered a superb example of the use of black humor. Other well-known authors who use black humor include Kurt Vonnegut, Edward Albee, Eugene Ionesco, and Harold Pinter. Also known as Black Comedy.

Blank Verse: Loosely, any unrhymed poetry, but more generally, unrhymed iambic pentameter verse (composed of lines of five two-syllable feet with the first syllable accented, the second unaccented). Blank verse has been used by poets since the Renaissance for its flexibility and its graceful, dignified tone. John Milton's *Paradise Lost* is in blank verse, as are most of William Shakespeare's plays.

Bloomsbury Group: A group of English writers, artists, and intellectuals who held informal artistic and philosophical discussions in Bloomsbury, a district of London, from around 1907 to the early 1930s. The Bloomsbury Group held no uniform philosophical beliefs but did commonly express an aversion to moral prudery and a desire for greater social tolerance. At various times the circle included Virginia Woolf, E. M. Forster, Clive Bell, Lytton Strachey, and John Maynard Keynes.

Bon Mot: A French term meaning ''good word.'' A *bon mot* is a witty remark or clever observation. Charles Lamb and Oscar Wilde are celebrated for their witty *bon mots.* Two examples by Oscar Wilde stand out: (1) ''All women become their mothers. That is their tragedy. No man does. That's his.'' (2) ''A man cannot be too careful in the choice of his enemies.''

Breath Verse: See *Projective Verse*

Burlesque: Any literary work that uses exaggeration to make its subject appear ridiculous, either by treating a trivial subject with profound seriousness or by treating a dignified subject frivolously. The word ''burlesque'' may also be used as an adjective, as in ''burlesque show,'' to mean ''striptease act.'' Examples of literary burlesque include the comedies of Aristophanes, Miguel de Cervantes's *Don Quixote,*, Samuel Butler's poem ''Hudibras,'' and John Gay's play *The Beggar's Opera.*

C

Cadence: The natural rhythm of language caused by the alternation of accented and unaccented syllables. Much modern poetry—notably free verse—deliberately manipulates cadence to create complex rhythmic effects. James Macpherson's ''Ossian poems'' are richly cadenced, as is the poetry of the Symbolists, Walt Whitman, and Amy Lowell.

Caesura: A pause in a line of poetry, usually occurring near the middle. It typically corresponds to a break in the natural rhythm or sense of the line but is sometimes shifted to create special meanings or rhythmic effects. The opening line of Edgar Allan Poe's ''The Raven'' contains a caesura following ''dreary'': ''Once upon a midnight dreary, while I pondered weak and weary. . . .''

Canzone: A short Italian or Provencal lyric poem, commonly about love and often set to music. The *canzone* has no set form but typically contains five or six stanzas made up of seven to twenty lines of eleven syllables each. A shorter, five- to ten-line ''envoy,'' or concluding stanza, completes the poem. Masters of the *canzone* form include

Petrarch, Dante Alighieri, Torquato Tasso, and Guido Cavalcanti.

Carpe Diem: A Latin term meaning "seize the day." This is a traditional theme of poetry, especially lyrics. A *carpe diem* poem advises the reader or the person it addresses to live for today and enjoy the pleasures of the moment. Two celebrated *carpe diem* poems are Andrew Marvell's "To His Coy Mistress" and Robert Herrick's poem beginning "Gather ye rosebuds while ye may. . . ."

Catharsis: The release or purging of unwanted emotions— specifically fear and pity—brought about by exposure to art. The term was first used by the Greek philosopher Aristotle in his *Poetics* to refer to the desired effect of tragedy on spectators. A famous example of catharsis is realized in Sophocles' *Oedipus Rex,* when Oedipus discovers that his wife, Jacosta, is his own mother and that the stranger he killed on the road was his own father.

Celtic Renaissance: A period of Irish literary and cultural history at the end of the nineteenth century. Followers of the movement aimed to create a romantic vision of Celtic myth and legend. The most significant works of the Celtic Renaissance typically present a dreamy, unreal world, usually in reaction against the reality of contemporary problems. William Butler Yeats's *The Wanderings of Oisin* is among the most significant works of the Celtic Renaissance. Also known as Celtic Twilight.

Celtic Twilight: See *Celtic Renaissance*

Character: Broadly speaking, a person in a literary work. The actions of characters are what constitute the plot of a story, novel, or poem. There are numerous types of characters, ranging from simple, stereotypical figures to intricate, multifaceted ones. In the techniques of anthropomorphism and personification, animals—and even places or things— can assume aspects of character. "Characterization" is the process by which an author creates vivid, believable characters in a work of art. This may be done in a variety of ways, including (1) direct description of the character by the narrator; (2) the direct presentation of the speech, thoughts, or actions of the character; and (3) the responses of other characters to the character. The term "character" also refers to a form originated by the ancient Greek writer Theophrastus that later became popular in the seventeenth and eighteenth centuries. It is a short essay or sketch of a person who prominently displays a specific attribute or quality, such as miserliness or ambition. Notable characters in lit-

erature include Oedipus Rex, Don Quixote de la Mancha, Macbeth, Candide, Hester Prynne, Ebenezer Scrooge, Huckleberry Finn, Jay Gatsby, Scarlett O'Hara, James Bond, and Kunta Kinte.

Characterization: See *Character*

Chorus: In ancient Greek drama, a group of actors who commented on and interpreted the unfolding action on the stage. Initially the chorus was a major component of the presentation, but over time it became less significant, with its numbers reduced and its role eventually limited to commentary between acts. By the sixteenth century the chorus—if employed at all—was typically a single person who provided a prologue and an epilogue and occasionally appeared between acts to introduce or underscore an important event. The chorus in William Shakespeare's *Henry V* functions in this way. Modern dramas rarely feature a chorus, but T. S. Eliot's *Murder in the Cathedral* and Arthur Miller's *A View from the Bridge* are notable exceptions. The Stage Manager in Thornton Wilder's *Our Town* performs a role similar to that of the chorus.

Chronicle: A record of events presented in chronological order. Although the scope and level of detail provided varies greatly among the chronicles surviving from ancient times, some, such as the *Anglo-Saxon Chronicle,* feature vivid descriptions and a lively recounting of events. During the Elizabethan Age, many dramas— appropriately called "chronicle plays"—were based on material from chronicles. Many of William Shakespeare's dramas of English history as well as Christopher Marlowe's *Edward II* are based in part on Raphael Holinshead's *Chronicles of England, Scotland, and Ireland.*

Classical: In its strictest definition in literary criticism, classicism refers to works of ancient Greek or Roman literature. The term may also be used to describe a literary work of recognized importance (a "classic") from any time period or literature that exhibits the traits of classicism. Classical authors from ancient Greek and Roman times include Juvenal and Homer. Examples of later works and authors now described as classical include French literature of the seventeenth century, Western novels of the nineteenth century, and American fiction of the mid-nineteenth century such as that written by James Fenimore Cooper and Mark Twain.

Classicism: A term used in literary criticism to describe critical doctrines that have their roots in ancient Greek and Roman literature, philosophy, and art. Works associated with classicism typically exhibit restraint on the part of the author, unity of design and purpose, clarity, simplicity, logical organization, and respect for tradition. Examples of literary classicism include Cicero's prose, the dramas of Pierre Corneille and Jean Racine, the poetry of John Dryden and Alexander Pope, and the writings of J. W. von Goethe, G. E. Lessing, and T. S. Eliot.

Climax: The turning point in a narrative, the moment when the conflict is at its most intense. Typically, the structure of stories, novels, and plays is one of rising action, in which tension builds to the climax, followed by falling action, in which tension lessens as the story moves to its conclusion. The climax in James Fenimore Cooper's *The Last of the Mohicans* occurs when Magua and his captive Cora are pursued to the edge of a cliff by Uncas. Magua kills Uncas but is subsequently killed by Hawkeye.

Colloquialism: A word, phrase, or form of pronunciation that is acceptable in casual conversation but not in formal, written communication. It is considered more acceptable than slang. An example of colloquialism can be found in Rudyard Kipling's *Barrack-room Ballads:* When 'Omer smote 'is bloomin' lyre He'd 'eard men sing by land and sea; An' what he thought 'e might require 'E went an' took—the same as me!

Comedy: One of two major types of drama, the other being tragedy. Its aim is to amuse, and it typically ends happily. Comedy assumes many forms, such as farce and burlesque, and uses a variety of techniques, from parody to satire. In a restricted sense the term comedy refers only to dramatic presentations, but in general usage it is commonly applied to nondramatic works as well. Examples of comedies range from the plays of Aristophanes, Terrence, and Plautus, Dante Alighieri's *The Divine Comedy,* Francois Rabelais's *Pantagruel* and *Gargantua,* and some of Geoffrey Chaucer's tales and William Shakespeare's plays to Noel Coward's play *Private Lives* and James Thurber's short story "The Secret Life of Walter Mitty."

Comedy of Manners: A play about the manners and conventions of an aristocratic, highly sophisticated society. The characters are usually types rather than individualized personalities, and plot is less important than atmosphere. Such plays were an important aspect of late seventeenth-century English comedy. The comedy of manners was revived in the eighteenth century by Oliver Goldsmith and Richard Brinsley Sheridan, enjoyed a second revival in the late nineteenth century, and has endured into the twentieth century. Examples of comedies of manners include William Congreve's *The Way of the World* in the late seventeenth century, Oliver Goldsmith's *She Stoops to Conquer* and Richard Brinsley Sheridan's *The School for Scandal* in the eighteenth century, Oscar Wilde's *The Importance of Being Earnest* in the nineteenth century, and W. Somerset Maugham's *The Circle* in the twentieth century.

Comic Relief: The use of humor to lighten the mood of a serious or tragic story, especially in plays. The technique is very common in Elizabethan works, and can be an integral part of the plot or simply a brief event designed to break the tension of the scene. The Gravediggers' scene in William Shakespeare's *Hamlet* is a frequently cited example of comic relief.

Commedia dell'arte: An Italian term meaning "the comedy of guilds" or "the comedy of professional actors." This form of dramatic comedy was popular in Italy during the sixteenth century. Actors were assigned stock roles (such as Pulcinella, the stupid servant, or Pantalone, the old merchant) and given a basic plot to follow, but all dialogue was improvised. The roles were rigidly typed and the plots were formulaic, usually revolving around young lovers who thwarted their elders and attained wealth and happiness. A rigid convention of the *commedia dell'arte* is the periodic intrusion of Harlequin, who interrupts the play with low buffoonery. Peppino de Filippo's *Metamorphoses of a Wandering Minstrel* gave modern audiences an idea of what *commedia dell'arte* may have been like. Various scenarios for *commedia dell'arte* were compiled in Petraccone's *La commedia dell'arte, storia, technica, scenari,* published in 1927.

Complaint: A lyric poem, popular in the Renaissance, in which the speaker expresses sorrow about his or her condition. Typically, the speaker's sadness is caused by an unresponsive lover, but some complaints cite other sources of unhappiness, such as poverty or fate. A commonly cited example is "A Complaint by Night of the Lover Not Beloved" by Henry Howard, Earl of Surrey. Thomas Sackville's "Complaint of Henry, Duke of Buckingham" traces the duke's unhappiness to his ruthless ambition.

Conceit: A clever and fanciful metaphor, usually expressed through elaborate and extended comparison, that presents a striking parallel between two seemingly dissimilar things—for example, elaborately comparing a beautiful woman to an object like a garden or the sun. The conceit was a popular device throughout the Elizabethan Age and Baroque Age and was the principal technique of the seventeenth-century English metaphysical poets. This usage of the word conceit is unrelated to the best-known definition of conceit as an arrogant attitude or behavior. The conceit figures prominently in the works of John Donne, Emily Dickinson, and T. S. Eliot.

Concrete: Concrete is the opposite of abstract, and refers to a thing that actually exists or a description that allows the reader to experience an object or concept with the senses. Henry David Thoreau's *Walden* contains much concrete description of nature and wildlife.

Concrete Poetry: Poetry in which visual elements play a large part in the poetic effect. Punctuation marks, letters, or words are arranged on a page to form a visual design: a cross, for example, or a bumblebee. Max Bill and Eugene Gomringer were among the early practitioners of concrete poetry; Haroldo de Campos and Augusto de Campos are among contemporary authors of concrete poetry.

Confessional Poetry: A form of poetry in which the poet reveals very personal, intimate, sometimes shocking information about himself or herself. Anne Sexton, Sylvia Plath, Robert Lowell, and John Berryman wrote poetry in the confessional vein.

Conflict: The conflict in a work of fiction is the issue to be resolved in the story. It usually occurs between two characters, the protagonist and the antagonist, or between the protagonist and society or the protagonist and himself or herself. Conflict in Theodore Dreiser's novel *Sister Carrie* comes as a result of urban society, while Jack London's short story "To Build a Fire" concerns the protagonist's battle against the cold and himself.

Connotation: The impression that a word gives beyond its defined meaning. Connotations may be universally understood or may be significant only to a certain group. Both "horse" and "steed" denote the same animal, but "steed" has a different connotation, deriving from the chivalrous or romantic narratives in which the word was once often used.

Consonance: Consonance occurs in poetry when words appearing at the ends of two or more verses have similar final consonant sounds but have final vowel sounds that differ, as with "stuff" and "off." Consonance is found in "The curfew tolls the knells of parting day" from Thomas Grey's "An Elegy Written in a Country Church Yard." Also known as Half Rhyme or Slant Rhyme.

Convention: Any widely accepted literary device, style, or form. A soliloquy, in which a character reveals to the audience his or her private thoughts, is an example of a dramatic convention.

Corrido: A Mexican ballad. Examples of *corridos* include "Muerte del afamado Bilito," "La voz de mi conciencia," "Lucio Perez," "La juida," and "Los presos."

Couplet: Two lines of poetry with the same rhyme and meter, often expressing a complete and self-contained thought. The following couplet is from Alexander Pope's "Elegy to the Memory of an Unfortunate Lady": 'Tis Use alone that sanctifies Expense, And Splendour borrows all her rays from Sense.

Criticism: The systematic study and evaluation of literary works, usually based on a specific method or set of principles. An important part of literary studies since ancient times, the practice of criticism has given rise to numerous theories, methods, and "schools," sometimes producing conflicting, even contradictory, interpretations of literature in general as well as of individual works. Even such basic issues as what constitutes a poem or a novel have been the subject of much criticism over the centuries. Seminal texts of literary criticism include Plato's *Republic*, Aristotle's *Poetics*, Sir Philip Sidney's *The Defence of Poesie*, John Dryden's *Of Dramatic Poesie*, and William Wordsworth's "Preface" to the second edition of his *Lyrical Ballads*. Contemporary schools of criticism include deconstruction, feminist, psychoanalytic, poststructuralist, new historicist, postcolonialist, and reader-response.

D

Dactyl: See *Foot*

Dadaism: A protest movement in art and literature founded by Tristan Tzara in 1916. Followers of the movement expressed their outrage at the destruction brought about by World War I by revolting against numerous forms of social convention. The Dadaists presented works marked by calculated madness and flamboyant nonsense. They stressed total freedom of expression, commonly through primitive displays of emotion and illogical, often senseless, poetry. The movement ended shortly after the war, when it was replaced by surrealism. Proponents of Dadaism include Andre Breton, Louis Aragon, Philippe Soupault, and Paul Eluard.

Decadent: See *Decadents*

Decadents: The followers of a nineteenth-century literary movement that had its beginnings in French aestheticism. Decadent literature displays a fascination with perverse and morbid states; a search for novelty and sensation—the ''new thrill''; a preoccupation with mysticism; and a belief in the senselessness of human existence. The movement is closely associated with the doctrine Art for Art's Sake. The term ''decadence'' is sometimes used to denote a decline in the quality of art or literature following a period of greatness. Major French decadents are Charles Baudelaire and Arthur Rimbaud. English decadents include Oscar Wilde, Ernest Dowson, and Frank Harris.

Deconstruction: A method of literary criticism developed by Jacques Derrida and characterized by multiple conflicting interpretations of a given work. Deconstructionists consider the impact of the language of a work and suggest that the true meaning of the work is not necessarily the meaning that the author intended. Jacques Derrida's *De la grammatologie* is the seminal text on deconstructive strategies; among American practitioners of this method of criticism are Paul de Man and J. Hillis Miller.

Deduction: The process of reaching a conclusion through reasoning from general premises to a specific premise. An example of deduction is present in the following syllogism: Premise: All mammals are animals. Premise: All whales are mammals. Conclusion: Therefore, all whales are animals.

Denotation: The definition of a word, apart from the impressions or feelings it creates in the reader. The word ''apartheid'' denotes a political and economic policy of segregation by race, but its connotations— oppression, slavery, inequality—are numerous.

Denouement: A French word meaning ''the unknotting.'' In literary criticism, it denotes the resolution of conflict in fiction or drama. The *denouement* follows the climax and provides an outcome to the primary plot situation as well as an explanation of secondary plot complications. The *denouement* often involves a character's recognition of his or her state of mind or moral condition. A well-known example of *denouement* is the last scene of the play *As You Like It* by William Shakespeare, in which couples are married, an evildoer repents, the identities of two disguised characters are revealed, and a ruler is restored to power. Also known as Falling Action.

Description: Descriptive writing is intended to allow a reader to picture the scene or setting in which the action of a story takes place. The form this description takes often evokes an intended emotional response—a dark, spooky graveyard will evoke fear, and a peaceful, sunny meadow will evoke calmness. An example of a descriptive story is Edgar Allan Poe's *Landor's Cottage,* which offers a detailed depiction of a New York country estate.

Detective Story: A narrative about the solution of a mystery or the identification of a criminal. The conventions of the detective story include the detective's scrupulous use of logic in solving the mystery; incompetent or ineffectual police; a suspect who appears guilty at first but is later proved innocent; and the detective's friend or confidant— often the narrator—whose slowness in interpreting clues emphasizes by contrast the detective's brilliance. Edgar Allan Poe's ''Murders in the Rue Morgue'' is commonly regarded as the earliest example of this type of story. With this work, Poe established many of the conventions of the detective story genre, which are still in practice. Other practitioners of this vast and extremely popular genre include Arthur Conan Doyle, Dashiell Hammett, and Agatha Christie.

Deus ex machina: A Latin term meaning ''god out of a machine.'' In Greek drama, a god was often lowered onto the stage by a mechanism of some kind to rescue the hero or untangle the plot. By extension, the term refers to any artificial device or coincidence used to bring about a convenient and simple solution to a plot. This is a common device in melodramas and includes such fortunate circumstances as the sudden receipt of a legacy to save the family farm or a last-minute stay of execution. The *deus ex machina* invariably rewards the virtuous and punishes evildoers. Examples of *deus ex machina* include King Louis XIV in Jean-Baptiste Moliere's *Tartuffe* and Queen Victoria in *The Pirates of Penzance* by William Gilbert and Arthur Sullivan. Bertolt Brecht parodies the abuse of such devices in the conclusion of his *Threepenny Opera.*

Dialogue: In its widest sense, dialogue is simply conversation between people in a literary work; in its most restricted sense, it refers specifically to the speech of characters in a drama. As a specific literary genre, a ''dialogue'' is a composition in which characters debate an issue or idea. The Greek philosopher Plato frequently expounded his theories in the form of dialogues.

Diction: The selection and arrangement of words in a literary work. Either or both may vary depending on the desired effect. There are four general types of diction: ''formal,'' used in scholarly or lofty writing; ''informal,'' used in relaxed but educated conversation; ''colloquial,'' used in everyday speech; and ''slang,'' containing newly coined words and other terms not accepted in formal usage.

Didactic: A term used to describe works of literature that aim to teach some moral, religious, political, or practical lesson. Although didactic elements are often found in artistically pleasing works, the term ''didactic'' usually refers to literature in which the message is more important than the form. The term may also be used to criticize a work that the critic finds ''overly didactic,'' that is, heavy-handed in its delivery of a lesson. Examples of didactic literature include John Bunyan's *Pilgrim's Progress,* Alexander Pope's *Essay on Criticism,* Jean-Jacques Rousseau's *Emile,* and Elizabeth Inchbald's *Simple Story.*

Dimeter: See *Meter*

Dionysian: See *Apollonian and Dionysian*

Discordia concours: A Latin phrase meaning ''discord in harmony.'' The term was coined by the eighteenth-century English writer Samuel Johnson to describe ''a combination of dissimilar images or discovery of occult resemblances in things apparently unlike.'' Johnson created the expression by reversing a phrase by the Latin poet Horace. The metaphysical poetry of John Donne, Richard Crashaw, Abraham Cowley, George Herbert, and Edward Taylor among others, contains many examples of *discordia concours.* In Donne's ''A Valediction: Forbidding Mourning,'' the poet compares the union of himself with his lover to a draftsman's compass: If they be two, they are two so, As stiff twin compasses are two: Thy soul, the fixed foot, makes no show To move, but doth, if the other do; And though it in the center sit, Yet when the other far doth roam, It leans, and hearkens after it, And grows erect, as that comes home.

Dissonance: A combination of harsh or jarring sounds, especially in poetry. Although such combinations may be accidental, poets sometimes intentionally make them to achieve particular effects. Dissonance is also sometimes used to refer to close but not identical rhymes. When this is the case, the word functions as a synonym for consonance. Robert Browning, Gerard Manley Hopkins, and many other poets have made deliberate use of dissonance.

Doppelganger: A literary technique by which a character is duplicated (usually in the form of an alter ego, though sometimes as a ghostly counterpart) or divided into two distinct, usually opposite personalities. The use of this character device is widespread in nineteenth- and twentieth- century literature, and indicates a growing awareness among authors that the ''self'' is really a composite of many ''selves.'' A well-known story containing a *doppelganger* character is Robert Louis Stevenson's *Dr. Jekyll and Mr. Hyde,* which dramatizes an internal struggle between good and evil. Also known as The Double.

Double Entendre: A corruption of a French phrase meaning ''double meaning.'' The term is used to indicate a word or phrase that is deliberately ambiguous, especially when one of the meanings is risque or improper. An example of a *double entendre* is the Elizabethan usage of the verb ''die,'' which refers both to death and to orgasm.

Double, The: See *Doppelganger*

Draft: Any preliminary version of a written work. An author may write dozens of drafts which are revised to form the final work, or he or she may write only one, with few or no revisions. Dorothy Parker's observation that ''I can't write five words but that I change seven'' humorously indicates the purpose of the draft.

Drama: In its widest sense, a drama is any work designed to be presented by actors on a stage. Similarly, ''drama'' denotes a broad literary genre that includes a variety of forms, from pageant and spectacle to tragedy and comedy, as well as countless types and subtypes. More commonly in modern usage, however, a drama is a work that treats serious subjects and themes but does not aim at the grandeur of tragedy. This use of the term originated with the eighteenth-century French writer Denis Diderot, who used the word *drame* to designate his plays about middle- class life; thus ''drama'' typically features characters of a less exalted stature than those of tragedy. Examples of classical dramas include Menander's comedy *Dyscolus* and Sophocles' tragedy *Oedipus Rex.* Contemporary dramas include Eugene O'Neill's *The Iceman Cometh,* Lillian Hellman's *Little Foxes,* and August Wilson's *Ma Rainey's Black Bottom.*

Dramatic Irony: Occurs when the audience of a play or the reader of a work of literature knows something that a character in the work itself does not know. The irony is in the contrast between the intended meaning of the statements or actions of a character and the additional information understood by the audience. A celebrated example of dramatic irony is in Act V of William Shakespeare's *Romeo and Juliet,* where two young lovers meet their end as a result of a tragic misunderstanding. Here, the audience has full knowledge that Juliet's apparent ''death'' is merely temporary; she will regain her senses when the mysterious ''sleeping potion'' she has taken wears off. But Romeo, mistaking Juliet's drug-induced trance for true death, kills himself in grief. Upon awakening, Juliet discovers Romeo's corpse and, in despair, slays herself.

Dramatic Monologue: See *Monologue*

Dramatic Poetry: Any lyric work that employs elements of drama such as dialogue, conflict, or characterization, but excluding works that are intended for stage presentation. A monologue is a form of dramatic poetry.

Dramatis Personae: The characters in a work of literature, particularly a drama. The list of characters printed before the main text of a play or in the program is the *dramatis personae.*

Dream Allegory: See *Dream Vision*

Dream Vision: A literary convention, chiefly of the Middle Ages. In a dream vision a story is presented as a literal dream of the narrator. This device was commonly used to teach moral and religious lessons. Important works of this type are *The Divine Comedy* by Dante Alighieri, *Piers Plowman* by William Langland, and *The Pilgrim's Progress* by John Bunyan. Also known as Dream Allegory.

Dystopia: An imaginary place in a work of fiction where the characters lead dehumanized, fearful lives. Jack London's *The Iron Heel,* Yevgeny Zamyatin's *My,* Aldous Huxley's *Brave New World,* George Orwell's *Nineteen Eighty-four,* and Margaret Atwood's *Handmaid's Tale* portray versions of dystopia.

E

Eclogue: In classical literature, a poem featuring rural themes and structured as a dialogue among shepherds. Eclogues often took specific poetic forms, such as elegies or love poems. Some were written as the soliloquy of a shepherd. In later centuries, ''eclogue'' came to refer to any poem that was in the pastoral tradition or that had a dialogue or mono-

logue structure. A classical example of an eclogue is Virgil's *Eclogues,* also known as *Bucolics.* Giovanni Boccaccio, Edmund Spenser, Andrew Marvell, Jonathan Swift, and Louis MacNeice also wrote eclogues.

Edwardian: Describes cultural conventions identified with the period of the reign of Edward VII of England (1901-1910). Writers of the Edwardian Age typically displayed a strong reaction against the propriety and conservatism of the Victorian Age. Their work often exhibits distrust of authority in religion, politics, and art and expresses strong doubts about the soundness of conventional values. Writers of this era include George Bernard Shaw, H. G. Wells, and Joseph Conrad.

Edwardian Age: See *Edwardian*

Electra Complex: A daughter's amorous obsession with her father. The term Electra complex comes from the plays of Euripides and Sophocles entitled *Electra,* in which the character Electra drives her brother Orestes to kill their mother and her lover in revenge for the murder of their father.

Elegy: A lyric poem that laments the death of a person or the eventual death of all people. In a conventional elegy, set in a classical world, the poet and subject are spoken of as shepherds. In modern criticism, the word elegy is often used to refer to a poem that is melancholy or mournfully contemplative. John Milton's ''Lycidas'' and Percy Bysshe Shelley's ''Adonais'' are two examples of this form.

Elizabethan Age: A period of great economic growth, religious controversy, and nationalism closely associated with the reign of Elizabeth I of England (1558-1603). The Elizabethan Age is considered a part of the general renaissance—that is, the flowering of arts and literature—that took place in Europe during the fourteenth through sixteenth centuries. The era is considered the golden age of English literature. The most important dramas in English and a great deal of lyric poetry were produced during this period, and modern English criticism began around this time. The notable authors of the period—Philip Sidney, Edmund Spenser, Christopher Marlowe, William Shakespeare, Ben Jonson, Francis Bacon, and John Donne—are among the best in all of English literature.

Elizabethan Drama: English comic and tragic plays produced during the Renaissance, or more narrowly, those plays written during the last years of and few years after Queen Elizabeth's reign. William Shakespeare is considered an Elizabethan dramatist in the broader sense, although most of his work was produced during the reign of James I. Examples of Elizabethan comedies include John Lyly's *The Woman in the Moone,* Thomas Dekker's *The Roaring Girl, or, Moll Cut Purse,* and William Shakespeare's *Twelfth Night.* Examples of Elizabethan tragedies include William Shakespeare's *Antony and Cleopatra,* Thomas Kyd's *The Spanish Tragedy,* and John Webster's *The Tragedy of the Duchess of Malfi.*

Empathy: A sense of shared experience, including emotional and physical feelings, with someone or something other than oneself. Empathy is often used to describe the response of a reader to a literary character. An example of an empathic passage is William Shakespeare's description in his narrative poem *Venus and Adonis* of: the snail, whose tender horns being hit, Shrinks backward in his shelly cave with pain. Readers of Gerard Manley Hopkins's *The Windhover* may experience some of the physical sensations evoked in the description of the movement of the falcon.

English Sonnet: See *Sonnet*

Enjambment: The running over of the sense and structure of a line of verse or a couplet into the following verse or couplet. Andrew Marvell's "To His Coy Mistress" is structured as a series of enjambments, as in lines 11-12: "My vegetable love should grow/Vaster than empires and more slow."

Enlightenment, The: An eighteenth-century philosophical movement. It began in France but had a wide impact throughout Europe and America. Thinkers of the Enlightenment valued reason and believed that both the individual and society could achieve a state of perfection. Corresponding to this essentially humanist vision was a resistance to religious authority. Important figures of the Enlightenment were Denis Diderot and Voltaire in France, Edward Gibbon and David Hume in England, and Thomas Paine and Thomas Jefferson in the United States.

Epic: A long narrative poem about the adventures of a hero of great historic or legendary importance. The setting is vast and the action is often given cosmic significance through the intervention of supernatural forces such as gods, angels, or demons. Epics are typically written in a classical style of grand simplicity with elaborate metaphors and allusions that enhance the symbolic importance of a hero's adventures. Some well-known epics are Homer's *Iliad* and *Odyssey,* Virgil's *Aeneid,* and John Milton's *Paradise Lost.*

Epic Simile: See *Homeric Simile*

Epic Theater: A theory of theatrical presentation developed by twentieth-century German playwright Bertolt Brecht. Brecht created a type of drama that the audience could view with complete detachment. He used what he termed "alienation effects" to create an emotional distance between the audience and the action on stage. Among these effects are: short, self-contained scenes that keep the play from building to a cathartic climax; songs that comment on the action; and techniques of acting that prevent the actor from developing an emotional identity with his role. Besides the plays of Bertolt Brecht, other plays that utilize epic theater conventions include those of Georg Buchner, Frank Wedekind, Erwin Piscator, and Leopold Jessner.

Epigram: A saying that makes the speaker's point quickly and concisely. Samuel Taylor Coleridge wrote an epigram that neatly sums up the form: What is an Epigram? A Dwarfish whole, Its body brevity, and wit its soul.

Epilogue: A concluding statement or section of a literary work. In dramas, particularly those of the seventeenth and eighteenth centuries, the epilogue is a closing speech, often in verse, delivered by an actor at the end of a play and spoken directly to the audience. A famous epilogue is Puck's speech at the end of William Shakespeare's *A Midsummer Night's Dream.*

Epiphany: A sudden revelation of truth inspired by a seemingly trivial incident. The term was widely used by James Joyce in his critical writings, and the stories in Joyce's *Dubliners* are commonly called "epiphanies."

Episode: An incident that forms part of a story and is significantly related to it. Episodes may be either self-contained narratives or events that depend on a larger context for their sense and importance. Examples of episodes include the founding of Wilmington, Delaware in Charles Reade's *The Disinherited Heir* and the individual events comprising the picaresque novels and medieval romances.

Episodic Plot: See *Plot*

Epitaph: An inscription on a tomb or tombstone, or a verse written on the occasion of a person's death. Epitaphs may be serious or humorous. Dorothy Parker's epitaph reads, "I told you I was sick."

Epithalamion: A song or poem written to honor and commemorate a marriage ceremony. Famous examples include Edmund Spenser's

''Epithalamion'' and e. e. cummings's ''Epithalamion.'' Also spelled Epithalamium.

Epithalamium: See *Epithalamion*

Epithet: A word or phrase, often disparaging or abusive, that expresses a character trait of someone or something. ''The Napoleon of crime'' is an epithet applied to Professor Moriarty, arch-rival of Sherlock Holmes in Arthur Conan Doyle's series of detective stories.

Exempla: See *Exemplum*

Exemplum: A tale with a moral message. This form of literary sermonizing flourished during the Middle Ages, when *exempla* appeared in collections known as ''example-books.'' The works of Geoffrey Chaucer are full of *exempla*.

Existentialism: A predominantly twentieth-century philosophy concerned with the nature and perception of human existence. There are two major strains of existentialist thought: atheistic and Christian. Followers of atheistic existentialism believe that the individual is alone in a godless universe and that the basic human condition is one of suffering and loneliness. Nevertheless, because there are no fixed values, individuals can create their own characters—indeed, they can shape themselves—through the exercise of free will. The atheistic strain culminates in and is popularly associated with the works of Jean-Paul Sartre. The Christian existentialists, on the other hand, believe that only in God may people find freedom from life's anguish. The two strains hold certain beliefs in common: that existence cannot be fully understood or described through empirical effort; that anguish is a universal element of life; that individuals must bear responsibility for their actions; and that there is no common standard of behavior or perception for religious and ethical matters. Existentialist thought figures prominently in the works of such authors as Eugene Ionesco, Franz Kafka, Fyodor Dostoyevsky, Simone de Beauvoir, Samuel Beckett, and Albert Camus.

Expatriates: See *Expatriatism*

Expatriatism: The practice of leaving one's country to live for an extended period in another country. Literary expatriates include English poets Percy Bysshe Shelley and John Keats in Italy, Polish novelist Joseph Conrad in England, American writers Richard Wright, James Baldwin, Gertrude Stein, and Ernest Hemingway in France, and Trinidadian author Neil Bissondath in Canada.

Exposition: Writing intended to explain the nature of an idea, thing, or theme. Expository writing is often combined with description, narration, or argument. In dramatic writing, the exposition is the introductory material which presents the characters, setting, and tone of the play. An example of dramatic exposition occurs in many nineteenth-century drawing-room comedies in which the butler and the maid open the play with relevant talk about their master and mistress; in composition, exposition relays factual information, as in encyclopedia entries.

Expressionism: An indistinct literary term, originally used to describe an early twentieth-century school of German painting. The term applies to almost any mode of unconventional, highly subjective writing that distorts reality in some way. Advocates of Expressionism include dramatists George Kaiser, Ernst Toller, Luigi Pirandello, Federico Garcia Lorca, Eugene O'Neill, and Elmer Rice; poets George Heym, Ernst Stadler, August Stramm, Gottfried Benn, and Georg Trakl; and novelists Franz Kafka and James Joyce.

Extended Monologue: See *Monologue*

F

Fable: A prose or verse narrative intended to convey a moral. Animals or inanimate objects with human characteristics often serve as characters in fables. A famous fable is Aesop's ''The Tortoise and the Hare.''

Fairy Tales: Short narratives featuring mythical beings such as fairies, elves, and sprites. These tales originally belonged to the folklore of a particular nation or region, such as those collected in Germany by Jacob and Wilhelm Grimm. Two other celebrated writers of fairy tales are Hans Christian Andersen and Rudyard Kipling.

Falling Action: See *Denouement*

Fantasy: A literary form related to mythology and folklore. Fantasy literature is typically set in non-existent realms and features supernatural beings. Notable examples of fantasy literature are *The Lord of the Rings* by J. R. R. Tolkien and the Gormenghast trilogy by Mervyn Peake.

Farce: A type of comedy characterized by broad humor, outlandish incidents, and often vulgar subject matter. Much of the ''comedy'' in film and television could more accurately be described as farce.

Feet: See *Foot*

Feminine Rhyme: See *Rhyme*

Femme fatale: A French phrase with the literal translation ''fatal woman.'' A *femme fatale* is a sensuous, alluring woman who often leads men into danger or trouble. A classic example of the *femme fatale* is the nameless character in Billy Wilder's *The Seven Year Itch,* portrayed by Marilyn Monroe in the film adaptation.

Fiction: Any story that is the product of imagination rather than a documentation of fact. characters and events in such narratives may be based in real life but their ultimate form and configuration is a creation of the author. Geoffrey Chaucer's *The Canterbury Tales,* Laurence Sterne's *Tristram Shandy,* and Margaret Mitchell's *Gone with the Wind* are examples of fiction.

Figurative Language: A technique in writing in which the author temporarily interrupts the order, construction, or meaning of the writing for a particular effect. This interruption takes the form of one or more figures of speech such as hyperbole, irony, or simile. Figurative language is the opposite of literal language, in which every word is truthful, accurate, and free of exaggeration or embellishment. Examples of figurative language are tropes such as metaphor and rhetorical figures such as apostrophe.

Figures of Speech: Writing that differs from customary conventions for construction, meaning, order, or significance for the purpose of a special meaning or effect. There are two major types of figures of speech: rhetorical figures, which do not make changes in the meaning of the words, and tropes, which do. Types of figures of speech include simile, hyperbole, alliteration, and pun, among many others.

Fin de siecle: A French term meaning ''end of the century.'' The term is used to denote the last decade of the nineteenth century, a transition period when writers and other artists abandoned old conventions and looked for new techniques and objectives. Two writers commonly associated with the *fin de siecle* mindset are Oscar Wilde and George Bernard Shaw.

First Person: See *Point of View*

Flashback: A device used in literature to present action that occurred before the beginning of the story. Flashbacks are often introduced as the dreams or recollections of one or more characters. Flashback techniques are often used in films, where they are typically set off by a gradual changing of one picture to another.

Foil: A character in a work of literature whose physical or psychological qualities contrast strongly with, and therefore highlight, the corresponding qualities of another character. In his Sherlock Holmes stories, Arthur Conan Doyle portrayed Dr. Watson as a man of normal habits and intelligence, making him a foil for the eccentric and wonderfully perceptive Sherlock Holmes.

Folk Ballad: See *Ballad*

Folklore: Traditions and myths preserved in a culture or group of people. Typically, these are passed on by word of mouth in various forms—such as legends, songs, and proverbs— or preserved in customs and ceremonies. This term was first used by W. J. Thoms in 1846. Sir James Frazer's *The Golden Bough* is the record of English folklore; myths about the frontier and the Old South exemplify American folklore.

Folktale: A story originating in oral tradition. Folktales fall into a variety of categories, including legends, ghost stories, fairy tales, fables, and anecdotes based on historical figures and events. Examples of folktales include Giambattista Basile's *The Pentamerone,* which contains the tales of Puss in Boots, Rapunzel, Cinderella, and Beauty and the Beast, and Joel Chandler Harris's Uncle Remus stories, which represent transplanted African folktales and American tales about the characters Mike Fink, Johnny Appleseed, Paul Bunyan, and Pecos Bill.

Foot: The smallest unit of rhythm in a line of poetry. In English-language poetry, a foot is typically one accented syllable combined with one or two unaccented syllables. There are many different types of feet. When the accent is on the second syllable of a two syllable word (con- *tort*), the foot is an ''iamb''; the reverse accentual pattern (*tor* -ture) is a ''trochee.'' Other feet that commonly occur in poetry in English are ''anapest'', two unaccented syllables followed by an accented syllable as in in-ter-*cept*, and ''dactyl'', an accented syllable followed by two unaccented syllables as in *su*-i- cide.

Foreshadowing: A device used in literature to create expectation or to set up an explanation of later developments. In Charles Dickens's *Great Expectations,* the graveyard encounter at the beginning of the novel between Pip and the escaped convict Magwitch foreshadows the baleful atmosphere and events that comprise much of the narrative.

Form: The pattern or construction of a work which identifies its genre and distinguishes it from other genres. Examples of forms include the different genres, such as the lyric form or the short story form, and various patterns for poetry, such as the verse form or the stanza form.

Formalism: In literary criticism, the belief that literature should follow prescribed rules of construction, such as those that govern the sonnet form. Examples of formalism are found in the work of the New Critics and structuralists.

Fourteener Meter: See *Meter*

Free Verse: Poetry that lacks regular metrical and rhyme patterns but that tries to capture the cadences of everyday speech. The form allows a poet to exploit a variety of rhythmical effects within a single poem. Free-verse techniques have been widely used in the twentieth century by such writers as Ezra Pound, T. S. Eliot, Carl Sandburg, and William Carlos Williams. Also known as *Vers libre.*

Futurism: A flamboyant literary and artistic movement that developed in France, Italy, and Russia from 1908 through the 1920s. Futurist theater and poetry abandoned traditional literary forms. In their place, followers of the movement attempted to achieve total freedom of expression through bizarre imagery and deformed or newly invented words. The Futurists were self-consciously modern artists who attempted to incorporate the appearances and sounds of modern life into their work. Futurist writers include Filippo Tommaso Marinetti, Wyndham Lewis, Guillaume Apollinaire, Velimir Khlebnikov, and Vladimir Mayakovsky.

G

Genre: A category of literary work. In critical theory, genre may refer to both the content of a given work—tragedy, comedy, pastoral—and to its form, such as poetry, novel, or drama. This term also refers to types of popular literature, as in the genres of science fiction or the detective story.

Genteel Tradition: A term coined by critic George Santayana to describe the literary practice of certain late nineteenth- century American writers, especially New Englanders. Followers of the Genteel Tradition emphasized conventionality in social, religious, moral, and literary standards. Some of the best-known writers of the Genteel Tradition are R. H. Stoddard and Bayard Taylor.

Gilded Age: A period in American history during the 1870s characterized by political corruption and materialism. A number of important novels of social and political criticism were written during this time. Examples of Gilded Age literature include Henry Adams's *Democracy* and F. Marion Crawford's *An American Politician.*

Gothic: See *Gothicism*

Gothicism: In literary criticism, works characterized by a taste for the medieval or morbidly attractive. A gothic novel prominently features elements of horror, the supernatural, gloom, and violence: clanking chains, terror, charnel houses, ghosts, medieval castles, and mysteriously slamming doors. The term ''gothic novel'' is also applied to novels that lack elements of the traditional Gothic setting but that create a similar atmosphere of terror or dread. Mary Shelley's *Frankenstein* is perhaps the best-known English work of this kind.

Gothic Novel: See *Gothicism*

Great Chain of Being: The belief that all things and creatures in nature are organized in a hierarchy from inanimate objects at the bottom to God at the top. This system of belief was popular in the seventeenth and eighteenth centuries. A summary of the concept of the great chain of being can be found in the first epistle of Alexander Pope's *An Essay on Man,* and more recently in Arthur O. Lovejoy's *The Great Chain of Being: A Study of the History of an Idea.*

Grotesque: In literary criticism, the subject matter of a work or a style of expression characterized by exaggeration, deformity, freakishness, and disorder. The grotesque often includes an element of comic absurdity. Early examples of literary grotesque include Francois Rabelais's *Pantagruel* and *Gargantua* and Thomas Nashe's *The Unfortunate Traveller,* while more recent examples can be found in the works of Edgar Allan Poe, Evelyn Waugh, Eudora Welty, Flannery O'Connor, Eugene Ionesco, Gunter Grass, Thomas Mann, Mervyn Peake, and Joseph Heller, among many others.

H

Haiku: The shortest form of Japanese poetry, constructed in three lines of five, seven, and five syllables respectively. The message of a *haiku* poem usually centers on some aspect of spirituality and provokes an emotional response in the reader. Early masters of *haiku* include Basho, Buson,

Kobayashi Issa, and Masaoka Shiki. English writers of *haiku* include the Imagists, notably Ezra Pound, H. D., Amy Lowell, Carl Sandburg, and William Carlos Williams. Also known as *Hokku.*

Half Rhyme: See *Consonance*

Hamartia: In tragedy, the event or act that leads to the hero's or heroine's downfall. This term is often incorrectly used as a synonym for tragic flaw. In Richard Wright's *Native Son,* the act that seals Bigger Thomas's fate is his first impulsive murder.

Harlem Renaissance: The Harlem Renaissance of the 1920s is generally considered the first significant movement of black writers and artists in the United States. During this period, new and established black writers published more fiction and poetry than ever before, the first influential black literary journals were established, and black authors and artists received their first widespread recognition and serious critical appraisal. Among the major writers associated with this period are Claude McKay, Jean Toomer, Countee Cullen, Langston Hughes, Arna Bontemps, Nella Larsen, and Zora Neale Hurston. Works representative of the Harlem Renaissance include Arna Bontemps's poems "The Return" and "Golgotha Is a Mountain," Claude McKay's novel *Home to Harlem,* Nella Larsen's novel *Passing,* Langston Hughes's poem "The Negro Speaks of Rivers," and the journals *Crisis* and *Opportunity,* both founded during this period. Also known as Negro Renaissance and New Negro Movement.

Harlequin: A stock character of the *commedia dell'arte* who occasionally interrupted the action with silly antics. Harlequin first appeared on the English stage in John Day's *The Travailes of the Three English Brothers.* The San Francisco Mime Troupe is one of the few modern groups to adapt Harlequin to the needs of contemporary satire.

Hellenism: Imitation of ancient Greek thought or styles. Also, an approach to life that focuses on the growth and development of the intellect. "Hellenism" is sometimes used to refer to the belief that reason can be applied to examine all human experience. A cogent discussion of Hellenism can be found in Matthew Arnold's *Culture and Anarchy.*

Heptameter: See *Meter*

Hero/Heroine: The principal sympathetic character (male or female) in a literary work. Heroes and heroines typically exhibit admirable traits: ideal-ism, courage, and integrity, for example. Famous heroes and heroines include Pip in Charles Dickens's *Great Expectations,* the anonymous narrator in Ralph Ellison's *Invisible Man,* and Sethe in Toni Morrison's *Beloved.*

Heroic Couplet: A rhyming couplet written in iambic pentameter (a verse with five iambic feet). The following lines by Alexander Pope are an example: "Truth guards the Poet, sanctifies the line,/ And makes Immortal, Verse as mean as mine."

Heroic Line: The meter and length of a line of verse in epic or heroic poetry. This varies by language and time period. For example, in English poetry, the heroic line is iambic pentameter (a verse with five iambic feet); in French, the alexandrine (a verse with six iambic feet); in classical literature, dactylic hexameter (a verse with six dactylic feet).

Heroine: See *Hero/Heroine*

Hexameter: See *Meter*

Historical Criticism: The study of a work based on its impact on the world of the time period in which it was written. Examples of postmodern historical criticism can be found in the work of Michel Foucault, Hayden White, Stephen Greenblatt, and Jonathan Goldberg.

Hokku: See *Haiku*

Holocaust: See *Holocaust Literature*

Holocaust Literature: Literature influenced by or written about the Holocaust of World War II. Such literature includes true stories of survival in concentration camps, escape, and life after the war, as well as fictional works and poetry. Representative works of Holocaust literature include Saul Bellow's *Mr. Sammler's Planet,* Anne Frank's *The Diary of a Young Girl,* Jerzy Kosinski's *The Painted Bird,* Arthur Miller's *Incident at Vichy,* Czeslaw Milosz's *Collected Poems,* William Styron's *Sophie's Choice,* and Art Spiegelman's *Maus.*

Homeric Simile: An elaborate, detailed comparison written as a simile many lines in length. An example of an epic simile from John Milton's *Paradise Lost* follows: Angel Forms, who lay entranced Thick as autumnal leaves that strow the brooks In Vallombrosa, where the Etrurian shades High over-arched embower; or scattered sedge Afloat, when with fierce winds Orion armed Hath vexed the Red-Sea coast, whose waves o'erthrew Busiris and his Memphian chivalry, While with perfidious hatred they pursued The sojourners of

Goshen, who beheld From the safe shore their floating carcasses And broken chariot-wheels. Also known as Epic Simile.

Horatian Satire: See *Satire*

Humanism: A philosophy that places faith in the dignity of humankind and rejects the medieval perception of the individual as a weak, fallen creature. ''Humanists'' typically believe in the perfectibility of human nature and view reason and education as the means to that end. Humanist thought is represented in the works of Marsilio Ficino, Ludovico Castelvetro, Edmund Spenser, John Milton, Dean John Colet, Desiderius Erasmus, John Dryden, Alexander Pope, Matthew Arnold, and Irving Babbitt.

Humors: Mentions of the humors refer to the ancient Greek theory that a person's health and personality were determined by the balance of four basic fluids in the body: blood, phlegm, yellow bile, and black bile. A dominance of any fluid would cause extremes in behavior. An excess of blood created a sanguine person who was joyful, aggressive, and passionate; a phlegmatic person was shy, fearful, and sluggish; too much yellow bile led to a choleric temperament characterized by impatience, anger, bitterness, and stubbornness; and excessive black bile created melancholy, a state of laziness, gluttony, and lack of motivation. Literary treatment of the humors is exemplified by several characters in Ben Jonson's plays *Every Man in His Humour* and *Every Man out of His Humour.* Also spelled Humours.

Humours: See *Humors*

Hyperbole: In literary criticism, deliberate exaggeration used to achieve an effect. In William Shakespeare's *Macbeth,* Lady Macbeth hyperbolizes when she says, ''All the perfumes of Arabia could not sweeten this little hand.''

I

Iamb: See *Foot*

Idiom: A word construction or verbal expression closely associated with a given language. For example, in colloquial English the construction ''how come'' can be used instead of ''why'' to introduce a question. Similarly, ''a piece of cake'' is sometimes used to describe a task that is easily done.

Image: A concrete representation of an object or sensory experience. Typically, such a representation helps evoke the feelings associated with the object or experience itself. Images are either ''literal'' or ''figurative.'' Literal images are especially concrete and involve little or no extension of the obvious meaning of the words used to express them. Figurative images do not follow the literal meaning of the words exactly. Images in literature are usually visual, but the term ''image'' can also refer to the representation of any sensory experience. In his poem ''The Shepherd's Hour,'' Paul Verlaine presents the following image: ''The Moon is red through horizon's fog;/ In a dancing mist the hazy meadow sleeps.'' The first line is broadly literal, while the second line involves turns of meaning associated with dancing and sleeping.

Imagery: The array of images in a literary work. Also, figurative language. William Butler Yeats's ''The Second Coming'' offers a powerful image of encroaching anarchy: Turning and turning in the widening gyre The falcon cannot hear the falconer; Things fall apart. . . .

Imagism: An English and American poetry movement that flourished between 1908 and 1917. The Imagists used precise, clearly presented images in their works. They also used common, everyday speech and aimed for conciseness, concrete imagery, and the creation of new rhythms. Participants in the Imagist movement included Ezra Pound, H. D. (Hilda Doolittle), and Amy Lowell, among others.

In medias res: A Latin term meaning ''in the middle of things.'' It refers to the technique of beginning a story at its midpoint and then using various flashback devices to reveal previous action. This technique originated in such epics as Virgil's *Aeneid.*

Induction: The process of reaching a conclusion by reasoning from specific premises to form a general premise. Also, an introductory portion of a work of literature, especially a play. Geoffrey Chaucer's ''Prologue'' to the *Canterbury Tales,* Thomas Sackville's ''Induction'' to *The Mirror of Magistrates,* and the opening scene in William Shakespeare's *The Taming of the Shrew* are examples of inductions to literary works.

Intentional Fallacy: The belief that judgments of a literary work based solely on an author's stated or implied intentions are false and misleading. Critics who believe in the concept of the intentional fallacy typically argue that the work itself is sufficient matter for interpretation, even though they may concede that an author's statement of purpose can be useful. Analysis of William Wordsworth's *Lyri-*

cal Ballads based on the observations about poetry he makes in his "Preface" to the second edition of that work is an example of the intentional fallacy.

Interior Monologue: A narrative technique in which characters' thoughts are revealed in a way that appears to be uncontrolled by the author. The interior monologue typically aims to reveal the inner self of a character. It portrays emotional experiences as they occur at both a conscious and unconscious level. images are often used to represent sensations or emotions. One of the best-known interior monologues in English is the Molly Bloom section at the close of James Joyce's *Ulysses*. The interior monologue is also common in the works of Virginia Woolf.

Internal Rhyme: Rhyme that occurs within a single line of verse. An example is in the opening line of Edgar Allan Poe's "The Raven": "Once upon a midnight dreary, while I pondered weak and weary." Here, "dreary" and "weary" make an internal rhyme.

Irish Literary Renaissance: A late nineteenth- and early twentieth-century movement in Irish literature. Members of the movement aimed to reduce the influence of British culture in Ireland and create an Irish national literature. William Butler Yeats, George Moore, and Sean O'Casey are three of the best-known figures of the movement.

Irony: In literary criticism, the effect of language in which the intended meaning is the opposite of what is stated. The title of Jonathan Swift's "A Modest Proposal" is ironic because what Swift proposes in this essay is cannibalism—hardly "modest."

Italian Sonnet: See *Sonnet*

J

Jacobean Age: The period of the reign of James I of England (1603-1625). The early literature of this period reflected the worldview of the Elizabethan Age, but a darker, more cynical attitude steadily grew in the art and literature of the Jacobean Age. This was an important time for English drama and poetry. Milestones include William Shakespeare's tragedies, tragi-comedies, and sonnets; Ben Jonson's various dramas; and John Donne's metaphysical poetry.

Jargon: Language that is used or understood only by a select group of people. Jargon may refer to terminology used in a certain profession, such as computer jargon, or it may refer to any nonsensical language that is not understood by most people. Literary examples of jargon are Francois Villon's *Ballades en jargon,* which is composed in the secret language of the *coquillards,* and Anthony Burgess's *A Clockwork Orange,* narrated in the fictional characters' language of "Nadsat."

Juvenalian Satire: See *Satire*

K

Knickerbocker Group: A somewhat indistinct group of New York writers of the first half of the nineteenth century. Members of the group were linked only by location and a common theme: New York life. Two famous members of the Knickerbocker Group were Washington Irving and William Cullen Bryant. The group's name derives from Irving's *Knickerbocker's History of New York.*

L

Lais: See *Lay*

Lay: A song or simple narrative poem. The form originated in medieval France. Early French *lais* were often based on the Celtic legends and other tales sung by Breton minstrels—thus the name of the "Breton lay." In fourteenth-century England, the term "lay" was used to describe short narratives written in imitation of the Breton lays. The most notable of these is Geoffrey Chaucer's "The Minstrel's Tale."

Leitmotiv: See *Motif*

Literal Language: An author uses literal language when he or she writes without exaggerating or embellishing the subject matter and without any tools of figurative language. To say "He ran very quickly down the street" is to use literal language, whereas to say "He ran like a hare down the street" would be using figurative language.

Literary Ballad: See *Ballad*

Literature: Literature is broadly defined as any written or spoken material, but the term most often refers to creative works. Literature includes poetry, drama, fiction, and many kinds of nonfiction writing, as well as oral, dramatic, and broadcast compositions not necessarily preserved in a written format, such as films and television programs.

Lost Generation: A term first used by Gertrude Stein to describe the post-World War I generation of American writers: men and women haunted by a sense of betrayal and emptiness brought about by the destructiveness of the war. The term is commonly applied to Hart Crane, Ernest Hemingway, F. Scott Fitzgerald, and others.

Lyric Poetry: A poem expressing the subjective feelings and personal emotions of the poet. Such poetry is melodic, since it was originally accompanied by a lyre in recitals. Most Western poetry in the twentieth century may be classified as lyrical. Examples of lyric poetry include A. E. Housman's elegy ''To an Athlete Dying Young,'' the odes of Pindar and Horace, Thomas Gray and William Collins, the sonnets of Sir Thomas Wyatt and Sir Philip Sidney, Elizabeth Barrett Browning and Rainer Maria Rilke, and a host of other forms in the poetry of William Blake and Christina Rossetti, among many others.

M

Mannerism: Exaggerated, artificial adherence to a literary manner or style. Also, a popular style of the visual arts of late sixteenth-century Europe that was marked by elongation of the human form and by intentional spatial distortion. Literary works that are self-consciously high-toned and artistic are often said to be ''mannered.'' Authors of such works include Henry James and Gertrude Stein.

Masculine Rhyme: See *Rhyme*

Masque: A lavish and elaborate form of entertainment, often performed in royal courts, that emphasizes song, dance, and costumery. The Renaissance form of the masque grew out of the spectacles of masked figures common in medieval England and Europe. The masque reached its peak of popularity and development in seventeenth-century England, during the reigns of James I and, especially, of Charles I. Ben Jonson, the most significant masque writer, also created the ''antimasque,'' which incorporates elements of humor and the grotesque into the traditional masque and achieved greater dramatic quality. Masque-like interludes appear in Edmund Spenser's *The Faerie Queene* and in William Shakespeare's *The Tempest.* One of the best-known English masques is John Milton's *Comus.*

Measure: The foot, verse, or time sequence used in a literary work, especially a poem. Measure is often used somewhat incorrectly as a synonym for meter.

Melodrama: A play in which the typical plot is a conflict between characters who personify extreme good and evil. Melodramas usually end happily and

emphasize sensationalism. Other literary forms that use the same techniques are often labeled ''melodramatic.'' The term was formerly used to describe a combination of drama and music; as such, it was synonymous with ''opera.'' Augustin Daly's *Under the Gaslight* and Dion Boucicault's *The Octoroon, The Colleen Bawn,* and *The Poor of New York* are examples of melodramas. The most popular media for twentieth-century melodramas are motion pictures and television.

Metaphor: A figure of speech that expresses an idea through the image of another object. Metaphors suggest the essence of the first object by identifying it with certain qualities of the second object. An example is ''But soft, what light through yonder window breaks?/ It is the east, and Juliet is the sun'' in William Shakespeare's *Romeo and Juliet.* Here, Juliet, the first object, is identified with qualities of the second object, the sun.

Metaphysical Conceit: See *Conceit*

Metaphysical Poetry: The body of poetry produced by a group of seventeenth-century English writers called the ''Metaphysical Poets.'' The group includes John Donne and Andrew Marvell. The Metaphysical Poets made use of everyday speech, intellectual analysis, and unique imagery. They aimed to portray the ordinary conflicts and contradictions of life. Their poems often took the form of an argument, and many of them emphasize physical and religious love as well as the fleeting nature of life. Elaborate conceits are typical in metaphysical poetry. Marvell's ''To His Coy Mistress'' is a well-known example of a metaphysical poem.

Metaphysical Poets: See *Metaphysical Poetry*

Meter: In literary criticism, the repetition of sound patterns that creates a rhythm in poetry. The patterns are based on the number of syllables and the presence and absence of accents. The unit of rhythm in a line is called a foot. Types of meter are classified according to the number of feet in a line. These are the standard English lines: Monometer, one foot; Dimeter, two feet; Trimeter, three feet; Tetrameter, four feet; Pentameter, five feet; Hexameter, six feet (also called the Alexandrine); Heptameter, seven feet (also called the ''Fourteener'' when the feet are iambic). The most common English meter is the iambic pentameter, in which each line contains ten syllables, or five iambic feet, which individually are composed of an unstressed syllable followed by an accented syllable. Both of the following lines from Alfred, Lord Tennyson's

"Ulysses" are written in iambic pentameter: Made weak by time and fate, but strong in will To strive, to seek, to find, and not to yield.

Mise en scene: The costumes, scenery, and other properties of a drama. Herbert Beerbohm Tree was renowned for the elaborate *mises en scene* of his lavish Shakespearean productions at His Majesty's Theatre between 1897 and 1915.

Modernism: Modern literary practices. Also, the principles of a literary school that lasted from roughly the beginning of the twentieth century until the end of World War II. Modernism is defined by its rejection of the literary conventions of the nineteenth century and by its opposition to conventional morality, taste, traditions, and economic values. Many writers are associated with the concepts of Modernism, including Albert Camus, Marcel Proust, D. H. Lawrence, W. H. Auden, Ernest Hemingway, William Faulkner, William Butler Yeats, Thomas Mann, Tennessee Williams, Eugene O'Neill, and James Joyce.

Monologue: A composition, written or oral, by a single individual. More specifically, a speech given by a single individual in a drama or other public entertainment. It has no set length, although it is usually several or more lines long. An example of an "extended monologue"—that is, a monologue of great length and seriousness—occurs in the one-act, one-character play *The Stronger* by August Strindberg.

Monometer: See *Meter*

Mood: The prevailing emotions of a work or of the author in his or her creation of the work. The mood of a work is not always what might be expected based on its subject matter. The poem "Dover Beach" by Matthew Arnold offers examples of two different moods originating from the same experience: watching the ocean at night. The mood of the first three lines— The sea is calm tonight The tide is full, the moon lies fair Upon the straights. . . . is in sharp contrast to the mood of the last three lines— And we are here as on a darkling plain Swept with confused alarms of struggle and flight, Where ignorant armies clash by night.

Motif: A theme, character type, image, metaphor, or other verbal element that recurs throughout a single work of literature or occurs in a number of different works over a period of time. For example, the various manifestations of the color white in Herman

Melville's *Moby Dick* is a "specific" *motif*, while the trials of star-crossed lovers is a "conventional" *motif* from the literature of all periods. Also known as *Motiv* or *Leitmotiv*.

Motiv: See *Motif*

Muckrakers: An early twentieth-century group of American writers. Typically, their works exposed the wrongdoings of big business and government in the United States. Upton Sinclair's *The Jungle* exemplifies the muckraking novel.

Muses: Nine Greek mythological goddesses, the daughters of Zeus and Mnemosyne (Memory). Each muse patronized a specific area of the liberal arts and sciences. Calliope presided over epic poetry, Clio over history, Erato over love poetry, Euterpe over music or lyric poetry, Melpomene over tragedy, Polyhymnia over hymns to the gods, Terpsichore over dance, Thalia over comedy, and Urania over astronomy. Poets and writers traditionally made appeals to the Muses for inspiration in their work. John Milton invokes the aid of a muse at the beginning of the first book of his *Paradise Lost:* Of Man's First disobedience, and the Fruit of the Forbidden Tree, whose mortal taste Brought Death into the World, and all our woe, With loss of Eden, till one greater Man Restore us, and regain the blissful Seat, Sing Heav'nly Muse, that on the secret top of Oreb, or of Sinai, didst inspire That Shepherd, who first taught the chosen Seed, In the Beginning how the Heav'ns and Earth Rose out of Chaos. . . .

Mystery: See *Suspense*

Myth: An anonymous tale emerging from the traditional beliefs of a culture or social unit. Myths use supernatural explanations for natural phenomena. They may also explain cosmic issues like creation and death. Collections of myths, known as mythologies, are common to all cultures and nations, but the best-known myths belong to the Norse, Roman, and Greek mythologies. A famous myth is the story of Arachne, an arrogant young girl who challenged a goddess, Athena, to a weaving contest; when the girl won, Athena was enraged and turned Arachne into a spider, thus explaining the existence of spiders.

N

Narration: The telling of a series of events, real or invented. A narration may be either a simple narrative, in which the events are recounted chronologically, or a narrative with a plot, in which the account is given in a style reflecting the author's artistic concept of the story. Narration is sometimes used as a synonym for ''storyline.'' The recounting of scary stories around a campfire is a form of narration.

Narrative: A verse or prose accounting of an event or sequence of events, real or invented. The term is also used as an adjective in the sense ''method of narration.'' For example, in literary criticism, the expression ''narrative technique'' usually refers to the way the author structures and presents his or her story. Narratives range from the shortest accounts of events, as in Julius Caesar's remark, ''I came, I saw, I conquered,'' to the longest historical or biographical works, as in Edward Gibbon's *The Decline and Fall of the Roman Empire,* as well as diaries, travelogues, novels, ballads, epics, short stories, and other fictional forms.

Narrative Poetry: A nondramatic poem in which the author tells a story. Such poems may be of any length or level of complexity. Epics such as *Beowulf* and ballads are forms of narrative poetry.

Narrator: The teller of a story. The narrator may be the author or a character in the story through whom the author speaks. Huckleberry Finn is the narrator of Mark Twain's *The Adventures of Huckleberry Finn.*

Naturalism: A literary movement of the late nineteenth and early twentieth centuries. The movement's major theorist, French novelist Emile Zola, envisioned a type of fiction that would examine human life with the objectivity of scientific inquiry. The Naturalists typically viewed human beings as either the products of ''biological determinism,'' ruled by hereditary instincts and engaged in an endless struggle for survival, or as the products of ''socioeconomic determinism,'' ruled by social and economic forces beyond their control. In their works, the Naturalists generally ignored the highest levels of society and focused on degradation: poverty, alcoholism, prostitution, insanity, and disease. Naturalism influenced authors throughout the world, including Henrik Ibsen and Thomas Hardy. In the United States, in particular, Naturalism had a profound impact. Among the authors who embraced its principles are Theodore Dreiser, Eugene O'Neill, Stephen Crane, Jack London, and Frank Norris.

Negritude: A literary movement based on the concept of a shared cultural bond on the part of black Africans, wherever they may be in the world. It traces its origins to the former French colonies of Africa and the Caribbean. Negritude poets, novelists, and essayists generally stress four points in their writings: One, black alienation from traditional African culture can lead to feelings of inferiority. Two, European colonialism and Western education should be resisted. Three, black Africans should seek to affirm and define their own identity. Four, African culture can and should be reclaimed. Many Negritude writers also claim that blacks can make unique contributions to the world, based on a heightened appreciation of nature, rhythm, and human emotions—aspects of life they say are not so highly valued in the materialistic and rationalistic West. Examples of Negritude literature include the poetry of both Senegalese Leopold Senghor in *Hosties noires* and Martiniquais Aime-Fernand Cesaire in *Return to My Native Land.*

Negro Renaissance: See *Harlem Renaissance*

Neoclassical Period: See *Neoclassicism*

Neoclassicism: In literary criticism, this term refers to the revival of the attitudes and styles of expression of classical literature. It is generally used to describe a period in European history beginning in the late seventeenth century and lasting until about 1800. In its purest form, Neoclassicism marked a return to order, proportion, restraint, logic, accuracy, and decorum. In England, where Neoclassicism perhaps was most popular, it reflected the influence of seventeenth- century French writers, especially dramatists. Neoclassical writers typically reacted against the intensity and enthusiasm of the Renaissance period. They wrote works that appealed to the intellect, using elevated language and classical literary forms such as satire and the ode. Neoclassical works were often governed by the classical goal of instruction. English neoclassicists included Alexander Pope, Jonathan Swift, Joseph Addison, Sir Richard Steele, John Gay, and Matthew Prior; French neoclassicists included Pierre Corneille and Jean-Baptiste Moliere. Also known as Age of Reason.

Neoclassicists: See *Neoclassicism*

New Criticism: A movement in literary criticism, dating from the late 1920s, that stressed close textual analysis in the interpretation of works of literature. The New Critics saw little merit in historical and biographical analysis. Rather, they aimed to examine the text alone, free from the question of how external events—biographical or otherwise—may have helped shape it. This predominantly American school was named ''New Criticism'' by one of its practitioners, John Crowe Ransom. Other important New Critics included Allen Tate, R. P. Blackmur, Robert Penn Warren, and Cleanth Brooks.

New Negro Movement: See *Harlem Renaissance*

Noble Savage: The idea that primitive man is noble and good but becomes evil and corrupted as he becomes civilized. The concept of the noble savage originated in the Renaissance period but is more closely identified with such later writers as Jean-Jacques Rousseau and Aphra Behn. First described in John Dryden's play *The Conquest of Granada,* the noble savage is portrayed by the various Native Americans in James Fenimore Cooper's "Leatherstocking Tales," by Queequeg, Daggoo, and Tashtego in Herman Melville's *Moby Dick,* and by John the Savage in Aldous Huxley's *Brave New World.*

O

Objective Correlative: An outward set of objects, a situation, or a chain of events corresponding to an inward experience and evoking this experience in the reader. The term frequently appears in modern criticism in discussions of authors' intended effects on the emotional responses of readers. This term was originally used by T. S. Eliot in his 1919 essay "Hamlet."

Objectivity: A quality in writing characterized by the absence of the author's opinion or feeling about the subject matter. Objectivity is an important factor in criticism. The novels of Henry James and, to a certain extent, the poems of John Larkin demonstrate objectivity, and it is central to John Keats's concept of "negative capability." Critical and journalistic writing usually are or attempt to be objective.

Occasional Verse: poetry written on the occasion of a significant historical or personal event. *Vers de societe* is sometimes called occasional verse although it is of a less serious nature. Famous examples of occasional verse include Andrew Marvell's "Horatian Ode upon Cromwell's Return from England," Walt Whitman's "When Lilacs Last in the Dooryard Bloom'd"— written upon the death of Abraham Lincoln—and Edmund Spenser's commemoration of his wedding, "Epithalamion."

Octave: A poem or stanza composed of eight lines. The term octave most often represents the first eight lines of a Petrarchan sonnet. An example of an octave is taken from a translation of a Petrarchan sonnet by Sir Thomas Wyatt: The pillar perisht is whereto I leant, The strongest stay of mine unquiet mind; The like of it no man again can find, From East to West Still seeking though he went. To mind unhap! for hap away hath rent Of all my joy the very

bark and rind; And I, alas, by chance am thus assigned Daily to mourn till death do it relent.

Ode: Name given to an extended lyric poem characterized by exalted emotion and dignified style. An ode usually concerns a single, serious theme. Most odes, but not all, are addressed to an object or individual. Odes are distinguished from other lyric poetic forms by their complex rhythmic and stanzaic patterns. An example of this form is John Keats's "Ode to a Nightingale."

Oedipus Complex: A son's amorous obsession with his mother. The phrase is derived from the story of the ancient Theban hero Oedipus, who unknowingly killed his father and married his mother. Literary occurrences of the Oedipus complex include Andre Gide's *Oedipe* and Jean Cocteau's *La Machine infernale,* as well as the most famous, Sophocles' *Oedipus Rex.*

Omniscience: See *Point of View*

Onomatopoeia: The use of words whose sounds express or suggest their meaning. In its simplest sense, onomatopoeia may be represented by words that mimic the sounds they denote such as "hiss" or "meow." At a more subtle level, the pattern and rhythm of sounds and rhymes of a line or poem may be onomatopoeic. A celebrated example of onomatopoeia is the repetition of the word "bells" in Edgar Allan Poe's poem "The Bells."

Opera: A type of stage performance, usually a drama, in which the dialogue is sung. Classic examples of opera include Giuseppi Verdi's *La traviata,* Giacomo Puccini's *La Boheme,* and Richard Wagner's *Tristan und Isolde.* Major twentieth- century contributors to the form include Richard Strauss and Alban Berg.

Operetta: A usually romantic comic opera. John Gay's *The Beggar's Opera,* Richard Sheridan's *The Duenna,* and numerous works by William Gilbert and Arthur Sullivan are examples of operettas.

Oral Tradition: See *Oral Transmission*

Oral Transmission: A process by which songs, ballads, folklore, and other material are transmitted by word of mouth. The tradition of oral transmission predates the written record systems of literate society. Oral transmission preserves material sometimes over generations, although often with variations. Memory plays a large part in the recitation and preservation of orally transmitted material. Breton lays, French *fabliaux,* national epics (including the Anglo- Saxon *Beowulf,* the Spanish *El Cid,* and the Finnish *Kalevala*), Native American myths and legends, and African folktales told by plantation slaves are examples of orally transmitted literature.

Oration: Formal speaking intended to motivate the listeners to some action or feeling. Such public speaking was much more common before the development of timely printed communication such as newspapers. Famous examples of oration include Abraham Lincoln's ''Gettysburg Address'' and Dr. Martin Luther King Jr.'s ''I Have a Dream'' speech.

Ottava Rima: An eight-line stanza of poetry composed in iambic pentameter (a five-foot line in which each foot consists of an unaccented syllable followed by an accented syllable), following the abababcc rhyme scheme. This form has been prominently used by such important English writers as Lord Byron, Henry Wadsworth Longfellow, and W. B. Yeats.

Oxymoron: A phrase combining two contradictory terms. Oxymorons may be intentional or unintentional. The following speech from William Shakespeare's *Romeo and Juliet* uses several oxymorons: Why, then, O brawling love! O loving hate! O anything, of nothing first create! O heavy lightness! serious vanity! Mis-shapen chaos of well-seeming forms! Feather of lead, bright smoke, cold fire, sick health! This love feel I, that feel no love in this.

P

Pantheism: The idea that all things are both a manifestation or revelation of God and a part of God at the same time. Pantheism was a common attitude in the early societies of Egypt, India, and Greece— the term derives from the Greek *pan* meaning ''all'' and *theos* meaning ''deity.'' It later became a significant part of the Christian faith. William Wordsworth and Ralph Waldo Emerson are among the many writers who have expressed the pantheistic attitude in their works.

Parable: A story intended to teach a moral lesson or answer an ethical question. In the West, the best examples of parables are those of Jesus Christ in the New Testament, notably ''The Prodigal Son,'' but parables also are used in Sufism, rabbinic literature, Hasidism, and Zen Buddhism.

Paradox: A statement that appears illogical or contradictory at first, but may actually point to an underlying truth. ''Less is more'' is an example of a paradox. Literary examples include Francis Ba-

con's statement, ''The most corrected copies are commonly the least correct,'' and ''All animals are equal, but some animals are more equal than others'' from George Orwell's *Animal Farm.*

Parallelism: A method of comparison of two ideas in which each is developed in the same grammatical structure. Ralph Waldo Emerson's ''Civilization'' contains this example of parallelism: Raphael paints wisdom; Handel sings it, Phidias carves it, Shakespeare writes it, Wren builds it, Columbus sails it, Luther preaches it, Washington arms it, Watt mechanizes it.

Parnassianism: A mid nineteenth-century movement in French literature. Followers of the movement stressed adherence to well-defined artistic forms as a reaction against the often chaotic expression of the artist's ego that dominated the work of the Romantics. The Parnassians also rejected the moral, ethical, and social themes exhibited in the works of French Romantics such as Victor Hugo. The aesthetic doctrines of the Parnassians strongly influenced the later symbolist and decadent movements. Members of the Parnassian school include Leconte de Lisle, Sully Prudhomme, Albert Glatigny, Francois Coppee, and Theodore de Banville.

Parody: In literary criticism, this term refers to an imitation of a serious literary work or the signature style of a particular author in a ridiculous manner. A typical parody adopts the style of the original and applies it to an inappropriate subject for humorous effect. Parody is a form of satire and could be considered the literary equivalent of a caricature or cartoon. Henry Fielding's *Shamela* is a parody of Samuel Richardson's *Pamela.*

Pastoral: A term derived from the Latin word ''pastor,'' meaning shepherd. A pastoral is a literary composition on a rural theme. The conventions of the pastoral were originated by the third-century Greek poet Theocritus, who wrote about the experiences, love affairs, and pastimes of Sicilian shepherds. In a pastoral, characters and language of a courtly nature are often placed in a simple setting. The term pastoral is also used to classify dramas, elegies, and lyrics that exhibit the use of country settings and shepherd characters. Percy Bysshe Shelley's ''Adonais'' and John Milton's ''Lycidas'' are two famous examples of pastorals.

Pastorela: The Spanish name for the shepherds play, a folk drama reenacted during the Christmas season. Examples of *pastorelas* include Gomez

Manrique's *Representacion del nacimiento* and the dramas of Lucas Fernandez and Juan del Encina.

Pathetic Fallacy: A term coined by English critic John Ruskin to identify writing that falsely endows nonhuman things with human intentions and feelings, such as "angry clouds" and "sad trees." The pathetic fallacy is a required convention in the classical poetic form of the pastoral elegy, and it is used in the modern poetry of T. S. Eliot, Ezra Pound, and the Imagists. Also known as Poetic Fallacy.

Pelado: Literally the "skinned one" or shirtless one, he was the stock underdog, sharp-witted picaresque character of Mexican vaudeville and tent shows. The *pelado* is found in such works as Don Catarino's *Los effectos de la crisis* and *Regreso a mi tierra.*

Pen Name: See *Pseudonym*

Pentameter: See *Meter*

Persona: A Latin term meaning "mask." *Personae* are the characters in a fictional work of literature. The *persona* generally functions as a mask through which the author tells a story in a voice other than his or her own. A *persona* is usually either a character in a story who acts as a narrator or an "implied author," a voice created by the author to act as the narrator for himself or herself. *Personae* include the narrator of Geoffrey Chaucer's *Canterbury Tales* and Marlow in Joseph Conrad's *Heart of Darkness.*

Personae: See *Persona*

Personal Point of View: See *Point of View*

Personification: A figure of speech that gives human qualities to abstract ideas, animals, and inanimate objects. William Shakespeare used personification in *Romeo and Juliet* in the lines "Arise, fair sun, and kill the envious moon,/ Who is already sick and pale with grief." Here, the moon is portrayed as being envious, sick, and pale with grief— all markedly human qualities. Also known as *Prosopopoeia.*

Petrarchan Sonnet: See *Sonnet*

Phenomenology: A method of literary criticism based on the belief that things have no existence outside of human consciousness or awareness. Proponents of this theory believe that art is a process that takes place in the mind of the observer as he or she contemplates an object rather than a quality of the object itself. Among phenomenological critics

are Edmund Husserl, George Poulet, Marcel Raymond, and Roman Ingarden.

Picaresque Novel: Episodic fiction depicting the adventures of a roguish central character ("picaro" is Spanish for "rogue"). The picaresque hero is commonly a low-born but clever individual who wanders into and out of various affairs of love, danger, and farcical intrigue. These involvements may take place at all social levels and typically present a humorous and wide-ranging satire of a given society. Prominent examples of the picaresque novel are *Don Quixote* by Miguel de Cervantes, *Tom Jones* by Henry Fielding, and *Moll Flanders* by Daniel Defoe.

Plagiarism: Claiming another person's written material as one's own. Plagiarism can take the form of direct, word-for- word copying or the theft of the substance or idea of the work. A student who copies an encyclopedia entry and turns it in as a report for school is guilty of plagiarism.

Platonic Criticism: A form of criticism that stresses an artistic work's usefulness as an agent of social engineering rather than any quality or value of the work itself. Platonic criticism takes as its starting point the ancient Greek philosopher Plato's comments on art in his *Republic.*

Platonism: The embracing of the doctrines of the philosopher Plato, popular among the poets of the Renaissance and the Romantic period. Platonism is more flexible than Aristotelian Criticism and places more emphasis on the supernatural and unknown aspects of life. Platonism is expressed in the love poetry of the Renaissance, the fourth book of Baldassare Castiglione's *The Book of the Courtier,* and the poetry of William Blake, William Wordsworth, Percy Bysshe Shelley, Friedrich Holderlin, William Butler Yeats, and Wallace Stevens.

Play: See *Drama*

Plot: In literary criticism, this term refers to the pattern of events in a narrative or drama. In its simplest sense, the plot guides the author in composing the work and helps the reader follow the work. Typically, plots exhibit causality and unity and have a beginning, a middle, and an end. Sometimes, however, a plot may consist of a series of disconnected events, in which case it is known as an "episodic plot." In his *Aspects of the Novel,* E. M. Forster distinguishes between a story, defined as a "narrative of events arranged in their time- sequence," and plot, which organizes the events to a ''sense of causality.'' This definition closely mirrors Aristotle's discussion of plot in his *Poetics.*

Poem: In its broadest sense, a composition utilizing rhyme, meter, concrete detail, and expressive language to create a literary experience with emotional and aesthetic appeal. Typical poems include sonnets, odes, elegies, *haiku,* ballads, and free verse.

Poet: An author who writes poetry or verse. The term is also used to refer to an artist or writer who has an exceptional gift for expression, imagination, and energy in the making of art in any form. Well-known poets include Horace, Basho, Sir Philip Sidney, Sir Edmund Spenser, John Donne, Andrew Marvell, Alexander Pope, Jonathan Swift, George Gordon, Lord Byron, John Keats, Christina Rossetti, W. H. Auden, Stevie Smith, and Sylvia Plath.

Poetic Fallacy: See *Pathetic Fallacy*

Poetic Justice: An outcome in a literary work, not necessarily a poem, in which the good are rewarded and the evil are punished, especially in ways that particularly fit their virtues or crimes. For example, a murderer may himself be murdered, or a thief will find himself penniless.

Poetic License: Distortions of fact and literary convention made by a writer—not always a poet—for the sake of the effect gained. Poetic license is closely related to the concept of ''artistic freedom.'' An author exercises poetic license by saying that a pile of money ''reaches as high as a mountain'' when the pile is actually only a foot or two high.

Poetics: This term has two closely related meanings. It denotes (1) an aesthetic theory in literary criticism about the essence of poetry or (2) rules prescribing the proper methods, content, style, or diction of poetry. The term poetics may also refer to theories about literature in general, not just poetry.

Poetry: In its broadest sense, writing that aims to present ideas and evoke an emotional experience in the reader through the use of meter, imagery, connotative and concrete words, and a carefully constructed structure based on rhythmic patterns. Poetry typically relies on words and expressions that have several layers of meaning. It also makes use of the effects of regular rhythm on the ear and may make a strong appeal to the senses through the use of imagery. Edgar Allan Poe's ''Annabel Lee'' and Walt Whitman's *Leaves of Grass* are famous examples of poetry.

Point of View: The narrative perspective from which a literary work is presented to the reader.

There are four traditional points of view. The ''third person omniscient'' gives the reader a ''godlike'' perspective, unrestricted by time or place, from which to see actions and look into the minds of characters. This allows the author to comment openly on characters and events in the work. The ''third person'' point of view presents the events of the story from outside of any single character's perception, much like the omniscient point of view, but the reader must understand the action as it takes place and without any special insight into characters' minds or motivations. The ''first person'' or ''personal'' point of view relates events as they are perceived by a single character. The main character ''tells'' the story and may offer opinions about the action and characters which differ from those of the author. Much less common than omniscient, third person, and first person is the ''second person'' point of view, wherein the author tells the story as if it is happening to the reader. James Thurber employs the omniscient point of view in his short story ''The Secret Life of Walter Mitty.'' Ernest Hemingway's ''A Clean, Well-Lighted Place'' is a short story told from the third person point of view. Mark Twain's novel *Huck Finn* is presented from the first person viewpoint. Jay McInerney's *Bright Lights, Big City* is an example of a novel which uses the second person point of view.

Polemic: A work in which the author takes a stand on a controversial subject, such as abortion or religion. Such works are often extremely argumentative or provocative. Classic examples of polemics include John Milton's *Aeropagitica* and Thomas Paine's *The American Crisis.*

Pornography: Writing intended to provoke feelings of lust in the reader. Such works are often condemned by critics and teachers, but those which can be shown to have literary value are viewed less harshly. Literary works that have been described as pornographic include Ovid's *The Art of Love,* Margaret of Angouleme's *Heptameron,* John Cleland's *Memoirs of a Woman of Pleasure; or, the Life of Fanny Hill,* the anonymous *My Secret Life,* D. H. Lawrence's *Lady Chatterley's Lover,* and Vladimir Nabokov's *Lolita.*

Post-Aesthetic Movement: An artistic response made by African Americans to the black aesthetic movement of the 1960s and early '70s. Writers since that time have adopted a somewhat different tone in their work, with less emphasis placed on the disparity between black and white in the United States. In the words of post-aesthetic authors such as Toni Morrison, John Edgar Wideman, and Kristin Hunter, African Americans are portrayed as looking inward for answers to their own questions, rather than always looking to the outside world. Two well-known examples of works produced as part of the post-aesthetic movement are the Pulitzer Prize-winning novels *The Color Purple* by Alice Walker and *Beloved* by Toni Morrison.

Postmodernism: Writing from the 1960s forward characterized by experimentation and continuing to apply some of the fundamentals of modernism, which included existentialism and alienation. Postmodernists have gone a step further in the rejection of tradition begun with the modernists by also rejecting traditional forms, preferring the anti-novel over the novel and the anti-hero over the hero. Postmodern writers include Alain Robbe-Grillet, Thomas Pynchon, Margaret Drabble, John Fowles, Adolfo Bioy-Casares, and Gabriel Garcia Marquez.

Pre-Raphaelites: A circle of writers and artists in mid nineteenth-century England. Valuing the pre-Renaissance artistic qualities of religious symbolism, lavish pictorialism, and natural sensuousness, the Pre-Raphaelites cultivated a sense of mystery and melancholy that influenced later writers associated with the Symbolist and Decadent movements. The major members of the group include Dante Gabriel Rossetti, Christina Rossetti, Algernon Swinburne, and Walter Pater.

Primitivism: The belief that primitive peoples were nobler and less flawed than civilized peoples because they had not been subjected to the tainting influence of society. Examples of literature espousing primitivism include Aphra Behn's *Oroonoko: Or, The History of the Royal Slave,* Jean-Jacques Rousseau's *Julie ou la Nouvelle Heloise,* Oliver Goldsmith's *The Deserted Village,* the poems of Robert Burns, Herman Melville's stories *Typee, Omoo,* and *Mardi,* many poems of William Butler Yeats and Robert Frost, and William Golding's novel *Lord of the Flies.*

Projective Verse: A form of free verse in which the poet's breathing pattern determines the lines of the poem. Poets who advocate projective verse are against all formal structures in writing, including meter and form. Besides its creators, Robert Creeley, Robert Duncan, and Charles Olson, two other well-known projective verse poets are Denise Levertov and LeRoi Jones (Amiri Baraka). Also known as Breath Verse.

Prologue: An introductory section of a literary work. It often contains information establishing the situation of the characters or presents information about the setting, time period, or action. In drama, the prologue is spoken by a chorus or by one of the principal characters. In the "General Prologue" of *The Canterbury Tales,* Geoffrey Chaucer describes the main characters and establishes the setting and purpose of the work.

Prose: A literary medium that attempts to mirror the language of everyday speech. It is distinguished from poetry by its use of unmetered, unrhymed language consisting of logically related sentences. Prose is usually grouped into paragraphs that form a cohesive whole such as an essay or a novel. Recognized masters of English prose writing include Sir Thomas Malory, William Caxton, Raphael Holinshed, Joseph Addison, Mark Twain, and Ernest Hemingway.

Prosopopoeia: See *Personification*

Protagonist: The central character of a story who serves as a focus for its themes and incidents and as the principal rationale for its development. The protagonist is sometimes referred to in discussions of modern literature as the hero or anti-hero. Well-known protagonists are Hamlet in William Shakespeare's *Hamlet* and Jay Gatsby in F. Scott Fitzgerald's *The Great Gatsby.*

Protest Fiction: Protest fiction has as its primary purpose the protesting of some social injustice, such as racism or discrimination. One example of protest fiction is a series of five novels by Chester Himes, beginning in 1945 with *If He Hollers Let Him Go* and ending in 1955 with *The Primitive.* These works depict the destructive effects of race and gender stereotyping in the context of interracial relationships. Another African American author whose works often revolve around themes of social protest is John Oliver Killens. James Baldwin's essay "Everybody's Protest Novel" generated controversy by attacking the authors of protest fiction.

Proverb: A brief, sage saying that expresses a truth about life in a striking manner. "They are not all cooks who carry long knives" is an example of a proverb.

Pseudonym: A name assumed by a writer, most often intended to prevent his or her identification as the author of a work. Two or more authors may work together under one pseudonym, or an author may use a different name for each genre he or she publishes in. Some publishing companies maintain "house pseudonyms," under which any number of authors may write installations in a series. Some authors also choose a pseudonym over their real names the way an actor may use a stage name. Examples of pseudonyms (with the author's real name in parentheses) include Voltaire (Francois-Marie Arouet), Novalis (Friedrich von Hardenberg), Currer Bell (Charlotte Bronte), Ellis Bell (Emily Bronte), George Eliot (Maryann Evans), Honorio Bustos Donmecq (Adolfo Bioy-Casares and Jorge Luis Borges), and Richard Bachman (Stephen King).

Pun: A play on words that have similar sounds but different meanings. A serious example of the pun is from John Donne's "A Hymne to God the Father": Sweare by thyself, that at my death thy sonne Shall shine as he shines now, and hereto fore; And, having done that, Thou haste done; I fear no more.

Pure Poetry: poetry written without instructional intent or moral purpose that aims only to please a reader by its imagery or musical flow. The term pure poetry is used as the antonym of the term "didacticism." The poetry of Edgar Allan Poe, Stephane Mallarme, Paul Verlaine, Paul Valery, Juan Ramoz Jimenez, and Jorge Guillen offer examples of pure poetry.

Q

Quatrain: A four-line stanza of a poem or an entire poem consisting of four lines. The following quatrain is from Robert Herrick's "To Live Merrily, and to Trust to Good Verses": Round, round, the root do's run; And being ravisht thus, Come, I will drink a Tun To my *Propertius*.

R

Raisonneur: A character in a drama who functions as a spokesperson for the dramatist's views. The *raisonneur* typically observes the play without becoming central to its action. *Raisonneurs* were very common in plays of the nineteenth century.

Realism: A nineteenth-century European literary movement that sought to portray familiar characters, situations, and settings in a realistic manner. This was done primarily by using an objective narrative point of view and through the buildup of accurate detail. The standard for success of any realistic work depends on how faithfully it transfers common experience into fictional forms. The realistic method may be altered or extended, as in stream of consciousness writing, to record highly subjec-

tive experience. Seminal authors in the tradition of Realism include Honore de Balzac, Gustave Flaubert, and Henry James.

Refrain: A phrase repeated at intervals throughout a poem. A refrain may appear at the end of each stanza or at less regular intervals. It may be altered slightly at each appearance. Some refrains are nonsense expressions—as with "Nevermore" in Edgar Allan Poe's "The Raven"—that seem to take on a different significance with each use.

Renaissance: The period in European history that marked the end of the Middle Ages. It began in Italy in the late fourteenth century. In broad terms, it is usually seen as spanning the fourteenth, fifteenth, and sixteenth centuries, although it did not reach Great Britain, for example, until the 1480s or so. The Renaissance saw an awakening in almost every sphere of human activity, especially science, philosophy, and the arts. The period is best defined by the emergence of a general philosophy that emphasized the importance of the intellect, the individual, and world affairs. It contrasts strongly with the medieval worldview, characterized by the dominant concerns of faith, the social collective, and spiritual salvation. Prominent writers during the Renaissance include Niccolo Machiavelli and Baldassare Castiglione in Italy, Miguel de Cervantes and Lope de Vega in Spain, Jean Froissart and Francois Rabelais in France, Sir Thomas More and Sir Philip Sidney in England, and Desiderius Erasmus in Holland.

Repartee: Conversation featuring snappy retorts and witticisms. Masters of *repartee* include Sydney Smith, Charles Lamb, and Oscar Wilde. An example is recorded in the meeting of "Beau" Nash and John Wesley: Nash said, "I never make way for a fool," to which Wesley responded, "Don't you? I always do," and stepped aside.

Resolution: The portion of a story following the climax, in which the conflict is resolved. The resolution of Jane Austen's *Northanger Abbey* is neatly summed up in the following sentence: "Henry and Catherine were married, the bells rang and every body smiled."

Restoration: See *Restoration Age*

Restoration Age: A period in English literature beginning with the crowning of Charles II in 1660 and running to about 1700. The era, which was characterized by a reaction against Puritanism, was the first great age of the comedy of manners. The finest literature of the era is typically witty and urbane, and often lewd. Prominent Restoration Age writers include William Congreve, Samuel Pepys, John Dryden, and John Milton.

Revenge Tragedy: A dramatic form popular during the Elizabethan Age, in which the protagonist, directed by the ghost of his murdered father or son, inflicts retaliation upon a powerful villain. Notable features of the revenge tragedy include violence, bizarre criminal acts, intrigue, insanity, a hesitant protagonist, and the use of soliloquy. Thomas Kyd's *Spanish Tragedy* is the first example of revenge tragedy in English, and William Shakespeare's *Hamlet* is perhaps the best. Extreme examples of revenge tragedy, such as John Webster's *The Duchess of Malfi,* are labeled "tragedies of blood." Also known as Tragedy of Blood.

Revista: The Spanish term for a vaudeville musical revue. Examples of *revistas* include Antonio Guzman Aguilera's *Mexico para los mexicanos,* Daniel Vanegas's *Maldito jazz,* and Don Catarino's *Whiskey, morfina y marihuana* and *El desterrado.*

Rhetoric: In literary criticism, this term denotes the art of ethical persuasion. In its strictest sense, rhetoric adheres to various principles developed since classical times for arranging facts and ideas in a clear, persuasive, appealing manner. The term is also used to refer to effective prose in general and theories of or methods for composing effective prose. Classical examples of rhetorics include *The Rhetoric of Aristotle,* Quintillian's *Institutio Oratoria,* and Cicero's *Ad Herennium.*

Rhetorical Question: A question intended to provoke thought, but not an expressed answer, in the reader. It is most commonly used in oratory and other persuasive genres. The following lines from Thomas Gray's "Elegy Written in a Country Churchyard" ask rhetorical questions: Can storied urn or animated bust Back to its mansion call the fleeting breath? Can Honour's voice provoke the silent dust, Or Flattery soothe the dull cold ear of Death?

Rhyme: When used as a noun in literary criticism, this term generally refers to a poem in which words sound identical or very similar and appear in parallel positions in two or more lines. Rhymes are classified into different types according to where they fall in a line or stanza or according to the degree of similarity they exhibit in their spellings and sounds. Some major types of rhyme are "masculine" rhyme, "feminine" rhyme, and "triple" rhyme. In a masculine rhyme, the rhyming sound falls in a single accented syllable, as with "heat"

and "eat." Feminine rhyme is a rhyme of two syllables, one stressed and one unstressed, as with "merry" and "tarry." Triple rhyme matches the sound of the accented syllable and the two unaccented syllables that follow: "narrative" and "declarative." Robert Browning alternates feminine and masculine rhymes in his "Soliloquy of the Spanish Cloister": Gr-r-r—there go, my heart's abhorrence! Water your damned flower-pots, do! If hate killed men, Brother Lawrence, God's blood, would not mine kill you! What? Your myrtle-bush wants trimming? Oh, that rose has prior claims— Needs its leaden vase filled brimming? Hell dry you up with flames! Triple rhymes can be found in Thomas Hood's "Bridge of Sighs," George Gordon Byron's satirical verse, and Ogden Nash's comic poems.

Rhyme Royal: A stanza of seven lines composed in iambic pentameter and rhymed *ababbcc.* The name is said to be a tribute to King James I of Scotland, who made much use of the form in his poetry. Examples of rhyme royal include Geoffrey Chaucer's *The Parlement of Foules,* William Shakespeare's *The Rape of Lucrece,* William Morris's *The Early Paradise,* and John Masefield's *The Widow in the Bye Street.*

Rhyme Scheme: See *Rhyme*

Rhythm: A regular pattern of sound, time intervals, or events occurring in writing, most often and most discernably in poetry. Regular, reliable rhythm is known to be soothing to humans, while interrupted, unpredictable, or rapidly changing rhythm is disturbing. These effects are known to authors, who use them to produce a desired reaction in the reader. An example of a form of irregular rhythm is sprung rhythm poetry; quantitative verse, on the other hand, is very regular in its rhythm.

Rising Action: The part of a drama where the plot becomes increasingly complicated. Rising action leads up to the climax, or turning point, of a drama. The final "chase scene" of an action film is generally the rising action which culminates in the film's climax.

Rococo: A style of European architecture that flourished in the eighteenth century, especially in France. The most notable features of *rococo* are its extensive use of ornamentation and its themes of lightness, gaiety, and intimacy. In literary criticism, the term is often used disparagingly to refer to a decadent or over-ornamental style. Alexander Pope's "The Rape of the Lock" is an example of literary *rococo.*

Roman a clef: A French phrase meaning "novel with a key." It refers to a narrative in which real persons are portrayed under fictitious names. Jack Kerouac, for example, portrayed various real-life beat generation figures under fictitious names in his *On the Road.*

Romance: A broad term, usually denoting a narrative with exotic, exaggerated, often idealized characters, scenes, and themes. Nathaniel Hawthorne called his *The House of the Seven Gables* and *The Marble Faun* romances in order to distinguish them from clearly realistic works.

Romantic Age: See *Romanticism*

Romanticism: This term has two widely accepted meanings. In historical criticism, it refers to a European intellectual and artistic movement of the late eighteenth and early nineteenth centuries that sought greater freedom of personal expression than that allowed by the strict rules of literary form and logic of the eighteenth-century neoclassicists. The Romantics preferred emotional and imaginative expression to rational analysis. They considered the individual to be at the center of all experience and so placed him or her at the center of their art. The Romantics believed that the creative imagination reveals nobler truths—unique feelings and attitudes—than those that could be discovered by logic or by scientific examination. Both the natural world and the state of childhood were important sources for revelations of "eternal truths." "Romanticism" is also used as a general term to refer to a type of sensibility found in all periods of literary history and usually considered to be in opposition to the principles of classicism. In this sense, Romanticism signifies any work or philosophy in which the exotic or dreamlike figure strongly, or that is devoted to individualistic expression, self-analysis, or a pursuit of a higher realm of knowledge than can be discovered by human reason. Prominent Romantics include Jean-Jacques Rousseau, William Wordsworth, John Keats, Lord Byron, and Johann Wolfgang von Goethe.

Romantics: See *Romanticism*

Russian Symbolism: A Russian poetic movement, derived from French symbolism, that flourished between 1894 and 1910. While some Russian Symbolists continued in the French tradition, stressing aestheticism and the importance of suggestion above didactic intent, others saw their craft as a form of mystical worship, and themselves as mediators between the supernatural and the mundane. Russian symbolists include Aleksandr Blok, Vyacheslav Ivanovich Ivanov, Fyodor Sologub, Andrey Bely, Nikolay Gumilyov, and Vladimir Sergeyevich Solovyov.

S

Satire: A work that uses ridicule, humor, and wit to criticize and provoke change in human nature and institutions. There are two major types of satire: "formal" or "direct" satire speaks directly to the reader or to a character in the work; "indirect" satire relies upon the ridiculous behavior of its characters to make its point. Formal satire is further divided into two manners: the "Horatian," which ridicules gently, and the "Juvenalian," which derides its subjects harshly and bitterly. Voltaire's novella *Candide* is an indirect satire. Jonathan Swift's essay "A Modest Proposal" is a Juvenalian satire.

Scansion: The analysis or "scanning" of a poem to determine its meter and often its rhyme scheme. The most common system of scansion uses accents (slanted lines drawn above syllables) to show stressed syllables, breves (curved lines drawn above syllables) to show unstressed syllables, and vertical lines to separate each foot. In the first line of John Keats's *Endymion,* "A thing of beauty is a joy forever:" the word "thing," the first syllable of "beauty," the word "joy," and the second syllable of "forever" are stressed, while the words "A" and "of," the second syllable of "beauty," the word "a," and the first and third syllables of "forever" are unstressed. In the second line: "Its loveliness increases; it will never" a pair of vertical lines separate the foot ending with "increases" and the one beginning with "it."

Scene: A subdivision of an act of a drama, consisting of continuous action taking place at a single time and in a single location. The beginnings and endings of scenes may be indicated by clearing the stage of actors and props or by the entrances and exits of important characters. The first act of William Shakespeare's *Winter's Tale* is comprised of two scenes.

Science Fiction: A type of narrative about or based upon real or imagined scientific theories and technology. Science fiction is often peopled with alien creatures and set on other planets or in different dimensions. Karel Capek's *R.U.R.* is a major work of science fiction.

Second Person: See *Point of View*

Semiotics: The study of how literary forms and conventions affect the meaning of language. Semioticians include Ferdinand de Saussure, Charles Sanders Pierce, Claude Levi-Strauss, Jacques Lacan, Michel Foucault, Jacques Derrida, Roland Barthes, and Julia Kristeva.

Sestet: Any six-line poem or stanza. Examples of the sestet include the last six lines of the Petrarchan sonnet form, the stanza form of Robert Burns's "A Poet's Welcome to his love-begotten Daughter," and the sestina form in W. H. Auden's "Paysage Moralise."

Setting: The time, place, and culture in which the action of a narrative takes place. The elements of setting may include geographic location, characters' physical and mental environments, prevailing cultural attitudes, or the historical time in which the action takes place. Examples of settings include the romanticized Scotland in Sir Walter Scott's "Waverley" novels, the French provincial setting in Gustave Flaubert's *Madame Bovary,* the fictional Wessex country of Thomas Hardy's novels, and the small towns of southern Ontario in Alice Munro's short stories.

Shakespearean Sonnet: See *Sonnet*

Signifying Monkey: A popular trickster figure in black folklore, with hundreds of tales about this character documented since the 19th century. Henry Louis Gates Jr. examines the history of the signifying monkey in *The Signifying Monkey: Towards a Theory of Afro-American Literary Criticism,* published in 1988.

Simile: A comparison, usually using "like" or "as", of two essentially dissimilar things, as in "coffee as cold as ice" or "He sounded like a broken record." The title of Ernest Hemingway's "Hills Like White Elephants" contains a simile.

Slang: A type of informal verbal communication that is generally unacceptable for formal writing. Slang words and phrases are often colorful exaggerations used to emphasize the speaker's point; they may also be shortened versions of an often-used word or phrase. Examples of American slang from the 1990s include "yuppie" (an acronym for Young Urban Professional), "awesome" (for "excellent"), wired (for "nervous" or "excited"), and "chill out" (for relax).

Slant Rhyme: See *Consonance*

Slave Narrative: Autobiographical accounts of American slave life as told by escaped slaves. These works first appeared during the abolition movement of the 1830s through the 1850s. Olaudah Equiano's *The Interesting Narrative of Olaudah Equiano, or Gustavus Vassa, The African* and Harriet Ann Jacobs's *Incidents in the Life of a Slave Girl* are examples of the slave narrative.

Social Realism: See *Socialist Realism*

Socialist Realism: The Socialist Realism school of literary theory was proposed by Maxim Gorky and established as a dogma by the first Soviet Congress of Writers. It demanded adherence to a communist worldview in works of literature. Its doctrines required an objective viewpoint comprehensible to the working classes and themes of social struggle featuring strong proletarian heroes. A successful work of socialist realism is Nikolay Ostrovsky's *Kak zakalyalas stal* (*How the Steel Was Tempered*). Also known as Social Realism.

Soliloquy: A monologue in a drama used to give the audience information and to develop the speaker's character. It is typically a projection of the speaker's innermost thoughts. Usually delivered while the speaker is alone on stage, a soliloquy is intended to present an illusion of unspoken reflection. A celebrated soliloquy is Hamlet's "To be or not to be" speech in William Shakespeare's *Hamlet.*

Sonnet: A fourteen-line poem, usually composed in iambic pentameter, employing one of several rhyme schemes. There are three major types of sonnets, upon which all other variations of the form are based: the "Petrarchan" or "Italian" sonnet, the "Shakespearean" or "English" sonnet, and the "Spenserian" sonnet. A Petrarchan sonnet consists of an octave rhymed *abbaabba* and a "sestet" rhymed either *cdecde, cdccdc,* or *cdedce.* The octave poses a question or problem, relates a narrative, or puts forth a proposition; the sestet presents a solution to the problem, comments upon the narrative, or applies the proposition put forth in the octave. The Shakespearean sonnet is divided into three quatrains and a couplet rhymed *abab cdcd efef gg.* The couplet provides an epigrammatic comment on the narrative or problem put forth in the quatrains. The Spenserian sonnet uses three quatrains and a couplet like the Shakespearean, but links their three rhyme schemes in this way: *abab bcbc cdcd ee.* The Spenserian sonnet develops its theme in two parts like the Petrarchan, its final six lines resolving a problem, analyzing a narrative, or applying a proposition put forth in its first eight lines. Examples of sonnets can be found in Petrarch's *Canzoniere,* Edmund Spenser's *Amoretti,* Elizabeth Barrett

Browning's *Sonnets from the Portuguese,* Rainer Maria Rilke's *Sonnets to Orpheus,* and Adrienne Rich's poem "The Insusceptibles."

Spenserian Sonnet: See *Sonnet*

Spenserian Stanza: A nine-line stanza having eight verses in iambic pentameter, its ninth verse in iambic hexameter, and the rhyme scheme ababbcbcc. This stanza form was first used by Edmund Spenser in his allegorical poem *The Faerie Queene.*

Spondee: In poetry meter, a foot consisting of two long or stressed syllables occurring together. This form is quite rare in English verse, and is usually composed of two monosyllabic words. The first foot in the following line from Robert Burns's "Green Grow the Rashes" is an example of a spondee: Green grow the rashes, O

Sprung Rhythm: Versification using a specific number of accented syllables per line but disregarding the number of unaccented syllables that fall in each line, producing an irregular rhythm in the poem. Gerard Manley Hopkins, who coined the term "sprung rhythm," is the most notable practitioner of this technique.

Stanza: A subdivision of a poem consisting of lines grouped together, often in recurring patterns of rhyme, line length, and meter. Stanzas may also serve as units of thought in a poem much like paragraphs in prose. Examples of stanza forms include the quatrain, *terza rima, ottava rima,* Spenserian, and the so-called *In Memoriam* stanza from Alfred, Lord Tennyson's poem by that title. The following is an example of the latter form: Love is and was my lord and king, And in his presence I attend To hear the tidings of my friend, Which every hour his couriers bring.

Stereotype: A stereotype was originally the name for a duplication made during the printing process; this led to its modern definition as a person or thing that is (or is assumed to be) the same as all others of its type. Common stereotypical characters include the absent- minded professor, the nagging wife, the troublemaking teenager, and the kindhearted grandmother.

Stream of Consciousness: A narrative technique for rendering the inward experience of a character. This technique is designed to give the impression of an ever-changing series of thoughts, emotions, images, and memories in the spontaneous and seemingly illogical order that they occur in life. The

textbook example of stream of consciousness is the last section of James Joyce's *Ulysses.*

Structuralism: A twentieth-century movement in literary criticism that examines how literary texts arrive at their meanings, rather than the meanings themselves. There are two major types of structuralist analysis: one examines the way patterns of linguistic structures unify a specific text and emphasize certain elements of that text, and the other interprets the way literary forms and conventions affect the meaning of language itself. Prominent structuralists include Michel Foucault, Roman Jakobson, and Roland Barthes.

Structure: The form taken by a piece of literature. The structure may be made obvious for ease of understanding, as in nonfiction works, or may obscured for artistic purposes, as in some poetry or seemingly "unstructured" prose. Examples of common literary structures include the plot of a narrative, the acts and scenes of a drama, and such poetic forms as the Shakespearean sonnet and the Pindaric ode.

Sturm und Drang: A German term meaning "storm and stress." It refers to a German literary movement of the 1770s and 1780s that reacted against the order and rationalism of the enlightenment, focusing instead on the intense experience of extraordinary individuals. Highly romantic, works of this movement, such as Johann Wolfgang von Goethe's *Gotz von Berlichingen,* are typified by realism, rebelliousness, and intense emotionalism.

Style: A writer's distinctive manner of arranging words to suit his or her ideas and purpose in writing. The unique imprint of the author's personality upon his or her writing, style is the product of an author's way of arranging ideas and his or her use of diction, different sentence structures, rhythm, figures of speech, rhetorical principles, and other elements of composition. Styles may be classified according to period (Metaphysical, Augustan, Georgian), individual authors (Chaucerian, Miltonic, Jamesian), level (grand, middle, low, plain), or language (scientific, expository, poetic, journalistic).

Subject: The person, event, or theme at the center of a work of literature. A work may have one or more subjects of each type, with shorter works tending to have fewer and longer works tending to have more. The subjects of James Baldwin's novel *Go Tell It on the Mountain* include the themes of father-son relationships, religious conversion, black life, and sexuality. The subjects of Anne Frank's

Diary of a Young Girl include Anne and her family members as well as World War II, the Holocaust, and the themes of war, isolation, injustice, and racism.

Subjectivity: Writing that expresses the author's personal feelings about his subject, and which may or may not include factual information about the subject. Subjectivity is demonstrated in James Joyce's *Portrait of the Artist as a Young Man,* Samuel Butler's *The Way of All Flesh,* and Thomas Wolfe's *Look Homeward, Angel.*

Subplot: A secondary story in a narrative. A subplot may serve as a motivating or complicating force for the main plot of the work, or it may provide emphasis for, or relief from, the main plot. The conflict between the Capulets and the Montagues in William Shakespeare's *Romeo and Juliet* is an example of a subplot.

Surrealism: A term introduced to criticism by Guillaume Apollinaire and later adopted by Andre Breton. It refers to a French literary and artistic movement founded in the 1920s. The Surrealists sought to express unconscious thoughts and feelings in their works. The best-known technique used for achieving this aim was automatic writing—transcriptions of spontaneous outpourings from the unconscious. The Surrealists proposed to unify the contrary levels of conscious and unconscious, dream and reality, objectivity and subjectivity into a new level of "super-realism." Surrealism can be found in the poetry of Paul Eluard, Pierre Reverdy, and Louis Aragon, among others.

Suspense: A literary device in which the author maintains the audience's attention through the build-up of events, the outcome of which will soon be revealed. Suspense in William Shakespeare's *Hamlet* is sustained throughout by the question of whether or not the Prince will achieve what he has been instructed to do and of what he intends to do.

Syllogism: A method of presenting a logical argument. In its most basic form, the syllogism consists of a major premise, a minor premise, and a conclusion. An example of a syllogism is: Major premise: When it snows, the streets get wet. Minor premise: It is snowing. Conclusion: The streets are wet.

Symbol: Something that suggests or stands for something else without losing its original identity. In literature, symbols combine their literal meaning with the suggestion of an abstract concept. Literary symbols are of two types: those that carry complex associations of meaning no matter what their con-

texts, and those that derive their suggestive meaning from their functions in specific literary works. Examples of symbols are sunshine suggesting happiness, rain suggesting sorrow, and storm clouds suggesting despair.

Symbolism: This term has two widely accepted meanings. In historical criticism, it denotes an early modernist literary movement initiated in France during the nineteenth century that reacted against the prevailing standards of realism. Writers in this movement aimed to evoke, indirectly and symbolically, an order of being beyond the material world of the five senses. Poetic expression of personal emotion figured strongly in the movement, typically by means of a private set of symbols uniquely identifiable with the individual poet. The principal aim of the Symbolists was to express in words the highly complex feelings that grew out of everyday contact with the world. In a broader sense, the term "symbolism" refers to the use of one object to represent another. Early members of the Symbolist movement included the French authors Charles Baudelaire and Arthur Rimbaud; William Butler Yeats, James Joyce, and T. S. Eliot were influenced as the movement moved to Ireland, England, and the United States. Examples of the concept of symbolism include a flag that stands for a nation or movement, or an empty cupboard used to suggest hopelessness, poverty, and despair.

Symbolist: See *Symbolism*

Symbolist Movement: See *Symbolism*

Sympathetic Fallacy: See *Affective Fallacy*

T

Tale: A story told by a narrator with a simple plot and little character development. Tales are usually relatively short and often carry a simple message. Examples of tales can be found in the work of Rudyard Kipling, Somerset Maugham, Saki, Anton Chekhov, Guy de Maupassant, and Armistead Maupin.

Tall Tale: A humorous tale told in a straightforward, credible tone but relating absolutely impossible events or feats of the characters. Such tales were commonly told of frontier adventures during the settlement of the west in the United States. Tall tales have been spun around such legendary heroes as Mike Fink, Paul Bunyan, Davy Crockett, Johnny Appleseed, and Captain Stormalong as well as the real-life William F. Cody and Annie Oakley. Literary use of tall tales can be found in Washington Irving's *History of New York,* Mark Twain's *Life on the Mississippi,* and in the German R. F. Raspe's *Baron Munchausen's Narratives of His Marvellous Travels and Campaigns in Russia.*

Tanka: A form of Japanese poetry similar to *haiku.* A *tanka* is five lines long, with the lines containing five, seven, five, seven, and seven syllables respectively. Skilled *tanka* authors include Ishikawa Takuboku, Masaoka Shiki, Amy Lowell, and Adelaide Crapsey.

Teatro Grottesco: See *Theater of the Grotesque*

Terza Rima: A three-line stanza form in poetry in which the rhymes are made on the last word of each line in the following manner: the first and third lines of the first stanza, then the second line of the first stanza and the first and third lines of the second stanza, and so on with the middle line of any stanza rhyming with the first and third lines of the following stanza. An example of *terza rima* is Percy Bysshe Shelley's ''The Triumph of Love'': As in that trance of wondrous thought I lay This was the tenour of my waking dream. Methought I sate beside a public way Thick strewn with summer dust, and a great stream Of people there was hurrying to and fro Numerous as gnats upon the evening gleam,. . .

Tetrameter: See *Meter*

Textual Criticism: A branch of literary criticism that seeks to establish the authoritative text of a literary work. Textual critics typically compare all known manuscripts or printings of a single work in order to assess the meanings of differences and revisions. This procedure allows them to arrive at a definitive version that (supposedly) corresponds to the author's original intention. Textual criticism was applied during the Renaissance to salvage the classical texts of Greece and Rome, and modern works have been studied, for instance, to undo deliberate correction or censorship, as in the case of novels by Stephen Crane and Theodore Dreiser.

Theater of Cruelty: Term used to denote a group of theatrical techniques designed to eliminate the psychological and emotional distance between actors and audience. This concept, introduced in the 1930s in France, was intended to inspire a more intense theatrical experience than conventional theater allowed. The ''cruelty'' of this dramatic theory signified not sadism but heightened actor/audience involvement in the dramatic event. The theater of

cruelty was theorized by Antonin Artaud in his *Le Theatre et son double* (*The Theatre and Its Double*), and also appears in the work of Jerzy Grotowski, Jean Genet, Jean Vilar, and Arthur Adamov, among others.

Theater of the Absurd: A post-World War II dramatic trend characterized by radical theatrical innovations. In works influenced by the Theater of the absurd, nontraditional, sometimes grotesque characterizations, plots, and stage sets reveal a meaningless universe in which human values are irrelevant. Existentialist themes of estrangement, absurdity, and futility link many of the works of this movement. The principal writers of the Theater of the Absurd are Samuel Beckett, Eugene Ionesco, Jean Genet, and Harold Pinter.

Theater of the Grotesque: An Italian theatrical movement characterized by plays written around the ironic and macabre aspects of daily life in the World War I era. Theater of the Grotesque was named after the play *The Mask and the Face* by Luigi Chiarelli, which was described as ''a grotesque in three acts.'' The movement influenced the work of Italian dramatist Luigi Pirandello, author of *Right You Are, If You Think You Are.* Also known as *Teatro Grottesco.*

Theme: The main point of a work of literature. The term is used interchangeably with thesis. The theme of William Shakespeare's *Othello*—jealousy—is a common one.

Thesis: A thesis is both an essay and the point argued in the essay. Thesis novels and thesis plays share the quality of containing a thesis which is supported through the action of the story. A master's thesis and a doctoral dissertation are two theses required of graduate students.

Thesis Play: See *Thesis*

Three Unities: See *Unities*

Tone: The author's attitude toward his or her audience may be deduced from the tone of the work. A formal tone may create distance or convey politeness, while an informal tone may encourage a friendly, intimate, or intrusive feeling in the reader. The author's attitude toward his or her subject matter may also be deduced from the tone of the words he or she uses in discussing it. The tone of John F. Kennedy's speech which included the appeal to ''ask not what your country can do for you'' was intended to instill feelings of camaraderie and national pride in listeners.

Tragedy: A drama in prose or poetry about a noble, courageous hero of excellent character who, because of some tragic character flaw or *hamartia*, brings ruin upon him- or herself. Tragedy treats its subjects in a dignified and serious manner, using poetic language to help evoke pity and fear and bring about catharsis, a purging of these emotions. The tragic form was practiced extensively by the ancient Greeks. In the Middle Ages, when classical works were virtually unknown, tragedy came to denote any works about the fall of persons from exalted to low conditions due to any reason: fate, vice, weakness, etc. According to the classical definition of tragedy, such works present the "pathetic"—that which evokes pity—rather than the tragic. The classical form of tragedy was revived in the sixteenth century; it flourished especially on the Elizabethan stage. In modern times, dramatists have attempted to adapt the form to the needs of modern society by drawing their heroes from the ranks of ordinary men and women and defining the nobility of these heroes in terms of spirit rather than exalted social standing. The greatest classical example of tragedy is Sophocles' *Oedipus Rex.* The "pathetic" derivation is exemplified in "The Monk's Tale" in Geoffrey Chaucer's *Canterbury Tales.* Notable works produced during the sixteenth century revival include William Shakespeare's *Hamlet, Othello,* and *King Lear.* Modern dramatists working in the tragic tradition include Henrik Ibsen, Arthur Miller, and Eugene O'Neill.

Tragedy of Blood: See *Revenge Tragedy*

Tragic Flaw: In a tragedy, the quality within the hero or heroine which leads to his or her downfall. Examples of the tragic flaw include Othello's jealousy and Hamlet's indecisiveness, although most great tragedies defy such simple interpretation.

Transcendentalism: An American philosophical and religious movement, based in New England from around 1835 until the Civil War. Transcendentalism was a form of American romanticism that had its roots abroad in the works of Thomas Carlyle, Samuel Coleridge, and Johann Wolfgang von Goethe. The Transcendentalists stressed the importance of intuition and subjective experience in communication with God. They rejected religious dogma and texts in favor of mysticism and scientific naturalism. They pursued truths that lie beyond the "colorless" realms perceived by reason and the senses and were active social reformers in public education,

women's rights, and the abolition of slavery. Prominent members of the group include Ralph Waldo Emerson and Henry David Thoreau.

Trickster: A character or figure common in Native American and African literature who uses his ingenuity to defeat enemies and escape difficult situations. Tricksters are most often animals, such as the spider, hare, or coyote, although they may take the form of humans as well. Examples of trickster tales include Thomas King's *A Coyote Columbus Story,* Ashley F. Bryan's *The Dancing Granny* and Ishmael Reed's *The Last Days of Louisiana Red.*

Trimeter: See *Meter*

Triple Rhyme: See *Rhyme*

Trochee: See *Foot*

U

Understatement: See *Irony*

Unities: Strict rules of dramatic structure, formulated by Italian and French critics of the Renaissance and based loosely on the principles of drama discussed by Aristotle in his *Poetics.* Foremost among these rules were the three unities of action, time, and place that compelled a dramatist to: (1) construct a single plot with a beginning, middle, and end that details the causal relationships of action and character; (2) restrict the action to the events of a single day; and (3) limit the scene to a single place or city. The unities were observed faithfully by continental European writers until the Romantic Age, but they were never regularly observed in English drama. Modern dramatists are typically more concerned with a unity of impression or emotional effect than with any of the classical unities. The unities are observed in Pierre Corneille's tragedy *Polyeuctes* and Jean-Baptiste Racine's *Phedre.* Also known as Three Unities.

Urban Realism: A branch of realist writing that attempts to accurately reflect the often harsh facts of modern urban existence. Some works by Stephen Crane, Theodore Dreiser, Charles Dickens, Fyodor Dostoyevsky, Emile Zola, Abraham Cahan, and Henry Fuller feature urban realism. Modern examples include Claude Brown's *Manchild in the Promised Land* and Ron Milner's *What the Wine Sellers Buy.*

Utopia: A fictional perfect place, such as "paradise" or "heaven." Early literary utopias were included in Plato's *Republic* and Sir Thomas More's

Utopia, while more modern utopias can be found in Samuel Butler's *Erewhon,* Theodor Herzka's *A Visit to Freeland,* and H. G. Wells' *A Modern Utopia.*

Utopian: See *Utopia*

Utopianism: See *Utopia*

V

Verisimilitude: Literally, the appearance of truth. In literary criticism, the term refers to aspects of a work of literature that seem true to the reader. Verisimilitude is achieved in the work of Honore de Balzac, Gustave Flaubert, and Henry James, among other late nineteenth-century realist writers.

Vers de societe: See *Occasional Verse*

Vers libre: See *Free Verse*

Verse: A line of metered language, a line of a poem, or any work written in verse. The following line of verse is from the epic poem *Don Juan* by Lord Byron: "My way is to begin with the beginning."

Versification: The writing of verse. Versification may also refer to the meter, rhyme, and other mechanical components of a poem. Composition of a "Roses are red, violets are blue" poem to suit an occasion is a common form of versification practiced by students.

Victorian: Refers broadly to the reign of Queen Victoria of England (1837-1901) and to anything with qualities typical of that era. For example, the qualities of smug narrowmindedness, bourgeois materialism, faith in social progress, and priggish morality are often considered Victorian. This stereotype is contradicted by such dramatic intellectual developments as the theories of Charles Darwin, Karl Marx, and Sigmund Freud (which stirred strong debates in England) and the critical attitudes of serious Victorian writers like Charles Dickens and George Eliot. In literature, the Victorian Period was the great age of the English novel, and the latter part of the era saw the rise of movements such as decadence and symbolism. Works of Victorian lit-

erature include the poetry of Robert Browning and Alfred, Lord Tennyson, the criticism of Matthew Arnold and John Ruskin, and the novels of Emily Bronte, William Makepeace Thackeray, and Thomas Hardy. Also known as Victorian Age and Victorian Period.

Victorian Age: See *Victorian*

Victorian Period: See *Victorian*

W

Weltanschauung: A German term referring to a person's worldview or philosophy. Examples of *weltanschauung* include Thomas Hardy's view of the human being as the victim of fate, destiny, or impersonal forces and circumstances, and the disillusioned and laconic cynicism expressed by such poets of the 1930s as W. H. Auden, Sir Stephen Spender, and Sir William Empson.

Weltschmerz: A German term meaning "world pain." It describes a sense of anguish about the nature of existence, usually associated with a melancholy, pessimistic attitude. *Weltschmerz* was expressed in England by George Gordon, Lord Byron in his *Manfred* and *Childe Harold's Pilgrimage,* in France by Viscount de Chateaubriand, Alfred de Vigny, and Alfred de Musset, in Russia by Aleksandr Pushkin and Mikhail Lermontov, in Poland by Juliusz Slowacki, and in America by Nathaniel Hawthorne.

Z

Zarzuela: A type of Spanish operetta. Writers of *zarzuelas* include Lope de Vega and Pedro Calderon.

Zeitgeist: A German term meaning "spirit of the time." It refers to the moral and intellectual trends of a given era. Examples of *zeitgeist* include the preoccupation with the more morbid aspects of dying and death in some Jacobean literature, especially in the works of dramatists Cyril Tourneur and John Webster, and the decadence of the French Symbolists.

Cumulative Author/Title Index

Nationality/Ethnicity Index

Subject/Theme Index